MOON HANDBOOKS

UTAH

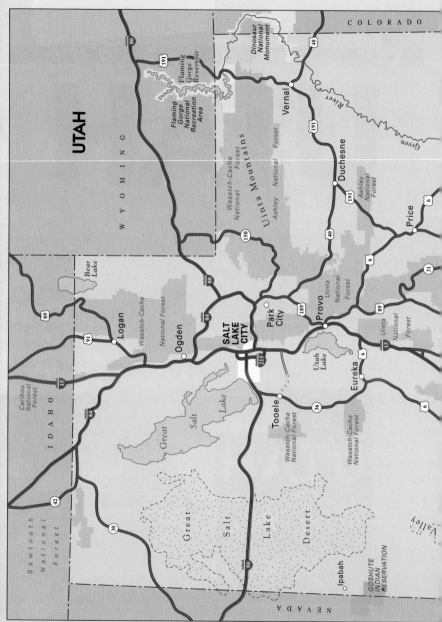

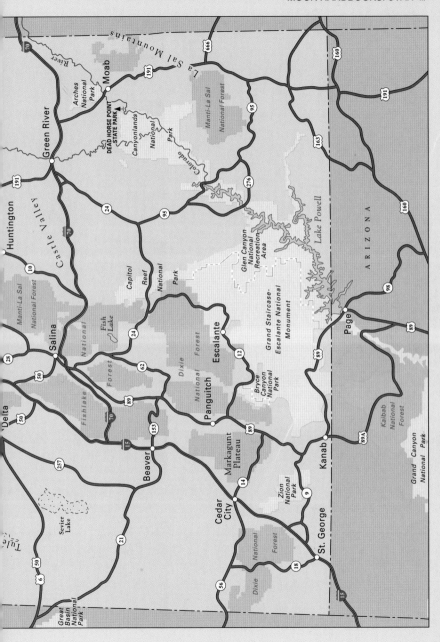

MOON HANDBOOKS

UTAH

SIXTH EDITION

**BILL WEIR
AND W. C. McRAE**

**AVALON
TRAVEL**
publishing

MOON HANDBOOKS: UTAH
SIXTH EDITION
BILL WEIR AND W. C. McRAE

Published by
Avalon Travel Publishing, Inc.
5855 Beaudry St.
Emeryville, CA 94608, USA

© Text and photographs copyright Bill Weir
and W. C. McRae, 2001. All rights reserved.

© Illustrations and maps copyright
Avalon Travel Publishing, Inc., 2001.
All rights reserved.

All photos by Bill Weir unless otherwise noted.
Some photos and illustrations are used by permission
and are the property of the original copyright owners.

ISBN: 1-56691-274-1
ISSN: 1531-5568

Editors: Grace Fujimoto, Erin Van Rheenen
Copyeditor: Marybeth Griffin
Production & Design: Carey Wilson, Kelly Pendragon
Illustrations: Bob Race
Map Editors: Naomi Dancis, Mike Ferguson
Cartography: Brian Bardwell, Chris Folks, Mike Morgenfeld, Doug Beckner
Index: Monica Smersh

Front cover photo: Skyline Arch, Arches National Park © Michael J. Gibbons

Distributed in the United States and Canada by Publishers Group West

Printed in the United States by R.R. Donnelley

Please send all comments,
corrections, additions,
amendments, and critiques to:

MOON HANDBOOKS: UTAH
AVALON TRAVEL PUBLISHING, INC.
5855 BEAUDRY ST.
EMERYVILLE, CA 94608, USA
e-mail: info@travelmatters.com
www.moon.com

Printing History
1st edition—1988
6th edition—March 2001

5 4 3 2 1

CONTENTS

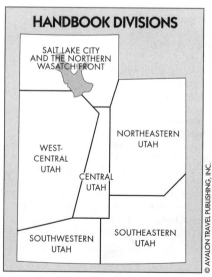

MAPS

MAP SYMBOLS

○ City

○ Town

★ Point of Interest

• Accommodation

▾ Restaurant/Bar

▪ Other Location

△ Campground

▲ Mountain

═══ Superhighway

══ Main Road

══ Other Road

====== Unpaved Road

·········· Trail

⬬ Interstate

⬭ U.S. Highway

○ State Highway

⚑ State/County Park

✕ Airport

✈ Military Airport

⛷ Ski Area

⚲ Golf Course

▨ Water

▦ Dry Lake

ACKNOWLEDGMENTS

Many thanks go to the hundreds of people who assisted in making *Moon Handbooks: Utah* complete and accurate. I am especially indebted to people of the National Park Service, U.S. Forest Service, Bureau of Land Management, and Utah State Parks, whose high standards help make Utah such a wonderful place to visit. Tourist offices everywhere from the tiniest communities to the largest cities supplied valuable maps, ideas, and advice. Most of the wonderful historic photos appear with the assistance of friendly librarians Bill Slaughter of the LDS Historical Department and Susan Whetstone of the Utah State Historical Society, both in Salt Lake City. And last but not least. . . the hard working crew at Avalon Travel Publishing deserves a round of applause for their patience in dealing with a fussy author!

—BILL WEIR

I'd like to thank Ken Kraus of the Utah Travel Council for his help, and give special thanks to the regional travel officials who gave advice and lent a hand. Thanks to Stuart and Janet, and Jeff and Kim for the Utah-sized hospitality.

—BILL MCRAE

IS THIS BOOK OUT OF DATE?

Nothing stays the same, it seems. Although this book has been carefully researched, Utah will continue to grow and change. New sights and places to stay and eat will open while others change hands or close. We'd appreciate comments and ideas for improving *Moon Handbooks: Utah*. If you find something new, discontinued, changed, or left out, please let us know so that we can include it in the next edition. Address your letters to:

Moon Handbooks: Utah
Avalon Travel Publishing
5855 Beaudry St.
Emeryville, CA 94608, USA

e-mail: info@travelmatters.com
(please put book title in the subject line)
www.travelmatters.com

ABBREVIATIONS

B&B—bed-and-breakfast
BLM—Bureau of Land Management
BYU—Brigham Young University
DUP—Daughters of Utah Pioneers
LDS—Latter-day Saints
NHS—National Historic Site
NRA—National Recreation Area
SLC—Salt Lake City
USFS—United States Forest Service
ZCMI—Zion's Cooperative Mercantile Institution

RATINGS KEY

Accommodation listings in this book use the following price ranges for room rates per room, based on double occupancy high season rates:

Under $50
$50–75
$75–100
$100–125
$125–150
$150–175
$175–200
$200 and up

INTRODUCTION

Lying in the heart of the American West, Utah combines spectacular terrain and unusual history that's unparalleled in the United States. The state hosts the majestic splendor of the Rocky Mountains, the colorful canyonlands of the Colorado Plateau, and the remote desert mountain ranges of the Great Basin. This region beckoned as the "Promised Land" to the struggling Mormon Church in the 1800s—a place where the faithful could survive and prosper. Today you can comfortably enjoy the scenic splendor of Utah, much of it little changed since the first pioneers arrived in 1847.

Salt Lake City in the north and the five national parks in the south rank at the top of most visitors' lists, but many other beautiful and intriguing places remain undiscovered. Utah's superb ski conditions and resorts are recognized as some of the best in North America, and in 2002 the Salt Lake area will host the Winter Olympics. Incredibly varied canyon country, rugged mountain ranges, glistening salt flats, Indian reservations, old mining towns—this handbook will help you discover these and many more attractions.

THE LAND

GEOGRAPHY

Utah's 84,990 square miles place it 11th in size among the 50 states. You could fit Maine, Vermont, New Hampshire, Connecticut, Massachusetts, New Jersey, and Maryland within its borders and still have room to squeeze in Rhode Island. The varied landscape is divided into three major physiographic provinces: the **Basin and Range Province** to the west; the **Middle Rocky Mountains Province** of the soaring Uinta, Wasatch, and Bear River Ranges to the north and northeast; and the **Colorado Plateau Province** of canyons, mountains, and plateaus in the southeast. Some physiographers argue for a fourth province, the **Basin and Range— Colorado Plateau Transition.** This area, also known as the High Plateaus, stretches from the Wasatch Range south into Arizona. Mountains and plateaus in this area share structural features with both neighboring provinces.

Basin and Range Province

Rows of fault-block mountain ranges follow a north-south alignment in this province in the Great Basin west of the Wasatch Range and the High Plateaus. Most of the province lies at elevations between 4,000 and 5,000 feet. Peaks in the Stansbury and Deep Creek Mountains rise more than 11,000 feet above sea level, creating "biological islands" inhabited by cool-climate plants and animals.

Erosion has worn down many of the ranges, forming large alluvial fans in adjacent basins. Many of these broad valleys lack effective drainage and none have outlets to the ocean. Terraces mark the hills along the shore of prehistoric Lake Bonneville, which once covered most of this province. Few perennial streams originate in these rocky mountains, but rivers from eastern ranges end their voyages in the Great Salt Lake, Sevier Lake, or barren silt-filled valleys.

Middle Rocky Mountains Province

The Wasatch Range and the Uinta Mountains, which form this province, provide some of the most dramatic alpine scenery in the state. In both mountainous areas, you'll find cirques, arêtes, horns, and glacial troughs carved by massive rivers of ice during periods of glaciation. Structurally, however, the ranges have little in common. The narrow Wasatch, one of the most rugged ranges in the country, runs north-south for about 200 miles between the Idaho border and central Utah. Slippage along the still-active Wasatch Fault has resulted in a towering western face with few foothills. Most of Utah's ski resorts lie in this area. The Uinta Mountains in the northeast corner of the state present a broad rise about 150 miles west to east and 30 miles across. Twenty-four peaks exceed 13,000 feet, with Kings Peak (elev. 13,528 feet) the highest mountain in Utah. An estimated 1,400 tiny lakes dot the glacial moraines of the Uintas.

Colorado Plateau Province

World-famous for its scenery and geology, the Colorado Plateau covers nearly half of Utah. Elevations lie mostly between 3,000 and 6,000 feet, but some mountain peaks reach nearly 13,000 feet. The Uinta Basin forms the northern part of this vast complex of plateaus; it's bordered on the north by the Uinta Mountains and on the south by the Roan Cliffs. Although most of the basin terrain is gently rolling, the Green River and its tributaries have carved some spectacular canyons into the Roan and Book Cliffs. Farther south, the Green and Colorado Rivers have

Colorado River, Fisher Towers, and the La Sal Mountains

W.C. McRAE

sculpted remarkable canyons, buttes, mesas, arches, and badlands. Uplifts and foldings have formed such features as the San Rafael Swell, Waterpocket Fold, and Circle Cliffs. The rounded Abajo, Henry, La Sal, and Navajo Mountains are examples of intrusive rock—an igneous layer that is formed below the earth's surface and later exposed by erosion. The High Plateaus in south-central Utah drop in a series of steps known as the Grand Staircase. Exposed layers range from the relatively young rocks of the Black Cliffs (lava flows) in the north, to the increasingly older Pink Cliffs (Wasatch Formation), Gray Cliffs (Mancos Shale), White Cliffs (Navajo Sandstone), and Vermilion Cliffs (Chinle and Wingate Formations) toward the south.

GEOLOGIC HISTORY

The land now contained in Utah began as undersea deposits when the North American continental plate sat near the equator, about 500 million years ago. The spectacular canyon country, now known as the Colorado Plateau, began as a basin of silt and sand deposits at the verge of a shallow sea. The continental plate on which this basin sat rose and fell; it was sometimes below the waters of ancient seas—at which time fossils of early marine life were encased in the deposits—and sometimes, during more arid periods, above sea level, with vast sand dunes covering the landscape.

Beginning about 200 million years ago, in the Mesozoic era, the North American continental plate broke away from Europe and Africa and began its westward movement over the top of the Pacific Ocean seafloor. This massive collision of tectonic plates resulted in the buckling of rock formations—which formed mountains including the Rockies and the Uintas—and in thrust faulting, where older formations were pushed up and onto younger rocks; one such range is the Oquirrh Mountains.

All of this activity happened at the verges of the Colorado Plateau, which by the Cretaceous period—the age of the dinosaurs, about 65 million years ago—had again sunk back to sea level, resulting in thick formations of sand, mud, and ancient vegetation. These formations would later be revealed in the region's mighty canyons and in the coal fields of northeastern Utah. In some places, fossilized mud footprints of dinosaurs provide unmistakable evidence of the era's far damper climate!

Basin and Range

In the Tertiary era, the new formations west of the old Colorado Plateau were shot through with volcanoes. Then, as the North American continental plate pivoted to the southwest, the earth's crust under this region—which would become the Basin and Range Province—stretched thinner and thinner. In fact, the Great Basin of Utah and Nevada is about twice as wide as it was about 18 million years ago. This stretching has resulted in a much thinner layer of underlying basement rock here than in other parts of the continent, and the entire area is riven by faults where parts of the crust have pulled apart. Given the differential forces at work in the earth's mantle, at times half of a fault would be pushed up to mountain heights while the other half would sink, caus-

ing a basin. The spectacular fault-block mountains of the Great Basin result from such parallel rising and falling along fault lines. The most famous instance of this type of formation is the rugged Wasatch Mountains, which rise directly above the basin of the Great Salt Lake.

To the east of this momentous fault-block mountain building, the old Colorado Plateau remained relatively undisturbed. However, within the last 10 million years the entire intermountain region bowed up in a broad arch, elevating the old sandstones of the Colorado Plateau; this corner of Utah has risen 5,000 feet during this time! The rivers that once wound across the surface of eastern Utah were forced to cut ever deeper canyons as the formations rose. The erosive power of the Green, Colorado, San Juan, and other rivers and streams have cut down through hundreds of millions of years of rock.

Ice Age Utah

During the geologically recent Pleistocene era, ice-age mountain glaciers and climatic changes brought an abundance of moisture to Utah. The runoff and meltwater flooded the basins of fault-block mountain ranges, forming enormous lakes. The largest of these was Lake Bonneville, the name given to the ice-age predecessor of the Great Salt Lake. At its greatest extent, Lake Bonneville covered nearly all of northern and west-central Utah and was nearly 900 feet deeper than the current Great Salt Lake. Even at that depth, finding an outlet to the sea was not simple. It was only after the lake waters breached Red Rock Pass in Idaho that the lake found an outlet into the Snake and Columbia River systems, about 16,000 years ago.

After the ice ages ended, about 10,000 years ago, Lake Bonneville diminished in size and dropped below the level necessary to cut through Red Rock Pass, resulting in the saline Great Salt Lake. You can easily see the old lake shorelines along the Wasatch Front, and cities like Logan, Provo, and Salt Lake City sprawl along these stairsteplike ledges. Much of the old lake bottom west of Salt Lake City is salt desert and extremely flat. In the Bonneville Salt Flats, the valley is so flat and unbroken that the curvature of the earth can be seen; a person of ordinary height can see for three miles simply by standing up.

CLIMATE

The hot summer sun awakens wildflowers in the mountains and turns desert areas brown. Autumn brings pleasant weather to all elevations until the snow line begins to creep down the mountain slopes. Winter snowfalls provide excellent skiing and add beauty to the landscape, but cause many mountain roads to close. On those roads that don't close, you'll need chains or snow tires. Spring tends to be unpredictable—wet and windy one day, sunny and calm the next—but it's then you'll find the deserts at their greenest.

Utah's mid-continent location brings wide temperature variations between the seasons. Only a small part of the south experiences winter temperatures that average above freezing. State records include a high of 116° F at St. George in 1892 and a low of -50° F at Woodruff in 1899 and at Strawberry East Portal in 1913.

Precipitation

Most of Utah is dry—evaporation exceeds precipitation. In fact, of the 50 states only Nevada receives less moisture annually than Utah's 13 inches. Precipitation varies greatly from place to place due to local topography and the irregularities of storm patterns. Deserts cover about 33 percent of the state; the driest areas are in the Great Basin, the Uinta Basin, and on the Colorado Plateau, where annual precipitation is around 5–10 inches. At the other extreme, the highest peaks of the Wasatch Range receive more than 50 inches of annual precipitation, most of it as snow; approximately 24 percent of Utah has a highland climate. About 40 percent of the state, classified as steppe, receives 8–14 inches of annual precipitation and supports grasslands suitable for ranching. Three percent of the state's land is humid continental—ideal for agriculture. This heavily populated strip lies along the Wasatch Front. Utah enjoys lots of sunshine, but storm systems can briefly darken the skies at any time.

Winter and Spring
Weather Patterns (Oct.–Apr.)

Periods of high-pressure systems broken by Pacific storm fronts shape most of Utah's winter weather. The high-pressure systems cause inversions when dense cold air flows down the snow-covered mountain slopes into the valleys, where it traps moisture and smoke. The blanket of fog or smog maintains even temperatures but is the bane of the Salt Lake City area. Skiers, however, enjoy bright, sunny days and cold nights in the clear air of the mountain peaks. The blankets of stagnant air in the valleys are cleaned out when cold fronts roll in from the Pacific. When skies clear, the daily temperature range is much greater until the inversion process sets in again.

Most winter precipitation arrives as snow, which all regions of the state expect. Fronts originating over the Gulf of Alaska typically arrive every six to seven days and trigger most of Utah's snowfall.

Summer and Autumn
Weather Patterns (May–Sept.)

During summer, the valleys still experience inversions of cold air on clear, dry nights, but with a much less pronounced effect than in winter. The canyon country in the south has higher daytime temperatures than do equivalent mountain elevations because there's no source of cold air in the canyons to replace the rising heated air. Also, canyon walls act as an oven, reflecting and trapping heat. Thunderstorms are most common in summer, when moist warm air rises in billowing clouds. The storms, though they can produce heavy rains and hail, tend to be erratic and concentrated in small areas less than three miles across. Southeastern Utah sees the first thunderstorms of the season, often in mid-June; by mid-July, these storms have spread across the entire state. They lose energy as autumn approaches and by October they're supplanted by "lows aloft" (low-pressure systems at high altitudes) and Pacific storm fronts. Lows aloft move in erratic patterns but can cause long periods of heavy precipitation. They're often the main source of weather disturbances during October, late April, and May. Surprisingly, most of Utah's moisture originates in the Gulf of California or the Gulf of Mexico. The Pacific fronts often lose most of their moisture by the time they reach Utah, yet their cold air can produce heavy precipitation when it meets moist warm air from the south. Hikers need to be aware that the highest mountain peaks can receive snow even in midsummer.

Storm Hazards

Rainwater runs quickly off the rocky desert surfaces and into gullies and canyons. Flash floods can sweep away anything in their path including boulders, cars, and campsites. Do not camp or park in potential flash-flood areas. If you come to a section of flooded roadway—a common occurrence on desert roads after storms—wait until the water goes down before crossing (it shouldn't take long). Summer lightning causes forest and brush fires, posing a danger to hikers foolish enough to climb mountains when storms threaten.

FLORA AND FAUNA

A wide variety of plants and animals find a home within Utah's great range of elevations (more than 11,000 feet). Regardless of the precipitation, the environment is harsh, and most plants and animals have had to adapt to endure the challenging climate. To help simplify and understand the different environments, some scientists use the Merriam system of life zones, which offers a concise way to get an overview of Utah's vegetation and animal life. Because plants subsist on rainfall, which is determined largely by elevation, each life zone can be identified with an elevation range. These ranges are not exact, however, due to the different rainfall patterns and evaporation rates.

Utah's lowest elevations lie in the Lower Sonoran Life Zone (below 3,500 feet). This zone is found in the Mojave Desert, which extends into the southwest corner of the state. Most of Utah's northern deserts and canyonlands are considered part of the Upper Sonoran Life Zone (3,500–5,500 feet). As rainfall increases near mountain ranges, the Transition Life Zone (5,500–8,000 feet) begins. The Transition Zone is best developed on the High Plateaus and the Uinta Mountains and less so in the Great Basin and the Wasatch Range. At successively higher elevations are the Canadian Life Zone (8,000–10,000 feet), the Hudsonian Life Zone (10,000–11,000 feet), and the Alpine Tundra Life Zone (above 11,000 feet).

DESERT FLORA

In the southern Lower Sonoran deserts near St. George, less than eight inches of rain falls yearly. Creosote bush dominates the plant life, though you're also likely to see rabbitbrush, snakeweed, blackbrush, saltbush, yucca, and cacti. Joshua trees grow on some of the higher gravel benches. Flowering plants tend to bloom either after the winter rains (the Sonoran or Mexican species) or the summer rains (the Mojave or Californian species).

In the more temperate Upper Sonoran Zones, shadscale—a plant resistant to both salt and drought—grows on the valley floors and the lower slopes of the Great Basin, Uinta Basin, and Canyonlands. Commonly growing with shadscale are grasses, annuals, Mormon tea, budsage, gray molley, and winterfat. In salty soils, more likely companions are greasewood, salt grass, and iodine bush. Nonalkaline soils, on the other hand, may have blackbrush as the dominant plant. Sagebrush, the most common shrub in Utah, thrives on higher terraces and in alluvial fans of nonalkaline soil. Grasses are commonly found mixed with sagebrush and may even dominate the landscape. Piñon pine and juniper, small trees often found together, can grow only where 12 inches of rain or more falls annually; the lower limit of their growth is sometimes called the "arid timberline." In the Wasatch Range, scrub oaks often grow near junipers.

MOUNTAIN FLORA

As elevation rises and rainfall increases, you'll see growing numbers of ponderosa pine and chaparral in the forest. The chaparral association includes oak, maple, mountain mahogany, and sagebrush. Gambel oak, juniper, and Douglas fir commonly grow among the ponderosa in the Uintas and the High Plateaus.

Douglas fir is the most common tree within the Canadian Zone in the Wasatch Range, the High Plateaus, and the northern slopes of the Great Basin Ranges. In the Uintas, however, lodgepole pine dominates. Other trees of the Canadian Zone include ponderosa pine, limber

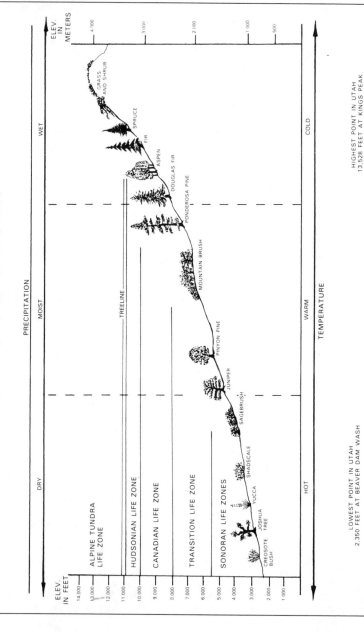

UTAH VEGETATION ZONES

© AVALON TRAVEL PUBLISHING, INC.

pine, white fir, blue spruce (Utah's state tree), and aspen.

Strong winds and a growing season of less than 120 days prevent trees from reaching their full size at higher elevations. The Hudsonian Zone receives twice as much snow as the Canadian Zone just below. Often gnarled and twisted, Engelmann spruce and subalpine fir grow in the cold heights over large areas of the Uintas and Wasatches. Limber and bristlecone pines live in the zone, too. Lakes and lush subalpine meadows are common.

Only grasses, mosses, sedges, and annuals can withstand the rugged conditions atop Utah's highest ranges. Freezing temperatures and snow can blast the mountain slopes even in midsummer.

DESERT FAUNA

Most desert animals retreat to a den or burrow during the heat of the day, when ground temperatures can reach 130° F! Look for wildlife in early morning, late afternoon, or at night. You may see kangaroo rat, desert cottontail, black-tailed jackrabbit, striped and spotted skunks, kit fox, ringtail cat, coyote, bobcat, mountain lion, and several species of squirrels and mice. Birds include the native Gambel's quail, roadrunner, red-tailed hawk, great horned owl, cactus wren, black-chinned and broad-tailed hummingbirds, and rufous-sided towhee. The endangered desert tortoise lives here, too, but faces extinction in a losing battle with livestock, which trample and graze on the tortoise's precious environment.

The rare Gila monster, identified by its beadlike skin with black and yellow patterns, is the only poisonous lizard in the United States. In Utah, it's found only in the state's southwest corner. Although slow and unaggressive, it has powerful

*Gambel's quail
(Lophortyx gambelii)*

jaws and excretes a potentially lethal venom from a gland in its lower jaw. Once the reptile gets a grip, it doesn't let go and the jaws must be pried loose—even if the head has been cut off. Sidewinder, Great Basin, and other Western rattlesnakes are occasionally seen. Also watch for other poisonous creatures; scorpions, spiders, and centipedes can inflict painful stings or bites. It's a good idea when camping to check for these unwanted guests in shoes and other items left outside. Be careful, too, not to reach under rocks or into places you can't see.

In the more temperate Upper Sonoran Zone, you'll see plenty of desert wildlife, though you might also see Utah prairie dog, beaver, muskrat, black bear, desert bighorn sheep, desert mule deer, and the antelope-like pronghorn. Marshes of the Great Basin have an abundance of food and cover that attract waterfowl; species include whistling swan, Great Basin Canada goose, lesser snow goose, great blue heron, seagull (Utah's state bird), common mallard, gadwall, and American common merganser. Chukar (from similar desert lands in Asia) and Hungarian partridge (from eastern Europe and western Asia) thrive under the cover of sagebrush in dry-farm areas. Sage and sharp-tailed grouse also prefer the open country. Rattlesnakes and other reptiles like the Upper Sonoran Zone best.

Not surprisingly, there aren't many fish that live in the desert. The Great Salt Lake is too salty to support fish life; the only creatures that can live in its extremely saline water are bacteria, a few insect species, and brine shrimp, which are commercially harvested. The Colorado River, which cuts through southeastern Utah, supports a number of fish species, several of which are endemic to the river and are now considered endangered. (See the special topic, Endangered Fish of the Colorado River, in the Southeastern Utah chapter.)

MOUNTAIN FAUNA

In the thin forests of the Transition Zone, squirrels and chipmunks rely on pine cones for food; other animals living here include Nuttall's cottontail, black-tailed jackrabbit, spotted and striped skunks, red fox, coyote, mule deer, Rocky Mountain elk (Utah's state mammal), moose, black

yellow belly marmot
(Marmota flaviventris)

bear, and mountain lion. Moose did not arrive until the 1940s, when they crossed over from Wyoming; now they live in northern and central Utah. Merriam's wild turkey, originally from Colorado, is found in oak and ponderosa pine forests of central and southern Utah. Other birds of the Transition Zone include Steller's jay, blue and ruffed grouse, common poorwill, great horned owl, black-chinned and broad-tailed hummingbirds, gray-headed and Oregon juncos, white-throated swift, and the common raven. Most snakes, such as the gopher, hognosed, and garter, are harmless, but you may also come across Western rattlers.

Utah has over 1,000 fishable lakes and numerous fishing streams. Species range from the rainbow and cutthroat trout to large mackinaw and Brown trout to striped bass, walleye, bluegill, and whitefish. Bear Lake in extreme northern Utah is home to the Bear Lake whitefish, Bonneville whitefish, Bonneville Cisco, and Bear Lake Sculpin—all are unique to Bear Lake and its tributaries. Because of their restricted range, they are vulnerable to extinction from habitat alteration due to water management of Bear Lake and its tributaries.

Deer and Rocky Mountain elk graze in the Canadian Zone but rarely higher. Smaller animals of the high mountains include northern flying squirrel, snowshoe rabbit, pocket gopher, yellow belly marmot, pika, chipmunk, and mice.

Even higher, in the Hudsonian Zone, on a bright summer day the trees, grasses, and tiny flowering alpine plants are abuzz with insects, rodents, and visiting birds. Come winter, though, most animals will have moved to lower and more protected areas. Few animals live in the true alpine regions. White-tailed ptarmigan, recently introduced to Utah, live in the tundra of the Uinta Mountains.

ENVIRONMENTAL ISSUES

Like many other western states, Utah is deeply conflicted about environmental issues. One of the most conservative states in the nation, Utah has always been very business oriented, especially toward the historic extractive industries such as mining, logging, and agriculture. Utah has also proved to be very friendly to the military; large portions of northeastern Utah are under Pentagon control as bases, weapons research areas, and munitions dumps.

On the other hand, tourism and high-tech industries are breathing life into Utah's economy. Tourism brings in 18 million visitors a year, making it the single largest employer in Utah. Wasatch Front cities are experiencing a phenomenal boom in population growth and new, low environmental-impact industry. A large part of the reason for this 20th-century migration is Utah's quality of life—pristine wilderness and world-class outdoor recreation is available right out the back door. The interests of the tourist industry and new residents are often at odds with the interests of the state's traditional power base.

GRAND STAIRCASE–ESCALANTE NATIONAL MONUMENT

In 1996, President Bill Clinton used provisions of the National Antiquities Act to establish the Grand Staircase–Escalante National Monument. This vast tract of land, which totals over 1.8 million acres, is the largest national monument land grouping in the lower 48 states. It brings under federal Interior Department management tracts of land previously administered by the Bureau of Land Management (BLM), the National Forest Service, and the state of Utah. Designation as a national monument means that the land is now off-limits to specific kinds of development and that the land will be managed to preserve its wilderness characteristics as much as possible.

The timing of the designation was apparently motivated by plans to develop a large strip coal mine in the slick rock Escalante River canyons, a well-loved destination for long-distance hikers and adventurers.

National monument status also puts to rest one of the most contentious public land debates in the American West. Earlier in the 1990s, Utah federal politicians introduced the Utah Public Lands Management Act into Congress. The bill, introduced into the Senate by Utah's Republican Senators Orrin Hatch and Bob Bennett and into the House by the state's Republican delegation, sought to ease restrictions on and transfer ownership of 22 million acres of publicly owned land currently administered by the BLM. Under the bill, 20 million acres of land currently protected by the BLM (including wilderness-study areas) would have been opened for development in return for granting wilderness status to two million acres. The federal government would have been barred forever from seeking wilderness designation for the newly released 20 million acres and, in fact, would transfer ownership of some federal land to the state of Utah. Additionally, the bill would allow broad exceptions to federal guidelines in the areas that would be designated as wilderness, opening the land to vehicular use, dam building, and road construction.

After a long and fractious debate, the bill died in the Senate. Voting followed a general east/west split, with some Republicans from eastern states voting with the minority Democrats to bury the bill. However, the Republican-led Utah delegation vowed to bring it up in the next congressional session.

With a stroke of his pen, President Bill Clinton effectively preempted any further discussion of the Utah Public Lands Act, utterly enraging the Utah delegation and many others in this deeply conservative state. Clinton signed the decree during a highly publicized outdoor media event, with the canyons of the Escalante in the background. However, what wasn't so well publicized was that Clinton was actually in the state of Arizona when he signed the declaration. Hostility from the Utah House delegation was so high that the president's advisers thought it unwise for him to journey inside the state boundaries to make the announcement.

Well, hostility to the declaration of the monument has hardly subsided in the years that have followed. In fact, the Grand Staircase–Escalante National Monument seems to have put a face onto a miasma of resentment, fear, and intimidation that's long been simmering beneath the surface in Utah—and in other western statesfor many years. The hostility is based in part on the fear of what the federal land changes will portend for small farmers and ranchers in southeastern Utah; agriculturists whose way of life and business has long depended on access to federal land. Other people have a strong aversion to any form of federal governmental authority, while others decry the fact that traditional rural families will be displaced to make room for hoards of eco-tourists, who are viewed with the same fear and distaste once reserved for cold war Communists.

Hostility to the changes in land use are very real and very strong, particularly in the small towns that surround the monument. Sentiment has been so strong that the BLM has been forced to revise its schedule for implementing changes in land access. In fact, despite all the sturm and drang, scarcely anything has changed in terms of agricultural or recreational access since the monument was declared.

What does this means to travelers who want to visit the monument? Keep in touch with the monument's official website to keep on top of changes that may occur and be mindful about what you say. Even though you may consider yourself a good global citizen with sound environmental opinions, to a resident of the Escalante area you may be the incarnation of his or her nightmare—a tree-hugging environmentalist with designs on the family farm.

NUCLEAR WASTE DISPOSAL ON THE GOSHUTE INDIAN RESERVATION

The disposal of nuclear waste from atomic energy generation plants has long been a problem, as the waste has typically been stored at the plants themselves, which don't have adequate or safe storage facilities. However, it's not exactly easy to get someone to open up his land to build a nuclear waste dump: it's the ultimate Not In My Back Yard (NIMBY) situation.

Scientists have isolated a number of sites in the Nevada Desert that they claim could be used to create a safe and stable storage facility—areas with little ground water to contaminate, few faults that could be triggered by an earthquake, and with almost no population centers around to irradiate if something did go wrong.

Although the siting of a long-term nuclear waste dump is being fought by many in Nevada, the Goshute Indian tribe and the federal government have arrived at an interim solution to the storage of nuclear waste. The Goshute invited the federal government and a consortium of eight power generation companies to build a temporary storage facility on their arid, west-central Utah reservation. In return, the Goshute, one of the poorest tribes in the United States, are expected to receive a windfall of money and infrastructure development.

The waste storage facility is due to break ground in 2001. However, potent opponents—including many from within the tribe and the state government—threaten to derail the project. Utah Governor Michael Leavitt has vowed to close state road access to the reservation if the plans go forward.

CHEMICAL WEAPONS AND THE TOOELE ARMY DEPOT

In the summer of 1996, the Army began burning part of the nation's store of chemical weapons at the Tooele Army Depot, located 10 miles south of the town of Tooele and 55 miles from Salt Lake City. The simultaneous incineration of the U.S. and Soviet stockpiles of poison gas and blistering agents was part of an agreement reached by the two countries in the late 1980s.

The Tooele Army Depot holds the nation's single largest cache of chemical weapons, with 44 percent of the arsenal stored in underground bunkers called igloos. Part of the reason for burning the weapons, besides treaty requirements, is that there is a far greater risk of leakage and environmental damage in leaving the chemical agents in the present bunkers than there is in incinerating them. Tooele is on a major earthquake fault zone, and a large temblor could cause a release from the bunkers. As it is, about three weapons leaks a week are detected—though contained—in the current igloos.

The Tooele incinerator was the first to go into operation in the United States (a total of eight chemical weapons depots are scattered across the country, and all will incinerate their weapons on site), and the plant is a prototype of the weapons-destruction factories to be erected elsewhere. The gases to be destroyed include sarin (the poison gas used by a Japanese cult in the notorious 1995 subway disaster), mustard gas, nerve gas, and lewisite, a skin-blistering agent.

The incineration of the chemical weapons has proved to be a hot issue, with many groups interested in public health and the environment seeking to prohibit operation of the burners. Opponents fear that the plants are unsafe and that there is a high risk of accidental release of toxins into the air. Proponents argue that there is a far greater risk to public health and the environment by leaving the chemical weapons in the bunkers.

The plant burned the first of its 1.1-million-item chemical weapon arsenal in August 1996. Within a week the plant had to close when traces of sarin were detected in the end-of-the-line air filters—the final stage before the air was released into the environment. After changing gaskets and fine-tuning the air pressure in the release chamber, the incineration began again after a week. Meanwhile, many residents of the area await more problems and fear a major release in the future.

HISTORY

PRE-SETTLEMENT UTAH

Utah in Prehistory

Archaeologists have evidence that Paleo-Indians began to wander across the region that would become Utah about 15,000 years ago—hunting big game and gathering plant foods. The climate was probably cooler and wetter when the first Indians arrived; food plants and game animals would have been more abundant than today. The early tribes continued their primitive hunting and gathering despite climate changes and the extinction of many big-game species about 10,000 years ago.

The first tentative attempts at agriculture were introduced from the south about 2,000 years ago and brought about a slow transition to a settled village life. The Fremont culture emerged in the northern part of the Colorado Plateau, the Anasazi in the southern part. Although both groups developed crafts such as basketry, pottery, and jewelry, only the Anasazi progressed to the construction of masonry buildings in their villages. Their corn, beans, and squash enabled them to be less reliant on migration and to construct year-round village sites. Thousands of stone dwellings, ceremonial kivas, and towers built by the Anasazi still stand. Both groups also left behind intriguing rock art, either pecked into the surfaces (petroglyphs) or painted on (pictographs). The Anasazi and the Fremont departed from this region about 800 years ago, perhaps because of drought, warfare, or disease. Some of the Anasazi moved south and joined the Pueblo tribes of present-day Arizona and New Mexico. The fate of the Fremont Indians remains a mystery.

About the same time, perhaps by coincidence, the nomadic Shoshoni in the north and the Utes and Paiutes in the south moved through Utah; none of these groups seemed to have knowledge of their more sophisticated predecessors. Relatives of the Athapascans of western Canada, the seminomadic Navajo, wandered into New Mexico and Arizona between A.D. 1300 and 1500. This adaptable tribe learned agriculture, weaving, pottery, and other skills from their Pueblo neighbors and became expert horsepeople and sheepherders with livestock obtained from the Spanish.

The size of prehistoric Indian populations has varied greatly in Utah. There were probably few inhabitants during the Archaic period (before A.D. 500), but many more during the time of the Anasazi and Fremont cultures (A.D. 500–1250), rising to a peak of perhaps 500,000. Except for the Athapascan-speaking Navajo, all of Utah's historic tribes spoke Shoshonian languages and had similar cultures.

Explorers and Colonizers

In 1776, Spanish explorers of the Dominguez-Escalante Expedition were the first Europeans to visit and describe the region during their unsuccessful attempt to find a route west to California. Utes guided the Spanish expedition through the Uinta Basin.

Anasazi bowl found near St. George

BUREAU OF AMERICAN ETHNOLOGY

Retreating to New Mexico, the explorers encountered great difficulties in the canyons of southern Utah before finding a safe ford across the Colorado River. This spot, known as the "Crossing of the Fathers," now lies under Lake Powell. Later explorers established the Old Spanish Trail through this area of Utah to connect New Mexico with California.

Mountain Men

Adventurous mountain men seeking beaver pelts and other furs entered northern Utah in the mid-1820s. They explored the mountain ranges, the rivers, and the Great Salt Lake and blazed most of the trails later used by wagon trains, the Pony Express, telegraph lines, and the railroads. By 1830, most of the mountain men had moved on to better trapping areas and left the land to the Indians; some, however, returned to guide government explorers and groups of pioneer settlers. The names of several mountain men are remembered on maps today: Peter Skene Ogden (Ogden), Etienne Provost (Provo), Jim Bridger (Bridgerland is the nickname of Cache and Rich Counties), John H. Weber (Weber River and County), and William Ashley (Ashley National Forest).

Joseph Walker, who served under Captain Benjamin Bonneville, crossed the northwest corner of Utah in 1833 on a trip to California. He reported such difficult conditions that no one else attempted the route for the rest of the decade. California-bound wagon trains took heed and followed a more northerly path through Idaho on the Oregon Trail. An exception was the Bartleson-Bidwell wagon train, which turned south into Utah in 1841 and skirted the northern edges of the Great Salt Lake and the Great Salt Lake Desert. Though members suffered immense hardships and later had to abandon their wagons, they eventually made it across. The group was the first to take wagons across Utah and included the first European women known to have crossed Utah and Nevada to California.

In 1843, John C. Frémont led one of his several government-sponsored scientific expeditions into Utah. Frémont determined the salinity of the Great Salt Lake and laid to rest speculation that a river drained the lake into the Pacific Ocean. Two years later, he led a well-prepared group across the heart of the dreaded Great Salt Lake Desert despite warnings from the local In-

dians that no one had crossed it and survived. His accounts of the region described not only the salty lake and barren deserts but also the fertile valleys near the Wasatch Range. Mormon leaders planning a westward migration from Nauvoo, Illinois, carefully studied Frémont's reports.

Langsford Hastings, an ambitious politician, seized the opportunity to promote Frémont's desert route as a shortcut to California. Hastings had made the trip on horseback but failed to anticipate the problems of a wagon train. On this route in 1846, the Donner-Reed wagon train became so bogged down in the salt mud that many wagons were abandoned. Moreover, an 80-mile stretch between waterholes proved too far for many of the oxen, which died from dehydration. Today, motorists can cruise in comfort along I-80 on a similar route between Salt Lake City and Wendover.

Native Americans vs. Settlers

The Paiutes and Utes befriended and guided the early explorers and settlers, but troubles soon began for these and other Indian groups when they saw their lands taken over by farmers and ranchers. None of the tribes proved a match for the white population, which eventually drove the Indians from the most desirable lands and settled them on the state's five reservations.

The Navajo's habit of raiding neighboring tribes and white settlements brought about their downfall. In 1863–1864 the U.S. Army rounded up all the Navajo they could find and forced the survivors on "The Long Walk" from Fort Defiance in northeastern Arizona to a bleak camp in eastern New Mexico. This internment was a dismal failure, and the Navajo were released four years later.

In 1868, the federal government "awarded" to the Navajo land that has since grown to a giant reservation spreading from northeastern Arizona into adjacent Utah and New Mexico.

THE MORMON MIGRATION

The Early Mormon Church

At the time of his revelations, the founder of the Mormon Church, Joseph Smith, worked as a farmer in the state of New York. In 1830, he and his followers founded the new religion and published the first edition of the Book of Mormon. But Smith's revelations evoked fear and anger in many of his neighbors, and in 1831 he and his new church moved to Kirtland, Ohio. They set to work building a temple for sacred ordinances, developing a missionary program, and recruiting new followers. Mormons also settled farther west in Missouri, where they made plans for a temple and a community of Zion.

Persecution by non-Mormons continued to mount in both Ohio and Missouri, fueled largely by the church's polygamist practices, the prosperity of its members, and the Latter-day Saint (LDS) claim that it was the "true" church. Many perceived the Mormons as a dire threat to existing political, economic, and religious systems; Missourians disliked the Mormons' anti-slavery views. Violence by gangs of armed men eventually forced church members to flee for their lives.

The dark winter of 1838–1839 found Joseph Smith in jail on treason charges and many church members without homes or legal protection. The Missouri Mormons made their way east to Illinois, not knowing where else to go. Brigham Young, a member of the Council of the Twelve Apostles, directed this exodus, foreshadowing the much longer migration he would lead eight years later.

Nauvoo the Beautiful

The Mormons managed to purchase a large tract of swampy land along the Mississippi River in Illinois and set to work draining swamps and building a city. Joseph Smith, allowed to escape

from the Missouri jail, named the Mormons' new home Nauvoo—a Hebrew word for "the beautiful location." Despite extreme poverty and the inability to secure reparations for the losses they had suffered in Missouri, the Mormons succeeded in building an attractive city that would one day rival any in the United States. A magnificent temple, begun in 1841, rose above Nauvoo. Despite their success, the Mormons continued to face virulent opposition from those who objected to their religion.

Smith, who had withstood tarring and feathering among other punishments, met his death in 1844 at Carthage, Illinois. He had voluntarily surrendered to the authorities to stand trial for treason, but a mob stormed the jail and killed both Smith and his brother Hyrum in a hail of bullets. Opponents thought that the Mormons would disband on the death of their leader. When they did not, their crops and houses were destroyed and their livestock was driven off. Brigham Young, who succeeded Smith, realized the Mormons would never find peace in Illinois. He and other leaders began looking toward the vastness of the West. They hoped the remote Rocky Mountains would provide a sanctuary from mobs and politicians. Plans for departure from Nauvoo began in the autumn of 1845.

The Mormon Exodus

Attacks against Nauvoo's citizens made life so difficult that they evacuated the following February despite severe winter weather. Homes, businesses, the temple, and most of their personal

KAREN McKINLEY

possessions were left behind as the Mormons crossed the Mississippi into Iowa. (Mobs later took over the town and desecrated the temple; not a single stone of the structure is in its original position today.) The group slowly pushed westward through the snow and mud. Faith, a spirit of sharing, and competent leadership enabled them to survive.

Brigham Young thought it best not to press on all the way to the Rocky Mountains that first year, so the group spent a second winter on the plains. Dugouts and log cabins housed more than 3,500 people at Winter Quarters, near present-day Omaha. By the early spring of 1847, the leaders had worked out plans for the rest of the journey. The Salt Lake Valley, an uninhabited and isolated region, would be its goal. Mountain men encountered on the journey gave discouraging descriptions of this place as a site for a major settlement. Samuel Brannan, a Mormon who had settled on the West Coast, rode east to meet Brigham Young and present glowing reports of California. But Young wouldn't be swayed from his original goal. On July 24, 1847, Young arrived at the edge of the Salt Lake Valley and announced, "This is the right place."

The City of Zion
The pioneers immediately set to work digging irrigation canals, planting crops, constructing a small fort, and laying out a city. Nearly 2,000 more immigrants arrived that same summer of 1847.

By necessity, these early citizens had to be self-sufficient; the nearest outposts of civilization lay 1,000 miles away. Through trial and error, farmers learned techniques of irrigating and farming the desert land. The city continued to grow—immigrants poured in; tanneries, flour mills, blacksmith shops, stores, and other enterprises developed under church direction; residential neighborhoods sprang up; and workers commenced raising the religious structures that still dominate the area around Temple Square.

The Colonization of Utah
Soon other areas in Utah were colonized: In 1849–1850, Mormon leaders in Salt Lake City took the first steps in exploring the rest of the state when they sent an advance party led by Parley P. Pratt to southern Utah. Encouraging re-

ports of rich iron ore west of Cedar Valley and of fertile land along the Virgin River convinced the Mormons to expand southward.

Calls went out for members to establish missions and to mine the iron ore and supply iron products needed for the expanding Mormon empire. In 1855, a successful experiment in growing cotton along Santa Clara Creek, near present-day St. George, aroused considerable interest among the Mormons. New settlements soon arose in the Virgin River Valley. However, poor roads hindered development of the cotton and iron industries, which mostly ended when cheaper products began arriving on the transcontinental railroad.

In the 1870s and early 1880s, the Mormon Church sent out calls for members to colonize lands east of the Wasatch Plateau. Though at first the land looked harsh and barren, crops and orchards eventually prospered with irrigation.

An Agrarian Paradise
By the end of the 19th century, the small agricultural settlements in Utah—mostly free of gentile influence—had by and large become the utopian religious communities envisioned by the religion's founders. Various tenets of the faith dictated nearly all aspects of life, from the width of the streets to social customs. Cultural homogeneity was greatly stressed; farmers and ranchers were discouraged from living on their land and encouraged instead to live in towns within range of the church. For a period, the Mormon Church encouraged full-fledged communal and cooperative farm towns as the ideal social structure.

The Mormons were hardworking farmers and managed to convert an unyielding desert into a land of abundance. Streams were diverted into irrigation canals, and acres of orchards and fields blossomed. Little farm towns, all laid out with uniform street grids, were planted with trees and flowers; substantial homes of stone announced the prosperity of the Mormon way of life.

The internal structure of the church—the ward (the parish) and stake (the diocese)—became the organizing principle of all religious and social life. Nearly all the social events of a small community were sponsored by the church, including dances, sports events, hay rides, swimming parties, and picnics. The overlap between church and civic authority was nearly complete.

The Road to Statehood

After many years of persecution, the early Mormons realized the importance of self-government. However, when the Mormon pioneers arrived in their new homeland of Zion, the land actually belonged to Mexico. However, after victory in the Mexican War in 1848, the United States took possession of a vast territory in the American West, including the land that would become Utah.

The Mormon Church quickly assessed the positive benefits that statehood would bring the new territory, and in 1849 called a convention "to consider the political needs of the community." The convention created the proposed state of Deseret that encompassed a great swath of the West, including all or parts of the current states of Utah, Nevada, Arizona, Wyoming, Colorado, New Mexico, Oregon, Idaho, and parts of southern California (San Diego was to be the state's port city). The convention wrote a constitution, elected officials (Brigham Young was elected governor), and sent a delegate to the U.S. Congress. However, the House of Representatives declined to admit the delegate from Deseret, and the statehood was effectively quashed. In fact, Mormon-dominated Utah would find it exceedingly difficult to attain statehood. Nearly 50 years would pass before Utah would finally become a state.

The federal Senate did pass legislation naming Utah as a territory in 1850; however, a number of factors—especially the thorny cultural and moral issues surrounding polygamy—worked to exacerbate tensions between the new territory and the federal government.

In 1857–1858, the U.S. government sent a 2,500-man army to occupy Salt Lake City and remove Brigham Young from the governorship (accompanying the army was Alfred Cummings, whom President Buchanan had selected as territorial governor). The army reached Salt Lake City to find it newly deserted, and Cummings assumed the governorship, ending at least in theory Utah's flirtation for theocracy. Cummings soon made peace with the Mormons and residents returned to Salt Lake City.

Second and third attempts at statehood for Deseret were met in Washington with defeat and actually seemed to stir up anti-Mormon sentiment: Congress quickly passed legislation prohibiting polygamy in the territories. The same legislation also sought to disincorporate the Mormon Church.

The building of the transcontinental railroad through Utah in the 1860s decreased Utah's isolation from the rest of the United States; however, greater contact with the outside world also meant increased Mormon-gentile hostility. In 1874, Congress passed a bill effectively disenfranchising Mormon-controlled district courts. In 1879, the U.S. Supreme Court upheld legislation that made the practice of plural marriage a criminal offense. Subsequent federal legislation made it illegal for polygamists to vote, hold public office, or serve on juries. The result was persecution and pursuit of avowed polygamists, many of whom were forced into hiding or exile in Mexico. The federal government's anti-Mormon campaigns also had the effect of empowering the territory's non-Mormon minority far beyond its small power base.

In 1890, LDS President Wilford Woodruff issued the startling proclamation that henceforward he advised his brethren "to refrain from contracting any marriage forbidden by the law of the land." The new doctrine was published across the country, and while many doubted the proclamation's sincerity, it signaled a major shift in direction for the statehood movement. Finally, in 1894 Congress passed the Enabling Act, which set forth the steps Utah had to follow in order to achieve statehood (the Act stipulated that the state constitution declare polygamy be banned forever). In 1896, President Cleveland proclaimed Utah as the 45th state.

It's helpful to remember the long and rancorous disputes between Utah's Mormon population and the federal government in the 19th century when trying to understand the state's fervid, ongoing anti-government tendencies. In some ways, the state's current anger over the establishment of the Grand Staircase–Escalante National Monument is just an example of Utah's long memory of perceived past injustice.

THE 20TH CENTURY

Utah's close-knit Mormon farm towns thrived from the late 19th century until the Depression years. The dust bowl years were particularly hard in Utah, as most farms were entirely dependent on irrigation and the decade-long drought greatly reduced the flow of already scarce water. Communities quickly rebounded during World War II, especially as federal money poured into military camps like Wendover Air Base in the deserts west of Salt Lake City.

The designation of five national parks (beginning with Zion in 1919), two huge national recreation areas, and the new and vast Grand Staircase–Escalante National Monument has brought an ever-increasing stream of tourists to the state. Today, tourism is the state's largest industry, dwarfing such stalwarts as mining and lumber.

Eighteen million people visit Utah annually (a full million of them from overseas). In 2002, the Winter Olympics will be held in the Salt Lake City area and the world spotlight will shine on the state as never before.

This surge of secular interest in the sacred homeland of the Mormon Church has led to concerns about the effect of the tourist boom on both the environment and traditional Mormon communities. Clashes between pro-growth business interests, environmentalists, and Mormon conservatives over the future of the state often make for some odd bedfellows.

GOVERNMENT AND ECONOMY

Utah became a territory in 1850 and a state in 1896. Utah is represented in Washington, D.C., by two senators and three representatives. Utah's two senators, Orrin Hatch and Bob Bennett, are both Republicans, as are all members of the house delegation.

The state legislature consists of 75 house members and 30 senators. Utah is generally considered to be one of America's most politically conservative states; it has the largest percentage of registered Republican voters of any state in the Union. In the 1992 presidential election, it was the only state in which Bill Clinton finished third.

Agriculture and mining have historically been considered the twin pillars of the Utah economy. Copper, tin, silver, lead, oil, and coal are among the primary minerals found in the state. Almost all agriculture is irrigated and includes a significant dairy industry, fruit orchards, grain, and hay production. Cattle and sheep graze the uplands and the mountain meadows.

Recently, tourism has overtaken these more traditional economic powerhouses to become the state's largest employer. Utah is also a center for the aerospace and military-related industries and has a number of military bases in the western deserts.

THE PEOPLE

One of the oddest statistics about Utah is that it's the most urban of America's western states. Eighty-five percent of the state's population of 2,129,836 citizens live in urban areas and a full 80 percent in the Wasatch Front area.

A relatively young population, combined with the Mormons' emphasis on family life and clean living, has resulted in Utah's having one of the highest birth rates and lowest death rates in the country. Racially, the state largely reflects the northern European origins of Mormon pioneers; in 1990 the state was 94 percent white. Small numbers of southern and eastern Europeans, many attracted by mining industries, also arrived during Utah's early years, but minorities form less than 7 percent of the state's population

today; they include Hispanics (3.9 percent), Native Americans (1.3 percent), Asians (0.9 percent), and African Americans (0.6 percent).

The state's Hispanic population live mostly along the fertile Wasatch Front, where they provide the backbone of the state's agricultural labor. There's also a sizeable Hispanic population in Salt Lake City.

UTAH'S NATIVE AMERICANS

Shoshoni

Nomadic bands of Shoshoni occupied much of northern Utah, southern Idaho, and western Wyoming for thousands of years. Horses ob-

UTAH STATE HISTORICAL SOCIETY

Shoshoni village

tained from the Plains Indians—who had obtained them from the Spanish—allowed hunting parties to cover a large range. The great Chief Washakie led his people for 50 years and negotiated the tribe's treaties with the federal government. The Washakie Indian Reservation, near Plymouth in far northern Utah, belongs to the Northwestern band of Shoshoni, though few Indians live there now. Tribal headquarters are in Rock Springs, Wyoming, south of the large Wind River Indian Reservation.

Goshute (or Gosiute)

This branch of the Western Shoshoni, more isolated than other Utah tribes, lived in the harsh Great Basin. They survived through intricate knowledge of the land and use of temporary shelters. These peaceful hunters and gatherers ate almost everything that they found—plants, birds, rodents, crickets, and other insects. Because the Indians had to dig for much of their food, early explorers called the tribe Digger Indians. White men couldn't believe these people survived in such a barren land of alkaline flats and sagebrush. Also known as the Newe, the tribe now

CHURCH OF JESUS CHRIST OF LATTER-DAY SAINTS

lives on the Skull Valley Indian Reservation in Tooele County and on the Goshute Indian Reservation along the Utah-Nevada border.

Ute

Several bands of Utes, or Núuci, ranged over large areas of central and eastern Utah and adjacent Colorado. Originally hunter-gatherers, they acquired horses in about 1800 and became skilled raiders. Customs adopted from Plains Indians included the use of rawhide, tepees, and the *travois* (a sled used to carry goods). The discovery of gold in southern Colorado and the pressures of farmers there and in Utah forced the Utes to move and renegotiate treaties many times. They now have the large Uintah and Ouray Indian Reservation in northeast Utah, the small White Mesa Indian Reservation in southeast Utah, and the Ute Mountain Indian Reservation in southwest Colorado and northwest New Mexico.

Southern Paiute

Six of the 19 major bands of the Southern Paiutes, or Nuwuvi, lived along the Santa Clara, Beaver, and Virgin Rivers and in other parts of

Ute mother and papoose

southwest Utah. Extended families hunted and gathered food together. Fishing and the cultivation of corn, beans, squash, and sunflowers supplemented the diet of most of the bands. Today, Utah's Paiutes have a tribal headquarters in Cedar City and scattered small parcels of reservation land. Southern Paiutes also live in southern Nevada and northern Arizona.

Navajo

Calling themselves Diné, the Navajo moved into the San Juan River area about 1600. The tribe has proved exceptionally adaptable in learning new skills from other cultures: many Navajo crafts, clothing, and religious practices have come from Indian, Spanish, and Anglo neighbors. As a tribe, the Navajo gave up their old hunting and gathering lifestyle, relying instead on the farming and shepherding techniques they had learned from the Spanish.

The Navajo have become one of the largest Native American groups in the country, occupying 16 million acres of exceptionally scenic land in southeast Utah and adjacent Arizona and New Mexico. Tribal headquarters is at Window Rock in Arizona.

THE MORMONS

If you're new to the "Beehive State," you'll find that you have plenty of opportunities to learn about Mormon history and religion. At least half of Utah's population actively participates in the Mormon Church; three quarters of the population was born into the faith. Temple Square in Salt Lake City offers excellent tours and exhibits about the church. You'll also find many other visitors' centers and historic sites scattered around the state.

The Church of Jesus Christ of Latter-day Saints, headquartered in Salt Lake City, has a worldwide membership of nearly 11 million, due largely to a vigorous missionary program. Members usually call themselves "Latter-day Saints". Nonmembers commonly use the nickname "Mormon" because of the emphasis the church puts on the Book of Mormon.

Members believe that God's prophets have restored teachings of the true Christian church to the world "in these latter days." Although the LDS church considers itself a Christian denomination, Mormons don't classify themselves as either Catholic or Protestant. They believe their church presidents, starting with Joseph Smith, to be prophets of God, and they hold both the Bible and the Book of Mormon as the sacred word of God. The latter, they believe, was revealed to Joseph Smith from 1823 to 1830. The text tells of three migrations from the Eastern Hemisphere to the New World and the history of the people who lived in the Americas from about 2200 B.C. to A.D. 500 421. The book contains 239 chapters, which include teachings Christ supposedly gave

Joseph Smith preaching to Native Americans in the Midwest

in the Americas, prophecy, doctrines, and epic tales of the rise and fall of nations. It's regarded by the church as a valuable addition to the Bible—but not a replacement.

Membership in the Mormon Church requires faith, a willingness to serve, tithing, and obedience to church authorities. The church emphasizes healthful living, moral conduct, secure family relationships, and a thoughtful approach to social services.

RELIGION

The Church of Jesus Christ of Latter-day Saints is by far the dominant religion in Utah; about 70 percent of the population belong to the church. Most major Christian denominations are represented in mid-sized towns, and in Salt Lake City there are small Jewish and Islamic congregations as well.

CONDUCT AND CUSTOMS

If you've never traveled in Utah before, you may find that Utahns don't initially seem as welcoming and outgoing as people in other western states. In many smaller towns, visitors from outside the community are a relatively new phenomenon, and not everyone in the state is anxious to have their towns turned into tourist or recreational meccas. The Mormons are very family- and community-oriented, and if certain individuals initially seem insular and uninterested in travelers, don't take it as unfriendliness.

Mormons are also very orderly and socially conservative people. Brash displays of rudeness or use of foul language in public will not make you popular.

Alcohol and Nightlife

Observant Mormons don't drink alcoholic beverages, and state laws have been drafted to make purchasing alcohol relatively awkward. If going out for drinks and nightclubbing is part of your idea of entertainment, you'll find that only Salt Lake City, Park City, and Moab offer much in the way of clubs and nightspots. Most towns have a liquor store; outside of the Wasatch Front and Moab, don't expect restaurants to have liquor licenses.

Private Clubs

Most drinking establishments—and certainly the ones that will seem most normal to outsiders—are private clubs. Clubs that serve hard liquor without

food and feature live music or other entertainment are almost all private clubs, which means you need to be a member to get in. Thankfully, it's not an overwhelming obstacle. You can buy a two-week membership, usually for $5.

Smoking

Smoking is taboo for observant Mormons, and in almost all public places smoking is prohibited. You're also not allowed to smoke on church grounds.

SAY IT RIGHT!

The following place names are easy to mispronounce. Say it like a local!

Duchesne	du-SHANE
Ephraim	E-from
Escalante	es-ka-LAN-tay
Hurricane	HUR-aken
Kanab	Ke-NAB
Lehi	LEE-hi
Manti	MAN-tie
Monticello	mon-ta-SELL-o
Nephi	NEE-fi
Panguitch	PAN-gwich
Salina	suh-LINE-uh
Tooele	Too-WIL-a
Uinta	u-INT-a
Weber	WE-ber

ON THE ROAD

RECREATION

OUTDOOR ACTIVITIES

By far the best place to begin looking for information on recreational opportunities in Utah is the comprehensive www.utah.com website. The site contains information on most sports and activities and it provides lots of links to yet more outfitters and sites.

Mountain Biking

More than any other single recreational activity, mountain biking has put Utah on the map. Trails in the Slickrock Canyon Country near Moab attract more than 150,000 biking enthusiasts a year, and now nearly all corners of the state promote their old Forest Service or mining roads as a biking paradise. If you're going to Utah with biking in mind, ask the state tourist office for a copy of its statewide *Bicycle Utah Vacation Guide,* which gives general information about biking paths throughout Utah and listings of tour operators, related organizations, and businesses. You can also contact the Bicycle Vacation Guide directly at P.O. Box 738, Park City, UT 84060, (435) 649-5806 or www.bicycleutah.com.

In general, Utah summers are too hot for mountain biking in the canyons. The peak season in Moab runs from March through May and again from September through November.

River Running

Rafting or canoeing Utah's rivers is another favorite activity for tourists and adventurers. The most notable float trip is down the Colorado River between Moab and the backwaters of Lake Powell. This multi-day trip passes through Cataract Canyon, and for spectacular adventure it's second only to trips through the Grand Canyon. The Green and San Juan Rivers are also popular. For these trips, you'll need to plan well in advance, as spaces are limited and demand more than outstrips availability. In towns like Moab, Green River, Vernal, and Bluff, a number of outfitters provide exciting day trips that can usually take people with only a day's notice. Ask state tourist offices for their *Utah Rivers* magazine or check out the official website at www.utah.com/raft.

Hiking, Backpacking, and Camping

Utah offers lots of backcountry for those interested in exploring the scenery on foot. One increasingly popular activity is canyoneering—exploring mazelike slot canyons. Hundreds of feet

THE 2002 OLYMPIC WINTER GAMES

The Winter Olympics come to northern Utah from February 8–24, 2002!

The Numbers

The games will be centered in Salt Lake City with events held in or near four other Utah cities. Salt Lake City is the largest city to have ever hosted the Winter Olympics, and organizers expect an estimated 2,345 athletes and 1,200 officials from 80 different countries. Approximately 9,000 media representatives will also be attending. The planning committee expects about a half-million spectators over the course of the 16-day event. Competition is scheduled for seven sports with 15 disciplines in 78 medal events.

In addition to the Winter Olympic Games, Salt Lake City will also host the Paralympic Winter Games, a winter sports competition for athletes with disabilities. The Paralympic Games will be held concurrent with the Olympics. Paralympic sports include Alpine skiing, Nordic skiing, short track racing, and ice sledge hockey; there will be 34 medal events. Event coordinators expect 1,100 parathletes from 40 different countries.

Venues

Olympic Village, where the athletes will be housed, is located on a 40-acre site on the University of Utah campus in Salt Lake City. Olympic Stadium (a.k.a., Rice-Eccles Stadium), where the opening and closing ceremonies take place, is also on campus. Medals ceremonies will take place in downtown Salt Lake City, at the Medals Plaza, between 200 West and 300 West on North Temple Street.

The Ice Sheet, Ogden: men's and women's curling competition.

Oquirrh Park Oval, Kearns: men's and women's speed skating.

Salt Lake Skating Arena (Delta Center), Salt Lake City: all figure skating events, short track speed skating.

Seven Peaks Hockey Arena, Provo: men's and women's ice hockey.

West Valley Hockey Arena ("E" Center), West Valley City: men's ice hockey, Paralympic ice sledge hockey, Paralympic short track racing.

Deer Valley Resort, Park City: men's and women's slalom and freestyle skiing.

Park City Mountain Resort, Park City: men's and women's snowboarding, men's and women's giant slalom skiing.

Snowbasin Ski Area, Ogden Valley: men's and women's downhill, combined downhill, and Super G skiing; Paralympic Alpine skiing.

Soldier Hollow, Wasatch State Park, Heber City: men's and women's biathlon, men's and women's cross-country skiing, Nordic combined skiing, and Paralympic Nordic skiing.

Utah Winter Sports Park, Park City: two-men, four-men, and two-women bobsleigh; men's, women's, and mixed luge; men's and women's skeleton, ski jumping, and Nordic combined ski jump.

Accommodations

The Salt Lake City Tourist and Visitor Information Center estimates that all available rooms within 50 miles of Salt Lake City will be reserved by mid-2000. That's not good news if you're reading this and haven't already made plans. However, many of the reservations are actually blanket bookings made by international Olympic committees, and many will be tentative. If you haven't already made reservations, this book is full of hotel listings and there's a no-charge on-line reservations website and toll-free phone number to help you find a room, courtesy of the Salt Lake Convention and Visitors Bureau. Contact them at (800) 847-5810 or www.saltlake.org/ reservations. However, expect to find many of the prices in this guide are doubled and the longer you wait to book a room, the longer your commute to the games will be. Good luck!

Information and Tickets

By far the best place to go for current information on the Winter Olympic Games is the official website, www.slc2002.org. Be sure to download the event schedule calendar. It's also the best place to go to find out about ticketing, as the information is quite fluid. Of the projected 700,000 tickets available to the general American public, at least 10 percent will be auctioned off on the Internet in the fall of 2000. Domestic Internet orders and mail-order sales will also begin in autumn 2000, with domestic over-the-counter sales beginning in 2001. A preference to Utah citizens will be given to 20 percent of all tickets for each event. Ticket prices vary, especially because of the ticket auctions, but the average price is below $82 and half the tickets are priced below $60. The system is quite confusing; it's best go to the website.

Contact the Salt Lake Organizing Committee, 299 South Main St., Ste. 1300, Salt Lake City, UT 84111, (801) 212-2002, www.slc2002.org.

SIGHTSEEING HIGHLIGHTS

Salt Lake City

Salt Lake City is home to the Church of Jesus Christ of Latter-day Saints, the Mormons. Temple Square preserves historic religious architecture, while the city booms with new businesses, restaurants, and the arts.

Every tourist should visit the sacred sights of Temple Square. Although the gleaming white temple is not open to non-Mormons, the tabernacle is. Plan to attend a free musical event (the 320-voice Mormon Tabernacle Choir has free concerts twice a week) to witness the structure's famed acoustics. Visitors' centers and museums explain the Mormon faith and display religious art. You can also visit Brigham Young's home, built in 1854.

The Utah State Capitol Building dominates the skyline just north of downtown. The building is modeled after the U.S. Capitol and sits amid 40 acres of lawns and gardens. Nearby is the Pioneer Memorial Museum, which tells the story of the 2,000-mile journey of the original Mormon pioneers in 1847.

Northern Utah

Park City and the other ski areas of the Wasatch Front have some of the finest powder snow skiing in North America and will host the 2002 Winter Olympics. Park City is also famed as a getaway for the rich and famous; this small town with a population of 6,500, has more art galleries than Salt Lake City and has one restaurant for every 60 inhabitants.

Ogden, just north of Salt Lake City, was once a thriving rail hub. Today it's practically subsumed as a suburb of Salt Lake City. The city's old downtown area, centered on 25th Street, retains its turn-of-the-20th-century storefronts, which are now home to good cafés and restaurants, plus antique stores and boutiques. Ogden's huge and handsome rail station at the head of 25th Street no longer receives rail passengers, but it does house four museums, a restaurant, and an art gallery.

Logan is one of the most attractive small cities in Utah: located in a green fertile valley and hedged round by towering peaks, its small downtown area has charming Victorian storefronts facing onto a park. Summer festivals make Logan a lively place. The nationally acclaimed Utah Festival Opera brings big voices to town for a three-opera season; Festival of the American West brings in buckskin-clad moun-

tain men and cowboy poets; and the Old Lyric Theater hosts a season of musicals and comedies. Bear Lake, on the Idaho border, is a large, high-altitude lake with good fishing and cool summer temperatures, and is popular with the motorboat set.

West-Central Utah

This is the part of Utah to visit if you want to get away from it all. The Great Basin desert alternates with arid mountain ranges, and only a few paved roads even cross this forlorn landscape. This is the best place in the state for rockhounding, and there's lots of history in the old mining ghost towns of Ophir, Gold Hill, and others. The Pony Express crossed this lonely stretch of desert, and remnants of old stations and inns can still be seen. If you're looking for solitude, backpacking trails lead into the little-visited Deep Creek and House Mountain Ranges. Just across the Utah border in Nevada is the Great Basin National Park, with Leman Caves (tours daily year-round), archeological sites, and alpine hiking.

Central Utah

Provo is Utah's second largest city and home to Brigham Young University. Provo is a good base for exploring the dramatic Wasatch peaks that rise directly behind the city. An especially nice back road is the Alpine Scenic Loop, which climbs up to 7,500 feet through dramatic mountain scenery. Along the way you'll pass Sundance Resort, owned by Robert Redford and noted for its skiing and good restaurants. Timpanogos Cave National Monument is on the north flank of Mt. Timpanogos and is open in summer for tours (it's an hour-long strenuous hike to the cave's entrance).

South of Provo are small sleepy towns that serve the needs of local ranchers and farmers. Fillmore was once the territorial capital of Utah, and the 1855 statehouse is preserved as a museum. The town of Beaver has over 200 historic homes and buildings, most from the 1870s.

To the east, U.S. 89 follows the Sanpete River, which lies in a lovely agricultural valley flanked by mountains. The little towns along the route are showcases of historic Mormon architecture.

Northeastern Utah

Dinosaur country! Vernal and Price each have dinosaur museums and easy access to dinosaur digs and paleontology labs. Dinosaur National Monument preserves a quarry with semi-excavated bones, plus a museum and research center; the Cleveland-Lloyd Dinosaur Quarry is less developed and features trails to dig sites.

The Green River cuts a mighty canyon through the Uinta Mountains, exposing cliffs of deep red and ochre. Called the Flaming Gorge, the canyon now contains a reservoir that's the center of a national recreation area and the focus of lots of boat-centric recreation. Rafting the Green River below the Flaming Gorge Dam is a popular summer adventure for families.

This region has a number of excellent ancient Native American rock art and petroglyph areas, particularly along the Nine Mile Canyon Backcountry Byway (east of Price) and at Dry Fork, northeast of Vernal. The lofty but rounded Uinta Mountains are noted for their high-country, trout-rich streams and lakes.

Southwestern Utah

St. George, located at the northern tip of the Sonoran Desert, makes the most of the year-round sun as a retirement and golf center. Just to the north, Cedar City is a pleasant town known for its summer Utah Shakespeare Festival, with eight plays a season. Kanab has a long history as a film-making center: tour the sets where *Gunsmoke* and *My Friend Flika,* plus nearly 150 other films and TV shows, were shot.

Zion National Park is one of the most popular in the park system: hiking trails lead up narrow canyons cut into massive stone cliffs, passing along quiet pools of water and groves of willows. Zion is so breathtaking and awe-inspiring that the early Mormons named these canyons for their vision of heaven.

Bryce Canyon National Park has famous vistas across an eroded amphitheater of pink sandstone hoodoos. Easy hikes lead down into a wonderland of fanciful formations and outcrops.

Other areas of southwestern Utah are not quite so busy. The Cedar Breaks National Monument preserves an area with formations similar to Bryce

Canyon, but without the rampaging tour bus crowds. Just below Bryce Canyon, Kodachrome Basin State Park is ringed by trademark pink cliffs, plus odd rock pillars called sand pipes. Red Canyon is also adjacent to Bryce Canyon and shares its geology, but since it's not a national park, you can mountain bike and ride horses amid the red rock formations.

Southeastern Utah

Moab is the center of the vast recreational area known as the Canyonlands. Mountain biking is spectacular here; rafting down the Colorado and Green Rivers is nearly mandatory. The Canyonlands is an exciting and vibrant destination filled with outdoor recreation, brewpubs, and large youthful crowds.

Vast chunks of the land here are preserved as national parks or monuments. Just up the road from Moab is Arches National Park, with its famous rock bridges. Capitol Reef and Canyonlands National Parks are remote and other-worldly, and a visit that involves more than just a drive to a vista point requires a little planning and forethought. This area offers a wealth of rock art, Anasazi ruins, and vertical desert landscapes—a perfect place for a multi-day backpacking trip.

The new Grand Staircase–Escalante National Monument preserves some of the Southwest's best canyon hiking. Numerous long-distance hiking trails follow the slot canyons of the Escalante River system. Off-road driving enthusiasts follow the Hole-in-the-Rock Road or the Burr Trail to visit some of the same landscape; just following scenic UT 12 across Escalante country in a car is an eye-popping experience to most travelers.

The far southeastern corner of Utah is home to the famed red rock towers at Monument Valley, plus the charming town of Bluff. From here explore side trips to rock-art sites, or take a rafting trip down the San Juan River. If all this desert has you hankering for water, go to Lake Powell, a massive reservoir on the Colorado River and a houseboating paradise.

---

deep but sometimes only wide enough for a hiker to squeeze through, these canyons are found in the southern part of the state, particularly near Escalante and in the Paria River area. You'll need to be fit and watch the weather carefully for flash floods to explore these regions.

Hikers will find great trails in almost all parts of the state. The rugged Wasatch Range near Salt Lake City is a popular day-hiking destination for urban residents of the Wasatch Front, while

the lofty, lake-filled Uintas in northeastern Utah are perfect for long-distance trips. The remote and little-explored deserts of western Utah make for great wilderness adventures. Much of the canyonlands of southern and southeastern Utah are accessible only by foot; visits to remote Anasazi ruins and petroglyphs reward the long-distance hiker.

Campers are in luck in Utah. The state has a highly developed network of campgrounds, both public and private. During peak tourist season, you'll need to make reservations or arrive at your destination early.

Skiing and Snowboarding

You may have noticed the legend on the license plates: "Ski Utah!" It is almost a command during the winter months. While skiing has always been excellent in the Wasatch Front ski areas near Salt Lake City and Park City, which provide some of the best powder skiing in North America, the state's recent promotional programs seem to be paying off. Winter tourism in Utah is way up, and Utah will host the 2002 Olympic Winter Games. If you've always wanted to have a chance to ski or board Olympic-quality slopes, plan a trip to Utah: all the runs and facilities for the Olympics are already in place.

Fishing

The Wasatch and Uinta Ranges are dotted with lakes and drained by streams that are rich in rainbow and cutthroat trout. Fly-fishing is a major sport in many mountain communities, and most towns will have at least one fly shop and an outfitter anxious to take you out to a stream. Favorite fishing spots include Bear Lake, with good fishing for lake and cutthroat trout; Flaming Gorge Reservoir on the Green River has good fishing for lake trout, smallmouth bass, and kokanee salmon; and Lake Powell has good fishing for catfish, striper, and bass.

Horseback Riding

While guest ranches are the best places to experience a Western-style vacation on horseback (see Guest Ranches under Accommodations, following), the ski areas at Park City also offer riding in summer. In winter, sleigh rides are featured.

Rockhounding

Utah is rich in curious stones, fossils, and gems. The lack of vegetation and the high level of erosion make rockhounding a relatively simple matter. One of the best places to plan a rock-hunting expedition is the Delta area, where you will want to explore for geodes, agates and garnets, and other treasures.

Golfing

There are dozens and dozens of golf courses across Utah. There are a number of notable

courses in the Salt Lake City area, and also near Ogden, Logan, Provo, and Park City. The state's greatest concentration of courses, though, is in St. George, in the southern part of the state. Perhaps it's rhetorical to wonder which comes first, retirees or golf courses, but St. George's excellent courses amid magnificent red-rock formations certainly have contributed mightily to the town's reputation as a retirement haven.

NATIONAL PARKS AND MONUMENTS

Utah is home to five major national parks, seven national monuments, two national recreation areas, and one national historic site. Three of the crown jewels of the national park system—Zion, Arches, and Bryce Canyon—are here, as well as the less traveled Capitol Reef and Canyonlands Parks. Just across the border in Nevada is the new Great Basin National Park, and just south in Arizona is the Grand Canyon. These national park areas are the state's largest tourist attractions, bringing in nearly 18 million people yearly.

The parks are all open year-round, though spring and fall are the best times to visit—you'll avoid the heat and crowds of high summer. The entry fee for the national parks has gone up greatly in the past few years; admission to Zion is now $20 per vehicle. If you're planning on making the rounds of the Utah national parks, it's an excellent idea to purchase the park system's Golden Eagle Passport ($65) or the National Parks Pass ($50), both of which cover admission costs at national parks.

STATE PARKS

Utah boasts 45 state parks, ranging from golf courses to fishing holes, from historic forts to Anasazi ruins. Entry fees to state parks vary, though in general there's a $4 or $5 per-vehicle charge at the recreational parks. Many of these have campgrounds; you can make reservations by calling (800) 322-3770. For general information on Utah's state parks, contact Utah State Parks, 1636 W. North Temple, Ste. 116, Salt Lake City, UT 84116-3456, (801) 538-7220. Or dial up the website at parks.state.ut.us.

WILDERNESS TRAVEL

As more people seek relief from the stress of urban life, wilderness areas are becoming increasingly popular. Fortunately, Utah has an abundance of this fragile and precious resource. The many designated wilderness areas have been closed to mechanized vehicles (including mountain bikes) to protect both the environment and the experience of solitude. Most designated areas lie within national forests or Bureau of Land Management lands and many are free to visit without a permit; others require permits and some have entrance fees. The national parks and monuments require backcountry permits for overnight stays.

Some of the most spectacular and memorable hiking and camping await the prepared outdoorsperson. If you are new to hiking, start with easy trips, then work up gradually. The following are suggestions for backcountry travel and camping:

- Before heading into the backcountry, ask a ranger about weather, water sources, fire danger, trail conditions, and regulations. Backpacking stores also provide good information.
- Tell rangers or other reliable people where you are going and when you expect to return; they'll alert rescuers if you go missing.
- Travel in small groups for the best experience (group size may also be regulated).
- Try not to camp on meadows, as the grass is easily damaged.
- Use a portable stove to avoid leaving fire scars.
- Resist the temptation to shortcut switchbacks; this causes erosion and can be dangerous.
- Avoid digging trenches or cutting vegetation.
- Help preserve old Indian and historic ruins.
- Camp at least 300 feet away from springs, creeks, and trails. Camp at least a quarter-mile from a *sole* water source to avoid scaring away wildlife and livestock.
- Avoid camping in washes at any time; hikers need to be alert to thunderstorms.
- Take care not to throw or kick rocks off trails—someone might be underneath you.
- Don't drink water directly from streams or lakes, no matter how clean the water appears; it may contain the parasitic protozoan *Giar-dia lamblia,* which causes giardiasis. Boiling water for several minutes will kill giardia as well as most other bacterial or viral pathogens. Chemical treatments and water filters usually work, too, although they're not as reliable as boiling (giardia spends part of its life in a hard shell that protects it from most chemicals).
- Bathe away from lakes, streams, and springs.
- Bring a trowel for personal sanitation; dig four to six inches deep.
- Bring plenty of feed for your horses and mules.
- Leave dogs at home if possible; they may disturb wildlife and other hikers and foul campsites. If you do bring a dog, please keep it under control at all times.
- Take home all your trash.
- If you realize you're lost, find shelter. If you're sure of a way to civilization and plan to walk out, leave a note with your departure time and planned route.

ARTS AND ENTERTAINMENT

Music
Generally speaking, Salt Lake City is the center of the state's arts scene. The state's Mormon heritage is reflected in the city's love of and support for fine music. The glittering Abravanel Concert Hall is home to the noted Utah Symphony, and the tabernacle at Temple Square is often filled with concerts and recitals. The famed Mormon Tabernacle Choir performs here, as do various other church-related music groups. Best of all, all performances at Temple Square are free, making this a great opportunity for travelers to soak up culture at a good price.

Salt Lake City is also the state's major venue for rock and alternative music. A number of lively clubs host both local bands and traveling acts from both coasts. In most cases, music clubs are private clubs and you'll either need to buy a temporary membership or get sponsored by a member. Despite the rigmarole, the music's usually good and the crowds are interesting.

Come summer, there's fine music at more out-of-the-way places. A number of venues at Park City offer a full summer schedule ranging from rock concerts at The Canyons Ski Area to the Utah Symphony at classy Deer Valley Resort. In Logan's sparkling Capitol Theatre, the

Utah Opera Company puts on a summer season of grand opera.

Theater

Again, Salt Lake City is the center of things theatrical in Utah. There are several year-round theatrical troupes dishing up everything from Broadway musicals to serious plays like Tony Kushner's *Angels in America.*

In the summer, Cedar City's Utah Shakespearean Festival (visit www.bard.org for more information) offers eight different plays performed by a professional repertory company. Both Shakespearean and contemporary plays are featured; the Bard is performed under the stars in an outdoor theater.

Dance

Salt Lake City supports a number of dance troupes, all with excellent reputations. Ballet West performs a mix of classical and contemporary pieces, while the Ririe-Woodbury Dance Company has a more eclectic approach to dance.

Cinema

While you'll be able to see most first-run films and some art-house fare in Salt Lake City and, to a lesser extent, in smaller cities in Utah, the real cinematic event in Utah is the Sundance Film Festival, held every January in Park City. Founded by actor Robert Redford as a forum for little-seen documentary and independent films, the festival has grown into a major showcase of new, high-quality cinema. Make lodging and ticket reservations well in advance if you want to attend. For more information and to get on the mailing list, call (801) 328-FILM.

Museums

Utahns are very proud of their pioneer past and nearly every community in the state will have a Daughters of Utah Pioneers (DUP) museum, which recounts the story of local Mormon settlement. In fact, church history and state history are so closely interconnected that the primary state history museums are the various Temple Square institutions and the Mormon-dominated Pioneer Memorial Museum. The museum at the Utah Historical Society isn't even in the same league.

Utah has a number of good museums dedicated to the dinosaurs and other forms of ancient life. The area around Price and Vernal is rich in fossils, and both towns have good dinosaur museums; additionally, there are fossil digs with visitors' centers at Dinosaur National Monument and at the Cleveland-Lloyd Dinosaur Quarry. The brand new Museum of Ancient Life at Lehi has one of the largest collections of complete dinosaur skeletons in the country.

Ogden has converted its large and handsome railroad depot into a four-museum complex with collections of minerals, fine art, firearms, and historic automobiles and train cars.

Art Galleries

Utah isn't exactly known for its fine art collections, but the Salt Lake Art Center has a changing lineup of traveling shows that focus on regional artists. The universities in Salt Lake City, Provo, and Logan each have art galleries, and Ogden boasts the Myra Powell Art Gallery in the historic train depot. If you're looking for commercial art galleries, the state's richest paydirt is in Park City. This small resort community has more fine art galleries than Salt Lake City.

ACCOMMODATIONS

Utah is a major tourist destination, and you can plan on finding high-quality, reasonably priced motels and hotels in most cities and towns. Reservations are a good idea in major centers like Salt Lake City, Park City, and Moab—especially on weekends. There are limited rooms available off-season along the national parks loop (some establishments are seasonal), so it's a good idea to call ahead to make sure there's a room at the inn.

Hostels

Hostels aren't available everywhere in Utah. Salt Lake City has a couple, as do Moab, Hurricane, and Kanab. Hostels are open to travelers of all ages, and most Utah hostels don't require membership cards. You may need to provide your own sleeping cloth. For locations of hostels in Utah and elsewhere in the United States, order a free hostelling map of the United States from Hostelling International (HI-AYH) Map Brochure,

733 15th St. NW, Ste. 840, Washington, D.C. 20005, www.hiayh.org.

B&Bs

With its wealth of pioneer-era homes and mansions, Utah also offers travelers some comfortable bed-and-breakfast accommodations. If you're only familiar with British-style B&Bs, you'll discover that in American B&Bs are more like small, well-appointed inns—usually in historically or architecturally significant homes. Smoking and pets are restricted, some inns have rules against young children, and others are reserved for couples only. Most require advance booking.

In Utah's B&Bs you'll find a friendly welcome, personalized advice on sites and recreation, a chance to meet fellow travelers, and, of course, a fine breakfast.

For more information on B&Bs, contact the visitors' centers in the regions you plan to visit; contact B&B Inns of Utah Incorporated, P.O. Box 3066, Park City, UT 84060-3066, (435) 645-8068, www.bbiu.org, a membership organiza-tion representing B&Bs across the state; or contact the Utah Travel Council, (801) 538-1030, for a more general list.

Guest Ranches

Utah has fewer guest ranches than other western states, but a number have sprung up here and there. Most are family ranches that take in guests during the summer. These tend to be authentic, horse-powered operations where you'll work alongside the family and stay in no-frills cabins or bunkhouses. Others are more upscale and offer a dude-ranch atmosphere with a number of recreational options.

Most guest ranches ask for minimum stays, and prices include all meals and lodging. Advance reservations are usually required. If you're contemplating staying at a guest ranch, be sure to ask specific questions about lodgings and work requirements. Expectations of the guest and host can vary widely. The Utah Travel Council can provide a full listing of Utah guest ranches; it's also available from the www.utah.com website.

FOOD AND DRINK

Utah is not one of the culinary capitals of the world. Outside of Salt Lake City, Park City, and Moab, you'll find restaurants in Utah generally serve standard American fare, with family restaurants and grills setting the standards in even midsize towns. Even the steak house, omnipresent elsewhere in the West, is curiously absent here. Most towns have a vintage American-Chinese restaurant, which is usually the best bet for a vegetarian. After a couple of days on the road, you may be glad to note that Pizza Hut usually offers a salad bar and that you can get a fresh salad at McDonalds.

The good news is that in the three towns noted above, you can eat quite well. Park City has some excellent high-end restaurants and plenty of hearty fare for those on a budget. Moab offers a varied selection of restaurants, including two excellent brewpubs with complete dining facilities. Salt Lake City has restaurants to satisfy most every taste, including some excellent ethnic options.

Travelers will also find that having a drink with your meal is easier in the above three cities than elsewhere in the state. Access to alcohol in restaurants varies quite a bit from community to community, and some towns are practically "dry"—alcohol-free.

Drinking Laws

The state's liquor laws are rather confusing and peculiar. Several different kinds of establishments are licensed to sell alcoholic beverages.

Taverns, which include brewpubs, can only sell 3.2 percent beer (not wine, which is classed as hard liquor in Utah). You don't need to purchase food or be a member of a private club to have a beer in a tavern. With the exception of brewpubs, taverns are usually fairly derelict and not especially cheery places to hang out.

Licensed restaurants are able to sell beer, wine, and hard liquor too. However, servers are not able to ask you if you care for a drink; such solicitation is barred by law. You'll need to specifically ask for a drink or the drink menu in order to begin the process. In Salt Lake City, Moab, and Park City, most restaurants have liquor licenses. In other cities and towns, very few eating establishments offer alcohol.

UTAH BREWPUBS

Utah is catching up with the rest of the West and the brewpub craze. Each of the following pubs brews its own beer and serves full meals. Brewpubs by and large escape the restrictions that apply to other bars (though all beer is 3.2 percent alcohol), and travelers will find them good places to meet the locals and eat light meals.

SALT LAKE CITY

Squatters Pub Brewery, 147 W. Broadway, (801) 363-2739. Utah's first brewpub, offers outdoor seating.

Marmot Mesa Brewery and Alehouse, 163 W. Pierpont, (801) 994-2800. Not your average pub grub: much better and more of it. Less of a scene than the other brewpubs.

Red Rock Brewing Company, 254 S. 200 West, (801) 521-7446. Very popular, great food.

Desert Edge Brewery, Trolley Square, at 700 East and 500 South, (801) 521-8917. Inexpensive food, post-industrial ambience.

OGDEN

Rooster's 25th Street Brewing Company, 253 25th St., (801) 627-6171. High-design pub in historic district.

MOAB

Eddie McStiff's, 57 S. Main in Western Plaza, (435) 259-BEER. Popular with young mountain bikers, garden patio in back.

Moab Brewery, 686 S. Main St., (435) 259-6333. Good food, classy atmosphere.

Private clubs are essentially the same as bars in other parts of the United States. You can have drinks with or without food during opening hours. However, you must be a member of the club in order to eat or drink in a private club. For the traveler, this doesn't present an insurmountable hurdle, as you can buy temporary memberships (a two-week membership usually costs around $5). If you're fond of a drink and nightlife, it might well be worth it. Most live music clubs are private clubs, for instance. Also, members of a club are able to sign in up to five friends on a nightly basis. You can either ask a friendly-looking stranger to sign you in, or, if you're part of a group, one of you can become a member and sign the others in.

A long-standing Utah law forbids the advertising of alcohol. No signs or notices are allowed to indicate that alcohol is available: you won't see many neon Spud McKenzies in Utah. (The law is only spottily enforced these days.) While it's pretty obvious that a brewpub will have beer, you won't know whether drinks are served at a restaurant until you ask.

Nearly all towns will have a state-owned liquor store, and 3.2 percent beer is available in most grocery stores. Many travelers will find that carrying a bottle of your favorite beverage to your room is the easiest way to enjoy an evening drink.

The state drinking age is 21.

TRANSPORTATION

GETTING THERE

By Air
More than a dozen major airlines serve Salt Lake City, which has the only major airport in the state. Salt Lake City is the western hub for Delta Airlines, which provides the most international and regional links (www.delta-air.com). Fares and schedules tend to change frequently—a travel agent can help find the best flights. Metropolitan newspapers usually run advertisements for discount fares and tours in their Sunday travel sections. You'll have the best chance of getting low fares by planning at least two weeks ahead.

By Rail
Amtrak now runs only one passenger train across Utah. The *California Zephyr* runs daily between Oakland and Chicago via Salt Lake City.

Amtrak charges more than Greyhound for one-way tickets but has far roomier seating, lounge cars, and sleepers. Special fares and round-trip discounts often make train travel a good value. For information and reservations, see a travel agent or call Amtrak at (800) 872-7245, www.amtrak.com. A **USA Railpass** is sold by travel agents outside the United States.

By Bus
The **Greyhound** bus line, (800) 229-9424, www.greyhound.com offers frequent service to Utah. Greyhound often features special deals on bus passes and one-way "anywhere" tickets. Outside the United States, residents may purchase a Greyhound **Ameripass** at additional discounts.

By RV
Many foreign travelers enter Utah in RVs, which they rent elsewhere and drive on a tour of the western national parks. It takes more planning to line up a rental RV than a car, but there are plenty of agencies in Los Angeles, Phoenix, Las Vegas, and Salt Lake City able to do the job. Most travel agents can help, or you can contact the local travel office in the city of your departure.

Driveaways
These are autos that need to be delivered to another city. If it's a place you're headed for, a driveaway can be like a free car rental (you pay for gas). To sign up, you must be at least 21 years old and make a refundable deposit of $75–150. There are time and mileage limits. Ask for an economy car if money's a consideration. Check the *Yellow Pages* under "Automobile Transporters & Driveaway Companies."

GETTING AROUND

By Air
Regional airlines connect Salt Lake City with other communities in the state. Regular scheduled flights link to Vernal, Moab, St. George, and Cedar City. The cost per mile of these short hops is high, but you'll often have excellent views!

climbing the Moki Dugway switchbacks on Hwy 261, with Muley Point in the background

W.C. McRAE

By Train

Amtrak can get you to Salt Lake City, but that's about all. There's a stop near Price but no further public transport from there.

By Bus

There's frequent Greyhound bus service up and down I-15 and along U.S. 40 to Vernal, but these routes really don't get you close to the sorts of sights that most people come to Utah to see. The Wasatch Front area (from Provo to Ogden and from Salt Lake City out to Tooele) is served by Utah Transit Authority (UTA), a regional bus company with excellent service. Park City and other Salt Lake City ski areas are accessible via a number of ski-bus operations, some of which pick up at the airport.

The only form of public ground transport to Moab and other towns in southeastern Utah is a once-daily van that provides transport to and from the Salt Lake City Airport.

By Car

Public transportation serves cities and some towns but very few of the scenic, historic, and recreational areas. Unless you're on a tour, you'll really need your own transportation. Cars are easily rented in any large town, though Salt Lake City offers by far the greatest selection. Four-wheel-drive vehicles can be rented, too, and will be very handy if you plan extensive travel on back roads.

Most tourist offices carry the Utah road map published by the Utah Department of Transportation; it's one of the best available and is free. Most regular-grade unleaded gasoline in Utah is only 85 octane. If your automobile owner's manual calls for a higher grade of octane you might need a higher grade of gasoline.

Hitchhiking

Opinions and experiences vary on hitching. It can be a great way to meet people despite the dangers and long waits. Offer to buy lunch or help with gas money to repay the driver's favor. Highway police tolerate hitchhiking as long as it doesn't create a hazard or take place on an interstate or a freeway. They do routinely check IDs, however. Rides can often be arranged with fellow travelers at youth hostels. Bulletin boards at universities and college ride lists are also good sources.

By Bicycle

Touring on a bicycle is to be fully alive to the land, skies, sounds, plants, and birds of Utah. The experience of gliding across the desert or topping out on a mountain pass goes beyond words. Some ef-

UTAH DRIVING DISTANCES

Logan
Ogden — 81mi
Wendover — 120mi
SALT LAKE CITY — 35mi
FLAMING GORGE NAT. REC. AREA
194mi
31mi
Park City — 144mi
45mi
Provo
Vernal
133mi
74mi
114mi
142mi
Price
179mi
63mi
Delta — 72mi
259mi
110mi
Green River
Salina — 56mi
303mi
Moab
117mi
118mi
136mi
CAPITOL REEF N.P.
CANYONLANDS N.P.
Cedar City — 174mi — 119mi — Escalante — 50mi
130mi
GLEN CANYON NAT. REC. AREA
BRYCE CANYON N.P.
100mi
53mi
ZION N.P.
Kanab
Monument Valley
St. George — 80mi — Page — 122mi

© AVALON TRAVEL PUBLISHING, INC.

HOW TO SELECT AN OUTFITTER

Utah has a number of outfitters, guides, trail-drive operators, and guest ranches, all of whom promise to get you outdoors and into an Old West adventure. However, all outfitting and recreational services are not created equal. The most important consideration in choosing an outfitter is safety, the second is your comfort. Make sure you feel confident on both counts before signing on.

Here are some points to ponder while you plan your adventure vacation.

All outfitters should be licensed or accredited by the state and be happy to provide you with proof. This means that they are bonded, carry the necessary insurance, and have the money and organizational wherewithal to register with the province. This rules out fly-by-night operations and college students who've decided to set up business for the summer. If you're just starting to plan an excursion, contact the Utah Travel Council at Capitol Hill, Salt Lake City, (801) 538-1030 or (800) 200-1160. The council's website, www.utah.com, contains an extensive network of outfitters and guides.

Often a number of outfitters offer similar trips. When you've narrowed down your choice, call and talk to the outfitters on your short list. Ask lots of questions, and try to get a sense of who these people are; you'll be spending a lot of time with them, so make sure you feel comfortable. If you have special interests, like bird- or wildlife-watching, be sure to mention them to your potential outfitter. A good outfitter will also take your interests into account when planning a trip.

If there's a wide disparity in prices between outfitters for the same trip, find out what makes up for the difference. The cheapest trip may not be the best choice for you. Food is one of the most common areas to economize in. If you don't mind having cold cuts each meal for your five-day pack trip, then maybe the cheapest outfitter is okay. If you prefer a cooked meal, or alcoholic beverages, or choice of entrées, then be prepared to pay more. On a long trip, it might be worth it to you. Also be sure you know what kind of accommodations are included in multiday trips. You may pay more to have a tent or cabin to yourself; again, it may be worth it to you.

Ask how many years an outfitter has been in business and how long your particular escort has guided this trip. While a start-up outfitting service can be perfectly fine, you should know what level of experience you are buying. If you have questions, especially for longer or more dangerous trips, ask for referrals.

Most outfitters will demand that you pay a portion (usually half) of your fee well in advance to secure your place, so be sure to ask about your outfitter's cancellation policy. Some lengthy float trips can cost thousands of dollars; if cancellation means the forfeiture of the deposit, then you need to know that. Also, find out what the tipping or gratuity policy is for your outfitter. Sometimes 15 or 20 percent extra is added to your bill as a tip for the "hands." While this is undoubtedly nice for the help, you should be aware that your gratuities for a week's stay can run into the hundreds of dollars.

---

fort, a lightweight touring or mountain bike, touring gear, and awareness of what's going on around you are all that's needed. Start with short rides if you're new to bicycle touring, then work up to longer cross-country trips. By learning to maintain and repair your steed, you'll seldom have trouble on the road. An extra-low gear of 30 inches or less will take the strain out of long mountain grades. Utah has almost every kind of terrain and road condition imaginable; mountain bicyclists find the Moab area in the southeast especially challenging and scenic. Note that designated wilderness areas are closed to cycling.

Most bookstores and bicycle shops have good publications on bicycle touring. *Bicycle Touring in Utah* and *The Mountain Bike Manual,* both by Dennis Coello, contain general information and details on various rides within the state. As when hiking, always have rain and wind gear and carry plenty of water. Cyclists with a competitive spirit can test themselves in a series of U.S. Cycling Federation-sanctioned races in the northern part of the state; local bicycle shops have schedules of races and training events. Even though, unlike other states, Utah as yet has no helmet law for cyclists, don't forget to wear a bicycling helmet.

THE GREAT WESTERN TRAIL

As its name implies, the Great Western Trail, when completed, will traverse some of the West's most spectacular country. The Utah stretch, approximately 350 miles long, will link trails in Arizona and Idaho with others in New Mexico, Wyoming, and Montana (the Utah section is now 90 percent complete). Planners envision a trail network stretching all the way from Mexico to Canada, providing travel possibilities for bicycles, horses, and motorized vehicles, as well as hikers. About 90 percent of the finished network will employ existing roads and trails.

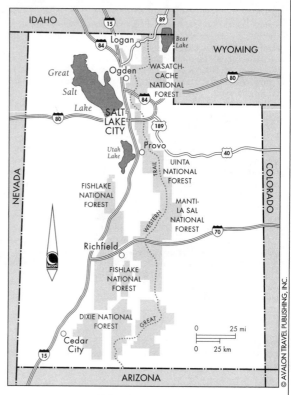

The southernmost Utah section follows washes and canyons across land administered by the Bureau of Land Management; elevations drop as low as 4,800 feet. The Dixie National Forest section skirts the western edge of Bryce Canyon National Park and continues across high plateaus to Boulder Top, where it reaches elevations topping 11,000 feet. Fishlake National Forest has more fine alpine country and expansive views from Thousand Lake Mountain, Windstorm Peak, and the UM Plateau areas. In the Manti–La Sal National Forest, the trail ascends the lofty Wasatch Plateau and extends for 75 miles through rolling meadows and forest country. Uinta National Forest features lush forests beneath the jagged summits of the Wasatch Range's Mount Timpanogos and Lone Peak. The ups and downs of the Wasatch Range continue as the trail winds through the Wasatch-Cache National Forest high above Salt Lake City and the Great Salt Lake. The northernmost trail section in Utah climbs into the Bear River Range and meets the Idaho border near Beaver Mountain.

Note that some trail sections are open to vehicles and pets and some aren't. You can obtain the latest amount of trail information from the agencies below. The **Great Western Trail Association** needs volunteers for trail construction and maintenance. If you'd like to help, contact the association at P.O. Box 1428, Provo, UT 84602. The group has a website at www.gwt.org.

Cedar District Office
Bureau of Land Management
176 E. DL Sargent Dr.
Cedar City, UT 84720
(801) 586-2401

Dixie National Forest
P.O. Box 580
82 N. 100 East
Cedar City, UT 84720
(801) 865-3700

Fishlake National Forest
115 E. 900 North
Richfield, UT 84701
(801) 896-9233

Manti–La Sal National Forest
599 W. Price River Dr.

Price, UT 84501
(801) 637-2817

Uinta National Forest
88 W. 100 North
Provo, UT 84601
(801) 377-5780

Wasatch-Cache National Forest
8230 Federal Bldg.
125 S. State St.
Salt Lake City, UT 84138
(801) 524-5030

INFORMATION AND SERVICES

General tourist literature and maps are available from the **Utah Travel Council,** Council Hall/Capitol Hill, Salt Lake City, UT 84114-7420, (801) 538-1030, fax (801) 538-1399, www.utah.com. Utah's many chambers of commerce also have free material and are happy to help with travel suggestions in their areas (see Information in the specific sections of this book). Also listed are national forest offices and other government agencies that have information on outdoor recreation in their areas.

GAY AND LESBIAN UTAH

Gay travelers will find Utah even less welcoming to openly gay people than many of the surrounding western states. There's a gay scene of sorts in Salt Lake City, but very little sign of support elsewhere in the state. In 1996, a bookstore owned by two gay men was burned in southern Utah and the owners were forced to leave town. Not surprisingly, Utah gays and lesbians tend to be extremely discreet.

Unfortunately, there aren't a lot of community resources for gay and lesbian travelers. Salt Lake City's *Pillar* newspaper carries gay news, and its website at www.pillarmag.com is a good place to get a flavor for the Utah gay scene. Many of the support groups that do exist in the state are concerned with supporting gay and lesbian Mormons.

TRAVELERS WITH DISABILITIES

Travelers with disabilities will find Utah quite progressive when it comes to accessibility issues, especially in Salt Lake City and the heavily traveled national parks in southern Utah. Most parks offer all-abilities trails, and many hotels advertise their fully accessible facilities. For skiers with disabilities, Park City Ski Area offers an all-ability ski program, which promises to get almost everyone out on the slopes.

HEALTH AND SAFETY

Utah has one of the lowest crime rates in the United States. Although parts of Salt Lake City look pretty scruffy, there's little reason to fear random violence unless you put yourself in unwise situations.

In emergencies, you can dial 911 in most communities in Utah; otherwise, use the emergency number listed on most telephones or dial a zero for an operator. Hospital emergency rooms offer the quickest help but cost more than a visit to a doctor's office or clinic. Hospital care is very expensive—medical insurance is recommended.

Animal Threats
Probably a greater threat to health are poisonous rattlesnakes and scorpions. When hiking or climb-

ing in desert areas, never put your hand onto a ledge or into a hole that you can't see. Both are lairs for snakes and scorpions. While snakebites are rarely fatal anymore, they're no fun, either. If you are bitten, immobilize the affected area and seek immediate medical attention.

If you do much hiking and biking in the spring, there's a good chance that you'll encounter ticks. While ticks in this part of the United States don't usually carry Lyme Disease, there is a remote threat of Rocky Mountain Spotted Fever, spread by the wood tick. If you find a tick has bitten you, pull it off immediately. Grasp the tick's head parts (as close to your skin as possible) with tweezers and pull slowly and steadily. Do not attempt to remove ticks by burning them or coating them with anything. Removing a tick as quickly as possible greatly reduces your chance of infection.

Utah is home to black bears, which aren't as menacing as their cousins the grizzly bear. However, black bears weigh more than most humans and have far sharper claws and teeth. An encounter with a black bear is rarely fatal, but it's something to be avoided.

If you encounter a bear, give it plenty of room and try not to surprise it. Wearing a fragrance while in bear country isn't a good idea because it attracts bears, as do strong-smelling foods. **Always store food items outside the tent,** and if you're in bear territory, sleep well away from the cooking area. Waking up with a bear clawing at your tent is to be avoided. Hanging food in a bag from a tree is a long-standing and wise precaution. If a bear becomes aggressive, try to drop something that will divert its attention while you flee. If that isn't possible, the next best bet is to curl up into a ball, clasp your hands behind your neck, and play dead, even if the bear begins to bat you around. Taking precautions and having respect for bears will ensure not only your continued existence, but theirs as well.

In recent years, as humans have increasingly moved into the mountain lions' habitat (and as their numbers have increased), they have become a threat to humans, especially small children. Never leave children unattended in forests and never allow them to lag far behind on a family hike. Nearly every summer newspapers in the western states carry tragic stories of children stalked and killed by mountain lions. Safety is in numbers.

Hypothermia

The greatest danger outdoors is one that can sneak up and kill with very little warning. Hypothermia—a lowering of the body's temperature below 95° F—causes disorientation, uncontrollable shivering, slurred speech, and drowsiness. The victim may not even realize what's wrong. Unless corrective action is taken immediately, hypothermia can lead to death. This is why hikers should travel with companions and always carry wind and rain protection. (Close-fitting rain gear works far better than ponchos.) Also, space blankets are lightweight and cheap and offer protection against the cold in emergencies. Remember that temperatures can plummet rapidly in Utah's dry climate—a drop of 40° F between day and night is common. Be especially careful at high elevations, where summer sunshine can quickly change into freezing rain or a blizzard. Simply falling into a mountain stream while fishing can also lead to hypothermia and death unless proper action is taken. If you're cold and tired, don't waste time! Seek shelter and build a fire, change into dry clothes, and drink warm liquids. If a victim isn't fully conscious, warm him or her by skin-to-skin contact in a sleeping bag. Try to keep the victim awake and offer plenty of warm liquids.

Hantavirus

Hantavirus is an infectious disease agent first isolated during the Korean War and then discovered in the Americas in 1993 by a task force of scientists in New Mexico. This disease agent occurs naturally throughout most of North and South America, especially in dry desert conditions. The infectious agent is airborne, and in the absence of prompt medical attention, its infections are usually fatal. This disease is called Hantavirus Pulmonary Syndrome (HPS). It can affect anyone, but given some fundamental knowledge, it can also be very easy to prevent.

The natural host of the hantavirus appears to be rodents, especially mice and rats. The virus is not usually transmitted directly from rodents to humans; rather, the rodents shed hantavirus particles in their saliva, urine, and droppings. Humans usually contract HPS by inhaling particles that are infected with the hantavirus. The virus becomes airborne when the particles dry out and get stirred into the air (especially

GIARDIA

It can be tough to resist: Picture yourself hiking in a beautiful area by the banks of a crystal-clear stream. The water in your canteen tastes stale, hot, and plastic; the nearby stream looks so inviting that you can't resist a cautious sip. It tastes delicious, clean, and cold, and for the rest of your hike you refresh yourself with water straight from the stream.

Days pass and you forget about drinking untreated water. Suddenly one evening after your meal you are terribly sick to your stomach. You develop an awful case of cramps and feel diarrhea beginning to set in. Food poisoning?

Nope—it's the effects of giardia, a protozoan that has become common in even the remotest mountain streams. Giardia is carried in animal or human waste that is deposited or washed into natural waters. When ingested, it begins reproducing, causing a sickness in the host that can become very serious and may not be cured without medical attention.

You can take precautions against giardia with a variety of chemicals and filtering methods or by boiling water before drinking it. The various chemical solutions on the market work in some applications, but because they need to be safe for human consumption they are weak and ineffective against the protozoan in its cyst stage of life (when it encases itself in a hard shell). Filtering may eliminate giardia, but there are other water pests too small to be caught by most filters. The most effective way to eliminate such threats is to boil all suspect water. A few minutes at a rolling boil will kill giardia even in the cyst stage.

---

from sweeping a floor or shaking a rug). Humans then inhale these particles, which leads to the infection.

Since HPS is not considered a highly infectious disease, people usually contract HPS from long-term exposure. Since transmission usually occurs through inhalation, it is easiest for a human being to contract hantavirus within a contained environment, where the virus-infected particles are not thoroughly dispersed. Being in a small house, a crawl space, or a barn where rodents can be found poses elevated risks for contracting the infection.

Environments that provide the greatest risk are unoccupied buildings, such as an abandoned house, a cabin, or the toolshed in your backyard. Also be wary of dusty caves where there is an accumulation of rat droppings. Rodents can thrive in such places, especially in cold weather. The gathering dust will only increase the infectiousness of the disease.

A very common scenario for contracting the infection is cleaning out a dirty shed: if the shed has been a long-standing home to any carrier rodents, then sweeping the floor will introduce the virus particles into the air and make their inhalation much more likely.

Simply traveling to a place where the hantavirus is known to occur is not considered a risk factor. Camping, hiking, and other outdoor activities also pose low risks, especially if steps are taken to reduce rodent contact.

The very first symptoms can occur anywhere between five days and three weeks after infection. They almost always include fever, fatigue, and aching muscles (usually in the back, shoulders, and/or thighs) and other flu-like conditions. Other early symptoms may include headaches, dizziness, chills, and abdominal discomfort (such as vomiting, nausea, and/or diarrhea). These are shortly followed by intense coughing and shortness of breath. If you have these symptoms, seek medical help immediately. Untreated infections of hantavirus are almost always fatal.

HIV

The Human Immunodeficiency Virus is the infectious agent that causes AIDS. The most common methods of transmission of HIV are having unprotected sexual contact with an infected person, exposure to infected blood or blood products, and sharing contaminated needles with infected IV drug users. While Utah has a relatively low occurrence of AIDS, always practice safe sex (i.e. use condoms) with anyone who's HIV status is unknown to you, and never reuse needles.

The Sun and Heat

Utah in summer is a very hot place. Be sure to use sunscreen, or else you risk having a very uncomfortable vacation. Heat exhaustion can also be a problem if you're hiking in the hot sun. Be sure to drink plenty of water; in midsummer, try to get an early start if you're hiking in full sun.

Getting Lost

Part of the attraction of Utah's vast wilderness backcountry is its remoteness. And if you're hiking in the canyon country in the southern part of the state, you'll find that you spend most of your time hiking at the bottom of narrow and twisting canyons. It's easy to get lost, or at least disorientated! You should always carry adequate and up-to-date maps and a compass—and you need know how to use them if you're heading off into the backcountry. Always plan a route. Planning usually saves time and effort. Always tell someone (like a family member or a ranger) where you are going and when you'll be back, so they know where and when to start looking for you in case you get into trouble. Always take at least one other person with you: DO NOT venture into the desert alone. Parties of four people (or two vehicles) are ideal, because one person can stay with the person in trouble, while the other two escort each other to get help. It's a good idea to carry your cell phone in case you need to make an emergency call or send an email.

Flash Floods

Thunderstorms can wash hikers away and bury them in the canyons and washes of the Southwest. Flash floods can happen almost any time of the year, but are most prevalent in the summer months. Before entering slot canyon areas like Paria or the Escalante Canyons, be sure to check with rangers or local authorities for weather reports. And while you're hiking you should read and heed the clouds. Many washes and canyons drain large areas, with their headwaters many miles away. The dangerous part is that sometimes you just can't tell what's coming down the wash or canyon due to the vast number of acres that these canyons drain, and because the cliff walls are too high to see out to any storms that may be creating flood potential upstream. With any sign of a threat, it's best to get out of the canyon bottom, at least 60 vertical feet up, to avoid water and debris. Since many of these canyons are narrow, there are places where it's not possible to get out of the canyon on short notice. Never drive a vehicle into a flooded wash. Stop and wait for the water to recede, as it usually will within an hour.

MONEY

Prices of all services mentioned in this book were current at press time. You're sure to find seasonal and long-term price changes, so *please,* don't use what's listed here to argue with the staff at a motel, campground, museum, airline, or other office!

Banking

You'll find cash machines or ATMs throughout Utah, even in the smallest towns. Foreign travelers will find it hard exchanging foreign currency or travelers checks outside of central Salt Lake City, so it's a good idea to exchange all you'll need before setting out for rural parts of the state. Credit cards are generally accepted at most businesses.

Taxes

A 6.125 percent sales tax is added to most transactions on goods, food, and services. Additional room taxes are added and vary by community.

Tipping

It's customary to tip 15–20 percent to food and drink servers; tips are almost never automatically added to the bill. Taxi drivers receive a 10–15 percent gratuity; bellmen get at least $1 a bag.

TIME ZONES

Travelers in Utah should remember that the state is in the Mountain Time zone and goes on daylight saving time (advanced one hour) April–October. Nevada is in the Pacific Time zone (one hour earlier); all other bordering states are in the Mountain Time zone. An odd exception is Arizona, which stays on Mountain Standard Time all year (except for the Navajo Reservation, which goes on daylight saving time to keep up with its Utah and New Mexico sections).

EVENTS

Utah has a full schedule of rodeos, parades, art festivals, historical celebrations, gem and mineral shows, and sporting events. Stop at a tourist office or chamber of commerce to see what's coming up. The offices should also have the annual *Utah! Travel Guide,* which lists major events.

MAJOR HOLIDAYS

Many museums, recreation areas, and other tourist attractions close on Thanksgiving, Christmas, New Year's, and other holidays (remember that nearly everything in Utah closes on Sundays!). These closings are not always mentioned in the text, so call ahead to check.

New Year's Day: January 1

Martin Luther King, Jr.'s Birthday (also called Human Rights Day): January 15, usually observed the third Monday in January

Presidents Day (honors Washington and Lincoln): third Monday in February

Easter Sunday: late March or early April

Memorial Day (honors veterans of all wars): last Monday in May

Independence Day: July 4

Pioneer Day: July 24, Utah's biggest summer event, with parades and fireworks in almost every Utah community

Labor Day: first Monday in September

Columbus Day: second Monday in October

Veterans Day: November 11

Thanksgiving Day: fourth Thursday in November

Christmas Day: December 25

LOCAL EVENTS AND FESTIVALS NOT TO MISS

January
Park City, Sundance Film Festival

February
Park City, Snow Sculpture Winterfest

March
Brian Head, Spring Carnival

Park City, National Freestyle Ski Jumping Championships

April
Ogden, Mountain Man Rendezvous

May
Green Valley, Green Valley–Moab Friendship Cruise
Kanab, Greyhound Gathering
Moab, Moab Arts Festival
Ogden, Taste of Ogden
Promontory, Golden Spike National Historic Site Re-enactment Event

June
Cedar City, Utah Shakespeare Festival (through Sept.)
Manti, Mormon Miracle Pageant
Price, Black Diamond Stampede PRCA Rodeo
Salt Lake City, Utah Art Festival

July
Deer Valley, Utah Symphony Summer Concert Series
Logan, Utah Festival Opera
Ogden, Street Festival
Vernal, Dinosaur Days

August
Bonneville Salt Flats, Speed Week
Park City, Park City Arts Festival
Wellsville, Festival of the American West

September
Brigham City, Peach Days Festival
Salt Lake City, Utah State Fair
Springdale, Southern Utah Folklife Festival

October
Moab, Canyonlands Fat Tire Mountain Bike Festival
St. George, Huntsman World Senior Games

November
Cedar City, Iron Mission Days

December
Logan/Hardware Ranch, Elk Feeding

POSTAL AND TELEPHONE SERVICES

Normal post office hours are Monday–Friday 8:30 A.M.–5 P.M. and sometimes Saturday 8:30 A.M.–noon; (800) 275-8777, www.usps.gov. U.S. post offices sell stamps and postal money orders. If you need to ship a package they can also offer overnight express service.

Utah has two area codes: 801 is the code to the greater Salt Lake City area, including suburbs as far south as Provo and as far north as Ogden. The rest of the state has the area code 435.

Toll-free numbers in the United States have **800, 888, or 877** area codes. To obtain a number within the state, dial 411; for another state or if you're calling from outside Utah, dial 1, the area code, then 555-1212. Many airlines and motel chains offer toll-free numbers; if you don't have it, dial 1-800-555-1212 for information.

The cost of a call from a pay phone is usually $.35.

BUSINESS HOURS

In Utah, most commercial businesses are open from 9 A.M.–6 P.M., Monday–Saturday. The biggest surprise to many travelers will be that nearly all businesses—and almost certainly those away from Salt Lake City, big recreational hubs, and the national parks—close on Sunday in Utah. **Again, almost all businesses in Utah, including restaurants, are closed on Sunday.** This also includes local public transportation. Even in Salt Lake City it can be difficult to find a place to eat on Sunday; even fast food restaurants are closed. Imagine how difficult it might be to find a bite to eat in—say—Monticello. If you're traveling outside the Wasatch Front on Sunday, ask your motel clerk if you'll be able to find a meal at your intended destination. Plan well ahead; it's easy to get stranded, hungry, and disappointed.

DRIVING HAZARDS

Summer heat in the desert puts an extra strain on both cars and drivers. It's worth double-checking your vehicle's cooling system, engine oil, transmission fluid, fan belts, and tires to make sure they are in top condition. Carry several gallons of water in case of a breakdown or radiator trouble. Never leave children or pets in a parked car during warm weather—temperatures inside can cause fatal heatstroke in minutes.

At times the desert has *too much* water, when late-summer storms frequently flood low spots in the road. Wait for the water level to subside before crossing. Dust storms can completely block visibility but tend to be short-lived. During such storms, pull completely off the road, stop, and turn off your lights so as not to confuse other drivers. Radio stations carry frequent weather updates when weather hazards exist. Continuous weather forecasts can be received on a VHF radio (162.4 or 162.55 MHz) in the Salt Lake City area (Wasatch Front), Logan (Cache Valley), Vernal (Uinta Basin), Cedar City, Glen Canyon National Recreation Area, and Las Vegas, Nevada, areas.

If stranded, either on the desert or in the mountains, stay with your vehicle unless you're *positive* of where to go for help, then leave a note explaining your route and departure time. Airplanes can easily spot a stranded car (tie a piece of cloth to your antenna), but a person walking is more difficult to see. It's best to carry emergency supplies: blankets or sleeping bags, first-aid kit, tools, jumper cables, shovel, traction mats or chains, flashlight, rain gear, water, food, and a can opener.

MAPS

The Utah Department of Transportation prints and distributes a free, regularly updated map of Utah. Ask for it when you call for information or when you stop at a visitors' information office. Also available are a series of five regional maps of Utah. Although the maps aren't regularly updated, they are still the best reference for off-road travel. If you're planning on extensive backcountry exploration, be sure to ask locally about conditions. Backcountry enthusiasts should also consider procuring the *Utah Atlas and Gazetteer,* the DeLorme map atlas to Utah.

ELECTRICITY

In all of the United States, electricity is 110–120 volts. Plugs have either two flat or two-flat-plus-one-round prongs. Older homes and hotels may have outlets that only have two-prong outlets, and you may well be traveling with computers or appliances that have three-prong plugs. Ask your hotel or motel manager for an adapter; if necessary, you may need to buy a three-prong adapter, but the cost is small.

SALT LAKE CITY AND THE NORTHERN WASATCH FRONT

INTRODUCTION

In 1847 the Mormon prophet Brigham Young proclaimed this site the "right place" for a new settlement. Today, many residents and visitors would still agree. Modern Salt Lake City offers an appealing mix of cultural activities, historic sites, varied architecture, shopping, sophisticated hotels, and elegant restaurants. About 174,000 citizens live in the city, making it by far the largest and most important urban center in Utah, while nearly one million people reside close by in sprawling suburbs.

By far the most popular tourist site in Salt Lake City is Temple Square, the spiritual center of the Mormon Church. You could easily spend a day just visiting the church's museums, religious and historical sites, and administrative buildings. Utah's political life centers on the imposing capitol, which overlooks the city from a hill just north of downtown. The University of Utah serves a major role in education and research

from its 1,500-acre campus in the foothills east of the city. Another high point of any visit to Salt Lake City should be a tour of the city's historic architecture. The early Mormons' pride in their City of Zion is clearly seen in the old residential districts, with their beautiful Victorian mansions, and the downtown's ornate storefronts and civic structures. Few cities in the West retain such a wealth of period architecture.

Once a prosperous though inward-looking trade center for local farmers and ranchers—and a virtual theocracy—Salt Lake City in the last 50 years has emerged from its isolation to join the ranks of the leading cities of the American West. A measure of the city's new prestige is the fact that Salt Lake City will host the 2002 Winter Olympics, the largest city to have ever hosted the winter games. As any pre-games visitor to Salt Lake City would readily note, the city is sparing no expense or trouble to ready itself for the games—construction cranes dominate the skyline and entire freeways have been rebuilt. After all, the capital city of Utah and the Mormon world has invited the world to come visit, and you can bet that it'll be quite a show.

THE SETTING

Salt Lake City lies on the broad valley floor and terraces once occupied by prehistoric Lake Bonneville. The Great Salt Lake, the largest remnant of that ancient inland sea, lies just northwest of the city. The Wasatch Range rises immediately to the east of the city; these rugged mountains, with many peaks exceeding 11,000 feet, are cut by steep canyons whose streams provide the area's drinking and irrigation water. In minutes from downtown you can be skiing on some of the world's best powder in winter, or hiking among wildflowers in summer. On the other side of the valley, to the west, Lewiston Peak (elev. 10,626 feet) crowns the Oquirrh Mountains.

ORIENTATION

The indisputable center of Salt Lake City is Temple Square, which sits at the north end of downtown. The Salt Palace Convention Center is south and west one block, and three blocks to the west is Delta Center, home of the National Basketball Association's Utah Jazz. The principle downtown retail core extends south of Temple Square along South Temple, Main, and State Streets. The handsome turn-of-the-century business precinct, called the Exchange District, sits at the corner of Main and 400 South Streets.

Dominating the skyline north of downtown is the Utah State Capitol; to the east, between downtown and the Wasatch Front, is the University of Utah. Most of the Salt Lake City's residential areas spread to the south in the wide valley of the Jordan River. West of the city is the airport and the southern shores of the Great Salt Lake.

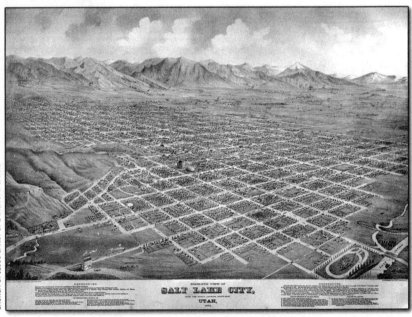

CHURCH OF JESUS CHRIST OF LATTER-DAY SAINTS

bird's-eye view of Salt Lake City, looking southeast, 1875

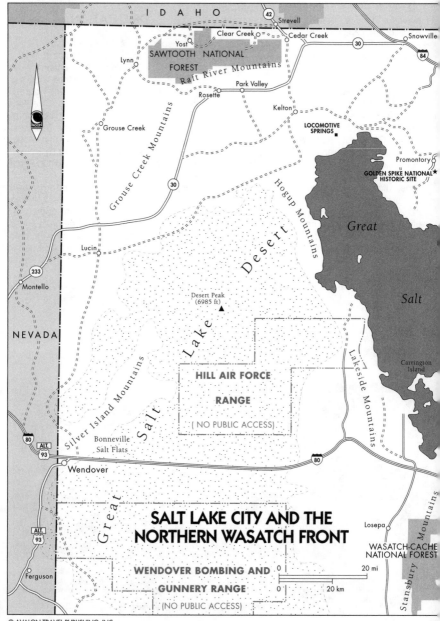

© AVALON TRAVEL PUBLISHING, INC.

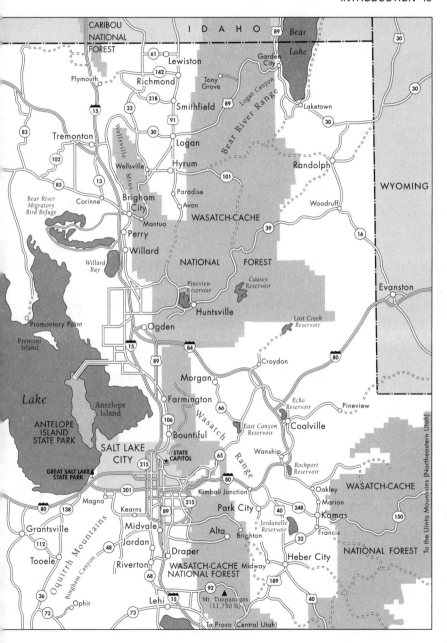

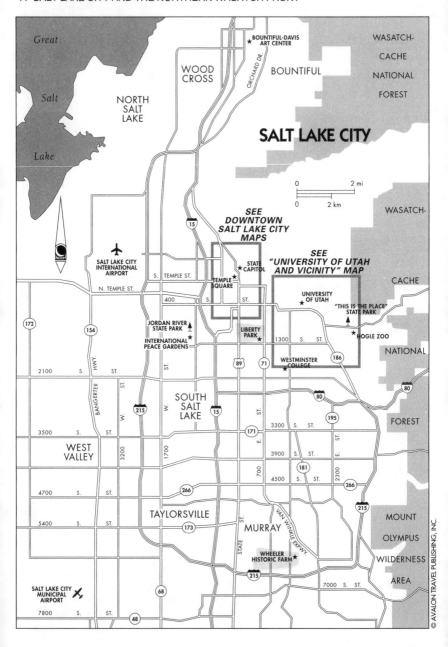

Getting Around

Although Salt Lake City's street system is the same as many other towns founded by Mormon settlers, it can be confusing to first-time visitors—mostly due to the scale of the city. Temple Square is the center of the city's address numbering grid. North, South, and West Temple are the streets that run along respective sides of the square, and Main Street flows along the east side; these streets effectively divide the city into quadrants. All further streets are numbered. For instance, West Temple is 100 West, then comes 200 West, and so on. One block south of South Temple is 100 South, 200 South, and so on (300 South is also called Broadway, by the way). In conversation many people will use the shorthand "4th South," "3rd West," and so on to indicate 400 South or 300 West.

While this street numbering system is a picture of precision, it's also confusing at first. For instance, all addresses have four parts. When you see the address 436 North 100 West, for instance, the system tells you that the address will be found four blocks north of North Temple, on 100 West. One rule of thumb is to remember that the last two segments of an address (300 South, 500 East, 2300 West) are the street's actual name—the equivalent of a single street signifier such as Oak Street or Front Street.

To add more confusion, there are several exceptions to the general rule. The one most likely to affect travelers involves the area just east of the capitol and north of South Temple, called The Avenues. This area was plotted by the city's non-Mormon population and is an island of addresses that follow their own numbering system. If you see an address for a numbered avenue (Fourth Ave., for instance) or on a letter street (J St.), then you know you are talking about The Avenues.

Blocks are very large in Salt Lake City: Brigham Young laid them out to resemble the heavenly City of Zion, which had been revealed to him in visions. At a full 10 acres each, each side of a block is 780 feet long! Streets are also Zion-sized: there's 132 feet between blocks—usually enough for four lanes of traffic and two parking strips. When making appointments or hotel reservations, remember that just six blocks make up a mile in Salt Lake City. It will take longer than you anticipate to get around on foot. Travelers from outside of Utah will also marvel at the audacity with which local drivers make U-turns in the middle of streets. It's a freedom you have if you're streets are all a divinely inspired eight rods across!

CLIMATE

The city experiences a full range of seasons at its 4,300-foot elevation. Rapidly moving storms can bring rain or snow one day and sunshine the next. Average temperatures range from highs in the upper 30s in January to the lower 90s in July. Total precipitation averages 15.3 inches for the year. Most of the winter moisture arrives as snow; average annual snowfall is 54 inches in town and considerably more in the mountains.

HISTORY

THE VISION

Salt Lake City began as a dream—a utopia in which the persecuted Mormons would have the freedom to create a Kingdom of God on earth. Their prophet, Brigham Young, led the first group of 143 men, three women, and two children to the valley of the Great Salt Lake in July 1847. The bleak valley, covered with sagebrush and inhabited mainly by lizards, could best be described as "the land nobody wanted." Many Mormon settlers wanted to continue under Young's leadership to the rich lands of California. But Young saw the value in staying: he had declared that the Kingdom of God should be independent of gentiles, and this land's remoteness would protect them from enemies.

SETTLEMENT

The pioneers put their doubts aside and set to work digging irrigation canals, planting crops, constructing a small fort, and laying out a city as nearly 2,000 more immigrants arrived that first summer.

Through trial and error, farmers learned techniques of irrigating and farming the desert land. Then, in 1848, disaster struck. A plague of "crickets" (actually a flightless grasshopper, *Anabrus simplex*) descended from the hills to the east and began devouring the crops, nearly ending chances for the community's survival. But flocks of California seagulls appeared out of the west to feed on the insects. Considered a miracle by the Mormons, the seagull intervention saved part of the crops and gave the pioneers hope that life in the Great Salt Lake Valley would eventually be fruitful.

Meanwhile, the city continued to grow. Immigrants from Europe and the eastern United States poured in, many under the sponsorship of the Perpetual Emigrating Fund Company. Tanneries, flour mills, blacksmith shops, stores, and other enterprises developed under church direction. Beautiful residential neighborhoods

sprang up, reflecting both the pride of craftsmanship and the sense of stability encouraged by the church. Workers commenced to raise the temple, the tabernacle, and the other religious structures that still dominate the area around Temple Square. Colonization of the surrounding country proceeded at a rapid pace.

As the Mormons' earthly City of Zion, Salt Lake City came close to its goal of being a community devoted to God. Nearly all aspects of political, economic, and family life came under the influence of the church during the first 20 years. Of all the utopian social experiments ever tried in the United States, the Mormon settlements at Salt Lake have had the greatest and most lasting success.

THE "MORMON WAR"

Even in distant Utah, the Mormons continued to have antagonistic relations with the U.S. government. Utah became a territory in 1850, but instead of incorporating American democratic in-

Brigham Young

stitutions as envisioned by Congress, the Mormon leadership arranged to hand the civil territorial titles to the LDS priesthood; church President Brigham Young was named territorial governor. The U.S. government, already chafing at the Utah Territory's refusal to outlaw polygamy, dismissed the territorial government as a theocracy. President James Buchanan, considering these acts rebellion, in 1857 dispatched the largest peacetime army ever assembled in the United States to settle the score.

The "Mormon War" never really materialized. Mormon "guerrillas" managed to delay the troops by driving off livestock and cutting supply lines. Meanwhile, nearly the entire population of Salt Lake City staged an orderly evacuation southward. When columns of soldiers marched down the deserted streets in June 1858, they found only a handful of men remaining, standing ready to torch the houses and buildings in case the U.S. Army chose to occupy the city. Level heads prevailed, and residents soon returned.

COMING OF THE GENTILES

The isolation that had shielded Salt Lake City from outside influence began to fade around 1870. The "Mormon War" had brought U.S. forts to the Salt Lake Valley; off-duty soldiers prospect-ed for gold and found enough of it to encourage a mini-gold rush. Completion of the transcontinental railroad through Utah in 1869 encouraged non-Mormons to seek opportunity in the territory.

Even in this new social climate, Mormons and gentiles remained largely segregated. Each group developed its own social and political organizations and its own schools. Political life had been very dull during the first decades, when only a single set of church-appointed candidates appeared on the ballots. Voters had the option of voting "no," but they knew that their numbered ballots could be traced. The church discouraged political parties, believing they would lead to corruption and disharmony, and that civil government should be an arm of the church.

With the rising power of the gentile population in the 1870s, the church founded the People's Party to counter the anti-church Liberal Party. Salt Lake City's two major newspapers date from this time, with the *Deseret News* stating Mormon views and the *Salt Lake Tribune* representing the gentiles. Such fine shades of the political spectrum as the Republican or Democratic Party rarely entered the picture. The Mormons steadily lost control of their city; from a 93 percent majority population in 1867, they slipped to only 50 percent by 1891. In 1889 the first non-Mormons were elected to city offices.

THE DONNER PARTY

Of all the harrowing stories of pioneer-era grit, determination, and tragedy, few can top the story of the Donner party. In July 1846, this group of California-bound emigrants reached Wyoming's Fort Bridger, located along the established Oregon Trail, and decided to take a piece of advice offered in a letter "To all California Emigrants now on the Road." The letter, by L.W. Hastings, spoke of a shortcut to the Golden State across the deserts near the Great Salt Lake.

Despite some misgivings (Hastings was not at Fort Bridger to lead the pioneers, having already left with an earlier party), the group of 81, led by George Donner, decided to follow Hastings' tracks into the desert. Although the wagon team was excellently provisioned, problems beset the group almost immediately. The previous party's tracks were quickly lost in the sand, but Donner and his group pressed on ever farther into the desert. Wagons bogged in the sand, livestock began to die, and the water ran out. By the time the group realized it was in trouble, it was too late in the season to turn back.

Finally, in October, the remains of the Donner party reached the Sierra Nevada, where an early snowstorm trapped the remaining pioneers. The group erected storm shelters and spent a desparate winter with no supplies or food. Dissent became rampant, and the party descended into illness, death, madness, and eventually cannibalism; the only food available for long periods was the flesh of party members who died of starvation and cold. In the end, only 30 of the Donner party made it down off the mountain later that winter to reach Sacramento.

The church leadership lost its grasp on Salt Lake City during the legal battles over polygamy in the 1880s. Embarking on a new course, the church ended the practice of multiple marriages, dissolved its People's Party, and sold off most of its businesses. Even the famed ZCMI—a Mormon co-op that is thought to be the first department store in America—became a private, profit-making concern. The end of the 19th century saw Salt Lake making the transition from a Mormon village to an American city.

THE 20TH CENTURY

Wealth from successful mining operations fueled much of the development in Salt Lake City's business district, located in the blocks south of Temple Square. As a rule, the blocks nearest the temple had affiliations with the church while those farther south belonged to non-Mormons. In the early 1900s, skyscrapers began sprouting high above East Temple Street—which was rechristened Main Street. Exchange Place became the non-Mormon financial center.

The Depression was hard on all of rural Utah, as the dust bowl droughts sapped an already precarious water supply. The local economies picked up during World War II, as federal spending began to pour in and military installations took shape in the deserts west of Salt Lake City. Suburban growth began, providing the first exodus from the city's older neighborhoods. By the 1970s, the LDS Church began to spend money on revitalization of the city's downtown core, and the church's renewed focus worked: the city center is graced by a profusion of towering office blocks, busy shoppers, and legions of tourists.

Like any major metropolitan area, Salt Lake City suffers its share of air pollution and traffic congestion. The amount of homelessness and vagrancy will surprise travelers who have overblown expectations of the City of the Saints. (However, SLC is on the whole a very safe city.)

On the brighter side, a new interest in historical conservation has preserved many graceful mansions, ornate churches, and stately turn-of-the-century office towers. New downtown parks provide open spaces for concerts, lunchtime picnics, and opportunities for getting out into the open air.

THE 2002 OLYMPIC WINTER GAMES

From February 8–24, 2002, Salt Lake City will host the Winter Olympics. Although many of the signature events will take place at the ski resorts of the Wasatch Front, other events such as figure skating and the opening and closing ceremonies will take place in Salt Lake City itself. The Olympic Village will be located on the University of Utah grounds.

Hosting the Olympic games is an incredibly big deal to Salt Lake City. Of course, playing host to the games is a huge honor and responsibility no matter where they are held, but it's hard to imagine that Lillehammer, Norway, or Albertville, France, had as much of their own pride and self-image invested in the success of the games as does Salt Lake City. You don't have to talk to many people in Salt Lake to realize that it's not just important that the city throw a good party to showcase the athletes and the games themselves. There's something more going on. After years of struggling with the reputation of being the insular capital city of Mormonism—a provincial and backward city run as a wholly owned fiefdom of the church elders—Salt Lake City seems anxious to reestablish itself anew, as a sparkling, thriving urban center of the New West. A "world-class city," to quote the sentiments of many of Salt Lake's boosters.

This is to say, to many in the city and the church, the 2002 games are as much about the city's self-identity and self-esteem as they are about athleticism. The city *really* wanted to host these games.

In late 1998, a Swiss member of the International Olympic Committee (IOC) alleged that the selection of Salt Lake City as the venue for the 2002 Winter Games was accompanied by pervasive bribery and vote buying on the part of the Salt Lake Olympic Bid Committee (the SLOC). Internal investigations by the IOC, the U.S. Olympic Committee, and the SLOC ensued. These inquiries and media investigations revealed a wide assortment of pay-off schemes that funneled money, scholarships, real estate, and other perquisites from the SLOC to influential members of the IOC. While members of the IOC denied that the payments and gifts—reportedly totaling more than $1 million—influenced their vote, and members of the SLOC stated that the payments were not meant to buy the votes of the committee, no one denies that the payments were made. Regardless, the games are coming to Salt Lake City.

In July 2000, two members of the SLOC were indicted on federal conspiracy, racketeering, and fraud charges. The defendants have promised to implicate others on the SLOC and the IOC, as well as prominent Utah politicians, when the case comes to trial. To many in Salt Lake, their greatest nightmare is a high-profile corruption trial taking place simultaneously with the games themselves, forever tarnishing Salt Lake City's moment in the sun.

SALT LAKE CITY SIGHTS

TEMPLE SQUARE AND MORMON HISTORIC SITES

Easily Salt Lake City's most famous attraction, this complex has a special meaning for Mormons: this is the Mecca or the Vatican of the LDS faith. Brigham Young chose this site for Temple Square in July 1847, just four days after arriving in the valley. Nearby, Young built his private residences; the tabernacle, museums, and a host of other buildings that play a role in LDS Church administration also line the streets around Temple Square. You're welcome to visit most of these buildings, the Assembly Hall, exhibits in the North and South visitors' centers, and historic monuments—all of which provide an excellent introduction to the Mormon religion and Utah's early history.

Enthusiastic guides offer several tours of Temple Square, which covers an entire block in the heart of the city. A 15-foot wall surrounds the square's 10 acres; you can enter through wrought-iron gates on the south, west, and north sides. Temple Square is open daily 9 A.M.–9 P.M. and in summer 8 A.M.–10 P.M. All tours, exhibits, and concerts are free. Foreign-language tours are available, too—ask at the North Visitor Center. Smoking is prohibited on the grounds.

Musical Concerts: Temple Square is the site for an ongoing series of free musical concerts. Organists demonstrate the sounds and versatility of the tabernacle's famous instrument in 25-minute recitals once daily. The renowned Tabernacle Choir sings on Sunday mornings and rehearses on Thursday evenings and early Sunday mornings. Occasionally when the choir is on tour, a youth choir, youth symphony, or other group replaces it. A concert series presents programs featuring soloists, small ensembles, or full orchestras on Friday and Saturday evenings throughout the year in Assembly Hall or in the tabernacle. Except for a few special events, you won't need tickets to attend performances. For additional activities check the bulletin boards as you enter Temple Square, ask the guides, or call (801) 240-2534 or (801) 240-2535, or visit www.lds.org.

Temple Square Historical Tour: Guides will greet you at the gates of the Square and offer an introduction to Salt Lake City's Mormon pioneers, the temple, tabernacle, Assembly Hall, and historic monuments. The free 40-minute tours begin every 10 minutes during the summer season and every 15 minutes the rest of the year; hours are usually 9 A.M.–9 P.M. Custom group tours can be scheduled in advance. Points of interest, which you may also visit on your own, include the Seagull Monument (commemorating the seagulls that devoured the plague of "crickets" in 1848); a bell from the abandoned Nauvoo Temple; sculptures of Christ, church leaders, and handcart pioneers; an astronomy observation site; and a meridian marker (outside the walls at Main and South Temple Streets) from which surveyors mapped out Utah. Although the tour leaders don't normally proselytize, the tours do give the guides a chance to witness their faith.

The Salt Lake Temple

Mormons believe that they must have temples within which to hold sacred rites and fulfill God's commandments. According to the Mormon faith, baptisms, marriages, and family-sealing ceremonies that take place inside a temple will last beyond death and into eternity (prior to entering a temple, members prepare for a spiritual experience by dressing in white clothing, which represents purity). The temple is used only for these special functions; normal Sunday services take place in local stake or ward buildings—in fact, the temple is closed on Sunday.

Only LDS members who meet church requirements of good standing may enter the sacred temple itself; others can learn about temple activities and see photos of interior rooms at the South Visitor Center. Non-Mormons are not allowed to enter the temple or the grounds. However, you can get a good look at the Temple's east facade from the Main Street gates.

The plan for Salt Lake City's temple came first as a vision to Brigham Young when he still lived in Illinois. Later, Young's concept became a reality with help from church architect Truman O. Angell; construction began in 1853. Workers

SALT LAKE CITY FOR KIDS

Children's Museum of Utah

None of the exhibits at this children's favorite display Do Not Touch signs; in fact, many of the displays are hands-on. Kids get to explore by "excavating" a saber-toothed tiger skeleton, piloting a 727 jet trainer, implanting an artificial heart in a dummy, creating art projects, and using computer exhibits. Handicap-awareness simulations allow youngsters to experience firsthand what it might feel like to be blind or to use a wheelchair. The museum is open Monday–Saturday 10 A.M.–6 P.M. (until 9 P.M. on Fri.). Admission is $3, free for children under three. Located north of downtown at 840 N. 300 West (U.S. 89), (801) 328-3383. The adjacent city park offers picnic tables, a playground, and tennis courts.

Lagoon Amusement Park and Pioneer Village

History, recreation, and thrilling rides come together at this attractively landscaped park 16 miles north of Salt Lake City, (801) 451-8000 or (800) 748-5246. Lagoon traces its own history back to 1887, when bathers came to Lake Park on the shores of the Great Salt Lake, two miles west of its present location. The vast Lagoon Amusement Park area includes roller coaster rides, a giant Ferris wheel, and other midway favorites. There are also musical performances. Other things to do include picnicking and playing miniature golf (extra charge). Lagoon A Beach provides thrilling water slides and landscaped pools.

Pioneer Village brings the past to life with authentic 19th-century buildings, stagecoach and steam-train rides, a Ute Indian museum, a carriage museum, a gun collection, and many other exhibits. Wild West shoot-outs take place several times daily. Food booths are scattered throughout the park or you can dine at the Gaslight Restaurant near the Opera House. Lagoon Amusement Park, Lagoon A Beach, and Pioneer Village open at 11 A.M. Sunday–Friday and 10 A.M. Saturday and close at 11 P.M. or midnight (depending on weather and day of week): Saturday and Sunday from early April–Memorial Day weekend, daily from Memorial–Labor Day weekends, then Saturday and Sunday through September. An all-day ride pass (the best deal, as individual rides cost $2–3.50) is $28.95 adults, $22.95 for children aged 4 to 50 inches in height, $14.95 for children 3 and under, and $15.95 for seniors. The all-day pass includes Lagoon A Beach privileges. An additional $5 is charged for parking. Take I-15 to the Lagoon Exit and follow signs. Adults also have the option of buying an $18 ticket that gains admission to the park without paying for the rides.

Wheeler Historic Farm

Kids enjoy a visit to this working farm to experience the rural life of milking cows, gathering eggs, churning butter, and feeding animals. Hay rides (sleigh rides in winter) take visitors around the farm. Henry and Sariah Wheeler started the farm in 1887 and developed it into a prosperous dairy and ice-making operation. Tour guides take you through the Wheeler's restored Victorian house, built 1896–1898, the first in the county to have an indoor bathroom. Signs on other farm buildings recount their history and use. The "Ice House" now sells crafts and snacks. The Salt Lake County Recreation Department operates the farm and offers special programs for both youngsters and adults; call or write for a schedule: 6351 S. 900 East, Salt Lake City, UT 84121, (801) 264-2241. There's no admission charge to the farm, but you'll pay for individual activities. A tour costs $1.50 adults, $1 children 3–11 and seniors 65 and up; milking the cow costs just $.50. Though once on the outskirts of town, suburbs now surround Wheeler Historic Farm. Open daily 9:30 A.M.–5:30 P.M. in spring and fall, 9:30 A.M.–8 P.M. in summer, and 1–5 P.M. in winter.

DOWNTOWN SALT LAKE CITY SIGHTS

CHILDRENS MUSEUM OF UTAH ★

VICTORY RD.

WALL ST.

CENTER ST.

CAPITOL ST.

COLUMBUS ST.

DESOTO ST.

CORTEZ ST.

EAST CAPITOL BLVD.

89

0   0.2 mi

0   0.2 km

600 N. ST.

500 N. ST.

400 N. ST.

MARMALADE

HISTORIC

DISTRICT ★

UTAH HERITAGE FOUNDATION ■

300 N. ST.

200 N. ST.

N. TEMPLE ST.

CITY

CANYON

(MEMORY

GROVE

PARK)

13TH   AVE.

12TH   AVE.

11TH   AVE.

10TH   AVE.

9TH   AVE.

8TH   AVE.

7TH   AVE.

THE AVENUES

6TH   DISTRICT   AVE.

5TH   AVE.

4TH   AVE.

3RD   AVE.

2ND   AVE.

1ST   AVE.

STATE CAPITOL BUILDING ★

PIONEER MEMORIAL MUSEUM ■

UTAH TRAVEL COUNCIL (COUNCIL HALL) ★

NEW ASSEMBLY BUILDING ★

LDS OFFICE BUILDING ■

MUSEUM OF CHURCH HISTORY AND ART ■

BRIGHAM YOUNG CEMETERY ■

TRIAD CENTER ■

FAMILY HISTORY LIBRARY ■

TEMPLE SQUARE

JOSEPH SMITH MEMORIAL BUILDING ★

BEEHIVE HOUSE ★

CATHEDRAL OF THE MADELEINE ■

FIRST PRESBYTERIAN CHURCH ■

KEARNS MANSION ■

UNION PACIFIC DEPOT ■

GREYHOUND BUS STATION ■

TEMPLE ST.

TRAX LIGHT RAIL LINE

DELTA CENTER ■

ABRAVANEL SYMPHONY HALL ★

SALT LAKE ART CENTER ★

BRIGHAM YOUNG MONUMENT ★

HANSEN PLANETARIUM ■

SOCIAL HALL ■

100   S.   ST.

CROSSROADS PLAZA SHOPPING CENTER ■

ZCMI SHOPPING CENTER ■

SALT PALACE CONVENTION CENTER AND VISITORS BUREAU ■

PROMISED VALLEY PLAYHOUSE ■

CAPITOL THEATER ■

200   S.   ST.

UTAH STATE HISTORY MUSEUM (DENVER AND RIO GRANDE DEPOT) ★

PERRY HALL COMPLEX ■

300   S.   ST.

PIONEER PARK

EXCHANGE PLACE HISTORIC DISTRICT

400   S.   ST.

TRAX LIGHT RAIL LINE

CITY AND COUNTY BUILDING ■

CITY LIBRARY ■

500   S.   ST.

TROLLEY CORNERS ■

TROLLEY SQUARE

600   S.   ST.

500 W.   400 W.   300 W.   200 W.   TEMPLE   MAIN   STATE   200   300   400   500   600   700

89

700   S.   ST.

© AVALON TRAVEL PUBLISHING, INC.

chiseled granite blocks from Little Cottonwood Canyon, 20 miles southeast of the city, then hauled them by oxen and later by railroad for final shaping at the temple site. The foundation alone required 7,478 tons of stone. Walls measure nine feet thick at the base and taper to six feet on the second story. The tallest of the six slender spires stands 210 feet and is topped by a glittering statue of the angel Moroni with trumpet in hand. The 12.5-foot statue is made of hammered copper covered with gold leaf. As with all Mormon temples, the interior was open to the public for a short time after completion. Dedication took place on April 6, 1893–1840 years to the day after work began.

The Tabernacle

Pioneers labored from 1863 to 1867 to construct this unique, dome-shaped building. Brigham Young envisioned a meeting hall capable of holding thousands of people in an interior free of obstructing structural supports. His design, drawn by bridge-builder Henry Grow, took shape in massive latticed wooden beams resting on 44 supports of red sandstone. Because Utah lacked many common building supplies, the workers often had to make substitutions. Wooden pegs and rawhide strips hold the structure together. The large organ pipes resemble metal, balcony pillars appear to be marble, and the benches look like oak, yet all are pine wood painted to simulate these materials.

The tabernacle has become known for its phenomenal acoustics, due to its smooth arched ceiling, and its massive pipe organ, regarded as one of the finest ever built. From 700 pipes when constructed in 1867, the organ has grown to about 12,000 pipes, five manuals, and one pedal keyboard. Daily recitals Monday–Saturday at noon and Sunday at 2 P.M., demonstrate the instrument's capabilities. Temple Square tours include a stop in the tabernacle for a short presentation on the history of the building; an acoustic demonstration shows that a dropped pin can be heard even in the back rows—170 feet away!

Important church conferences take place in the tabernacle every spring and autumn, but the seating capacity of about 6,500—considered huge when it was built—is now far too small, despite the addition of a balcony. The renowned Mormon Tabernacle Choir, 320 voices strong, sings on Sunday mornings over national radio (CBS) and regional TV networks. The choir's radio broadcast, which dates back to 1929, is the longest-running broadcast in the world. Visitors may also attend choir rehearsals Thursday evenings at 8 P.M. or the broadcast performance on Sunday at 9:30 A.M. (be seated by 9:15 A.M.); both are free. Families with infants can sit in a glassed-in room at the rear without fear of disturbing other listeners. For information on performances in the tabernacle, call (801) 240-3318.

Assembly Hall

Thrifty craftspeople built this smaller, Gothic Revival structure in 1877–1882 using granite left over from the temple construction. The truncated spires, reaching as high as 130 feet, once functioned as chimneys. Inside the hall, there's seating for 1,500 people and a choir of 100. The baroque-style organ, installed in 1983, has 3,500 pipes and three manuals; of particular note are the organ's horizontal pipes, called trumpets. Initially, the Salt Lake Stake Congregation met here; now the building serves as a concert hall and hosts a variety of church functions.

North Visitor Center

Wander around on your own or ask the ever-present tour guides for help. Murals on the lower floor depict Old Testament prophets; head upstairs to see paintings of the life of Christ. A spiraling ramp leads to the upper level where

Tabernacle under construction, ca. 1867

CHURCH OF JESUS CHRIST OF LATTER-DAY SAINTS

Cristus, an 11-foot replica of a sculpture by Bertel Thorvaldsen, stands in a circular room whose wall mural depicts the universe. The Resource Center, near the bottom of the ramp, offers touch-screen video programs. Downstairs display areas and theaters have other offerings, which change periodically.

South Visitor Center

Two 30-minute tours begin here: **Book of Mormon** and **Purpose of Temples.** Things to see on the main level include paintings of prophets and church history, a baptismal font supported by 12 life-size oxen (representing the 12 tribes of Israel) as used in temples, photos of the Salt Lake Temple interior, and a scale model of Solomon's Temple. Head downstairs to see replicas of the metal plates inscribed with the Book of Mormon, which Mormons believe were revealed to Joseph Smith in 1823. Ancient plates of Old World civilizations and stone boxes from the Americas are exhibited to support the claim that the plates are genuine. Mormon literature can be obtained at a desk near the entrance.

Museum of Church History and Art

Brigham Young encouraged the preservation of church history, especially when he saw that Salt Lake City's pioneering era was drawing to a close. The collection of church artifacts, begun by the Deseret Museum in 1869, includes the plow that cut the first furrows in the Salt Lake Valley. Exhibits document each of the past church presidents and religious paintings and sculpture. Perhaps the most striking piece is the gilded 11.5-foot statue of Moroni, which crowned a Washington, D.C., chapel from 1933 to 1976. Temporary exhibits also display Mormon artistry and themes in photography, abstract art, textiles, furniture, and woodworking.

Step outside to see the 1847 log cabin, one of only two surviving from Salt Lake City's beginnings. The interior has been furnished as it might have been during the first winter here. The free Museum of Church History and Art is open Monday–Friday 9 A.M.–9 P.M. and Saturday, Sunday, and holidays 10 A.M.–7 P.M. April–December and daily 10 A.M.–7 P.M. (until 9 P.M. Monday and Wednesday) January–March. It's located just west of Temple Square at 45 N. West Temple, (801) 240-3310.

Family History Library

This new building houses the largest collection of genealogical information in the world. Library workers have made extensive travels to many countries to microfilm documents and books. More than 500 employees are assisted by over 400 volunteers to keep track of the records. The Mormon Church has gone to this effort to enable members to trace their ancestors, who can then be baptized by proxy. In this way, according to Mormon belief, the ancestors will be sealed in the family and the church for eternity. However, the spirits for whom these baptisms are performed have a choice of accepting or rejecting the baptism.

The library is open to the public. If you'd like to research your family tree, bring what information you have and get the library's *A Guide to Research* booklet. A brief slide presentation explains what types of records are kept and how to get started. Staff will answer questions. In most cases the files won't have information about living persons because of rights to privacy. The Mormon Church leaves nothing to chance in preserving its genealogical records and history—master copies on microfilm rest in vaults deep within the mountains southeast of Salt Lake City. The Family History Library opens Monday–Saturday at 7:30 A.M. and closes Monday at 6 P.M., Tuesday–Saturday at 10 P.M.; it's closed Sunday and federal holidays. Located just west of Temple Square at 35 N. West Temple, (801) 240-2331.

New Assembly Building

Completed in 2000, this block-square, ten-acre building is used both as a performance space and a place of worship. The main auditorium, which seats 21,000, serves as a meeting hall for large LDS assemblies. The building is fronted by white granite. The many-tiered design incorporates four acres of landscaping, with trees, flowers, fountains, and waterfalls. From a distance the building looks like the Hanging Gardens of Babylon.

Brigham Young Monument

This monument stands in the middle of Main between North and South Temple Streets. Brigham Young, in bronze, stands atop a granite pedestal with figures below representing an

Indian, a fur trapper, and a pioneer family. Unveiled on July 24, 1897, it celebrates the first 50 years of settlement in Salt Lake City. A plaque lists the names of the first group of 148 Mormon pioneers. The statue is also the originating point for the city's street numbering system.

Joseph Smith Memorial Building/Hotel Utah

Built of white terra-cotta brick in modern Italian Renaissance style, this building was opened in 1911 as a first-class hotel for church and business leaders. However, in 1987 the LDS Church, which owned the hotel, converted it into an office building and a memorial to LDS founding father, Joseph Smith. The opulent lobby, with its massive marble columns, chandeliers, and stained-glass ceiling, remains intact; you definitely should walk through the lobby and admire the grand architecture.

On the ground floor the **Family Search Center** has 200 computers available to trace family ancestry; (801) 240-4400. Also on the ground floor is a large-screen theater showing the 53-minute film *Legacy*, which traces a Mormon family's experiences from conversion through years of persecution, relocation, war, and settlement in Utah; admission is free, but you'll need a ticket for entry; one can be obtained at the information desk at the building's Main Street entrance; (801) 240-2205. The 10th floor offers observation areas, the formal **Roof Restaurant,** (801) 539-1911, and the less formal **Garden Restaurant** (same phone). The building is open Monday–Saturday but is closed on Sunday except to those attending worship services.

LDS Office Building

Day-to-day running of the massive church organization is centered in the 28-story tower east of Temple Square. Such a volume of correspondence takes place that the building has its own zip code. Free tours begin in the main lobby and explain a bit about the work here, but the big attraction is a visit to the 26th-floor observation deck. You'll see Temple Square and the whole city spread out below like a map. Weather permitting, the valley, the Great Salt Lake, and the surrounding mountains stand out clearly. Tours last about 30 minutes, depending on how long you want to take in the panorama. The main lobby has some noteworthy artwork including a giant 66- by 16-foot mural of Christ appearing to his apostles just prior to his ascension. Gardens and fountains grace a small park behind the building. You can take tours Monday–Friday (and Sat. mornings in summer only) 9 A.M.–4:30 P.M.; closed Sunday and holidays. The address is 50 E. North Temple, (801) 240-2842.

Beehive House

This former house of Brigham Young was built in 1854 and occupied by him until his death in 1877. The adobe and brick structure stood out as one of the most ornate houses in early Salt Lake City. Free tours lasting 30–40 minutes take visitors through the house and tell of family life within the walls. The interior has been meticulously restored with many original furnishings. A beehive symbol, representing industry, caps the house and appears in decorative motifs inside. Brigham Young had about 27 wives, but only one stayed

Beehive House and Eagle Gate, ca. 1869

in this house at a time; other wives and children lived next door in the Lion House. Downstairs in the main house, Young's children gathered in the sitting room for evenings of prayer, talks, and music. Upstairs, he entertained guests and dignitaries in a lavish reception room called the Long Hall. Other rooms to see include the kitchen, family store, bedrooms, playroom, and the "fairy castle," where small children could peer through a window at grown-ups in the hallway below.

The Beehive House is located in the shadow of the LDS Church office building, at 67 E. South Temple, (801) 240-2671. Tours leave Monday–Saturday 9:30 A.M.–4:30 P.M. (until 6:30 P.M. Mon.–Fri. in summer) and Sunday 10 A.M.–1 P.M.; closed on Thanksgiving, Christmas, and New Year's Day; open other holidays but usually only until 1 P.M.

The **Lion House,** next door at 63 E. South Temple, was built in 1855–1856 of stuccoed adobe; a stone lion guards the entrance. Brigham Young used the dwelling as a supplementary dwelling for his many wives and their children. Today, the pantry and basement of the building are open to the public as the Lion House cafeteria.

Brigham Young Cemetery
Church president, founder of Utah, colonizer, and territorial governor, Brigham Young rests here with five of his wives and his eldest son. Several monuments on the grounds honor the pioneers and Young's family. From State Street near Beehive House, travel one-half-block east on First Avenue.

Eagle Gate
This modern replacement of the original 1859 gate spans State Street just north of South Temple Street. It once marked the entrance to Brigham Young's property, which included City Creek Canyon. The bronze eagle has a 20-foot wingspan and weighs two tons. The present gate, designed by Brigham Young's grandson, architect George Cannon Young, was dedicated in 1963.

OTHER DOWNTOWN SIGHTS

Abravanel Concert Hall
Easily the most striking modern building in Salt Lake City, Abravanel Hall glitters with gold leaf,

Abravanel Concert Hall

crystal chandeliers, and more than a mile of brass railing. Careful attention to acoustic design has paid off: the concert hall is one of the best in the world. The Utah Symphony Orchestra inaugurated its new home in 1979 after $12 million and three years of construction. An illuminated fountain flows outside on the plaza during concerts. The hall is located at 123 W. South Temple (next to the Salt Palace); call the box office for concert dates at (801) 533-5626.

Salt Lake Art Center
This civic gallery hosts a changing lineup of traveling and thematic exhibits including displays of painting, photography, sculpture, ceramics, and conceptual art. Diverse art classes and workshops are scheduled along with films, lectures, poetry readings, musical concerts, and theater. A gift shop offers art books, posters, crafts, and artwork. The center, located at 20 S. West Temple (between Abravanel Concert Hall and the Salt Palace Convention Center), (801) 328-4201, is open Monday–Saturday 10 A.M.–5 P.M. (Friday

till 9 P.M.) and Sunday 1–5 P.M.; admission is free, but a donation is requested.

Salt Palace Convention Center

This enormous structure, between 200 South and South Temple along West Temple, (801) 534-4777, just keeps on getting larger. After its expansion in 2000, the Salt Palace encompasses 370,000 square feet of exhibit space, a 45,000-square-foot ballroom, and 53 individual meeting rooms. Even in the sprawling scale of downtown Salt Lake City, this is a big building. The center also houses the Salt Lake Convention and Visitors Bureau and the **Visitor Information Center,** 90 S. West Temple, (801) 521-2822.

Hansen Planetarium

This planetarium and science center is a popular family destination. In the museum, exhibits include the planetarium's original Spitz star projector, meteorites, Apollo displays, a rock from the moon, a Foucault pendulum, and hands-on interactive displays. The museum exhibit halls are open Monday–Saturday 9 A.M.–5:15 P.M. and 7–9 P.M. and Sunday 1–4 P.M.; free.

The Star Chamber Planetarium, with its simulated space journey, laser/music shows, images of the night skies projected on a 50-foot domed ceiling, and special events, is open Monday–Thursday 9 A.M.–9 P.M., Friday–Saturday 9 A.M.–midnight, and Sunday noon–4 P.M. Call ahead as the schedule of events and the pricing change for individual shows. Hansen Planetarium is in a historic building at 15 South State Street (just east of ZCMI Shopping Center) downtown, (801) 538-2104 (recording).

For upcoming astronomical events and telescope viewings throughout northern Utah, call (801) 532-STAR.

Social Hall Heritage Museum

Early settlers built Utah's (and the West's) first theater between 1852–1853 under the direction of Brigham Young. Recent excavations have unearthed the foundation and sandstone walls of the venerable building, which was torn down and buried in 1921. The ruins and historic exhibits lie within a glass enclosure south of Hansen Planetarium at 39 South State Street, (801) 321-8743. An underground passage connects Social Hall with ZCMI Shopping Center; both are open daily. Free admission.

Utah State Historical Society Museum

The Denver and Rio Grande Railroad built this grand terminal in 1910 while in keen competition with Union Pacific, which kept a depot two blocks away. Displays outline state history in the museum's spacious lobby. The museum, located at the west end of 300 South at 455 West, (801) 533-3500, is open Monday–Friday 8 A.M.–5 P.M. and Saturday 10 A.M.–3 P.M.; free. The Utah State Historical Society operates a bookstore just off the lobby with an excellent selection of Utah history and travel books. Upstairs, the society offers a research library containing thousands of books and photos about Utah's past. The depot is also the local Amtrak station.

UTAH STATE CAPITOL AND VICINITY

The State Capitol

Utah's granite capitol occupies a prominent spot on a hill just north of downtown. The architectural style may look familiar; the building was patterned after the national capitol. The interior, with its Ionic columns, is made of polished marble from Georgia. Murals depict early explorers and pioneers; smaller paintings and statues show all of the territorial and state governors and prominent Utah figures of the past. The Gold Room, used for receiving dignitaries, provides a formal setting graced by chandeliers, wall tapestries, elegant furniture, and cherubs on the ceiling. Enter the chambers of the House of Representatives, Senate, and Supreme Court from the mezzanine. Photo exhibits of the state's scenic and historic spots, beehive memorabilia, mining, and agriculture line hallways on the ground floor.

Forty acres of manicured parks and monuments surround the capitol. From the steps leading to the building, you can look out over Salt Lake City and straight down State Street, which runs south about 28 miles without a curve. From near the Mormon Battalion Monument, east of the capitol, steps lead down into a small canyon and **Memory Grove,** another war memorial, and a series of streamside parks.

The Utah State Capitol, 300 North and State Sts., (801) 538-3000, is open daily 8 A.M.–6 P.M.

(extended in summer to 8 P.M.). Free tours in summer depart every half hour Monday–Friday 9 A.M.–4 P.M.; meet in front of the large map on the first floor. Visitors are welcome to dine at the circular cafeteria (open Mon.–Fri. 7 A.M.–4 P.M.) behind the capitol. Annual legislative sessions begin in January and last about 45 days.

Pioneer Memorial Museum

Descendants of Utah's Mormon pioneers have packed all four levels of this museum with a huge collection of pioneer artifacts, portraits, and memorabilia that tell the story of the 2,000-mile exodus from Nauvoo, Illinois, to Salt Lake City. A video shown on request introduces the collection.

While some exhibits here are of interest mostly to Mormons (for example, the personal effects of Brigham Young), other displays in the museum's four floors provide insights into the daily life of frontier Utah. The two-story **Carriage House,** connected to the museum by a short tunnel, displays pioneer-era conveyances including a mule-drawn streetcar, stagecoaches, and the wagon in which Brigham Young is believed to have arrived in the Salt Lake Valley. The Pioneer Memorial Museum, 300 N. Main St. (near the State Capitol), (801) 538-1050, is open Monday–Saturday 9 A.M.–5 P.M. and closed major holidays; donation appreciated. Free parking is available at a lot between the museum and the State Capitol.

Council Hall

The venerable Council Hall lies across the street from the capitol. Dedicated in 1866, the brick building served as the city hall and a meeting place for the territorial and early state legislatures. Council Hall used to stand downtown before being moved here in 1963.

It is now the home of the **Utah Travel Council.** Drop in to see the staff of the **Utah Tourism and Recreation Information Center** on the main floor for information on sights, services, and events in the state. Council Hall and the information center, (801) 538-1030 or (800) 200-1160, are open Monday–Friday 8 A.M.–6 P.M., Saturday 9 A.M.–5 P.M. The 1883 Gothic Revival building just to the east was also moved here. Formerly the 18th Ward Chapel of the LDS Church, it's now the **White Memorial Chapel** and is used for community events.

UNIVERSITY OF UTAH AND VICINITY

University of Utah

Mormon pioneers established a university in their short-lived town of Nauvoo, Illinois, and they brought its books with them to Utah. The University of Deseret opened in 1850, just 2.5 years after the first colonizers reached the Salt Lake Valley. It was renamed the University of Utah in 1892 and moved to its present site on a terrace east of town in 1900. The state-assisted institution now sprawls across a 1,500-acre campus. A giant "U" on the hillside lights up during sporting events and if the university team wins, the lights flash.

About 26,000 students study a wide range of fields including the liberal arts, business, medicine, science, engineering, and architecture—some 16 colleges and schools in all. The adjacent Research Park is a partnership of the university and private enterprise involving many students and faculty. A center of culture, the

Kearns Mansion

University of Utah is home to the Utah Museum of Natural History, the Utah Museum of Fine Arts, musical concerts, and theater groups. Visitors are welcome at cultural and sporting events, libraries, bookstore, movie theater, and Olpin Union food services. Most recreational facilities are reserved for students. For a campus map, a list of scheduled events, and other information, drop by the Park Building at the top of President's Circle, (801) 581-6515, or the Olpin Union, (801) 581-5888. On-campus parking is available at metered spaces around the grounds and in pay lots next to the Olpin Union and the Marriott Library; free parking can be found off campus on residential streets. The general information number for the university is (801) 581-7200.

Utah Museum of Natural History

This large and varied collection of geology, biology, and anthropology exhibits tells the natural and early Native American history of Utah. Impressive natural history models include dinosaurs, early mammals, and the varied wildlife of the present day. Look for the exhibit of California gulls *(Larus californicus)* devouring the plague of grasshoppers. Exhibits display artifacts and trace the development of prehistoric cultures and their replacement by modern tribes such as the Ute and the Navajo. A reproduction of the huge Barrier Canyon Mural pictograph shows early Indian art. Other exhibits illustrate Utah's mining history and feature specimens of the state's more than 600 minerals. A gift shop sells animal souvenirs for the kids, fossil and

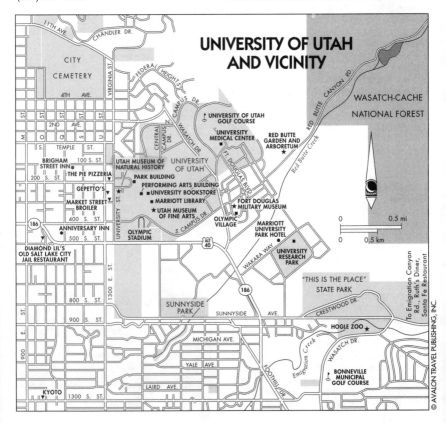

mineral specimens, books on Utah and natural history, and posters. The museum, located on the University of Utah campus on President's Circle; turn in off University St. (1350 East) between 200 and 300 South Sts., (801) 581-4303 (recording),is open Monday–Saturday 9:30 A.M.–5:30 P.M. and Sunday and holidays noon–5 P.M.; $4 adults, $2.50 children 3–12 and seniors 65 and up (special exhibits may cost more). Free validated parking is available in front.

Utah Museum of Fine Arts

Though of modest size, this museum displays a little of everything, from 5,000-year-old Egyptian art to works by contemporary artists. Permanent exhibitions include art of China, India, Southeast Asia, Europe, Africa, pre-Columbia, and the early American West. Three large galleries host visiting exhibitions. The Museum of Fine Arts, 1650 E. South Campus Pl. (located just south of the Marriott Library on the university campus at 1530 E. South Campus Dr.), (801) 581-7332, is open Monday–Friday 10 A.M.–5 P.M. and Saturday and Sunday noon–5 P.M.; free. Metered parking is available near the museum or at the library; both are off South Campus Drive, an extension of 400 South Street.

Red Butte Garden and Arboretum

Utah's largest botanical garden offers 30 acres of floral displays, ponds, waterfalls, and four miles of mountain nature trails in a 200-acre natural area. The garden visitors' center features botanical gifts and books, and the Courtyard Garden is an excellent place for a family picnic. To reach the garden from I-15, take the Sixth South exit, which will take you east, then turn north two blocks to Fourth South and head east past where Fourth merges into Fifth South. After rising up a hill, take the left onto Wakara Way and continue east to the Red Butte Garden and Arboretum exit. The garden is open year-round with irregular hours and days. For times, call (801) 581-4747 (recording) or (801) 581-5322. Entrance fees to the gardens are $3 adults, $2 seniors and children under 16. Free access to hiking trails in the natural area.

Fort Douglas Military Museum

Artifacts and historical photos take the visitor back to the days of the Nauvoo Legion, the Mormon Battalion, and U.S. Army life in Utah during pioneer days. In late 1862, Colonel Patrick Connor marched to this site with his California-Nevada volunteers and built Camp Douglas. Officially the post defended the mail route and kept check on local tribes of Indians. Connor also felt it necessary to keep an eye (and cannon) on the Mormons, whom he and other federal officials distrusted. The colonel wasted no time in seeking Indians to fight. In January 1863, just months after his arrival, Connor's troops ambushed several hundred Shoshoni on the Bear River in northern Cache Valley. The event advanced Connor's career but ranks as one of the bloodiest slaughters in the history of U.S.-Native American conflicts. Later, in a more peaceable mood, the colonel and some of his soldiers pioneered the development of Utah's minerals near Park City and elsewhere in the territory.

Fort Douglas Museum's exhibits show the unique histories of Fort Douglas and other military bases in Utah. A World War I room includes photos of German POWs once interned here. Other exhibits illustrate the big military buildup during World War II, when Utah even had a naval base. The Fort Douglas Museum, (801) 581-1710, is open Tuesday–Saturday, 10 A.M.–noon and 1–4 P.M.; free.

The museum building, officers' row, and some of the other structures at Fort Douglas date from the 1870s and 1880s and are built in an architectural style termed Quartermaster Victorian. Pick up a walking-tour leaflet of the fort at the museum; a map shows the nearby post cemetery, where Colonel Connor, soldiers, and German POWs are buried. Fort Douglas, formerly used by the military as administration and recruitment offices, is now part of the University of Utah; turn north on Wasatch Drive from 500 South and travel one-half mile to the museum.

"This Is The Place" State Park

Brigham Young gazed onto the Salt Lake Valley for the first time from this spot, it's believed, and spoke the famous words, "This is the right place. Drive on." Exactly 100 years later, on July 24, 1947, a crowd gathered to dedicate the massive *This Is the Place* monument. Twelve-foot bronze statues of Brigham Young flanked by Heber C. Kimball and Wilford Woodruff stand atop a central pylon. The park has a pleasant picnic area, and the monument honors not only the Mormon pioneers but also the Catholic missionaries from Spain, fur trappers and traders, government explorers, and California immigrants who contributed to the founding of an empire in "the top of the mountains." Sculptures, bas-reliefs, and plaques around the base of the monument illustrate Utah's beginnings. A visitors' center contains a mural depicting major events on the migration of the "Saints" from Nauvoo, Illinois, to their promised land. An eight-minute narration recounts the journey; narration in a foreign language can be requested, too. "This is the Place" State Park is southeast of the University of Utah near the mouth of Emigration Canyon, at 2601 Sunnyside Ave., (801) 584-8392 (recording). The visitors' center is open daily 11 A.M.–5 P.M. (Thursday until 8 P.M.); free.

Old Deseret, in the grounds near the monument, re-creates a Utah pioneer village. During the summer it comes alive with farming and craft demonstrations and wagon rides. Most of the dozen buildings that were moved here are original, some of the first in the valley. Some notable structures include Brigham Young's forest farmhouse, the 1847 Levi Riter cabin, and the Charles Rich house, designed in the 1850s for polygamous family living.

Old Deseret is open daily from early April–early October 11 A.M.–5 P.M. and Thursday until 8 P.M. Admission is $8 adults, $6 children and seniors; a family pass is available for $30.

Hogle Zoo

Utah's state zoo, an especially popular spot with the kids, is on the eastern edge of town and across from "This Is The Place" State Park. Children like to ride the miniature train ($.75; closed in winter) and see exhibits in the Discovery Center. Many of the large-animal enclosures have natural settings; here you'll see the familiar elephants, rhinos, and hippos. The apes and monkeys carry on almost all the time, though mornings are best to hear the songs of the white-handed gibbons of Southeast Asia. Exhibits on tropical, temperate, and desert zones contain deadly cobras and vipers, aardvarks, Australian kookaburras, brightly colored birds in a walk-in aviary, and dozens of other exotic species. The cats include lions, leopards, tigers, and ocelots.

Though zoos don't normally display taxidermied animals, Hogle Zoo's unusual "liger" can be seen in the cat area. Shasta the liger was born of a Bengal tigress and an African lion father, the result of a mating that couldn't happen in nature because the animals' territories don't overlap. Hogle Zoo, 2600 E. Sunnyside Ave. (one-half-mile east of Wasatch Dr.), (801) 582-1631, www.hoglezoo.com, is open daily 9 A.M.–5 P.M. Entrance fees are $6 adults, $4 children 3–12 and seniors 65 and over. Snack bars and strollers are available.

SOUTH OF DOWNTOWN

Liberty Park

This large park is the jewel of the city's public park system and contains abundant recreational facilities in addition to an excellent aviary, an arts center, and 80 acres of grass and shady boulevards. A fun new addition to the park is a conceptual "map" of northern Utah that re-creates the rivers, lakes, and mountains as a series of fountains and wading pools.

The Children's Garden—playground, amusement park, snack bar, and large pond with rental boat—sits in the southeast corner of the park (all closed in winter). The tennis center on the western side of the park offers 16 lighted courts and instruction; an outdoor swimming pool adjacent to the tennis center is open in summer. Liberty Park is southeast of downtown and bordered by 900 and 1300 South and by 500 and 700 East.

Birds have taken over the southwest corner of Liberty Park. **Tracy Aviary** houses over 1,000 individual birds of 240 species and offers the "Birds of a Feather" show, with trained free-flying birds such as falcons. Birds on display include majestic golden and bald eagles, showy flamingos and peacocks, the hyacinthine macaw (the world's largest parrot), the golden pheasant of China, and hundreds of other feathered friends. Emus from Australia prance across fields while ducks, geese, swan, and other waterfowl keep to the ponds. You'll also get to meet Utah's only native vulture, the turkey vulture.

The "Birds of a Feather" show is presented during the summer Tuesday–Friday at noon and 2 P.M. and Saturday, Sunday, and holidays at noon, 2 P.M., and 4 P.M.; shows are also scheduled during weekends in spring and fall. Tracy Aviary is located in Liberty Park at 589 E. 1300 South, (801) 596-8500; enter the aviary from the east side. The aviary is open daily 9 A.M.–6 P.M. in summer and 9 A.M.–4:30 P.M. the rest of the year; adults pay $3, children 4–12 and seniors $2.

The Chase Mill, just north of the aviary entrance, was built by Isaac Chase in 1852 and is one of the oldest buildings in the valley. Free flour from the mill saved many families during the famine of 1856–1857. The interior is closed to the public but you can view the exterior and an old millstone. Formal gardens lie north of the mill.

Chase's adobe brick house (built 1853–1854), farther to the north, has been restored. Go inside to see exhibits of the **Chase Home Museum of Utah Folk Art,** sponsored by the Utah Arts Council. On display is contemporary Utah folk art including quilts, rugs, woodcarvings, ethnic arts, and Native American works. You'll find horseshoe pits to the north of the Chase house. The museum, (801) 533-5760, is open weekends noon–5 P.M. from mid-April–mid-October and daily Memorial Day–Labor Day; free.

Westminster College

The Salt Lake Collegiate Institute, founded in 1875 by the Presbyterian Church as a boys preparatory school, became Westminster College about the turn of the century. By 1944 it had grown to be a four-year college, and in 1974 it became independent. Converse Hall, constructed in 1906 as the first building on the present campus, is a registered National Historic Site.

This private four-year college provides a liberal arts education with training in business, computer science, education, and nursing. Postgraduate programs are offered in business and education. Westminster College has approximately 2,200 students and 90 faculty members. Shaw Center in the middle of the campus, serves as a student meeting place with snack bar, cafeteria, and small bookstore. Concerts, theater performances, poetry series, lectures, art exhibits, and other cultural activities are open to the public. Westminster College is located at 1840 South 1300 East, (801) 488-4200.

International Peace Gardens

With wishes for world peace, the Salt Lake Council of Women created this unusual garden in the northwest corner of Jordan Park. Members of Salt Lake City's various ethnic and national groups were invited to design and plant a garden that reflected their cultural heritage. Currently, nearly 25 groups have taken part; you'll find Dutch windmills, pagodas, and Buddhist temples scattered around the grounds. The Peace Gardens, located near 900 West and 1000 South, are a lovely place for a stroll in summer.

SALT LAKE CITY ACCOMMODATIONS

Salt Lake City has the best selection of accommodations in Utah, and with the Olympics coming in 2002, even more lodgings are on the way. Unless you're on a real budget, you'll probably be more comfortable if you avoid the cheapest motels along West Temple or State Street. Many of these older motor-court units have become residential lodgings and the owners don't put much effort into upkeep. However, you should have a pleasant stay at all of the following accommodations.

There are several major lodging centers. Downtown Salt Lake City has the advantage of being close to Temple Square, Delta Center, the Salt Palace, and most other visitor attractions. South of downtown, near 600 South and West Temple, you'll find a clutch of hotels and motels including several business-oriented hotels. While these lodgings are only six blocks from the center of the city at Temple Square, remember that blocks are very long in SLC. Another cluster of hotels and motels is found west along North Temple, the primary surface street leading to the airport. If your trip to Salt Lake City involves visiting students or conducting business at the university, there are a couple good lodging options near the campus.

In general, room rates are rather high, though quality is good. Because SLC is a major convention site and a winter recreation center, there really isn't much seasonal variation in the price of rooms. However, at the downtown business hotels, weekend rates can be very favorable. Reservations are strongly suggested, especially if you want to stay in central Salt Lake City.

SALT LAKE CITY'S HISTORIC ARCHITECTURE

Salt Lake City contains some of the best-preserved historic architecture in the American West. From the magnificent public buildings to the craftsmanship of humble workers' cottages, the city's structures say a lot about the early citizens' pride in their earthly City of Zion.

The **Utah Heritage Foundation,** located at 355 Quince Street, has information and self-guided tour brochures on Salt Lake City's historic districts. In addition to Temple Square and the State Capitol, any tour of the city's historic architecture should include the following:

South Temple Street was probably the most prestigious street address in all of early Utah. Many religious and business leaders owned stately mansions along South Temple, once known as Brigham Street. (A number of these homes are now B&Bs.) Twin towers and gargoyles embellish the imposing Catholic **Cathedral of the Madeleine,** 331 E. South Temple, (801) 328-8941; open daily year-round and for concerts Sunday evenings in spring and summer. Adjacent is the equally impressive **First Presbyterian Church,** 347 E. South Temple. The palatial **Kearns Mansion,** 603 E. South Temple, now serves as the official governor's residence. Thomas Kearns, noted for his silver-mining wealth, became a U.S. senator and publisher of the *Salt Lake Tribune.* The Kearns Mansion is open for free tours Monday–Saturday in summer and on a limited schedule the rest of the year; (801) 538-1005.

Just north of South Temple Street is the district known as **The Avenues,** where the majority of Salt Lake City's (SLC's) early Catholics lived. While most of these homes aren't grand mansions, they are excellent examples of Victorian workers' homes. Streets in the **Marmalade District** on the hillside west of the capitol bear the names of fruit trees—hence the term "marmalade." Many residences date from the 19th century. The **McCune Mansion** at 200 N. Main, is one of the city's most eye-catching old houses. The turn-of-the-century turreted structure features a tiled roof and exceptional interior woodwork.

Downtown's grandest building is undoubtedly the **City and County Building,** at 400 South and State Street. This confection of a building resembles a fanciful Scottish castle right out of *Brigadoon* and once served as the Utah State Capitol; it's now the seat of SLC's local government. Across the street at Main and 400 South is the **Exchange District,** a clutch of grandly handsome office towers that served as the banking center for turn-of-the-century Salt Lake City.

DOWNTOWN SALT LAKE CITY ACCOMMODATIONS

0   0.2 mi

0   0.2 km

VICTORY RD.

WALL ST.

CENTER ST.

CAPITOL ST.

COLUMBUS ST.

DESOTO ST.

CORTEZ ST.

EAST CAPITOL BLVD

CITY

CANYON

(MEMORY

GROVE

PARK)

600 N. ST.

500 N. ST.

400 N. ST.

300 N. ST.

200 N. ST.

N. TEMPLE ST.

MARMALADE

HISTORIC

DISTRICT

TEMPLE VIEW MOTEL ●

STATE CAPITOL BUILDING ★

WOLFE KREST BED & BREAKFAST ●

INN ON CAPITOL HILL ●

THE AVENUES DISTRICT

13TH AVE.

12TH

11TH
10TH
9TH
8TH
7TH
6TH
5TH
4TH

3RD
2ND
1ST

AVE.
AVE.
AVE.
AVE.
AVE.
AVE.
AVE.
AVE.
AVE.
AVE.
AVE.

HOWARD JOHNSON EXPRESS INN ●

CITY CREEK INN ●

TRAVELODGE AT TEMPLE SQUARE ●

THE AVENUES HOSTELLING INTERNATIONAL HOSTEL AVE.

BEST WESTERN SALT LAKE PLAZA HOTEL ●

TEMPLE SQUARE

TEMPLE

UNION PACIFIC DEPOT ■

TRAX LIGHT RAIL LINE

GREYHOUND BUS STATION ■■

WYNDHAM HOTEL ●

INN AT TEMPLE SQUARE ●

MARRIOTT HOTEL ●

CARLTON HOTEL ●

ANTON BUXRUD B&B ●

ARMSTRONG MANSION ●

HOTEL MONACO ●

SHILO INN SALT LAKE CITY ●

DOUBLETREE HOTEL ●

To Saltair B&B

PEERY'S HOTEL ●

PIONEER PARK

COURTYARD BY MARRIOTT DOWNTOWN ●

EXCHANGE PLACE HISTORIC DISTRICT

To Chase Suite Hotel

HAMPTON INN ●

SALT LAKE CITY SHERATON ●

LITTLE AMERICA HOTEL & TOWERS ●

CRYSTAL INN ●

QUALITY INN CITY CENTER ●

EMBASSY SUITES HOTEL ●

GRAND AMERICA HOTEL AND SUITES ●

TROLLEY SQUARE

MOTEL 6 DOWNTOWN ●

SUPER 8 ●

CAVANAUGH'S OLYMPUS HOTEL ●

To International Ute Hostel and Holiday Inn Downtown

© AVALON TRAVEL PUBLISHING, INC.

If you have trouble locating a room, consider using the state's free reservation service by calling (800) SEE-UTAH (733-8824).

DOWNTOWN NEAR TEMPLE SQUARE

Under $50

There aren't many good budget-class accommodations in this prime area, but if cheap is what you're looking for, try the **Temple View Motel,** 325 N. 300 West, (801) 521-9525, slightly north of the city center; there are three kitchen units. The **City Creek Inn,** 230 W. North Temple, (801) 533-9100, has just undergone a face-lift; it's a little motor court motel just two blocks from the Temple.

$50–75

You can find a couple of good moderately priced motels near Temple Square. The **Howard Johnson Express Inn,** 121 N. 300 West, (801) 521-3450 or (800) 541-7639, is an older but well-maintained motor-court motel with a pool, complimentary continental breakfast, and free HBO. The **Travelodge at Temple Square,** 144 W. North Temple, (801) 533-8200 or (800) 255-3050, is kitty-corner to the temple. It also has four two-bedroom units.

$75–100

Just east of Temple Square is the pleasant, well-maintained **Carlton Hotel,** 140 E. South Temple, (801) 355-3418 or (800) 633-3500. The Carlton offers a guest laundry, exercise room, sauna, and hot tub, and in-room VCRs with free movies; there are also five suites.

Overlooking Temple Square is the **Best Western Salt Lake Plaza Hotel,** 122 W. South Temple, (801) 521-0130 or (800) 366-3684, which offers a pool in addition to its great location.

$100–125

Directly across from Temple Square is the **Inn at Temple Square,** 71 W. South Temple, (801) 531-1000 or (800) 843-4668. Owned by the LDS Church, the Inn was upgraded after the grand Hotel Utah was closed as a lodging; the Inn is now the city's premier historic luxury hotel. Rooms are very well appointed and the entire facility is nonsmoking.

The **Shilo Inn Salt Lake City,** 206 S. West Temple, (801) 521-9500 or (800) 222-2244, is just south of the Salt Palace. This hotel has been remodeled recently, and in addition to the usual pool and fitness facilities offers microwaves, refrigerators, and videocassette players in all rooms, free continental breakfast, restaurant and lounge on the premises, and a guest laundry.

One of SLC's best hotels, the **DoubleTree Hotel,** 255 S. West Temple, (801) 328-2000 or (800) 222-TREE, is a huge complex with an indoor pool, fitness facilities, valet laundry, and convention facilities for small groups. There's a fine dining restaurant on the premises, as well as a private club. Pets are accepted.

The first of SLC's historic older hotels to be refurbished into a natty, upscale lodging was the **Peery Hotel,** 110 W. 300 South, (801) 521-4300 or (800) 331-0073. Its 1910 vintage style is preserved in the comfortable lobby, while the guest rooms are completely updated, nicely furnished, and quite spacious. There's a notable restaurant on the premises, as well as an exercise room.

Some of Salt Lake's most grand heritage homes sit on Capitol Hill, just below the State Capitol Building. Surely one of the most eye-catching is the red sandstone mansion now called the **Inn on Capitol Hill,** 225 N. State St., (801) 575-1112 or (888) 8THEINN. Built in 1906 by a local captain of industry, the inn has 13 guestrooms decorated with period detail, but all with modern amenities like private bathrooms. Practically every room has views over all of Salt Lake City. Full gourmet breakfasts included.

$150–175

One block west of the temple is the **Wyndham Hotel,** 215 W. South Temple, (801) 531-7500 or (800) 553-0075. At this modern, 15-story hotel, you'll find a pool and conference, business, and exercise facilities; children under 12 stay free. Rack rates are high but often discounts are available that bring that price down substantially.

The **Marriott Hotel,** 75 S. West Temple, (801) 531-0800 or (800) 345-4754, is located directly across from the Salt Palace Convention Center. At this high-quality hotel there's an indoor/outdoor pool, sauna, fitness center, a good restaurant, lounge, and private nightclub (available to hotel guests). Weekend rates are often deeply discounted.

In 2001, the **Marriott Hotel Salt Lake City at Gallivan Plaza,** 220 South State St., (801) 715-6685, will open with 370 rooms in the very center of the city.

$200 and up

Perhaps the grandest of all the fantastic homes on Capitol Hill is a three-story Georgian Revival Mansion built in 1905 and now converted into the **Wolfe Krest Bed & Breakfast,** 273 NE Capitol Blvd., (801) 521-8710 or (800) 669-4525, www.wolfekrest.com. The inn's 13 rooms, all with private baths, are decorated with luxury fabrics, Oriental carpets, and antiques. Views over the city and City Canyon are fantastic, as are the many-course breakfasts. Also of note: the proprietress is Mrs. Kay Malone, wife of Utah Jazz star Karl.

SOUTH DOWNTOWN

Just south of the religious sites and convention areas downtown is a large complex of hotels and motels (mostly representatives of large chains) with rooms in almost every traveler's price range. These lodgings aren't entirely convenient for travelers on foot, but if you have a car or intend to ride buses (unfortunately, the free bus zone doesn't extend this far south, but the zone is just a short walk from these hotels), then these are some of the newest and nicest places to stay in the city.

Under $50

Directly south of downtown a couple miles is the **International Ute Hostel,** 21 East Kelsey Ave., (801) 595-1645. Beds in dorm-style rooms are $15, private rooms are $35, and there's full access to kitchen facilities and common areas. Kelsey Avenue is the equivalent of 1160 South, just east off State Street.

$50–75

Best Inn and Suites, 1009 S. Main St., (801) 355-4567 or (888) 500-4419, isn't walking distance from downtown, but the TRAX light rail stops a block away. There's a pool, fitness facility, guest laundry, and free continental breakfast.

Motel 6 Downtown, 176 W. 600 South, (801) 531-1252 or (800) 4MOTEL6, has a pool. Pets are allowed at the **Super 8 Motel,** 616 S. 200 West, (801) 534-0808 or (800) 800-8000. The **Salt Lake City Center Travelodge,** 524 S. West Temple, (801) 531-7100 or (800) 578-7878, offers nicely maintained rooms, all with coffeemakers and access to a heated pool and hot tub. Pets are accepted.

$75–100

The best location of all the south downtown motels is held by **Courtyard by Marriott Downtown,** 130 W. 400 South, (801) 531-6000. It's very central to all the restaurants and happenings in the city's fast-changing warehouse/loft district. There's a pool, hot tub, fitness facility, and airport shuttle.

If you're looking for comfortable rooms without breaking the bank, the **Little America Hotel & Towers,** 500 S. Main St., (801) 363-6781 or (800) 453-9450, is a great place to stay. In this large lodging complex (with nearly 850 rooms) are three room types. Courtside rooms and Garden Suites are scattered around the hotel's nicely manicured grounds, with most rooms overlooking a pool or fountain. Tower Suites are executive-level suites in a 17-story block offering some of SLC's best views. All guests share the hotel's elegant public areas, two pools, health club, and workout facility. The restaurant here is better than average, and there is free airport transport.

The **Quality Inn City Center,** 154 W. 600 South, (801) 521-2930 or (800) 521-9997, has a number of brand new rooms and offers a pool, fitness room, two restaurants, guest laundry, and free airport shuttle.

One of the nicer-for-the-money hotels in this part of Salt Lake City is the **Crystal Inn,** at 230 W. 500 South, (801) 328-4466 or (800) 366-4466. Rooms here are very large and nicely furnished; all come with refrigerators and microwaves. There's a free hot breakfast buffet for all guests. For recreation, there's an indoor pool, exercise room, sauna, and hot tub.

If you're in Salt Lake for an extended time, or are traveling with a family, consider the **Embassy Suites Hotel,** at 110 W. 600 South, (801) 359-7800 or (800) 362-2779. All rooms have efficiency kitchens (with coffeemakers) and separate living and sleeping areas; there are two two-bedroom units. Facilities include a pool, sauna, exercise area, a restaurant, and a lounge.

Hampton Inn, 425 S. 300 West, (801) 741-1110 or (800) HAMPTON, has a free continental breakfast and free local calls.

$100–125

Cavanaugh's Olympus Hotel, 161 W. 600 South, (801) 521-7373 or (800) 524-0354, has a pool, spa, exercise facilities, room service, guest laundry, and free airport transportation. **Salt Lake Hilton,** 150 W. 500 South, (801) 532-3344 or (800) 421-7602, is one of the city's best addresses for high-quality comfort and service. The lobby areas are very pleasant, and facilities include a great pool, exercise room, and spa. The rooftop restaurant and lounge are also notable. The Hilton offers free airport and downtown shuttles.

Holiday Inn Downtown, 999 South Main, (801) 359-8600, (800) 933-9678, is three blocks farther south than the other lodgings in this listing but offers a number of facilities that make it stand out. The Holiday Inn offers a putting green, tennis courts, basketball court, and a playground for children in addition to the usual pool and exercise facilities. Besides, there's a free downtown shuttle service to whisk guests to the center of things (free airport transportation is offered as well). Rooms are very nicely appointed.

The most exciting thing to happen to Salt Lake City lodging in years is the **Hotel Monaco,** 15 West 200 South, (801) 595-0000 or (877) 294-9710. The hotel occupies a grandly renovated historic office building in a very convenient spot in the middle of downtown; on the main floor is **Bambara,** one of the most sophisticated restaurants in Utah. Rooms are sumptuously furnished with real élan: this is no anonymous up-scale hotel in beige and mauve. Expect wild colors and contrasting fabrics, lots of flowers, and excellent service. Facilities include on-site fitness center, meeting rooms, plus concierge and valet services. Each room comes with two-line phones, CD stereo, in-room fax, printer and copier, plus an iron and board. Pets are welcome, and if you forgot your own pet, the hotel will deliver a companion goldfish to your room. If you want to splurge on a hotel in Salt Lake, make it this one.

$150–175

Another new addition to the Salt Lake hotel scene—and to the skyline—is the new-in-2001

Grand America Hotel and Suites, 75 E. 600 South, (800) 533-3525. This behemoth of a hotel is a full Salt Lake City block square (remember, that's 10 acres), and its 24 stories contains 775 rooms, over half of them suites. Rooms have luxury level amenities; expect all the perks and niceties that modern hotels can offer.

EAST OF DOWNTOWN

There aren't many lodging choices in this part of the city, but this is a pleasantly residential area without the distinct urban jolt of much of the rest of central Salt Lake City.

This is also where most of the city's **B&Bs** are located. Salt Lake City contains a wealth of beautiful residential architecture, especially in the historic neighborhoods east of downtown and near the capitol. Early politicians, Mormon leaders, and wealthy merchants especially favored South Temple Street, east of downtown. Many of their mansions have been restored, and some are now high-quality B&Bs.

Most B&Bs have a range of room prices, so use the rate headings as just a guideline; most will have suites at a higher price.

Under $50

The Avenues, one mile east of Temple Square, offers dorm rooms with use of a kitchen, TV room, and laundry. Information-packed bulletin boards list city sights and goings-on, and you'll meet travelers from all over the world. Year-round rates for the dorm are $12–14 per person (cost includes sheets), while private rooms are $25–40 (only half have private baths). Reservations (with first night's deposit) are advised in the busy summer-travel and winter-ski seasons. The hostel is on the corner of 107 F St. and Second Ave., Salt Lake City, UT 84103, (801) 363-3855; open 8 A.M.–10 P.M. year-round. From downtown, head east on South Temple Street to F Street, then turn north two streets.

$50–75

The **Anton Boxrud Bed and Breakfast,** 57 S. 600 East, (801) 363-8035 or (800) 524-5511, offers seven guest rooms (with a mix of private and shared baths) in a grand 1901 Victorian brick home. The house has been restored to its original splendor and features hardwoods, wood-paneled walls, stained glass, and period furnishings. There's also a hot tub, and breakfasts are notably good. Anton Boxrud B&B is one-half-block south of South Temple on 600 East, near the governor's mansion.

The **Saltair B&B/Alpine Cottages and Condos,** 164 S. 900 East, (801) 533-8184 or (800) 733-8184, www.saltlakebandb.com, is the oldest continuously operating bed-andbreakfast in Utah. Located in a pleasant neighborhood between downtown and the university, the property was built in 1903 and is on the National Historic Registry. In addition to the five comfortable and moderately priced rooms in the inn (with a mix of shared and private baths), there are two adjacent cottages available for families or for longer stays. Each of these totally renovated 1870s cottages comes with a full kitchen (though breakfast in the main inn is included), a fireplace, cable TV, and private phones; each sleeps up to four. Additionally, the Saltair has nine refurbished turn-of-the-century condos for rent on a weekly or monthly basis.

$75–100

The **Brigham Street Inn** is a fabulous Queen Anne mansion at 1135 E. South Temple, (801) 364-4461 or (800) 417-4461. When the architect-owners refurbished the home, they engaged 12 local designers and gave each a room to make over—the result is an eclectic showcase of sensitive historic renovation. There are nine guest rooms, each with private bath. One deluxe room has private garden entrance, kitchen, and whirlpool.

The **Armstrong Mansion,** 667 E. 100 South, (801) 531-1333 or (800) 708-1333, is another Queen Anne mansion converted to a comfortable B&B. Each of the 14 rooms has a private bath and is decorated with full Victorian flair.

$100–125

Right on the University of Utah's research park, the **Marriott University Park Hotel & Suites,** 480 Wakara Way, (801) 581-1000 or (800) 637-4390, is one of the city's best-kept secrets for luxurious lodgings in a lovely setting. You can't miss with the views: all rooms either overlook the city or look onto the soaring peaks of the Wasatch Range directly behind the hotel. Rooms

are very nicely appointed—the suites are some of the nicest in the city. All rooms have mini-bars, refrigerators, and coffeemakers; there's a pool and exercise room, and bicycles are available for rent.

A block from the recent commercial development at Trolley Square is the **Chase Suite Hotel by Woodfin,** 765 E. 400 South, (801) 532-5511 or (800) 237-8811. All rooms have separate sleeping and living spaces and come with full kitchens—just the thing if you're in town for a few days or traveling with a family. There's also a pool, hot tub, and sport court.

The **Anniversary Inn,** 460 S. 1000 East, (801) 363-4900 or (800) 324-4152, caters to couples and newlyweds interested in a romantic getaway. All 32 rooms are imaginatively decorated according to theme: beds may be in a covered wagon or a vintage rail car, and bathrooms may be in a "sea cave." Chances are good that your room will have its own private waterfall. You get to pick your suite from choices that include "the lighthouse," "the opera house," "South Pacific," and "Venice." These rooms aren't just filled with kitsch: they are luxury-class rooms, each with big-screen TVs, hot tubs, stereos, and private bathrooms. Rates vary widely according to room. If you'd like to check out these clever theme rooms before signing up, call the inn for information on tours, which are held on Tuesday and Thursday afternoons.

WEST DOWNTOWN TO THE AIRPORT

Nearly all of the following will offer some form of transportation to the Salt Lake City Airport. Hotels with the smallest address on W. North Temple are closest to downtown.

$50–75

Although it's on the road to the airport, the **Econo Lodge,** 715 W. North Temple, (801) 363-0062 or (800) BE ECONO, is also convenient to downtown, as it's just west of the railroad overpass. The motel offers a courtesy car to downtown or the airport and has a pool and guest laundry. Of the many older motor-court motels along North Temple, the best maintained is the **Overniter Motor Inn,** 1500 W.

North Temple, (801) 533-8300 or (800) 914-8301, with an outdoor pool and clean rooms. Moderately priced rooms are also available at **Days Inn,** 1900 W. North Temple, (801) 539-8538 or (800) 329-7466, and at the **Motel 6 Airport,** 1990 W. North Temple; (801) 364-1053, where there's a pool. Closer to the airport, the **Airport Inn,** 2333 W. North Temple, (801) 539-0438, has a pool and guest laundry.

$75–100

The **Holiday Inn Airport,** 1659 W. North Temple, (801) 533-9000, offers more luxury and a pool and spa.

Practically next door to the terminal are the **Holiday Inn & Suites,** 5575 W. Amelia Earhart Dr., (801) 537-7020 or (800) 522-5575, with a pool and spa. At the **Airport Hilton,** 5151 Wiley Post Way, (801) 539-1515 or (800) 999-3736, rooms are very spacious and nicely furnished, and facilities include two pools, a putting green, sports court, and an exercise room and spa. The hotel even has its own lake.

$100–125

The **Radisson Hotel Salt Lake City Airport,** 2177 W. North Temple, (801) 364-5800 or (800) 333-3333, is a very attractive, lodgelike building with nicely furnished rooms. Guests receive a complimentary continental breakfast and newspaper, and in the evenings there's a "manager's reception" with free beverages. Facilities include a pool, spa, and fitness room. Suites come with a loft bedroom area. There's quite a range in room rates, though package rates and promotions can bring down the rates dramatically.

COMMERCIAL CAMPGROUNDS

Camp VIP offers tent and RV sites year-round with showers, swimming pool, game room, playground, store, and laundry. Rates are $23.95 for tents or RVs without hookups, $26.45 with. The campground is between downtown and the airport at 1350 W. North Temple, (801) 328-0224. From I-15 northbound, take Exit 311 for I-80, go west 1.3 miles on I-80, exit north one-half mile on Redwood Rd. (UT 68), then turn right another one-half mile on North Temple. From I-15 southbound, take Exit 313 and turn

south 1.5 miles on 900 West, then turn right 0.8 mile on North Temple. From I-80 either take the North Temple exit or exit on Redwood Rd. (UT 68) and go north one-half mile, then right one-half mile on North Temple.

Hidden Haven Campground, 18 miles east of Salt Lake City near Park City, (435) 649-8935, has showers, store, laundry, and a trout stream. Tent and RV sites are open year-round; $14.50 without hookups, $19.75 with. Take I-80 Exit 143, then go east 1.6 miles on the north frontage road (or take Park City Exit 145 and go west one mile on the north frontage road).

Pioneer Village Campground, 16 miles north of Salt Lake City in Farmington, at Lagoon Amusement Park, (801) 451-8100, is open mid-April–mid-October with showers, store, laundry, and discounts on rides; tent and RV sites cost $19 without hookups, $23–25 with. Take I-15 Lagoon Exit and follow signs.

Cherry Hill Recreation Park, 18 miles north of Salt Lake City, (801) 451-5379, features a water slide, inner-tube ride, swimming pool, Pirates Cove (for young children), restaurant, miniature golf, and a variety of games, as well as a large campground with showers, store, and laundry. The season lasts mid-April–mid-October, though some activities operate only Memorial Day–Labor Day weekends. Tent or RV sites cost $19 without hookups, $23 with. Take I-15 Lagoon/Farmington Exit 327 and go north two miles on U.S. 89.

FOREST SERVICE CAMPGROUNDS

There are three campgrounds in Big Cottonwood Canyon about 15 miles southeast of downtown Salt Lake City. All have drinking water and cost $14 a night. Groups can reserve **Jordan Pines Campground** (elev. 7,400 feet) by calling (800) 280-CAMP; it's 8.8 miles up the canyon. **Spruces Campground** (elev. 7,400 feet, 9.1 miles up the canyon) is open early June–mid-October. Some sites can be reserved by calling (800) 280-CAMP. The season at **Redman Campground** (elev. 8,300 feet) lasts mid-June–early October. It's located between Solitude and Brighton, 13 miles up the canyon.

Little Cottonwood Canyon, about 19 miles southeast of downtown Salt Lake City, has two campgrounds with drinking water. **Tanners Flat Campground** (elev. 7,200 feet, 4.3 miles up the canyon) is open mid-May–mid-October; $12. Some sites can be reserved by calling (800) 280-

CAMP. **Albion Basin Campground** lies high in the mountains (elev. 9,500 feet) and is open early July–late September; $12; go 11 miles up the canyon (the last 2.5 miles are gravel).

SALT LAKE CITY RESTAURANTS

Travelers will be pleased with the quality of food in Salt Lake City. If you've been traveling around the more remote areas of the state, the abundance of ethnic restaurants especially will be a real treat; the number of Chinese restaurants alone is astonishing.

Most of the following restaurants serve alcohol, though you'll need to ask specifically to see the drinks menu. At the time of publication, none of the restaurants below were private clubs (meaning that you'd need to buy a membership to get in), but these things change. Several of the more popular restaurants have private clubs adjacent to the dining areas.

The free *Salt Lake Visitors Guide* also lists dining establishments. Dinner reservations are advisable at the more expensive restaurants; also check to see if coat and tie are required for men at the posher restaurants. Also note that most restaurants are closed Sunday; if you're going to be in Salt Lake over the weekend, it's a good idea to ascertain that your hotel has a restaurant, or else you may be wandering the streets looking for an eating establishment that's open on the Sabbath.

COFFEEHOUSES AND BREAKFAST

If you've fallen victim to the nation's obsession with gourmet coffees, you'll discover lattes and cappuccinos are more scarce in Utah than elsewhere because of Mormon strictures on caffeine. However, several fine coffeehouses exist in Salt Lake City, though at some distance from Temple Square. The **Salt Lake Roasting Co.,** 329 East 400 South, (801) 363-7572, offers a wide selection of coffees, fresh baked European-style pastries, a vaguely "alternative" atmosphere, and a pleasant outdoor patio in good weather. At **Cup of Joe,** 353 W. 200 South, (801) 363-8322, the atmosphere is sleek and industrial; however, you'll also find comfortable

couches and stacks of reading material. Joe's also serves lunchtime Panini sandwiches and is open till midnight with entertainment—poetry slams, acoustic music—most evenings.

For one of Salt Lake's favorite breakfasts, drive (or ride your bike) a couple of miles east of the city to **Ruth's Diner,** 2100 Emigration Canyon, (801) 582-5807. The restaurant's namesake was a cabaret singer in the 1920s who opened her own restaurant in 1931. Ruth's Diner has been in continuous operation ever since (the ads read "70 years in business. . . Boy am I tired!"). Ruth's is full of atmosphere and overlooks a rushing stream. It's a great place to go for an old-fashioned breakfast or a hearty lunch. Live music is featured at Sunday brunch.

La Caille at Quail Run

LA CAILLE AT QUAIL RUN

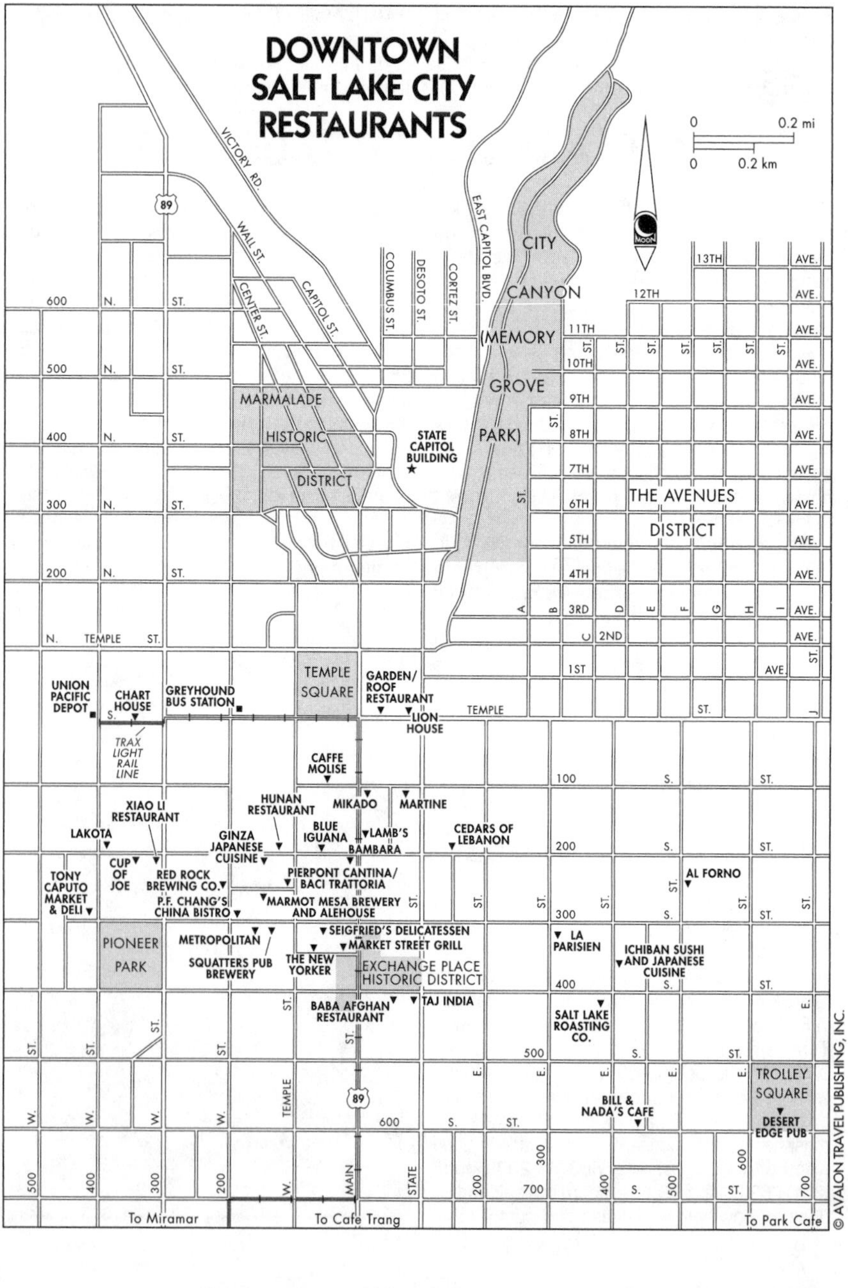

DOWNTOWN SALT LAKE CITY RESTAURANTS
0 0.2 mi
0 0.2 km
MOON
CITY CANYON (MEMORY GROVE PARK)
MARMALADE HISTORIC DISTRICT
STATE CAPITOL BUILDING
THE AVENUES DISTRICT
TEMPLE SQUARE
PIONEER PARK
EXCHANGE PLACE HISTORIC DISTRICT
TROLLEY SQUARE
VICTORY RD.
WALL ST.
CENTER ST.
CAPITOL ST.
COLUMBUS ST.
DESOTO ST.
CORTEZ ST.
EAST CAPITOL BLVD.
600 N. ST.
500 N. ST.
400 N. ST.
300 N. ST.
200 N. ST.
N. TEMPLE ST.
S. TEMPLE ST.
100 S. ST.
200 S. ST.
300 S. ST.
400 S. ST.
500 S. ST.
600 S. ST.
700 S. ST.
13TH AVE.
12TH AVE.
11TH AVE.
10TH AVE.
9TH AVE.
8TH AVE.
7TH AVE.
6TH AVE.
5TH AVE.
4TH AVE.
3RD AVE.
2ND AVE.
1ST AVE.
A ST.
B ST.
C
D
E
F
G
H
I
J
500 W. ST.
400 W. ST.
300 W. ST.
200 W. ST.
W. TEMPLE ST.
MAIN ST.
STATE ST.
200 E. ST.
300 E. ST.
400 E. ST.
500 E. ST.
600 E. ST.
700 E. ST.
89
UNION PACIFIC DEPOT
CHART HOUSE
GREYHOUND BUS STATION
TRAX LIGHT RAIL LINE
GARDEN/ROOF RESTAURANT
LION HOUSE
CAFFE MOLISE
XIAO LI RESTAURANT
HUNAN RESTAURANT
MIKADO
MARTINE
LAKOTA
GINZA JAPANESE CUISINE
BLUE IGUANA
LAMB'S
BAMBARA
CEDARS OF LEBANON
CUP OF JOE
RED ROCK BREWING CO.
TONY CAPUTO MARKET & DELI
PIERPONT CANTINA/ BACI TRATTORIA
P.F. CHANG'S CHINA BISTRO
MARMOT MESA BREWERY AND ALEHOUSE
AL FORNO
SEIGFRIED'S DELICATESSEN
METROPOLITAN
MARKET STREET GRILL
LA PARISIEN
SQUATTERS PUB BREWERY
THE NEW YORKER
ICHIBAN SUSHI AND JAPANESE CUISINE
BABA AFGHAN RESTAURANT
TAJ INDIA
SALT LAKE ROASTING CO.
BILL & NADA'S CAFE
DESERT EDGE PUB
To Miramar
To Cafe Trang
To Park Cafe
© AVALON TRAVEL PUBLISHING, INC.

Another pleasant place for a traditional breakfast is the **Park Cafe,** 604 E. 1300 South, (801) 487-1670. The Park is located directly across from Liberty Park, which makes a great pre- or post-breakfast destination. Closer to downtown, in the Exchange District, the **Market Street Grill,** 48 Market St., (801) 322-4668, is best known for its excellent seafood dinners but is also a favored spot for stylish and delicious breakfasts. If you're up late in Salt Lake City (not that easy to do) it's good to know about **Bill and Nada's Cafe,** 479 S. 600 East, (801) 359-6984, whose old-fashioned breakfasts are served anytime, 24 hours a day.

If you're looking for Sunday brunch, most of the hotel restaurants have buffets, but for the brunch of champions, head to the lodges and resorts up nearby Wasatch Front Canyons. The **Silver Fork Lodge,** (435) 649-9551, 11 miles up Big Cottonwood Canyon, and the **Log Haven,** (801) 272-8255, four miles up Mill Creek Canyon, are both favorite destinations for a scenic brunch, perhaps followed by a hike. The brunch at **La Caille at Quail Run,** at the mouth of Big Cottonwood Canyon, (801) 942-1751, is where to head if you feel like putting on the Ritz.

DELIS AND HEALTH FOOD

Siegfried's Delicatessen, downtown at 69 W. 300 South, (801) 355-3891, closed Sunday, has a great selection of sausages, cold cuts, breads, pastries, and cheeses. Another good place to stop to provision a picnic is **VonKomen's European Foods,** 418 E. 200 S., (801) 363-7352. One of Salt Lake's favorite delis is **Tony Caputo Market & Deli,** 308 West Broadway, (801) 531-8669, with great sandwiches, Italian-style sausage and cheese, loads of olives and other Mediterranean temptations, and a park nearby where you can have an impromptu picnic.

AMERICAN FARE

Lamb's, downtown at 169 S. Main, (801) 364-7166, claims to be Utah's oldest restaurant; it started in Logan in 1919 and moved to Salt Lake City in 1939. You can still enjoy the classic 1930s diner atmosphere as well as the tasty food. The menu offers seafood, steak, chops, chicken, and

sandwiches; Lamb's is an especially good place for breakfast. Dinner entrées range between $13 and $15. Open for breakfast, lunch, and dinner; closed Sunday.

For moderately priced food and history of a different sort, try the **Lion House,** 63 East South Temple, (801) 363-5466. Built in 1856, this was one of Brigham Young's homes, where his 26 wives and 56 children spent most of their time. High-quality cafeteria-style meals are available for lunch and dinner in the basement dining room, formerly the household pantry.

Travelers will find steak houses and supper clubs—the dining mainstays in much of the West, where beef is king—in curiously short supply. There's a Wild West theme at **Diamond Lil's,** 1528 W. North Temple, (801) 533-0547. Prime rib is the specialty ($15), though you can also pick from a selection of eight steak cuts, plus chicken and seafood. **Diamond Lil's Old Salt City Jail Restaurant,** two blocks east of Trolley Square near the University of Utah at 460 S. 1000 East, (801) 355-2422, offers steak, prime rib, and seafood in an authentic Old West jailhouse. Open daily for dinner.

FINE DINING

Salt Lake City has several upscale restaurants where high-rollers can flex their credit cards and eat world-class cuisine.

Metropolitan, 173 W. Broadway, (801) 364-3472, is easily Salt Lake City's most ambitious restaurant, taking "fusion cuisine" to new lengths. In this high-design dining room (reserve tables near the fireplace-cum-water-sculpture), the foods of the world meet and mingle on your plate in preparations that are sometimes unexpected but always stylish. Seared venison medallions appear with tempura vegetables, venison-laced spring rolls, morel mushrooms, and a reduced sake sauce. A crabmeat Napoleon is served with caviar and fresh lobster sauce. Cuisine like this doesn't come cheap; expect to pay upwards of $10 for appetizers and $25–30 for entrées. Metropolitan is open nightly for dinner, Monday–Friday for lunch.

Bambara, in the Hotel Monaco, 202 S. Main, (801) 363-5454, is another exciting addition to the Salt Lake dining scene. The menu emphasizes the freshest and most flavorful of local meats and produce, with preparations in a wide-awake New American style that's equal parts tradition and innovation; entrées range from $20–25. This is easily the most beautiful dining room in the city. Highly recommended.

Martine, 22 E. 100 South, (801) 363-9328, offers equally delicious food in a less formal atmosphere. The antique high-ceilinged dining room is coolly elegant, and the cooking and presentation subtly continental. You have a choice of ordering tapas-style—from $6.50 to $7.50 for lime and garlic calamari or tarragon halibut cakes with saffron aioli—or ordering full meals. For $26, you can order a tapas appetizer plus an entrée, which may be grilled halibut with a *Pernod chervil beurre blanc.*

Lakota, 380 W. 200 South, (801) 519-8300, is in Salt Lake's trendy warehouse district and features New American dining. The menu is a combination of updated American classics like blackened meatloaf, crab cakes, baby back ribs, and roast chicken, plus more forward-looking dishes like braised coconut halibut with papaya mint salsa. Entrées range between $14 and $19.

BREWPUBS

Many visitors to Utah will find that brewpubs are the most convenient places to enjoy good food and drink. There's no private-club rigmarole or furtive passing of drinks menus. Each of the following pubs is open for both lunch and dinner.

The state's oldest brewpub is **Squatters Pub Brewery,** 147 W. Broadway, (801) 363-2739. In addition to fine beers and ales, the pub serves sandwiches, burgers, and other light entrées in a handsome old warehouse. In summer, there's seating on the back deck.

Very popular and kind of a scene, the **Red Rock Brewing Company,** 254 S. 200 West, (801) 521-7446, offers pasta, salads, and sandwiches, including an excellent variation on the hamburger (baked in a wood-fired oven inside a bread pocket). There's often a wait to get in the door, but the food and brews are worth it. The Red Rock is unusual for Salt Lake in that it serves food late—till midnight on weekends.

Right downtown, **Marmot Mesa Brewery and Alehouse,** 163 W. Pierpont, (801) 994-2800,

has excellent brews and a wide menu selection. The roast lamb sandwich is notable.

Desert Edge Brewery, (801) 521-8917, also known simply as "The Pub," is located in Trolley Square at 700 East and 500 South. The menu is inexpensive, with sandwiches and salads available all day; some of the ales are cask-conditioned. In the evening, several zippy entrées such as grilled salmon with spinach and chicken with citrus *chipotle* chili glaze appear on the menu; best of all, nothing costs more than $10. The atmosphere is retro industrial chic, and there's a second-floor outdoor veranda.

PIZZA

Gepetto's, near the University of Utah at 230 S. 1300 East, (801) 583-1013, presents pizza, lasagna, sandwiches, and salads. Live entertainment is offered Thursday–Saturday; open Mon.–Sat. for lunch and dinner.

The Pie Pizzeria, downstairs from the University Pharmacy, 1320 E. 200 South, (801) 582-0193, offers New York-style hand-thrown pizza. Live music Monday and Tuesday evenings; open daily for lunch and dinner.

STEAK AND SEAFOOD

Two sister restaurants with confusingly similar names offer the best fish and seafood in SLC. The **Market Street Grill,** downtown at 48 Market St., near Main and Broadway, (801) 322-4668, features fresh seafood plus steak, prime rib, chops, chicken, and pasta. Entrées run $14–22, though if you arrive before 7 P.M. you can order the early-bird specials for $12. Open daily for breakfast, lunch, and dinner and for brunch on Sunday.

Market Street Broiler, 260 S. 1300 East, (801) 583-8808, specializes in fresh fish and seafood, which you can enjoy in the dining room, pick up at the take-out counter, or purchase at the fresh fish market. Most of the fish is mesquite grilled; steaks, hickory-smoked ribs, and chicken are also available. An in-house bakery creates tempting pastries; open Mon.–Sat. for lunch (daily in summer) and daily for dinner.

For steaks, prime rib, and seafood in a historical atmosphere, the local **Chart House,** 334

West South Temple, (801) 596-0990, is located in the ornate Devereaux Mansion, built in the 1870s and exquisitely refurbished. Prices range $18–21 for entrées; open daily for dinner only.

The New Yorker, 60 Market St., (801) 363-0166, is yet another fine dining house in a historic storefront. Here the emphasis is on seafood and excellently prepared certified Angus beef and fresh American lamb. If you're not up to a full meal, there's also a café menu; or just go to the oyster bar and fill up on bivalves. The atmosphere is lively; located in Salt Lake's financial district, expect an audience of stock brokers and businessmen.

DINING WITH A VIEW

Some of the best views in the city are from the top of the 10-story Joseph Smith Memorial Building (the former Hotel Utah), 15 East South Temple, where you'll find two excellent restaurants. The **Garden Restaurant,** (801) 539-1911, offers unparalleled views onto Temple Square and downtown Salt Lake City. What's more, the restaurant is reasonably priced, offering sandwiches and salads for lunch ($8 and under) and steaks, seafood, and continental dishes at dinner (under $15). With even better views onto Temple Square, the **Roof Restaurant,** (801) 539-1911, offers an upscale buffet (dinner only) with prime rib, salmon, ham, shrimp, salads, desserts, and all the trimmings. The price for this all-you-can-eat extravaganza is $24 adults, $15 children. Reservations are recommended; no alcohol is served.

MEXICAN AND SOUTHWESTERN

Red Iguana, 736 West North Temple, (801) 322-1489, is one of the city's favorite Mexican restaurants and offers excellent south-of-the-border cooking with a specialty in Mayan and regional foods. Best of all, flavors are crisp, fresh, and earthy. The Red Iguana is very popular, so arrive early—especially at lunch—to avoid the lines. Entrées on the extensive menu average $10.

A sister restaurant, the **Blue Iguana** 165 S. West Temple, (801) 533-8900, brings the famous Iguana *molés* to downtown. Not only is the Mexican cooking here outstanding, but the

Blue Iguana and the **Express-O Coffee House,** with which it shares space, is open 24 hours, a real breakthrough in somnolent Salt Lake City.

Miramar, 342 W. 1300 South, (801) 484-2877, serves traditional Mexican tortilla-based dishes, but its real focus is the excellent cuisines of other Latin and South American regions. Seafood dishes are a specialty. The food is authentic (for example, they offer *menudo*—tripe soup), so expect exciting and unusual flavors.

Right downtown, the **Pierpont Cantina,** 122 W. Pierpont, (801) 364-1222, offers a large selection of traditional Mexican dishes plus salads, fajitas, and grilled meats. Nearly all entrées are priced under $10. Located next to popular Baci Trattoria, the atmosphere is equally high-voltage, in an airy, wood-paneled room that rises in tiers toward the ribboned ceiling fans. There's seating outdoors in good weather. (Pierpont is an alley between 200 and 300 South.)

For the city's best Southwestern cooking plus scenic views, drive up Emigration Canyon two miles to the **Santa Fe Restaurant,** 2100 Emigration Canyon Rd., (801) 582-5888. The menu is comprehensive and blends Creole, Mexican, and New Mexican flavors with worldly savvy. Dishes like *pollo asada* are served with jalapeño fettuccini ($13); shrimp come sautéed in lime juice and tequila with cilantro relish and succotash ($15).

For Mexican fast food, the local chain **La Frontera,** 1236 W. 400 South, (801) 532-3158, 1434 S. 700 West, (801) 974-0172, and other metro locations, serves burritos, enchiladas, tacos, *huevos rancheros,* and other Mexican favorites. Open daily for breakfast, lunch, and dinner.

FRENCH

For classic French cuisine, **La Caille at Quail Run,** near Little Cottonwood Canyon at 9565 Wasatch Blvd., (801) 942-1751, offers superb pastry, crepes, egg, seafood, and meat dishes in an 18th-century rural French atmosphere. Vineyards, gardens, ponds, and manicured lawns surround the re-created French chateau—hard to believe it's Utah. Antique furnishings grace the dining rooms and halls. Expect to pay $30–40 per person for dinner. Dress is semiformal; reservations advised. Dinner is served daily, brunch and a Basque-style dinner are served on Sunday.

La Parisien, 417 S. 300 East, (801) 364-5223, isn't nearly so atmospheric, but the simple French classics offered here (flip the menu and you can order equally well-loved Italian favorites) are well prepared and modestly priced. Dishes like *coq au vin* or *escalope de veau Savoyarde* each weigh in at under $15. Open Mon.–Sat. for lunch and dinner, Sun. for dinner only.

ITALIAN

Right downtown at 55 W. 100 South, **Caffe Molise,** (801) 364-8833, offers a bistro atmosphere and tasty mid-priced Italian specialties. Pasta dishes are in the $10 range, with grilled chicken and beef dishes from $13 to $17. Another good value for classic Italian pasta dishes is **Al Forno,** 239 S. 500 East, (801) 359-6040.

Baci Trattoria, 134 West Pierpont Ave., (801) 328-1500, with its zippy, high-tech decor and lively clientele, is near both the Delta Center and the Salt Palace. Most nights it gets busy and boisterous, and the regulars like it that way. The food is good, including boutique pizza, updated pasta dishes from $12 to $18, grilled meats ranging from $15 for chicken preparations to $27 for three different veal dishes, and fresh fish specials nightly.

Many people feel that **Fresco Italian Cafe,** 1513 S. 1500 East, (801) 486-1300, is SLC's finest Italian eatery, if not the city's best overall restaurant. The pleasant setting features an intimate dining room entered through a garden, and the property is on a quiet street a few miles south of the city center. The entrées are full-flavored yet subtle: cheese tortellini is served with fresh peas, roasted red peppers, sage, and tomato butter ($16), and the house specialty is grilled lamb medallions served with roasted garlic-rosemary demi-glacé ($19).

MIDDLE EASTERN AND INDIAN

For something unusual, try **Baba Afghan Restaurant,** 55 E. 400 South, (801) 596-0786. Afghani food is like a mix of Indian and Middle Eastern cuisines and, with entrées from $9 to

$12 dollars, it's a good value. There are a number of vegetarian dishes.

Cedars of Lebanon, downtown at 152 E. 200 South, (801) 364-4096, has exotic Mediterranean flavors from Lebanon, Morocco, Armenia, Greece, and Israel—many vegetarian items, too. Belly dancers enliven the scene on Friday and Saturday nights. Open Mon.–Sat. for lunch and dinner.

Tandoori and northern Indian cooking is the specialty at **Taj India,** 73 E. 400 South, (801) 596-8727. The nan breads are wonderful, and there is a large selection of vegetarian dishes. Near the university is a good Indian restaurant, the **Bombay House,** 1615 S. Foothill Dr., (801) 581-0222, open for lunch and dinner. The **Star of India,** 177 E. 200 South, (801) 363-7555, is another favorite for tandoori-roasted meats and full-flavored curries.

ASIAN

An amazing number of Chinese restaurants dot Salt Lake City. Most feature rather old-fashioned Mandarin/American cooking. If you're looking for more spice, try the **Hunan Restaurant,** downtown in Arrow Press Square at 165 S. West Temple, (801) 531-6677, which serves Szechwan-style preparations. Open Mon–Fri. for lunch, daily for dinner.

Two new restaurants bring updated Chinese food to Salt Lake City. The best of these is **P.F. Chang's China Bistro,** 174 W. 300 South, (801) 539-0500, in a historic building just south of the convention center. The cuisine is a split between traditional Chinese and modern ingredients cooked in a Chinese method. You'll find inventive salads, wonderful little *yon-ton* nuggets, and aggressively spiced combos that feature all your favorite up-to-the-minute vegetables and meats. This is a busy place, so reservations are a good idea. Dinner entrées are $12–20.

Another new Chinese restaurant is **Xiao Li Restaurant,** 307 W. 200 South. Located in a vintage warehouse, Xiao Li prepares traditional northern Chinese cuisine but to a standard almost never observed in Western-influenced Asian restaurants. This is a good place to come if you want carefully prepared classics like orange chicken, sesame beef, or General Tso's Chicken.

Thai food is popular in SLC. **Bangkok Thai,** 1400 S. Foothill Dr., (801) 582-8424, is a ways from downtown, but worth the drive for intensely flavored red curries and other Thai specialties.

There are several good Japanese restaurants. At **Kyoto,** 1080 E. 1300 South, (801) 487-3525, chefs and servers take pride in the authentic food and atmosphere. Try their sukiyaki or teriyaki. Dinner reservations requested. Open Mon.–Sat. for lunch and daily for dinner. At **Mikado,** 67 W. 100 South, (801) 328-0929, include *shabu shabu,* steak teriyaki, sushi, and shrimp tempura. Open Mon.–Sat. for dinner only; reservations recommended.

Ginza Japanese Cuisine and Sushi Bar, 209 W. 200 South, (801) 322-2224, has a big local reputation for its sushi bar; best, it's within walking distance of most downtown hotels. **Ichiban Sushi and Japanese Cuisine,** 336 S. 400 East, (801) 532-7522, is a transplant from Park City, where it had a huge reputation as a superlative sushi house. Its reputation has only grown since its move to Salt Lake.

Cafe Trang, south of downtown at 818 S. Main, (801) 539-1638, is a top-rated Vietnamese restaurant with wonderful food, though don't expect much in the way of decor. Open daily for lunch and dinner.

SALT LAKE CITY ARTS AND ENTERTAINMENT

Salt Lake City offers a wide variety of high-quality arts and cultural institutions; classical and religious music venues are particularly noteworthy. Some of the "lower" forms of art and entertainment, such as alternative music clubs and dance bars, have taken a little longer to get a toe-hold in the city, but there's a lot more going on here than you might think at first glance.

Local publications are the best places to check for information on what's happening. The *City Weekly* is the largest and most comprehensive free newspaper with lots of arts and entertainment coverage. Good listings for restaurants, too. *The Event* newspaper, published weekly, also gives detailed coverage of local films, concerts, theater, dance, art exhibits, art classes, and nightspots. If you're into the youthful music scene, pick up self-published 'zines like *Slug* or *Grid* to find out what's going on at the clubs. All of the above are free and are distributed at coffee shops and bookstores. It's harder to find *The Pillar,* Salt Lake City's gay newspaper; its distribution is pretty much limited to the city's gay bars.

Another good source is the *Salt Lake Visitors Guide* (available free at the Salt Lake Convention and Visitors Bureau). The daily papers, *Deseret News* and *Salt Lake Tribune,* both have listings in their Friday "weekend" and Sunday "art and entertainment" sections.

You can also phone one of several events and information lines. **Area Entertainment,**

(801) 544-1313, is a free comprehensive events information service that gives travelers prerecorded information about movies, live theater, concerts, community events, skiing and recreation, dining suggestions, flower shops and hair salons, and local historic sites and museums. The push-button menu system requires quite a bit of patience from the user, as well as some basic knowledge of Salt Lake City business districts and neighborhoods. It's recommended if you know exactly what movie, show, or ski resort you're after, but not as a way to find directions or addresses or to browse general entertainment offerings. There are a number of websites that offer information about Salt Lake events. A good place to start is www.saltlake.org.

Tickets to most concerts and performances are available from **Fastix** at (801) 355-ARTS.

Venues of Note

Most of Salt Lake City's top-flight music and arts performances take place in a handful of venues, themselves world-class facilities worthy of a visit. When you know the dates of your visit to Salt Lake City, contact the following concert halls and performance spaces to find out what's going on while you're here.

The city's main performance space is the **Capitol Theatre,** 50 West 200 South, (801) 534-6364, a glittering vaudeville house from the turn of the century that's been refurbished into an elegant concert hall. The Utah Opera, Ballet West, other dance troupes, and traveling Broadway shows are staged here. The **Abravanel Concert Hall,** between the Salt Palace and Temple Square at 123 West South Temple, (801) 533-5626, has fantastic acoustics and is home to the Utah Symphony and other classical music performances. In **Temple Square,** the Mormon Tabernacle and the Assembly Hall host various classical and religious musical concerts including performances by the famed Mormon Tabernacle Choir; call (801) 240-3318 for information. The **Promised Valley Playhouse,** 132 S. State, (801) 364-5696, was built in 1905 and has been used as a vaudeville hall, a movie palace, and, now, one of the city's leading stages for theater performances.

CLASSICAL MUSIC AND DANCE

From its modest beginnings in 1940, the **Utah Symphony,** www.utahsymphony.org, has grown to be one of the best-regarded orchestras in the country. Each season, the symphony performs in the glittering Abravanel Hall in Salt Lake City and travels to Snowbird, Deer Valley, Ogden, Provo, Logan, and other cities. Abravanel Hall and ticket offices are at 123 W. South Temple; call (801) 533-5626 for information or (801) 355-ARTS for tickets.

The **Utah Opera Company,** www.utahopera. org, founded in 1978, stages four operas during its October–May season. Ticket offices and performances are in the restored Capitol Theatre. Call (801) 736-6868 for information, (801) 355-ARTS for tickets.

Another center for classical music and performance is the **University of Utah.** The university's Symphony Orchestra, Chamber Orchestra, jazz ensembles, opera, bands, and ballet, dance, and choral groups present regular concerts and performances on and off campus; the season runs September–May. Call the university's Public Relations office at (801) 581-6772, or check the website at www.utah.edu/artsmuseums.

Ballet West began in Salt Lake City in 1963 as the Utah Civic Ballet, but as the group gained fame and began traveling widely it chose its present name to reflect its regional status. This versatile group's repertoire includes classical, modern, and foreign works. Most Utah performances

take place at downtown's Capitol Theatre, September–April. For information, call (801) 323-6900, for tickets call (801) 355-ARTS, or check the website: www.balletwest.org.

The professional **Ririe-Woodbury Dance Company,** (801) 323-6801, www.ririewoodbury.com, has one of the most active dance programs outside New York City. The varied repertoire includes mixed media, eye-catching choreography, and humor. The group also shares its expertise by teaching production and dance skills to students and professionals. Ririe-Woodbury Dance Company is based at the Capitol Theatre. Also performing at the Capitol is the **Repertory Dance Theatre,** a professional company focusing on classical American and contemporary dance. For information, call (801) 534-1000.

CONCERT SERIES AND MUSIC FESTIVALS

The **Concert Series at Temple Square** presents hundreds of performances a year for the public; all are free. The LDS Church sponsors the varied musical fare to provide a common meeting ground of great music for people of all faiths. You might hear chamber music, a symphony, operatic selections, religious choral works, piano solos, organ works, a brass band, or a percussion ensemble. Programs last about an hour and usually take place Friday and Saturday evenings at 7:30 P.M. in either the Assembly Hall or the tabernacle. Organists present 25-minute **Organ Recitals** in the tabernacle Monday–Saturday at noon (and at 2 P.M. in summer) and Sunday at 2 P.M. The **Mormon Tabernacle Choir** sings in the tabernacle on Sunday mornings at 9:30 A.M. (be seated 15 minutes before) for a 30-minute radio broadcast. You're also welcome to attend rehearsals by the Mormon Tabernacle Choir on Thursday evenings at 8 P.M. At the same hour on Wednesday evenings, the Mormon Youth Symphony rehearses in the tabernacle, and on Tuesday evenings the Youth Chorus rehearses. Schedules of all musical events are posted in Temple Square; or call (801) 240-3318 or (801) 240-2534.

The **Madeleine Arts & Humanities Program** is held in the historic Cathedral of the Madeleine, 331 East South Temple, (801) 328-8941. This series of choral, organ, and chamber music concerts takes place on Sunday evenings throughout the spring and summer. Lectures, theatrical performances, and dance concerts are also held. All events are free.

In June, the **Gina Bachauer International Piano Competition** takes over Salt Lake City. Over 60 young pianists from around the world gather to perform a week-long series of performances both as solos (early in the competition) and with the Utah Symphony (only the finalists). The winners compete for recording contracts, a Steinway piano, and thousands of dollars in cash. It's a good chance to enjoy the musicianship of tomorrow's rising piano stars and to savor the thrill of musical competition. For information, call (801) 521-9200, or check the website at www.bachauer.com.

THEATER

Pioneer Theatre Company, (801) 581-6961, one of Salt Lake City's premier theater troupes, offers a seven-show season running from September to May. The company performs a mix of contemporary plays, classics, and musicals. Although the company operates from the University of Utah's **Pioneer Memorial Theatre,** 300 South and University St., it is not part of the university itself. The Pioneer Memorial Theater is also the site of University of Utah student productions and the Young People's Theatre, which produces plays for children.

The city's cutting-edge theater group is the **Salt Lake Acting Company.** This well-established troupe doesn't shy away from controversy: their excellent production of Tony Kushner's *Angels in America* raised eyebrows and stirred strong reactions. Besides presenting new works from around the world, the company is also committed to staging plays by local playwrights; there are performances year-round. This professional troupe has two theater spaces at 168 W. 500 North; for information, call (801) 363-0526 or (801) 355-ARTS for tickets.

The **Grand Theatre,** located on the Salt Lake City Community College campus at 1575 South State Street, (801) 957-3459 or (801) 957-3263, is home to a year-round program of theatrical performances by both student and semiprofessional troupes. The **Hale Centre Theater,** 3333 S. Decker Lake Dr. (2200 South), (801) 984-9000, offers family-oriented musicals and stage plays throughout the year.

For something spoofier, the **Off Broadway Theatre,** 272 South Main, (801) 355-4628, is the place for "improv" competitions, Broadway comedies, and topical farces. At the **Desert Star Playhouse,** 4861 South State, (801) 266-7600, you'll find old-fashioned melodramas and cabaret-style comedy skits.

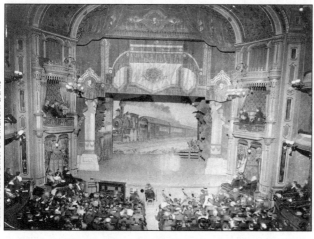

CHURCH OF JESUS CHRIST OF LATTER-DAY SAINTS

Lightning Express, Salt Lake Theatre, ca. 1900

NIGHTLIFE

Nearly all nightclubs and music bars that serve alcohol in Salt Lake are private clubs, and you'll end up paying a temporary membership charge (usually $5) in addition to the cover charge (even if you don't have a drink). Clubs open to the public (no membership needed) are so noted. The best place to check out the club scene is to pick up a copy of **City Weekly** or **The Slug,** both free and widely available.

If you're just looking for a beer and a chance to chat with the locals, try one of the brewpubs listed above under restaurants. There's no membership charge at Salt Lake brewpubs.

To explore the live-music club scene, start at the **Zephyr,** 301 South West Temple, (801) 355-CLUB. The Zephyr is perhaps SLC's premier music club, with live music (often national acts) performing in an intimate, friendly setting. The **O'Shucks Bar & Grill,** 22 E. 100 South, (801) 596-8600, combines a comfortable pub atmosphere with nightly live music, mostly acoustic. **D.B. Cooper's,** 19 E. 200 South, (801) 532-2948, also offers live music (usually jazz) nightly. If you're looking for a singles-oriented, collegiate crowd, some danceable live music, and high spirits, check out the **Port O' Call,** 78 W. 400 South, (801) 521-0589, or **Green Street,** 602 Trolley Sq., (801) 532-4200.

If you like more aggressive, post-grunge music, the **Dead Goat Saloon,** 165 South West Temple, in Arrow Press Square, (801) 328-GOAT (open to the public), or the **Cinema Bar,** 45 West Broadway, (801) 359-1200, are both good places to begin your exploration of SLC's alternative music scene. If you just want to dance, SLC offers a number of options. The most popular dance clubs are **DV8,** 115 South West Temple, (801) 539-8400, both a disco and a dance-band venue, and **Axis,** 108 S. 500 West, (801) 519-AXIS, which has a DJ and cutting-edge music; Friday evening is Gay Night, live bands on Saturday nights. **Area 51,** 400 W. 451 South, (801) 534-0819, has theme nights (Gothic, Techno, DiverseCity, etc.)

Salt Lake City isn't known for its vibrant gay scene, to put it mildly, and what gay life there is here is pretty well disguised. A good place to start the evening is at **Zipperz,** 155 W. 200 South, (801) 521-8300, with couches and chairs in a book-lined "library" and video screens in the back. **Bricks,** 579 W. 200 South, has contests and activities (drag shows, karaoke), plus disco dancing. **Club Blue,** 60 E. 800 South, (801) 517-4074, combines a boots and leather scene with great dance music.

If you don't drink alcohol but want to experience the SLC scene, try **The Bay,** 400 South West Temple, (801) 363-2623, with two floors of dance music. There's no smoking at The Bay, either, and it's open to the public. **Cup of Joe,** 353 W. 200 South, (801) 363-8322, has a comfortable coffee shop atmosphere and evening poetry readings and live music; open to the public.

MOVIES

There are a number of first-run multiplexes in downtown Salt Lake City; check the daily newspapers for listings. The city is lucky to have a couple of excellent art and revival cinemas as well. The **Tower Theatre,** 876 E. 900 South, (801) 328-1645 is the city's premier showcase for new foreign and independent films as well as revivals of the classics. The **Avalon Theatre,** 3605 S. State (5.5 miles south of downtown), (801) 266-0258, offers similar but less avant-garde films and tends to maintain a more family-oriented lineup. Both the Tower and the Avalon offer a fine selection of art and foreign videos for rent. The **Utah Film and Video Center,** 20 S. West Temple (Salt Lake Art Center), (801) 534-1158, also screens independent documentaries, animation, and experimental films.

Brewvies, 677 S. 200 West, (801) 355-5500, is a brewpub/cinema combo where you can buy an ale and a burger and watch a first-run or cult favorite film.

For a selection of major release first-run movies, check out the following multiplexes in the downtown area: **Cineplex Odeon,** 111 E. 300 South, (801) 359-2112, **Crossroads Cinema,** 50 S. Main, (801) 355-3883, and **Trolley Corners Theatre,** 515 S. 700 East, (801) 364-6183.

SPORTS

Pro Sports

Utah professional sports fans love their **Utah Jazz,** which are usually strong contenders in the NBA's Western Division. The team plays at the Delta Center at 300 West and South Temple. Tickets are hard to come by at the last minute, but it's worth a call to the team's box office, (801) 355-DUNK, to inquire. Otherwise, you'll need to rely on scalpers or ads in the classifieds. The **Salt Lake Buzz,** (801) 485-3800, is the AAA affiliate of baseball's Minnesota Twins. Games are played at the impressive Franklin Quest Field from April through September; it's hard to imagine a more astonishing backdrop to a game of baseball than the craggy Wasatch Front. The **Utah Grizzlies,** (801) 988-8000, are Salt Lake City's professional ice-hockey team and recently won the International League championships. The Grizzlies skate at the Delta Center.

University of Utah

University athletic teams compete in football, basketball, baseball, softball, tennis, track and field, gymnastics, swimming, golf, skiing, and other sports. Contact the Jon M. Huntsman Special Events Center, on campus near 400 South and 2000 East, (801) 581-3542.

Bonneville Raceway Park

For roaring engines, smoking tires, and checkered flags, visit the raceway during its April–October season. Located in West Valley City at 6555 W. 2100 South, (801) 250-2600.

EVENTS

Concerts, festivals, shows, rodeos, and other special events happen here nearly every day, and the Salt Lake Convention and Visitors Bureau, 180 S. West Temple, (801) 521-2822, can tell you what's going on. Also check the Visitors Bureau's *Salt Lake Visitors Guide,* for some of the best-known annual happenings:

In **April,** the annual **World Conference of the Church of Jesus Christ of Latter-day Saints** is held the first weekend of the month at Temple Square. The church president (believed to be a prophet of God) and other church leaders give guidance to members throughout the world.

(Hotel rooms are in short supply at this time.) Call (801) 240-2531 for more information.

Cinco de Mayo is celebrated in **May** with a party and concerts at the Utah State Fairgrounds on the week of May 5th. For information, call (801) 538-FAIR. A larger celebration of multiculturalism comes the third weekend of the month, when the grounds of the Salt Lake City and County Building at State Street and 400 South erupts with the **Living Traditions Festival.** Enjoy dances, food, and entertainment of the many different cultures that make up the Utah mosaic. For more information, call (801) 596-5000.

The **Scottish Festival & Highland Games** starts **June** off on a lively step with manly contests, bagpipe music and dancing, and ethnic food; held at Fort Douglas, off Wasatch Drive east of the University of Utah. Call (801) 969-7030 for more information. The **Utah Arts Festival,** (801) 322-2428, www.uaf.org, takes place the last weekend in June and includes lots of music, dance, literary readings, arts demonstrations, crafts sales, and food booths. The event is held at the state Fairpark west of the city off North Temple.

The summer's single largest festival is in **July.** The **Days of '47 Celebration,** commemorates the arrival of Mormon pioneers here on July 24, 1847. The city celebrates with three parades, including the huge 24th of July Pioneer Parade (the day is a state holiday), a marathon, lots of fireworks, and the year's biggest rodeo, held at the Delta Center. For information, call (801) 560-0047.

The **Greek Festival** in **September** celebrates Greek culture with food, music, folk dancing, and tours of the historic Holy Trinity Greek Orthodox Cathedral. The festival is held at the Hellenic Center at 300 South and 300 West on the weekend after Labor Day. Call (801) 328-9681 for more information. The **Utah State Fair** is a celebration of the state's agricultural heritage and features rodeos, livestock shows and judging, art and craft exhibits, musical entertainment, and a midway, all at the state fairgrounds, North Temple and 1000 West, (801) 538-FAIR.

SALT LAKE CITY RECREATION

Salt Lake City's stunning physical location at the base of the craggy, snow-covered Wasatch Mountains gives tangible evidence of the region's stellar recreational and sporting opportunities. Even on a short visit to the Salt Lake area, you'll want to get outdoors and enjoy a hike or ride a bike up a mountain canyon. You won't be alone: the city's newest flood of emigrants, young professionals, are as attracted to the city's right-out-the-back-door access to the great outdoors as to the region's vibrant economy.

Skiing has always been Utah's biggest recreational draw, and as host of the 2002 Winter Olympics the Salt Lake City area is set to command the stage of international skiing and winter sports. Summer visitors will find lots to like after the snow melts: most ski areas remain open for warm-weather recreation including mountain biking, hiking, trail rides, tennis, and plain old relaxing. The U.S. Forest Service manages Mill Creek and Big and Little Cottonwood Canyons as part of the Wasatch National Forest. Located just east of the city, these canyons provide easy access to hiking and biking trail systems and to popular fishing streams.

DOWNHILL SKIING

Utah's "Greatest Snow on Earth" lies close at hand. Within an hour's drive from Salt Lake City you can be at one of seven downhill areas in the Wasatch Range, each with its own character and distinctive skiing terrains. (Coverage of each of the individual resorts follows in the Wasatch Canyons and Ski Resorts section.) The snow season runs from about mid-November to April or May. Be sure to pick up the free *Utah Ski Vacation Planner* from Ski Utah, Inc., 150 W. 500 South, Salt Lake City, UT 84101, (801) 534-1779 or 800-SKI-UTAH, fax (801) 521-3722, or from most tourist offices in Utah. Or check out the website at www.skiutah.com. The planner lists most Utah resorts and has diagrams of the lifts and runs, lift ticket rates, and detailed information on lodging. Call (801) 521-8102 for Utah snow conditions.

Salt Lake City-area ski resorts are grouped quite close together. Although they are in different drainages, Solitude and Brighton Ski Areas in Big Cottonwood Canyon and Snowbird and Alta Ski Areas in Little Cottonwood Canyon, they all share the high country of the Wasatch Divide with Park City, Deer Valley, and The Canyons Ski Areas. There is no easy or quick route between the three different valleys, however, and traffic and parking can be a real hassle. Luckily, there are plenty of options for convenient public transport between Salt Lake City and the ski areas and between the resorts themselves.

Alternatively, you can ski between the various ski areas with **Interconnect Ski Tours,** which provides a guide service for extensive tour-

---

SALT LAKE CITY AREA WINTER OLYMPIC VENUES

Olympic Village, where the athletes will be housed, is located on a 40-acre site in the Fort Douglas area on the University of Utah campus in Salt Lake City. Olympic Stadium (a.k.a., the Rice-Eccles Football Stadium), where the opening and closing ceremonies take place, is also on campus. Medals ceremonies will take place nightly in downtown Salt Lake City, with a presentation of gold, silver, and bronze medals at the Medals Plaza, between 200 West and 300 West on North Temple Street. There's no admission charge to attend the medals presentation.

For the purposes of the Olympics, **Delta Center,** home of the Utah Jazz, has been renamed the **Salt Lake City Skating Arena,** at 300 West and South Temple Street. Events held here are **all figure skating events** and **short track speed skating.**

Oquirrh Park Oval, in the suburb of Kearns at 5624 South 4800 West, is host to the men's and women's speed skating.

West Valley Hockey Arena is the Olympic name for the "E" Center, 3200 Decker Lake Dr., in the suburb of West Valley Center. The majority of the men's ice hockey competition will take place here.

ing to the high country between Wasatch Front Ski Areas. Skiers should be experienced and in good physical condition because of the high elevations (around 10,000 feet) and the need for some walking and traversing. Touring is with downhill equipment. Trips include Snowbird-Alta-Brighton-Solitude and Park City-Brighton-Solitude-Alta-Snowbird (both $150 a day). For details, contact Ski Utah, Inc., 150 W. 500 South, Salt Lake City, UT 84101, (801) 534-1907.

Transportation to Ski Areas

Salt Lake City's public bus system, the UTA, (801) 287-4636, will take you to the four resorts on the west side of the Wasatch Range: Solitude, Brighton, Snowbird, and Alta. You can get on the buses downtown, at the University of Utah, or at the bottoms of the canyons.

Lewis Brothers Stages offers a "Ski Express" from the Salt Lake City Airport and downtown hotels to all Wasatch Front Ski Areas, including Park City, Deer Valley, Wolf Mountain, Brighton, Solitude, Snowbird, and Alta. Book a $22 round-trip ticket through a hotel or call Lewis Brothers directly at (801) 359-8677 or (800) 826-5844. For the same price, Lewis Brothers also operates the "Canyon Jumper," which connects Park City to Snowbird, Alta, Solitude, and Brighton. Optional ski packages include transportation and lifts at a discount. Similar services are offered by a number of other transportation companies including All Resort Express, (435) 649-3999 or (800) 457-9457, and Park City Transportation, (435) 649-8567 or (800) 637-3803.

CROSS-COUNTRY SKIING

During heavy snowfalls, Salt Lake City parks and streets become impromptu cross-country ski trails, and any snowed-under Forest Service road in the Wasatch Range is fair game for Nordic skiers. The Mill Creek Canyon road is a favorite. If you don't mind cutting a trail or skiing ungroomed snow, ask at ski rental shops for hints on where the backcountry snow is good.

Otherwise, there are a number of organized cross-country ski areas in the Salt Lake City area. The Mountain Dell Golf Course in Parley's Canyon (off I-80 toward Park City) is a favorite place to make tracks. There are cross-country facilities at Alta and Solitude (see under Wasatch Range Canyons and Ski Resorts) as well as at the White Pine Touring Center in Park City.

OTHER SPORTS AND RECREATION

Parks

Salt Lake City has lovely parks, many of which have facilities for recreation. For information about the city's park system, contact the Parks and Recreation office at (801) 972-7800; for county park information, call (801) 468-2560.

There are abundant reasons to spend time at **Liberty Park,** (801) 538-2062, including the Tracy Aviary, the children's play area, and the acres of shade and lawn. The park also affords plenty of opportunity for recreation. The tennis

paddleboats in Liberty Park

center on the western side offers 16 lighted courts. The outdoor swimming pool adjacent to the tennis center is open in summer. During the sweltering Salt Lake summer, the shady boulevards provide a cool environment for jogging. You'll find horseshoe pits to the north of the park's historic Chase House. Liberty Park is southeast of downtown and bordered by 900 and 1300 South and by 500 and 700 East.

Mormon pioneers manufactured beet sugar at **Sugarhouse Park,** (801) 467-1721, beginning in 1851; the venture later proved unprofitable and was abandoned. Today, expanses of rolling grassland in the 113-acre park are ideal for picnics, strolling, and jogging. The facility has a playground and fields for baseball, soccer, and football. In winter, the hills provide good sledding and tubing. A lake attracts seagulls and other birds for bird-watching. Sweet smells rise from the Memorial Rose Garden in the northeast corner. Sugarhouse Park is on the southeast edge of Salt Lake City at 1300 East and 2100 South (access is from 2100 South).

Swimming Pools and Gymnasiums
Fourteen public swimming pools in Salt Lake City offer places to splash. For outdoor pools in summer, two of the best and most central are found at **Liberty Park,** 1300 South and 700 East, and **Fairmont Park,** 2361 S. 900 East. **Steiner Aquatic Center,** 645 South Guardsman Way, (801) 583-9713, has both an indoor and an outdoor pool.

For an even bigger splash, try **Raging Waters,** 1200 W. 1700 South, (801) 973-8300, a water-sport theme park that features water slides and a Wild Wave pool. The children's area has waterfalls, geysers, a "dinosaur beach," and a small wave pool.

Tennis
Seventeen city parks have courts; call the Salt Lake City Parks and Recreation Department, (801) 972-7800, for the one nearest you. **Liberty Park,** 1300 South and 500 East, has 16 courts.

Hiking, Biking, and Jogging Trails
For hiking trails in the nearby Wasatch Range, simply drive up Mill Creek, Big or Little Cottonwood Canyon and look for trailheads. Contact the Salt Lake Ranger District, (801) 943-1794, at

the base of Big Cottonwood Canyon for maps and advice. Also see the Wasatch Range Canyons and Ski Resorts section.

In the city itself, a pleasant and relaxing route for a stroll or a jog follows **City Creek Canyon,** a shady, stream-filled ravine just east of the State Capitol. The road that runs up the canyon is now closed to most traffic and extends five miles from its beginnings at **Memory Grove,** just northeast of the intersection of E. North Temple and State Street, to Rotary Park at the top of the canyon.

Another quiet place for a walk or a jog are the four miles of trails outside **Red Butte Gardens** east of the University of Utah. The hiking trails wind through wildflower meadows and past old sandstone quarries. You don't need to pay the admission to the gardens proper to hike the trails.

Joggers also favor the shady oasis of **Liberty Park** and the rolling terrain of **Sugarhouse Park.**

Golf
Salt Lake City has plenty of places to tee off. The following lie close to town and are open to the public. **Bonneville** is an 18-hole, par-72 course east of downtown at 954 Connor Street (2130 East off Sunnyside Ave. near the Hogle Zoo), (801) 583-9513. **University** is a nine-hole, par-33 executive course on the University of Utah campus at 100 S. 1900 East, (801) 581-6511. **Mountain Dell** is a 36-hole, par-71 or -72 course east in Parleys Canyon; take I-80 East Canyon/Emigration Canyon Exit 134, (801) 582-3812. Mountain Dell will be the site of the Olympic Cross-country Ski Competition in 2002. **Forest Dale** is a nine-hole, par-36 course at 2375 S. 900 East (near Sugarhouse Park), (801) 483-5420. **Nibley Park** is a nine-hole, par-34 course at 2730 S. 700 East, (801) 483-5418. **Glendale** is an 18-hole, par-72 course at 1603 W. 2100 South, (801) 974-2403. **Rose Park** is an 18-hole, par-72 course northwest of downtown at 1386 N. Redwood Rd., (801) 596-5030.

Horseback Riding
East Canyon Outfitters lead hourly, day, breakfast, sunset, and overnight rides on the Mormon Pioneer Trail and in other areas in the Wasatch Range east of Salt Lake City; located 20 miles from Salt Lake City via I-80 and UT 65 (one-half-mile south of East Canyon Reservoir), (801) 355-3460.

Skating
Cottonwood Heights Recreation Center 7500 S. 2700 East, (801) 943-3160, offers year-round ice-skating and lessons, indoor and outdoor pools, racquetball courts, and a weight room. Roller-skate at the Utah Fundome, 4998 S. 360 West in Murray, (801) 293-0800, and **Classic Roller Skating Centers,** 9151 S. 255 West in Sandy, (801) 561-1791.

Canoeing
A canoe trip through **Jordan River State Park** reveals birds and other wildlife in a peaceful setting that you wouldn't expect so close to downtown Salt Lake City. A green canopy of willow, Russian olive, and Siberian elm overhangs the river for much of its length. Canoeists can stop at the International Peace Gardens and other parks along the way. The state park office can advise on boating conditions and places to rent canoes, paddles, and life jackets. Park rangers enforce the rule that each boater must wear a Coast Guard-approved life jacket.

You'll need two cars or someone to pick you up at trip's end. Put-in is at 1200 W. 1700 South (across from Raging Waters), take-out at 1000 N. 1525 West; allow at least 2.5 hours (without

stops) for the six-mile route. This is the only section of the river open to boats. The Jordan River State Park office is at 1084 N. Redwood Rd., Salt Lake City, UT 84116, (801) 533-4496 (open Mon.–Fri. 8 A.M.–5 P.M.). It's a good idea to call the park before a trip to check on possible river obstructions. Off-season boating isn't recommended because of the greater likelihood of hazards blocking the way.

Rock Climbing
Rockreation, 2074 E. 3900 South, (801) 278-7473, offers instruction, equipment rental, and a massive rock gym with 6,700 square feet of climbing terrain. Day passes are available; there's also a weight and fitness room at the complex.

Equipment Rental
Utah Ski & Golf, 134 W. 600 South, (801) 355-9088, rents golf clubs in summer and ski equipment when the snow falls. Rent bicycles at **Canyon Bicycle,** 3969 S. Wasatch Blvd., (801) 278-1500. For hiking, camping, climbing, and ski rentals, try **REI,** 3285 East 3300 South, (801) 486-2100. Another all-sport rental outfit is **Bike, Board, and Blade,** 703 E. 1700 South, (801) 467-0992.

The rock squirrel (Citellus variegatus) is a large ground squirrel that lives in rocky areas from high plateaus to the edge of the desert.

OTHER PRACTICALITIES IN SALT LAKE CITY

SHOPPING

As in most large U.S. cities, shoppers in Salt Lake take much of their business to suburban malls. Cottonwood Mall, at Highland and Murray Holiday Roads south of the city, and Valley Fair Mall, at I-215 Exit 18 southwest of the city, are two popular malls, each containing over 100 stores. Salt Lake City also boasts several unique shopping areas and unusual stores including some excellent boutique centers and two large downtown malls. **Remember that many shops will be closed on Sunday.**

Trolley Square

Salt Lake City's most unusual shopping center came about when developers cleverly converted the city's old trolley barn. Railroad magnate E.H. Harriman built the barn in 1908 as a center for the city's extensive trolley system. The vehicles stopped rolling in 1945, but their memory lives on in Trolley Square. Inside, you'll see several trolleys, a large stained-glass dome, salvaged sections of old mansions and churches, and many antiques. More than 100 shops and restaurants call this gigantic barn home. Watch movies at Cineplex-Odeon Theatres (four screens, 801-363-1183) and Flick 2 (two screens, 801-521-6113). Trolley Square is open daily, including Sunday afternoons, at the corner of 500 South and 700 East, (801) 521-9877. **Trolley Corners,** across the street at 515 S. 700 East, is a smaller shopping area with shops, restaurants, and Trolley Corners Theatres, (801) 364-6183.

Crossroads Plaza

Located at 50 S. Main across from Temple Square in the heart of downtown, (801) 531-1799, this modern shopping center on four levels has more than 100 shops, fast-food restaurants, banks, and Crossroads Cinemas (three screens, 801-355-3883). Waldenbooks on the main floor and B. Dalton Bookseller on the second level have good selections of Utah books. Crossroads Plaza is open daily, including Sunday afternoons.

ZCMI Mall

What may be America's oldest department store, Zion's Cooperative Mercantile Institution, downtown at the corner of South Temple and State Sts., (801) 321-8743, began in 1869 as a church-owned operation. The old facade graces the Main Street side, but the more than 90 shops and restaurants inside are new. There are six ZCMI stores in the Salt Lake City metro area. ZCMI Mall is open Monday–Saturday.

TP Gallery

Crafts and art by Native Americans are featured here. Look for beadwork and leather items (Ute Indians), jewelry (Navajo, Hopi, and Zuni tribes), pottery (Hopi and New Mexico Pueblo tribes), kachina dolls (Hopi), baskets (Papago), sand-paintings, books, and cassettes. The gallery, located downtown at 252 S. Main Street, (801) 364-2961, is open Monday–Saturday.

Recreational Equipment, Inc. (REI)

This large store has an outstanding array of outdoor recreational gear for hiking, camping, bicycling, skiing, river running, rock-climbing, and travel. Gear can be rented, too. The book section is a good place to look for regional outdoor guides. Topo maps cover the most popular hiking areas of Utah. REI memberships (optional) allow you to receive annual dividends on your purchases. Open daily at 3285 East 3300 South, (801) 486-2100.

Gardner Village

This attractive shopping village offers a restaurant and craft shops in the refurbished Gardner Mill, built in 1877. Old houses and cabins have been moved to the grounds and restored for additional shops. Step into the silo to dine at **Archibald's Restaurant,** (801) 566-6940 (American and continental food), open daily for lunch and dinner (and Saturday and Sunday for breakfast). The village also has a small museum of historic exhibits. Village and museum, (801) 566-8903, are located in West Jordan, 12 miles south of downtown Salt Lake City; take I-15 Midvale Exit 301 (7200 South), turn west, and follow signs to the Gardner Mill at 1095 W. 7800 South.

OTHER PRACTICALITIES IN SALT LAKE CITY 85

Bookstores

Sam Weller's Zion Book Store, 254 S. Main, (801) 328-2586, claims to be one of the West's largest, with more than half a million new and used books covering many topics. **Borders Books and Music** in the Crossroads Plaza, 50 S. Main, (801) 363-1271, has a good selection of general reading and Utah books. **Deseret Book Co.** specializes in LDS literature, but it also has many general reading and Utah books; 36 S. State (ZCMI Mall), (801) 328-8191 and other locations. The **University of Utah's Bookstore,** (801) 581-6326, has a varied selection on many subjects.

SERVICES

Post

The main **downtown post office** is at 230 W. 200 South in the Expo Mart, (801) 974-2200. The University of Utah has a post office in the bookstore.

Banking and Exchange

Salt Lake City is a major regional banking center, and you'll have no trouble with most common financial transactions. If you are depending on foreign currency, consider changing enough for your trip around Utah while in Salt Lake City. Exchanging currency will be much more difficult in smaller, rural towns. Change foreign currency at **Zions First National Bank,** downtown at Main and South Temple, (801) 524-4873; **First Security Bank of Utah,** 41 East 100 South, (801) 246-5629; or the airport's Terminal 1, (801) 524-4711. **American Express** is at 175 S. West Temple, (801) 328-9733.

Health and Medical

Minor medical emergencies can be treated by **IHC,** just west of downtown at 55 N. Redwood Rd. and at six other area locations, (801) 321-2490. Hospitals with 24-hour emergency care include **Salt Lake Regional Medical Center,** 1050 E. South Temple, (801) 350-4111; **LDS Hospital,** Eighth Ave. and C St., (801) 350-4111; **St. Mark's Hospital,** 1200 E. 3900 South, (801) 268-7111; and **University Hospital,** 50 N. Medical Dr. (1800 East), (801) 581-2121. For a physician referral, contact one of the hospitals or the Utah State Medical Association, (801) 355-7477.

For a 24-hour pharmacy, try the **Rite Aid** at 5540 S. 900 East, (801) 262-2981. If you're looking for a drug store, check the phone book for **Smith's Pharmacy;** there are over 25 in the Salt Lake metro area.

Child Care

Guardian Angel offers bonded and licensed baby- and child-sitters at your hotel room. Call (801) 598-1229.

AAA

The **American Automobile Association** offices are at 560 E. 500 South, (801) 541-9902.

Employment

Low on dough? The **Job Service Center** offers free services at 720 S. 200 East, (801) 536-7000, and 5735 S. Redwood Rd., (801) 269-4700.

PHONE NUMBERS

Emergencies (fire, police, medical): 911.
Highway Emergency Assistance: (801) 576-8606 or *71 (mobile phones).
Lawyer Referral Service (Utah State Bar Association): (801) 531-9075.
Physician Referral Service (Utah State Medical Association): (801) 355-7477.
Police (Salt Lake City): (801) 799-3000.
Road Conditions: (801) 964-6000.
Salt Lake Convention and Visitors Bureau (local travel information): (801) 521-2822 or (800) 541-4955.
Sheriff (Salt Lake County): (801) 535-5441.
Utah Division of Wildlife Resources: (801) 538-4700.
Utah Recreation/Ski Report: (801) 521-8102.
Utah State Parks: (801) 538-7220.
Utah Transit Authority (UTA): (801) 287-4636.
Utah Travel Council (statewide travel information): (801) 538-1030.

INFORMATION

Tourist Offices

Volunteers at the **Salt Lake Convention and Visitors Bureau,** downtown in the Salt Palace at 90 S. West Temple, Salt Lake City, UT 84101,

(801) 521-2822 or (800) 541-4955, www.visit-saltlake.com, will tell you about the sights, facilities, and goings-on in town. The office also has many helpful magazines and brochures. Open Mon.–Fri. 8 A.M.–5 P.M. (to 6 P.M. in summer) and Sat. 9 A.M.–4 P.M.; you can park in spaces behind the office. The Visitors Bureau has a branch in Terminal 2 at the airport (Concourse D is open 24 hours daily and staffed only during the day, and an information kiosk near the baggage claim area is also staffed only during the day).

The **Utah Travel Council,** www.utah.com, publishes a well-illustrated *Utah Travel Guide,* travel maps (both state maps and a series of five detailed maps covering the state), and other helpful publications. There are specialized guides to biking and rafting holidays as well. (You can also find these publications at the Salt Lake Convention and Visitors Bureau and local chambers of commerce.) The staff at the information desk provide advice and literature about Utah's national parks and monuments, national forests, Bureau of Land Management areas, and state parks as well as general travel in the state. You can stop by the Utah Travel Council offices in historic Council Hall, across the street from the Capitol, or write Council Hall/Capitol Hill, Salt Lake City, UT 84114. Open Mon.–Fri. 8 A.M.–5 P.M. and weekends and holidays 10 A.M.–5 P.M., (801) 538-1900, fax (801) 538-1399, or (800) 200-1160.

Wasatch-Cache National Forest

The **supervisor's office,** downtown on the eighth floor of the Federal Building, 125 S. State St., Salt Lake City, UT 84138, (801) 524-3900, has general information and forest maps for all the national forests in Utah; some forest and wilderness maps of Nevada, Idaho, and Wyoming; and regional books. Open Mon.–Fri. 7:30 A.M.–4:30 P.M. (to 5 P.M. in summer). The website is also a fountain of information: www.fs.fed.us/wcnf.

For detailed information on hiking and camping in the nearby Wasatch Range, visit the **Salt Lake Ranger District office,** 6944 S. 3000 East., Salt Lake City, UT 84121, (801) 943-1794. The district includes the popular Mill Creek, Big Cottonwood, and Little Cottonwood Canyons in the Wasatch Range, the Wasatch Range east of Bountiful and Farmington, and the Stansbury Mountains west of Tooele. Large reference books cover nearly every recreational activity and trail. The foresters here will likely have personal knowledge of the area you're heading to. Open Mon.–Fri. 8 A.M.–5 P.M.

Bureau of Land Management

The state office has general information on BLM areas in Utah and sells recreation and land-status maps of the state. Open Mon.–Fri. 8 A.M.–4 P.M. Located downtown on the fourth floor at 324 S. State Street, Salt Lake City, UT 84111-2303, (801) 539-4001.

Utah State Parks and Recreation

Obtain literature and the latest information on all of Utah's state parks here, or check the website: parks.state.ut.us. If you're planning a lot of state park visits, ask about the $65 annual park pass or the $45–55 annual pass for a specific park (these cover only day-use fees). Open Mon.–Fri. 8 A.M.–5 P.M. Located west of downtown at 1594 W. North Temple, Salt Lake City, UT 84116, (801) 538-7220 (information line). Reservations for campgrounds and some other services can be made by calling (801) 322-3770 or (800) 322-3770; a reservation fee of $5 per family or $10 per group applies.

Utah Division of Wildlife Resources

The staff here issues fishing and hunting licenses and information. Open Mon.–Fri. 8 A.M.–5 P.M. Located at 1596 W. North Temple, Salt Lake City, UT 84116, (801) 538-4700, or at www.nr.state.ut.us/dwr/dwr.htm.

Libraries

The large **city library** contains a wealth of reading material, a children's library, records, and audio and video tapes. Special collections include Western Americana and Mormon history. The Atrium Gallery hosts art exhibits. Puppet shows and story hours entertain children. Large bulletin boards on the main floor list upcoming art shows, entertainment, local events, classes, volunteer opportunities, and bus routes. Open Mon.–Thurs. 9 A.M.–9 P.M. and Fri. and Sat. 9 A.M.–6 P.M. The main library is at 209 E. 500 South, (801) 524-8200. See the telephone blue pages or call for locations of the five branch libraries.

The **Marriott Library** at the University of Utah ranks as one of the leading research libraries of the region. You'll find more than two million volumes and over 14,000 periodical titles inside. Special collections include the Middle East, United Nations, Western Americana, and Utah manuscripts. The large map collection has topo maps of all 50 states as well as maps and atlases of distant lands. Hikers can photocopy maps of areas they plan to visit. The public is welcome to use the library; a Library Permit Card can be purchased to use materials outside of the library. Open Mon.–Thurs. 7 A.M.–10 P.M., Fri. 7 A.M.–5 P.M., and Sat. 9 A.M.–5 P.M. (shorter hours during summer and school breaks); (801) 581-6085 (hours) or (801) 581-8558 (information).

Media

The Salt Lake Tribune morning daily reflects the city's liberals. The LDS-owned *Deseret News* comes out daily in the afternoon with a conservative viewpoint and greater coverage of Mormon Church news. *Utah Highways* is a travel magazine reporting on back roads, hiking and biking, recreation, and other topics of interest to the Utah traveler. *City Weekly* and *The Event* describes the latest on art, entertainment, events, and social spots as well as covering local politics and issues.

Salt Lake City has a number of good public radio stations. KUER 90 FM offers a good musical mix along with National Public Radio news. KCPW, at both 88.3 and 105.1 FM, offers more NPR news and programming as well as foreign news programs. KRCL, at 91 FM, is a community radio station with progressive news and locally produced programming.

TRANSPORTATION

Tours

A free **Pioneer Trolley** circles the Mormon historic and religious sites at Temple Square. Guides point out significant sites. Pick up the trolley at any point around Temple Square.

The **Gray Line,** 553 W. 100 South, Salt Lake City, UT 84101, (801) 521-7060 or (800) 309-2352, offers a 2.5-hour city tour in the morning (afternoons, too, in summer) for $18 adults, $9 ages 5–12. A four-hour Utah Copper Mine and Great Salt Lake tour visits the Bingham Canyon open-pit mine and a beach on the Great Salt Lake for $25 adults, $13 ages 5–12. Both tours can be combined for $40 adults, $20 ages 5–12. Gray Line will pick up at most large hotels. Three-day tours head south to Bryce, Zion, and Grand Canyon National Parks or northeast to Yellowstone and Grand Teton National Parks.

Great Western Aviation, Salt Lake Air Service, 180 N. 2400 W., Salt Lake City, UT 84116, (801) 359-4840 or (800) 748-5454, will show you any part of this scenic state. Tours are as follows: Salt Lake City area (one hour, 25 minutes); the Uinta Range, Flaming Gorge, and Dinosaur National Monument (two hours, 20 minutes); Canyonlands and Arches National Parks (three hours); Capitol Reef, Bryce Canyon, Lake Powell, and Monument Valley (four hours, 20 minutes); and Zion, Grand Canyon, and Bryce Canyon (four hours, 30 minutes). Flights operate from Salt Lake City, Ogden, and Logan.

Classic Helicopter Service, (801) 295-5700 or (800) 444-9220, has flights to and between ski areas, helicopter skiing, and tours of the Salt Lake City area.

Local Bus and Light Rail

Utah Transit Authority (UTA) provides inexpensive bus and light rail train service in town and to the airport, the University of Utah, and surrounding communities. Buses go as far north as Ogden, as far south as Provo and Springville, and as far west as Tooele. The new TRAX light rail trains connect the Delta Center, downtown Salt Lake City, and the southern suburbs. No charge is made for travel downtown within the "Free-Fare Square" area (bounded by North Temple, 400 South, West Temple, and 200 East). During the winter ski season, skiers can hop on the Ski Bus Service to Solitude, Brighton, Snowbird, and Alta Ski Areas from downtown, the University of Utah, and other locations. A bus route map and individual schedules are available from the ground transportation information desk at the airport, the Salt Lake Convention and Visitors Bureau downtown, Temple Square visitors' centers, the Crossroads Mall, and the ZCMI Mall or by calling UTA at (801) 287-4636 (BUS-INFO) Monday–Saturday 6 A.M.–7 P.M. Free transfers are given on request when the fare is paid. On Sunday, only the airport, Ogden, Provo, and a few other destinations are served. UTA shuts down on holidays.

Fares are $1 for two hours of travel on both TRAX and the buses; a day pass is $2.

Lewis Brothers Stages offers "Red Horse Express" service during ski season to Park City from the Salt Lake City Airport ($18 one-way, $34 round-trip). The "Ski Express" from Salt Lake City serves Solitude, Brighton, Snowbird, Alta, and the Park City Ski Areas ($22 round-trip). The "Canyon Jumper" shuttle operates during the ski season connecting the Park City Ski Areas with Snowbird, Alta, Brighton, and Solitude ($22 round-trip). Ski packages with transportation and lift tickets can be purchased, too. Reservations 12 hours in advance are advised for these trips; (801) 359-8677 (Salt Lake City), (801) 649-2256 (Park City), or (800) 826-5844.

Park City Transportation provides year-round service to Park City from downtown Salt Lake City and the airport for $23 one-way; ski shuttles depart from Salt Lake City and Park City in winter to Solitude, Brighton, Snowbird, Alta, Sundance, Snowbasin, and Powder Mountain Ski Areas; call a day in advance for reservations and to check if a passenger minimum applies; (801) 364-8472 (Salt Lake City), (801) 649-8567 (Park City), or (800) 637-3803.

Long-Distance Bus

Salt Lake City sits at a crossroads of several major freeways and has good **Greyhound** bus service. Generally speaking, buses go north and south along I-15 and east and west along I-80. One bus daily leaves from Salt Lake City for Yellowstone National Park (summer only). The Greyhound station is downtown at 160 W. South Temple, (801) 355-9579 or (800) 231-2222.

Auto Rentals

You'll find all the major companies and many local outfits eager to rent you a set of wheels. In winter you can find "skierized" vehicles with snow tires and ski racks ready to head for the slopes. Many agencies have an office or delivery service at the airport: Avis Rent A Car, Salt Lake International Airport, (801) 575-2847 or (800) 331-1212; Budget Rent A Car, 641 N. 3800 West, (801) 575-2586 or 800-527-0700; Dollar Rent-A-Car, 601 N. 3800 West, Salt Lake International Airport, (801) 575-2580 or (800) 421-9849; Enterprise Rent-A-Car, 151 E. 5600 South, (801) 266-3777 or (801) 534-1888, (800) RENT-A-CAR; Hertz, Salt Lake International Airport, 775 North Terminal Dr., (801) 575-2683 or (800) 654-3131; National Car Rental, Salt Lake City International Airport, (801) 575-2277 or (800) 227-7368; and Payless Car Rental, 1974 West North Temple, (801) 596-2596 or (800) 327-3631.

Taxis

The following have 24-hour service: City Cab, (801) 363-8400; Ute Cab, (801) 359-7788; and Yellow Cab, (801) 521-2100.

Train

Amtrak trains stop at a new depot at 340 S. 600 West. In the last two years, Salt Lake has lost two of its transcontinental routes. The only train that currently passes through the city is the

stained-glass
window in the
Union Pacific Station

California Zephyr, which heads west to Reno and Oakland and east to Denver and Chicago four times a week. Call for fares, as Amtrak now prices tickets as airlines do, with advance booking, special seasonal, and other discounts available. Amtrak office hours (timed to meet the trains) are irregular, so call first, (800) 872-7245 (information and reservations).

Air

Salt Lake City International Airport is conveniently located seven miles west of downtown; take North Temple or I-80 to reach it. All major U.S. carriers fly into Salt Lake City. Salt Lake City is the western hub for Delta Airlines, which is the region's air-transport leader.

SkyWest Airlines, (800) 453-9417, Delta's commuter line, flies to Vernal, Cedar City, and St. George in Utah and to towns in adjacent states.

Sunrise Air, (800) 842-8211, provides several flights daily to Moab.

The **airport** has three terminals; in each you'll find a ground-transportation information desk, a cafeteria, motel/hotel courtesy phones, auto rentals (Hertz, Avis, National, Budget, and Dollar), Morris Travel office, and a ski-rental shop. Terminal 1 also houses Zion's First National Bank (currency exchange), an ice cream parlor, and gift shops. The Utah Information Center (Salt Lake Convention and Visitors Bureau) is upstairs in Terminal 2 and open 24 hours daily (but staffed only during the day), (801) 575-2800. Terminal 3 is dedicated to foreign arrivals and departures. Staff at the ground-transportation information desks will know the bus schedules into town and limousine services direct to Park City, Sundance, Provo, Ogden, Brigham City, Logan, and other communities. UTA Bus #50 is the cheapest way into town. It leaves the airport daily except holidays every hour from about 6:30 A.M. to about 11:30 P.M. (less frequently and only to about 5:30 P.M. on Sun.).

DAY TRIPS FROM SALT LAKE CITY

THE GREAT SALT LAKE

Since its discovery by fur trappers in the 1820s, the lake has both mystified and entranced visitors. Early explorers guessed that it must be connected to the ocean, not realizing that they had come across a body of water far saltier. Only the Dead Sea has a higher salt content. When Mormon pioneers first tried evaporating the lake water, they found the residue bitter tasting—it's only 84 percent sodium chloride (table salt); the remaining 16 percent is sulfates and chlorides of magnesium, calcium, and potassium. Mining companies have extracted salt, magnesium, lithium, chlorine, gypsum, potassium sulfate, and sodium sulfate from the water, which yields up to 27 percent solids. The lake's northern arm, isolated by a railroad causeway, contains the highest mineral concentrations—about twice those of the southern arm. The lowest salt levels occur on the south and east sides at river inlets. Bacteria grow in such numbers that they sometimes give a red tint to water in the northern arm, as do the reddish-orange algae *Dunaliella salina.* The blue-green algae *Dunaliella viridis* occasionally give their own hue to the lake's southern arm. A tiny brine shrimp *(Artemia salina)* and two species of brine fly *(Ephydra sp.)* live in the lake, too. The harmless flies emerge from the lake near the end of their life cycle to lay eggs, then die several days later. Until recently, no fish had ever been found alive in the Great Salt Lake. By the spring of 1986, however, unusually heavy runoff from tributaries had diluted the lake so that small rainwater killifish could survive.

The lake has always been changing—rising with spring snowmelt, then falling due to evaporation that peaks in late summer and autumn. These annual variations result in differences in lake levels of six to as much as 18 inches. Long-term changes have affected the lake, too: climate variations and diversion of river water for irrigation have caused a 21-foot difference between record low and high levels. Because the lake lies in a very shallow basin, its area has varied dramatically between 900 square miles at the lowest water level and 2,500 square miles at the highest. The record low surface elevation of 4,191 feet was reached in 1963, and the "experts" thought the lake might shrink to nothing. Unfortunately, at that time much construction was going on near the shore without thought that the waters could rise. The lake's previous record high had occurred in 1873, causing concern to Brigham Young and other church leaders. They devised a plan to pump lake water into the desert to the west, but receding levels eliminated the need for the pumping project.

Present-day Utahns haven't been so lucky. In just five years, from 1982 to 1987, the lake rose 12 feet to record elevations. The spreading waters threatened to inundate parts of Salt Lake City, nearby towns and farms, the airport, rail lines,

and I-80. High levels also upset the lake's ecology and ruined much of the surrounding marshland. Seven of the state's nine bird refuges were flooded including world-famous Bear River Migratory Bird Refuge. An emergency session of the Utah Legislature in May 1986 authorized a pumping project with an initial price tag of $60 million to transfer water to the West Pond site in the Great Salt Lake Desert. From a peak elevation of 4,212 feet in January 1987, the lake level subsided, soon eliminating the need for pumping. The Great Salt Lake continues to confound the experts.

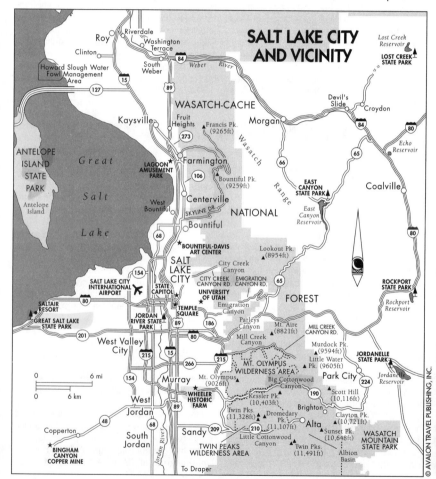

Antelope Island State Park

Though just a short distance offshore from Salt Lake City, Antelope Island seems a world away. Its rocky slopes, rolling grasslands, marshes, sand dunes, and lake views instill a sense of remoteness and rugged beauty. An extension of the Oquirrh Mountains, Antelope Island is the largest of the lake's eight islands. It measures 15 miles long and five wide; Frary Peak (elev. 6,596 feet) rises in the center. Archaeologists have found prehistoric sites showing that Indians came here long ago, perhaps on a land bridge during times of low lake level. In 1843, explorers John Frémont and Kit Carson rode their horses across a sandbar to the island and named it after the antelope (pronghorn) herds that the party hunted for food. In 1849, Brigham Young established a ranch here for the church's herds of cattle, sheep, and horses. Ranching has continued to be a major activity, though the Mormons lost ownership of the island in 1884.

Today the entire island is a state park. Buffalo, deer, and other wildlife live here. You drive to the island on a seven-mile paved causeway (entrance fee is $7 per vehicle). Park trails for hiking, bicycling, and horseback riding allow access to much of the island. Campsites run $9 (including the toll and day-use fee), with an extra $1 charge on Saturday, Sunday, and holidays. Showers and restrooms are available in the swimming area in the northwest corner of the island. Take I-15 Exit 335 (two thirds of the way north to Ogden), then drive nine miles west to the start of the causeway and the entrance booth; 4528 W. 1700 South, Syracuse, UT 84075, (801) 773-2941.

Salt Island Adventures, (801) 583-4400, www.gslcruises.com, offers a variety of cruiseboat excursions on the Great Salt Lake. Cruises leave from the state park marina at the northern point of the island and sail to remote Fremont Island and back via the west shore of Antelope Island. There are several cruise options including one-hour sight-seeing tours ($12 adults, $10 seniors, and children 2–12, and free for ages under two); six-hour lake tours ($70 adult, $67 seniors, and $30 children); and sunset/dinner cruises ($43 adult, $41 senior, and $32 children).

Great Salt Lake State Park

Bathers have enjoyed hopping into the lake ever since the 1847 arrival of Mormon pioneers. Extreme buoyancy in the dense water makes it impossible for a bather to sink—no swimming ability is needed! But anyone who puts his head underwater quickly realizes that the salty water causes great irritation to the eyes, throat, and nose. During summer algae blooms, the odor of the water will prove an irritant to the nose.

Beginning in the 1880s, several resorts popped up along the lake's east and south shores. Besides bathing, guests could enjoy lake cruises, dances, concerts, bowling, arcade games, and roller-coaster rides. **Saltair Resort** stood as the last and grandest of the old resorts. Completed in 1893, the Moorish structure rose five stories and contained a huge dance floor where as many as 1,000 couples could enjoy the orchestra's rhythms. A rail line from Salt Lake City ran out on a 4,000-foot pier to the resort, which stood on pilings over the water. After 1930, low water levels, the Great Depression, fires, and fewer visitors gradually brought an end to Saltair. Its buildings burned for the second time in 1970.

A developer has recently built a smaller replica of the Saltair Resort on the Great Salt Lake's southern shore near I-80 Exit 104. Despite floods

Saltair Resort, ca. 1900

of rising lake waters and wind damage, this Saltair is still open, though it is nowhere near as glamorous as the resort's earlier incarnations. The main structure has a smattering of gift shops (Christmas tree ornaments made of salt), food concessions, and a small museum; videos detail the history of the lake and promote the race course at Bonneville Salt Flats. A short causeway leads out into the lake, where you can get a good whiff of the brackish water. Saltair is also a popular site for concerts; for information on events, call (801) 250-4400.

The adjacent **Great Salt Lake State Park beaches,** (801) 250-1898, are popular in summer; free entry. Stop in at the nearby **Great Salt Lake Visitor Center,** (801) 533-4083, to see a video and exhibits about the lake; free. A good selection of local travel information is available, too. Open daily year-round 9 A.M.–4 P.M. From Salt Lake City, drive west nine miles on I-80, take Exit 111 (7200 West), and follow the north frontage road west to the beaches; or take I-80 Exit 104 (Magna) and turn east on the north frontage road.

ringtail cat
(Bassariscus astutus)

LOUISE FOOTE

SOUTH OF SALT LAKE CITY

Bingham Canyon Copper Mine

An overlook within the world's largest and oldest open-pit copper mine provides a close look at the nonstop excavation work taking place on the terraced slopes. Signs and exhibits explain the mining process. Prospectors discovered the mineral wealth in 1863, though the Mormon rancher for whom the canyon was named never took part in the mining. Most of the early production concentrated on gold, silver, and lead. Attention shifted to copper in 1906 as mining companies began excavation of an open-pit mine. Today, five billion tons of rock later, the pit measures 2.5 miles in diameter at its top and one-half-mile deep. The "richest hole on earth" has yielded 12 million tons of copper and significant amounts of gold, silver, and molybdenum. Efficient mining, smelting, and refining techniques can make a profit even though Bingham Canyon ore now averages only 0.7 percent copper. Miners once lived in the town of Bingham Canyon, famed for being one street wide and seven miles long! Expanding operations gradually destroyed

the town in the 1950s; by 1961 nothing remained. Company officials lived in the attractive town of Copperton, which survives today.

The mine overlook and visitors' center are in the Oquirrh Mountains 25 miles southwest of Salt Lake City. Because of the distance, it's a good idea to call ahead before going out; (801) 252-3234 (recording). Open daily from 8 A.M. until 8 P.M. from mid-Apr. to Oct. 31; admission is $3 car, $2 motorcycle. Take I-15 Midvale Exit 301 and follow UT 48 west through Copperton to the mine. Stop at the mine gate for a pass, then follow signs to the overlook. For a bird's-eye view of the mine from the crest of the Oquirrh Mountains, follow the winding unpaved roads from Tooele or the Salt Lake Valley (see Oquirrh Overlook under Sights in the Tooele section of the West-Central Utah chapter).

NORTH OF SALT LAKE CITY

Bountiful-Davis Art Center

Exhibits by Utah artists and art classes take place at this gallery eight miles north of Salt Lake City. Open Mon. 5–9 P.M., Tues.–Fri. 10 A.M.–6 P.M., and Sat. 2–5 P.M.; closed Sun. and holidays; free. A gift shop is open during gallery hours. Located at 2175 S. Main in Bountiful (84010); take I-15 North Salt Lake/Woods Cross Exit 318, go east 0.3 mile on 2600 South to 500 West (which becomes Main Street), then turn left (north) 0.2 mile; (801) 292-0367.

Utah Botanical Gardens

The gardens have closed to make way for a new highway interchange. The beautiful array of flowers and other plants may open as early as Spring 2004 at a nearby location in Farmington; (801) 451-3204.

WASATCH RANGE CANYONS AND SKI RESORTS

Spectacular mountains and canyons of the Wasatch Range begin right at the edge of Salt Lake City. The name Wasatch comes from an Indian word meaning "high mountain pass," of which the range has a great abundance. The range is about 200 miles long, extending from Mt. Nebo in central Utah to the Bear River in southern Idaho. Geologic forces over the last 20 million years have uplifted and twisted these block-faulted mountains into a confusing jumble of rock layers. Intrusions of molten granitic rock and volcanic eruptions then added to the complexity. Massive rivers of ice carved knife-edged ridges and U-shaped valleys during at least three major periods of glaciation in the last 500,000 years. None of the glaciers remain, though some snowfields persist through years of heavy precipitation.

Recreation

City Creek, Mill Creek, Big Cottonwood, and Little Cottonwood Canyons beginning on the edge of Salt Lake City hold a special attraction for visitors. Paved roads lead up each canyon to idyllic picnic spots and trailheads for dozens of hiking paths. Brilliant autumn colors of maple, aspen, and oak trees decorate hillsides from mid-September to early October. Big and Little Cottonwood Canyons also contain campgrounds, lodges, and ski resorts. Canyon streams and alpine lakes harbor elusive trout. Hikers will find detailed trail descriptions in *Hiking the Wasatch* by John Veranth (trails and major routes). Other good books with Wasatch hikes include *Utah's Favorite Hiking Trails* by J. David Day. For firsthand information on recreation in the range, contact the **Salt Lake Ranger District office** of the Wasatch-Cache National Forest. The office is in Salt Lake City at 594 S. Grant Boulevard, (801) 524-5042, and is open Monday–Friday 8 A.M.–4 P.M.

Camping is allowed only at designated sites or in the backcountry. Camps must be at least 200 feet from trails and water sources and one-half mile from any road, but because of the steep terrain nearly all camping is near the top of trail. Dogs are prohibited in City Creek, Big Cottonwood, and Little Cottonwood Canyons to protect drinking water sources. Don't forget to bring wind and rain gear in case a sudden storm appears; hypothermia is a serious danger in the mountains. Poison ivy, with its shiny leaves in groups of three, grows along streams at lower elevations. Rattlesnakes live in many areas as high as 8,000 feet; look for them before reaching or stepping over rocks and logs.

SKYLINE DRIVE

This 28-mile scenic drive north of Salt Lake City climbs nearly 5,000 feet for impressive views west across the Great Salt Lake and east over the Weber River Valley; allow two to three hours. **Bountiful Peak Overlook,** just below the peak's 9,259-foot summit, has the most sweeping panorama. The forest road is narrow and mostly unpaved; it's not recommended for trailers or those who fear heights. Begin the drive in either Bountiful or Farmington. From Bountiful (I-15 Exit 321), go east two miles on 400 North, turn left (north) two blocks on 1300 East, turn right (east) on 600 North. Then, take 1375 East (Skyline Drive) to Ward Canyon; look closely for the switchback below the giant "B"—don't take the road past a large gravel pit. From Farmington (I-15 Exit 327), go east one mile on State, then turn left (north) on 100 East into Farmington Canyon.

Bountiful Peak Campground (elev. 7,500 feet) is north of the overlook and 8.5 miles up Farmington Canyon; open mid-June to early October with drinking water; free. **Sunset Campground** (elev. 6,400 feet) is 5.3 miles up Farmington Canyon; open early May–mid-Oct.; no

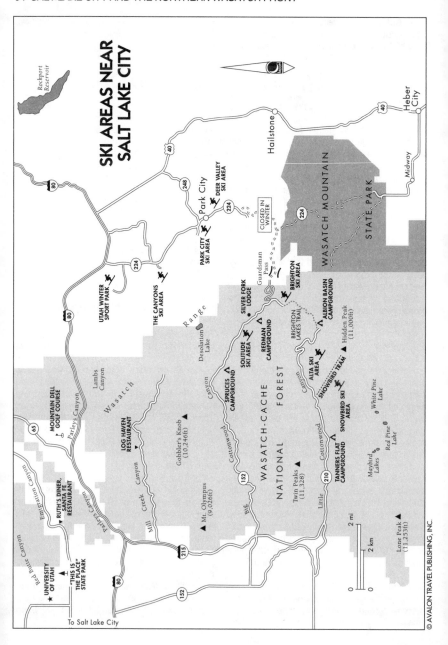

SKI AREAS NEAR
SALT LAKE CITY

© AVALON TRAVEL PUBLISHING, INC.

water or charge; a hiking trail climbs to Sunset Point. The Francis Peak Road turns off near Bountiful Peak Campground to an overlook eight miles away with more good views.

CITY CREEK CANYON

This pretty canyon begins just east of the State Capitol and winds northeast into the Wasatch Range. Since pioneer days, people have obtained precious water here and enjoyed the diverse vegetation, wildlife, and scenery. Because City Creek is still part of the city's water supply, regulations prohibit dogs, horses, and overnight camping. A paved road through City Creek Canyon extends six miles past picnic areas to a trailhead. Hikers and joggers may travel on the road every day. In summer (Memorial Day weekend–September 30), bicyclists may enter only on odd calendar days, motorized vehicles may drive up only on even calendar days and only with reservations (usually for a picnic); a gate at the bottom controls entry. No motorized vehicles are allowed the rest of the year, but bicycles can use the road daily then. A $3 charge applies if you drive through to the trailhead at the upper end (no reservation needed).

The big attraction for many visitors is a stop at one of the picnic areas along the road. Picnickers can reserve sites with the Water Department; obtain the required receipt at least a day ahead by visiting the accounting office in the Public Utilities Building at 1530 S. West Temple (Salt Lake City, UT 84115), (801) 483-6797. Mark your envelope "Attn. City Creek Reservations" and allow one week or more to obtain reservations by mail. Sites are sometimes available on a first-come, first-served basis (midweek is best). Picnic permits cost $3 and up depending on size of group. The entrance to City Creek Canyon is reached via Bonneville Boulevard, a one-way road. From downtown Salt Lake City, head east on North Temple, which becomes Second Avenue after crossing State Street, then turn left (north) 1.3 miles on "B" Street, which becomes Bonneville Boulevard after 11th Avenue, to City Creek Canyon Road. Returning from the canyon, you have to turn right on Bonneville Boulevard to the State Capitol. Bicyclists and joggers may approach City Creek Canyon from either direction.

Hiking

A popular hiking destination from the trailhead at road's end (elev. 6,050 feet) is City Creek Meadows, four miles away and 2,000 feet higher. After 1.5 miles, you'll pass Cottonwood Gulch on the left; a side trail leads up the gulch to an old mining area. After another one-half mile on the main trail, a spring off to the right in a small meadow is the last reliable source of drinking water. During the next mile, the trail steepens and winds through aspen groves and then passes two shallow ponds. The trail becomes indistinct here, but you can continue one mile northeast to the meadows (elev. 8,000 feet); a topo map and compass help. For splendid views of the Wasatch Range, climb north one-half mile from the meadows up the ridge to where Davis, Salt Lake, and Morgan Counties meet. Hikers also enjoy shorter strolls from the trailhead along the gentle lower section of trail.

MILL CREEK CANYON

Plentiful picnic areas and many hiking possibilities lie along Mill Creek just outside Salt Lake City. The canyon entrance is at Wasatch Boulevard and Mill Creek Road (3800 South). You may bring your dog along, too—this is one of the few canyons where pets are welcome. Picnic sites are free and available on a first-come, first-served basis; most lack water. The first one, **Church Fork Picnic Area,** is three miles in at an elevation of 5,700 feet; **Big Water Picnic Area** is the last, 8.8 miles up at an elevation of 7,500 feet. A small usage fee applies (except on winter weekdays) to visitors in Mill Creek Canyon.

Hiking

Salt Lake Overlook on Desolation Trail is a good hiking destination for families. The trail climbs 1,200 feet in two miles for views of the Salt Lake Valley. Begin from the lower end of Box Elder Picnic Area (elev. 5,760 feet) on the south side of the road. Energetic hikers can continue on Desolation Trail beyond the overlook to higher country near timberline and go all the way to Desolation Lake (19 miles). The trail runs near the ridgeline separating Mill and Big Cottonwood Canyons, connecting with many trails from both canyons. Much of this high country lies in the Mount Olympus Wilderness. See Mt. Aire and Park City West 7½-minute topo maps.

Alexander Basin Trail winds to a beautiful wooded glacial bowl below Gobblers Knob; the trailhead (elev. 7,080 feet) is on the south side of the road eight miles up Mill Creek Canyon, 0.8 miles beyond Clover Springs Picnic Area. The moderately difficult trail begins by paralleling the road northwest for a few hundred feet, then turns southwest and switchbacks one mile to the beginning of Alexander Basin (elev. 8,400 feet). The trail to Bowman and Porter Forks turns right here, but continue straight one-half mile for the meadows of the upper basin (elev. 9,000 feet). The limestone rock here contains many fossils, mostly shellfish. From the basin it's possible to rock-scramble to the summit of Gobblers Knob (elev. 10,246 feet). (The name comes from an attempt by mine owners to raise turkeys after their ore played out; the venture ended when bobcats ate all the birds.) See the Mt. Aire 7½-minute topo map.

BIG COTTONWOOD CANYON

Cliffs towering thousands of feet form the gateway to Big Cottonwood Canyon. Skiers come in season to try the downhill slopes at Solitude and Brighton and to cross-country ski at the Solitude Nordic Center. Enter the canyon from Wasatch Boulevard and 7000 South, about 15 miles southeast of downtown Salt Lake City. The 14-mile drive to Brighton Basin reveals splendid vistas at each turn while climbing to an elevation of 8,700 feet. Guardsman Pass Road turns off just before Brighton and winds up to Guardsman Pass (elev. 9,800 ft.) at the crest of the Wasatches, then drops down into either Park City or Heber City on the other side; the mostly unpaved road is usually open late June to mid-October.

Eight picnic areas lie along Big Cottonwood Creek. You'll come first to **Oak Ridge Picnic Area,** one mile from the entrance, followed by **Dogwood Picnic Area** (elev. 5,200 feet), 1.1 miles from the entrance, and finally to **Silver Lake Picnic Area** (elev. 8,720 feet) near road's end, 14.5 miles up the canyon. Silver Lake offers full access to fishing and picnic sites. All picnic areas are first-come, first-served except the **Jordan Pines** group area (8.8 miles from the canyon entrance; has water), with picnic sites and campgrounds by reservation only; (800) 280-CAMP.

Solitude Ski Resort

Skiers come here for the wide variety of runs—some highly challenging even for experts, others ideal for beginners and intermediate skiers. Honeycomb Canyon, on the back side of the resort, contains over 400 acres of ungroomed powder skiing. In all, there's over 1200 skiable acres, rated 20 percent beginner, 50 percent intermediate, and 30 percent advanced. Seven lifts (one quad, two triple chair, and four double chair) service the 63 named runs and three bowls. Skiers enjoy a vertical drop of 2,047 feet from the top of the highest lift. One run makes a loop with nearby Brighton Ski Area for even more skiing. Solitude has a ski school, rentals, ski shops, a Nordic center (see below), and six restaurants. Adult lift tickets cost $39. Lift tickets for children (11–13) and seniors (60–69) are $32. Up to two kids under 10 can ski free with each paying adult; seniors 70 and over ski free anytime. For more information, check the website at www.skisolitude.com.

Solitude Nordic Center

Plenty of snow and groomed tracks make this one of the best places in Utah for cross-country skiers. The 21 kilometers of groomed trails range from easy level loops to varied rolling terrain. Most trails have both compacted snow for skating and set tracks. The center is based in the Silver Lake Day Lodge (immediately after the highway joins the Brighton loop); open daily 9 A.M.–4:30 P.M. from mid-Nov.–mid-Apr. Trail fee is $10 ($7 after 12:30 P.M.), and free for children under 10 and seniors 70 and over. Staff at the shop offer rentals (touring, racing, telemark, and snowshoes), sales, instruction, day tours, and advice on backcountry touring and avalanche hazards. Tickets can also be purchased at Solitude Ski Area. For more information, contact P.O. Box 21350, Salt Lake City, UT 84121-0350, (801) 536-5774 or (800) 748-4754, ext. 5774. The ski area is 12 miles up Big Cottonwood Canyon and only a 28-mile drive southeast of downtown Salt Lake City.

Brighton Ski Resort

This is a favorite with local families for the excellent skiing and friendly, unpretentious atmosphere. While 21 percent of the runs are beginner and 40 percent intermediate, Brighton does offer some difficult powder-bowl skiing and steep runs as well. Two quads, two triple chairlifts, and three double chairs climb as high as 10,500 feet for a 1,745-foot vertical descent to the base. In addition to the more than 60 runs and trails at Brighton, you can hop on the Sol Bright run to visit Solitude Ski Area; a lift there will put you back on a trail to Brighton. Night skiing is offered Monday–Saturday, too. Brighton has a ski school with a learn-to-ski package, rentals, two shops, and three cafeterias. Adults ski for $35 a day, $28 afternoon only, and $20 at night. Children 10 and under go free with a paying adult.

Contact Brighton Ski Resort at Brighton, UT 84121, (801) 532-4731 or (800) 873-5512, www.skibrighton.com. Brighton is at road's end, two miles past Solitude in Big Cottonwood Canyon.

Hiking

Mineral Fork Trail follows an old mining road past abandoned mines, cabins, and rusting equipment to a high glacial cirque. Waterfalls, alpine meadows, wildflowers, and abundant birdlife make the steep climb worthwhile. The signed trailhead is on the south side of the road six miles up the canyon (0.8 miles past Moss Ledge Picnic Area). You'll climb 2,000 feet in three miles to the Wasatch Mine, whose mineralized water makes up much of the flow of Mineral Fork Creek. Another two miles and 1,400 feet of climbing lead to Regulator Johnson Mine. A loop trip can be made by climbing the ridge west of Regulator Johnson (no trail) and descending Mill B South Fork Trail to Lake Blanche and the main road, coming out 1.5 miles west of the Mineral Fork Trailhead. See Mt. Aire and Dromedary Peak 7½-minute topo maps.

Brighton Lakes Trail winds through some of the prettiest lake country in the range. Families enjoy outings on this easy trail, which begins in Brighton behind the Brighton Lodge. Silver Lake has a boardwalk giving full access to fishing docks. The first section follows Big Cottonwood Creek through stands of aspen and evergreens. The trail continues south across meadows filled with wildflowers, then climbs more steeply to Brighton Overlook, one mile from the start. Dog Lake, surrounded by old mine dumps, lies 200 yards to the south. Continue on the main trail one-half mile to Lake Mary, a large, deep lake below Mt. Millicent. Lake Martha is another one-half mile up the trail. Another mile of climbing takes you to Lake Catherine, bordered by a pretty alpine meadow on the north and by the steep talus slopes of Sunset and Pioneer Peaks on the south. Total elevation gain for the three-mile hike to Lake Catherine is 1,200 feet. Hikers can also go another one-half mile to Catherine Pass and descend 1.5 miles to Albion Basin in Little Cottonwood Canyon. Sunset Peak (elev. 10,648 feet) can be climbed by following a half-mile trail from the pass. See the Brighton 7½-minute topo map.

Accommodations

$50–75: The **Brighton Lodge,** below, offers hostel lodging at $70 per night.

$100-125: Room prices at the following Brighton accommodations vary considerably, depending on season, day of week, and room size. Each has entry level rooms within this price range. Winter weekend rates can easily double these prices.

Adjacent to the slopes is resort-owned **Brighton Lodge,** which offers accommodations with a heated outdoor pool and spa; restaurant adjacent. Call (800) 873-5512 for information. Individual private chalets can be arranged through **Brighton Chalets,** 2750 E. 9800 South, Sandy, UT 84092, (801) 942-8824 or (800) 748-4824. Each chalet comes with a furnished kitchen, fireplace, and cable TV. The **Silver Fork Lodge,** (801) 649-9551, 11 miles up Big Cottonwood Canyon, offers eight rustic B&B rooms. The Silver Fork is also the area's most popular restaurant (especially for Sunday brunch) and roadhouse.

$150-175: Most lodgings at Solitude are in the European-style ski village at the base of the slopes and have very wide price ranges. The **Inn at Solitude** has hotel rooms, restaurants, private club bar, movie theater, and other amenities, while the **Village at Solitude Condominiums** offer condo units in three different developments. All have fireplaces, full kitchens, TVs and VCRs, private decks, and come with one-, two-, three-, or four-bedrooms. For reservations or information on the rooms or the ski area, contact Solitude Ski Resort at P.O. Box 21350, Salt Lake City, UT 84121-0350, (801) 534-1400 or (800) 748-4754.

Campgrounds: At an elevation of 7,400 feet, **Spruces Campground** has family sites 9.1 miles up the canyon. The campground is open with water and a $12 fee from early June to mid-October. Some sites can be reserved, (800) 280-CAMP. **Redman Campground** lies 13 miles up between Solitude and Brighton at an elevation of 8,300 feet; open from mid-June to early Oct. with water, family sites cost $12.

LITTLE COTTONWOOD CANYON

The road through this nearly straight glacial valley ascends 5,500 feet in 11 miles. Splendid peaks rise to more than 11,000 feet on both sides. In winter and spring, challenging terrain attracts skiers to Snowbird and Alta Ski Areas. Enter Little Cottonwood Canyon from the junction of UT 209 and UT 210, four miles south of the entrance to Big Cottonwood Canyon.

Granite rock for the Salt Lake Temple came from quarries one mile up the canyon on the left. Here, too, are the Granite Mountain Record Vaults, containing genealogical and historical records of the LDS Church stored on millions of rolls of microfilm. Neither site is open to the public.

Snowbird Ski and Summer Resort

This highly developed resort lies in Little Cottonwood Canyon on the west side of the Wasatch Range. Snowbird had a difficult time getting started back in the early '70s—not everyone wanted to see high-rise hotels among the mountains. Today, the complete resort facilities, excellent snow conditions, varied terrain, and large lift capacity entice plenty of skiers and boardheads.

The resort underwent another major expansion in 2000, opening up another 500 acres of backcountry skiing into Mineral Basin. With this additional acreage (the resort now offers more than 2,500 skiable acres)—plus masses of hotel and retail development in advance of the 2002 Olympics—Snowbird is a busy place, more like a small city than a mountain village.

Twenty-five percent of the runs are classed as beginner, 30 percent as intermediate, and 45 percent as advanced. Plenty of ungroomed areas lie in the backcountry, too. Snowbird's ski and snowboard schools and separate "bunny

skiing on Hidden Peak at Snowbird Ski Resort

hill" make it a good place to learn. Seven double chairlifts, two quads, and a large aerial tram serve the 89 named runs. The longest run is 3.5 miles and drops 3,200 feet.

The exceptionally long season at Snowbird continues to mid-May, though most lifts close by May 1. Adult chairlift tickets to all the lifts cost $52. Seniors and children (12 and under) are $39 (two children 12 and under ski free with each adult, however). All skiers can use the beginners' Chickadee Chairlift free of charge. Guided ski tours of about two hours (free with lift-ticket purchase) introduce new customers to the resort's skiing; groups divide up according to ability. Advanced skiers may take the Snowbird Mountain Experience, a five-hour guided excursion on steeper, more challenging terrain including powder and off-trail skiing (extra cost). Wasatch Powderbird Guides offers helicopter skiing in the peaks above the regular runs; call (801) 742-2800 for information.

Snowbird also offers a number of **adaptive ski programs.** Sit-skis, mono-skis, and outriggers make skiing possible for athletes with mobility impairments. Instruction and programs are available for both children and adults.

In addition to its ski school, Snowbird offers rentals, a wide selection of shops, restaurants, snack bars, four lodges, swimming pools, health spa, and child-care services. For reservations and information on the skiing and year-round resort facilities, contact Snowbird Ski and Summer Resort, Snowbird, UT 84092, (800) 385-2002, www.snowbird.com. The resort at Snowbird is six miles up Little Cottonwood Canyon and 25 miles southeast of downtown Salt Lake City.

Tram rides: Nonskiers can enjoy the heights aboard the tram as it climbs 2,900 vertical feet to the summit of Hidden Peak (elev. 11,000 feet) for a fantastic panorama of the Wasatches, the surrounding valleys, and the distant Uinta Mountains. The tram runs year-round; wear a warm jacket and hat in winter. Round-trip tickets are $14 adults, $8 children under 12 and seniors 62 and up, and $30 for families.

Summer Programs: Snowbird offers a full array of family recreation and resort facilities to summer visitors. All lodging, spa, and recreational facilities remain open, as do all restaurants and retail outlets. The resort's summer emphasis is on fitness and outdoor activities. The Activity Center (near the tennis courts), ext. 4147, rents mountain bikes and offers tours for hiking, climbing, backpacking, and mountain biking. A hiking map available at the center shows local trails and jogging loops. Guided hikes are available, and there's a nature trail adapted to guests with disabilities.

Tennis, mountain biking, hiking, and rentals are available. If your looking to relax, there's also the Cliff Spa and Salon, with a variety of beauty and massage treatments. Snowbird is also the site of ongoing musical and arts events. A summer favorite is the tram ride to Hidden Peak.

Alta Ski Area

The little town of Alta owes its original reputation to rich silver veins and the mining camp's riproaring saloon life. Mining started in 1865 with the opening of the great Emma Mine and peaked in 1872, when Alta had a population of 5,000 served by 26 saloons and six breweries. Crashing silver prices the following year and a succession of deadly avalanches ended the boom. Little remains from the old days except abandoned mine shafts, a few shacks, and the cemetery.

Ski enthusiasts brought Alta back to life: today, Alta is probably the most highly regarded of Utah's ski areas, with deep powder, wide-open terrain, and charming accommodations. In 1937, when some skiers decided to try the revolutionary concept of using ski lifts, detractors complained that the $1.50 per day lift tickets reserved the sport just for the rich. Some of the original Collins single chairs are still around; look for them at the bus stop beside Goldminer's Daughter Lodge and in the Shallow Shaft Steak House.

Alta likes to think of itself as a haven of serious skiing: the number of skiers allowed on the slopes on any given day is limited in order to protect "the quality of the experience." Also, Alta

Alta City during its early years

is for *skiers;* snowboards aren't allowed. Today Alta offers two triple and six double chairlifts serving more than 40 named runs of which 25 percent are rated beginner, 40 percent intermediate, and 35 percent advanced. The longest run is 3.5 miles and drops 2,500 feet. Beginners can use the free rope tows beside Alta Lodge and Snowpine Lodge or the three beginners' lifts. Lift tickets cost $33 ($25 half day), $24 ($18 half day) for the beginners' lifts. Skier Services offers a ski school, rentals, shops, child-care services, and restaurants (two on the slopes). Alta doesn't offer any summer programs, though a number of area Forest Service trails attract hikers and bikers; the Alta Lodge and the Alta Peruvian Lodge remain open. For more information, contact Alta Ski Area, P.O. Box 8007, Alta, UT 84092, (801) 742-3333 (office) or (801) 572-3939 (snow conditions), or dial up the website at www.alta.com. Alta is eight miles up Little Cottonwood Canyon.

Alta Cross–Country Skiing
Both beginning and experienced skiers enjoy cross-country skiing at Alta. There are no groomed tracks, but you can head up the unplowed summer road to Albion Basin. Sno-Cats often pack the snow. The road begins at the upper end of the Albion parking lot, then climbs gently to the top of Albion Lift, where skiers can continue to Albion Basin. Intermediate and advanced skiers can also ski to Catherine Pass and Twin Lakes Pass. Cross-country skiers may ski the beginner (green) Alta trails. Those heading for the backcountry should have proper equipment and experience; the Alta ski school office at the Albion ticket building can advise on avalanche conditions. There's no charge for skiing at Alta unless you use the lifts. Rent track and telemark cross-country skis at the Albion Day Lodge near the trailhead.

Hiking
White Pine, Red Pine, and **Maybird Gulch Trails** lead to pretty alpine lakes. Red Pine and Maybird Gulch lie in the Lone Peak Wilderness. All three trails begin from the same trailhead, then diverge into separate valleys. On any one of them, you'll enjoy wildflowers and superb high-country scenery. Start from White Pine Trailhead (elev. 7,700 feet) 5.3 miles up the canyon

Red Pine Trail in Little Cottonwood Canyon

and one mile beyond Tanners Flat Campground. The trail crosses a bridge over Little Cottonwood Creek and contours west, then southwest to White Pine Fork. The effects of several avalanches can be seen along this section. The trails divide after one mile, just before crossing White Pine Fork; turn sharply left for White Pine Lake or continue straight across the stream for Red Pine Lake and Maybird Gulch. Red Pine Trail contours around a ridge, then parallels Red Pine Fork to the lake (elev. 9,680 feet); a beautiful deep pool ringed by conifers and alpine meadows. Energetic hikers can rock-scramble along the stream another one-half mile (no trail) to Upper Red Pine Lake. The upper lake sits in a glacial cirque devoid of trees. Trout lurk in the waters, though the lake may remain frozen until late June. Maybird Gulch Trail begins two miles up Red Pine Trail from White Pine Fork and leads to tiny Maybird Lakes. From the trailhead, White Pine Lake is 3.5 miles (2,300-foot elevation gain), Red Pine Lake is the same (1,920-foot elevation gain), and Maybird Lakes are 4.5 miles (2,060-foot elevation gain). See the Dromedary

Peak 7¹/2-minute topo map. This whole area is heavily used by hikers, so take great care with the environment. Please follow the Forest Service regulation that prohibits wood fires within one mile of the lakes.

Peruvian Gulch–Hidden Peak Trail gives you the advantage of hiking just one-way from either the top or bottom by using the Snowbird tram. From the top of Hidden Peak (elev. 11,000 feet), the trail crosses open rocky country on the upper slopes and spruce- and aspen-covered ridges lower down, then follows an old mining road down Peruvian Gulch. Elevation change along the 3.5-mile trail is 2,900 feet. The Dromedary Peak 7¹/2-minute topo map covers this area.

Cecret Lake Trail begins from the west side of Albion Basin Campground and climbs glacier-scarred granite slopes to a pretty alpine lake (elev. 9,880 feet) below Sugarloaf Mountain. Wildflowers put on colorful summer displays along the way. The trail is just one mile long and makes a good family hike; elevation gain is 360 feet. Continue another mile for fine views south to Mt. Timpanogos from Germania Pass. It's no secret that early miners had trouble spelling Cecret Lake; you'll see two versions on maps!

Accommodations

Both Snowbird and Alta are very expensive places to spend the night. If you're on a budget, inquire at the Snowbird resort about hostel rooms. Most are used by staff, but sometimes (especially in summer) there are bunks available. Most accommodations at Snowbird are owned by the resort itself, and the best way to find out about the many options is simply to call the central reservation line, (800) 385-2002 or check the website at www.snowbird.com. Prices vary wildly according to season, day of week, and view. Alta boasts excellent though pricey accommodations: even bunk beds in a dorm room at the Alta Lodge are over $100! There are five grand lodges, several condominium developments, and a number of private homes available. Note, however, that room rates include three meals a day. The easiest way to find a room is simply to call **Alta Reservation Service,** (801) 942-0404 or (888) 782-9258, which can make reservations at all lodgings and arrange transportation rentals and ski packages.

$150–175: The poshest place to stay in Snowbird is the ski-in/ski-out **Cliff Lodge,** with 532 rooms, four restaurants (including the highly regarded **Steak Pit** and the **Wildflower Ristorante**), conference facilities, and retail shops (there are a total of 12 restaurants at the resort). The lodge's Cliff Spa and Salon is a full-service health and beauty facility with an outdoor heated pool, weight-training rooms, and spa treatment rooms with various beauty and massage therapies. At the resort's Racquet Club are indoor and outdoor tennis courts, racquetball courts, an indoor climbing wall, and other recreational facilities.

$200 and up: The Snowbird resort rents out a number of condominium properties in four different developments. Most are one-bedroom units, with prices ranging from $259 to $459; studio and efficiency rooms are sometimes available for less.

More condos are available through **Canyon Services,** P.O. Box 920025, Snowbird, UT 84092, (801) 943-1842 or (800) 562-2888. These upscale accommodations are found between Snowbird and Alta, and are available in four different complexes and in units with two to five bedrooms.

In Alta, one of the nicest and most central places to stay is the **Alta Lodge,** (801) 742-3500 or (800) 707-2582, with saunas and hot pools, good restaurants, and a country-inn atmosphere. The **Alta Peruvian Lodge,** (801) 742-3000 or (800) 453-8488, is another good choice, with its heated outdoor therapy pool and grand lobby. There's a good restaurant and a private club for guests. Alta's most luxurious place to stay is **Rustler's Lodge,** (801) 742-2200 or (800) 451-5223, with heated outdoor pool, fine-dining restaurant, and spacious rooms.

The lodges operate only on the modified or full American plan, with two or three meals included or added to the price; there's usually an additional 15 percent service charge added to your lodging and dining total as well. There is a bewildering array of room types, but all of the facilities generally charge about the same price for each type of room: expect to pay around $100 for a dorm, $125–$200 *per person* for a standard room, and upwards of $250 for a room with extras like fireplace, balcony, or hot tub. In summer, room rates drop by nearly half.

Campgrounds: There aren't any picnic areas in the canyon, but the U.S. Forest Service offers two places to camp. **Tanners Flat Campground** is 4.3 miles up the canyon at an elevation of 7,200 feet; sites cost $8 and have water from mid-May to early September, then no water or fee to mid-October. Some sites can be reserved, (800) 280-CAMP. **Albion Basin Campground** lies 11 miles up near the head of the canyon at an elevation of 9,500 feet (the last 2.5 miles are gravel road); sites cost $8 and have water from early July to early September, then no water or fee to late September or early October.

PARK CITY

Park City is without a doubt the recreational capital of Utah. With three ski areas and a new Winter Sports Park located in the valley, the city (pop. 6,800) is noted worldwide for its snow sports: the U.S. national ski team trains here, and many of the 2002 Winter Olympic competitions will take place in the valley. In summer, guests flock to the resorts to golf and explore the scenic mountain landscapes on horseback, mountain bike, or foot.

However, there's a lot more to Park City than recreation: the well-heeled clientele that frequent the resorts have transformed this old mining town into the most sophisticated shopping, dining, and lodging center in Utah. However, such worldly comforts come at a cost. Condominium developments stretch for miles, encroaching on the beauty that brought people here in the first place.

Even if you're not a skier or hiker, you should plan to explore Park City's historic downtown. Turn-of-the-century buildings along Main Street and on the hillsides recall Park City's colorful and energetic past. Here you'll find a historical museum, art galleries, specialty shops, and fine restaurants. A busy year-round schedule of arts and cultural events (including the Sundance Film Festival), concerts, and sporting contests also help keep Park City hopping.

Orientation

Park City lies in a mountain valley at an elevation of 7,000 feet on the eastern side of the Wasatch Range 31 miles east of Salt Lake City via I-80 and UT 224. The principal exit for Park City is called Kimball Junction, and although Park City proper is seven miles south, the condominiums and shopping centers begin immediately. Just south of Kimball Junction is The Canyons Ski Area, with its mammoth new lodges, and the Utah Winter Sports Park, the new ski-jump facility. In Park City proper, the Park City Ski Area is just west of downtown; most businesses stretch along historic Main Street. Two miles west of Park City is Deer Valley, both an upscale condo development and the state's most exclusive ski resort. Deer Valley's most expensive addresses are in Silver Lake Village, a development perched 1,000 feet above the town on a rocky bluff.

HISTORY

In October 1868, with winter fast approaching, three off-duty soldiers from Fort Douglas discovered a promising outcrop of ore on a hillside two miles south of the present town site. Their sample assayed at 96 ounces of silver per ton, with lesser values of lead and gold. Two years later, the Flagstaff Mine began operation at that first discovery, and development of one of the West's richest mining districts took off. What had been a peaceful valley with grazing cattle now swarmed with hordes of fortune hunters and rang with the sound of pickaxes. The famed Ontario Mine and dozens of other strikes soon followed. Silver from the Ontario—as much as 400 ounces in a ton—started the fortunes of U.S. Senator Thomas J. Kearns of Salt Lake City and George

CHURCH OF JESUS CHRIST OF LATTER-DAY SAINTS

Park City looking south, ca. 1900

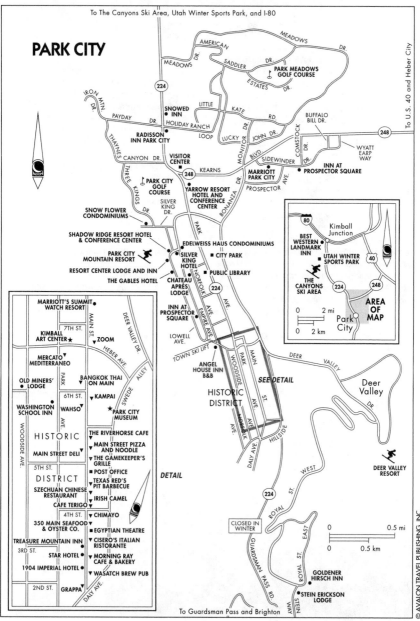

PARK CITY

To The Canyons Ski Area, Utah Winter Sports Park, and I-80

To U.S. 40 and Heber City

MEADOWS DR.

AMERICAN DR.

MEADOWS DR.

SADDLER DR.

PARK MEADOWS GOLF COURSE

MEADOWS DR.

ESTATES DR.

224

IRON MTN DR.

PAYDAY DR.

LITTLE KATE RD.

HOLIDAY RANCH LOOP

SNOWED INN

RADISSON INN PARK CITY

THAINES CANYON DR.

THREE KINGS DR.

LUCKY DR.

JOHN DR.

MONITOR DR.

BUFFALO BILL DR.

COMSTOCK DR.

248

WYATT EARP WAY

VISITOR CENTER

248

KEARNS

SIDEWINDER

INN AT PROSPECTOR SQUARE

MARRIOTT PARK CITY

PARK CITY GOLF COURSE

SILVER KING DR.

YARROW RESORT HOTEL AND CONFERENCE CENTER

BONANZA DR.

PROSPECTOR

SNOW FLOWER CONDOMINIUMS

SHADOW RIDGE RESORT HOTEL & CONFERENCE CENTER

PARK CITY MOUNTAIN RESORT

RESORT CENTER LODGE AND INN

THE GABLES HOTEL

EDELWEISS HAUS CONDOMINIUMS

SILVER KING HOTEL

CITY PARK

PUBLIC LIBRARY

PARK AVE.

NORFOLK AVE.

CHATEAU APRES LODGE

224

INN AT PROSPECTOR SQUARE

EMPIRE AVE.

LOWELL AVE.

TOWN SKI LIFT

ANGEL HOUSE INN B&B

WOODSIDE AVE.

PARK AVE.

MAIN ST.

NORFOLK AVE.

SEE DETAIL

DEER VALLEY DR.

Deer Valley

HISTORIC DISTRICT

DAILY AVE.

HILLSIDE AVE.

WEST

DEER VALLEY RESORT

DETAIL

224

CLOSED IN WINTER

ROYAL ST.

WEST

ROYAL ST. EAST

GUARDSMAN PASS RD.

STEIN WAY

GOLDENER HIRSCH INN

STEIN ERICKSON LODGE

0   0.5 mi

0   0.5 km

Inset map (AREA OF MAP)

80

Kimball Junction

BEST WESTERN LANDMARK INN

UTAH WINTER SPORTS PARK

THE CANYONS SKI AREA

224

40

248

AREA OF MAP

Park City

0   2 mi

0   2 km

Detail (Historic District)

MARRIOTT'S SUMMIT WATCH RESORT

7TH ST.

MAIN ST.

DEER VALLEY DR.

KIMBALL ART CENTER

ZOOM

MERCATO MEDITERRANEO

HEBER AVE.

OLD MINERS' LODGE

PARK AVE.

BANGKOK THAI ON MAIN

SWEDE ALLEY

WASHINGTON SCHOOL INN

6TH ST.

KAMPAI

WAHSO

PARK CITY MUSEUM

HISTORIC

WOODSIDE AVE.

MAIN STREET DELI

THE RIVERHORSE CAFE

MAIN STREET PIZZA AND NOODLE

THE GAMEKEEPER'S GRILLE

5TH ST.

POST OFFICE

DISTRICT

TEXAS RED'S PIT BARBECUE

SZECHUAN CHINESE RESTAURANT

CAFE TERIGO

IRISH CAMEL

4TH ST.

CHIMAYO

350 MAIN SEAFOOD & OYSTER CO.

EGYPTIAN THEATRE

TREASURE MOUNTAIN INN

CISERO'S ITALIAN RISTORANTE

3RD ST.

STAR HOTEL

MORNING RAY CAFE & BAKERY

1904 IMPERIAL HOTEL

WASATCH BREW PUB

2ND ST.

GRAPPA

DAILY AVE.

To Guardsman Pass and Brighton

© AVALON TRAVEL PUBLISHING, INC.

Hearst, father of publisher William Randolph Hearst. By 1880, Park City had grown into a substantial town with an ethnically diverse population of 10,000. The *Park Mining Record,* later the *Park Record,* began weekly publication that continues today. Scandinavian miners introduced skiing to the community, though the heavy 10-foot boards used then have little in common with today's equipment. A lively red-light entertainment district sprang up in Deer Valley Gulch, but it's long gone today.

The great hotel fire of 1898 nearly brought an end to the young city. The fire raced along Main Street and reduced 200 businesses and houses to ashes and left much of the population homeless. Determined citizens immediately set to work rebuilding and constructed a new downtown within three months. Many of the businesses you see along Main Street date from that time. In the early 1900s, Park City's mining economy began seeing more depressions than upswings. Mine flooding, labor troubles, and a big drop in metal prices during the Great Depression caused many residents to leave. By the early 1960s the town looked ready to fold up, but then the big skiing and resort boom brought it to life again!

SIGHTS

No matter what else you do in Park City, spend a hour or two wandering along the historic Main Street. Even with the inrush of galleries, gift shops, and trendy restaurants, there's still considerable Old West charm here.

Park City Museum

Drop in here to see historic exhibits on Park City's colorful past. The museum, (435) 649-6104, is at 528 Main Street in the old City Hall Building, built in 1885 and rebuilt after the 1898 fire. Go downstairs to see the original jail, known as the "dungeon." Open Mon.–Sat. 10 A.M.–7 P.M., Sun. noon–6 P.M., daily noon–5 P.M. in May and Oct.; free. The **Visitor Information Center,** (435) 649-6100, is here, too, and open the same hours; staff can answer your questions and provide literature on the area. Ask for a historic walking-tour leaflet. Groups can arrange guided walking tours.

Kimball Art Center

This large civic art center exhibits works of noted artists and sponsors classes and workshops. Two galleries display monthly-changing shows of paintings, prints, sculptures, ceramics, photography, and other media. The gift shop has many items for sale. Open Mon.–Sat. 10 A.M.–6 P.M., Sun. noon–6 P.M. Located at the corner of Heber and Park near the bottom of Main Street, (435) 649-8882. Look for other art galleries along Main Street, too.

SUNDANCE INSTITUTE FILM FESTIVAL

Robert Redford began this noted film festival in 1981 as a venue for independent films that otherwise had a difficult time reaching the screen or a mass audience. In subsequent years, the Sundance Festival has become the nation's foremost venue for new and innovative cinema. The festival is held the second half of January, at the height of the ski season, so Park City is absolutely packed and then some (as the festival has grown, some films are now shown at the Tower Theatre in Salt Lake City). Definitely make plans well in advance if you want to attend any of the screenings or festival activities.

Tickets to the screenings can be hard to come by, especially for films with advance reputations or big stars; if you can't get tickets, put your name on waiting lists or join the lines at the theaters for canceled tickets. However, tickets to less well-known films are usually available at the last minute. If you are coming to Park City expressly to see the films, inquire about package tours that include tickets.

Park City is exciting during the festival, as the glitterati of New York and Hollywood descend on the town. You'll see movie stars, some wild clothing, and lots of deal-making. For information on the Sundance Festival, call its information number, (435) 328-FILM, or check the website at www.sundance.org.

WINTER SPORTS

Park City Mountain Resort

Located in Park City proper, this is Utah's most famous and popular ski area. One high speed

PARK CITY WINTER OLYMPIC VENUES

The **Deer Valley Resort,** Deer Valley Drive South, will be the site for men's and women's slalom and freestyle skiing.

Park City Mountain Resort, Lowell Ave., will host men's and women's snowboarding, men's and women's giant slalom skiing.

Utah Winter Sports Park, 3000 Bear Hollow Drive, is to host two-men, four-men, and two-women bobsleigh; men's, women's, and mixed luge; men's and women's skeleton, ski jumping, and Nordic combined ski jump.

quad, four six-passenger high-speed lifts, a gondola, four quad chairs, five triple chairs, and four double chairs carry up to 27,200 skiers *per hour* high onto the eastern slope of the Wasatch Range. More than 100 trails range in length from one-quarter to 3.5 miles (16 percent easier, 45 percent more difficult, and 39 percent most difficult). Also, experienced skiers can enjoy the powder in five open bowls near the top of the mountain—a total of 650 acres. The total drop is 3,100 feet in elevation from the top of Jupiter Bowl to the Resort Center. Ski season usually runs from mid-November to mid-April.

Park City Ski Area and the adjacent resort village offer night skiing, a ski school, rentals, ski shops, ice-skating, and restaurants (three are on the slopes). The Town Lift and two runs allow skiers staying in downtown Park City to connect directly with the ski area.

Adult lift tickets cost $55 all day, $44 for the afternoon, $22 for night skiing. Children 12 and under go for $32, $25, and $12. Contact Park City Resort at P.O. Box 39, Park City, UT 84060, (435) 649-8111 (office), (435) 647-5335 (snow report), or (435) 649-0493 or (800) 222-PARK (lodging reservations). Or dial up the website at www.parkcitymountain.com. You'll find accommodations right at the ski center and many other places close by in town.

Skiing is one of several outdoor activities that people with disabilities can learn with the help of the **National Ability Center,** located on Level One at Park City Ski Area. The center provides special equipment and instruction at affordable rates, offers programs to people of all ages, and

is open for summer programs, as well. For more information, contact the center at P.O. Box 682799, Park City UT 84068, (435) 649-3991 (Voice/TDD).

Summer Programs: Although the Park City Ski Area shuts most of its lifts down for the summer, the resort remains open and maintains 30 miles of trails for mountain bikers, hikers, and horseback riders; for $8 you can ride up the Payday Lift with your bike or picnic hamper. A free map of designated mountain-biking trails is available from the resort, local bike shops, and grocery stores.

The ski area's **Alpine Slide** gives the thrill of a toboggan ride for summer visitors. A chairlift takes you to the start of a half-mile track that twists and winds down the hillside. No special skills are needed to ride the sled. Open late May to late Sept.: weekdays noon–10 P.M., weekends 10 A.M.–10 P.M. (shorter hours after Labor Day); $8 adult per plunge, $2.50 children.

Deer Valley Ski Resort

This is the crème de la crème of Utah ski areas. Here you'll find good uncrowded skiing with all the extras of posh accommodations, gourmet dining, attentive service, and polished brass everywhere. Attendants meet you in the parking lot to assist in unloading your skis and to guide you; help is never far away.

The slopes are served by 19 lifts: one four-passenger high-speed gondola, five detachable quads, three quad chairlifts, eight triples, and two double chairs carry skiers to the top of Bald Eagle Mountain, Bald Mountain, Empire Canyon, and Flagstaff Mountain, providing 87 runs, three bowls, and a vertical drop of 3,000 feet. The longest run is two miles. Fifteen percent of the skiing is rated easier, 50 percent more difficult, and 35 percent most difficult. The majestic Snow Park Lodge (elev. 7,200 feet) contains the ticket office, ski school, rentals, ski shop, child-care service, gift shop, and restaurant. You can drive 1,000 feet higher to Silver Lake Lodge, which offers two more restaurants.

Adult lift tickets cost $60 full day, $42 afternoon; children 12 and under cost $32 full day, $24 afternoon. Deer Valley will reserve accommodations, lift tickets, restaurants, flights, and local transportation for you. Contact Deer Valley Central Reservations, P.O. Box 3149, Park City,

UT 84060, (435) 649-1000 or (800) 558-3337 (skiing information and reservations) or (435) 649-2000 (snow report). The website is at www.deervalley.com. Deer Valley is 1.5 miles south of downtown Park City (33 miles east of Salt Lake City).

Multi-million-dollar expansion projects have prepared Deer Valley for the 2002 Olympic slalom, aerial, and mogul events. The resort built a 40,000-square-foot addition to its massive Snow Park Lodge, increased parking, and improved visitor facilities. Lifts have been upgraded to high-speed quads, snowmaking capacity has been doubled, two new restaurants have opened.

Summer Programs: Mountain bikers, hikers, and sight-seers can catch the Sterling Lift up to the top of Bald Mountain Wednesday–Sunday 10 A.M.–5:30 P.M., where they can explore more than 50 miles of trails running from the peak. Cost is $16 for a full-day pass, $9 for a single-ride bike pass, and $8 for hikers or sight-seers. Riders must wear helmets. Instruction, rentals, and tours are available; call the resort at (800) 424-3337 for more information. Summer is also the season for off-road cycling events, Utah Symphony concerts, and music festivals. For horseback rides, call Deer Valley Stables at (435) 645-6530.

The Canyons Ski Area

Talk about infinitely expanding ski areas! (And in Utah, everyone is.) The Canyons Ski Area (formerly Wolf Mountain) is growing so fast that from year to year entire cities' worth of buildings go up near the bottom of the lifts. In the past few years over $33 million has been spent on expanding and renovating the resort. Lifts now reach up to seven separate peaks along the Wasatch Mountains, serving more than 3,700 skiable acres—that makes The Canyons one of the largest ski areas in the United States. Brand new and at the base of the slopes are two of the largest lodge hotels in all of Utah. And the building continues.

The Canyons is the first ski area you'll reach coming from Salt Lake City. The resort has 19 lifts, including an eight-passenger gondola and five high-speed quads. The 125 ski trails are rated 14 percent beginner, 44 percent intermediate, 42 percent advanced and expert. The longest run is 2.5 miles and drops 3,100 feet. High season adult lift tickets cost $60, $46 half

day; children 12 and under pay $33, $25 half day. Tickets are slightly cheaper in the shoulder season. The resort offers day care, supervised lunches, ski lessons, and rentals for the younger set. The Canyons includes a ski school, rental and sales shop, a half dozen restaurants (two mid-slope), and a free shuttle service from lodges and hotels in Park City. For skiing information, contact The Canyons, 4000 The Canyons Dr., Park City, UT 84098, (435) 649-5400 or (888) CANYONS; www.thecanyons.com. The Canyons is 27 miles east of Salt Lake City via I-80 and UT 224.

Summer Programs: The Flight of the Canyons Gondola ($10 adult, $7 seniors, $5 children) lifts you up to the Red Pine Lodge, where you can eat lunch or embark on a day hike. The resort also can arrange backcountry horseback rides and hot-air balloon rides.

Accommodations $200 and up: A major portion of the expansion at The Canyons has been the building of the **Grand Summit** and the **Sundial Lodges,** which sit at the base of the ski slopes. Completed just in time for the Olympics, these enormous hotels are built to a scale unlike any other lodgings in Park City, and vie with Canadian national park resorts in terms of grandness and scope. The Grand Summit offers fully furnished hotel rooms, suites, penthouses, and studio apartments. One-, two-, and three-bedroom units are available. Facilities include a full-service health club including indoor/outdoor pool, three on-sight restaurants, and bar and brewpub. The Sundial Lodge is a luxury-level condominium development. All units have full kitchens and nearly all have fireplaces and balconies. Make inquiries through the central reservation numbers or website, above.

Utah Winter Sports Park

Built for the upcoming Olympics, the Utah Winter Sports Park has four Nordic jumps to serve the training needs of athletes competing in the Nordic Ski Jumping and Freestyle events, plus a course for the Luge and Bobsled events. Jumps are available to the public three days a week in the winter (Dec.–Mar.) for recreational jumping. Helmets are required; the park has a limited amount of rental equipment. The park is open Wednesday–Sunday 10 A.M.–4 P.M. for viewing, but actual training times vary. For schedule information contact the Utah Winter Sports Park at Bear Hollow, 3000 Bear Hollow Dr., P.O. Box 682382, Park City, UT 84068, (435) 658-4200.

Summer Programs: The park's summer season runs from July to September; Friday through Sunday spectators can usually watch athletes train on the Nordic jumps and make freestyle landings in a 750,000-gallon splash pool. There's also a Freestyle and Nordic Air Show at noon on Saturday during July and August. Admission fees help to support training. Call the park for specific flight times.

White Pine Touring

Park City's cross-country ski center offers rentals, instruction, and guided snowshoe tours. It has a touring center and 18 kilometers of groomed trails during the winter at the **Park City Golf Course,** Park Ave. and Thaynes Canyon Dr., (435) 649-8701. The season runs from about mid-November to early April. Trail fee is $10 adults; children 12 and under ski free. Year-round office is on Main Street at Heber Avenue in Park City, (435) 649-8710.

Adventure Skiing

Sno-Cat skiing is available from **Park City Powder Cats,** (435) 649-6596 or (800) 635-4719. Experienced skiers can explore the backcountry between the ski areas in Big and Little Cottonwood Canyons and Park City with **Interconnect Ski Tours,** which provides a guide service for extensive touring of Wasatch Front Ski Areas. Touring is with downhill equipment. Begin at Park City and move onto Brighton-Solitude-Alta-Snowbird ($150). For details, contact Ski Utah, Inc., 150 W. 500 South, Salt Lake City, UT 84101, (435) 534-1907.

Sleigh Rides

Riding a horse-drawn sleigh to a Western dinner or an evening of entertainment is quickly becoming a Park City tradition. One of the more elaborate activities is offered by **Snowed Inn Sleigh Company,** (435) 647-3310, which takes guests on a sleigh ride into the forest, where cooks prepare a Dutch-oven meal; while you wait, singers entertain. Costs are $45 adults, $28 children; reservations a must; (435) 647-3310. Snowed Inn also offers daytime rides to their deer park. For other sleigh possibilities, contact **Park City Sleigh Company,** (435) 649-3359 or (800) 820-2223.

Snowmobiling

A number of outfitters offer snowmobile tours around the Park City high country. You get to drive your own snowmobile and follow a guide into the backcountry; lunch and dinner excursions are the norm. **High Country Snowmobile Tours** offers snowmobile excursions to Deer Valley's Silver Lake Lodge with a meal included for $95. For information or reservations call (435) 645-7533. Other outfitters include **Snowest Snowmobile Tours,** (435) 645-7669, and **Park City Snowmobile Adventures,** (435) 645-7256 or (800) 303-7256.

OTHER SPORTS AND RECREATION

Mountain Biking

This is a favorite summer activity in the Park City area. Some of the local landowners, including ski resorts and mining companies, have offered access to their land and have even built trail sections at their own expense. Helmets are always required when riding on private land. The Chamber of Commerce publishes an annual summer booklet, *Park City Mountain Bike Trails,* which gives descriptions and maps of the trails open that summer. Both Deer Park and Park City Resorts keep a lift open for bikers and hikers during the summer. Deer Park offers 55 miles of single and double track trails while Park City has 35 miles of trails. After its building boom is completed, The Canyons will also offer lifts to mountain bikers.

In addition, Park City is on the route of the **Historic Union Pacific Rail Trail,** which runs 29 miles from Echo Reservoir to Jordanelle Reservoir State Park.

Bikes are rented by nearly every resort and sports store. (See Equipment Rental, below.)

Golf

Park City has two 18-hole courses. The **Park City Municipal Golf Course** is at Park Avenue and Thaynes Canyon Drive, (435) 615-5800. Designed by Jack Nicklaus, **Park Meadows Golf Club** is one of the longest in the state—7,338 yards; 2000 Meadows Dr., (435) 649-

2460. Play the **Silver Putt Miniature Golf Course** at Park City Ski Area, (435) 649-8111.

Hiking

The ski areas open their trails to hikers in summer; pick up a trail map and just head out. Deer Valley, Park City, and The Canyons Resorts all offer lift-assisted hiking that takes walkers up to the high country without a painful foot ascent; see individual resorts (above) for information. *Park City Trails,* by Raye Ringholz, describes many hiking and ski-touring possibilities in the area and offers a history and walking tour of Park City.

When hiking around Park City, stay clear of relics of the mining past that lie scattered about. You're likely to come across miners' cabins in all states of decay, hoist buildings, aerial tramway towers, rusting machinery, and great piles of mine tailings. Unlike other parts of the Wasatch Range, most of the land here belongs to mining companies and other private owners. Visitors need to keep a distance from mineshafts—which can be hundreds of feet deep—and respect No Trespassing signs.

Horseback Riding

For trail rides and riding lessons, contact **Park City Stables,** with three locations in the Park City area, (435) 645-7256 or (800) 303-7256. Additionally, Deer Valley operates its own stables, open to nonguests, (435) 645-6530.

Ballooning

Though expensive, a flight aboard a hot-air balloon is an exhilarating experience. Balloons take off in the early morning year-round, weather permitting, and trips typically include a continental breakfast and post-flight champagne toast. Cost is $50 for 30 minutes, $100 for one hour with either **Park City Balloon Adventures,** (435) 645-8787 or (800) 396-8787, or **Park City Adventure Center,** (435) 649-1217 or (800) 287-9401.

Fishing

Fly-fishing is a favorite pastime in the mountain streams and lakes of the Wasatch Mountains. The Weber and Provo Rivers are well known for their wily native cutthroat, wild brown, and rainbow trout and Rocky Mountain whitefish. Get your fishing license at **Park City Fly Shop,**

2065 Sidewinder Dr., (435) 645-8382. For guide service and instruction, contact **Local Waters Fly Fishing,** (435) 748-5329 or (800) 748-5329

Other Sports and Activities

Two-hour **rafting** trips down the Provo River Canyon are offered by **High Country Tours,** (435) 645-7679. Trips start at Frazier Park, 30 minutes from Park City, and cost $30 for adults, $15 for children. With similar prices, white-water trips down the Weber River, north of Park City, are offered by **Park City Rafting. Boating, water-skiing,** and **sailboarding** are popular activities at the Jordanelle, Rockport, and Echo Reservoirs.

The **Norwegian School of Nature Life,** (435) 649-5322, is a nonprofit organization offering cross-country ski tours and instruction, snowshoeing, hiking, backpacking, canoeing, and mountain-bike treks for people of all ages. For a schedule, contact the school at 1912 Sidewinder Dr., P.O. Box 4036, Park City, UT 84060.

The **city park** next to the former miners' hospital (1904) has picnic tables, a playground, volleyball and basketball courts, and ball fields. **Park City Recreation Department,** (435) 645-5112, organizes classes in art, music, folk dancing, gymnastics, aerobics, karate, and a variety of sports.

Prospector Athletic Club, at the Inn at Prospector Square, 2200 Sidewinder Dr., (435) 649-6670, has an indoor pool, ski conditioning, racquetball and tennis courts, gym, weight room, saunas, hot tub, classes, and massage and physical therapies; open daily. **Park City Racquet Club,** 1200 Little Kate Rd., (435) 645-5400, features two outdoor pools, indoor and outdoor tennis, racquetball, basketball, volleyball, aerobics, saunas, and massage.

Equipment Rental

Most sports stores in Park City rent skis and related equipment in winter and bicycles and camping gear in summer.

White Pine Touring, 201 Heber Ave. (Park City Golf Course), (435) 649-8710, rents cross-country skis, mountain-climbing equipment, camping gear, and mountain bikes.

Gart Brothers Sporting Goods, in Holiday Village Mall, 1780 Park Ave., (435) 649-6922 or (800) 284-4754, carries downhill skis and equipment.

Cole Sport, 1615 Park Ave. and at Deer Valley and Park City Ski Areas, (435) 649-4806 or (800) 345-2938, rents downhill skis and equipment, snowboards, mountain bikes, in-line skates, and tennis rackets. There's also a downtown location at 518 Main Street, (435) 655-3032

Jans Mountain Outfitters, 1600 Park Ave. and Wolf Mountain, Deer Valley, and Park City Ski Areas, (435) 649-4949 or (800) 745-1020, has downhill, telemark, and cross-country rentals, snowboards, mountain bikes, in-line skates, and fly-fishing gear.

ACCOMMODATIONS

Park City offers more than 30 B&Bs and hotels, plus nearly 60 condo developments; guest capacity far exceeds the town's permanent population! Rates peak at dizzying heights during the ski season, when accommodations may also be hard to find. Most lodgings will have four different winter rates, which peak at the Christmas holidays and in February and March; there will be different rates for weekends and weekdays as well. Many lodgings will have rooms in a wide range of prices (from hostel rooms, multi-room suites to penthouses), so remember that **the following price categories are for a standard double room in the winter high season.** Summer rates will usually be about half of the listed rates below. During ski season, many lodgings will ask for minimum stays—sometimes a weekend, sometimes a full week.

The following accommodations are mostly in addition to the lodges and hotels operated by and located at the Deer Valley, Park City, and The Canyons Resorts. For rooms at these resort facilities, contact the central reservation phone numbers listed above in Winter Sports.

See the *Vacation Planner* published by the Park City Area Chamber of Commerce for a complete listing of accommodations (P.O. Box 1630, Park City, UT 84060); there are separate summer and winter editions. You can print a copy off from the website: www.parkcityinfo.com. Skiers will also want to check accommodation-and-ski package listings in the *Utah Ski Vacation Planner,* Ski Utah, Inc., 150 W. 500 South, Salt Lake City, UT 84101, www.skiutah.com.

Reservation Services
Undoubtedly the easiest way to find a room or condo in Park City is to call one of the many reservation services; most also offer ski, golf, or other recreational packages. For reservations in Deer Valley condos and private homes, contact **Deer Valley Central Reservations** (435) 649-1000 or (800) 558-3337, www.deervalley.com; they also represent some properties in Park City. Other Deer Valley properties are available through **Deer Valley Lodging,** 1375 Deer Valley, P.O. Box 3000 (84060), (435) 649-4040 or (800) 453-3833, www.deervalleylodging.com.

Park City Custom Vacations, (435) 645-7902 or (800) 646-7333, www.parkcityvacations.com, and **Park City Mountain Reservations,** (435) 649-0493 or (800) 222-7275, www.parkcitymountain.com, represent most of the available hotel and condo rooms in the Park City area. **ABC Reservations,** (435) 649-2223 or (800) 820-ABCD, offers a wide selection of lodgings as well as a good recreation reservation service. **AAA Lodging & Ski Reservations,** (435) 649-2526 or (800) 522-7669, www.ski-res.com, represents that rarity in Park City—a moderately priced accommodation.

Another good place to start your lodging search is **David Holland's Resort Lodging and Conference Services,** P.O. Box 905, Park City, UT 84060, (435) 645-3315 or (800) SKI 2002, www.davidhollands.com. This service owns 10 different inns, condos, and lodges in Park City, and represents other units and private homes, which makes it able to offer a variety of prices and facilities.

$75–100
One of the few moderately priced lodgings in the area is the **Star Hotel,** 227 Main St., (435) 649-8333, one of Park City's older hotels that hasn't gone through an all-out renovation. Still, it's cozy and comfortable enough and offers a location right on Main Street. Somewhat incredibly, the tariff also includes both breakfast and dinner.

Designating itself as a "skier's ski lodge" **Chateau Après Lodge,** 1299 Norfolk Ave., (435) 649-9372, offers some of the least-expensive lodgings in Park City. The lodge offers basic hotel rooms and even cheaper beds in the men's or women's dorm.

$100–125

Out at the Kimball Junction freeway exit is the **Best Western Landmark Inn,** 6560 N. Landmark Dr., (435) 649-7300 or (800) 548-8824, with a pool, spa, and a free ski shuttle. Also by the freeway and with similar facilities is the **Holiday Inn Express,** 1501 West Ute, (435) 658-1600.

Near the Park City lifts, the **Edelweiss Haus Condominium Hotel,** 1482 Empire Ave., (435) 649-9342 or (800) 438-3855, has a mix of hotel-style rooms and one- and two-bedroom condos with full kitchens. The complex includes a swimming pool, hot tub, fitness room, sauna, and guest laundry.

As its name implies, the **Old Miners' Lodge,** 615 Woodside Ave., (435) 645-8068 or (800) 648-8068, started out as a miners' boardinghouse in 1889. The old inn was refurbished to period authenticity but with added luxuries—private baths in all rooms, a hot tub, and down comforters—which Utah's early miners likely had to do without. All rooms are individually decorated and named for characters from Park City's past. Stone steps lead to the lodge, and access to the inn may be difficult for guests with mobility problems.

Adjacent to the Park City Ski Area is the **Shadow Ridge Resort Hotel & Conference Center,** 50 Shadow Ridge St., (435) 649-4300 or (800) 451-3031. The Shadow Ridge offers a mix of hotel-style rooms and kitchen-equipped condos with one to three bedrooms. Facilities include a heated outdoor pool, spa, sauna, and fitness center.

The **Inn at Prospector Square,** 2200 Sidewinder Dr., (435) 649-7100 or (800) 453-3812, is another upscale conference hotel and condominium complex; it also includes a full athletic club and Park City's best steak house, the Grub Steak. There are seven room types scattered through eight different buildings.

$150–175

The comfortable and friendly **1904 Imperial Hotel,** 221 Main St., (435) 649-1904 or (800) 669-8824, began its life as a boardinghouse during Park City's mining boom. Today, the venerable structure has been carefully refurbished and now serves as a homey B&B inn with modern conveniences. All 10 rooms are decorated with period furnishings and have private baths.

The hotel's Main Street address means that guests are in easy walking distance to restaurants, shopping, and nightlife. Prices vary quite a bit between seasons.

Another landmark Park City B&B is the **Washington School Inn,** 543 Park Ave., (435) 649-3800 or (800) 824-1672. The quarried limestone inn was built in 1889 as the town's elementary school; after a complete remodel in the 1980s, the old Washington School emerged as one of the most luxurious lodgings in Park City. There are 12 large standard rooms and three suites, all with private baths and each uniquely decorated. There's an indoor hot tub, sauna, and ski lockers. Children 12 and over are welcome. The inn closes for the month of May. **Angel House Inn B&B,** (435) 647-0338 or (800) ANGEL-01, is a Victorian mansion built in 1889 and converted into an eight-room B&B. Rooms are decorated in period style but have private baths. Guests share a parlor with fireplace, TV, and VCR; the Angel House is just two blocks from Main Street.

Also right downtown is the **Treasure Mountain Inn,** 255 Main St., (435) 649-7334 or (800) 344-2460. Treasure Mountain is a large complex of three buildings with several room types. The Treasure Mountain has seen a lot of use, but you can't argue with its location.

There are a number of lodging options clustered around the Park City Ski Area lifts. The resort itself operates the **Resort Center Lodge and Inn,** 1415 Lowell Ave., (435) 649-0800 or (800) 824-5331, and **The Gables Hotel,** 1345 Lowell Ave., (435) 647-3160 or (800) 443-1045; both located right at the base of the lifts. All guests have use of an indoor/outdoor swimming pool, hot tubs, saunas, steam rooms with massage, and free covered parking; the resort has a number of shops, nightclubs, and good restaurants on the premises. The inn offers simple hotel rooms in the $150–175 range, plus studios, and one-bedroom units complete with kitchens. The lodge offers studio to four-bedroom condo units.

The **Silver King Hotel,** 1485 Empire Ave., (435) 649-5500 or (800) 331-8652, is a top-quality condominium hotel with studio, one-, and two-bedroom units. All units have full kitchens (including microwaves and dishwashers), washers and dryers, whirlpool tubs, and fireplaces; some rooms have private hot tubs. Facilities include year-round indoor/outdoor pool, ski lockers, covered parking, and sauna. The Silver King requests a five- to seven-day minimum stay during the ski season and weekend stays in summer.

Another deluxe condo hotel next to the lifts at Park City is **Snow Flower Condominiums,** 400 Silver King Dr., (435) 649-6400 or (800) 852-3101, with balconies, fully-equipped kitchens, fireplaces, and jetted tubs. Facilities include outdoor soaking tubs and, in summer, tennis courts and a barbecue area.

Marriott Park Hotel & Convention Center, 1895 Sidewinder Dr., (435) 649-2900 or (800) 234-9003, is one of Park City's plushest hotels and is located in a newer business development northeast of downtown. Designed with the small conference trade in mind, the Olympia offers swimming pool and spa facilities, two restaurants, and a lounge; in addition to hotel rooms, there are one- and two-bedroom units with kitchens.

The **Radisson Inn Park City,** 2346 Park Ave., (435) 649-5000 or (800) 333-3333, sits two miles below the lifts at Park City. Facilities include an indoor/outdoor pool, hot tubs, and sauna.

$175–200

If historic buildings aren't your style but you fancy the coziness of a B&B, consider the **Snowed Inn,** 3770 N. UT 224, (435) 649-5713 or (800) 545-SNOW. Located midway between Kimball Junction and Park City, the Snowed Inn is a large Victorian-style mansion set in a five-acre meadow, and although it looks authentic it is newly built, thus avoiding the squeaky floorboards and cramped quarters of some older B&Bs. All rooms have private baths, there's transportation to the ski slopes and daily maid service, and the inn has an excellent on-site restaurant.

The **Yarrow Resort Hotel and Conference Center,** 1800 Park Ave., (435) 649-7000 or (800) 927-7694, is located just below historic Main Street and close to the ski lifts. This large and attractive hotel offers high-quality rooms, a good restaurant, outdoor heated pool, hot tub, and exercise room. Some rooms have kitchens, and there are eight suites.

If you're looking for a more intimate luxury hotel, the **Goldener Hirsch Inn** located in exclusive Silver Lake Village at 7570 Royal Street East, (435) 649-7770 or (800) 252-3373, is one

of the area's best. The inn maintains the atmosphere of an Austrian ski lodge with a grand lobby, beautifully furnished rooms, and personalized service. The restaurant here is one of the best in Park City.

The new **Marriott's Summit Watch Resort,** 780 Main St., (435) 647-4100 or (800) 845-5279, is a cluster of condominium hotels at the base of Main Street near the Town Lift. They are easily the nicest lodging options in the downtown district, with rooms ranging from studios to two-room villas. All rooms have kitchen facilities and luxury level amenities; there's a central pool, and all the dining that downtown Park City offers within a five-minute stroll.

$200 and up

The **Stein Erickson Lodge,** 7700 Stein Way, (435) 649-3700 or (800) 453-1302, is one of the area's most luxurious lodgings. Located mid-mountain at Silver Lake in the Deer Mountain District, the lodge is like a Norwegian fantasy castle built of log and stone. Rooms are exquisitely appointed, and the restaurant here is one of the highest rated in Park City.

Campgrounds

Hidden Haven, (435) 649-8935, offers seasonal tent and year-round RV sites with showers and laundry; guests may cast for trout in a stream running beside the campground; $14.50 without hookups, $19.75 with. Drive to I-80 Park City Exit 145 (five miles north of town on UT 224) and turn west one mile on the north frontage road.

RESTAURANTS

Park City has the greatest concentration of good restaurants in Utah. The five blocks of historic Main Street alone offer dozens of fine places to eat, and each of the resorts, hotels, and lodges offers more options including moderately priced buffets. Note that many of the restaurants close in May and November—the so-called "mud season." On ski-season weekends, reservations are strongly suggested for any of the restaurants.

American Fare and Steak Houses

A favorite place for a traditional breakfast is the **Morning Ray Cafe & Bakery,** 268 Main, (435)

649-5686, with fresh pastries, omelets, and hot-cakes served till noon. For lunch, there's salads and sandwiches. At night, the Morning Ray becomes the Acme Late Nite Diner, serving American classics like meatloaf and mashed potatoes; open till 1 A.M. on weekends. Another good choice for breakfast, bagels, and deli sandwiches is the **Main Street Deli,** 525 Main St., (435) 649-1110.

For a Western steak house atmosphere, go to the **Grub Steak Restaurant,** in the Inn at Prospector Square Hotel, Kearns Blvd. and Sidewinder Ave., (435) 649-8060. The steaks, prime rib, grilled chicken, and seafood are excellent, and dinners come with a trip to the salad bar. Open Sun. for brunch, Mon.–Fri. for lunch, and daily for dinner. **Texas Red's Pit Barbecue,** 440 Main St., (435) 649-7337, dishes out ribs, beef, pork, chicken, two-alarm chili, and catfish in a Western setting; open daily for lunch, dinner, and takeout.

American Regional Cuisine
New American cooking is the order of the day at **Zoom,** 660 Main St., (435) 649-7614. The grilled meats are excellent, as is the trout, and lamb kebabs ($12–18). At lunch you'll find boutique pizzas and sandwiches. Zoom has perhaps the nicest patio dining in Park City. Zoom is owned by Robert Redford, and the walls are festooned with photos from the Sundance Film Festival.

The **Gamekeeper's Grille,** 505 Main, (435) 647-0327, makes the case for a Mountain West cuisine style, with an emphasis on local beef, lamb, trout, and game. Maple pecan-crusted trout join pan-seared venison medallions on the menu ($19–29). The dining room is rustic, while the second-floor deck is flanked by potted flowers.

Seafood
Fresh seafood is flown in daily to **350 Main Seafood & Oyster Co.,** 350 Main St., (435) 649-3140. Diners can choose the informal oyster bar or opt for fine dining on daily fresh specials and house favorites like lobster thermidor, bouillabaisse, paella, and seafood pasta dishes ($15–30). Open daily for dinner only. The **Seafood Buffet** at Deer Valley's Snow Park Lodge, (435) 645-6632, offers an outstanding smorgasbord of salmon, crab, grilled tuna, shrimp, and other fish as well as prime rib, vegetables, and desserts. Open Mon.–Sat. during the ski season for dinner; $38 adults, $17 children under 12.

Brewpubs
Park City's sole brewpub is **Wasatch Brew Pub,** 250 Main St., (435) 649-0900. In addition to excellent beers and ale, the Wasatch offers sandwiches, fish and chips, and soups for lunch and grilled fish, chicken, and steaks for dinner. A lighter snack and appetizer menu is available throughout the day; in good weather, there's a patio for outdoor dining. Open for lunch and dinner.

Mexican and Southwestern
The **Baja Cantina,** at the Resort Center at Park City Ski Area, (435) 649-2252, serves zippy, full-flavored Mexican food in a colorful and airy dining room. Besides the usual tortilla-based favorites ($5–10), there are more substantial options like carne asada ($16) and chicken molé ($11).

One of Park City's most noted restaurants is **Chimayo,** 368 Main St., (435) 649-6222, the area's leading purveyor of contemporary Southwest cuisine. Entrées like adobe chicken, herb-crusted trout, and piñon crab cakes make for exciting, highly flavored dining. Most entrées are $15–22; open daily for dinner only.

Asian
Bangkok Thai on Main, 605 Main St., (435) 649-8424, has Thai barbecue ($11), curries ($12–15), and other specialties including many vegetarian options. Save room for the home-made coconut ice cream; open daily for dinner only. **Szechuan Chinese Restaurant,** 438 Main St., (435) 649-0957, offers both spicy and mild dishes ($9–17); open daily for lunch and dinner. **Taste of Saigon,** 580 Main St., (435) 647-0688, brings Vietnamese cuisine to Park City. A filling bowl of noodle soup is under $9. **Kampai,** 586 Main, (435) 649-0655, has sushi, tempura, plus an assortment of noodle dishes. Entrées range $15–23 in the evening.

One of the most exciting new restaurants in Park City is **Wahso,** 577 Main, (435) 615-0300. It's name is both Chinese and French (oiseau, meaning "bird"), as is the cuisine at this stylish, slightly formal restaurant. French sauces meet Chinese cooking techniques, and vice versa. It's a wonderful blend of cuisines; highly recommended. Entrées range $15–32.

Pizza and Italian

Try **Davanza's Pizza,** at 1776 Park Avenue in the Holiday Village Mall, (435) 649-9700, fixes old-fashioned pizza, subs, burgers, and salads; open Mon.–Sat. (daily in ski season) for lunch, and dinner, with free delivery in Park City and Deer Valley. Right downtown, **Park City Pizza Company,** 430 Main St., (435) 649-1591, prepares pizza (whole-wheat crust optional), hot sandwiches, pasta dishes, and salads for sit-down or take out; open daily for lunch and dinner. For a choice of pizza or pasta in a pleasant dining room, try the **Main Street Pizza & Noodle,** 530 Main St., (435) 645-8878.

Cisero's Italian Ristorante, 306 Main St., (435) 649-6800, offers a large selection of pasta dishes ($12–18), veal, seafood, and chicken entrées ($12–19) and the house specialty, cioppino ($23); open daily for lunch and dinner.

If you enjoy sunny Mediterranean flavors, you're in luck. The following are among Park City's best restaurants. Plan to spend $15–25 for most entrees. Up in Silver Lake Village, the **Olive Barrel Food Company,** Mount Cervin Plaza, (435) 647-7777, offers terrific wood-fired pizzas as well as high-quality, full-flavored Italian dishes like *osso buco,* gnocchi with salmon and gorgonzola, and spicy roast chicken *Calabrese.* At **Grappa,** 151 Main St., (435) 645-0636, the cuisines of southern France and Italy meet in a lovely plant-filled dining room (and in summer, a beautiful deck) above the bustle of Main Street. Entrées range from wood-fired pizza to pasta (five-cheese mushroom lasagna), and horse-radish-crusted salmon. The Mediterranean focus is even wider at **Mercato Mediterraneo,** 628 Park Ave., (435) 647-0030, located at the base of Main Street in a colorful, light-filled dining room. The menu is a tempting mélange of dishes from the sun-drenched cuisines of North Africa, Spain, Greece, southern France, and Italy. A selection that includes couscous, cassoulet, paella, seafood pasta, and wood-fired pizza precludes easy dining decisions.

International

The inspiration for the food at pleasant **Cafe Terigo,** 424 Main St., (435) 645-9555, is Italian, but dishes such as seared duck breast with polenta, rosemary, and brandy and almond salmon with horseradish potatoes ($15–27) show that ingredients and techniques have been substantially updated. Open for lunch and dinner.

The Riverhorse Cafe, in the old Masonic building at 540 Main Street, (435) 649-3536, is considered one of Park City's best restaurants, with a variety of fresh fish and seafood, poultry, lamb, porterhouse steak, and pasta dishes ($18–32). The Riverhorse also features live musical entertainment; open daily for dinner. The **Mariposa,** Deer Valley Resort, Silver Lake Lodge, (435) 645-6715, prepares "classic and current" cuisine; fresh fish, rack of lamb, steaks, chicken, and other meats receive internationally savvy sauces and preparations ($20–30). Open daily (winter only) for dinner (reservations suggested).

At the **Goldener Hirsch Inn,** in Silver Lake Village, (435) 649-7770, diners have a choice of a European Ski Buffet ($19 adults, $17 children) or sit-down service in the dining room. Dishes reflect both an Austrian heritage and New World pizzazz: steaks are served with mushroom strudel ($32), sturgeon fillets are pan-seared ($28). The Stein Eriksen Lodge, also at Silver Lake Village, (435) 649-3700, offers two fine dining restaurants. The **Forest Room** offers adventuresome dining options including ostrich, wild boar, and other game as well as steaks, chicken, and fish ($30–40). The elegant **Glitretind Restaurant** serves contemporary European cuisine ($25–35). Both are open for dinner only.

ENTERTAINMENT

Musical Concerts

Summer is music-festival time in Park City. The Utah Symphony and other classical performers take the stage at Deer Valley's outdoor amphitheater for a summer concert series, (435) 649-1000, while The Canyon offers rock, country, and jazz concerts, (801) 536-1234. The Park City International Music Festival offers chamber music at Kimball Art Center and Park City Community Church from mid-July to mid-August; call (435) 649-5309 for more information. And there are free concerts on Wednesday evenings 6–8 P.M. in summer at the City Park bandstand; (435) 649-6100.

Cinema

Catch first-release films at **Holiday Village Cinemas III** in Holiday Village Mall, 1776 Park Ave. (north edge of town), (435) 649-6541. The **Park City Film Series,** (435) 615-8291, offers art, foreign, and classic films at the Carl Winters Auditorium in the Park City Library, 1225 Park Ave.

Theater

Park City Performances puts on dramas, comedies, musicals, and children's theater year-round in the historic Egyptian Theatre, 328 Main St., (435) 649-9371.

Nightlife

As you'd expect in a youthful ski resort, nightlife centers on bars and dance clubs. The principal hangouts are on Main Street, though all the lodges and resorts and most of the larger hotels have bars and clubs of their own. **The Alamo,** 447 Main St., (435) 649-2380, has darts, pool, and live music nightly; **The Club,** 449 Main St., (435) 649-6693, features two bars and DJs spinning the hits on the weekends. **The Cozy,** 438 Main St., (435) 649-6038, has live music and a sports bar atmosphere. **Cisero's,** 306 Main St., (435) 649-6800, has live music Wednesday–Saturday and a big-screen TV for sports. All are private clubs, so you'll need to pay a small membership fee (usually around $5) to enter.

Jazz and pop singers entertain nightly at the **Riverhorse Cafe,** 540 Main St., (435) 649-3536. You can drink a microbrew and chat with friends at **Wasatch Brew Pub,** 250 Main St., (435) 645-9500.

EVENTS

Contact the Park City Area Chamber/Bureau for the latest news on happenings around town, (435) 649-6100/6104. Major annual events include in **January** the **Utah Winter Games,** which features Alpine and Nordic Skiing and Ice-Skating. January is also the month the stars come to town for the **Sundance Film Festival.**

In **June,** cyclists speed toward the finish line in the **Park City Pedalfest,** a major bicycle event including a road race, criterion, and time-trial stages.

Cowboys and cowgirls compete in the **Oakley Rodeo** Thursday–Saturday on the Fourth of July weekend 15 miles east of Park City. In **August,** over 200 artists exhibit their work on Main Street for the **Art Festival. Summit County Fair** in nearby Coalville has a parade, rodeo, horse show, roping, demolition derby, entertainment, and exhibits. Golfers meet for the **Franklin Quest Championship,** a senior PGA tournament held at Park Meadows Golf Club.

September means the **Miners' Day Celebration** is here, including a parade and mucking and drilling contests over Labor Day weekend. Dozens of balloons take flight over Park City for the **Autumn Aloft Hot-Air Balloon Festival.**

Ski areas open in **November.** In celebration, there's a big street dance, ski racing, and fireworks, usually near Thanksgiving.

Christmas in the Park presents carols, the lighting of a community tree, and a visit by Santa in **December.** Skiers descend the slopes with torches at Park City Ski Area for the **Christmas Eve Torchlight Parade.** In **Santa Claus on the Mountain,** Santa takes to skis to give treats to kids at Park City Ski Area. Well-known personalities compete in the **Celebrity Ski Classic** and the **Tournament of Champions** at Deer Valley in mid-December.

SHOPPING

Park City's primary shopping venue is the historic Main Street, which is lined with upscale boutiques, gift shops, galleries, craft shops, and sporting-goods stores. Many shoppers enjoy a visit to the new **Factory Stores@Park City,** a complex of about 50 factory outlets at 6699 Landmark Drive, just south of I-80 Park City Exit 145, (435) 645-7078.

SERVICES

For **emergencies** (police, fire, or medical), dial 911.

Post

The **post office** is downtown at 450 Main Street, (435) 649-9191.

Health and Medical
University of Utah Park City Family Health Center provides care 24 hours a day at 1665 Bonanza Drive, (435) 649-7640.

Child Care
Guardian Angel, (435) 640-1229, and **Mzzz Poppins Child Care,** (435) 649-6463, offers in-room licensed and bonded child care. Deer Valley, Wolf Mountain, and Park City Resorts all have day-care facilities at the lodges; or put the kids on skis and enroll them in the children's instructional programs offered at all resorts.

Information
The **Park City Area Chamber/Bureau** has excellent vacation planners and other free literature; the staff knows of upcoming events and will answer your questions. The Visitors Information Center is at 750 Kearns Avenue, Park City, UT 84060, (435) 658-4541 or (800) 453-1360, www.parkcityinfo.com. Park City's **public library,** 1255 Park Ave., (435) 645-5600, has a good collection of regional books and maps; open Mon.–Thurs. 10 A.M.–9 P.M., Fri. and Sat. 10 A.M.–6 P.M., and Sun. 1–5 P.M.

Transportation
Park City Transit operates a trolley bus up and down Main Street (about every 10 minutes daily) and has several bus routes to other parts of town including Park City and Deer Valley Ski Areas (about every 10–20 minutes daily). All buses are free; pick up a transit guide from the Visitor Information Center, on any of the buses, or by calling Park City Transit, (435) 645-5130 (recording). **The Canyons,** (435) 649-5400, runs a free shuttle to its ski area during the ski season from lodges at the other ski resorts. **Park City Transportation** provides year-round service to downtown Salt Lake City and the SLC Airport for $23 one-way; ski shuttles depart from Park City and Salt Lake City in winter to Brighton, Solitude, Snowbird, Alta, Sundance, Snowbasin, and Powder Mountain Ski Areas; call 24 hours in advance for reservations and to check if a passenger minimum applies; (435) 649-8567 (Park City), (435) 364-8472 (Salt Lake City), (800) 356-7384 in Utah, or (800) 637-3803 out of state.
    Lewis Brothers Stages operates a "Red Horse Express" during the ski season between Park City and Salt Lake City Airport or down-

town ($18 one-way, $34 round-trip). A shuttle during the ski season connects the Park City Ski Areas with Solitude, Brighton, Snowbird, Alta, and Sundance ($22 round-trip). Ski packages with transportation and lift tickets can be purchased, too. Reservations two days in advance are advised for these trips, (435) 359-8677 (Salt Lake City), (435) 649-2256 (Park City), or (800) 826-5844.

Taxi
Call **Ol' Miner Taxi,** (435) 649-4185, for cabs. **All Resort Express,** runs a shuttle bus service around the Park City region, (435) 649-3999.

Auto Rentals
The following rental outfits feature cars, 4X4s, and vans; most come with ski racks. Each will deliver cars to and pick them up from Park City area addresses. All Resort Car Rental, (435) 649-3999 or (800) 457-9457; Budget Rent-A-Car, (435) 645-7555 or (800) 237-7521; Mountain Car Rental, (435) 645-9772.

NORTH OF PARK CITY

Old ranching and mining communities dominate the mountain valleys that now serve as the I-80 and I-84 corridor east of Salt Lake City. The little towns out here don't offer much for the traveler, though Coalville does have inexpensive lodging alternatives to pricey Park City. The reservoirs here are popular with RV campers, boaters, and anglers.

Coalville and Vicinity
In 1858, when William Smith noticed that wheat that had spilled from wagons here had grown to maturity, he decided that this area would be a good place to settle. Smith returned the following spring with several families to begin farming. Coal mines discovered by the pioneers provided additional income and gave the community its name. Today coal has lost importance, but a large oil and gas field discovered in the 1970s holds future promise. Coalville (pop. 1,282), the Summit County seat, lies 19 miles northeast of Park City on I-80 near the confluence of Chalk Creek and the Weber (pronounced WEE-ber) River.
    Accommodations Under $50: Frugal skiers can choose to stay at unfussy motels in Coalville

like **A Country Place,** 99 S. Main, (435) 336-2451 or (800) 371-2451, or **Moore's Motel,** 90 S. Main, (435) 336-5991. **Holiday Hills RV Park** offers tent and RV sites (all $16), showers, and a store; located just off I-80 Coalville Exit 164, (435) 336-4421.

Rockport State Park

Rockport Reservoir (1,189 surface acres) is tucked in the Weber River Valley 13 miles south of Coalville. Visitors enjoy fishing, water-skiing, sailing, windsurfing, and swimming. Anglers come to reel in rainbow, cutthroat, and German brown trout, and smallmouth bass. The Weber River above and below the lake also has good fishing for trout and whitefish. During freeze-up, December–April, anglers try their luck through the lake ice. Like most high-country lakes, Rockport (elev. 6,100 feet) is usually calm in the mornings and evenings but windy in the afternoons. The state park facilities are along the eastern shore and include a paved boat ramp, docks, three picnic areas with covered tables, eight primitive campgrounds, and the modern Juniper Campground (with showers). Reservations are recommended for Juniper Campground on summer weekends, though there's usually plenty of space in the primitive campgrounds. The main season runs April–October, but a camping area (no water) is kept open for winter visitors. Entrance fees are $5 for day use, $7–14 for camping. Anglers may park in highway pullouts on the lake's west side without charge. Contact the park at 9040 N. UT 302, Peoa, UT 84061, (435) 336-2241 (ranger), (435) 538-7221 (Salt Lake City), or (800) 322-3770 (reservations). Rockport State Park is 45 miles east of Salt Lake City; take I-80 Wanship Exit 156 and go south five miles on U.S. 189.

Echo Reservoir

This privately owned reservoir between Coalville and Echo averages about 1,000 surface acres. **Echo Resort,** (435) 336-9894 or 336-2247, in a grove of large cottonwood trees on the eastern shore, has a boat ramp, picnicking, camping, and a snack bar. The resort has a second camping area two miles south. Fishing, mostly for rainbow and brown trout and channel catfish, is fair to good. Water-skiing and sailing are the most popular lake activities. Open early May–Sept.; fees are $5 parking, $5 boat launch, $9 tents or RV camping with hookups. Take I-80 Coalville Exit 164 and go north 3.5 miles (or take I-80 Echo Exit 169 and go south two miles).

Morgan and Vicinity

Mormons settled here along the Weber River in 1852 and named their community after one of its members. The town (pop. 2,478) is the Morgan County seat and a center for farming, livestock raising, and dairying. Die-hard hot-springs fans can check out the pools at the old **Como Springs Resort,** (435) 829-3489, where there's also a motel and an RV Park. Look for **Devil's Slide** 7.5 miles east of Morgan on the south side of I-84; the natural rock formation resembles a giant playground slide.

Lost Creek State Park

Steep hillsides covered with grass, sage, and groves of evergreens surround the 365-acre reservoir. Anglers catch mostly rainbow trout; winter visitors come to ice fish. The east arm has a paved boat ramp. Picnicking and camping are primitive; there are outhouses but no established sites, tables, drinking water, or fees. Elevation is 6,000 feet. For information, contact East Canyon State Park, (801) 829-6866 (538-7221 in Salt Lake City). The road is paved to the dam, then turns to gravel. Take I-84 Devil's Slide/Croydon Exit 111, go northeast two miles past a cement plant to the small farming town of Croydon, then turn left 13 miles to Lost Creek Reservoir. Or take I-84 Henefer Exit 115 and turn northwest 4.5 miles to Croydon, then right 13 miles to the reservoir.

brown trout (Salmo trutta)

East Canyon State Park

East Canyon Reservoir is one of the closest mountain lakes to Salt Lake City (38 miles). It's also close to Ogden (33 miles) and Morgan (12 miles). The 600-acre lake is about six miles long and a half-mile wide; elevation is 5,700 feet. Power boating, water-skiing, and angling are the most popular activities. Fishing is good for rainbow trout in the lake and in East Canyon Creek. You'll find a marina and most of the state park facilities at the lake's north end. The marina is open from late May to mid-September with a store, snack bar, boat storage, slips, and boat rentals (fishing boats with or without motors, canoes, personal watercrafts, paddle boats, and ski boats), (435) 829-6157. A beach east of the marina is popular with swimmers and picnickers. The state park is open year-round; facilities at the north end of the lake include a paved boat ramp, picnic area, and campground (water and showers). Parking areas with outhouses are along the east side and at the south end. Camping reservations are recommended for summer weekends. The **park office** can be reached at 5535 S. UT 66, Morgan, UT 84050, (801) 829-6866 (538-7221 in Salt Lake City) or (800) 322-3770 (reservations). Entrance fees are $4 for day use at the recreation area and at the south end of the lake, $11 for camping. **East Canyon Resort,** a quarter mile south of the reservoir, has a restaurant open to the public.

OGDEN

Located at the northern edge of the Wasatch Front urban area, Ogden remains very much its own city even as it is engulfed by suburbs. Ogden was one of the West's most important rail hubs at the turn of the century, and in the downtown area you'll notice vestiges of the city's affluence in the grand architecture and the impressive Union Pacific Depot.

Today, Ogden is Utah's third largest city, with a population of 65,500, housing over 125,000 people in the metro area. The city is worth exploring for its museums, historic sites, and access to scenic spots in the Wasatch Range, which looms precipitously just behind the city. Ogden Canyon, beginning on the east edge of town and leading into the Wasatch, leads up to lakes, campgrounds, hiking trails, and three downhill ski areas. Several 2002 Winter Olympic events are slated for the Ogden area, including the downhill and Super-G ski races and the men's and women's curling competition. Ogden lies 35 miles north of Salt Lake City off I-15.

History
Tribes of nomadic Shoshoni Indians chose the confluence of the Weber and Ogden Rivers as a winter camp because of its relatively mild climate, good fishing and hunting, and plentiful grass for their horses. This same location, the site of present-day Ogden, was also used in the winter of 1825–1826 by a group of American fur trappers and their Indian wives and children. The Shoshoni maintained friendly relations with the new Americans and continued to camp in the area.

Peter Skene Ogden of the British Hudson's Bay Company explored and trapped in the upper reaches of the Ogden and Weber Valleys, but he never descended to the site of the city that bears his name. In 1846, Miles Goodyear established an out-of-the-way trading post and stockade here, one of the first permanent settlements in Utah, and named it Fort Buenaventura.

When Mormons arrived at the site of Salt Lake City in 1847, Goodyear, a former mountain man, felt too crowded, so he sold out to the Mormons and left for California. Captain James Brown of the Mormon Battalion, who negotiated the purchase, moved in with his family. In 1849, Brigham Young visited the site, then known as Brownsville, and thought it favorable for settlement. The following year he sent 100 families to found the town of Ogden. The pioneer community suffered floods, drought, early frosts, insects, cholera, and Indian attacks but managed to survive. At times residents had to supplement their meager harvests with the roots of sego lilies, thistles, and other wild plants.

Arrival of the transcontinental railroad in 1869 changed Ogden forever. Although the railroad's Golden Spike had been driven at Promontory Summit, 55 miles to the northwest, Ogden earned the title "Junction City" as lines branched from it through Utah and into surrounding states. New industries and an expanding non-Mormon population transformed the sleepy farm town into a bustling city. Today, Ogden serves as a major administrative, manufacturing, and livestock center for the intermountain West.

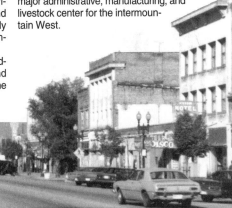

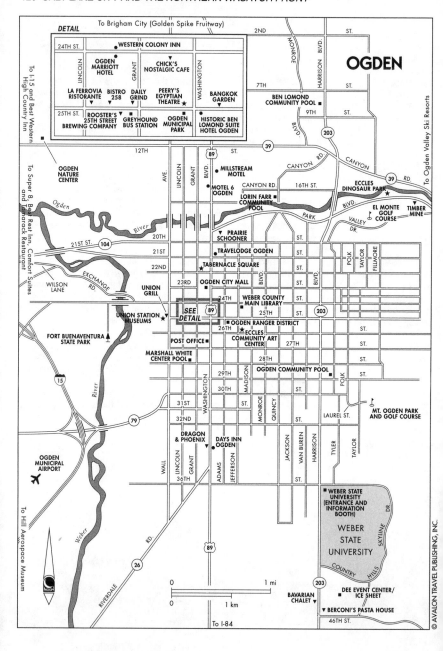

OGDEN

DETAIL

To Brigham City (Golden Spike Fruitway)

24TH ST.

WESTERN COLONY INN

OGDEN MARRIOTT HOTEL

CHICK'S NOSTALGIC CAFE

LA FERROVIA RISTORANTE

BISTRO 258

DAILY GRIND

PEERY'S EGYPTIAN THEATRE ★

BANGKOK GARDEN

25TH ST.

ROOSTER'S 25TH STREET BREWING COMPANY

GREYHOUND BUS STATION

OGDEN MUNICIPAL PARK

HISTORIC BEN LOMOND SUITE HOTEL OGDEN

To I-15 and Best Western High Country Inn

To Super 8, Best Rest Inn, Comfort Suites and Tamarack Restaurant

OGDEN NATURE CENTER

Ogden River

12TH

MILLSTREAM MOTEL

MOTEL 6 OGDEN

LORIN FARR COMMUNITY POOL

PRAIRIE SCHOONER

BEN LOMOND COMMUNITY POOL

CANYON RD.

ECCLES DINOSAUR PARK ★

EL MONTE GOLF COURSE

TIMBER MINE

To Ogden Valley Ski Resorts

21ST ST.

WILSON LANE

EXCHANGE RD.

UNION GRILL

UNION STATION MUSEUMS ★

SEE DETAIL

FORT BUENAVENTURA STATE PARK

POST OFFICE

MARSHALL WHITE CENTER POOL

TRAVELODGE OGDEN

TABERNACLE SQUARE

OGDEN CITY MALL

WEBER COUNTY MAIN LIBRARY

OGDEN RANGER DISTRICT ★

ECCLES COMMUNITY ART CENTER

OGDEN COMMUNITY POOL

20TH

21ST

22ND

23RD

24TH

25TH

26TH

27TH

28TH

29TH

30TH

31ST

32ND

MT. OGDEN PARK AND GOLF COURSE

OGDEN MUNICIPAL AIRPORT

To Hill Aerospace Museum

River

Weber

DRAGON & PHOENIX

DAYS INN OGDEN

36TH

LAUREL ST.

WEBER STATE UNIVERSITY (ENTRANCE AND INFORMATION BOOTH)

WEBER STATE UNIVERSITY

RIVERDALE RD.

0   1 mi

0   1 km

BAVARIAN CHALET

DEE EVENT CENTER/ ICE SHEET

BERCONI'S PASTA HOUSE

46TH ST.

To I-84

© AVALON TRAVEL PUBLISHING, INC.

Orientation

Mormon pioneers laid out the city in their typically neat fashion but adopted an unusual street system. Streets running east-west are numbered, from 1st Street in the north of town to 47th Street in the south; streets running north-south commemorate U.S. presidents and other historical figures. The streets were laid out before the city had found its center—today, the intersection of 25th Street and Washington Boulevard is usually considered the center.

SIGHTS

Union Station Museums

Travelers thronged into the cavernous Union Station Building during the grand old days of railroading. Completed in 1924, it saw more than 120 trains daily during the peak World War II years. Now, though, Union Station echoes mostly with memories. Visit the main lobby to see murals painted in 1978, when the city restored the station to its former glory. The South Mural shows workers of the Central Pacific (many of them immigrants from China) building the first transcontinental railroad from Sacramento; the North Mural pictures the Union Pacific crew laying its line from Omaha. Special shows and performances occasionally take place in the lobby or at the M.S. Browning Theatre.

Union Station houses the **Ogden-Weber Convention and Visitors Bureau Information Center,** supplier of local travel information; open Mon.–Sat. 8 A.M.–8 P.M. and Sun. 10 A.M.–7 P.M. from Memorial Day weekend–Labor Day weekend and Mon.–Fri. 8 A.M.–5 P.M. the rest of the year; (801) 627-8288 or (800) ALL-UTAH, www.ogdencvb.org. Located in the same office,

the **Forest Service Information Center,** (801) 625-5306, provides recreation information for forested areas in the Wasatch Range; open Mon.–Fri. 8 A.M.–4:30 P.M. (and Sat. in summer). The station also houses the Union Grill Restaurant, a model train store, and a gift shop.

The museums and art gallery in the station are well worth a visit. A single ticket gives admission to all exhibitions—$3 adults, $1.50 children 3–12, and $2 ages 65 and over. Open Mon.–Sat. 10 A.M.–5 P.M. (also Sun. 1–3 P.M. in summer). Union Station is at 25th Street and Wall Avenue, (801) 629-8444.

The **Browning-Kimball Car Museum** displays a glittering collection of about a dozen antique autos ranging from a one-cylinder 1901 Oldsmobile to a 16-cylinder 1930 Cadillac sports sedan. Chicago gangsters once owned the 1931 Pierce Arrow, probably the museum's most famous car; note the built-in gun holster. Car exhibits rotate about three times a year. The Utah License-Plate Exhibit shows every tag from 1915, when they were first issued, to the present.

Wattis-Dumke Railroad Museum uses highly detailed dioramas to illustrate railroad scenes and construction feats. Eight model trains (HO scale) roll through the Ogden rail yard, wind through a model of the Sierra and Humboldt Palisades, cross the Great Salt Lake on the Lucin Cutoff, and descend Weber Canyon. Exhibits and photos show railroading history and great trains, such as the "Big Boys," which weighed more than one million pounds and pulled heavy freights up the mountain ranges. A documentary film about the first transcontinental railroad is shown on request. Outside, just to the south of the station, you can visit giant diesel locomotives and some cabooses; ask for tour times.

The **Natural History Museum** displays beautiful rocks, minerals, and gemstones. Fossils reveal imprints of dinosaurs and other prehistoric life forms, and you can look at Indian artifacts and crafts. On display is a smoky quartz specimen weighing 19 pounds—over 44,000 carats—said to be the world's largest faceted stone.

Browning Firearms Museum (upstairs) contains the gun shop of and many examples of firearms invented by the Browning family. John M. Browning (1855–1926), a genius in his field, held 75 major gun patents. He developed the world's first successful automatic firearms, which

---

OGDEN WINTER OLYMPIC VENUES

The **Ogden Ice Sheet,** 4390 Harrison Blvd., will host the men's and women's curling competition.

In Ogden Valley, **Snowbasin Ski Area,** 17 miles east of Ogden in Huntsville, will host men's, women's, and combined downhill, Super-G, and the Paralympic Alpine skiing.

used gases from the bullet to expel the old shell, load a new one, and cock the mechanism. The skillfully done exhibitions display both military and civilian handguns, automatic weapons, rifles, and shotguns. A 17-minute slide show illustrates the Browning family's story and advancement of firearms design.

Myra Powell Art Gallery (also upstairs) displays paintings, sculpture, and photography in a former pigeon roost. Exhibitions rotate monthly.

Historic 25th Street

When Ogden was the railroad's main transport hub, 25th was the city's main street. Running like a wide boulevard between Washington Avenue and the palatial Union Pacific Depot, the street attracted the city's first grocery and hardware stores, blacksmith shops, livery stables, hotels, and restaurants, many of them run by immigrants attracted by the railroads. Most of the buildings were built for posterity in red brick and handsome vernacular styles.

After the city's residents came to rely less on the railway and more on the motor car, the city's orientation changed, and this historic precinct fell into disrepair and ill-repute. In the last decade, artists and small cafés have colonized the street because of its cheap rents, and a younger generation finds aesthetic value in the lovely historic commercial architecture. Twenty-fifth Street now serves as a combination of gallery and restaurant row, while still functioning as the city's bowery. It's a pleasant place for a stroll, and many of the shops and cafés are worth a detour. Pick up a brochure detailing histories of many of these buildings from the tourist office in Union Station.

Peery's Egyptian Theatre

You can't miss the unusual facade of this venerable building at 2415 Washington Boulevard, near the corner of 25th Street and Washington Avenue. Looking suspiciously like an Egyptian sun temple, this old-time movie palace and vaudeville theater was built in 1924 in the "atmospheric" style during the fit of Egyptomania that followed the discovery of King Tut's tomb. After falling into disrepair for many years, the old theater has been completely refurbished and serves as Ogden's performing arts center. The interior of the hall is equally astonishing, with a sun that moves across the ceiling, floating clouds, and glittering stars. With columns, hieroglyphs, and mummies everywhere, the theater looks like the set for *Aida*. The Egyptian keeps very busy with a series of top-notch musical performances and regional theatre productions. For information on current performances, call (801) 395-3200 or (800) 337-2690.

Adjacent to the Egyptian Theater is the **David Eccles Conference Center,** a handsome new building designed to harmonize architecturally with the theater. Together the conference center and the theater form the core of Ogden's convention facility.

Pioneer Museum and the Miles Goodyear Cabin

Drop in to examine the furnishings, clothes, and crafts of Mormon pioneers. Walk behind the museum to see the Goodyear cabin, probably the oldest non-Indian structure in Utah. It was built in about 1845 of cottonwood logs and later moved here from its original site near the Weber River. The cabin can be seen even when the museum is closed. Pioneer Museum, (801) 393-4460, is open Monday–Saturday 10 A.M.–5 P.M. from Memorial Day through Labor Day; free. The former Weber Stake Relief Society Building (1902), housing the museum, is at 2148 Grant Avenue.

Ogden Temple and Tabernacle

The modern temple of white cast stone and reflective glass has a central gold spire much like that of the Provo Temple. In fact, both temples were designed by the same architect. Dedicated in January 1972, the Ogden Temple contains 283 rooms on four levels and efficiently accommodates many people while retaining a reverent atmosphere; only Mormons engaged in sacred ordinance work may enter. The white-steepled Ogden Tabernacle, 2133 Washington Blvd. on Tabernacle Square, completed in 1956, sits just to the north. Visitors are welcome inside the tabernacle when it's open, 9 A.M.–5 P.M. Mon.–Sat. in the summer.

Fort Buenaventura State Park

Miles Goodyear built the original Fort Buenaventura in 1846 to serve as a trading post and way station for travelers crossing the remote Great Basin region. Now a replica of the tiny fort at 2450 South A Avenue provides a link with Utah's mountain-man past. Researchers excavated the original site and pored through historical documents so that reconstruction would be authentic. The location, dimensions, and materials used for the stockade and three cabins inside closely follow the originals. Volunteers often have displays and presentations inside the cabins daily in the summer and on weekends in spring and autumn. Special programs are scheduled throughout the year: you can catch the mountain-man rendezvous on Easter and Labor Day weekends or the pioneer skill show held on July 24. Check program schedules with the park office (801) 621-4808, or the Ogden-Weber Convention and Visitors Bureau Information Center (801) 392-5581. Trees and grass surrounding the fort provide a peaceful setting near downtown. The park has a picnic area and a pond popular for canoeing in summer (rentals are available). Open daily 8 A.M. until dark except in winter; $4 per vehicle or $1 per person to walk in. From downtown Ogden, take 24th Street west across the rail yard and Weber River, turn left on A Avenue, and follow signs to 2450 A Avenue.

Eccles Community Art Center

A series of monthly changing exhibitions in this historic mansion display the best of regional paintings, sculpture, photography, and mixed media. The ornate mansion, once owned by the philanthropic Eccles family (whose name attaches to many arts centers in northern Utah) is an attraction in itself. Turrets, cut glass, and carved woodwork decorate the brick and sandstone structure, built in 1893 in a Richardsonian-Romanesque style. The carriage house in back contains a sales gallery. Open Mon.–Fri. 9 A.M.–5 P.M. and Sat. 10 A.M.–4 P.M.; free; 2580 Jefferson Ave., (801) 392-6935.

Ogden Nature Center

The 127 acres of wildlife sanctuary on the outskirts of Ogden provide a place for children and adults to enjoy nature while learning. Hiking trails lead through woods, wetlands, and open fields. Deer, porcupines, muskrats, rabbits, snakes, and about 130 species of birds have been spotted here. Injured or orphaned animals are cared for at the center's rehabilitation center and then released into the wild. The new visitors' center offers classes, workshops, displays, and activities year-round; the pillars used in construction are recycled from the railroad trestle that once spanned the Great Salt Lake. Visitors are welcome to use the picnic area. Call (801) 621-7595 or write the center at 966 W. 12th Street, Ogden, UT 84404, for information on summer camps and other children's programs or to arrange a tour. Open Mon.–Sat. 10 A.M.–4 P.M.; $1 ages 4 and up, $5 per family. Located northwest of downtown; just follow W. 12th Street from downtown.

Eccles Dinosaur Park

Paths at this leafy park lead to 115 life-size, realistic replicas of dinosaurs, making this a favorite with children. Exhibitions are based on the most up-to-date studies of paleontologists, and the replicas are created by the same folks who build "dino-stars" for Hollywood films. Real fossils are on display at the park entrance, and casts of fossils are used in a children's study area where even the youngest can enjoy brushing dirt off "fossils" or participating in programs for children of all ages. Open Mon.–Sat. 10 A.M.–6 P.M. and Sun. noon–6 P.M.; $3.50 adults, $2.50 seniors (62 and older), $1.50 ages 3–17. Located near the entrance to Ogden Canyon at 1544 E. Park Blvd., (801) 393-DINO.

Hill Aerospace Museum

Construction of Hill Field began in 1940, just in time to serve the aircraft maintenance and storage needs of the military during the hectic World War II years. The decades since have seen a parade of nearly every type of bomber, fighter, helicopter, trainer, and missile belonging to the U.S. Air Force. About 50 of these can be seen close-up in outdoor and indoor exhibits at Hill Aerospace Museum, from the Stearman bi-wing trainer—which helped many servicemen and women learn to fly during the late 1930s and early 1940s—to the super-fast (Mach 3.5) SR-71 Blackbird strategic reconnaissance plane. The Engine Room displays cutaway models of a 28-cylinder Pratt & Whitney R-4360 and several jet engines. Other exhibits inside include flight simulators, missiles, a Norden bombsight, uniforms, aircraft art, and model aircraft. Chances are you'll see jets from the adjacent Air Force base streaking overhead on training missions. Open

B-29 at Hill Aerospace Museum

daily year-round 9 A.M.–4:30 P.M. and Sat. and Sun. 9 A.M.–5:30 P.M.; donation; (801) 777-6868 or (801) 777-6818. Located five miles south of Ogden on I-15; take Roy Exit 341 and follow signs east.

WEBER STATE UNIVERSITY

Weber (WEE-ber) State University lies southeast of downtown on a bench of prehistoric Lake Bonneville; the Wasatch Range rises steeply behind. The university emphasizes undergraduate education, though the four-year school also offers a few graduate programs in education and business. The school began in 1889 as Weber State Academy under the Mormon Church, became a state-supported community college in 1933, Weber State College in 1963, and Weber State University in 1991. It now operates on a four-quarter system with a student population of about 15,000 and faculty and staff of 1,200. The institution serves largely as a commuter university for Weber and Davis Counties. Visitors are welcome on campus for the **Museum of Natural History,** (801) 626-6653, Collett Art Gallery, library, student union with bookstore, and a variety of cultural and sporting events. **Swenson Gymnasium,** on the south end of campus, (801) 626-6466, provides swimming, racquetball, tennis, basketball, indoor track, and weight-room facilities to the public. **Wilderness**

Recreation Center, (801) 626-6373, rents bicycles, white-water kayaks, rafts, cross-country skis, camping gear, and other sports equipment; located next to Swenson Gymnasium; open year-round Mon.–Fri. 9 A.M.–5 P.M., Sat. 8 A.M.–5 P.M., and Sun. 2–5 P.M. The Olympic curling competitions will take place at the campus' new **Ice Sheet,** an ice rink and stadium; call (801) 399-8750 for public skating schedule.

Obtain a free parking permit and map at the **information booth** along the main entrance road off 3750 Harrison Boulevard Campus tours can be arranged by calling (801) 626-6844. A clock tower at the center of campus makes a handy landmark, so it's hard to get lost. The general information number for the university is (801) 626-6000.

ACCOMMODATIONS

Rooms are relatively inexpensive in Ogden, which makes it a good base for exploring the area (remember, Salt Lake City is only 35 miles south).

Under $50
You'll find the city's cheapest rooms along Washington Boulevard, which was the main highway before the freeway went in. Quite a number of older motor-court motels still operate here, but caveat emptor: some are in fairly grim shape, and for the same money you could find better values. If you're looking for an inexpensive room,

try the **Millstream Motel,** 1450 Washington Blvd., (801) 394-9425; almost half the rooms have kitchenettes and there's a restaurant on the premises. Right across the street is the new **Motel 6 Ogden,** 1455 Washington Blvd., (801) 627-4560 or (800) 466-8356, with a pool.

West of the freeway is the **Super 8 Motel of Ogden,** 1508 W. 2100 South, (801) 731-7100 or (800) 800-8000.

$50–75

Closer to the center of the city is **Travelodge Ogden,** 2110 Washington Blvd., (801) 394-4563, a nicely maintained older motel with a pool, guest laundry, and an exercise room. Pets are accepted for a $10 fee. For an affordable stay in the city center, try the **Western Colony Inn,** 234 24th St., (801) 627-1332, with kitchenettes and nicely maintained motel rooms.

Most other Ogden mid-range lodgings are located near freeway exits. At I-15 Exit 347 is the **Best Western High Country Inn,** 1335 W. 12th St., (801) 394-9474 or (800) 594-8979, with a pool, spa, and fitness room—plus guests get free membership at Gold's Gym just down the street. Pets are accommodated, and there's a good restaurant in the motel. At I-15 Exit 346 is **Best Rest Inn,** 1206 W. 21st St., (801) 393-8644 or (800) 343-8644, with a pool, 24-hour restaurant, and a convenience store. All rooms are newly remodeled and come equipped with microwaves and fridges.

The **Comfort Suites of Ogden,** 1150 W. 2100 South, (801) 621-2545 or (800) 462-9925, is new and has an indoor pool and fitness center; all rooms have efficiency kitchens, coffeemakers, and include continental breakfast.

$75–100

Near the city center is **Ogden Marriott Hotel,** 247 24th St., (801) 627-1190 or (800) 421-7599, with an indoor pool, hot tub, guest laundry, and a business center; there's a lounge and restaurant on the premises. A few blocks south of downtown is **Days Inn Ogden,** 3306 Washington Blvd., (801) 399-5671 or (800) 999-6841. This comfortable hotel offers nicely decorated rooms (some poolside rooms are quite large), a restaurant, and a private club. Facilities include an indoor pool, spa, and fitness room.

$100–125

The city's finest and most central hotel is undoubtedly the **Historic Ben Lomond Suite Hotel Ogden,** 2510 Washington Blvd., (801) 627-1900 or (800) 333-3333. The Ben Lomond is one of Ogden's most noteworthy architectural specimens, facing Union Pacific Station across 25th Street's boulevard of turn-of-the-century storefronts. The rooms are very nicely furnished—most units include wet bars and mini-refrigerators. The hotel provides two good restaurants, a private club for guests, and services for business and convention travelers.

For a unique lodging experience, consider the **Alaskan Inn,** six miles east of Ogden at 435 Ogden Canyon, (801) 621-8600 or (888) 707-8600, www.alaskaninn.com. A new log lodge and cabin complex, the Alaska Inn sits along the banks of a mountain stream. Lodging is either in suites in the central lodge building, or in individual log cabins. The decor—handhewn pine furniture, brass lamps, Western art—is rustic and elegant. Breakfast is included in the rates.

Campgrounds

Century Mobile Home and RV Park, 1399 W. 21st St. South (I-15 Exit 346, then one block west on Wilson Ln.), (801) 731-3800, has showers, swimming pool, game room, store, and laundry. Sites are open year-round: $17 tents or RVs without hookups, $23 with. There are a number of more rural campgrounds up Ogden Canyon; see Vicinity of Ogden later in this chapter.

FOOD

Starting the Day and Light Meals

For breakfast, **Chick's Nostalgic Cafe,** 319 24th St., (801) 621-9159, is a favorite spot; open Mon.–Sat. for breakfast and lunch. The **Tamarack Restaurant,** 1254 W. 21st St., near I-15 21st St. exit, (801) 393-8691, is good to know about; it's open 24 hours daily. If your idea of breakfast is strong coffee, fresh pastries, and the option of an omelet, plan on frequenting **Daily Grind,** 252 25th St., (801) 629-0909, the city's best coffee shop; there's often entertainment in the evening.

Historic 25th Street

Quite a number of good restaurants are found along 25th Street, the slowly gentrifying Main Street of turn-of-the-20th-century Ogden. In addition to the following are a number of bakery cafés, a Greek restaurant, taverns with burgers, and home-style Mexican food. And don't forget the fine dining room at the elegant Ben Lomond Hotel, at 25th and Washington (see Accommodations, above).

One of the most youthful and lively places along 25th is **Rooster's 25th Street Brewing Company,** 253 25th St., (801) 627-6171, a brewpub with good food (burgers, pizza, ribs, fresh fish, and sandwiches) and good microbrews. In summer there's a pleasant shady deck that's lightly misted to keep diners cool. Entrées range $8–$15; open daily. **La Ferrovia Ristorante,** 234 25th St., (801) 394-8628, offers an inexpensive selection of pasta, pizza, and calzone in the $10 range; dinner entrées edge up to $15. Open Tues.–Sat. for lunch and dinner.

Bistro 258, 258 25th St., (801) 430-4287, is probably Ogden's best fine dining restaurant. The dishes are continental-influenced, though there's also a good selection of good, honest Utah beef. A house specialty is roasted Balsamic herb chicken; filet mignon stuffed with spinach and Montrachet cheese is a stand-out. Open for dinner only; closed Sun. Entrées range $11–$21.

If you're looking for modern American-style food—grilled fish, gourmet sandwiches, and salads—head to the Union Pacific Station and try the **Union Grill,** 2501 Wall Ave., (801) 621-2830. Dinner entrées range $11–16; closed Sun.

Western-Theme Restaurants

For good beef, seafood, and American-style dining, Ogden has a number of interesting choices; entrées at the following three restaurants will run $13–18. The **Graycliff Lodge,** 508 Ogden Canyon, five miles up Ogden Canyon on the left, (801) 392-6775, serves old-fashioned steak, lamb, prime rib, and seafood in a romantic creekside setting; open for Sunday brunch and Tues.–Sun. for dinner.

Prairie Schooner, 445 Park Blvd., (801) 392-2712, serves steak, prime rib, and seafood in an informal Western atmosphere (dine in a covered wagon); open daily for dinner. For another take on the Western theme, try the **Timber Mine,** 1701 Park Blvd., (801) 393-2155, which serves steak and seafood to diners in a mine shaft; open daily for dinner.

Ethnic Restaurants

As befits a town at the base of towering mountains, Ogden has a good and very popular German restaurant, the **Bavarian Chalet,** 4387 Harrison Blvd., across from the Dee Event Center, (801) 479-7561. All your German favorites are here, including schnitzels, sauerbraten, and strudels. This is one of the city's most beloved restaurants; reservations are suggested; open Tues.–Sat. for dinner.

Ogden's best Chinese food by far is at **Dragon and Phoenix,** 3303 Washington Blvd., (801) 399-0786. This is also the only place in Ogden where you can find dim sum. You'll find the standard Cantonese dishes here, but the locals swear by the fiery Northern Chinese entrées.

Bangkok Garden, has a good selection of spicy Thai cuisine, and it also serves up high quality Chinese cooking.

Berconi's Pasta House, 4850 Harrison Blvd., (801) 479-4414, has a long menu of veal, seafood, and chicken specialties, pasta dishes, and pizza; open Mon.–Sat. for lunch and daily for dinner.

OTHER PRACTICALITIES

Entertainment and Events

Ogden has a busy calendar of theater, dance, festivals, shows, and sporting events. To find out what's going on, contact the Ogden-Weber Convention and Visitors Bureau Information Center in Union Station, (801) 627-8288 or (800) 255-8824, www.ogdencvb.org.

In **January,** the **Winterfest/Hof Sister City Festival** celebrates winter and Ogden's German sister city, Hof, with ski and dogsled races and German food, music, and dancing.

June brings the **Taste of Ogden,** which takes place in mid-month at Municipal Park, and is a celebration of Ogden's restaurants.

Two of summer's biggest civic events are in July. **Pioneer Days** has a parade, rodeo, and crowning of Miss Rodeo Utah, while **Ogden Street Festival** takes over 25 Street with a 10-K run, dog-trick contests, chili cook-off, and a huge garage sale in the lot in front of Union Station.

August brings the **Weber County Fair,** with horse shows and racing, livestock sale, and exhibits. Every Saturday morning, there's a lively **Farmer's Market** on historic 25th Street.

The **Golden Spike Bicycle Classic** is a road race of about 85 miles from Promontory Summit to Ogden the weekend after Labor Day in **September.** Late in the month is the **Greek Festival,** which celebrates Ogden's Greek heritage with food, dancing, and entertainment at the Greek Orthodox Church of the Transfiguration (674 42nd St.).

Recreation

Year-round **swimming** is offered at Ben Lomond Community Pool, 1049 7th St., (801) 625-1100; Ogden Community Pool, 2875 Tyler Ave., (801) 625-1101; and Marshall White Center Pool, 222 28th St., (801) 629-8346. The outdoor Lorin Farr Community Pool, 1691 Gramercy Ave., (801) 629-8691, is open in summer. **Holiday Island Event Park,** 1750 S. 1350 West, (801) 394-3232, has waterslides to provide still more ways to get wet in summer.

Tennis courts are located at many parks around the city; call the Ogden Parks Department for the one nearest you at (801) 629-8284. The Ogden City Recreation Department, (801) 629-8253, organizes many sports and crafts programs for children and adults.

Total Fitness Gym, 550 25th St., (801) 399-5861, features an indoor pool, track, weight room, basketball, racquetball, handball, and volleyball; by daily admission or membership. **Classic Skating Center Waterpark,** 4181 Riverdale Rd.; (801) 394-0822, has a roller-skating rink and water slides.

Hikers with time and a vehicle should head up into the Wasatch Range for **wilderness hikes** amongst the aspen forests and cliff-hung canyons; check with the Forest Service Information Center in Ogden's Union Station, (801) 625-5306, for trail maps. However, the city of Ogden provides its own excellent trail system, the Ogden River Parkway. This 3.1-mile trail system links a number of the city's major parks and attractions along the Ogden River including Eccles Dinosaur Park and the Utah State University Botanical Gardens. Join the trail at any number of points along Park Avenue, Big D Sports Park,

the Botanical Gardens, or off Valley Drive.

Enjoy **golfing** at any of these courses: 18-hole Ben Lomond, 1800 N. U.S. 89, (801) 782-7754; nine-hole El Monte, 1300 Valley Dr. at the mouth of Ogden Canyon, (801) 629-8333; nine-hole Golf City Family Fun Center, 1400 E. 5600 South, (801) 479-3410 (also has a lighted 18-hole miniature golf course); 18-hole Mount Ogden Park and Golf Course, 1787 Constitution Way, (801) 629-8700; nine-hole Nordic Valley, 15 miles east at 3550 Nordic Valley Way in Eden, (801) 745-0306; 18-hole Schneiter's Riverside, 5460 S. Weber Dr., (801) 399-4636; 18-hole Valley View, 2501 E. Gentile in Layton, (801) 546-1630; 18-hole The Barn Golf Course, 305 W. Pleasant View Dr. in North Ogden, (801) 782-7320; and 18-hole Wolf Creek, 15 miles east at 3900 N. Wolf Creek Dr. in Eden, (801) 745-3365.

You'll find good **downhill skiing** in the Wasatch Range 15–19 miles east of Ogden at Nordic Valley, Snowbasin, and Powder Mountain; see East of Ogden, below. **Cross-country skiers** can use the easy set tracks in Mount Ogden Park and Golf Course at 30th and Taylor or head into the mountains for more challenging terrain. The Ogden Ranger District office of the U.S. Forest Service, 25th and Adams Ave., (801) 625-5112, has a list of popular cross-country and snowshoeing areas; the *Wasatch Ski Touring and Hiking Map #3* published by Alpentech details routes near Ogden.

Shopping

Ogden City Mall, downtown at 24th and Washington Blvd., (801) 399-1314, is a giant indoor shopping area with five department stores and about 60 smaller shops and restaurants; open daily including Sun. afternoons. The **Newgate Mall,** in the southwest part of town at Wall Ave. and Riverdale Rd., (801) 621-1161, has more than 60 stores and restaurants; open daily including Sun. afternoons. Obtain outdoor supplies for camping, backpacking, mountain-biking, and skiing (and rentals for both downhill and cross-country) at **Alpine Sports,** 1165 Patterson, (801) 393-0066.

Services

In **emergencies** (police, fire, ambulance/paramedic) dial 911. Hospital care and physician referrals are provided by **McKay-Dee Hospital**

Center, 3939 Harrison Blvd., (801) 627-2800, and **Columbia Ogden Regional Medical Center,** 5475 S. 500 East, (801) 479-2111. Minor medical problems can be handled at **NowCare,** 698 12th, (801) 394-7753. The downtown **post office** is at 2641 Washington Boulevard, (801) 627-4184.

Information

The **Ogden-Weber Convention and Visitors Bureau Information Center** in Union Station at Wall Avenue and 25th Street, Ogden, UT 84401, (801) 627-8288 or (800) ALL-UTAH, can tell you about the sights, facilities, and goings-on for Ogden and surrounding communities including Davis, Morgan, and Box Elder Counties; open Memorial Day–Labor Day weekends Mon.–Sat. 8 A.M.–8 P.M. and Sun. 10 A.M.–7 P.M., Mon.–Fri. 8 A.M.–5 P.M. the rest of the year.

Visit the **Forest Service Information Center** at Union Station or the **Ogden Ranger District office** of the U.S. Forest Service, 507 25th St. and Adams Ave., to find out about local road conditions (or call 801-625-5112 or 800-492-2400), camping, hiking, horseback riding, ski touring, snowshoeing, and snowmobiling. The district comprises the Wasatch Range from Kaysville to just south of Brigham City; both offices have maps and books for sale. They're open Monday–Friday 8 A.M.–4:30 P.M. (and Sat. in summer at Union Station).

Weber County's **main library,** 2464 Jefferson Ave., provides good reading; open Mon.–Thurs. 10 A.M.–9 P.M., Fri.–Sat. 10 A.M.–6 P.M., and Sun. (Oct.–May) 1–5 P.M. Call (801) 627-6913 for information on the county's two branch libraries. Weber State University has the large **Stewart Library,** (801) 626-6415 or 626-6403; hikers can make photocopies of topo maps; open during the semester Mon.–Thurs. 7:30 A.M.–midnight, Fri. 7:30 A.M.–8 P.M., Sat. 9 A.M.–5 P.M., and Sun. noon–8 P.M.; open in summer and during school breaks Mon.–Thurs. 7:30 A.M.–8 P.M., Fri. 7:30 A.M.–6 P.M., and Sat. and Sun. 2–5 P.M.

Transportation

Utah Transit Authority (UTA) buses serve many areas of Ogden and head east to Huntsville and south to Salt Lake City and Provo; buses operate Monday–Saturday and offer some late-night runs. UTA has an **information booth** at its main downtown bus stop in Ogden Municipal Park at the corner of 25th and Washington Boulevard; open weekdays noon–5 P.M., (801) 621-4636. **Greyhound** provides long-distance service from the terminal at 25th and Grant Avenue, (801) 394-5573.

Air travelers use the Salt Lake City International Airport, just 35 miles away.

Yellow Cab, (801) 394-9411, provides 24-hour taxi service.

VICINITY OF OGDEN

EAST OF OGDEN

Ogden Canyon

Cliffs rise thousands of feet above narrow Ogden Canyon, just barely allowing UT 39 and Ogden River to squeeze through. In autumn, the fiery reds of maples and the golden hues of oaks add color to this scenic drive deep within the Wasatch Range. Ogden Canyon begins on the eastern edge of Ogden and emerges about six miles farther, at Pineview Reservoir in the broad Ogden Valley.

This fertile agricultural basin is a crossroads for recreationalists. In winter, skiers turn south from the reservoir to Snowbasin Ski Area and

north to Nordic Valley and Powder Mountain Ski Areas. Summer visitors have a choice of staying at swimming beaches and campgrounds on the shore of Pineview Reservoir or heading to canyons and mountain peaks in the Wasatch. For recreation and road information, contact the Forest Service Information Center in Union Station at Wall Avenue and 25th Street in Ogden, (801) 625-5306, or the Ogden Ranger District office at 507 25th Street and Adams Avenue, (801) 625-5112. Reach the canyon from Ogden by heading east on 12th Street (take I-15 Exit 347).

Pineview Reservoir

This many-armed lake on the Ogden River provides excellent boating, fishing, water-skiing, and

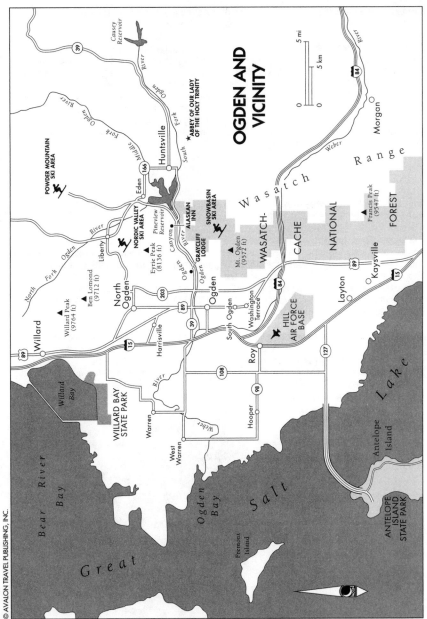

OGDEN AND VICINITY

swimming at an elevation of 4,900 feet. Campgrounds, picnic areas, and marinas ring the shore of this four-mile-long reservoir. The USFS' **Anderson Cove,** a large campground with a swimming beach on the southern shore, is eight miles east of Ogden. The campground is open Memorial Day to Labor Day weekends; camping costs $12, and sites have drinking water but no showers. Reservations can be made for family and group sites by calling (800) 280-CAMP. Slightly cheaper, the **Jefferson Hunt Campground** is on the South Fork of the Ogden River where it meets Pineview Reservoir, one mile east of Anderson Cove; all sites and facilities are wheelchair accessible, have drinking water, and cost $11 from Memorial Day to Labor Day. For day tripping, the **Bluffs Swim Area** offers sandy beaches and shaded picnic areas at Cemetery Point on the lake's east side ($4 per vehicle, $1 per pedestrian; day use only); a marina with boat ramp, docks, and snack bar is nearby ($3 boat launch); follow UT 39 to the Huntsville turnoff (10.5 miles east of Ogden), then turn west two miles. **Middle Inlet** is another beach area 1.5 miles north of Huntsville ($4 per vehicle). **Port Ramp,** (801) 745-8089, on the lake's western shore, has a boat ramp, small store, dock, slips, fuel, and storage ($3 to launch or park); open daily late Apr.–Sept. 30. **North Arm Wildlife Viewing Trail** makes a 0.4-mile loop at the north end of the reservoir, where the North Fork of the Ogden River joins the reservoir; the trail, built especially for wildlife viewing, lies off UT 162.

Abbey of Our Lady of the Holy Trinity

This community of 30 Trappist monks welcomes visitors to its chapel and reception room. The monks explain the monastery's work and sell locally produced bread, honey, and farm products. Although no tours are given, a slide show illustrates the religious life and work of the community. You may attend the Mass and chants held daily in the chapel. Quonset buildings, originally just temporary, have proved both practical and unique for nearly all the monastery's needs. The founders chose this location for its seclusion and beautiful setting. The reception room is open Monday–Saturday 8 A.M.–noon and 1–5 P.M.; (801) 745-3784. Located four miles southeast of Huntsville at 1250 S. 9500 East; follow signs for "Monastery" from UT 39.

Ogden Valley Accommodations

$50–75: The **Jackson Fork Inn** also offers rooms starting at $60, each with private baths and unique decor—not bad for a barn. On the northern arm of Pineview Reservoir is a charming log B&B, the **Snowberrry Inn,** 1315 N. Hwy. 158 (P.O. Box 795), Eden, UT 84310, (801) 745-2634. The inn provides access for water sports and swimming, while Ogden-area ski resorts are only 15 minutes away. All five guest rooms come with private baths; guests share a hot tub, billiard table, and TV room.

$75–100: Between Eden and the Powder Mountain Ski Resort are several condominium developments. The **Wolf Creek Village,** 3720 N.

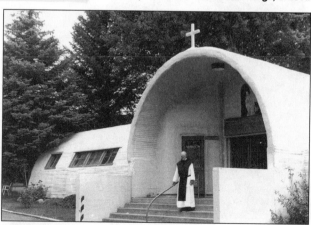

Father David Kinney at Abbey of Our Lady of the Holy Trinity

Wolf Creek Dr., Eden, UT 84310, (801) 745-0223 or (800) 933-9653, has condos and an 18-hole golf course. In ski season, the rates are substantially more expensive.

Also see the **Alaskan Inn,** under Ogden Accommodations, which is near the top of Ogden Canyon near Ogden Valley.

Campgrounds: The free **Maples Campground** (elev. 6,200 feet) is nestled among maples and aspens in the mountains near Snowbasin Ski Area. The season lasts from late May to early September; no drinking water. Drive to the ski area's lower parking lot (marked "Lower Shop"), then turn west 1.5 miles on a gravel road.

Travel UT 39 east from Huntsville and you'll find eight USFS campgrounds within 10 miles. Most of these campgrounds have water; charges range $8–11. **Perception Park,** 7.5 miles east of Huntsville, was specially built to accommodate people with disabilities. Some sites can be reserved by calling (800) 280-CAMP.

The free (first-come, first-served) **Weber County Memorial Park,** (801) 399-8491, is one mile down the paved road to Causey Reservoir, a narrow crescent-shaped lake in the upper South Fork of the Ogden River. A paved road in the park crosses the river to individual sites; three group sites can be reserved through Weber County Parks and Recreation. Water is available from late May to late September. Turnoff for Causey Reservoir is one mile east of Willows Campground on UT 39. **Monte Cristo Campground** sits high in mountain forests of spruce, fir, and aspen at an elevation of 8,400 feet (between Mileposts 48 and 49, 40 miles east of Ogden, 21 miles west of Woodruff on UT 39); sites are open early July–late September with drinking water ($9). Two group sites can be reserved by calling (800) 280-CAMP.

Food

You'll find some of the Ogden area's favorite places to eat in the bucolic Ogden Valley, just minutes from downtown Ogden. The **Jackson Fork Inn,** on UT 39 at Milepost 18 (7345 E. 900 South), (801) 745-0051, used to be a dairy barn, though it's now a popular supper club with steaks, chicken, and pasta ($12–18), open for Sunday brunch and daily for dinner.

Also located in the valley, the little town of Huntsville offers a couple of places to eat and

Utah's oldest bar—in business since 1879—the **Shooting Star Saloon,** at 7345 E. 200 South, (801) 745-2002. This is a favorite place to come for burgers; TV's *Good Morning America* named it one of the top five places for burgers in the United States. Interesting graffiti in the restrooms.

A fun place to eat near Eden is **Eats of Eden,** 2529 N. Hwy. 162, (801) 745-8618, serving good pizza, pasta, and sandwiches; open for lunch and dinner.

OGDEN AREA SKIING

Snowbasin Ski Area

Skiers have been gliding down the varied terrain here since the early 1940s. In the 2002 Winter Olympics, the men's and women's downhill, Super-G, and combined competitions will take place at Snowbasin.

Four triple and one double chairlifts plus one quad and two gondolas serve 55 runs, of which 20 percent are rated beginner, 50 percent intermediate, and 30 percent expert; snowboarding is allowed. The longest run is three miles and drops 2,400 feet in elevation. Snowbasin's season usually lasts from Thanksgiving until mid-April. Adult lift tickets cost $34 for a full day. Snowbasin offers a ski school, ski shop, rentals, and a day lodge. Snowbasin is 17 miles southeast of Ogden; go through Ogden Canyon, continue 2.5 miles past Pineview Dam, then turn right on Snowbasin Road. From the Salt Lake City area, take I-15 and U.S. 89 to I-84, then UT 167. Contact Snowbasin at P.O. Box 460, Huntsville, UT 84317, (801) 399-1135 or (801) 399-1136 (main office), (801) 399-0198 (snow report), (801) 399-4611 (ski school), or (801) 399-0197 (ski shop). Or dial up the website at www.snowbasin.com.

Nordic Valley Ski Area

This downhill ski area is the closest to Ogden and is especially popular with families (Mon. is family night). Two double chairlifts serve 19 runs, of which 30 percent are beginner, 50 percent intermediate, and 20 percent expert. Elevation drop is 1,000 feet. You can ski at night, too—all runs are under lights Monday–Saturday until 10 P.M. Day skiing takes place Friday–Sunday and all school holidays. Nordic Valley's season runs from early December to late March. Adult lift tickets cost $18 full day, $14 half day, and $12 night. Nordic Valley has a ski school, ski shop, and a day lodge. Located 15 miles northeast of Ogden; go through Ogden Canyon, turn left at Pineview Dam, and follow signs; P.O. Box 478, Eden, UT 84310, (801) 745-3511.

Powder Mountain Ski Area

Two double and one triple chairlifts, plus one quad, reach two different peaks, and serve more than 80 runs (10 percent beginner, 50 percent intermediate, and 40 percent expert). Three surface tows supplement the chairlifts. High elevations of 6,895–8,900 feet catch plentiful powder snow. You can ski at night from the Sundown Lift until 10 P.M. Powder Mountain's season lasts from mid-November to late April. Adult lift tickets cost $33 full day, $30 for half day and night skiing. Facilities include a ski school, ski shops, rentals, and three day lodges. Located 19 miles northeast of Ogden; drive through Ogden Canyon, turn left at Pineview Dam, and follow signs; P.O. Box 450, Eden, UT 84310, (801) 745-3771 (recording) or (801) 745-3772 (office), www.powdermountain.com. In summer, mountain bikers are free to use the trails, but there is no lift-assisted hiking or biking.

Accommodations: A number of condo developments are located between Eden and the resort along Highway 158 (see above). At the ski area itself, you'll find rooms and suites at the **Columbine Inn,** (801) 745-3772, and condos at **Powder Ridge MTA Resort,** (801) 531-9011 or (800) 272-UTAH. One-bedroom units begin at $125–140 a night.

NORTH OF OGDEN

Golden Spike Fruitway

Following old U.S. 89 north to Brigham City, you'll pass many orchards. Fruit stands, open during the July–mid-September season, offer a bountiful supply of cherries, apples, peaches, pears, apricots, plums, berries, and vegetables.

Willard

This small community (pop. 1,535) is known for its fine pioneer houses. The city park has picnic tables and a playground. Willard lies at the foot of the Wasatch Range 11 miles north of Ogden on U.S. 89 (take I-15 Exit 360).

Willard Bay State Park

Two separate recreation areas along the eastern shore of Willard Bay provide opportunities for a variety of water sports, camping, and opportunities for nature study. More than 200 species of birds have been observed near the park; common ones include the white pelican, California gull, snowy egret, Western grebe, killdeer, black-necked stilt, and American avocet; eagles visit in winter. Conditions are great for water-skiing and power boating, but only fair for sailing. Anglers catch channel catfish, smallmouth bass, bluegill, crappie, and walleye. Winter visitors find good ice fishing in the bay from mid-December to late February. Only two miles of Willard Bay's 15-mile circumference are natural shoreline; dikes enclose nearly all of the bay to keep out saltwater from the Great Salt Lake just to the west. Canals carry water into the bay during winter and spring, then out for irrigation during the growing season. Park fees are $5 for day use, $11 for camping. Contact Willard Bay State Park at 900 W. 650 North, P.O. Box A, Willard, UT 84340, (435) 734-9494 (ranger) or (800) 322-3770 (reservations).

North Marina features a sandy swimming beach, campground with showers, boat ramp, and dock. The developed campground's season is normally April 1 (or Easter, if it falls in Mar.) to October 31, but an overflow area on the shore stays open year-round. Reservations are recommended on summer weekends and holidays. North Marina is just west of I-15 Willard Exit 360.

South Marina has a boat ramp, docks, and campground with showers. The area is set up mostly for day use, as the open grassy areas used for camping lack designated sites. The dikes on this part of the bay prevent beaches and lake views, but you won't be so crowded here on summer weekends and the campground nearly always has room. South Marina is open April 1 (Easter if it falls in Mar.) to October 31; no reservations are taken here. Access is from I-15 Exit 354, then follow signs west 2.5 miles.

BRIGHAM CITY

Peaks of the Wasatch Range exceeding 9,000 feet form the backdrop to this city of 16,960 people 21 miles north of Ogden. Pioneers settled along Box Elder Creek in 1851, naming both the creek and the town for the trees growing here. Five years later they renamed their community to honor Mormon Church President Brigham Young. Brigham City serves as Box Elder County seat and a center for surrounding fruit orchards, truck farms, and ranches.

Historic displays on view in the **Brigham City Museum–Gallery** show how residents lived in the 19th century. The art gallery, 24 N. 300 West, (435) 723-6769, features changing shows by local artists and artists from all over Utah; open Tues.–Fri. 11 A.M.–6 P.M. and Sat. 1–5 P.M.; free. The **Brigham City Depot**, 833 W. Forest, (435) 723-2989, a turn-of-the-century railroad station, has been lovingly restored to its original condition, with separate waiting rooms for each gender and many antiques from railroading in the past.

Many people think the Mormon **Box Elder Tabernacle**, 251 S. Main St., (435) 723-5376, is Utah's most beautiful building. Construction took place from 1865 to 1890. Six years later the tabernacle burned; the present structure dates from 1897. Gothic-arched windows and doors, a soaring white steeple, and 16 smaller spires make the stone and brick structure distinctive. Non-Mormons are welcome; tours are conducted in the tabernacle daily 9 A.M.–9 P.M. from May 1 to October 31.

The **Chamber of Commerce**, 6 N. Main St., (435) 723-3931, will answer your questions about the area and offers a three-hour tour of the historic city and surrounding area; open Mon.–Fri. 9 A.M.–noon and 1–4 P.M.

Accommodations

Main Street, which runs north-south through Brigham City, is where most of the town's businesses are located. Toward the south end, off I-15 Exit 364, is a clutch of motels and restaurants.

Under $50: The **Galaxie Motel**, 740 S. Main St., (435) 723-3439, is an older motor court motel with inexpensive rooms.

$50–75: For more comfort, try the **Howard Johnson Brigham City**, 1167 S. Main St., (435) 723-8511, or (800) 1 GO HOJO, with a pool, hot tub, and restaurant. The **Crystal Inn**, 480 Westland Dr., (435) 723-0440 or (800) 408-0440, offers all suite units with efficiency kitchens, complimentary continental breakfast, guest laundry, indoor pool; children under 16 stay free. For

the business traveler, there are easily accessed modem jacks and three phones in each room.

Campgrounds: Golden Spike RV Park, 905 W. 1075 South, (435) 723-8858, offers camping sites at $16 for tents, vans, or campers and $19 for RVs with hookups. Grounds include showers, store, and laundry; may close in winter. **Brigham City KOA,** four miles south of Brigham City on U.S. 89 (near I-15 Willard Exit 360), (435) 723-5503, offers sites for tents and RVs ($15.50 without hookups, $20.25 with) with showers, pool, a store, and laundry; open Mar. 1–Nov. 15. Other nearby places to camp are at Willard Bay State Park (see above) and Mantua Reservoir (see below).

Food

Amid the taco stands and fast-food restaurants along Main Street are a couple of unique places to eat. The **Idle Isle Restaurant,** 24 S. Main St., (435) 734-2468, is an ice-cream parlor, candy store, and diner little changed from the 1920s when it first opened. At lunch, there's soup, homemade rolls, and various sandwiches on the menu; in the evening, all meals—good American-style dishes like roast pork and chicken-fried steak—come with a piece of pie. The atmosphere is splendid.

Another restaurant with an illustrious past is the **Maddox Ranch House,** 1900 S. U.S. 89, (435) 723-8545, just south of Brigham City. Established during the 1940s, this restaurant is the epitome of the classic steak house. The dining room used to overlook a feedlot—how's that for atmosphere? Besides steaks, diners come for burgers and fried chicken—and they come from miles around to eat here; reservations are a good idea on weekends.

Events

During **Golden Spike Days** in May, the city has historic art exhibits in the museum, the Golden Spike Parade, and other festivities. Brigham City celebrates the harvest during **Peach Days** (the weekend after Labor Day) with a parade, entertainment, carnival, art show, Peach Queen Pageant, and a footrace.

Recreation

Box Elder Natatorium, 380 S. 600 West, (435) 723-2622, has an indoor pool, basketball court, and weight room at Box Elder High School. There's an outdoor swimming pool in **Pioneer Park** at 800 W. Forest, (435) 723-2711. **John Adams Park,** 100 North and 500 East, has picnicking, playground, and tennis courts.

The 18-hole **Eagle Mountain Golf Course** is at 960 E. 700 South, (435) 723-3212. **Brigham City Community Hospital** is at 950 S. 500 West, (435) 734-9471.

VICINITY OF BRIGHAM CITY

Bear River Migratory Bird Refuge

Millions of birds drop in to feed or nest in the freshwater marshes created by the intersection of the Bear River and the Great Salt Lake; about 60 species nest in the refuge. In pioneer days, reports told of flocks of waterfowl blackening the sky. Flooding in the late 1980s closed the area and displaced many birds until receding waters allowed it to reopen in 1990. A four-mile loop gravel road is open to visitors. Head west 15 miles on Forest Street from Brigham City on a partly paved road. The refuge office in town, 866 S. Main, in Breitenbeker's Plaza, Brigham City, UT 84302, (435) 723-5887, offers a bird list, a short video shown on request, and information; open Mon.–Fri. 8 A.M.–4:30 P.M.

Mantua Reservoir

This 554-acre reservoir beside the town of Mantua is popular for fishing, boating, and picnicking. From Brigham City, follow U.S. 89/91 east four miles up Box Elder Canyon. Visitors are welcome to view the native cutthroat and lake trout at **Mantua Fish Hatchery,** one mile southeast of Mantua; open daily 8 A.M.–5 P.M. Exhibits show how the trout are obtained as eggs at Bear Lake and returned a year later after growing to a five-inch length. All of the one million trout produced annually go to Bear Lake.

The U.S. Forest Service's **Box Elder Campground** is just west of the reservoir; open with drinking water from mid-May to late Sept. ($9); some sites can be reserved by calling (800) 280-CAMP. The adjacent picnic areas are free.

Inspiration Point

Beginning as Main Street in Mantua, unpaved Forest Route 084 leads south 14 miles to Inspi-

ration Point (elev. 9,422 feet) and dizzying views across the Great Salt Lake and much of northern Utah; you can spy mountains in Nevada, Idaho, and Wyoming on a clear day. Limber pine grow near the summit and subalpine fir lower down. The road is rough in spots, though cars with good clearance can make it to the top in dry weather. Keep left at the three-way fork 2.5 miles from Mantua; see the Wasatch–Cache National Forest map.

Willard Basin Campground (elev. 9,000 feet) lies two miles before Inspiration Point; open about early June to mid-Sept.; no water or fee. **Skyline Trail** begins from Willard Basin and winds south to the summit of Ben Lomond (elev. 9,712 feet) and other peaks, then to North Ogden Pass, and finally Pineview Reservoir, 22 miles away. Or you could start hiking from Inspiration Point. Other trails branch off Skyline, too; see the Mantua, North Ogden, and Huntsville 7½-minute topo maps. For more information, contact the **Ogden Ranger District office** at 507 25th Street and Adams Avenue in Ogden, (435) 625-5112.

Tremonton

This agricultural center 15 miles northwest of Brigham City was settled in 1888 and named for Tremont, Illinois. The **North Box Elder County Museum,** 150 S. Tremont, (435) 257-3371, displays historic exhibits and Indian artifacts; open in summer Mon.–Fri. 8 A.M.–4 P.M., Mon.–Fri. 9 A.M.–5 P.M. the rest of the year; free. For information about the area, visit the **information desk** in the Tremonton Community Center, 150 S. Tremont, Tremonton, UT 84337, (435) 257-3371.

Box Elder County Fair and Rodeo in late August features a parade, rodeo, horse pulling, livestock judging, and varied exhibits. **Bear River Valley Hospital** provides medical services at 440 W. 600 North, (435) 257-7441.

Accommodations

Under $50: The **Marble Motel,** 116 N. Tremont, (435) 257-3524, is a small, homey motel in the center of town in Tremonton; it accepts pets and offers five two-bedroom units.

$50–75: Also in the town center is the red-brick **Sandman Motel,** 585 W. Main, (435) 257-5675. The large and modern **Western Inn,** is lo-

horse pull (pony class) at the Box Elder County Fair

cated at I-84 Exit 40, (435) 257-3399; $44 single, $49 double.

Belmont Springs

Hot springs have been developed into a swimming pool and hot tubs, a nine-hole golf course, and a campground. Volleyball and horseshoe equipment are available, too. Belmont Springs, (435) 458-3200, lies 10 miles north of Tremonton and one mile south of Plymouth. The season at this small resort runs early May to early October; open 9 A.M.–9 P.M.; golf hours are 8:30 A.M. until dark. Admission to the pool and hot tubs is $4 adults, $2.50 children; camping costs $8 without hookups and $15 with (ask about tent rates).

Corinne

The location beside the Bear River and along the transcontinental railroad seemed ideal in 1869, when Corinne's founders laid out the town. Banks, freight companies, and mining concerns based themselves at the promising new site. A steamboat service began ferrying ore across the Great Salt Lake to a mill and smelter at Corinne. The population swiftly rose to the 2,000 mark as business boomed. Saloons, dance halls, and prostitutes entertained the largely non-Mormon population and prompted Brigham Young to declare the town off-limits to his followers. Corinne became the gentile capital of Utah and a center for political opposition to the Mormon Church.

But the "curse of Corinne" kept the town from realizing its dreams. Receding lake levels grounded the steamboat business, a diphtheria epidemic killed many citizens, appeals for po-litical support from the U.S. Congress failed, and, finally, the railroads chose the Mormon city of Ogden as their junction point. Today Corinne is a sleepy farm town haunted by a few old buildings from its past. The Methodist Church, corner of S. Sixth St. and Colorado, dates from 1870 and is believed to be the first non-Mormon Church built in Utah. Corinne lies five miles west of Brigham City on the way to the Golden Spike National Historic Site.

GOLDEN SPIKE NATIONAL HISTORIC SITE

At 12:47 P.M. on May 10, 1869, rails from the East and the West met for the first time. People across the country closely followed telegraph reports as dignitaries and railway officials made their speeches and drove the last spikes, then everyone broke out in wild celebration. The joining of rails at this windswept pass in Utah's Promontory Mountains marked a new chapter in the growth of the United States. A transcontinental railroad at last linked both sides of the nation. The far western frontier would be a frontier no more. Swift-moving Army troops would soon put an end to Indian troubles. Vast resources of timber, mineral wealth, and farmland lay open to development.

History

The Central Pacific and Union Pacific Railroads, eager for land grants and bonuses, had been laying track at a furious pace and grading the lines far ahead. So great was the momentum that the grader crews didn't even stop when they met but laid parallel grades for 250 miles across Utah. Finally Congress decided to join the rails at Promontory Summit and stop the wasteful duplication of effort. A ragged town of tents, boxcars, and hastily built wooden shacks sprang up along a single muddy street. Outlaws and crooked gam-

bling houses earned Promontory Summit an awful reputation as a real "hell-on-wheels" town. The party ended six months later when the railroads moved the terminal operations to Ogden. Soon only a depot, roundhouse, helper engines, and other rail facilities remained. The Lucin Cutoff across the Great Salt Lake in 1904 bypassed the long twisting grades of Promontory Summit and

GOLDEN SPIKE CEREMONY

In grade school, many of us learned that when the Union Pacific and Central Pacific Railroads met, a solid-gold ceremonial stake was driven to mark the spot. One yearns to go to Promontory and pry out that golden spike. But the real story tells us the event was marked with no fewer than two golden spikes, both from California—a silver spike contributed by the state of Nevada—and an iron spike with its body plated in silver and its cap plated in gold, courtesy of the state of Arizona.

A polished myrtlewood tie was placed at the site to receive the spikes, protecting the precious metals

from the damage of driving them into the earth. At the ceremony, Central Pacific President Leland Stanford (founder of Stanford University) took the first swing at the final spike and missed it entirely—but did hit the tie. Union Pacific Vice President and General Manager Thomas C. Durant next tried his hand and missed not only the spike but the rail and the tie as well. A bystander was finally summoned from the crowd to tap the stake home.

Shortly after the formal ceremony concluded, the valuable spike and tie were removed and standard fittings were substituted to link the nation by rail.

Bottled spirits help celebrate the laying of the Golden Spike.

GOLDEN SPIKE NATIONAL HISTORIC SITE

GOLDEN SPIKE NATIONAL HISTORIC SITE

119 and Jupiter at Golden Spike NHS

dramatically reduced traffic along the old route. The final blow came in 1942, when the rails were torn up for scrap to feed wartime industries.

Visitor Center and Events

The Golden Spike National Historic Site, authorized by Congress in 1965, re-creates the momentous episode of railroad history that took place here. The visitors' center offers a few scant exhibits and programs that illustrate the difficulties of building the railroad and portray the officials and workers who made it possible. A short slide show introduces Promontory Summit's history. The 20-minute program, *The Golden Spike,* presents a more detailed account of building the transcontinental railroad. Rangers give talks several times a day in summer. An exhibit room has changing displays on railroading, and historic markers behind the visitors' center indicate the spot where the last spike was driven.

The two locomotives that met here in 1869, Central Pacific's Jupiter and Union Pacific's 119, succumbed to scrap yards around the turn of the century. However, they have been born again in authentic replicas. Every day in summer the trains steam along a short section of track from the Engine House to the historic spot. You can't ride on the engines; they're here mostly for photo ops.

The annual Last Spike Ceremony reenacts the original celebration every May 10th with great fanfare. The Railroaders' Festival in August has special exhibits, a spike-driving contest, reen-

actments, handcar races, and entertainment. The visitors' center is open daily 8 A.M.–6 P.M. Memorial Day–Labor Day weekends and 8 A.M.–4:30 P.M. the rest of the year; closed Thanksgiving, Christmas, and New Year's Day. Admission is $7 per vehicle or $3.50 per adult, whichever is less. A sales counter offers a good selection of books on railroading, Utah history, and natural history, as well as postcards and souvenirs. Motels and restaurants are nearby in Brigham City and Tremonton. From the I-15 Brigham City Exit 368, head west on UT 13 and UT 83 and follow signs 29 miles. (Mailing address: P.O. Box 897, Brigham City, UT 84302, 801-471-2209; www.nps.gov/gosp.)

Promontory Trail Auto Tour

Imagine you're riding the rails across Utah a century ago. This scenic drive follows the old grades past many construction feats of hardy railway workers. You'll see the parallel grades laid by the competing Union Pacific and Central Pacific, clearings for sidings, original rock culverts, and many cuts and fills. Wildflowers, grass-covered hills, and views over the blue Great Salt Lake appear much the same as they did to early train travelers. A booklet available at the visitors' center describes the features and history at numbered stops on the drive. Allow about 1.25 hours for the complete tour. If time is short, drive along just the west section (45 minutes) or the east section (30 minutes).

Big Fill Walk

An easy 1.5-mile round-trip at the east end of the driving tour leads farther down a railroad grade to the famous Big Fill and Big Trestle sites. Rugged terrain on this side of the Promontory Mountains posed some of the greatest construction challenges to both lines. The Central Pacific tackled an especially deep ravine here with a massive fill, 170 feet deep and 500 feet long, requiring about two months of work by 500 men and 250 teams of animals. The Union Pacific, pressed for time, threw together a temporary trestle over the gorge, paralleling the Big Fill.

VICINITY OF GOLDEN SPIKE NATIONAL HISTORIC SITE

Promontory Point

This peninsula that juts into the Great Salt Lake has no connection with the first transcontinental railroad but does make a pleasant scenic drive. A paved road follows the eastern shore of the peninsula below the Promontory Mountains for 22.5 miles, then becomes gravel for the last 17.5 miles around to the west side. There are good views of the Great Salt Lake, the Wasatch Range, and the Lucin Cutoff railroad causeway. Lake Crystal Salt Co. at road's end was a salt extraction plant (it's no longer in operation). There's no hiking or camping on Promontory Point as the land has been fenced and signed No Trespassing. The Promontory Point turnoff is six miles east of the Golden Spike Visitor Center.

Thiokol

Many buildings of this giant aerospace corporation lie scattered across the countryside about six miles northeast of the historic site. You're not likely to be allowed to tour the facility, but you can see a group of missiles, rocket engines, and a space-shuttle booster casing in front of administrative offices. Turn north two miles on UT 83 at the junction with the Golden Spike National Historic Site road (eight miles east of the visitors' center).

**Promontory Branch
of the Central Pacific Railroad**

Adventurous motorists, mountain bikers, and hikers can follow sections of the historic railroad

grade west 89 miles from Golden Spike National Historic Site to Lucin, near the Nevada border. Signs along the way describe histories of town sites, sidings, and natural features in this austerely beautiful land. You may see small herds of pronghorn. Only cemeteries, foundations, and debris remain at such former towns as Kelton (1869–1942), Terrace (1869–1910), and historic Lucin (1875–1907).

Cars can make the 11-mile section of unpaved county road between the junction near Locomotive Springs (20 miles southwest of Snowville) and Kelton, but you'll need dry weather and a four-wheel drive, high-clearance vehicle for further sections of the railroad grade. If you are planning on exploring this remote region, contact the Bureau of Land Management's Salt Lake District office, (801) 977-4300, or ask the staff at Golden Spike National Historic Site about road conditions. Sections of the road may be closed, and bridges and trestles that have not been maintained may be dangerous.

THE NORTHWEST CORNER

**Raft River Mountains
(Sawtooth National Forest)**

Few Utahns know about these mountains in the northwest corner of the state, despite their pretty alpine scenery. Panoramic views from the top of the Raft River Range take in the Great Salt Lake, barren desert, farmlands, and mountains in Utah, Nevada, and Idaho. The range runs east-west—something of a rarity in the region. The summit ridge isn't what you'd expect, either—it's a long ridge of gently rolling grasslands. Bull Mountain (elev. 9,931 feet) crowns the range, though it's hard to pick out from all the other grassy knolls.

Hikers haven't yet discovered the range—you'll find pristine forests and canyons but no real trails. Aspen, Douglas and subalpine fir, and limber pine thrive in the canyons and on the northern slopes below the summit ridge. Ranchers run cattle on the top and in other meadow areas. A road that requires a four-wheel-drive vehicle climbs into the mountains from Yost.

Clear Creek Campground (elev. 6,400 feet) offers sites in a beautiful setting below the north slope of the Raft River Range. The roads leading to the campground also offer access to the range's best hiking. For information, contact the **Burley Ranger District office** of the Sawtooth National Forest, 2621 S. Overland Ave., Burley, ID 83318, (208) 678-0430.

Park Valley
Travelers can easily cross the lonely country of Utah's northwest corner on paved highways UT 42 and UT 30. Park Valley, south of the Raft River Mountains, has a small store and gas station, and a café (all closed Sun.).

LOGAN AND VICINITY

Without question one of the most appealing towns in Utah, Logan (pop. 40,272) lies surrounded by the lush dairy and farmlands of the Cache Valley and by the lofty peaks of the Bear River Range. Of all the mountain communities in the American West that advertise their Swiss or Bavarian aspirations, Logan comes closest to actually looking alpine.

The town itself is built on stair-like terraces, which mark ancient shorelines of Lake Bonneville. Utah State University lends a youthful energy to the town, and residents are notably trim and attractive (the fact that some are performers from New York City doesn't hurt). Logan is also one of the state's festival centers: theater, music, and performance series enliven the town in summer. As everywhere in Utah, the outdoors is never far away: the mountains provide abundant year-round recreation including scenic drives, boating on nearby Bear Lake, camping, fishing, hiking, and skiing.

History
Mountain men tramped through Utah's northernmost lands in search of beaver and other furbearing animals as early as 1819. They found good trapping near Cache Valley and stayed for several seasons, holding one rendezvous here and two at nearby Bear Lake. The fur trappers often stored their valuable pelts in a cache (French for "hiding place"), an underground pit for which the valley was later named.

Cold winters and hostile Indians discouraged permanent settlement in the area until 1856, when a small group of Mormons established Maughan's Fort (now Wellsville). Uncertainties caused by the "Mormon War" delayed the founding of Logan and other communities another three years. Farms, a dairy industry, and livestock raising begun in those early years continue to be an important part of Logan's economy today. High-tech industries have moved to the area in recent years, most notably the Utah State University Space Dynamics Lab, which designs projects for the Space Shuttle.

SIGHTS

Logan has a lovely little downtown filled with handsome architecture, lined with trees, and flanked by parks. A walk along Main Street is a pleasant diversion, as there are a number shops to visit, including bookstores, recreation stores, old-fashioned shops, and the mandatory Bluebird Restaurant, a traditional soda fountain.

Mormon Temple and Tabernacle
The distinctive castellated temple rises from a prominent hill just east of downtown. After Brigham Young chose this location in 1877, church members labored for seven years to complete the temple. Architect Truman O. Angell,

Mormon Temple

designer of the Salt Lake Temple, oversaw construction. Timber and blocks of limestone came from nearby Logan Canyon. Only Mormons engaged in sacred work may enter the temple, but visitors are welcome on the grounds to view the exterior. Located two blocks east of Main Street at 175 N. 300 East.

The tabernacle also stands as a fine example of early Mormon architecture. Construction of the stone structure began in 1865, but other priorities—building the temple and ward meeting-houses—delayed dedication until 1891. The public may enter the tabernacle, which is located downtown at Main and Center Streets.

At the **Cache Valley Historical Museum** (Daughters of Utah Pioneers Museum), exhibits show how Logan's early settlers lived. You'll see their tools, household furnishings, clothing, art, and photographs; open Tues.–Fri. 10 A.M.–4 P.M. in summer and by appointment the rest of the year; free. The museum (and Bridgerland tourist office) are downtown at 160 N. Main,

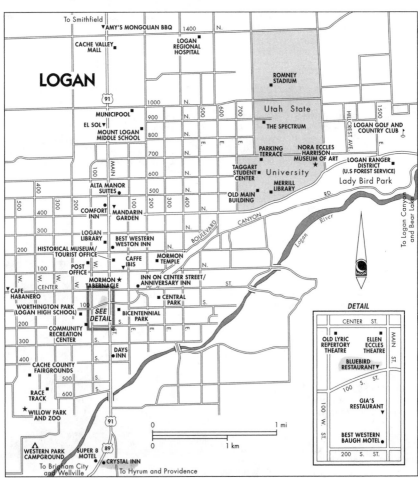

(435) 753-5139. More of Logan's history can be seen on a walking tour; ask for the self-guided, 45-minute Logan's Historic Main Street at the Bridgerland office.

Willow Park and Zoo
This small free zoo displays exotic birds such as an Andean condor, a golden pheasant, a mitered conure, and more familiar golden and bald eagles, peacocks, swans, and ducks. Animals you might meet include capuchin monkeys and coatimundis. Willow Park also has picnic areas and a playground in amongst its large shady trees. The zoo, located at 419 W. 700 South, is open daily from 8 A.M. until dark year-round except on some holidays.

American West Heritage Center
This brand new institution combines the function of a visitors' center with the history and culture of the Old West. This center, closely tied to the popular **Festival of the American West,** is quite ambitious, and plans call for building a permanent living history installation that will highlight the lives and lifestyles of the Native peoples of the Cache Valley as well as the fur-trapping explorers who arrived here in the 1840s. The center really comes alive in August when the festival hits: mountain men clad in buckskin throw tomahawks, cowboy poets rhapsodize about the Open Range, and bonneted homestead wives give cooking lessons. (For information, see below.)

Adjacent to the center and incorporated into it is the **Ronald V. Jensen Living Historical Farm,** an outdoor museum that re-creates life on a Cache Valley family farm in 1917. Workers dress in period clothing to plow soil, thresh grain, milk cows, shear sheep, and butcher hogs. The men mostly worked in the fields while women stayed closer to home to cook, can, quilt, gather eggs from the henhouse, and pick vegetables from the garden. You'll see breeds of animals representative of early farms, a lineup of steam tractors, a giant early gasoline tractor, and many other pieces of farm machinery. Buildings here include an 1875 farmhouse, summer kitchen, root cellar, smokehouse, blacksmith shop, horse barn, sheep shed, and a privy or two. Special demonstrations take place all through the year, usually on Saturday; these range from planting the garden to shearing the sheep and harvesting the grain. In fall, the cornfield is converted into a maze. Call to have a schedule sent. The farm is open Tuesday–Saturday 10 A.M.–4 P.M. June–August; $5 adults, $3 seniors, $3 children, or $15 family. Utah State University operates the farm, located six miles southwest of Logan on U.S. 89/91, (435) 245-4064.

PERFORMING ARTS

One of the best reasons to visit Logan is to catch the community's high-quality arts and music festivals. People from all over Utah and the Mountain West come to Logan to take in an opera, a chamber music concert, or an evening of theater in this scenic alpine valley.

Utah Festival Opera Company
This professional opera troupe, (435) 750-0300 or (800) 830-6088, www.ufoc.org, takes over the beautifully restored Ellen Eccles Theatre, 43 S. Main, in July and August. The fact that a small Utah agricultural college town has its own prominent opera company is slightly unusual. Two factors account for the opera and its hearty success. Michael Ballam, a Logan-area native and professional opera singer, decided in 1993 to start an opera company in Utah; at the same time, Logan's old movie palace and vaudeville hall, the Capitol Theatre, was remodeled and transformed into a world-class performing arts center. Renamed the Ellen Eccles Theatre, the theater has excellent acoustics and an intimate yet formal atmosphere that perfectly suited Ballam's operatic vision. Utah Festival Opera currently stages three performances during its month-long season. For more information, write P.O. Box 3489, Logan, UT 84323-3489.

Old Lyric Repertory Theatre
The Old Lyric, 28 W. Center, (435) 797-1500 or (888) 878-2931, provides a summer season of musicals, comedies, and dramas in a historic theater in downtown Logan at 28 W. Center. Visiting equity actors lead the shows produced by the Utah State University's drama department. A number of other Logan-area summer stock theaters also present light comedies and musicals in addition to the Old Lyric.

Musical Events

Utah State University and Logan jointly sponsor a **Music in the Parks** series throughout the summer. The university also sponsors a **summer performing arts series** which brings the Utah Symphony, dance troupes, and chamber musicians to the campus. For information on both series, call (435) 797-0305. The **Capitol Arts Alliance,** (435) 752-0026, brings in musicals, events, and performances to the Ellen Eccles Theatre throughout the year.

Festival of the American West

This unusual festival, (435) 797-1143 or (800) 225-FEST, is a full-strength celebration of Western heritage held the last week of July and the first week of August at the new American West Heritage Center in Wellsville, five miles south of Logan on Highway 89.

The festival and the center are a hybrid of a number of interesting ideas. The center and the Jensen Living Historical Farm (see above) are a living museum of farm life in the early 20th century.

However, in late July and early August, the center is the site of the eight-day Festival of the American West. There's a wide mix of events during the festival ranging from shootouts and a mountain-man encampment to a Dutch-oven cook-off; however, the various musical and arts events generally draw the biggest crowds. Cowboy poetry readings here bring together some of the most noted bards in the West, and the festival's musical pageant, *The West: America's Odyssey,* is a huge production of song, dance, and narration featuring over 200 performers. There's also a display of Western art, performances of folk ballet, and a number of concerts. For more information, check out the website at www.americanwestcenter.org.

UTAH STATE UNIVERSITY

In 1888, a federal land-grant program opened the way for the territorial legislature to establish the Agricultural College of Utah. The school grew to become Utah State University (USU) in 1957 and now has eight colleges, 45 departments, and a graduate school. USU's "Aggies" number more than 20,000, led by 2,300 faculty and staff.

The university has continued its original purpose of agricultural research while diversifying into atmospheric and space sciences, ecology, creative arts, social sciences, and other fields.

Attractions on campus include the **Nora Eccles Harrison Museum of Art,** (435) 797-1414, one of the largest permanent collections of art in Utah, the student center, and several libraries. **Old Main Building,** with its landmark bell tower, was begun one year after the college was founded and has housed nearly every office and department in the school at one time or another. The oak-shaded campus sits northeast of downtown on a bench left by a northern arm of prehistoric Lake Bonneville.

A full schedule of concerts, theater, lecture series, art exhibits, and sports competitions fills the calendar. The University Relations Department can provide information on upcoming cultural events; contact them at (435) 797-1158. Park free along streets off campus or for a small charge at the Parking Terrace on 700 North (between 800 and 900 East). Try USU's famous Traditional Aggie Ice Cream, available in the student center and at the USU Dairy Sales outlet, 8710 University Blvd., (435) 797-2109.

ACCOMMODATIONS

$50–75

Logan's motels are generally well maintained and moderately priced. For a basic, inexpensive room, try the **Super 8 Motel,** 865 S. U.S. 89/91, (435) 753-8883 or (800) 800-8000. The **Days Inn,** 364 S. Main, (435) 753-5623 or (800) 325-2525, provides a pool, some kitchen rooms, and a guest laundry. Right downtown, the **Best Western Baugh Motel,** 153 S. Main, (435) 752-5220 or (800) 462-4154, offers large rooms, outdoor swimming pool, and exercise room. There's also a restaurant adjacent. Also downtown, **Best Western Weston Inn,** 250 N. Main, (435) 752-5700 or (800) 532-5055, has a pool, two hot tubs, a weight room, and a free breakfast. **Comfort Inn,** 447 N. Main, (435) 752-9141 or (800) 228-5150, has a guest laundry, complimentary continental breakfast, pool, hot tub, and exercise room. The **Crystal Inn,** 850 S. Main, (435) 531-0500 or (800) 280-0707, offers a pool, hot tub, and nicely furnished rooms with efficiency kitchens.

South of Logan, near Wellsville and the American West Heritage Center, is the new **Logan Travelodge and RV Park,** 2002 S. U.S. Hwy. 89, (435) 787-2060.

$75–100

History and luxury meet at **Providence Inn B&B,** located three miles south of Logan at 10 S. Main in Providence, (435) 752-3432. The inn is listed on the National Registry of Historic Places; parts of the building were built as a stone church in 1869. Each of the grandly refurbished 15 rooms offers a private bath, a TV and a VCR, and a phone.

North of town, **Alta Manor Suites,** 45 E. 500 North, (435) 752-0808, offers units with fireplaces, full kitchens, and whirlpool baths in a handsome apartment-like structure.

$100–125

One of the more unusual places to stay in Logan is **Inn on Center Street/Anniversary Inn,** 169 E. Center, (435) 752-3443, www.anniversaryinn.com, a complex of heritage homes with 22 theme rooms. Designed as a special occasion destination (hence the name), each room has private baths with jetted tubs, big screen TVs, and breakfast delivered to your room. No children; reservations only.

Campgrounds

To reach **Riverside RV Park,** (435) 245-4469, turn east on 1700 South from U.S. 89/91, (435) 245-4469; open year-round just south of town with showers and laundry; $14 tents or RVs without hookups, $18.50 RVs with. **Country Cuzzins RV Park,** 1936 N. Main, (435) 752-1025, is open year-round with campsites, a Laundromat, convenience store, and hot showers; $9 RVs without hookups, $17 with; no tenting. **Hyrum State Park** offers camping, swimming, fishing, and boating seven miles south near the town of Hyrum (see Hyrum State Park, below) and the U.S. Forest Service operates many campgrounds beginning six miles east of town on U.S. 89 in Logan Canyon (see Logan Canyon, below).

FOOD

If you're looking for a cup of coffee, a pastry, or perhaps a salad for lunch, then head to **Caffe Ibis,** 52 Federal Ave., (435) 753-4777. The atmosphere is pleasantly alternative, and the adjacent bakery and health food store a nice plus.

Like any college town, Logan has a full array of pizza and fast-food places; you'll find most of them along North Main. **Mandarin Garden,** 432 N. Main, (435) 753-5789, is the best of the many Chinese restaurants in town; open Mon.–Fri. for lunch, daily for dinner. At **Amy's Mongolian BBQ,** 1537 N. Main, (435) 753-3338, you can enjoy Mongolian barbecue or a Chinese buffet, or order from the menu; open Mon.–Sat. for lunch and dinner. For Mexican food, try **El Sol,** 871 N. Main, (435) 752-5743, open daily for lunch and dinner.

For something uniquely Loganesque, try the **Bluebird Restaurant,** 19 N. Main, (435) 752-3155, a beautifully maintained soda fountain, chocolatier, and restaurant that appears unchanged from the 1930s. Open Mon.–Sat. for breakfast, lunch, and dinner.

Also a Logan tradition, **Gia's Restaurant,** 119 S. Main, (435) 752-8384, open Monday–Saturday for lunch and dinner, has an atmospheric dining room and is Logan's best bet for a traditional Italian meal; entrées between $8–14. For a more traditional steak house, go to **DeVerle's Juniper Inn,** 4088 N. Main, (435) 563-3622; open Tues.–Sat. for lunch and dinner.

For more up-to-date dining, **Cafe Habanero,** at the west end of Center Street at 600 W. Center, (435) 753-8880, offers tasty Mexican and Southwest fare in Logan's old train depot. The tortillas and salsas are all made fresh on premises; there's outdoor dining on the shaded passenger platforms. Traditional Mexican dishes are $7–9; grilled chicken, fish, and beef entrées are $8–14.

OTHER PRACTICALITIES

Entertainment

Watch films at **Cache Valley 3,** Cache Valley Mall, 1300 N. Main, (435) 753-3312 (recording); **Cinema Theatre,** 60 W. 100 North, (435) 753-1900; or the **Utah Theatre,** 18 W. Center, (435) 752-3072.

Events

Check out the Bridgerland Travel Region/ Cache-Rich Tourist Council, (435) 752-2161, www.

bridgerland.com, where you can find current information on what's happening in the area. In addition to the major summer festivals noted above, annual events include:

The **Mendon May Day Festival** takes place 11 miles west of Logan and features a Maypole dance and other festivities.

June brings the **Summerfest Art and Jazz Festival** to downtown Logan, which features works by local artists, concerts, food, and a home tour.

The **Cache County Fair and Rodeo** has agricultural and craft exhibits along with PRCA rodeo action at the fairgrounds in Logan during **August.** At the Clarkstor Amphitheatre, 21 miles northwest of Logan, the **Martin Harris Pageant** re-creates pioneer and Mormon history.

In Wellsville, seven miles southwest of Logan, **Wellsville Founders Day Celebration** on Labor Day in early **September** commemorates the first pioneers to settle in Cache Valley.

Parks and Swimming

Willow Park, 450 W. 700 South, is a good place for a picnic and has the added attractions of a small zoo, playground, volleyball courts, and a softball field. **Bicentennial Park** offers picnic spots downtown at 100 S. Main. Swim year-round at the indoor **Municipool,** 114 E. 1000 North, (435) 750-9890. The **Community Recreation Center,** 195 S. 100 West, (435) 750-9877, features tennis and handball/racquetball courts, basketball, volleyball, weight room, indoor track, table tennis, sauna, and whirlpool. **Tennis courts** are also available at Mount Logan Middle School, 875 N. 200 East; Central Park, 85 S. 300 East; and Worthington Park, Logan High School, 162 W. 100 South.

Golf

The cool and verdant Cache Valley is especially suited to golf, and there are some dandy courses in the Logan area. Play at the 18-hole **Logan Golf and Country Club,** 710 N. 1500 East, (435) 753-6020; the **Logan River Golf Course,** 550 W. 1000 South, (435) 750-0123; the 18-hole **Birch Creek Golf Course,** 600 E. Center in Smithfield, seven miles north, (435) 563-6825; or nine-hole **Sherwood Hills,** in Sardine Canyon, 13 miles southwest on U.S. 89/91, (435) 245-6055. Sherwood Hills also offers a hotel, (435)

245-6424, one indoor and two outdoor pools, horseback riding, cross-country ski trails, racquetball, and tennis.

Winter Sports

Ice-skating is popular in winter at Central Park, 85 S. 300 East. The Logan Ranger District office, (435) 755-3620, has lists of cross-country ski tours in the area.

The **Beaver Creek Lodge,** 28 miles east of Logan on UT 39, (435) 753-1707 or (435) 753-1076, offers snowmobile rentals plus cross-country ski trails in winter. Just next door is the **Beaver Mountain Ski Area** (see Logan Canyon, below).

Equipment

Trailhead Sports, 117 N. Main, (435) 753-1541, has hiking and camping gear, cross-country ski rentals and sales, canoe and kayak rentals and sales, and topo maps. Outdoor sporting goods are also sold at **The Sportsman,** 129 N. Main, (435) 752-0211, and **Gart's Sporting Goods,** 585 N. Main, (435) 752-4287.

Services

In an **emergency** (police, fire, or medical), dial 911. **Logan Regional Hospital** provides 24-hour emergency care at 1400 N. 500 East, (435) 752-2050. The **post office** is at 151 N. 100 West, (435) 752-7246.

Information

The **Bridgerland Travel Region/Cache-Rich Tourist Council,** downtown at 160 N. Main, Logan, UT 84321, (435) 752-2161 or (800) 882-4433, www.bridgerland.com, has maps and travel information for Cache and Rich Counties, including Logan and Bear Lake; open Mon.–Fri. 8 A.M.–5 P.M. (and sometimes Sat. in summer). To learn more of local history and architecture, ask for *Logan's Historic Main Street,* a brochure outlining a self-guided, 45-minute walking tour. For recreation information and maps of the surrounding mountain country, visit the **Logan Ranger District office,** on U.S. 89 at the east edge of town (1500 E. U.S. 89, Logan, UT 84321), (435) 755-3620; open Mon.–Fri. 8 A.M.–4:30 P.M. (until 5 P.M. in summer and some Sat.). The district covers Logan Canyon, the Bear River Range, and the Wellsville Mountains.

Logan's **public library,** 255 N. Main, (435) 750-9870, is open Monday–Thursday 10 A.M.–9 P.M., Friday–Saturday 10 A.M.–6 P.M. Good places for regional and general reading include the simply named **A Bookstore,** 130 N. 100 East, (435) 752-9089, and **The Book Table,** 29 S. Main, (435) 752-3055.

Transportation

Greyhound, 2500 N. 900 West, (435) 752-4921, runs buses daily south to Ogden and Salt Lake City and northeast to Idaho Falls (and West Yellowstone in summer). **Logan Cab,** (435) 753-3663, provides taxi service. No scheduled airlines serve Logan.

VICINITY OF LOGAN

Hyrum City Museum

The attractive small town of Hyrum has a museum that houses exhibitions on local history, gems and minerals, and dinosaurs. Open Tues., Thurs., and Sat. 2–6 P.M. in the city offices at 83 W. Main, (435) 245-6033.

Hyrum State Park

The Little Bear River feeds this popular 450-acre reservoir beside the town of Hyrum. Boaters come to water-ski, sail, or paddle across the waters. Sandy beaches can be found at several places along the shore, though no lifeguards watch over the area. Fishing for bluegill, perch, and largemouth bass tends to be only fair, but trout fishing can be excellent. Anglers sometimes have good luck in the river just below the spillway during spring runoff. Winter visitors fish through the ice, ice-skate, and sail iceboats during freeze-up from about mid-December to late March.

The park has two developed areas on the north shore. The launch and campground area has picnic grounds, a beach, a boat ramp, docks, and the ranger office, but most park visitors head for the day-use area farther east along the shore for picnicking, lying on the beach, and swimming. It's reached by one- half-mile drive (follow signs) or a one-half-mile foot trail from the campground. The main season at Hyrum Lake (elev. 4,700 feet) runs mid-April–late September; water and outhouses are available off-season at the campground. Day use costs $3, camping $10. Camp-ground reservations are advised on summer weekends. The park makes a good base for exploring the Cache Valley area; rangers can suggest places to go and provide snowmobiling information. The ranger office at the main entrance is open daily 8 A.M.–5 P.M. during the warmer months and 8 A.M.–noon the rest of the year; 405 W. 300 South, Hyrum, UT 84319, (435) 245-6866 (ranger) or (800) 322-3770 (reservations). From Logan, drive south seven miles on the Hyrum Road (UT 165), which branches off U.S. 89/91 on the south edge of town, or go southwest six miles on U.S. 89/91, then turn east three miles on UT 101 and follow signs.

Hardware Ranch
and Blacksmith Fork Canyon

The Utah Division of Wildlife Resources operates this ranch in the midst of the northern Wasatch Range to provide winter feed for herds of elk; call (435) 753-6168 for general information. In winter, concessionaires offer sleigh rides for a closer look at the elk and wagon rides if there's not enough snow. A visitors' center, (435) 753-6168, with displays and a café, (435) 753-6768, is also open in winter. You can also rent snowmobiles from the café. During the spring calving season, you might see newborn baby elk. You're not likely to see elk here in the summer months, but the drive in is still pretty.

The 16-mile paved road from Hyrum east to Hardware Ranch follows the scenic Blacksmith Fork Canyon past fishing spots (trout and whitefish), **Shenoah Picnic Area,** and **Pioneer Campground.** Pioneer's sites are open late May to late September with water; $9. Two small campgrounds, **Friendship** and **Spring,** are to the north along the Left Hand Fork of Blacksmith Canyon; they're open mid-May–late October (no water; $5 fee). An extensive snowmobile trail system extends from Hardware Ranch as far as Logan Canyon to the north and the Monte Cristo area to the south, with many side trails.

LOGAN CANYON

From its mouth on the east edge of Logan, Logan Canyon, with its steep limestone cliffs, winds more than 20 miles into the Bear River Range, a northern extension of the Wasatch

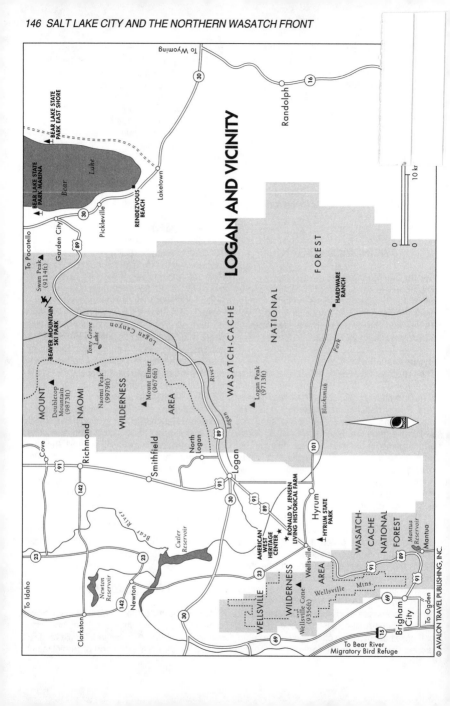

LOGAN AND VICINITY

To Wyoming

Randolph

30
16

BEAR LAKE STATE PARK EAST SHORE

BEAR LAKE STATE PARK MARINA

Bear Lake

RENDEZVOUS BEACH

Laketown

To Pocatello

Garden City

Pickleville

30

89

Swan Peak (9114ft)

BEAVER MOUNTAIN SKI PARK

Tony Grove Lake

Logan Canyon

MOUNT

Doubletop Mountain (9873ft)

RICHMOND

NAOMI

Naomi Peak (9979ft)

WILDERNESS

Mount Elmer (9676ft)

AREA

River

Logan

WASATCH-CACHE

NATIONAL

FOREST

Logan Peak (9713ft)

HARDWARE RANCH

Blacksmith Fork

Cove

91

142

Bear River

Smithfield

North Logan

89

Logan

91

30

Newton Reservoir

Cutler Reservoir

Clarkston

Newton

142

23

23

To Idaho

30

91

89

101

RONALD V. JENSEN LIVING HISTORICAL FARM

AMERICAN WEST HERITAGE CENTER

Hyrum

HYRUM STATE PARK

Wellsville

23

WELLSVILLE

WILDERNESS

Wellsville Cone (9356ft)

AREA

Wellsville Mtns

WASATCH-CACHE NATIONAL FOREST

Mantua Reservoir

Mantua

89

91

69

69

15

Brigham City

To Ogden

To Bear River Migratory Bird Refuge

0   10 km

© AVALON TRAVEL PUBLISHING, INC.

Mountains. Paved U.S. 89 follows the canyon and is a designated Scenic Byway. If you're looking for a daytrip out of Logan, just head up the canyon; you'll pass lots of picnic areas, campgrounds, fishing spots, and trailheads where you can easily spend a few blissful hours.

Steep slopes on the west rise to rolling plateau country across the top of the range, and moderate slopes descend to Bear Lake on the east. The route climbs to an elevation of 7,800 feet at Bear Lake Summit, from which there's a good view of the lofty Uintas of northeastern Utah. In autumn, maples of the lower canyon turn a brilliant crimson while aspens in the higher country are transformed to gold. Roadside geologic signs explain features in Logan Canyon. Picnicking is free at picnic areas, but you have to pay to picnic at some campgrounds.

A mile-by-mile guide to the canyon is available from the Bridgerland travel office in Logan. Contact the Logan Ranger District office for information on picnicking, camping, fishing, hiking, cross-country skiing, snowmobiling, and road conditions; it's open Monday–Friday 8 A.M.–5 P.M. near 1500 East and U.S. 89 in Logan, (435) 753-2772. Some campsites can be reserved by calling (800) 283-CAMP.

Skiing

Beaver Mountain Ski Area operates three double chairlifts serving 22 runs, the longest of which is 2.25 miles and drops 1,600 vertical feet. A cafeteria, ski shop, rentals, and lessons are available at the day lodge. Adult lift tickets cost $24 full day, $17 half day; children under 12 and seniors over 65 ski for $16 full day, $13 half day. Open daily 9 A.M.–4 P.M. early Dec.–Mar.; (435) 753-4822 (snow and road conditions) and (435) 753-0921 (office, ski school, and lift tickets). Go northeast 28 miles on U.S. 89, then north 1.5 miles on UT 243.

Hiking

A number of easy to moderate hikes makes Logan Canyon a lovely and convenient destination for a little exercise and an eyeful of nature. Four miles up the canyon, **Riverside Nature Trail** winds along the Logan River between Spring Hollow and Guinavah Campgrounds, a 1.5 mile (one-way) stroll with good bird-watching opportunities. From Guinavah, you can loop back to Spring Hol-

low via the **Crimson Trail;** this more strenuous trail takes you up the limestone cliffs and down in another two miles. It takes its name from the autumn colors visible along the way. Five miles up is the **Wind Cave Trailhead.** Wind Cave, with eroded caverns and arches, is one mile and a 1,100-foot climb from the trailhead.

Jardine Juniper Trail begins at the Wood Camp Campground, 10 miles up the canyon. The trail climbs 1,900 feet in 4.4 miles to Old Jardine, a venerable Rocky Mountain juniper tree. Still alive after 1,500 years, it measures about 27 feet in circumference and 45 feet high. The name honors a USU alumnus. A mile farther up the canyon is **Logan Cave,** a 2,000-foot-long cavern, which hardy spelunkers can explore; bring at least two light sources.

At **Bear Lake Summit,** 30 miles from Logan, the **Limber Pine Nature Trail** originates at the parking area on the right and terminates at a massive limber pine 25 feet in circumference and 44 feet high. At one time this tree was thought to be the world's oldest and largest limber pine, but a forestry professor at USU discovered that it is really five trees grown together and "only" about 560 years old. The easy self-guided walk takes about an hour; Bear Lake can be seen to the east.

Accommodations

$75–100: A handsome timber and stone lodge, **Beaver Creek Lodge,** (435) 753-1707 or 753-1076, not only offers rooms daily but also has horseback trail rides, snowmobile rentals, and cross-country ski trails in winter. The lodge is about 28 miles northeast on U.S. 89, just past the turnoff for Beaver Mountain Ski Area.

Campgrounds: There are 10 USFS campgrounds along U.S. 89 in Logan Canyon, so finding a place to pitch a tent shouldn't be difficult. The closest to Logan are **Bridger** and **Spring Hollow** Campgrounds, three and four miles respectively from town. Most campgrounds charge $9–11. You can reserve a campsite by calling (800) 283-CAMP.

BEAR LAKE

More than 28,000 years ago, faulting in massive blocks of the earth's crust created a basin

50 miles long and 12 miles wide. Bear Lake filled the entire valley during the last ice age but has now receded to cover an area 20 miles long and eight miles wide at an elevation of 5,900 feet. About half the lake lies in Utah and half in Idaho. The lake's famed turquoise color is thought to be caused by limestone particles suspended in the water.

The ecology of Bear Lake has been upset somewhat by an enterprising irrigation system. In recent centuries, Bear Lake has dwindled in size so greatly that Bear River, which once fed the lake, now totally bypasses it. The lake is kept from becoming saline by farmers who canal water from the river back to the lake during spring runoff and then pump it back into the river during the summer irrigation season.

David McKenzie, an early fur trapper, named the lake after the black bears once found here. Nomadic Indian tribes and groups of trappers frequented the shores during the 1820s and held two large gatherings here. Mormons arrived beginning in 1863 to start farms and ranches.

In recent years, thousands of summer cabins have sprouted along the shore and hillsides to take advantage of the scenery and water sports. Bear Lake State Park offers a marina and campground on the west shore, a large camping area on the south shore at Rendezvous Beach, and undeveloped campgrounds on the east shore. For information on Bear Lake, dial up the website www.bearlake.org.

Bear Lake National Wildlife Refuge

This wetlands refuge occupies 17,600 acres of marshlands north of the lake and is a favored stopping place for sandhill cranes, herons, white pelicans, egrets, and many species of ducks. Four species of fish evolved in Bear Lake that are not found any other place in the world. One of these, the Bonneville cisco, attracts anglers by the thousands. During spawning in January, nets are used to dip the small (six to eight inches long), tasty fish from the icy water. Ice fishing is very popular; fish sought year-round by anglers include the native Bear Lake cutthroat and Bonneville whitefish and the introduced rainbow and Mackinaw trout and yellow perch. Keep an eye out for the Bear Lake Monster—a dark dragonlike creature 90 feet long that spouts water!

Bear Lake State Park: Marina

The 71,000 acres of Bear Lake give plenty of room to water-ski, sail, or fish. The marina offers boat slips (protected by a breakwater), a boat ramp, a swimming area, picnic tables, a campground with showers, and ranger offices. Season is year-round; $5 day use, $13 camping. On busy summer weekends it's a good idea to make reservations for the marina or Rendezvous Beach areas. The marina is one mile north of Garden City on U.S. 89, P.O. Box 184, Garden City, UT 84028, (435) 946-3343 or (800) 322-3770 (reservations).

Bear Lake State Park: Rendezvous Beach

A wide sandy beach attracts visitors to the lake's southern shore. The park has a day-use area with a boat-rental concession and several campgrounds with showers. Ask at the entrance station for recommended places to camp; some sites have lake views, some offer hookups, and some are set up mainly for RVs. Open early May–late Sept.; $5 day use, $13 camping, $17 camping with hookups. Located eight miles south of Garden City near Laketown, P.O. Box 184, Garden City, UT 84028, (435) 946-3343 or (800) 322-3770 (reservations).

Bear Lake State Park: East Shore

Primitive campgrounds and day-use areas are located on the east side of Bear Lake. From south to north are First Point, Second Point (day use only), South Eden, Cisco Beach, Rainbow Cove, and North Eden. Sites stay open year-round; outhouses are provided but only South Eden has drinking water; $4 day-use, $7 camping. First Point and Rainbow Cove offer boat ramps. Scuba divers like the steep underwater drop-offs near Cisco Beach. Turn north from Laketown.

Garden City and Vicinity

This small town (year-round pop. 300) on the east shore at the junction of U.S. 89 and UT 30 comes to life in summer. You can learn about the area at a **tourist information center** at the highway junction; open daily 10 A.M.–6 P.M. May–Sept. **Pickleville Playhouse,** 2.8 miles south of Garden City, (435) 946-2918 (Garden City) or (435) 755-0961 (Logan), features family entertainment on summer evenings—call for days and times; a Western-style cookout precedes the show.

Events: The town celebrates the harvest of its most famous crop during the **Raspberry Days Festival** on the first weekend in August with a parade, the crowning of Miss Raspberry, a Little Buckaroo Rodeo, crafts, and entertainment. The **Mountain Man Rendezvous** reenacts the big gatherings of fur trappers and Indians that took place at Bear Lake in the summers of 1826 and 1827; the modern event is held the second weekend of September at Rendezvous Beach in Bear Lake State Park; (435) 946-3343.

Accommodations

$50–75: Bear Lake Motor Lodge, just south of the highway junction at 50 S. Bear Lake Blvd., (435) 946-3271, is open year-round and has a restaurant. **Ideal Beach Resort,** 2144 S. Bear Lake Blvd. (3.3 miles south of Garden City), (435) 946-3364 or (800) 634-1018 in Utah, offers motel and condo accommodations (half-week or longer) year-round, plus camping and a restaurant. The Ideal also offers boat rentals, a beach, swimming pools, tennis, and miniature golf. The adjacent nine-hole **Bear Lake Golf Course,** (435) 946-8742, is open to the public.

$100–125: Harbor Village Inn, 900 N. Bear Lake Blvd., (435) 946-3448 or (800) 324-6840, is open year-round and offers suites with full kitchens and fireplaces, plus use of tennis courts, lap pool, and hot tub.

Campgrounds: In addition to the state park campgrounds, there's the **Bear Lake KOA,** 0.8 mile north of Garden City on U.S. 89 near the state park marina, (435) 946-3454. It offers a swimming pool, miniature golf, tennis, store, showers, and laundry; open May 1–Oct. 31; $14.50 tents or RVs without hookups, $18.50 RVs with, $26 cabins.

Food

Each of the above three lodgings (Bear Lake Motor Lodge, Ideal Beach Resort, Harbor Village Inn) has it's own restaurant. Additionally, **Bear Lake West** is 4.5 miles north of Garden City, just across the Idaho border (three miles south of Fish Haven), (208) 945-2222, and has a nine-hole golf course and a steak and seafood restaurant; open in summer for Sunday brunch and Thurs.–Sat. for dinner.

Minnetonka Cave

Just after the turn of the century a grouse hunter retrieved a fallen bird after climbing a steep slope and noticed a cave entrance. Returning a few

---

BEAR LAKE MONSTER

When white settlers first arrived in the Bear Lake area, the local Indians warned them that a monster lived in the lake. The beast was described as being of the "legged serpent" variety and was said to have carried humans away. Few Indians of the area would bathe in the lake or camp nearby, but settlers scoffed—even after a few sightings by whites.

In 1868, no fewer than 20 people reported seeing the monster, all within a period of a few weeks. These included a few citizens of local repute and a wagonload of eight travelers. The monster gained fame and many believers, both in the area and beyond. Soon monsters were "spotted" in other lakes, including a 45-foot-long alligator that came out of the Great Salt Lake and smashed a campsite as the residents fled. This proliferation of tall tales began to cast doubts on the existence of Bear Lake's monster, and fewer sightings were reported.

There were even a few legends explaining the monster's demise. One farmer told of a huge creature from the lake that hungrily devoured part of his flock of sheep. As the surviving animals fled, the monster's eye caught a coil of barbed wire about the size and shape of huddled prey and swallowed it whole. By the farmer's account, the resulting pain drove the beast back into the lake and it was never seen again.

Rangers at Minnetonka Cave offer another story. They maintain the monster was intimidated by the surrounding human population and sought refuge in the cave where it survived on cave popcorn and coral. In this version, the monster was felled by a collapsing cave wall, with all but a clenched claw buried under rubble. The existing trail was built over that rockfall and rangers today still point out a piece of flowstone just under the trail that strangely does resemble a large dragon claw.

days later with friends and lights, he discovered an extensive and beautiful cave. Now you can visit this cave with a U.S. Forest Service ranger as your guide through its nine rooms.

Wear comfortable shoes with good soles—the tour is 1,800 feet long, involves 484 stair steps (some of them muddy and slick), and the route is repeated on the way out. Wear a light jacket and long pants; the temperature is 40° F and the humidity gives the cold a bite. Tours last 1–5 hours (depending on group size); from the cave's sign at St. Charles, Idaho, go west 10 miles to the cave entrance parking lot.

There are several USFS campgrounds along the route and a few free camping sites. Tours of the cave are given every half-hour 10 A.M.–5:30 P.M. daily mid-June–Labor Day; $4 adults, $3 children (6–15); (208) 945-2407.

Randolph

Rich County seat, Randolph (pop. 800) is a quiet rural town 19 miles south of Bear Lake. Farming and ranching have been the main activities here ever since Randolph H. Stewart led the first settlers here from Idaho in 1870. **Rich County Round-Up Days,** held in August, feature a rodeo, parade, and exhibits. No accommodations in town—just a drive-in.

WEST-CENTRAL UTAH

INTRODUCTION

Utah's Wild West remains nearly as wild as ever. Rugged mountain ranges and barren desert valleys have discouraged all but the most determined individuals. Explorers, pioneers in wagon trains, Pony Express riders, and telegraph linemen crossed this inhospitable land with only the desire to reach the other side. It took the promise of gold and silver to lure large numbers of people into the jagged hills. Fading ghost towns still show the industry of the early miners. Hardy ranchers also braved the isolation to grow hay and run their cattle and sheep. Shortage of water has always been the limiting factor to development. Travelers, however, can enjoy the solitude and the thrill of exploring a land little changed since white men first arrived. Roads provide surprisingly good access for such a remote region. Paved I-80, U.S. 50/6, and UT 21 cross it, while dirt roads branch off in all directions. Following the Pony Express and Stage Route from Fairfield to Ibapah might be the most unique driving tour; you experience some of the same unfenced wilderness as did the tough young Pony Express riders. You can negotiate this and many other back roads by car in dry weather. For the adventurous, the wildly beautiful mountain ranges offer countless hiking pos-sibilities—though you'll have to rough it. Hardly any developed trails exist.

THE LAND

Located in the Great Basin, west-central Utah consists of nearly equal amounts of valley and mountain terrain. Geologic forces have worked here on a grand scale. Great sections of the earth's crust rising along faults formed the mountains—all of which run north-south. Volcanic activity has left well-preserved craters, cinder cones, and lava flows. The massive sandbars that once lined the southern shore of Lake Bonneville have blown northeastward to form impressive dunes at Little Sahara. Streambeds in west-central Utah actually drain into several different subbasins, the two largest of which are Great Salt Lake and Sevier Lake.

Clouds moving in from the Pacific Ocean lose much of their moisture to the Sierra Nevada and other towering mountain ranges in California and Nevada. By the time the depleted clouds reach west-central Utah, only the Deep Creek, Stansbury, and southern Wah Wah Mountains reach high enough to gather sufficient rain and

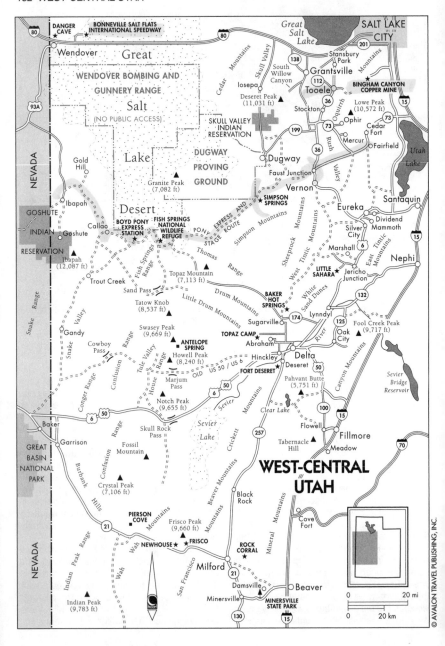

snow to support permanent streams. Notable summits of the region include Ibapah (12,087 feet) and Haystack (12,020 feet) Peaks of the Deep Creek Range, Deseret Peak (11,031 feet) of the Stansbury Mountains, Swasey (9,669 feet) and Notch (9,655 feet) Peaks of the House Range, Frisco Peak (9,660 feet) of the San Francisco Mountains, and Crystal Peak (7,106 feet) of the Wah Wah Range.

Though west-central Utah is now one of the driest parts of the Great Basin, a far different scene existed some 10,000 years ago. Freshwater Lake Bonneville then covered 20,000 square miles—one-fourth of Utah. Forests blanketed the mountains that poked above the lake waters. With time, the giant inland sea gradually shrank to much smaller remnants such as the Great Salt Lake, leaving behind the glistening salt flats of the Great Salt Lake Desert. Rainfall variations over time have caused Sevier Lake, southwest of Delta, to fluctuate between being a dry lakebed and the state's third-largest body of water.

Climate

Precipitation averages 8–10 inches annually over most of the region, which ranges from 4,000 to 6,000 feet in elevation. The rain and snow that do fall soon disappear because of the low humidity and abundant sunshine. Rainfall peaks in spring and again during the late summer–early autumn thunderstorm season. In this harsh semidesert, winter temperatures can drop into the subzeros, but the summer sun can send the thermometer climbing above 100 degrees. Visibility to 70 miles or more in the clean, dry air rewards mountain climbers with incredible views.

FLORA AND FAUNA

Vegetation in the valleys consists of sparse, low-growing plants such as saltbush, greasewood, black and bud sagebrush, shadscale, little rabbitbrush, Mormon tea, and grasses. Big sagebrush, juniper, and piñon pine grow higher up.

The highest peaks support mountain shrubs, aspen, and a variety of conifers, including the long-lived bristlecone pine.

Availability of water determines the quantity and variety of wildlife. Of the larger animals, mule deer and pronghorn are most widespread. Elk can be found in mountainous areas east of Delta. Rocky Mountain bighorn sheep have been reintroduced in the Deep Creek Range. Herds of wild horses roam the Confusion and House Ranges. Other wildlife includes coyote, mountain lion, bobcat, kit fox, spotted and striped skunks, and black-tailed jackrabbit. Vast numbers of birds visit Fish Springs National Wildlife Refuge and other desert oases. Waterfowl and marsh birds stop over in greatest numbers during their early spring and late autumn migrations. Many smaller birds nest near water sources in late spring and early summer.

HISTORY

Indian Peoples

Paleo-Indians entered this region about 15,000 years ago to collect wild plants and to pursue the now-extinct mammoth and other big game. After 5,000 years or so, the drying climate and changing environment caused many of the large animals to disappear. Still nomadic, the Indian groups adapted by relying more on small game and wild plant foods. New technologies including the bow and arrow, pottery, and small-scale agriculture distinguished the Fremont people around A.D. 550. When the Fremont culture faded, about 1300—perhaps because of drought and depletion of resources—the culturally distinct Shoshoni Indians moved in. These nomadic hunters and gatherers proved well suited to the dry environment. It's likely the modern Goshute—or Gosiutes—and Ute Indians descended from them. Within the first decades of Utah's settlement by white men, all tribes suffered great losses of population and land. Even today the Indians struggle to adapt

beautiful thistle (Cirsium pulchellum)

LOUISE FOOTE

to modern ways. The Goshutes once occupied northwest Utah and adjacent Nevada; they now live in the Goshute and Skull Valley Indian Reservations. The Utes had the greatest range of all of Utah's tribes, extending from west-central Utah into Colorado and New Mexico; they now have reservations in northeast Utah and southwest Colorado.

Explorers and Overland Trails
Imposing terrain and a scarcity of water discouraged early explorers from crossing the Great Basin region. In 1776, the Spanish became the first non-Indians to visit west-central Utah when members of the Dominguez-Escalante Expedition left the Utah Lake area and headed southwest, passing near the present-day towns of Delta and Milford.

Most American mountain men of the 1820s also kept to the Great Basin's edge—but not Jedediah Smith. With a party of 17 men, Smith set out in 1826 from northern Utah for Spanish California, searching for new fur-trapping areas. When Smith returned to Utah with two companions, the little group nearly perished in deep snows in the Sierra Nevada and from thirst in the desert.

Government explorer John C. Frémont named and made the first scientific studies of the Great Basin in 1845, putting to rest myths about the Great Salt Lake's monsters, whirlpools, and subterranean outlets to the Pacific.

In the following year, travelers began crossing the Great Basin as a shortcut to California. Horses and mules made the crossing safely, but the Donner-Reed wagon train met with disaster. Mud in the Great Salt Lake Desert slowed the group so much that they ran out of water and lost some of their wagons and oxen. The exhausted and demoralized group reached the Sierra Nevada late in the season, when snowstorms trapped and killed 40 of the 87 emigrants.

In 1859, Captain J.H. Simpson surveyed a military road to the south of the treacherous desert to connect Camp Floyd in central Utah with Carson Valley in western Nevada. Swift riders of the Pony Express used the road, known as the South-Central Overland Route, in 1860–1861, before the telegraph ended this brief chapter of American history. The Lincoln Highway, America's first designated transcontinental motoring route, included part of this road from 1910 to 1927.

Gold!
Prospectors found placer gold deposits in the early 1860s, though significant production had to wait for the arrival of the transcontinental railroad in 1869. Deposits of gold, silver, copper, lead, and zinc were found in quick succession. Major mining districts included Ophir, Mercur, and Tintic to the southwest of Salt Lake City; Gold Hill, Clifton, and Willow Springs in the far west of Utah; Detroit near Delta; and the San Francisco Mountains near Milford. Active gold mining continues in the Mercur, Tintic, and Detroit districts.

Bombs Away!
Much of the Great Salt Lake Desert is off-limits to visitors because of military activities. Jet aircraft and helicopters occasionally break the silence in flights above the Wendover Bombing and Gunnery Range. Scientists and engineers at Dugway Proving Grounds work on chemical and biological weapons. The base received some notoriety in 1968 after 6,500 sheep died on neighboring ranches. The military never admitted that it had released toxic warfare chemicals but it did compensate the ranchers. Just south of Tooele you'll see the neat rows of buildings across the vast Tooele Army Depot, which functions as a storage, maintenance, repair, and training center. In 1996, the Army began incineration of part of the U.S. chemical weapons cache at the depot.

WENDOVER AND VICINITY

Wendover began in 1907 as a watering station during construction of the Western Pacific Railroad. The highway went through in 1925, marking the community's beginnings as a travelers' stop. Wendover Air Force Base got its start in 1940 and soon grew to become one of the world's largest military complexes. During World War II, crews of bombers and other aircraft learned their navigation, formation flying, gunnery, and bombing skills above the 3.5 million acres of desert belonging to the base. Only after the war ended did the government reveal that one of the bomber groups had been training in preparation for dropping atomic bombs on Japan. Little remains of the base—once a city of nearly 20,000 people. Hill Air Force Base, near Ogden, continues to use the vast military reserve for training air crews.

Practicalities

This desert oasis has a split personality—half the town lies in Utah and half in Nevada. On both sides you'll find accommodations and restaurants where you can take a break from long drives on I-80. Five casino hotels, eight motels, and two campgrounds offer places to stay. Six casinos on the Nevada side provide a chance to lose your money in the usual gambling games. Most of the town's visitor facilities line Wendover Boulevard, also known as State Highway, which parallels the interstate. For information about the area stop in at the **Nevada-Wendover Welcome Center,** on the Nevada side at 937 Wendover Boulevard (P.O. Box 2468, Wendover, NV 89883), (775) 664-3414 or (800) 426-6862. Open daily 8:30–11:30 A.M. and noon–5 P.M.; look for the World War II Memorial capped by a B-29 model in front. Major annual events near Wendover include the **Wendover Bordertown Bike Challenge,** held over three days in late April or early May for both mountain and road bikes. During the **Land Speed Opener** in July, attempts are made to set new speed records. **Wendover Air Show** takes place in August or October, **Speed Week** in the third week of August, the smaller **World of Speed** in late September, and the **Bonneville World Finals** in mid-October at the Bonneville Salt Flats International Speedway.

Bonneville Salt Flats International Speedway

A brilliant white layer of salt left behind by prehistoric Lake Bonneville covers more than 44,000 acres of the Great Salt Lake Desert. For much of the year, a shallow layer of water sits atop the salt flats. Wave action planes the surface almost perfectly level—some say you can see the curvature of the earth here. The hot sun usually dries out the flats enough for speed runs in summer and autumn. Cars began running across the salt in 1914 and continue to set faster and faster times. Rocket-powered vehicles have exceeded 600 mph. Expansive courses can be laid out; the main speedway is 10 miles long and 80 feet wide.

A small tent city goes up near the course during the annual **Speed Week** in August; vehicles in an amazing variety of styles and ages take off individually to set new records in their classes. The salt flats, just east of Wendover, are easy to access: take I-80 Exit 4 and follow the paved road five miles north, then east. Signs and markers indicate if and where you can drive on the salt. Soft spots underlain by mud can trap vehicles venturing off the safe areas. Take care not to be on the track when racing events are being held!

Silver Island Mountains

These rugged mountains rise above the salt flats northeast of Wendover. You can visit them and their rocky canyons on a 54-mile loop drive. Take I-80 Exit 4, go north 1.2 miles, turn left 0.8 mile on a gravel road, then turn right at the sign

*Jenkins's
Mormon Meteor*

for the Silver Island Mountains. The road loops counter-clockwise around the mountains, crosses Lebby Pass, and returns to the junction near I-80. Another road goes north from Lebby Pass to Lucin in the extreme northwest corner of Utah. High-clearance vehicles do best on these roads, though cars can often negotiate them in dry weather. The Northern Utah map in the Utah Travel Council series shows approximate road alignments and terrain.

Danger Cave
Archaeologists from the University of Utah discovered thousands of prehistoric Indian artifacts in this cave. The five distinct layers of debris—the oldest dating back at least 10,000 years—have provided a wealth of new information on the region's early inhabitants. During field work in the 1950s, a huge piece of the cave's ceiling came crashing down. No one was hurt, but "Danger Cave" seemed an appropriate name. No exhibits or signs exist, so there's not much to see. If you'd like to visit the cave anyway, take I-80 Exit 4, turn north 0.4 mile, turn left (west) 1.4 miles on a paved road, then turn right (northwest) 1.8 miles on a gravel road (keep left past the gravel pits) to the cave. The road curves southwest along the face of the Silver Island Mountains. The cave entrance is easy to locate, about 200 feet from the road. You'll find excavation work and the collapsed ceiling in the large room that was once home to ancient Indians. A bit farther down the road is another undeveloped cave once used by off-duty military personnel for recreation. The cave floor was paved with concrete and a jukebox was powered by a generator to create a dance area that could be used even during blackouts. Juke Box Cave and Danger Cave are both part of an undeveloped Utah state park.

TOOELE

To sound like a native, pronounce the town's name "too-ILL-uh." Origin of the word is uncertain, but it may honor the Goshute Chief Tuilla. The attractive town (pop. 16,748) lies 34 miles southwest of Salt Lake City in the western foothills of the Oquirrh (pronounced OH-ker) Mountains. At its 4,900-foot elevation, Tooele offers fine views of the Great Salt Lake to the north and Tooele Valley and Stansbury Mountains to the west. Mormon pioneers settled here in 1849 to farm and raise livestock, but today the major industries are the nearby Tooele Army Depot—site of ongoing chemical-weapons incineration—the Dugway Proving Ground, and mining. Visitors wanting to know more about the region's history will enjoy the Tooele County Museum's exhibits on mining, smelting, and railroading; the pioneer mill and historic park at Benson Grist Mill; the Daughters of Utah Pioneers Museum of pioneer history in Tooele; and the Donner-Reed Pioneer Museum in nearby Grantsville. Other attractions in the area include a scenic drive and overlook in the Oquirrhs, the ghost town of Ophir, and hiking and camping in the South Willow Canyon Recreation Area in the Stansbury Mountains.

SIGHTS

Tooele Railroad Museum
A steam locomotive and a collection of old railroad cars surround Tooele's original (1909) train station. Step inside to see the restored station office and old photos showing railway workers, steam engines, and trestle construction. You might also meet and hear stories from retired railway men who volunteer as museum guides. Mining photos and artifacts illustrate life and work in the early days at Ophir, Mercur, Bauer, and other booming communities now faded to ghosts. Much of the old laboratory equipment and tools on display came from the Tooele Smelter, built by International Smelter & Refining Company in 1907–09. The smelter processed copper, lead, and zinc until 1972. Ore came over the Oquirrh Mountains by aerial tramway from the Bingham Mine. More than 3,000 people worked here during the hectic World War II years. A highly detailed model shows the modern Carr Fork Mill, built near Tooele but used only 90 days before being dismantled and shipped to a more profitable site in Papua, New Guinea. Two

railroad cars, once part of an Air Force mobile ballistic missile train, contain medical equipment and antique furniture. Outside, kids can ride the scale railway (Sat. only), check out a caboose, or explore a replica of a mine. Tooele County Museum is open Tuesday–Saturday 1–4 P.M. from Memorial Day to Labor Day weekends. Admission is by donation. From downtown Tooele go east a half mile on Vine Street; the museum is at 33 N. Broadway, (435) 882-2836.

Daughters of Utah Pioneers Museum

Meet Tooele's pioneers through 128 framed pictures and see their clothing and other possessions at this museum; downtown at 39 E. Vine St., just a half-block east of Main. The small stone building dates from 1867 and once served as a courthouse for Tooele County. The little log cabin next door, built in 1856, was one of the town's first residences. The Daughters of Utah Pioneers Museum (DUP) is open some Saturdays in summer and for groups on request; call the numbers on the front (the small DUP

DUP Museum

museums are run by volunteers and those who are on call to open the museums change from season to season and year to year).

Benson Grist Mill

Pioneers constructed this mill—one of the oldest buildings in western Utah—in 1854. Wooden pegs and rawhide strips hold the timbers together. E.T. Benson, grandfather of LDS President Ezra Taft Benson, supervised its construction for the Mormon Church. The mill produced flour until 1938, then ground only animal feed until closing in the 1940s. Local people began to restore the exterior in 1986. Much of the original machinery inside is still intact. Antique farm machinery, a granary, log cabin, blacksmith shop, and other buildings stand on the grounds to the east. Ruins of the Utah Wool Pullery, which once removed millions of tons of wool annually from pelts, stand to the west. The mill and historic park are open regularly Tuesday–Saturday 10 A.M.–4 P.M. from Memorial Day to Labor Day, though tours can be arranged at any other time on request. Benson Grist Mill is one block west of Mills Junction (UT 36 at UT 138), eight miles north of Tooele, four miles south of I-80 Exit 99, and 10 miles east of Grantsville, (435) 882-7678.

Oquirrh Overlook

A look into the world's largest open-pit copper mine, panoramic views, and canyon scenery reward those who drive to this spot atop the Oquirrh Mountains. Views take in much of northern and western Utah: Great Salt Lake, Wasatch Range, Salt Lake City, Tooele Valley, and the Stansbury Mountains. The intricate patterns of the terraced **Bingham Canyon Copper Mine** lie directly below. To reach the overlook, 10.5 miles from town, head east on Vine Street and enter Middle Canyon. Forests of box elder and maple dominate the lower canyon, with firs and aspen farther up. After seven miles you'll see a picnic and parking area on the right. The pavement ends here, and large RVs and vehicles with trailers should not go beyond. The gravel road begins a steep one-mile climb with sharp curves to Butterfield Pass (elev. 8,400 feet). Turn left at the pass and continue 2.5 miles to the overlook (elev. 9,400 feet). Ice and snow close the road in winter.

Continue east at the pass and you'll descend on a gravel road through Butterfield Canyon into the Salt Lake Valley; ask about conditions—this road is sometimes closed. After seven miles, the road meets a bend in a paved highway—though this junction may not be signed. Continue straight (east) 11 miles to I-15 (Exits 294 and 295) or turn left (north) five miles to UT 48 and the Bingham Canyon Copper Mine entrance.

Sailboarding
Ten miles south of Tooele is the small town of Stockton on the shore of Rush Lake, where sailboarding has gained great popularity in recent years. Rush Lake's location between two mountain ranges and its proximity to Salt Lake guarantee sailboarders steady currents of south winds, with plenty of strong 8–15 mph blasts on hot days.

Mountain Biking
Soldier Canyon, six miles south of Tooele, draws mountain bikers. It's a four-mile climb to the mining ghost town of Jacob City, 9,000 feet above sea level.

Other Recreation
The **city park** offers picnicking, playground, and an indoor swimming pool (open year-round) at the corner of Vine and Second West, (435) 882-3247. During the summer months it may be more fun to swim in the **outdoor pool** at the Stansbury Park Golf Course, (435) 882-5067. **Elton Park** at Second North and Broadway has tennis courts and ball fields. **Middle Canyon** has a picnic area seven miles from town (head east on Vine St.). **Settlement Canyon** contains a small reservoir (a local fishing and swimming spot) a half mile up and **Legion Park,** a picnic area 1.5 miles up. Play golf at the nine-hole **Oquirrh Hills Golf Course** at Seventh and Edgemont on the east side of town, (435) 882-4220, or the 18-hole course in **Stansbury Park** eight miles north on UT 36, (435) 882-4162.

ACCOMMODATIONS

Under $50
All motels lie conveniently along Main Street (UT 36). On the north end, the **Villa Motel,** 475 N. Main, (435) 882-4551 or (800) 882-4551, has basic rooms, some with kitchenettes.

$50–75
The **Best Western Inn Tooele,** 365 N. Main, (435) 882-5010 or (800) 448-5010, has an indoor pool, a spa, and a couple of rooms with kitchenettes. **Comfort Inn,** 491 S. Main, (435) 882-6100 or (800) 228-5150, offers free full breakfasts, kitchenettes and efficiency kitchens, laundry facilities, and a pool and spa. Rates are discounted on weekends. The new **Hampton Inn,** 461 S. Main, (435) 882-6102 or (800) HAMP-TON, has a pool, hot tub, a free breakfast bar, and each room has an efficiency kitchen.

You won't find any developed campgrounds in town, but campers sometimes head east on Vine Street to Middle Canyon or southeast on Settlement Canyon Road (one-third mile south of Valleyview Motel) into Settlement Canyon. Other possibilities are the BLM **Clover Creek Campground** 20 miles southwest (go 12 miles south on UT 36, then eight miles west on UT 199) and the Forest Service campgrounds in **South Willow Canyon Recreation Area** and the **Grantsville Reservoir** 20 miles west of town (see Stansbury Mountains, below); none of the areas has water or a fee.

OTHER PRACTICALITIES

Food
Francesco's of Tooele, 411 N. Main, (435) 882-6579, has Italian-American cooking, and is a good bet for a steak. Otherwise, somewhat oddly in this prototypically Old West town, all the other good eating options are ethnic. Eat Chinese-Polynesian-American at the **Sun Lok Yuen,** 615 N. Main, (435) 882-3003; open Mon.–Sat. for lunch and dinner. **Tooele Pizza & Restaurant,** 21 E. Vine, (435) 882-8035, also has Greek food; open Mon.–Sat. for lunch and dinner.

For Mexican and American food try **La Frontera,** 494 S. Main (across from the Comfort Inn), (435) 882-0888; open daily for breakfast, lunch, and dinner, or **Los Laureles,** 23 N. Main, (435) 882-2860; open Mon.–Sat. for lunch and dinner.

Entertainment and Events
Catch movies at the **Ritz,** 111 N. Main, (435) 882-2273. Summer events in Tooele include the

Arts Festival in early June. July 4th marks the opening of rodeo season with the **Bit 'N Spur Rodeo,** held at the rodeo grounds at 200 West and 600 North. A morning Fourth of July parade of cowboys, cowgirls, and public safety vehicles highlights the event; the location of the evening fireworks display alternates yearly between Tooele and Grantsville. A demolition derby and Quarterhorse Show draw a crowd to the Tooele City Recreation Complex for the **Tooele County Fair** in early August. In late September, Tooele hosts the **Festival of the Old West,** a Native American powwow and cultural event, and the long-running **Tooele Gem & Mineral Show.**

Services and Information

In **emergencies** (police, fire, or paramedic), dial 911. The **post office** is downtown at 65 N. Main, (435) 882-1429. **Tooele Valley Regional Medical Center** has 24-hour emergency services at 211 S. First East, (435) 882-1697.

The **Tooele Chamber of Commerce** can tell you about the sights and services here. Its office is upstairs in the Key Bank at 201 N. Main (Tooele, UT 84074), (435) 882-0690 or (800) 378-0690; open Mon.–Fri. about 9 A.M.–4 P.M. The **public library** is at 47 E. Vine Street, (435) 882-2182; open Tues.–Sat.

Transport

Utah Transit Authority (UTA) buses connect Tooele with Salt Lake City and other towns of the Wasatch Front Monday–Saturday. The main bus stop is at Main and Fourth South, (435) 882-9031.

WEST OF TOOELE

GRANTSVILLE

Old buildings and tall Lombardy poplars reflect the pioneer heritage of this rural community, first settled in 1851 and named Willow Creek Fort. The museum in town offers a look at local history. Grantsville stretches along UT 138 nine miles northwest of Tooele. For hiking and camping in the Stansbury Mountains, crowned by 11,031-foot Deseret Peak, head south 10 miles to South Willow Canyon Recreation Area.

Donner-Reed Pioneer Museum

Early residents built this one-room adobe schoolhouse within the old fort walls in 1861. Today it's a museum honoring the Donner-Reed wagon train of 1846. These pioneers crossed the Great Salt Lake Desert to the west with great difficulty, then became trapped by snow while attempting to shortcut through the Sierra Nevada to California. Of the 87 people who started the trip, only 47 desperate people survived the harsh winter—by eating boiled boots and harnesses and the frozen flesh of dead companions. Museum displays include a large collection of guns and pioneer artifacts found abandoned on the salt flats, pottery, arrowheads, and other Indian artifacts. Outside you can try out Grantsville's original iron jail and see an early log cabin, black-smith shop, and old wagons. Another adobe building across the street served as a church and dates from 1866. The museum is open on request during the summer; free. To view the exhibits, visit or call Grantsville City Hall; open Mon.–Fri. 8:30 A.M.–5 P.M. at the corner of Park and Main, (435) 884-3411. From the city hall, go two blocks west on Main to Cooley Street, then one block north to the museum.

Bonneville Seabase

Scuba divers can enjoy ocean-type diving in the desert. A natural pool here was found to have salinity so close to that of the ocean that marine creatures could thrive in it. Several dozen species have been introduced including groupers, triggerfish, damsel fish, clown fish, and lobsters. The springs are geothermally heated, so winter cold is no problem. The original pool has been expanded and new pools were created by dredging. User fees run $15 per person; you can rent full equipment for scuba diving ($21) or snorkeling ($11). Located five miles west of Grantsville at 2445 S. 900, (435) 884-3874.

Practicalities

The **city park** at 100 E. Cherry Street offers picnicking, a playground, and a baseball diamond. Big events include the **Fourth of July** parade and fireworks (the show alternates between here and Tooele each year) and the **Tooele County Livestock Show and Rodeo** in mid-July.

STANSBURY MOUNTAINS

Not all of western Utah is desert, as a visit to this section of the Wasatch National Forest southwest of Grantsville will show. Trails lead to Deseret Peak and other good day-hiking and backcountry destinations. Grantsville Reservoir, South Willow Canyon Recreation Area, and trailheads into the Deseret Peak Wilderness are accessed via the South Willow Canyon on the southeast slope of the Stansbury Mountains. Signs for Willow Creek Recreation Areas on the west end of Grantsville will guide you south onto South Willow Road. Turn right onto a paved road after four miles and continue west up South Willow Canyon. For more information about the area, contact the Salt Lake Ranger District office, 6944 S. 3000 East, Salt Lake City, UT 84121, (435) 524-5042.

Follow the paved road only a few miles from the South Willow Road Junction to reach the **Grantsville Reservoir,** popular for water sports, trout fishing, picnicking, and camping; campsites begin to appear after three miles. Reach an alternate part of the reservoir by continuing on the dirt road at the first curve. Five miles from South Willow Road is the **South Willow Canyon Recreation Area,** on the east slope of the mountains—six small, free campgrounds along the South Fork of Willow Creek are open from early June to mid-September; no drinking water. Cot-

tonwood, box elder, Douglas fir, and aspen thrive in the canyon. Elevations range from 6,080 feet at the first campground to 7,400 feet at the last one, Loop, at the end of the road. Sites can be crowded on summer weekends.

If these campgrounds are full, you'll find more sites at the BLM's **Clover Creek Campground,** located at the southern end of the Stansbury Mountains on a spring-fed creek. There's no developed water or fee. From Grantsville head out South Willow Canyon Road and continue past the recreation area turnoff to UT 199 at Rush Valley. Turn right onto UT 199 and travel west; the campground is located eight miles from the junction with UT 36.

Deseret Peak Wilderness Area

Hikers enjoy expansive views amidst alpine forests and glacial cirques in the Deseret Peak Wilderness Area in the central portion of the Stansbury Mountains. The moderately difficult 3,600-foot climb to the summit is 7.5 miles roundtrip. Most of the way is easy to follow, though it's recommended that you carry the USGS topo maps Deseret Peak West and Deseret Peak East (7 1/2-minute) or Deseret Peak (15-minute). The trail begins at Loop Campground at the end of the road up South Willow Canyon and connects to make a loop to the summit. After three quarters of a mile the main summit trail turns left and follows Mill Fork (the trail forking right leads to an alternate summit trail and North Willow Canyon). The main trail ascends two more miles through meadows, aspen, Douglas fir, limber pine, and a glacial cirque to a high ridge at

descending Deseret Peak

10,000 feet. Follow the ridge west three quarters of a mile to Deseret Peak (elev. 11,031 feet). On a clear day atop the summit you can see much of the Wasatch Range on the eastern horizon, the Great Salt Lake to the north, Pilot Peak in Nevada to the northwest, the Great Salt Lake Desert to the west, and countless desert ranges to the southwest. To make a loop, follow the trail along the north ridge about 1.5 miles, contouring on the west side of three smaller peaks, then drop east a half mile into Pockets Fork. At the junction with the trail connecting North and South Willow Canyons, turn right 1.5 miles back to the trail junction in Mill Fork, three-quarters of a mile from the start.

For other trails and access roads in the Stansburys, see the topo and Wasatch-Cache National Forest maps. Only foot and horse travel are permitted in the wilderness area (west of Mack Canyon-Big Hollow Trail, north of Dry Canyon, and south of Pass Canyon).

SKULL VALLEY

Iosepa

Now a ghost town with little more than a cemetery, foundations, and a few houses, Iosepa once had a population of 226 Polynesian settlers. Devout Hawaiian Mormons who desired to live in the promised land of Utah began the settlement in 1889. All the good farmland around Salt Lake City had been taken, so the group wound up in this desolate valley west of the Stansbury Mountains. Undaunted by the harsh climate and scarcity of water, the Hawaiians laid out a townsite and named it Iosepa ("Joseph") after the sixth president of the LDS Church, Joseph F. Smith. Livestock was raised, crops and trees were planted, and roses bloomed in the new desert home. The islanders celebrated Pioneer Day on August 28, the date they arrived in Skull Valley, with feasts of poi and roast pig. Not all harvests produced a profit, however, and life here was hard. Leprosy appeared in 1896 and its several victims were forced to live in a separate building—Utah's only known leper colony. News in 1916 of plans to build a Mormon temple in Hawaii brought a wave of homesickness, and within a year the struggling settlement disbanded.

Today Iosepa is a large ranch along the road 15 miles south of I-80 Timpie Springs Exit 77. There's no sign at the ranch, but it's the largest in the area, with four houses along the road and several farm buildings. The two small frame houses belonged to the original Hawaiian settlement; two other surviving buildings are farther back. Residents don't mind people visiting the old townsite, but ask first. To see the cemetery, turn east past a group of mailboxes and the northernmost house, go through a gate, then keep left at a fork. The cemetery, marked by six flagpoles, is three quarters of a mile in; the road may be too rough for cars. Time and the elements have reduced the graves to mounds of gravel with just a few marble headstones. Their Hawaiian names seem out of place in this lonely desert valley.

Skull Valley Indian Reservation

From prehistoric times, Goshute Indians have ranged over this region to hunt and gather wild plant foods. And since the 1860s, they have been ranching and farming. If you've seen the hogans and sweat lodges in the Four Corners area, you'll find this reservation something of a change: there are no culturally distinctive houses or outbuildings here.

SOUTH OF TOOELE

OQUIRRH MOUNTAINS GHOST TOWNS

Ophir

Picturesque old buildings and log cabins line the bottom of Ophir Canyon, which once boomed with saloons, dance halls, houses of ill repute, hotels, restaurants, and shops. In the 1860s, soldiers under General Patrick Connor heard stories of Indians mining silver and lead for ornaments and bullets. The soldier-prospectors tracked the Indian mines to this canyon and staked claims. By 1870 a town was born—named after the biblical land of Ophir, where King Solomon's mines were located. Much of the ore went to General Connor's large smelter at nearby Stockton. Later the St. John & Ophir Railroad entered the canyon to haul away the rich ores of silver, lead, and zinc and small amounts of gold and copper. Ophir's population peaked at 6,000 but, unlike most other mining towns of the region, Ophir never quite died. People still live here and occasionally prospect in the hills. The city hall and some houses have been restored, and the **Ophir Gophir** sells groceries and refreshments, (801) 882-9903, but canyon vegetation has claimed the rest of the old structures.

Paved roads go all the way into town. From Tooele, head south 12 miles on UT 36 through Stockton, turn left five miles on UT 73, then left 3.5 miles to Ophir. Tailings and foundations of a flotation mill built in 1930 are near the mouth of Ophir Canyon. The road to Ophir follows an old railroad grade; part of an abandoned passenger car still lies on the right just before the town. A gravel road continues up the canyon beyond Ophir, crossing Ophir Creek and weaving through forests of box elder and aspen before ending 2.5 miles farther. You can camp here, but you won't find any facilities. Hikers can continue upstream and ascend Lowe Peak (elev. 10,572 feet) and other summits in the Oquirrh Mountains.

Barrick Mercur Gold Mine

General Connor's soldiers also discovered silver in the canyon southeast of Ophir during the late 1860s. After a slow start, prospectors made rich strikes and the rush was on. The mining camp of Lewiston boomed in the mid-1870s, then busted by 1880 as the deposits worked out. Arie Pinedo, a prospector from Bavaria, began to poke around the dying camp and located the Mercur Lode of gold and mercury ore. He and other would-be miners were frustrated when all attempts to extract gold from the ore failed. Then in 1890, a

Golden Gate Mill at Mercur, ca. 1898

new cyanide process proved effective, and a new boomtown arose around the Golden Gate Mill five years later. Though fire wiped out the business district in 1902, Mercur was rebuilt and had an estimated population of more than 8,000 by 1910. Only three years later, the town closed up when ore bodies seemed depleted. Mining revived in the 1930s and again in the 1980s. Barrick Mercur Gold Mines now owns the ghost town site, of which little remains. Current technology allows profitable mining of both the massive old tailing piles (heaps of refuse pulled from the mines) and new deposits.

The **Barrick Mercur Visitors Center,** a company-operated mining museum and information center, provides a narrative of mining technology and displays equipment and historic photos from the early mining days. It's located near the entrance gate and is open Thursday–Monday from

Memorial Day weekend to Labor Day 10 A.M.–8 P.M.; (435) 822-4356. From the Ophir turnoff, continue southeast four miles on UT 73, then turn left 3.5 miles on a paved road. A sign at the turnoff indicates whether the center is open. If it's closed, there's no reason to drive in, as the mining and ghost town site can't be accessed without special permission. Tours of the operations can sometimes be arranged by calling in advance.

Other Ghost Towns
Stories of several other historic mining sites and the famous Ajax underground store make fascinating reading, but little remains at these sites. Good sources of information include *The Historical Guide to Utah Ghost Towns,* by Stephen L. Carr, and *Some Dreams Die: Utah's Ghost Towns and Lost Treasures,* by George A. Thompson.

PONY EXPRESS AND STAGE ROUTE

In 1860, Pony Express officials put together a chain of stations between St. Joseph, Missouri, and Sacramento, California. Relays of frontier-toughened men covered the 1,838-mile distance in 10 days. Riders stopped at stations spaced about 12 miles apart to change horses. Only after changing horses about six times did the rider complete his day's work. Despite the hazards of frontier travel, only one mail pouch was ever lost, and Indian wars held up service for only a single month. Historians credit the daring enterprise with providing communications vital to keeping California aligned with the Union during the Civil War and proving that the West could be crossed in all kinds of weather—thus convincing skeptical politicians that a transcontinental railroad could be built. The Pony Express operated for only 18 months; completion of the transcontinental telegraph in October 1861 put the riders out of work. The company, which received no government assistance, failed to make a profit for its owners.

Relive some of the Old West by driving the Pony Express route across western Utah. The scenic route goes from spring to spring as it winds through several small mountain ranges and across open plains, skirting the worst of the Great Salt Lake Desert. Interpretive signs and

monuments along the way describe how Pony Express riders rode swiftly on horseback to bring the country closer together. The 140 miles between Fairfield in the east and Ibapah near the Nevada border provide a sense of history and appreciation for the land lost to motorists speeding along I-80.

Allow at least a full day for the drive and bring food, water, and a full tank of gas. The Bureau of Land Management has campgrounds at Simpson Springs and south of Callao. No motels or restaurants line the road, but Ibapah has two gas station/grocery stores. You can travel the well-graded gravel road by car; just watch for the usual backcountry hazards of wildlife, rocks, and washouts. Adventurous travelers may want to make side trips for rockhounding, hiking, or visiting old mining sites. Always keep vehicles on existing roads—sand and mud flats can be treacherously deceptive!

You can begin your trip down the historic route from the Stagecoach Inn at Fairfield (from Salt Lake City or Provo, take I-15 to Lehi, then go 21 miles west on UT 73). You can also begin at Faust Junction, 30 miles south of Tooele on UT 36, or Ibapah, 51 miles south of Wendover off U.S. 93A. The BLM has an information kiosk and small picnic area 1.8 miles west of Faust

Junction. For the latest road conditions and travel information, contact the BLM Salt Lake District office, 2370 S. 2300 West, Salt Lake City, UT 84119, (801) 977-4300. The following are points of interest along the route.

Stagecoach Inn at Fairfield

The inn was built for travelers in 1858 by John Carson, who had arrived as one of the first white settlers in the area around 1855. Now it's a state park. Inside the restored structure you can see where weary riders slept and sat around tables swapping stories. Stagecoach Inn is 36 miles northwest of Provo.

Simpson Springs

Indians had long used these excellent springs before the first white men came through. The name is in honor of Captain J.H. Simpson, who stopped here in 1859 while leading an Army survey across western Utah and Nevada. About the same time, George Chorpenning built a mail station here later used by the Pony Express and Overland Express companies. A reconstructed stone cabin on the old site shows what the station looked like. Ruins of a nearby cabin built in 1893 contain stones from the first station. Foundations of a Civilian Conservation Corps camp lie across the road. In 1939, the young men of the CCC built historic markers, improved roads, and worked on conservation projects. The BLM campground higher up on the hillside has water (except in winter) and good views across the desert. A $3 per-vehicle fee is charged; do not drink the water. Sparse juniper trees grow at the 5,100-foot elevation. Simpson Springs is 25 miles west of Faust Junction and 67 miles east of Callao.

Fish Springs National Wildlife Refuge

The Pony Express station once located here no longer exists, but you can visit the 10,000 acres of marsh and lake that attract abundant bird- and wildlife. Waterfowl and marsh birds stop over in greatest numbers during their early-spring and late-autumn migrations. Many smaller birds nest here in late spring and early summer, though they're difficult to see in the thick vegetation. Opportunistic hawks and other raptors circle overhead. A self-guided auto tour makes an 11.5-mile loop through the heart of the refuge. Most of the route follows dikes between the human-made lakes and offers good vantage points from which to see ducks, geese, egrets, herons, avocets, and other water birds. The tour route and a picnic area near the entrance are open from sunrise to sunset; no camping is allowed in the refuge. Stop at the information booth near the entrance to pick up a brochure, see photos of birds found at the refuge, and read notes on the area's history. Fish Springs National Wildlife Refuge is 42 miles west of Simpson Springs and 25 miles east of Callao, (435) 831-5353.

*Stagecoach Inn,
built by John Carson
in 1858*

Boyd Pony Express Station

Portions remain of the station's original rock wall, and signs give the history of the station and the Pony Express. Find the station 13 miles west of Fish Springs and 12 miles east of Callao.

Callao

This cluster of ranches dates from 1859, when several families decided to take advantage of the desert grasslands and good springs here. The original name of Willow Springs had to be changed when residents applied for a post office—too many other Utah towns had the same name. Then someone suggested Callao (locally pronounced CAL-ee-o), because the Peruvian town of that name enjoys a similar valley-backed-by-high-mountain setting. Residents raise cattle, sheep, and hay. Children go to Callao Elementary School, one of the last one-room schoolhouses in Utah. Local people believe that the Willow Springs Pony Express Station site was located off the main road at Bagley Ranch, but a BLM archaeologist contends that the foundation is on the east side of town. Callao is 67 miles west of Simpson Springs and 28 miles east of Ibapah (via the Pony Express and Stage Route). A BLM campground at the site of a former CCC camp is four miles south beside Toms Creek; no water or fee. The tall Deep Creek Range rises to the west.

Canyon Station

To get here, follow signs for Sixmile Ranch, Overland Canyon, and Clifton Flat between Callao and Ibapah. The original station used by Pony Express riders was in Overland Canyon northwest of Canyon Station. Indians attacked in July 1863, burned the first station, and killed the Overland agent and four soldiers. The new station was built on a more defensible site. You can see its foundation and the remnants of a fortification. A signed fork at Clifton Flat points the way to Gold Hill, a photogenic ghost town six miles distant (see below). Canyon Station is north of the Deep Creek Range, 13 miles northwest of Callao and 15 miles northeast of Ibapah.

Ibapah

Pronounce Ibapah "EYE-buh-paw" to avoid sounding like a tourist! Ibapah is about the same size as Callao—little more than a group of some 20 ranches. **Ibapah Trading Post,** (435) 234-1166, offers gas and groceries.

VICINITY OF IBAPAH

Continuing south a short way, the main road forks left to the Goshute Indian Reservation, while the right fork crosses into Nevada to U.S. 93 (58 miles) on the old Pony Express and Stage Route. From Ibapah you can also go north to Gold Hill ghost town (14 miles) and Wendover (58 miles) or south to U.S. 50/6 near Great Basin National Park via Callao, Trout Creek, and Gandy (90 miles).

Goshute Indian Reservation

Goshute Indians mastered living in the harsh desert by knowing of every edible seed, root, insect, reptile, bird, and rodent, as well as larger game. Their meager diet and possessions appalled early white settlers, who referred disparagingly to the Indians as "diggers." Loss of land to ranchers and dependence on manufactured food put an end to the old nomadic lifestyle.

In recent times the Goshute have gradually begun to regain independence by learning to farm and ranch. Several hundred members of the tribe live on the Goshute Indian Reservation, which straddles the Utah-Nevada border. Most of the reservation is off-limits to nonmembers without special permission.

The isolated Goshute Reservation has been in the national news in the last few years. Tribal elders have tentatively agreed to build a repository on their reservations for the nuclear waste from several out-of-state atomic energy generation facilities, in return for tens of millions of dollars in payments and infrastructure development. The Federal Government and Private Fuel Storage, a consortium of eight nuclear power companies, have worked out an agreement with the Goshute tribal leadership to lease reservation land for the nuclear storage facility, which could house up to 40,000 metric tons of highly-radioactive fuel rods. The Utah governor—and a number of vocal Goshute opponents—have vowed to fight the facility's placement. Meanwhile, plans call for breaking ground at the facility in 2001. (Officially, the storage site is deemed temporary, to be used until a permanent storage facility is sited in neighboring Nevada.)

Gold Hill

Miners had been working the area for three years when they founded Gold Hill in 1892. A whole treasure trove of minerals came out of the ground here—gold, silver, lead, copper, tungsten, arsenic, and bismuth. A smelter along a ridge just west of town processed the ore. But three years later Gold Hill's boom ended. Most people lived only in tents anyway, and soon everything but the smelter foundations and tailings was packed up. A rebirth occurred during World War I, when the country desperately needed copper, tungsten, and arsenic. Gold Hill grew to a sizable town with 3,000 residents, a railroad line from Wendover, and many substantial buildings. Cheaper foreign sources of arsenic knocked the bottom out of local mining in 1924, and Gold Hill began to die again. Another frenzied burst of activity occurred in 1944–1945, when the nation called once more for tungsten and arsenic. The town again sprang to life, only to fade just as quickly after the war ended. Determined prospectors

still roam the surrounding countryside awaiting another clamor for the underground riches. Decaying structures in town make a picturesque sight. (Several year-round residents live here; no scavenging allowed.) Visible nearby are the cemetery, mines, railroad bed, and smelter site. The smaller ghost town of **Clifton** lies over the hill to the south but little remains; No Trespassing signs make visitors unwelcome. Good roads (partly dirt) approach Gold Hill from Ibapah, Wendover, and Callao.

DEEP CREEK RANGE

The range soars spectacularly above the Great Salt Lake Desert. Few people know about the Deep Creeks despite their great heights, diverse wildlife, and pristine forests. Ibapah Peak (elev. 12,087 feet) and Haystack Peak to the north (elev. 12,020 feet) crown the range. Glacial cirques and other rugged features have been carved into the nearly white granite that makes up most of the summit ridge. Prospectors have found gold, silver, lead, zinc, copper, mercury, beryllium, molybdenum, tungsten, and uranium. You'll occasionally run across mines and old cabins in the range, especially in Goshute Canyon. Of the six perennial streams on the east side, Birch and Trout Creeks still contain Lake Bonneville cutthroat trout that originated in the prehistoric lake; both creeks were closed to fishing at press time. Wildlife includes Rocky Mountain bighorn sheep (reintroduced), deer, pronghorn, mountain lion, coyote, bobcat, and many birds. Vegetation ranges from grass and sagebrush in the lower foothills to piñon pine and juniper, then to montane forests of aspen, Engelmann spruce, Douglas fir, white fir, subalpine fir, ponderosa pine, and limber pine. Bristlecone pine grows on some of the high ridges. Alpine tundra covers the highest peaks. The Deep Creek Range gets plenty of snow in winter, so the climbing season runs from about late June to late October. Aspen and some mountain shrubs put on colorful displays in September and early October. Streams in the range have good water (purify first), but the lower canyons are often polluted by the organisms that accompany cattle excrement. Carry water while hiking on the dry ridges.

Main Climbing Routes

Most of the canyons have roads into their lower reaches. Four-wheel-drive vehicles will be able to get farther up the steep grades than cars. Most hikers start up Granite or Indian Farm Creek and head for Ibapah or Haystack Peak. A trail along **Granite Creek** offers the easiest approach to Ibapah Peak, about 12.5 miles round-trip and a 5,300-foot elevation gain from the beginning of the jeep trail. The road to Granite Creek turns west off Snake Valley Road 10 miles south of Callao (7.8 miles north of Trout Creek Ranch). Keep left at a junction about one mile in, then follow the most-used track. The road enters Granite Canyon after three miles. The first ford of Granite Creek, a half mile into the canyon, requires a high-clearance vehicle; the second, 0.8 mile farther, may require four-wheel drive. The road deteriorates into a jeep track in another 0.6 mile at the border of Deep Creek Wilderness Study Area. Four-wheel-drive vehicles can climb the steep grade another two miles. Continue two miles on a pack trail to the beginning of a large meadow at the pass, then head cross-country 1.5 miles to the small peak (11,385 feet) just before Ibapah. You should find a small trail on the east side of this peak that continues three quarters of a mile to the summit of Ibapah. (This small trail probably once connected with the pack trail but is little used today.)

Impressive panoramas take in the rugged canyons and ridges of the Deep Creek Range below and much of western Utah and eastern Nevada beyond. Remains of a heliograph station sit atop Ibapah. Early mapmakers measured the highest point in the range at 12,101 feet and named it "Haystack." A later survey determined the correct height to be 12,087 feet and renamed the peak "Ibapah;" the second-highest peak was given the old Haystack name by default. Hikers can head cross-country two miles north from Ibapah to Haystack Peak (12,020 feet). The 7 1/2-minute Ibapah Peak topo map covers the entire hike to the summit of both peaks via Granite Creek.

Other Climbing Routes

Red Mountain (11,588 feet) can also be climbed from the pass above Granite Creek. The jeep trail to **Toms Creek** leads to a route to the head of the creek, from which Haystack Peak is about three miles south along the crest of the range; turnoff for Toms Canyon is 1.6 miles south of Callao and 8.4 miles north of the Granite Creek turnoff. A more direct route to Haystack Peak goes up through **Indian Farm Canyon.** Turnoff for this canyon is 4.3 miles south of Callao and 5.7 miles north of the Granite Creek turnoff. **Red Cedar Creek** in the heart of the Deep Creeks remains pristine—no trails, roads, or other developments. It's also very rugged; allow a day or two just to hike through one-way. Early ranchers mistook the Rocky Mountain juniper for red cedar. **Trout Creek** is another good hiking area. A trail goes most of the way up the valley.

Approaches to the peaks from the **Goshute Indian Reservation** have been used less because of travel restrictions and because this western slope is much drier. Probably the easiest way up from here is to drive though Goshute village to Fifteen Mile Creek and to hike the pack trail to the ridge between Ibapah Peak and Red Mountain, meeting the trail coming up from Granite Creek. To visit the west side you need to plan ahead and get permission from the Tribal Council, which meets once a month. Write to them at P.O. Box 6104, Ibapah, UT 84034, explaining the purpose of your trip, what you'll be doing, dates, roads and trails to be used, and the organization you're with, if any. Then, on arrival, check in at the tribal offices. For more information call the executive secretary at (435) 234-1138 or the law enforcement office at (435) 234-1139.

Information

Hikers venturing into this remote range must be self-sufficient and experienced in wilderness travel. You'll need the 7 1/2-minute Ibapah Peak and Indian Farm Creek topo maps for the central part of the range, the 7 1/2-minute Goshute and Goshute Canyon maps for the northern part, and the 15-minute Trout Creek map for the southern part. The metric 1:100,000 Fish Springs quad covers the whole area, but with less detail. For firsthand information, contact the BLM House Range Resource Area, 35 E. 500 North, Fillmore, UT 84631, (435) 743-6811. The Sierra Club book *Hiking the Great Basin,* by John Hart, has detailed trail descriptions.

All approaches to the Deep Creeks involve dirt-road travel and generally sizable distances. Some of the ways in (to the Granite Creek Road

Junction) start from Wendover and continue via Gold Hill (92 miles), from Provo via the Pony Express and Stage Route (158 miles), from Delta via the Weiss Highway (93 miles), and from U.S. 50/6 near the Utah-Nevada border via Gandy and Trout Creek (52 miles). Ibapah has the nearest gas and groceries (38 miles from the Granite Creek turnoff).

EUREKA AND TINTIC MINING DISTRICT

The lucky prospectors who cried "Eureka! I've found it!" had stumbled onto a fabulously rich deposit of silver and other valuable metals. Eureka sprang up to be one of Utah's most important cities and the center of more than a dozen mining communities. Much can still be seen of the district's long history—mine headframes and buildings, shafts and glory holes, old examples of residential and commercial architecture, great piles of ore tailings, and forlorn cemeteries. Exhibits at the Tintic Mining Museum in Eureka show what life was like. Paved highways provide easy access: from I-15 Santaquin Exit 248 (south of Provo), go west 21 miles on U.S. 6, from Delta go northeast 48 miles on U.S. 6, and from Tooele go south 54 miles on UT 36.

History

Mormon stockherders began moving cattle here during the early 1850s to take advantage of the good grazing lands. Ute Indians under Chief Tintic, for whom the district was later named, opposed the newcomers but couldn't stop them. Mineral deposits found in the hills remained a secret of the Mormons, as church policy prohibited members from prospecting for precious metals. In 1869, though, George Rust, a gentile cowboy, noted the promising ores. Soon the rush was on—ores assaying up to 10,000 ounces of silver per ton began pouring out of the mines. Silver City, founded in 1870, became the first of many mining camps. New discoveries kept the Tintic District booming. Gold, copper, lead, and zinc added to the riches. By 1910 the district had a population of 8,000 and the end was nowhere in sight. The hills shook from underground blasting and the noise of mills, smelters, and railroads. Valuable Tintic properties kept the Salt Lake Stock Exchange busy, while Salt Lake City office buildings and mansions rose with Tintic money. Mining began a slow decline in the 1930s but has continued, sporadically, to the present. Most of the old mining camps have dried up and blown away. Eureka and Mammoth drift on as sleepy towns—monuments to an earlier era.

The ghosts of former camps can be worth a visit, too, though most require considerable imagination to see them as they were. Do not go near decaying structures or mine shafts. You'll also find sites of towns that exist mostly as memories. Diligent searching through the sagebrush may uncover foundations, tailings piles, broken glass, and neglected cemeteries. Yet behind many of the sites linger dramatic stories of attempts to win riches from the earth. History buffs may want to look at the book *Faith, Hope and Prosperity: The Tintic Mining District,* by Philip Notarianni, available at the Tintic Mining Museum. Also see *The Historical Guide to Utah Ghost Towns,* by Stephen L. Carr, and *Some Dreams Die,* by George A. Thompson.

EUREKA

Mines and tailing dumps surround weather-beaten buildings. Eureka lacks the orderliness of Mormon towns; the main street snakes through the valley with side streets branching off in every direction. Few recent buildings have been added, so the town retains an authentic atmosphere from an earlier time. Eureka now has a population of about 600, down from the 3,400 of its peak years.

Tintic Mining Museum

The varied exhibits in this small museum will give you an appreciation of the district and its mining pioneers. A mineral collection from the Tintic area has many fine specimens. You'll see early mining tools, assay equipment, a mine office, courtroom, blacksmith shop, a 1920s kitchen, many historic photos, and displays that show social life in the early days. One display is dedicated to the influence of Jessie Knight, a

CHURCH OF JESUS CHRIST OF LATTER-DAY SAINTS

Eureka Mines, ca. 1900

Mormon financier and philanthropist. Knightsville, now a ghost town site near Eureka, gained fame as one of the few mining towns in Utah without a saloon or gambling hall. Knight also promoted mine safety and closed his mines for a day of rest on Sunday—both radical concepts at the time. You'll find the museum galleries upstairs in City Hall (built in 1899) and next door in the former railroad depot (1925). The *Tintic Tour Guide* sold here describes a 35-mile loop to some of the nearby ghost towns and mines. The Tintic Mining Museum, (435) 433-6842 or (435) 433-6869, is open sporadically—usually on summer weekends and some weekdays and on request at other times. Admission is free.

Bullion-Beck Mine

A large timber headframe on the west edge of town beside the highway marks one of the most productive mines in the district. John Beck arrived in 1871 and began sinking a shaft. At first people called him the "Crazy Dutchman," but the jeers ended when he hit a huge deposit of rich ore 200 feet down. The present 65-foot-high headframe dates from about 1890; originally a large wooden building enclosed it.

EUREKA VICINITY GHOST TOWNS

Dividend

Emil Raddatz bought this property on the east slope of the Tintic Mountains in 1907, believing that the ore deposits mined on the west side of

the Tintics extended to here. Raddatz nearly went broke digging deeper and deeper, but the prized silver and lead ore 1,200 feet below proved him right. After his 1916 discovery, a modern company town grew up complete with hotel, movie theater, golf course, and ice plant. The miners, whose wages had been paid partly in stock certificates, chose the name Dividend because they had been so well rewarded. Mining continued until 1949, producing $19 million in dividends, but today only foundations, mine shafts, and large piles of tailings remain. A loop road east of Eureka will take you to this site and other mining areas. Walking or driving off the road is forbidden because of mine shafts and other hazards. Though the road is paved, some sections are badly potholed and need to be driven slowly. From downtown Eureka, go east 1.5 miles on U.S. 6 and turn right on the Dividend road (0.1 mile east of Milepost 141); the road climbs into hills and passes the Eureka Lily headframe and mine on the left after 2.5 miles. Continue 0.3 mile to Tintic Standard #1 shaft on right, then 0.3 mile more to the site of Dividend and the #2 shaft (signed); the road ends at a junction 0.9 mile farther; turn left 0.7 mile to U.S. 6 (four miles east of Eureka). The Sunshine Mining Company currently operates the Burgin Mine about one mile east of Dividend.

Mammoth

Prospectors made a "mammoth" strike over the hill south of Eureka in 1870. The town of Mammoth, more mines, mills, and smelters followed.

The eccentric mining engineer George Robinson built a second town, immodestly named after himself, one mile down the valley. Both towns prospered, growing together and eventually becoming just Mammoth. Nearly 3,000 people lived here when activity peaked in 1900–1910. Then came the inevitable decline as the high-grade ores worked out. By the 1930s, Mammoth was well on its way to becoming a ghost town. People still live here and have preserved some of the old buildings. The Mammoth glory hole and mine buildings overlook the town at the head of the valley. Ruins of smelters and mines cling to hillsides. From Eureka, go southwest 2.5 miles on U.S. 6, then turn left (east) one mile on a paved road. Upper and lower towns can now be distinguished.

black-tailed jackrabbit
(Lepus californicus)

Silver City

Optimistic prospectors named their little camp for the promising silver ore, but a city it was not to be. The cost of pumping water out of the mines cut too deeply into profit margins, and a 1902 fire nearly put an end to the town. At that point Mormon financier Jessie Knight stepped in to improve the mines and rebuild the town. He also built a smelter and later a mill. Silver City reached its peak about 1908 before declining to ghost town status in the 1930s. You can't miss the giant piles of tailings (light colored) and slag (dark colored) from the smelter and mill at the old townsite. Extensive concrete foundations show the complexity and size of the operations. Sagebrush has reclaimed the rest of the town, of which only debris and foundations survive. Some diehards still mine and prospect in the area, though; a new mining operation is currently reprocessing the old smelter waste products. Silver City ghost town site lies 3.3 miles southwest of Eureka (0.8 mile past the Mammoth turnoff) just off U.S. 6.

SHEEPROCK MOUNTAINS

Black Crook Peak (elev. 9,275 feet) tops this little-known range northwest of Eureka. Sheeprock Mountain Trail (Forest Trails #051 and #052) follows the crest of the mountains for most of their length. Several other trails connect from each side. See the Uinta National Forest map and the 7¹/₂-minute Erickson Knoll, Dutch Peak,

Lookout Pass, and Vernon topo maps. Mining, which peaked in the early 1900s, still continues on a small scale for silver, lead, and zinc. Bald eagles winter here from about December to March; their numbers appear to fluctuate with the rabbit population. Anglers can try for brook and brown trout in Vernon Reservoir and Vernon and Bennion Creeks.

The small **Little Valley Campground** is open May–November; no water or charge. Benmore Experimental Pastures, northeast of the mountains, date from 1933 as a cooperative state and federal program to develop techniques of restoring and managing rangelands. Although the Sheeprock Mountains are in the Wasatch National Forest, the Spanish Fork Ranger District office of the Uinta National Forest manages this area, known as the Vernon Division, 44 W. 400 North, Spanish Fork, UT 84660, (435) 798-3571. Follow UT 36 northwest 17 miles from Eureka (or south 42 miles from Tooele) to a junction signed Benmore, just east of Vernon; turn south five miles to Benmore Guard Station, then left 2.5 miles for Vernon Reservoir. Little Valley Campground is off to the right in a side valley 2.3 miles past the reservoir. A road in via Lofgreen is a bit rough for cars. None of these roads are recommended in wet weather.

LITTLE SAHARA RECREATION AREA

Sand dunes have made a giant sandbox between Eureka and Delta. Managed by the BLM, the recreation area covers 60,000 acres of free-moving sand dunes, sagebrush flats, and juniper-covered ridges. Elevations range from about 5,000 to 5,700 feet. Varied terrain provides challenges for dune buggies, motorcycles, and four-wheel-drive vehicles. While off-road vehicles can range over most of the dunes, areas near White Sands and Jericho Campgrounds have been set aside for children. The Rockwell Natural Area in the western part of the dunes protects 9,150 acres for nature study.

The dunes originated 150 miles away as sandbars along the southern shore of Lake Bonneville roughly 10,000 years ago. After the lake receded, prevailing winds pushed the exposed sands on a slow trek northeastward at a rate of about 18 inches per year. Sand Mountain, however, deflected the winds upward, and the sand grains piled up into large dunes downwind. Lizards and kangaroo rats scamper across the sands in search of food and, in turn, are eaten by hawks, bobcats, and coyotes. Pronghorn and mule deer live here all year. Juniper, sagebrush, greasewood, saltbush, and grasses are the most common plants. An unusual species of fourwing saltbush *(Atriplex canescens)* grows as high as 12 feet and is restricted to the dunes area.

A visitors' center near the entrance is open irregular hours. Three developed **campgrounds** with water (White Sands, Oasis, and Jericho) and a primitive camping area (Sand Mountain) are open all year. In winter, water is available only at the visitors' center on the way in. Visitors to Little Sahara pay a daily $6 fee per vehicle (a pickup truck or trailer carrying off-road vehicles counts as one vehicle), which includes use of campgrounds. For more information or group camping permits, contact the BLM at 15 E. 500 North, Fillmore, UT 84631, (435) 743-6811.

The entrance road is 4.5 miles west of Jericho Junction, which lies 17 miles south of Eureka, 31 miles west of Nephi (I-15 Exits 222 and 228), or 32 miles northeast of Delta.

pronghorn (Antilocapra americana)

DELTA TO MILFORD

The barren Pahvant Valley along the lower Sevier River had long been considered a wasteland. Then, in 1905, some Fillmore businessmen purchased water rights from Sevier River Reservoir and 10,000 acres of land. The farm and town lots they sold became the center of one of Utah's most productive agricultural areas. Other hopeful homesteaders who settled farther from Delta weren't as fortunate. Thousands of families bought cheap land in the North Tract but found the going very difficult. Troubles with the irrigation system, poor crop yields, and low market prices forced most to leave by the late 1930s. A few decaying houses and farm buildings mark the sites of once-bustling communities. Farmers near Delta raise alfalfa seed and hay, wheat, corn, barley, mushrooms, and livestock. The giant coal-burning Intermountain Power Project (IPP) and the Brush Wellman beryllium mill have helped boost Delta's population to about 4,000. Miners have been digging into the Drum Mountains northwest of Delta since the 1870s for gold, silver, copper, manganese, and other minerals; some work still goes on there. The beryllium processed near Delta comes from large deposits of bertrandite mined in open pits in the Topaz and Spors Mountains farther to the northwest.

DELTA

For travelers, Delta (pop. 3,123) makes a handy base for visiting the surrounding historic sites, rockhounding, and exploring nearby mountain ranges. In downtown Delta, the **Great Basin Museum** presents a varied collection of pioneer photos and artifacts, Indian arrowheads, a Topaz Camp exhibit, fossils, and minerals; antique farm machinery stands outside. The museum is located at 328 W. 100 North (turn north one block on 300 West from Main St.), (435) 864-5013; open during the summer Mon., Wed., and Sat. 10 A.M.–4 P.M. and Tues., Thurs., and Fri. 1–4 P.M.; free.

A **pioneer log cabin** (built 1907–1908), now on Main Street in front of Delta's Municipal Building, was the second house and the first post office in Melville, which was later known as Burtner and finally as Delta in 1910. Historical markers near the cabin commemorate the Spanish Dominguez-Escalante Expedition, which passed to the south in 1776, and the Topaz Camp for Japanese Americans interned during World War II.

Rockhounding

Beautiful rock, mineral, and fossil specimens await discovery in the deserts surrounding Delta. Sought-after rocks and minerals include topaz, bixbyite, sunstones, geodes, obsidian, muscovite, garnet, pyrite, and agate. Some fossils to look for are trilobites, brachiopods, horn coral, and crinoids. The chamber of commerce in Delta is a good source of local information.

You can see gemstones from the area at **West Desert Collectors** and **Tina's Jewelry & Minerals** (see Recreation, Shopping, and Services below). Useful publications include *Guide to Rocks and Fossils,* available at the chamber of commerce, and *Collector's Guide to Mineral and Fossil Localities,* published by the Utah Geological and Mineral Survey (June 1977). A hat and plenty of water will add to your comfort and safety when enjoying the outdoors. Always be watchful when hiking to avoid rattlesnakes and mine shafts. Both are occasionally found in caves, where the dim light makes them harder to see.

Accommodations

Under $50: All of Delta's motels are on or close to Main Street. **Vans Motel,** 127 W. Main, (435) 864-2906; **Delta Inn Motel,** 347 E. Main, (435) 864-5318; and the **Budget Motel,** a half-block south of Main on 350 East, (435) 864-4533; each offer inexpensive, no-fuss rooms.

$50–75: At the east edge of town, the **Best Western Motor Inn Motel,** 527 E. Topaz Blvd. just north on U.S. 6, (435) 864-3882 or (800) 354-9378, has an indoor pool and allows pets.

Campgrounds: Kitten Klean RV Park, 181 E. Main, (435) 864-2614, has showers and is open all year; $8 tents, $15 RVs with hookups. **Antelope Valley RV Park,** 760 W. Main, (435) 864-1813, has showers and is open April 1–December 1; $12 tents, $14 RVs without hookups, $20 RVs with. **Oak Creek Campground** lies in a pretty wooded canyon in the Fishlake National Forest; sites have drinking water late May–early

October; $7. Head east 14 miles on U.S. 50 and UT 125 to Oak City, then turn right four miles on a paved road.

Food

Tops City Cafe, 313 W. Main, (435) 864-2148, serves standard American fare daily for breakfast, lunch, and dinner. The **Rancher Motel,** 171 W. Main, (435) 864-2741, has a café with American and Mexican food and a dining room upstairs serving steak and seafood; open daily for breakfast, lunch, and dinner. **Chef's Palace,** 225 E. Main, (435) 864-2421, offers steak, seafood, chicken, and a salad bar; open Mon.–Sat. for dinner only. **Jade Garden,** at the Best Western Plaza Motel, just north on U.S. 6 at the east edge of town, (435) 864-2947, has American and Chinese food; open daily for breakfast, lunch, and dinner.

Delta Valley Farms has a family restaurant two miles northeast of Delta on U.S. 6; open Mon.–Sat. for lunch. Call in advance if you'd like a tour of their cheese-making plant, (435) 864-3566.

Entertainment and Events

Catch movies at **T&T Twin Theatres** in Pendray Plaza (east end of town just north of U.S. 6 and U.S. 50 Junction), (435) 864-4551. Annual events include **Fourth of July** fireworks and demolition derby, **Pioneer Day** (parade, rodeo, games) on July 24 in Hinckley, and **Millard County Fair** (parade, horse show, games, demolition derby, and street dance) at the fairgrounds on the east side of town in early August. In September enjoy the **Classy Chassy Car Show** and the **West Millard High School Rodeo** with hundreds of contestants.

Recreation, Shopping, and Services

The indoor **West Millard County Swimming Pool** is open year-round at the corner of 200 East and 300 North, (435) 864-3133. A **city park** with picnic facilities and tennis courts is at the corner of Main and 100 West; restrooms are in the nearby municipal building. **Sunset View Golf Course** offers nine holes three miles northeast of town on U.S. 6, (435) 864-2508. **Gunnison Bend Park** west of town has picnicking, waterskiing, and fishing (catfish and largemouth bass); go west 2.5 miles on U.S. 50/6, then right two miles. **West Desert Collectors,** 278 W. Main, (435) 864-2175, has beautiful rocks, minerals,

and fossils. **Tina's Jewelry & Minerals,** 320 E. Main, (435) 864-2444, offers beautiful gems.

The **post office** is at the corner of 300 East and 100 South, (435) 864-2811. **Delta Community Medical Center** provides emergency care at 126 S. White Sage Avenue (south off U.S. 50 on the east side of town), (435) 864-5591. In **emergencies** (police, fire, or medical), call 911.

Information

Delta Chamber of Commerce will tell you about services in town and sights in the surrounding area. The office is in the municipal building at Main and 200 West (80 N. 200 West, Delta, UT 84624), (435) 864-4316; open Mon.–Fri. 10 A.M.–5 P.M. The **public library,** also in the municipal building, (435) 864-4945, is open Monday–Friday 2–8 P.M. and Saturday 1–5 P.M.

BAKER HOT SPRINGS

Though Crater Springs Health Resort, north of Delta, has closed, local people still come here to soak in the hot springs. Water emerges from the ground at near boiling temperatures and flows into two surviving concrete tubs. The springs also feed shallow ponds that feature colorful mineral deposits and strange-looking algae growths. Easiest way from Delta is to go northeast 11 miles on U.S. 6, turn left (west) 19 miles on the paved Brush Wellman Road, then right (north) seven miles on a dirt road along a large black lava flow. Springs are on the right. Ruts may make this dry-weather-only road difficult for cars. (You can save about nine miles from Delta if you can navigate the maze of farm roads between the west edge of Delta and the Brush Wellman Road.) Adventurous motorists can also follow dirt roads from Baker Hot Springs north and east 35 miles to Little Sahara Recreation Area.

CANYON MOUNTAINS

East of Delta, the **Oak Creek Campground** lies along the creek amid Gambel oak, cottonwood, maple, and juniper on the west side of the mountains. Canyon walls cut by Oak Creek reveal layers of twisted and upturned rock. This Forest Service Campground (elev. 5,900 feet) has water from late May to early October ($6 for family sites). Groups can reserve a large area with amphitheater, sports area, and shelter. Oak Creek usually has good fishing for rainbow trout. Much of its flow comes from a spring at the upper end of the campground. From Delta go east 14 miles on U.S. 50 and UT 125 to the small farming town of Oak City, then turn right four miles on a paved road. A gravel road continues upcanyon past the campground to other forest roads and hiking trails; see the Fishlake National Forest map. Unpaved roads also provide access to the steeper east side of the Canyon Mountains. Fool Creek Peak tops this small range at 9,717 feet. For more information, contact the Fillmore Ranger District office at 390 S. Main in Fillmore (P.O. Box 265, Fillmore, UT 84631), (435) 743-5721.

WEST OF DELTA

Topaz Camp
Topaz is easily Utah's most dispirited ghost town site. Other ghost towns had the promise of precious metals or good land to lure their populations, but those coming to Topaz had no choice—they had the bad fortune to be of the wrong ancestry during the height of World War II hysteria. About 9,000 Japanese—most of whom were American citizens—were brought from the West Coast to this desolate desert plain in 1942. Topaz sprang up in just a few months and included barracks, communal dining halls, post office, hospital, schools, churches, and recreational facilities. Most internees cooperated with authorities; the few who caused trouble were shipped off to a more secure camp. Barbed wire and watchtowers with armed guards surrounded the small city—which was actually Utah's fifth-largest community for a time. All internees were released at war's end in 1945 and the camp came down almost as quickly as it had gone up. Salvagers bought and removed equipment, buildings, barbed wire, telephone poles, and even street paving and sewer pipes. An uneasy silence pervades the site today. Little more than the streets, foundations, and piles of rubble remain. You can still walk or drive along the streets of the vast camp, which had 42 neatly laid-out blocks. A concrete memorial stands at the northwest corner of the site.

One way to get here is to go west six miles from Delta on U.S. 50/6 to the small town of Hinckley, turn right (north) 4.5 miles on a paved road (some parts are gravel) to its end, turn left (west) 2.5 miles on a paved road to its end in Abraham, turn right (north) 1.5 miles on a gravel road to a stop sign, then turn left three miles on a gravel road; Topaz is on the left.

Drum Mountains
Strange subterranean noises can sometimes be heard in these desert mountains; some say the sounds are like the thumps or rumblings of a drum. Prospectors began combing the parched hillsides in 1872 but did little mining development. Harry Joy and Charles Howard, mining engineers from Michigan, organized the Detroit Mining District here in 1879. They dug for gold, silver, and copper and built a smelter. Mining centered on the small town of **Joy.** Crumbling foundations are all that remain of the townsite, though you can find dilapidated mine buildings in nearby canyons. Western States Minerals has an active gold mine in the Drums. You can reach the mountains by continuing west from Topaz or from U.S. 6 on the paved Brush Wellman Road.

House Range
This range about 45 miles west of Delta offers great vistas, scenic drives, wilderness hiking,

on their way to Topaz

and world-famous trilobite fossil beds. Swasey Peak (elev. 9,669 feet) is the highest point. From a distance, however, Notch Peak's spectacular 2,700-foot face stands out as the most prominent landmark in the region. What the 50-mile-long range lacks in great heights, it makes up for in massive sheer limestone cliffs and rugged canyons. Precipitous drops on the western side contrast with a gentler slope on the east. Hardy vegetation such as juniper, piñon pine, mountain mahogany, and sagebrush dominates the dry slopes. Bristlecone pines grow on the high ridges of Swasey and Notch Peaks; the long-lived trees are identified by inward-curving bristles on the cones and by needles less than 1.5 inches long in clusters of five. Some of the high country also harbors limber pine, ponderosa pine, white fir, Douglas fir, and aspen.

Wildlife includes mule deer, pronghorn, chukar partridge, bald and golden eagles, and peregrine falcon. Wild horses roam Sawmill Basin to the northeast of Swasey Peak. Permanent water supplies are found only at a few scattered springs in the range. Limestone caves attract spelunkers, especially Antelope Spring Cave near Dome Canyon Pass (ask directions at the BLM office in Fillmore or from the Speleological Society of Utah). Council Cave on Antelope Peak (between Notch and Swasey Peaks) has an enormous opening, visible for more than 50 miles.

Mining in the range has a long history. Stories tell of finding old Spanish gold mines with iron tools in them that crumbled at a touch. More recent mining for tungsten and gold has occurred on the east side of Notch Peak. Outlaws found the range a convenient area to hide out; Tatow Knob (north of Swasey Peak), for example, was a favorite spot for horse thieves. Death Canyon got its name after a group of pioneers became trapped and froze to death; most maps now show it as Dome Canyon.

Driving in the House Range: The dirt roads here can be surprisingly good. Often you can zip along as if on pavement, but watch for loose gravel, large rocks, flash floods, and deep ruts that sometimes appear on these backcountry stretches. Roads easily passable by car connect to make a 43-mile loop through Marjum and Dome Canyon Passes. You'll have good views of the peaks and go through scenic canyons on the west side of both passes. Drivers with high-clearance vehicles can branch off on old mining roads or drive past Antelope Spring to Sinbad Overlook for views and hiking near Swasey Peak.

Shale beds near Antelope Spring have given up an amazing quantity and variety of **trilobite fossils** dating from about 500 million years ago. Professional collectors have leased a trilobite quarry, so you'll have to collect outside. Trilobites can also be found near Swasey Spring and near Marjum Pass. Flat-edged rock hammers work best to split open the shale layers.

During World War I, a hermit took a liking to the House Range and built a one-room cabin in a small cave, where he lived until his death. He entertained visitors with a special home brew. Walk a quarter-mile up a small side canyon from the road to see the cabin, which is on the right side of the road that comes down to the west from Marjum Pass.

Several roads connect U.S. 50/6 with the loop through Marjum and Dome Canyon Passes. Going west from Delta on U.S. 50/6, you have the choice of the following turnoffs: after 10 miles, turn right 25 miles at the fork for the unpaved old U.S. 50/6; or after 32 miles, turn right 10 miles on a road signed Antelope Spring; or after 42 miles, turn right 16 miles on a road also signed Antelope Spring; or after 63 miles (30 miles east of the Utah-Nevada border), turn right 14 miles on a road signed Painter Spring.

Hiking in the House Range: Most hiking routes go cross-country through the wilderness. Springs are very far apart and sometimes polluted, so carry water for the whole trip. Bring topo maps and a compass; help can be a long way off if you make a wrong turn. Because of the light precipitation, the hiking season at the high elevations can last from late April to late November. You can visit most destinations, including Swasey and Notch Peaks, on a day hike. These peaks offer fantastic views over nearly all of west-central Utah and into Nevada. For more information on the House Range, contact the BLM office at 35 E. 500 North in Fillmore (P.O. Box 778, Fillmore, UT 84631), (435) 743-6811.

The trip to **Swasey Peak** makes a good half-day hike and is usually done as a loop. Total distance for the moderately difficult trip is about 4.5 miles with a 1,700-foot elevation gain to the summit (elev. 9,669 feet). Drive to the Antelope Spring turnoff, 2.5 miles east of Dome Canyon

view north from Swasey Peak

Pass, and follow the well-used Sinbad Overlook road 3.3 miles, passing the spring and trilobite area, up a steep grade to a large meadow below Swasey Peak. Cautiously driven cars might be able to get up this road, though it's safer to park low-clearance vehicles and walk the last 1.5 miles. (Nonhikers with suitable vehicles will enjoy driving to Sinbad Overlook for views at the end of the road.) From the large meadow at the top of the grade, head northeast on foot up the ridge, avoiding cliffs to the left. After one and a quarter miles you'll reach a low summit; continue one-half mile along the ridgeline, curving west toward Swasey Peak. To complete the loop, descend one-half mile to the northwest along a ridge to bypass some cliffs, then head southwest three quarters of a mile to the end of Sinbad Overlook road.

From here it's an easy 1.5 miles by road back to the start; Sinbad Spring and a grove of ponderosa pines are about halfway. No signs or trails mark the route, but hikers experienced with maps shouldn't have any trouble. Topo maps for this hike are the 7 1/2-minute Marjum Pass and Swasey Peak. Route-finding is easier when hiking the loop in the direction described. You'll get a close look at the mountain mahogany on Swasey Peak—some thickets of this stout shrub have to be crossed; wear long pants to protect your legs.

The 2,700-foot sheer rock wall on the western face of prominent **Notch Peak** is only 300 feet shorter than El Capitán in Yosemite. Most hikers prefer the far easier summit route on the other side via Sawtooth Canyon. This moderately difficult canyon route is about nine miles round-trip and has a 1,700-foot elevation gain. Bring water, as no springs are in the area. Like the Drum Mountains, Notch Peak has a reputation for strange underground noises. The 15-minute Notch Peak topo map is needed as much for navigating the roads to the trailhead as for the hiking. First take Antelope Spring Road to the signed turnoff for Miller Canyon, 4.5 miles north of Milepost 46 on U.S. 50/6 (42 miles west of Delta) and 11.5 miles south of old U.S. 50/6 (35 miles west of Delta). Turn west 5.3 miles on Miller Canyon Road, then bear left to Sawtooth Canyon at a road fork.

A stone cabin 2.5 miles farther on the right marks the trailhead. The cabin is owned and used by people who mine in the area. Follow a rough road on foot into Sawtooth Canyon. After three quarters of a mile the canyon widens where two tributaries meet; take the left fork in the direction of Notch Peak. A few spots in the dry creekbed require some rock-scrambling. Be on the lookout for flash floods if thunderstorms threaten.

After about three miles the wash becomes less distinct; continue climbing to a saddle visible ahead. From there, a short but steep quarter-mile scramble takes you to the top of 9,655-foot Notch Peak and its awesome drop-offs. Other ways up Notch Peak offer challenges for the adventurous. The other fork of Sawtooth Canyon can be used, for example, and a jeep road through Amasa Valley provides a northern approach.

Confusion Range

The Confusions lie in a long, jumbled mass west of the House Range. The sparse vegetation consists largely of piñon pine, juniper, sagebrush, shadscale, and cheatgrass. Some Douglas fir grow on the King Top Plateau, the highest area in the Confusion Range, where elevations reach

8,300 feet. Shortages of water and feed allow only small numbers of wild horses, pronghorn, deer, and smaller animals to eke out an existence.

Fossil Mountain in the southeast part of the Confusions has an exceptional diversity of marine fossils, many very rare. Thirteen fossil groups of ancient sea creatures have been found in rocks of early Ordovician age (350–400 million years ago). Fossil Mountain stands 6,685 feet high on the west edge of Blind Valley. A signed road to Blind Valley turns south off U.S. 50/6 between Mileposts 38 and 39 (54 miles west of Delta). Fossil Mountain is about 14 miles south of the highway.

SOUTH OF DELTA

Fort Deseret

What remains of this fort represents a fading piece of pioneer history. Mormon settlers hastily built the adobe-walled fort in only 18 days in 1865 for protection against Indians during the Black Hawk War. The square fort had walls 550 feet long and 10 feet high with gates in the middle of each side. Bastions were located at the northeast and southwest corners. Indians never attacked the fort, but it came in handy for penning up cattle at night. Parts of the wall and stone foundation still stand. From Delta go west five miles on U.S. 50/6, then turn left (south) 4.5 miles on UT 257. The site is on the west side of the road near Milepost 65, about 1.5 miles south of the town of Deseret.

Great Stone Face

A natural rock formation seven miles southwest of Deseret bears a striking resemblance to the Mormon prophet Joseph Smith. To see the profile you have to view the rock from the west. From the town of Deseret, go south three miles on UT 257, then turn right (west) four miles (should be signed) on a dirt road. A short hike at road's end leads up a lava flow to the stone face.

Clear Lake State
Waterfowl Management Area

Lakes and marsh country offer ducks, Canada geese, and other birds a refreshing break from the desert. Roads cross Clear Lake on a causeway and lead to smaller lakes and picnic areas to the north. The Utah Division of Wildlife Re-

sources manages the area. From the junction of U.S. 50/6 and UT 257 west of Delta, go south 15.5 miles on UT 257, then turn left (east) seven miles on a good gravel road.

Pahvant Butte

Locally known as Sugar Loaf Mountain, this extinct volcano rises 1,000 feet above the desert floor. Waters of prehistoric Lake Bonneville leveled off the large terrace about halfway up. Remnants of a crater, now open to the southwest, are on this level. Another terrace line is at the bottom of the butte. Hikers can enjoy the volcanic geology, expansive panoramas, and a visit to the curious ruins of a windmill. Construction of the wind-powered electric power station began in 1923 but was never completed. A large underground room and two concentric rings of concrete pylons give an eerie Stonehenge-like atmosphere to the butte.

Easiest way up is an old road on the south side that goes to the windmill site. From Clear Lake, continue east 3.3 miles to the second signed turn on the left for Pahvant Butte (Pahvant Butte Road: 3 miles, Sugarloaf Well #1: 8 miles). Turn left 3.5 miles at the sign, then turn left one-half mile on Pahvant Butte Road. Park before the road begins a steep climb. Daredevils in four-wheel drives have tried going straight up the slope from here, but the real road turns right and follows switchbacks 0.7 mile to the windmill site. This last 0.7 mile is closed to vehicles because of the soft volcanic rock, but it's fine for walking; elevation gain is about 400 feet. Pahvant Butte's highest point is about a half mile to the north and 265 feet higher; you'll have to find your own way across if headed there. Dirt roads encircle Pahvant Butte and go northeast to U.S. 50 and southeast to Tabernacle Hill and Fillmore. The Tabernacle Hill area provides good examples of volcanic features.

MILFORD

Miners on their way to Frisco and Newhouse crossed the Beaver River at a ford below a stamp mill, so Milford seemed the logical name for the town that grew up here. Most of Milford's businesses in the early days supplied the mining camps. Today the town serves as a center for the railroad, nearby farms, and a geothermal plant. Steam from wells at the Blundell Geothermal Plant, 13 miles northeast of town, produces electricity for Utah Power and Light. Travelers heading west will find Milford their last stop for supplies before the Nevada border. Milford (pop. 1,305) is at the junction of UT 21 and UT 257, 77 miles south of Delta and 32 miles east of Beaver. Baker, Nevada, is 96 miles northwest.

Accommodations
Under $50: In Milford, the **Station Motel,** at the corner of 100 West and 500 South, (435) 387-2482, has basic rooms, and the **Station Restaurant,** (435) 387-2804, is open daily for breakfast, lunch, and dinner.

Other Practicalities
The **city park** at 300 South and 200 West has a picnic area. An **outdoor pool** is behind the high school at 141 N. 200 West, (435) 387-2315. **Pavilion Park** has a free camping area just beyond the high school grounds on 300 West, open year-round with water. Milford's five-hole **golf course,** on the west edge of town (about 1000 South and 700 West), (435) 387-2711 (city office), is open April 1–October 31. The **post office** is at 458 S. Main. **Milford Valley Memorial Hospital** is at 451 N. Main, (435) 387-2411. **Milford City office,** 302 S. Main (P.O. Box 69, Milford, UT 84751), (435) 387-2711, can answer questions about the area Monday–Friday 8 A.M.–3 P.M. During the summer you can obtain area information in the old caboose at 46 S. Main. The **public library,** 400 S. 100 West, (435) 387-5039, is open weekday afternoons.

Rock Corral Campground and Pass Road
The BLM has a campground and picnic area east of Milford in the Mineral Mountains, a popular area for rockhounding; no water or fee. From UT 21 on the southeast edge of Milford, turn east 5.5 miles on Pass Road, then left (north) 5.2 miles. Returning to Pass Road, you can continue east 13.4 miles over the Mineral Mountains and loop back to UT 21 between Mileposts 102 and 103 4.8 miles west of Beaver. Pass Road has a gravel surface with a dirt section near the pass.

MINERSVILLE STATE PARK

The 1,130-acre reservoir here has good year-round fishing for rainbow trout and smallmouth bass (ice fishing in winter). Be sure to check with the rangers for information about fishing regulations for the park. Bait fishing is not allowed and there are special catch limits. Most people come here to fish, though some visitors go sailing or water-skiing. Park facilities include picnic tables, campsites (all with electric and water hookups), restrooms with showers, paved boat ramp, fish-cleaning station, and dump station. Fees are $4 for day use, $13 for sites in the campground with water and electric hookups, $11 for sites in the overflow area. Reservations are a good idea on summer holidays. In winter the restrooms may be closed but water is available. For information about the park, write P.O. Box 1531, Beaver, UT 84713, (435) 438-5472 or (800) 322-3770 (reservations). Minersville Reservoir lies just off UT 21 in a sage- and juniper-covered valley eight miles east of Minersville, 18 miles southeast of Milford, and 14 miles west of Beaver.

SAN FRANCISCO MOUNTAINS AND GHOST TOWNS

Frisco Peak (elev. 9,660 feet) crowns this small range northwest of Milford. The Wah Wah Valley and Mountains lie to the west. Silver strikes in the San Francisco Mountains in the 1870s led to the opening of many mines and the founding of the towns of Newhouse and Frisco. By 1920 the best ores had given out and both communities turned to ghosts. A jeep road goes to the summit of Frisco Peak.

Frisco
The Horn Silver Mine, developed in 1876 at the south end of the San Francisco Mountains, was the first of several prolific silver producers. Smelters, and charcoal ovens to fuel them, sprouted up to process the ore. A wild boomtown developed as miners flocked to the new diggings. The railroad reached Frisco in 1880 and later extended to nearby Newhouse. Frisco's population of 6,000 included quite a few gamblers and other

shady characters. Twenty-three saloons labored to serve the thirsty customers. Gunfights became almost a daily ritual for a while, keeping the cemetery growing. But it all came to an end early in 1885, when rumblings echoed from deep within the Horn Silver Mine between shifts. The foreman luckily delayed sending the next crew down, and a few minutes later the whole mine collapsed with a deafening roar that broke windows in Milford, 15 miles away. Out of work, most of the miners and business people moved on. More than $60 million in silver and other valuable ores had come out of the ground in the mine's 10 frenzied years. Some mining has been done on and off since, but Frisco has died.

Today Frisco is one of Utah's best-preserved mining ghosts, with about a dozen stone or wood buildings surviving. A headframe and mine buildings, still intact, overlook the town from the hillside. Five beehive-shaped charcoal kilns stand on the east edge of Frisco. You can see the kilns and the townsite if you look north from UT 21 (between Mileposts 62 and 63) 15 miles west of Milford. Dirt roads wind their way in. A historical marker for Frisco is at the turnoff for the town; turnoff for the beehive kilns is 0.3 mile east. Hiking off the roads can be very dangerous near the old mines and time-worn buildings.

Newhouse

Prospectors discovered silver deposits in 1870 on the southwest side of the San Francisco Mountains but lacked the funds to develop them. Mining didn't take off until 1900, when Samuel Newhouse financed operations. A sizable town grew here as ore worth $3.5 million came out of the Cactus Mine. Citizens maintained a degree of law and order not found in most mining towns: even the saloon and the working girls had to operate outside the community. Deposits of rich ore ran out only 10 years later and the town's inhabitants departed. The railroad depot was moved to a nearby ranch and other buildings went to Milford. Today, Newhouse is a ghostly site with about half a dozen concrete or stone buildings standing in ruins. Foundations of a smelter, mill, other structures, railroad grades, and lots of broken glass remain. A good dirt road turns north two miles to the site from UT 21 (between Mileposts 57 and 58) 20 miles west of Milford.

WAH WAH MOUNTAINS

Beyond the San Francisco Mountains, the Wah Wah Mountains extend south about 55 miles in a continuation of the Confusion Range. Elevation ranges from 6,000 to more than 9,000 feet. The name comes from a Paiute Indian term for salty or alkaline seeps. Sparse sagebrush, juniper, and piñon pine cover most of the land. Aspen, white fir, ponderosa pine, and bristlecone pine grow in the high country. Mule deer, pronghorn, and smaller animals roam the mountains. Carry water, maps, and a compass into this wild country. Few people visit the Wah Wahs despite their pristine ecosystem. A 1986 BLM publication reported an estimated 155 visitor days per year for recreation in the Wah Wah Mountains Wilderness Study Area, which includes the northern and central parts of the range. That's an average of less than half a person per day!

Crystal Peak

This snow-white pinnacle in the north end of the Wah Wah Mountains stands out as a major landmark. The soft white rock of the peak is tuff from an ancient volcano thought to predate the block-faulted Wah Wahs. The best way to climb the peak (elev. 7,106 feet) is to ascend the ridge just south of it from the east, then follow the ridge northeast up the peak. Be careful of soft, crumbly rock. See the 15-minute Crystal Peak topo map for details.

Central Section

The heart of the Wah Wahs has some fine scenery and opportunities for nature study. Rugged cliffs mark the west edge of the range. A good hiking route begins at about 6,600 feet in elevation at the end of a dirt road going up Pierson Cove. Follow the dry wash upstream a short way to a split in the drainage, then take the left fork north through a canyon. After about two miles you'll come out of the canyon onto a high plateau. For the best views, turn northwest and continue climbing three quarters of a mile to the summit of an 8,918-foot peak. See the 15-minute Wah Wah Summit topo map for back roads and hiking routes.

GREAT BASIN NATIONAL PARK

Lehman Caves and Wheeler Peak lie just across the Nevada border in Nevada's only national park. Lehman Caves, a national monument since 1922, has long been known for its beautiful formations. Wheeler Peak (elev. 13,063 feet), with its glacial features, alpine lakes, forests, and great views, stands as one of the best examples of the Great Basin Mountains. Legislation in 1986 joined the caves and peak to form Great Basin National Park. The 6,200-foot difference in elevation between the upper Sonoran Desert and the alpine tundra on Wheeler Peak encompasses the region's full spectrum of plant and wildlife habitats.

Lehman Caves

Long ago, underground heat turned layers of limestone on the east side of Wheeler Peak into marble. Much later, the caves formed as water containing carbon dioxide slowly worked into cracks and dissolved the rock. After the under-

ground chambers had partly drained, stalactites, stalagmites, and other features typical of limestone caves began to grow. Indians knew about the caves in times past but didn't venture beyond the entrance room. A rancher named Absalom Lehman became the first to explore the wonders within. He'd come to the area about 1869 to try his hand at ranching and raising fruit, knowing that nearby mining camps would provide a good market. Some trees from his orchard still grow in front of the park's visitors' center. Word of the cave system spread quickly after its discovery in 1885; hundreds of sight-seers arrived in the first year. Lehman guided many of the visitors until his death in 1891.

Visitors' Center

Cave entrance, exhibits, bookshop, café/gift shop, and park headquarters sit in a piñon pine and juniper woodland on the east slope of Wheeler Peak. Views at the 6,825-foot elevation look over valleys and ranges of western Utah. A short film and exhibits introduce the geology of Lehman Caves and illustrate cave formations, flora, wildlife, and human history of the park. You can purchase books, topo maps, postcards, slides, and other interpretive materials here. **Rhodes Cabin,** just north of the visitors' center, has additional historical and natural history exhibits. **Mountain View Nature Trail** begins a half-mile loop here; pick up a trail guide at the visitors' center. You can plan your own nature hikes with materials in Family Adventure Packs available at the visitors' center information desk. In summer, rangers give evening programs nightly in two of the campgrounds and lead nature walks and hikes; check the posted schedule for locations and times. The visitors' center is open daily 8 A.M.–5 P.M. (7:30 A.M.–6 P.M. Memorial Day–Labor Day weekends) except on New Year's Day, Thanksgiving, and Christmas. The only fees charged are for the cave tour and campsites. From Baker, Nevada (just west of the Utah-Nevada line and five miles south of U.S. 50/6), head west five miles to the visitors' center. The park is about 106 miles west of Delta. Contact the Great Basin National Park at Baker, NV 89311, (775) 234-7331.

Cave Tours

Ranger-led tours begin daily (except on the holidays noted above) from the visitors' center 8 A.M.–5 P.M. The schedule has frequent departures (hourly, on the hour) in summer, decreasing to four tours a day in winter. In summer you can also take a daily candlelight tour of the cave and see it much as Ab Lehman did. The cave's cool interior (50° F) comes as a welcome relief from desert heat, and a jacket or sweater is recommended.

There are three tours offered, 30 minutes (which visits the front cave only), 60 minutes, and 90 minutes. Adults tickets are $2/$4/$6 respectively. Don't forget that Nevada is on Pacific time, one hour earlier than Utah.

Wheeler Peak Scenic Drive

Cars can drive this 12-mile paved road from near the visitors' center to Wheeler Peak Campground (elev. 9,880 feet) from about late May–October. It's not recommended for trailers or large RVs to go past Upper Lehman Creek Campground. You'll pass Lower Lehman Creek Campground two miles in and Upper Lehman Creek Campground 0.6 mile farther. Once past the camps, you'll enjoy great panoramas to the east and north, then, as the road swings around, of Wheeler Peak itself. Attractions include the Osceola gold mining ditch (reached by a one-third-mile trail), Mather Overlook, Wheeler Peak Overlook, and hiking trails. Wildflowers bloom profusely beginning at lower elevations in spring and progressing to the high country by late summer.

Hiking Trails

Glaciers and streams have carved sheer cliffs and rugged canyons into lofty **Wheeler Peak.** A ridge that extends north and south from the sum-

mit has many peaks exceeding 11,000 feet. Hikers can climb to Wheeler Peak's summit on the **Wheeler Peak Trail** from Summit Trailhead (elev. 10,161 feet), just before Wheeler Peak Campground. The strenuous trip takes 6–8 hours for the 10 miles to the top and back. **Alpine Lakes Loop Trail** offers an easier hike of three miles past beautiful Stella and Teresa Lakes. The trail, great for families, begins near the entrance to Wheeler Peak Campground; elevation gain is 400 feet.

Bristlecone Pine Trail branches off the Alpine Lakes Loop Trail between the trailhead and Teresa Lake, then winds around to a glacial moraine and a pine grove, four miles round-trip from the trailhead with a 500-foot elevation gain. **Wheeler Peak Rock Glacier & Icefield Trail** continues about one mile past the bristlecone-

© AVALON TRAVEL PUBLISHING, INC.

pine grove to a spectacular cirque below Wheeler Peak. A layer of broken rock covers the lower icefield—hence the term "rock glacier." A sign warns where hiking farther would be dangerous due to rock avalanches. The hike is six miles round-trip from the trailhead with about a 1,000-foot elevation gain. Hikers on the easy, four-mile (one-way) **Lehman Creek Trail** cross four life zones from spruce, fir, and aspen forests to cactus and sage 2,100 feet lower; most people arrange to be dropped off at the upper trailhead on the far side of Wheeler Peak Campground and picked up in Upper Lehman Creek Campground below. The **Baker and Snake Creek drainages** in the park's central section have longer trails, good for day hikes or backpacking trips.

Lexington Arch spans an opening 120 feet wide and 75 feet high in the southern section of the park; the arch has the unusual feature of being limestone instead of the sandstone found in most other arches of the Southwest. Drive to Garrison, Utah, continue southeast on UT 21 to Milepost 6, and turn right 12 miles on a dirt road (high-clearance vehicles recommended) to the trailhead. The hike to Lexington Arch in Arch Canyon is two miles round-trip with a 1,000-foot elevation gain; trailhead elevation is 7,440 feet. Maps, trail descriptions, and backcountry permits are available at the visitors' center; you can purchase the colorful book *Trails to Explore in Great Basin National Park* here; it contains trail descriptions, topo maps, flora and fauna illustrations, and background information.

Baker Village Archaeology Site

Fremont Indians lived in the Snake Valley about 1,000 years ago, leaving what appears to be an exceptionally large village at this site seven miles east of Great Basin National Park. Full-scale excavations began in the summer of 1991 by the Brigham Young University Archaeological Field School in a cooperative effort with the Ely District of the BLM and White Pine Public Museum (Ely). Visitors have been able to tour the site and see archaeologists at work during past summers and may be able to visit in the future, too. Ask at the Great Basin National Park or the Ely District BLM office, (775) 289-1800.

Accommodations

Under $50: The small town of **Baker** has a few accommodations and restaurants. **Silver Jack Motel,** (775) 234-7323, is open April–October. **Whispering Elm Motel & RV Park,** (435) 234-7343, has rooms, campsites, and a gas station/grocery store. The **"Y,"** on U.S. 50/6 at the NV 487 turnoff for Baker, (775) 234-7223, has RV spaces and a restaurant open Monday–Saturday for breakfast, lunch, and dinner.

Campgrounds: In the park, with distances from the visitors' center, are the following campgrounds: Lower Lehman Creek (two miles; open year-round; elev. 7,500 feet); Upper Lehman Creek (2.6 miles; open mid-May–mid-Oct.; elev. 7,800 feet); Wheeler Peak (12 miles; open mid-June–mid-Sept.; 9,880 feet); Baker Creek (3 miles; open mid-May–mid-Sept.; elev. 8,000 feet); and Snake Creek (23 miles; open mid-May–late Sept.; elev. 7,800 feet). All the campgrounds except Snake Creek have drinking water and charge a $7 fee.

Other Practicalities

Lehman Caves Gifts and Cafe at the visitors' center is open for breakfast and lunch April–October. Picnic grounds are just a short distance away.

The **Outlaw Cafe** serves lunch and dinner daily.

CENTRAL UTAH

In many ways, the geography and history of central Utah are extensions of the northern part of the state. The rugged Wasatch Range continues to act as an eastern boundary to the spread of the state's largest municipalities, which cluster at the base of the range. Here, smaller mountains and hills form a transition to the basin and range terrain to the west. The mountains of the Wasatch Range are steeper and higher than those to the north, perhaps even more majestic, and likely to be coated with snow. Just two years after the founding of Salt Lake City, Mormon pioneers began settling both this area and the Wasatch Plateau south of the range. Quiet Mormon villages occupy much of the lower country today.

PROVO

Utah's second-largest city (pop. 110,000) has a striking setting on the shore of Utah Lake beneath the west face of the Wasatch Range. Provo is best known as the home of Brigham Young University (BYU), a large, dynamic school sponsored by the Mormon Church. Museums and cultural events on the BYU campus make it a popular destination.

Provo also contains a rich architectural heritage. At the turn of the 20th century, this hardworking young city constructed its civic buildings with style and substance, and its residential areas are filled with Victorian mansions and vernacular workers' homes. The visitors' center can provide two self-guided tour brochures to the city's historic architecture.

Provo boasts one of the most majestic views of any of the Wasatch Front cities, perhaps contributing to the city's high marks in many publications' "livability" ratings. It also offers a university town's full selection of cultural and sporting events, easy access to water sports, fishing, hiking, and skiing, and a relatively low crime rate.

History
In 1776, members of the Dominguez-Escalante Expedition visited the Utah Valley, where Provo now sits, and sent back glowing reports of fertile soil, plentiful game, and beautiful countryside. The Spanish friars who led the group had hoped to return and establish missions for the local Indians, but political decisions prevented them from doing so. The expedition had friendly relations with the Ute Indians (known here as the "Timpanogotzis"), as did most later mountain men and early Mormon settlers. Fur trappers included

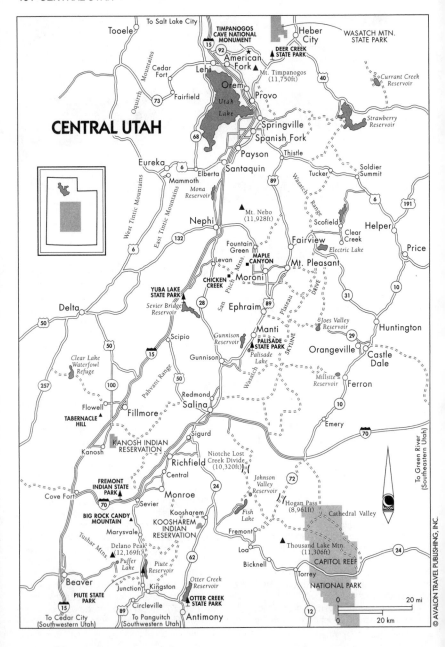

CENTRAL UTAH

To Salt Lake City

Tooele

TIMPANOGOS CAVE NATIONAL MONUMENT

WASATCH MTN. STATE PARK

Heber City

DEER CREEK STATE PARK

American Fork

Mt. Timpanogos (11,750ft)

Currant Creek Reservoir

Cedar Fort

Lehi

Oquirrh Mountains

Fairfield

Orem

Provo

Utah Lake

Strawberry Reservoir

Springville

Spanish Fork

Eureka

Payson

Thistle

Santaquin

Tucker

Soldier Summit

Elberta

Mammoth

Mona Reservoir

Mt. Nebo (11,928ft)

Scofield

Clear Creek

Helper

Nephi

Fountain Green

Fairview

Electric Lake

Price

Levan

MAPLE CANYON

MT. PLEASANT

CHICKEN CREEK

Moroni

San Pitch Mtns.

YUBA LAKE STATE PARK

Sevier Bridge Reservoir

Ephraim

Joes Valley Reservoir

Delta

Scipio

Gunnison Reservoir

Manti

PALISADE STATE PARK

Huntington

Gunnison

Palisade Lake

Orangeville

Castle Dale

Clear Lake Waterfowl Refuge

Pahvant Range

Redmond

Millsite Reservoir

Ferron

Flowell

Salina

Sigurd

Fillmore

TABERNACLE HILL

KANOSH INDIAN RESERVATION

Emery

Kanosh

Richfield

Niotche Lost Creek Divide (10,320ft)

Johnson Valley Reservoir

Central

FREMONT INDIAN STATE PARK

Cove Fort

Monroe

Sevier

Koosharem

Fish Lake

Hogan Pass (8,961ft)

Cathedral Valley

BIG ROCK CANDY MOUNTAIN

KOOSHAREM INDIAN RESERVATION

Marysvale

Tushar Mtns.

Delano Peak (12,169ft)

Fremont

Loa

Thousand Lake Mtn. (11,306ft)

CAPITOL REEF

Puffer Lake

Piute Reservoir

Bicknell

Beaver

PIUTE STATE PARK

Junction

Kingston

Otter Creek Reservoir

Torrey

NATIONAL PARK

To Green River (Southeastern Utah)

To Cedar City (Southwestern Utah)

Circleville

OTTER CREEK STATE PARK

Antimony

To Panguitch (Southwestern Utah)

0   20 mi

0   20 km

© AVALON TRAVEL PUBLISHING, INC.

PROVO WINTER OLYMPIC VENUES

The **Seven Peaks Hockey Arena,** 1330 East 300 North, plays host to the women's and some of the men's ice hockey competition.

Etienne Provost, a French Canadian who passed through in 1824 and 1825. His Anglicized name was adopted in 1849 when Mormons arrived in the Utah Valley to start their first settlement. Within the next two years, the communities of Lehi, Pleasant Grove, American Fork, Springville, and Payson also sprang up in the valley. Geneva Steel and other major industries established during the World War II years transformed the Provo area from an agrarian landscape to the major urban center it is today. The downtown business district, though, still features many distinctive buildings from the turn of the century and earlier.

BRIGHAM YOUNG UNIVERSITY

The university had a modest beginning in 1875 as the Brigham Young Academy, established under the direction of Mormon Church President Brigham Young. Like the rest of Provo, BYU's population and size have grown dramatically in recent decades. BYU is one of the largest church-affiliated schools in the world. Students aren't required to be Mormons, but about 95 percent of the student body of 29,000 do belong to the LDS Church. High academic standards upheld by students and faculty have made the university a leader in many fields. Everyone attending the school must follow a strict dress and grooming code—something you'll notice immediately on a stroll across the modern campus.

Exhibits and concerts are held in the **Harris Fine Arts Center** (just north of the Wilkinson Center) and other locations on campus, (801) 378-7444 (music ticket office) or (801) 378-4322 (theater performances). BYU also goes all out to support its Cougars football and other athletic teams. Major sporting events take place in the 65,000-seat Cougar Stadium and the indoor 23,000-seat Marriott Center, (801) 378-2981 (ticket office).

You're welcome to visit the more than 600 acres of BYU's vast campus. The **visitors' cen-**ter provides literature and advice about things to see, events, and facilities open to the public. It's open Monday–Friday 8 A.M.–5 P.M. on the brow of the hill near the Maeser Building, south on Campus Drive, (801) 378-4678, www.byu.edu. Campus tours, either walking or in small open-air vehicles, introduce the university; student guides point out features of interest and tell about student life and research work. The free tours last about 45 minutes and depart Monday–Friday 9 A.M.–4 P.M. by reservation; tours also depart the same days at 11 A.M. and 2 P.M. on a walk-in basis from the visitors' center. Free parking is available in front of the center for those taking guided tours or needing information about the campus. Additional free parking (signed) is near the north end of Campus Drive, near the Wilkinson Center (east across the street), and north of the Museum of Art.

Wilkinson Center serves as the social center for BYU. The main level has a choice of cafeterias and snack bars (open Mon.–Sat. for breakfast, lunch, and dinner), the Varsity Theater (current movies), an art gallery, lounge areas, and an information desk. The **Skyroom Restaurant** on the sixth floor, (801) 378-2049, offers great views and fine dining (open Mon.–Fri. for lunch and Fri. for dinner). The lower level has **Outdoors Unlimited** (rentals of bicycles and equipment for camping, boating, snowshoeing, cross-country and downhill skiing, and other sports), (801) 378-2708, and a **post office.** Some of the other recreation facilities are open only to university students, faculty, and staff.

The **BYU Bookstore** occupies three levels on the west side of the Wilkinson Center with a good selection of general books, textbooks, LDS titles, art supplies, and BYU clothing and souvenirs. The **Harold B. Lee Library,** just west of the bookstore, has an impressive collection of books and maps on five levels; the genealogical library on the fourth floor ranks second in size only to the one in Salt Lake City, which is the largest in the world; main collections are open Monday–Saturday 7 A.M.–midnight; (801) 378-2926.

BYU MUSEUMS

Small collections on campus include a series of salt- and freshwater aquariums in the basement of the Widtsoe Building, and Earth Science

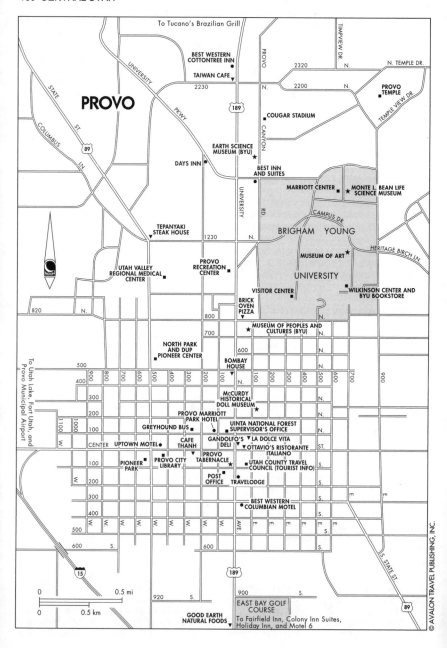

exhibits and a Foucault pendulum in the lobby and hallways of the Eyring Science Center. The Summerhays Planetarium in the Eyring Science Center presents programs to the public for a small charge; (801) 378-4361.

Museum of Art

This is one of the largest art museums in the west, displaying famous works of art including Rembrandt's *Raising of Lazarus,* Gifford's *Lake Scene,* and Andy Warhol's *Marilyn.* These are just of few of the museum's 14,000 works ranging from Renaissance to modern, Asian to local. The building itself is a work of art, with a polished granite exterior, hardwood floors, and high-ceilinged galleries bathed in natural light. Special exhibits have entrance fees; otherwise, admission is free; open Mon.–Sat. 9 A.M.–9 P.M., (801) 378-2787.

Monte L. Bean Life Science Museum

Mounted animals and dioramas realistically depict wildlife of Utah and distant lands. The exhibits not only identify the many species on display but also show how they interact within their environments. The Children's Discovery Room has cages of insects and small animals. Special presentations include movies, talks, workshops, and live-reptile, animal-adaptation, and other demonstrations; call for the schedule. The research library is located southeast of the Marriott Center on 1430 North, (801) 378-5051; open Mon.–Fri. 10 A.M.–5 P.M.; natural history items can be purchased in the gift shop. Museum exhibits are open Monday 1–9 P.M. and Tuesday–Saturday 10 A.M.–5 P.M.; free.

Earth Science Museum

This small museum features excellent exhibits of dinosaurs and early mammals. A popular dinosaur video program both entertains and educates. A viewing window lets you observe researchers cleaning and preparing bones. The museum is located on 1683 N. Provo Canyon Road (across from Cougar Stadium), (801) 378-3680; open Mon.–Fri. 9 A.M.–5 P.M. (til 9 P.M. on Mon.) and Sat. noon–4 P.M.; free.

Museum of Peoples and Cultures

This museum's purpose is to communicate knowledge about both modern and ancient peoples of the world. Exhibits reflect research in the Great Basin in Utah, the American Southwest, Mesoamerica, South America, the Near East, and Polynesia. The museum is located at the corner of 700 North and 100 East, (801) 378-6112; open Mon.–Fri. 9 A.M.–5 P.M.; free.

OTHER PROVO SIGHTS

McCurdy Historical Doll Museum

Mrs. Laura McCurdy Clark, who started the collection, often used her dolls to teach history to students. The original collection has been expanded to about 4,000 dolls, representing U.S. presi-

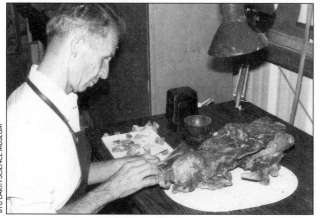

Head Preparator Dee Hall assembling skull of a female Uintatherium, *an Eocene herbivore; this prehistoric mammal had an exceptionally small brain in relation to its body size.*

BYU EARTH SCIENCE MUSEUM

dents and their wives, other historical figures, and diverse nationalities. Private parties can be arranged here. The museum shop sells dolls, doll supplies, toys, and books. Located at 246 N. 100 East, (801) 377-9935; open Tues.–Sat. noon–5 P.M. (1–5 P.M. Jan.–Mar.); $3 adults, $2 ages under 12.

Provo Tabernacle
Architect William Folsom, who designed the St. George and Manti Temples, patterned this English-style structure after a Presbyterian Church he had visited in Salt Lake City. Construction, begun in 1883, required 15 years. Organ recitals and other concerts take place here; located at 100 S. University Ave.

Provo Temple
This modern building of white cast stone incorporates floral elements and a central golden spire. It's particularly impressive lit up against the sky at night. Dedication took place in 1972 with 75,000 people in attendance. Church members carry out sacred work within the 283 rooms. Visitors can't go inside but are welcome to visit the landscaped grounds; 2200 N. Temple Dr. (turn east on 2230 North from University Ave. or drive north on 900 East).

Utah Lake State Park
The largest body of fresh water completely within the state, Utah Lake is 24 miles long and 11 miles wide. Average depth is only 9.4 feet. Mountains form the skyline in all directions. Swans, geese, pelicans, ducks, and other migratory birds stop by. Best bird-watching is at the south end of the lake and near the Provo Airport. The state park provides recreation facilities on the east shore, just a short drive from downtown Provo. Boaters come for water-skiing, sailboarding, and fishing; four paved boat ramps, docks, and slips are available.

The swimming beach offers another way to cool off. Anglers catch white and black bass, channel catfish, walleyed pike, carp, and other warm-water fish during most of the year. The lake usually freezes over by late December and has good ice fishing; trout descend from the mountain rivers during this season. A visitors' center has ice-skating in winter. The campground is open mid-March–October 31 with water and showers; $5 per vehicle for day use, $10–12 for camping. The park is open year-round at 4400 W. Center, Provo, UT 84601, (801) 375-0733 (recording), (801) 375-0731 (office), or (800) 322-3770 (reservations). Head west four miles on Center from downtown Provo or take the I-15 exit for West Center and go west three miles.

Springville Museum of Art
The museum started in the early 1900s as the collection of Springville High School, but when it began to receive gifts of major works from artists Cyrus Dallin and John Hafen, townspeople decided that a special building was needed. They built this fine Spanish-style structure during the Depression with federal and LDS Church assistance. The town is now also known as "Art City" for its patronage. The permanent collection contains 1,200 American works including some of the best by early Utah pioneers and Native Americans as well as the state's modern artists. Eleven galleries display visiting exhibits down-

Appeal to the Great Spirit; *Cyrus Dallin (1912)*

stairs; a permanent collection is housed upstairs. The annual April Salon is a major show of Utah contemporary artists. The museum is at 126 E. 400 South in Springville, (801) 489-2727. From Provo, drive seven miles south on U.S. 89 (South State St.) or take I-15 Exit 263 and go east. The museum is open Tuesday–Saturday 10 A.M.–5 P.M. (until 9 P.M. on Wednesday) and Sunday 2–5 P.M.; closed Monday and state holidays and two weeks prior to the April Salon; free.

ACCOMMODATIONS

Most of Provo's newer hotels and motels are chain motels that lie along South University Avenue, the long commercial strip that runs from I-15 Exit 266 to downtown. The downtown area has a number of older but well-maintained properties.

Under $50
Motel 6, 1600 S. University Ave., (801) 375-5064 or (800) 4-MOTEL-6, has a pool and a guest laundry and allows pets. The **Colony Inn Suites,** 1380 S. University Ave., (801) 374-6800 or (800) 524-9999, is an especially good deal, with suite-style rooms—all with kitchens and living and dining areas—for the price of a motel room. Facilities include a sauna, pool, and hot tub.

For a comfortable, inexpensive room downtown, try the **Uptown Motel,** 469 W. Center, (801) 373-8248. There's a pool, and some rooms have kitchenettes.

$50–75
The **Fairfield Inn by Marriott,** 1515 S. University Ave., (801) 377-9500 or (800) 228-2800, has an indoor pool, spa, and a complimentary continental breakfast. In addition to the nicely furnished standard rooms, there are six suites with kitchens. The **Holiday Inn,** 1460 S. University Ave., (801) 374-9750, is a new complex with a good restaurant, pool, and nicely furnished rooms.

The **Travelodge,** 124 S. University Ave., (801) 373-1974 or (800) 255-3050, is in the center of town and has a pool. The Travelodge has some larger family units that sleep up to six. The **Best Western Colombian Motel,** 70 E. 300 South, (801) 373-8973 or (800) 321-0055, has a pool.

Another clutch of motels sits north of downtown near the university. The **Days Inn,** 1675 N.

200 West, (801) 375-8600 or (800) 325-2525, has a pool. The **Best Inn and Suites,** 1555 N. Canyon Rd., (801) 374-0015, is nicely landscaped and has an indoor pool, spa, and a complimentary continental breakfast. The **Best Western Cottontree Inn,** 2230 N. University Pkwy., (801) 373-7044 or (800) 662-6886, has an indoor and outdoor pool, plus large rooms with lots of extras.

$75–100
Provo's finest hotel is the **Provo Marriott Park Hotel,** 101 W. 100 North, (801) 377-4700 or (800) 777-7144, an upscale business and conference hotel. Rooms are large, very nicely appointed, and come with minibars and coffeemakers; facilities include a pool, spa, and weight room.

Campgrounds
Lakeside RV Campground has sites for tents ($19) and RVs ($21 with hookups) with showers, pool, laundry, store, and canoe rentals; open year-round at 4000 W. Center (just before Utah Lake State Park), (801) 373-5267. **Provo KOA** has sites for tents ($15) and RVs ($18 without hookups, $21 with) with showers, pool, laundry, and store; open year-round at 320 N. 2050 West (a quarter mile west of I-15 on Center, then one block north), (801) 375-2994. **Frazier Park** lies along the Provo River, five miles up Provo Canyon, (801) 225-5346; $16 tents or RVs with hookups and showers; closed in winter. **Deer Creek Park** lies along the Provo River farther upstream near the dam for Deer Creek Reservoir, (801) 225-9783; $14 tents or RVs without hookups, $16 RVs with water, electricity, and showers. Open April 15–October 15. You'll find **Forest Service Campgrounds** near Provo along the Alpine Scenic Loop to the northeast, Squaw Peak Road to the east, and Hobble Creek-Diamond Fork Loop to the southeast.

FOOD

You'll notice a strong collegiate influence at Provo area eateries. Food tends to be fairly simple and cheap—liquor licenses, in the hometown of BYU, are rare. A drive along North University Drive will reveal dozens of perfectly good fast-food restaurants.

Otherwise, with a couple exceptions, the food scene here is rather restrained. **Good Earth Natural Foods,** 1045 S. University Ave., (801) 375-7444, has a café (open Mon.–Sat. for lunch and dinner), a bakery, and groceries. **Gandolfo's Deli,** 18 N. University, (801) 375-3354, is a popular spot for sandwiches. One of Provo's few fine dining restaurants is **Ottavios Ristorante Italiano,** 69 E. Center St., (801) 377-9555, with a wide selection of excellent pasta and roast meat dishes ($12–18) served in a historic hotel lobby. In a side café is a coffee shop with fresh pastries that will enliven your Provo morning. Open daily for breakfast, lunch, and dinner; it also has a liquor license.

For less expensive Italian food, try **La Dolce Vita,** 61 N. 100 East, (801) 373-8800; open Mon.–Sat. for lunch and dinner, or **Brick Oven Pizza,** 111 E. 800 North, (801) 374-8803; open Mon.–Sat. for lunch and dinner.

For ethnic food, Provo has a surprising number of Asian and South Asian restaurants. Try the **Taiwan Cafe,** 2250 N. University Parkway in the Plum Tree Shopping Center, (801) 373-0389, which specializes in Mandarin cuisine and Mongolian barbecue; open Mon.–Sat. for lunch and daily for dinner. For Vietnamese food, head to **Cafe Thanh,** 278 W. Center, (801) 373-8373, offering a good variety of Vietnamese and some Chinese food; open Mon.–Sat. for lunch and dinner. **Tepanyaki Steak House,** 1240 N. 500 West, (801) 374-0633, prepares Japanese cuisine daily for dinner. The **Bombay House,** 463 N. University Ave., (801) 373-6677, is a good Indian restaurant with lunchtime buffet and Tandoori-baked meats.

If you're looking for Mexican food, consider driving south of Provo to Springville. There, **La Casita Mexican Restaurant,** 333 N. Main St., (801) 489-9543, is the area's best bet for good traditional south of the border cooking; the restaurant also has a liquor license. For a different Latin American twist, go to **Tucano's Brazilian Grill,** 4801 N University Ave., (801) 224-4774.

MORE PRACTICALITIES

Entertainment and Events

For current happenings not only in Provo but also in nearby towns, check with the Utah County Travel Council at 51 S. University Avenue, Suite 111, (801) 370-8393.

Brigham Young University has a busy calendar of cultural and sporting events; (801) 378-7444 (music ticket office), (801) 378-4332 (theater performances), or (801) 378-2981 (sporting events). Catch movies at **Carmike Cinemas,** 175 W. 200 North, (801) 374-6061; **Movies 8,** Plum Tree Shopping Center at 2424 N. University Parkway, (801) 375-5667; or BYU's **Varsity Theatre,** Wilkinson Center, (801) 378-3311.

In Orem, **SCERA** offers family entertainment movies year-round inside the Show House at 745 S. State and summer plays and musicals in an outdoor shell at 699 S. State; (801) 225-2560 (recorded info) or (801) 225-2569 (office).

Major annual events in the area include the **Art City Days,** which takes place in Springville in **June.** The City of Orem Family Summerfest presents a parade, talent show, five-K run, Dutch-oven cook-off, and other entertainment. Also in June, Sundance holds a **Bluegrass Festival.** Cowboys show their skills at the **Lehi Round-up and Rodeo.**

In **July,** Provo celebrates the Fourth with a **Freedom Festival** grand parade, freedom run, sports events, concerts, arts festival, and fireworks. **Provo Arts Festival** has performing and visual arts and special programs for kids. Springville presents groups of dancers from many countries in the **Springville World Folkfest. Pioneer Day** brings a parade and other entertainment to Provo and other towns on July 24. **Fiesta Days** in Spanish Fork has a parade, rodeo, pioneer activities, 10-K run, and entertainment for three days near July 24. Highland lets loose in its **Highland Fling** with a parade, 10-K run, carnival, fireworks, entertainment, and children's games.

In **August,** the Utah County Fair features a horse show, exhibits, and entertainment in Spanish Fork. The town of Payson puts on a **Scottish Festival.** Nationally recognized storytellers present traditional and new pieces in the **Timpanogos Storytelling Festival.**

Parks, Gyms, and Waterparks

North Park, 500 W. 500 North, contains Veterans' Memorial Pool & Waterslide Park, (801) 379-6614, picnic areas, playground, and a **Daughters of Utah Pioneers Pioneer Museum;** open Mon.–Fri. 2–5 P.M. in summer. **Fort**

Utah City Park has picnic tables, playground, and a replica of the fort built by Provo's first settlers; from downtown, head west on Center past the I-15 interchange and turn north one block on UT 114 (2050 West). **Pioneer Park** has picnicking and a playground at Center and 500 West. **Provo Recreation Center** next to Provo High School at 1155 N. University Avenue, (801) 379-6610, has an indoor pool, racquetball and volleyball courts, and weight rooms.

The big **Seven Peaks Resort Water Park** contains two huge waterslides, twisting tubes, and a variety of pools to cool off in; guests can also picnic or play games including volleyball, basketball, softball, and horseshoes. Other attractions include ice-skating in winter and an 18-hole executive golf course. Open late May–early Sept.; admission is $15.95 ages 12–59, $11.95 ages 3–12, and free for toddlers (ages 3 and under) and seniors (60 and over); turn east on Center St. to its end and follow signs; (801) 373-8777. **Trafalga Family Fun Center,** 168 S. 1200 West in Orem (take I-15 Exit 274), (801) 224-6000, features a water-tube slide, mini golf, bumper boats, and arcade games.

Other Recreation

Play golf at the 27-hole **East Bay Golf Course,** (801) 373-6262 (turn east on East Bay Blvd. from South University Ave. near the I-15 interchange), or the nine-hole **Cascade Fairways Public Golf Course,** 1313 E. 800 North in Orem, (801) 225-6677.

In winter, skiers hit the slopes at **Sundance Ski Area** 14 miles northeast of town, (801) 225-4107. **Hansen Mountaineering,** 757 N. State, Orem, UT 84057, (801) 226-7498, leads trips and provides instruction and sales for rock-climbing, winter camping, and cross-country skiing.

Services

In **emergencies** (police, fire, medical), call 911. The **post office** is at 95 W. 100 South, (801) 275-8777. The **U.S. Forest Service** provides avalanche/mountain weather information during the snow season at (801) 374-9770. **Utah Valley Regional Medical Center** is at 1034 N. 500 West, (801) 373-7850.

Information

Utah County Travel Council, Ste. 111, 51 S. University Ave. in the old county courthouse (P.O. Box 912, Provo, UT 84601), (801) 370-8393 or (800) 222-UTAH out of state, www.utahvalley.org, offers advice on sights and services in Provo and the Utah Valley; open Memorial Day–Labor Day weekends Mon.–Fri. 8 A.M.–8 P.M. and Sat.–Sun. 10 A.M.–6 P.M., then Mon.–Fri. 8 A.M.–5 P.M. the rest of the year.

The U.S. Forest Service has three offices in the area. The **Uinta National Forest Supervisor,** 88 W. 100 North, Provo, UT 84601, (801) 377-5780, has general information about all districts in the forest and some books and maps for sale; open Mon.–Fri. 8 A.M.–5 P.M. Contact the **Pleasant Grove Ranger District office,** 390 N. 100 East, Pleasant Grove, UT 84062, (801) 785-3563, for specific information about the Alpine Scenic Loop and other areas in the Uinta National Forest north of Provo; open Mon–Fri. 8 A.M.–5 P.M. (plus Sat. 8 A.M.–5 P.M. in summer). The **Spanish Fork Ranger District office**, 44 W. 400 North, Spanish Fork, UT 84660, (801) 798-3571, covers the Uinta National Forest east and southeast of Provo and the Wasatch National Forest, Vernon Division, southwest of town; open Mon.–Fri. 8 A.M.–5 P.M. (daily 8 A.M.–4:30 P.M. in summer).

Provo City Library, 425 W. Center, (801) 379-6650, is open Monday–Thursday 9:30 A.M.–9 P.M. and Friday–Saturday 9:30 A.M.–6 P.M. BYU's **Harold B. Lee Library,** just west of the Wilkinson Center, (801) 378-2926, has an impressive collection of books and maps on five levels; open Mon.–Fri. 7 A.M.–midnight and Sat. 8 A.M.–midnight. The **BYU Bookstore** at the Wilkinson Center, (801) 378-3584, has one of the best and largest selections in the state. For a good selection of books plus a coffee bar, head to **Border's Books,** 4801 N. University Blvd., (801) 224-2720.

Transportation

Utah Transit Authority (UTA), (801) 375-4636, provides local bus service in Provo and connects with Springville, Salt Lake City, Ogden, and other towns; buses don't run on Sunday and holidays except for a few lines on Sunday in Salt Lake City and Ogden. **Greyhound Bus,** 124 N. 300 West, (801) 373-4211, has at least two northbound and two southbound departures daily. **Amtrak** trains serve Provo, (800) 872-7245. **Yellow Cab** provides taxi service, (801) 377-7070. Scheduled airline flights leave from the Salt Lake City Airport.

NORTHWEST OF PROVO

Hutching's Museum of Natural History

This amazingly diverse collection in the town of Lehi (LEE-high) began as a family museum. Highlights include pioneer rifles, Indian crafts, glittering minerals, ancient fossils, mounted birds of Utah, and colorful tropical shells. Located at 53 N. Center St. in Lehi (16 miles northwest of Provo on I-15), (801) 768-7180; open Mon.–Sat. 9:30 A.M.–5:30 P.M.; $3 adults, $1.50 children under 12.

Museum of Ancient Life

Also near Lehi, this brand new museum opens completely in 2001. When complete, nearly 50 dinosaur skeletons will be on display, with hands-on displays, research facilities, and a theater to show IMAX films. Most of the featured dinosaurs will represent species that once strode across the alluvial sands of ancient Utah, including the first-ever displayed skeleton of a Supersaurus, super-sized at 110 feet long. The museum is part of the development at Thanksgiving Point, 2095 N. Thanksgiving Way. The provisional phone number is (801) 768-2300.

Camp Floyd Stagecoach Inn State Park

A restored inn, an old U.S. Army building, and a military cemetery preserve a bit of pioneer history at Fairfield, a sleepy village on the other side of Utah Lake from Provo. John Carson, who had been one of the first settlers of the site in 1855, built a family residence and hotel three years later. About the same time, troops of the U.S. Army under Colonel Albert Johnston marched in and established Camp Floyd nearby.

The soldiers had been sent by President Buchanan to put down a rumored Mormon rebellion. Upon finding that no "Mormon War" existed, the colonel led his men to this site so as not to intimidate the major Mormon settlements. Fairfield jumped in size almost overnight to become Utah's third-largest city, with a population of about 7,000—including the 3,000 soldiers. Even for the times, it was rowdy—17 saloons served the Army men. The camp (later named Fort Crittenden) served no real purpose, however, and was abandoned in 1861 so that troops could return east to fight in the Civil War. Carson's hotel, later known as the Stagecoach Inn, continued to serve travelers on the dusty main road across Utah. Pony Express riders, stagecoach passengers, miners, sheepherders, and every other kind of traveler stopped here for the night until the doors closed in 1947.

Now the inn is a state park, furnished as in the old days and full of exhibits on frontier life. A shaded picnic area is beside it. The only surviving building of Camp Floyd has been moved across the street and contains a diorama of the fort and some excavated artifacts. Camp Floyd's well-kept cemetery is a three-quarter-mile drive west and south of Fairfield. The Stagecoach Inn is open daily 11 A.M.–5 P.M. from about Easter weekend to the end of September. The season may be extended depending on visitation; it's a good idea to call ahead, especially if you are driving out just to see the exhibits, (801) 768-8932. Admission is $4 per vehicle, $2 per individual. From Provo or Salt Lake City, take I-15 to Lehi and turn west 21 miles on UT 73.

whiptail lizard
(Cnemidophorus sp.)

LOUISE FOOTE

NORTH OF PROVO

TIMPANOGOS CAVE NATIONAL MONUMENT

Beautiful cave formations reward visitors who hike the trail to the cave entrance on the north side of Mt. Timpanogos. Branching helictites, icicle-like stalactites, rising stalagmites, and graceful flowstone formations appear snow white or in delicate hues of green, yellow, or red. Tunnels connect three separate limestone caves, each of which has a different character. The first was discovered by Martin Hansen in 1887 while tracking a mountain lion. Middle and Timpanogos Caves weren't reported until 1921–22. Timpanogos Cave so impressed early explorers that a trail, lighting, and national monument protection came soon afterward.

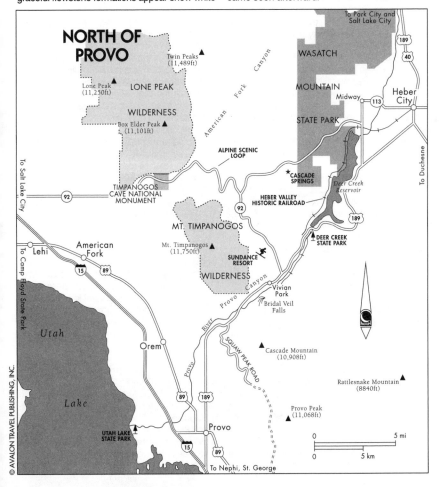

Exhibits and a short slide show in the visitors' center introduce the formation, history, and ecology of the caves. The staff provides information on special cave tours and on wildlife and plants of the area. A brochure available here identifies plants and trees along the trail to the caves and illustrates the geology and formation of the caves. Related books, hiking maps, posters, and slides are sold. Be sure to obtain tickets here for the cave tour before starting up the trail. Rangers schedule nature walks on the trail to the caves. There's a $3 per vehicle entry fee.

Allow about three hours for the complete trip, including 45–60 minutes for the cave tour. The three-mile round-trip hike from the visitors' center to the caves is moderately difficult; you'll climb 1,065 feet to an elevation of 6,730 feet. Points along the way have fine views up and down American Fork Canyon and out onto the Utah Valley. People with breathing, heart, or walking difficulties shouldn't attempt the trail; wheeled vehicles (including strollers) and pets aren't allowed. Rangers enforce safety rules that prohibit running, throwing rocks, or shortcutting; children under 16 must stay with their parents.

Ranger-led tours wind about one-third mile through the caves. Underground temperature is about 45° F all year, so bring a sweater or jacket. The caves close during winter because snow and ice make the trail too hazardous. The season lasts from about mid-May–mid-October; tickets are sold (in the visitors' center only) 8 A.M.–3:30 P.M. (extended to 7 A.M.–5:30 P.M. in the peak summer season). On Saturday (all day), Sunday afternoons, holidays, and mid-summer weekdays, you may have a long wait. It's a good idea to call ahead to check hours and find out how busy the caves are. Tickets can also be purchased two to three weeks in advance by calling and paying with a credit card. Tours often sell out from mid-June–mid-August, when advance reservations are strongly recommended. Admission fees for the cave tours are $6 adults, $5 children 6–15, $3 for kids 3–5, and free for infants; Golden Age card holders pay $3.

A snack bar at the visitors' center is open in summer. Picnickers can use tables across the

black-chinned hummingbird
(Archilocus alexandri)

road from the visitors' center and at a site a quarter-mile west. The U.S. Forest Service has several campgrounds nearby. Contact the monument at R.R. 3, Box 200, American Fork, UT 84003, (801) 756-5238. The visitors' center is two miles up American Fork Canyon on the Alpine Scenic Loop (UT 92). You can take I-15 American Fork Exit 279 if you're coming north from Provo or the I-15 Alpine Exit 287 if coming south from Salt Lake City.

ALPINE SCENIC LOOP

The narrow paved highway twists and winds through some of the most beautiful alpine terrain in Utah. Mount Timpanogos rises to 11,750 feet in the center of the loop and presents sheer cliff faces and jagged ridges in every direction. More than a dozen campgrounds and several picnic areas line the way. Anglers can try for trout in swift clear streams. Autumn brings brilliant golds to the aspen and scarlets to the maples. Winter snows close the loop at its higher elevations and attract skiers to Sundance Resort. The most scenic sections of the loop lie along American Fork Canyon and its South Fork, Provo Canyon and its North Fork, and on the high pass between these drainages. A drive on U.S. 89 or I-15 completes the approximately 40-mile loop. With a few stops, a full day can easily be spent on the drive. If you'd like to see Timpanogos Cave on the way, it's recommended to begin the loop there to avoid waiting in ticket lines, especially on weekend afternoons.

Most of the picnic areas and campgrounds lie along American Fork Canyon at elevations of 5,400 to 6,200 feet; their season begins in early May and lasts to late October. Higher recreation areas are **Granite Flat Campground** (elev. 6,800 feet), **Altamont Group Campground** (elev. 6,600 feet), **Timpooneke Campground** (elev. 7,400 feet), **Mt. Timpanogos Campground** (elev. 6,800 feet), and **Theatre in the Pines Picnic Area** (elev. 6,800 feet). The season runs from about Memorial Day weekend to the third week in September. Nearly all the recreation areas have water and charge a $13 fee (except Timpooneke and Mt. Timpanogos Campgrounds, which charge $10). Some areas can be reserved by calling (800) 280-CAMP. **Pleasant Grove Ranger District office** of the Uinta National Forest has information and maps for recreation areas along the Alpine Scenic Loop and for the Lone Peak and Mount Timpanogos Wildernesses; open Mon.–Fri. (daily in summer) 8 A.M.–5 P.M. at 390 N. 100 East, Pleasant Grove, UT 84062, (801) 785-3563. (You'll pass the office if taking U.S. 89 and UT 146 between Provo/Orem and the mouth of American Fork Canyon.)

Lone Peak Wilderness

The summit of Lone Peak rises to 11,250 feet on the divide between Little Cottonwood and American Fork Canyons. Despite its closeness to Provo and Salt Lake City, the wilderness (30,088 acres) offers good opportunities for solitude. Hikers sometimes spot mountain goats. A climb to the summit is a very strenuous day hike; many people prefer taking two days. Some routes have dangerous drop-offs and require mountaineering skills. Lower elevations have fine scenery as well as easier hiking. Lake Hardy (southeast of the summit) is a popular destination. Four main trailheads provide access to the wilderness: Bells Canyon from lower Little Cottonwood Canyon to the north, Draper Ridge to the west, Alpine to the south, and Granite Flat Campground (off American Fork Canyon) to the southeast. Topo maps for the wilderness are the 7 1/2-minute Lehi, Draper, Dromedary Peak, and Timpanogos Cave. Trail descriptions are given in *Wasatch Trails, Volume Two,* by Daniel Geery, and *The Hiker's Guide to Utah,* by Dave Hall. Contact the Salt Lake City Ranger District office for hiking information on the north slope, the Pleasant Grove Ranger District office for the south side.

Mount Timpanogos Wilderness

Sheer cliffs of Mt. Timpanogos tower 7,000 feet above the Utah Valley and present one of the most dramatic sights of the Wasatch Range. Trails to the heights lead past waterfalls, flower-filled alpine meadows, lakes, and permanent snowfields. One trail continues to the 11,750-foot summit for superb vistas of central Utah. The climb is strenuous, especially the last three miles,

Mt. Timpanogos

but requires no special skills. You'll see whole families—from grandchildren to grandparents—on this popular mountain. Even short hikes can be very rewarding. Take care to bring storm gear in case the weather suddenly turns bad. A shelter at Emerald Lake provides a refuge from storms. Hike either the **Timpooneke Trail** from Timpooneke Campground or the **Aspen Grove Trail** from the Theatre in the Pines Picnic Area; both trailheads lie just off the Alpine Scenic Loop. One-way distances to the summit are 9.1 miles on the Timpooneke Trail (4,350-foot elevation gain) and 8.3 miles on the Aspen Grove Trail (4,900-foot elevation gain). A hike on both trails (highly recommended) can be done with a car shuttle. If a trip to the summit sounds too ambitious, you can stick to the 12 miles between the trailheads via Emerald Lake (elev. 10,300 feet).

The **Summit Trail** branches off west of Emerald Lake, climbs a steep slope to the jagged summit ridge, then follows the ridge southeast to the top. A large snowfield and the deep blue waters of Emerald Lake lie directly below.

W. C. McRAE

Chunks of ice break off the snowfield and float in the lake during even the hottest summer days. Local people often refer to the snowfield as a glacier, but technically it's just a snowfield. Some climbers continue southeast along the summit ridge and drop down onto the snowfield and slide or walk to Emerald Lake, but this can be a bit hazardous. Hiking season is from about mid-July–mid-October. In winter and spring, hikers must be equipped and experienced for snow travel. Topo maps are the 7¹/₂-minute Timpanogos Cave and Aspen Grove, though you're not likely to need them unless snow covers the trails. The Pleasant Grove Ranger District office can advise on hiking conditions.

Cascade Springs

Crystal-clear water emerges amidst lush vegetation and flows down a long series of travertine terraces at this beautiful spot. The springs produce more than seven million gallons of water daily. Boardwalks (some accessible for people with disabilities) and short trails with interpretive signs allow a close look at the stream and pools. Trout can be seen darting through the water (though fishing is prohibited). Plant life includes maple, oak, aspen, willow, water birch, box elder, cattails, watercress, and wildflowers. The drive to Cascade Springs is also very pretty, either from the Alpine Scenic Loop or from Heber Valley. A paved road (Forest Route 114) branches off the Alpine Scenic Loop near its summit (between Mileposts 18 and 19) and winds northeast seven miles to the springs. An unpaved road, passable by car if the road is dry, begins on the west edge of Heber Valley and climbs high above the valley with good views, then drops down to the springs; turn west seven miles on UT 220 from UT 113 (between Midway and Charleston) and follow signs.

Sundance Resort

Since actor/director Robert Redford purchased this land in 1969, he has worked toward obtaining an ideal blend of recreation, the arts, and natural beauty. Musicals and other entertainment of the **Sundance Summer Theatre** take place outdoors. Tickets can be purchased the day of the show or reserved by calling (801) 223-4110. Redford founded the **Sundance Institute** in 1980 as a laboratory for independent filmmakers; the actual Sundance Film Festival is held in Park City.

Downhill skiing begins in mid-December and lasts into April. One quad, two double chairlifts, and two triple chairs take skiers high on the southeast slopes of Mt. Timpanogos. The 41 runs on 450 acres provide challenges for people of all abilities; total elevation drop is 2,150 feet. Ski instruction, rentals, accommodations, restaurants, and packages are available at the resort. Adult lift tickets cost $39 full day, $30 half day; children 12 and under ski for $22 full day, $16 half day. **Sundance Nordic Center** offers 15 kilometers of Nordic track, lessons, and rentals.

Accommodations: Cottages start at $185 in summer, $205 in winter; mountain houses start at $475 in summer, $660 in winter.

Food: Sundance has three dining facilities in the main compound, including the **Foundry Grill,** which serves breakfast, lunch, and dinner daily, and the **Tree Room** prepares elegant dinners daily and a Sunday brunch. A barbecue is held prior to performances of the Sundance Summer Theatre. Reservations are recommended for all dining. Contact Sundance at R.R. 3, Box A-1, Sundance, UT 84604, (801) 225-4100 (recording of summer theater, events, and winter skiing) or (801) 225-4107 or (800) 892-1600 (office). The website is www.sundanceresort.com. The resort can be easily reached by taking U.S. 189 from Provo, Orem, or Heber City, then turning northwest 2.5 miles on UT 92 (Alpine Scenic Loop).

Squaw Peak Road

This scenic drive follows the Wasatch Range east of Provo and offers many fine views over Utah Valley. The road turns south from U.S. 189 in Lower Provo Canyon, then climbs high into the mountains. Pavement ends after five miles at the turnoff for **Hope Campground** (has water from late May–mid-October; $7; elev. 6,600 feet). The road continues south eight miles to **Rock Canyon Campground** (a group area with water from late May–mid-October) and on to the Left Fork of Hobble Creek east of Springville for a total of 26 miles one-way. Squaw Peak Road has some rough spots in the middle section, but cars with good clearance can usually be driven through in dry weather. The Pleasant Grove Ranger District office can advise on camping, hiking, road conditions, and Rock Canyon group reservations.

HEBER CITY

Its setting in a lush agricultural valley surrounded by high mountains has earned Heber City the title "Switzerland of America." Many of its people work at farming, raising livestock, and dairying—as their families have done since pioneer days. A massive snowslide blocked passage of the first settlers making their way up Provo Canyon in 1859, but they simply disassembled their wagons and portaged them to the other side. The town's name honors Heber C. Kimball, a counselor to church President Brigham Young. Heber City (pop. 5,872) makes a handy stop for travelers exploring the nearby Wasatch and Uinta Ranges or visiting the large Deer Creek and Strawberry Reservoirs. It also offers reasonably priced accommodations a short drive from Park City.

Heber Valley Historic Railroad

Ride a turn-of-the-century train pulled by steam locomotive #618 past Deer Creek Lake into scenic alpine Provo Canyon. The round-trip to Vivian Park and back to Heber City takes 3.5 hours; adult fare is $19, senior $17, and children $12. One-way rates are available and diesel locomotive rides cost $2 less. The depot is located at 450 South 600 West, (435) 654-5601 or (800) 982-3257.

Midway Fish Hatchery

Visitors are welcome at this state-run trout hatchery. It's open daily 8 A.M.–4:30 P.M.; located one mile south of Midway just off UT 113 (Charleston Road).

Accommodations

$50–75: Heber City motels are generally very well-maintained and pleasant places to stay. All of the following have pools, and most also have spas with saunas and whirlpools. Rooms at the **National Nine High Country Inn,** 1000 S. Main, (435) 654-0201 or (800) 345-9198, all come with refrigerators and microwaves. The **Danish Viking Lodge,** 989 S. Main, (435) 654-2202 or (800) 544-4066, has a grassy playground, guest laundry, and two two-bedroom units. **Hylander Motel,** 425 S. Main, (435) 654-2150 or (800) 932-0355, is clean and attractive and has one suite. The **Swiss Alps Inn,** 167 S. Main, (435)

HEBER CITY WINTER OLYMPIC VENUES

Soldier Hollow, Wasatch State Park, three miles north of Midway, is host to the men's and women's biathlon, men's and women's cross-country skiing, Nordic combined skiing, and Paralympic Nordic skiing.

654-0722, has a playground and two suites with full kitchens.

$75–100: Undoubtedly the most unique place to stay in the Heber City area is the **Homestead Resort,** 700 N. Homestead Dr. (Midway, UT 84049), (435) 654-1102 or (800) 327-7220. This hot-spring resort is three miles west of town near Midway and features mineral baths, swimming, and accommodations. The natural hot-spring water is believed to be good for the skin.

The spacious grounds and stately buildings of the Homestead may remind you of an age long past, but the facilities are modern. A large volcano-like cone called the Crater sits alongside the resort. The Crater is actually composed of travertine deposited by the springs; water once flowed out of the top, but it's now piped to indoor and outdoor pools and hot tubs (open only to hotel guests). The Crater is accessible for scuba diving, snorkeling, bathing, and tours; reservations are recommended.

Golfers can play at the resort's 18-hole course. Stables offer horseback and hay rides (and sleigh rides in winter) and bicycle rentals, (435) 654-1102 ext. 440. Rooms should be reserved well in advance, especially for summer weekends. The resort's own **Simon's** restaurant serves dinner and Sunday brunch in an elegant country setting (reservations are recommended), and **Fanny's Grill** offers breakfast, lunch, and dinner daily; open year-round.

$100–125: In Midway, the **Kastle Inn,** 1220 Interlaken Ln., (435) 654-2689, is a massive castle-like home with five guest rooms, all with private baths.

Food

There are a number of American-style cafés along Main Street, and plenty of fast food to serve the skiing crowds. For something a little different, try **Yodels,** (435) 654-5370, 79 E. Main

St. in Midway, with Swiss and American cuisine for lunch and dinner Monday–Saturday. For a steak, go to **The Claimjumper,** 1267 S. Main, (435) 654-4661. The best place to eat in the area is **Simon's,** out at the Homestead Resort, (435) 654-1102, with steaks, prime rib, seafood, and high-quality American cuisine.

Events

Horse shows and rodeos take place through the summer in the Heber City area. A **powwow** in June brings Indian tribes for dances and craft sales. The **Utah High School Rodeo Finals** are held in June. **Wasatch Fair Days** features a parade, rodeo, exhibits, livestock show, entertainment, and demolition derby in early August. **Swiss Days** celebrates with a parade, entertainment, food, and flea market on the Friday and Saturday before Labor Day. The Experimental Aircraft Association sponsors the **E.A.A. Fly In** of experimental and vintage aircraft in September.

Services

The **city park** at Main and 300 South has picnic tables and a playground. **Wasatch Community Pool** has indoor swimming and racquetball at Wasatch Middle School, 200 E. 800 South (turn east from Main onto 600 South, then right on 200 East), (435) 654-3450. Wasatch County High School has **tennis courts** at 600 South and 200 East. The **post office** is at 125 E. 100 North, (435) 654-0881. **Wasatch County Hospital** is at 55 S. 500 East, (435) 654-2500. In **emergencies** (police, fire, paramedic), dial 911.

Information

The **Heber Valley Chamber of Commerce** has an information center at 475 N. Main (P.O. Box 427, Heber City, UT 84032), (435) 654-3666; open Mon.–Fri. 9 A.M.–5 P.M. (also on Sat. and Sun. from June to Sept.). **Heber Ranger District office,** 2460 S. U.S. 40 (P.O. Box 190, Heber City, UT 84032), (435) 654-0470, manages the Uinta National Forest lands east and southeast of Heber City. The staff provides literature and advice on camping, hiking, horseback riding, boating, fishing, cross-country skiing, snowmobiling, and back-road travel; open Mon.–Fri. 8 A.M.–5 P.M. (also some Sat. and Sun. June–Sept.). The

Wasatch County Library, 188 S. Main, (435) 654-1511, is open Monday–Saturday.

VICINITY OF HEBER CITY

Wasatch Mountain State Park

Utah's largest state park encompasses 22,000 acres of valleys and mountains on the east side of the Wasatch Range. An excellent 27-hole golf course in the park has a pro shop and a café. Unpaved scenic drives lead north through Pine Creek Canyon to Guardsman Pass Road (turn right for Park City or left over the pass for Brighton), northwest through Snake Creek Canyon to Pole Line Pass and American Fork Canyon, and southwest over Decker Pass to Cascade Springs. Only a short nature trail has been developed, but you can set out on your own. Winter brings snow depths of three to six feet from about mid-December–mid-March. Separate cross-country ski and snowmobile trails begin near the golf course. **Homestead Cross-Country Ski Center,** (435) 654-1102, provides equipment for both sports.

The large **Pine Creek Campground** has showers and hookups from late April or early May to late October; located just north of the golf course at an elevation of 5,600 feet. A 1.5-mile **nature trail** begins near site #21 on the Oak Hollow Loop in Pine Creek Campground. The staff offers **campfire programs,** usually on Friday and Saturday evenings, at the campground's amphitheater. **Little Deer Creek Campground** is a smaller, more secluded area in an aspen forest; open with water from June–mid-Sept. It's also open earlier and later without water; check with the park office first; groups often reserve all the sites. You can get here by driving the seven-mile unpaved road to Cascade Springs, then turning north four miles on another unpaved road. The park visitors' center, just before the golf course, has an information desk open daily year-round daily 8 A.M.–5 P.M.; P.O. Box 10, Midway, UT 84049, (435) 654-1791 or (800) 322-3770 (reservations). Make golf course reservations at (435) 654-0532 (local) or (435) 266-0268 (Salt Lake City). There's a $14–16 fee for camping at the Pine Creek sites; it's $10 per vehicle overnight at Little Deer Creek Campground. From Heber

City, drive west three miles to Midway, then follow signs north two miles.

Deer Creek State Park

The seven-mile-long Deer Creek Reservoir lies in a very pretty setting below Mt. Timpanogos and other peaks of the Wasatch Range. A developed area near the lower end of the lake has a campground with showers, picnic area, paved boat ramp, dock, and fish-cleaning station; elevation is 5,400 feet. Island Beach Area, 4.5 miles to the northeast, has a gravel swimming beach and a marina (open in summer with a store, snack bar, boat ramp, and rentals of fishing boats, ski boats, and personal watercrafts); ice fishers can park here in winter. Rainbow trout, perch, largemouth bass, and walleye swim in the lake. Good winds for sailing blow most afternoons. You'll often see a lineup of catamarans at the sailboat beach near the campground and crowds of sailboarders at the Island Beach Area. Deer Creek State Park is open mid-April–late October; P.O. Box 257, Midway, UT 84049, (435) 654-0171 or (800) 332-3770 for reservations (advised Memorial Day–Labor Day weekends). Admission fee is $5 per vehicle for day use (includes Island Beach Area), $11 per vehicle for camping at the campground area. The campground is just off U.S. 189, 11 miles southwest of Heber City and 17 miles northeast of Provo.

Deer Creek Island Resort, at the Island Beach Area, (435) 654-4779, has boat rentals (fishing, ski, sport) and a snack bar in summer; a restaurant offers fine dining Friday and Saturday evenings year-round. **Snow's Marina,** on Wallsburg Bay 1.2 miles northeast of the state park campground, has a small store, snack bar, boat ramp ($3), RV park ($8 without hookups), and fishing-boat rentals (with or without motors). Snow's is open daily May–October.

Jordanelle State Park

This large reservoir upstream on the Provo River provides recreation for boaters and anglers. It's located east of U.S. 40 six miles north of Heber. There are two recreation areas. **Rock Cliff Recreation Site** is located at the upper end of the east arm of the reservoir and has walk-in camping sites with restrooms and hot showers, a nature center, boardwalks with interpretive displays, and pavilions for day use. Admission is $5 per carload, $2 per individual for day use; sites cost $11 tents or RVs without hookups, $15 with. **Hailstone Recreation Site** is a camping area with 230 campsites, restrooms and showers, day-use shaded pavilions, a modern marina with 80 boat slips, a general store, a Laundromat, and a small restaurant; tent sites are $11, full hookups are $15. Facilities include wheelchair access with raised tent platforms. The season is April–mid-October; P.O. Box 309, Heber City, UT 84032, (435) 783-3030.

Heber Valley RV Park Resort offers camping sites, hot showers, a country store, and a Laundromat just below the Jordanelle Reservoir dam, about six miles north of Heber City, (435) 654-4049, open year-round; $15 tents, $17 RVs without hookups, $21 RVs with.

Historic Union Pacific Rail Trail State Park

Utah's new state park consists of a multi-use, nonmotorized trail built to accommodate hikers, bicyclists, horseback riders, and cross-country skiers. The trail runs 27 miles from Echo Reservoir to Park City with trailheads and information kiosks at Echo Reservoir, Coalville, Wanship, Star Pointe, and Park City. Other staging areas will be added as well as spurs connecting to the Mormon Pioneer Historic Trail, Rockport Lake State Park, and the Jordanelle State Park's proposed trail system. There are campgrounds near the trailheads and spurs but not on the trails. The state park office can be reached at P.O. Box 309, Heber City, UT 84032, (435) 645-8036.

Strawberry Reservoir

This 17,000-acre reservoir lies on a high rolling plateau 23 miles southeast of Heber City. Creation of the original Strawberry Reservoir began in 1906 as a federal reclamation project to divert water from the Colorado Basin west to the Utah Valley. Soldier Creek Dam (constructed in 1973) greatly increased the reservoir's size. A section of lake called "The Narrows" separates Strawberry Arm on the west from the smaller Soldier Creek Arm on the east. The water at this 7,600-foot elevation is cold for water-skiing, but hardy souls in wet suits often brave it. Fishing is good all year (through the ice in winter) for rainbow and cutthroat trout and some brook trout and kokanee salmon. Several winter parking areas along U.S. 40 provide access for cross-country skiing, snowmobiling, and ice fishing. Check with the Heber Ranger District office for information on recreation at the reservoir and in surrounding Uinta National Forest; (435) 654-0470.

The **Strawberry Visitor Center/Fish Hatchery** not only sells maps and books but also functions as a small museum with interactive displays explaining the history of the reservoir from its construction to its present-day fish-breeding programs. A 200-yard boardwalk with interpretive stations leads to the hatchery and an information kiosk. Open Mon.–Thurs. 9 A.M.–5 P.M. and Fri.–Sun. 9 A.M.–6 P.M. from Memorial Day through the last weekend of Oct., (435) 548-2321.

The U.S. Forest Service maintains four campgrounds and three marinas around the lake; all are open with water from late May to late October; $11 without hookups, $20 (Loop B) with.

**Other Recreation Areas
in the Heber Ranger District**
Whiskey Springs Picnic Area is near the mouth of Daniels Canyon, eight miles southeast of Heber City on U.S. 40; water is available in summer. Elevation is 6,400 feet; signs along the short **Whiskey Springs Nature Trail** identify plants. **Lodgepole Campground** lies in upper Daniels Canyon, 16 miles southeast of Heber City on U.S. 40; open late May–late Oct. with water; $11. Lodgepole pine and aspen grow at the 7,800-foot elevation.

Currant Creek Recreation Complex, on the southwest shore of **Currant Creek Reservoir** (elev. 8,000 feet), has a campground (with water from late May to late Oct.; $11 fee), paved boat ramp, fish-cleaning station, and fishing access for people with disabilities. Anglers catch rainbow, cutthroat, and brook trout; ice fishing is good in winter. **Currant Creek Nature Trail** begins from Loop D of the campground and climbs 400 feet in a 1.25-mile loop; signs tell about the ecology. The best way to get here from Heber City is to drive southeast 42 miles on U.S. 40 past Strawberry Reservoir, just before **Currant Creek Lodge** (motel and café, 801-548-2226), turn northwest 19.5 miles along Currant Creek on Forest Route 083. High-clearance vehicles can take a slow, scenic route over Lake Creek Summit (elev. 9,900 feet); from Heber City, head east 31 miles on Center Street, which becomes Lake Creek/Currant Creek Road (Forest Route 083).

Mill Hollow Campground sits on the shore of small Mill Hollow Reservoir at an elevation of 8,800 feet in an Engelmann spruce forest 37 miles from Heber City. It's open with water from mid-June–late October; $11; the reservoir has trout fishing. Take U.S. 189 to Francis (northeast of Heber City), then UT 35 and Forest Route 054 (gravel).

Wolf Creek Campground is in an Engelmann spruce forest at 9,500 feet near Wolf Creek Pass 38 miles from Heber City; open with water from early July–mid-Oct.; $7; also group sites. From Heber City, drive north and east to Francis, then head southeast about 22 miles on UT 35 (part gravel); this scenic road continues on to Hanna and Duchesne in northeastern Utah.

SOUTH OF PROVO ALONG I-15

HOBBLE CREEK–DIAMOND FORK LOOP

Pleasant canyon and mountain views line this 34-mile scenic drive east of Springville. The road is open from about mid-May–late October and is normally fine for cars—all but about the middle eight miles are paved. Along the way you'll pass picnic spots, campgrounds, hiking trailheads, and fishing holes. Back roads branch off to Squaw Peak Road, Strawberry Reservoir, and other destinations. Hikers can choose from a trail network totaling about 100 miles. Contact the **Spanish Fork Ranger District office** for maps and recreation information at 44 W. 400 North, Spanish Fork, UT 84660, (435) 798-3571. Open Mon.–Fri. 8 A.M.–5 P.M. (daily in summer). Family and group sites at some campgrounds can be reserved by calling (800) 280-CAMP; sites cost $7–10 a night. To drive the loop from Main Street in Springville (take I-15 Exit 263), head east three miles on 400 South to the mouth of Hobble Creek Canyon and follow Forest Routes 058 and 029.

NEBO SCENIC LOOP

This mountain drive loops off I-15 and winds into the heights of the southern Wasatch Range. You'll enjoy alpine forests, fine panoramas of the valleys below, and a close look at Mt. Nebo—highest peak in the range. The entire 43-mile length from Payson to Nephi is paved; it's open from about mid-June–late October. In winter and spring, cross-country skiers and snowmobilers come up to glide across the snow. You can begin the drive from Payson in the north (I-15 Exit 254) or Nephi in the south (take I-15 Exits 222 or 228 and go east six miles on UT 132). A partly paved road from Santaquin (I-15 Exit 248) goes southeast 11 miles via Santaquin Canyon to connect with the main drive.

More than 100 miles of trails lead into the backcountry. **Devil's Kitchen Geologic Area** lies at the end of a quarter-mile trail, 28 miles south of Payson; eroded layers of red-tinted river gravel and silt form spires and sharp ridges. **Mount Nebo Wilderness** is west of the drive and can be reached by several trails. Strong hikers can climb the south summit (elev. 11,877 feet) by trail on a day or overnight trip. The higher north summit (elev. 11,928 feet) is two peaks farther north along a knife-edged ridge (no trail). *The Hiker's Guide to Utah,* by Dave Hall, has hiking descriptions for Mt. Nebo and Santaquin Peak.

The U.S. Forest Service maintains recreation facilities, trailheads, and overlooks along the Nebo Scenic Loop. Contact the **Spanish Fork Ranger District office** for maps and information at 44 W. 400 North, Spanish Fork, UT 84660, (435) 798-3571; open Mon.–Fri. (daily in summer) 8 A.M.–5 P.M. If you're coming from the south, you can stop at the Forest Service's **Nephi Ranger District office,** 740 S. Main, (435) 623-2735, for info on the scenic loop; open Mon.–Fri. 8 A.M.–5 P.M. You can reserve sites at Payson, Blackhawk, Ponderosa, and Bear Canyon by calling (800) 280-CAMP; sites cost between $8–13.

NEPHI

This small town (pop. 4,519) serves as the commercial center for the region and the seat of Juab County. The first settlers arrived in 1851 and named the place for a patriarch in the Book of Mormon. Pleasant scents fill the air at the **Nephi Rose Garden,** one block east of Main on 100 North.

Nephi's annual events are the **Ute Stampede and Rodeo** in July and the **Juab County Fair** in August. The **city park** has picnic tables, playground, and an outdoor pool at Main and 500 North.

Accommodations

Under $50: The **Safari Motel,** 413 S. Main, (435) 623-1071, has clean, inexpensive rooms plus a pool. The **Motel 6,** 2195 S Main, (435) 623-0666, is out by freeway Exit 222.

$50–75: You can't miss the **Whitmore Mansion Bed & Breakfast,** an ornate Eastlake/Queen Anne-style structure built in 1898 at 110 S. Main, (435) 623-2047. Five rooms are decorated with period antiques, and all have private baths.

Several modern motels lie just off I-15 Exit 222 including the **Super 8,** 1901 S. Main, (435) 623-0888, and **Roberta's Cove Motor Inn,** 2250 S. Main, (435) 623-2629 or (800) 456-6460. Closer to downtown is the **Best Western Paradise Inn,** 1025 S. Main, (435) 623-0624.

Campgrounds: There's a very pleasant campground just east of Nephi. The **Nephi-KOA Horseshoe Ranch,** five miles east of town on UT 132, (435) 623-0811, has a pool, fishing, game room, and pleasant shady sites in a rural setting.

Food

The favorite place to eat in Nephi is **J.C. Mickelson's Restaurant,** at I-15 Exit 222, with good American-style home cooking. The area's best Mexican restaurant is **Mi Rancherito Restaurant,** 390 S. Main, (435) 623-4391.

Other Practicalities

Canyon Hills Park Golf Course (nine holes) lies up a canyon at 1200 E. 100 North, (435) 623-9930. **Central Valley Medical Center** is at 549 N. 400 East, (435) 623-1242. The **Nephi Ranger District office** of the Uinta National Forest has information on the Nebo Scenic Loop at 740 S. Main (Nephi, UT 84648), (435) 623-2735; open Mon.–Fri. 8 A.M.–5 P.M. The **public library** is at 21 E. 100 North, (435) 623-0822.

YUBA LAKE STATE PARK

Sevier Bridge Reservoir, 26 miles south of Nephi, is 22 miles long and 11,000 acres when full; its elevation is 5,014 feet. Minerals give the lake a turquoise tint that varies with the light. There's plenty of space for both water-skiers and anglers. Sailboarders often find good wind conditions here and warmer water in springtime than at most other Utah lakes. Anglers catch yellow perch, walleye, channel catfish, and northern pike; ice fishing, mostly for yellow perch, is done from January to early March. North Sandy Beach (on the main road to the campground) and East Beach (reached from UT 28) have the best swimming, but there's also a beach at the campground (see below).

For many years the reservoir and state park were known as Yuba Lake, despite the fact that no such thing existed! The name "Yuba" refers to the dam, begun in 1902 and originally named "U.B." Farmers who helped to build the dam received water rights from the Deseret Irrigation Company in payment for their labor; if they stopped working they lost their stock; if they kept working they had to do additional work to pay for an assessment. An old song lamented that "U.B. damned if you do and U.B. damned if you don't."

The campground (with showers), picnic area, and a paved boat ramp lie on the west shore; take I-15 Exit 202 and follow signs 4.3 miles. North Beach is off to the left 2.2 miles in; a small store here is open on summer weekends. If driving to the campground from the south, you can save eight miles by taking the I-15 frontage road (west side) from Scipio. East Beach and Painted Rocks Pictograph Site, both on the east shore, can be reached by boat or from UT 28 (an unpaved road from North Beach provides a shortcut to UT 28). Boaters can also use a boat ramp near Painted Rocks Pictograph Site. The park and campground stay open all year, though the campground showers close November–March. It's a good idea to reserve campsites for summer weekends. If the campground is full, ask a ranger about other areas around the lake. Admission fees are $4 per vehicle for day use, $7 per vehicle for camping at Painted Rocks (no water), $8 per vehicle in the overflow area, or $12–14 per vehicle camping at the main campground; group

day-use and camp areas can also be reserved. Write P.O. Box 159, Levan, UT 84639, or call (435) 758-2611 (ranger) or (800) 322-3770 (reservations).

FILLMORE

In 1851, Brigham Young and the Utah Territorial Legislature designated Fillmore as the territorial capital, even before the town was established. They chose this site in the Pahvant Valley because it lay in the approximate geographic center of the territory. Their plans didn't work out, but Fillmore (pop. 2,000) has become the center of a large agricultural region and the Millard County seat. A state historical museum in the Territorial Statehouse contains a wealth of pioneer history.

Territorial Statehouse State Park

Completed in 1855, the statehouse is Utah's oldest government building. Architect Truman O. Angell designed the three-story sandstone structure, originally planned to have four wings capped by a large Moorish dome. Only the south wing was completed, though, because antagonism between the U.S. government and the Mormons blocked the appropriation of expected federal funds. Several legislatures met here, but only the fifth session, in 1855, stayed for its full term; the sixth and eighth sessions opened here, then quickly adjourned to Salt Lake City's better-suited facilities.

Rooms are furnished to represent a typical pioneer bedroom, parlor, and kitchen. Other exhibits display clothing, tools, and Indian artifacts. Lawbreakers spent time in the jail—one of the building's many uses. Historic photos and paintings show pioneer families and leaders of the church and government in early Utah. Open daily 9 A.M.–5 P.M. (to 6 P.M. in summer season); $3 adults, $1 ages 3–15, or $6 per vehicle. Guided tours can be arranged with advance notice at no additional charge. You can visit a pair of 1880s log cabins on the grounds; one has pioneer furnishings, the other a wagon. Peek in the windows of the restored 1867 Little Rock School House nearby. The cabins and schoolhouse can be opened on request. Rose gardens surround the statehouse, which is located downtown at

50 W. Capitol Avenue (behind the Millard County Courthouse), (435) 743-5316. Also part of this parklike complex are the municipal swimming pool and some lovely shaded picnic spots.

Accommodations

Under $50: Several motels lie along or near the I-15 Business Loop through town. The **Fillmore Motel,** 61 N. Main, (435) 743-5454, has economy rooms and three two-bedroom units. The **Best Western Paradise Inn** is located at I-15 Exit 167, (435) 743-6895, and has a heated pool and a good restaurant, the **Garden of Eat'n.**

$50–75: The really unique place to stay in Fillmore is **Suite Dreams,** 172 North Main, (435) 743-6862, a newly built B&B inn with wraparound porches. The inn was built as a guesthouse, so rooms are large and well-furnished; each has a private bath; suites have hot tubs, refrigerators, and king-size beds.

Campgrounds: Open year-round, **Wagons West RV Campground,** 545 N. Main, (435) 743-6188, has showers, laundry, and a store; $12 tents or RVs without hookups, $18 with. **Fillmore KOA,** a half mile off the south end of the business loop near I-15 Exit 163, (435) 743-4420, has showers, laundry, and store; $18 tents or RVs without hookups, $20 with.

Services

For **emergencies** (police, fire, paramedic), dial 911. The **city park** in front of the Territorial Statehouse has picnic tables and a playground. An indoor **swimming pool** is just west of the statehouse. **North Park,** at 500 N. Main, offers picnicking and a tourist information booth (open in summer). **Fillmore Community Medical Center** is at 674 S. UT 99, (435) 743-5591.

Information and Transportation

An **information booth** is open in summer at North Park, 500 N. Main. **Millard County Tourism** provides year-round information on the county and the Paiute ATV Trail; open variable hours at 195 N. Main (P.O. Box 1082, Fillmore, UT 84631), (435) 743-7803 or (800) 441-4ATV. The **Fillmore Ranger District office** of the Fishlake National Forest has information about camping, fishing, hiking, horseback riding, and back-road travel in the nearby Pahvant Range and Canyon Mountains; open Mon.–Fri.

8 A.M.–5 P.M. at 390 S. Main (P.O. Box 265, Fillmore, UT 84631), (435) 743-5721. Visit the office of the **BLM's Warm Springs and House Range Resource Areas** to learn about the valleys and rugged mountains of west-central Utah; open Mon.–Fri. 7:45 A.M.–4:30 P.M. at 35 E. 500 North (P.O. Box 778, Fillmore, UT 84631), (435) 743-5123. The **public library** is at 25 S. 100 West, (435) 743-5314.

VICINITY OF FILLMORE

Pahvant Range

These mountains east of Fillmore have seven summits over 10,000 feet; Mine Camp Peak (elev. 10,222 feet) is the highest. Elk, deer, and other wildlife live here. A network of trails and forest roads leads into the high country; contact the Fillmore Ranger District office for a Fishlake National Forest map, recreation information, and group campground reservations. Turn east six miles on 200 South from downtown Fillmore to reach four **picnic areas** along wooded Chalk Creek. They have water in summer; free; elevations are 5,700–6,100 feet. Anglers catch rainbow and German brown trout in the creek. **Adelaide Campground** lies along Corn Creek farther south near Kanosh; open with water from late May to early Oct.; $8. Cottonwood, piñon pine, juniper, spruce, and maple grow at the 5,500-foot elevation. From the southernmost east-west street in Kanosh, turn east five miles on a gravel road (Forest Route 106). The road continues through pretty country and descends Mud Spring Hollow to I-70. Corn Creek has fishing for rainbow and German brown trout. Two recreation areas are in the northern part of the range: **Maple Hollow Picnic Area,** on the west side, has water from late May to early October (elev. 6,900 feet); take the I-15 South Holden Exit 174 and go east six miles; box elder, maple, oak, and fir trees grow in the hollow. **Maple Grove Campground** is open with water from late May to early October (elev. 6,400 feet); $6; turn west four miles on the signed paved road from U.S. 50 (near Milepost 47 between Scipio and Salina); maple, water birch, oak, piñon pine, juniper, and aspen grow in the valley; Ivie Creek has fishing for rainbow trout.

Tabernacle Hill

Volcanic eruptions in the desert 15 miles south-west of Fillmore have covered the land with cinder cones, a tuff ring, a collapsed caldera, spatter cones, pit craters, pressure ridges, and squeeze-ups. The first eruptions occurred 12,000–24,000 years ago, when Lake Bonneville covered the region. Explosive cinder and ash eruptions built a circular ring of tuff 3,000 feet across and 200 feet or more high, which rose above the lake waters. In a second period of eruptions 11,000–12,000 years ago, molten lava filled the tuff ring and spilled out to the north, forming a seven-square-mile island of black lava in the receding lake. About two-thirds of the tuff ring survives today. When viewed from the north, it resembles the Mormon Tabernacle in Salt Lake City—hence the name Tabernacle Hill. The collapsed caldera inside is 1,000 feet across and 60 feet deep. Two spatter cones near the hill represent the last gasps of the final eruption. A lava-tube cave, most of which lies west of the caldera, can be traced (on the surface) for about a mile. Bats live in some of the cave sections. You can enter the cave where its roof has col-lapsed, though rock falls commonly block the passages. Watch for Great Basin rattlesnakes when exploring the caves and other features here.

You can visit Tabernacle Hill any time of the year, but in summer try to visit early in the day. From Fillmore, go west six miles on 400 North (UT 100) to Flowell, turn left (south) one mile, turn right two miles (pavement ends), turn left (south) 3.5 miles at the junction (the other road continues to cinder pits). Continue on the main track to-ward Tabernacle Hill in the distance; at a major gravel road, turn west, then immediately turn south again on a narrow dirt road—Tabernacle Hill is 2.5 miles farther. You may have to walk the last two miles, depending on road conditions. Tabernacle Hill can also be reached from Mead-ow, eight miles to the southeast. The BLM office in Fillmore has maps and information helpful in exploring this and other areas of Utah's Great Basin; (435) 743-5123.

Cove Fort

In 1867, during the Black Hawk War, Mormon Church President Brigham Young ordered con-struction of this fort to protect travelers on the overnight journey between Fillmore and Beaver. Walls of volcanic basalt 13 feet high contained 12 rooms and a cistern and enclosed an area 100 feet square. Gunports at the two entrances and along the upper walls discouraged Indians from ever attacking the fort. Now furnished and re-stored to its 1877 specifications, the fort is open daily 10 A.M.–dusk from about early April to mid-October; free. The south row of rooms contains the telegraph, stagecoach, post offices, dining room, kitchen, and laundry. North rooms con-stitute the sleeping accommodations. Outbuild-ings that have been reconstructed or relocated to the site include a barn, blacksmith shop, pig-pen, and cabin. An icehouse is scheduled to be constructed. A picnic area is across the street. Volunteers of the LDS Church lead informal tours and relate the fort's history. Cove Fort stands near the junction of I-15 and I-70; take I-15 Exit 135 and go southeast two miles or take I-70 Exit 1 and go northwest one mile.

BEAVER

Mormon pioneers settled near the mouth of Beaver Canyon in 1856 to farm and raise live-stock. Large flocks of sheep kept a woolen mill busy. The pastoral tranquility came to an end four years later when prospectors discovered silver and gold in the San Francisco Mountains to the west. The flood of rambunctious miners, fric-tion with the staid Mormon community, and fear of Indian attacks caused the community to call for federal troops. The Army arrived in 1872, built a fort (later named Fort Cameron), and stayed until 1882. Today, Beaver (pop. 2,300) is a handy travelers' stop just east of I-15. Main Street (the I-15 Business Loop) has a good selection of mo-tels and restaurants. Center Street (UT 21) goes west to Minersville State Park (fishing and boat-ing) and the desert country of west-central Utah. An entirely different world lies just to the east on UT 153 (200 North St.)—wooded canyons, alpine lakes, and a ski area in Utah's third-high-est mountain range, the Tushars.

Historic Buildings

More than 200 historic houses of architectural in-terest lie scattered around town. You'll see many of them by driving along the side streets. A large stone building remaining from Fort Cameron still stands on the east edge of town across the high-

Beaver County's old courthouse

way from the golf course. The old **Beaver County Courthouse,** with an ornate clock tower, represents the architectural splendor of its period. Building started in 1877, and the courthouse served Beaver County from 1882 until 1975. It now houses a historical museum; drop by Tues.–Thurs. noon–6 P.M. between Memorial Day and Labor Day weekends to see pioneer portraits, historic documents, an 1892 wedding cake, other artifacts, and mineral specimens. Visit the courtroom on the top floor, then head down to the dungeonlike jail cells in the basement (check out the graffiti). The adjacent Historical Park has a statue of Philo T. Farnsworth (1906–1971), the "Father of Television," who was born in a log cabin near Beaver. Located on Center one block east of Main.

Accommodations

Under $50: A dozen motels lie along the business route through town between I-15 Exits 109 and 112. For an inexpensive room, try the **Delano Motel,** 480 N. Main, (435) 438-2418 or (800) 537-2165, a well-maintained older motel. The **Sleepy Lagoon Motel,** 882 S. Main, (435) 438-5513, is an attractive motel with nice landscaping and a small pond.

$50–75: Best Western's **Paice Inn,** 161 S. Main, (435) 438-2438, and **Paradise Inn,** 1451 N. 300 West, (435) 438-2455, are both very pleasant and have pools and spas. The **Beaver Super 8,** 626 W. 1400 North, (435) 438-3888, and the **Days Inn,** 645 N. Main, (435) 438-2409, are both new and comfortable.

Campgrounds: At the north edge of town, **Beaver KOA** has showers, store, laundry, and pool (take I-15 Exit 112, go south 0.6 mile on the Business Loop, then turn left on Manderfield Rd.), (435) 438-2924, sites cost $15 tents, $17 RVs without hookups, $20 with; open Feb. 1–Nov. 30. **Beaver Canyon Campground,** on the east side of town at 1419 E. Canyon Road (200 North), (435) 438-5654, has showers, laundry, and a Mexican restaurant (open daily for dinner); $12 tents or RVs without hookups, $15 with; open May 1–Nov. 1. **United Beaver Camperland** offers showers, store, laundry, and pool at the south edge of town (near I-15 Exit 109), (435) 438-2808; sites cost $11 tents, $13 RVs without hookups, $18 with; open year-round. **Minersville State Park** has a campground 14 miles west on UT 21. The Tushar Mountains have good camping, too (see below).

Food

You'll find good old-fashioned American food at **Arshel's Cafe,** 711 N. Main, (435) 438-2977. A fixture in Beaver since the 1930s, this is the kind of diner where you ought to save room for homemade pie after your meal. Also good for standard American food is the **Garden of Eat'n Restaurant,** at Paradise Inn on the north edge of town.

Entertainment and Events

Beaver City Birthday celebrates with historic programs on February 6. **Summer Theater** performances take place from late June to late July in the Opera House Civic Center across from the old county courthouse. **Horse races** run through the summer. Beaver celebrates **Pioneer Day** on July 24 with a parade, fireworks, rodeo, horse racing, and games. The **Beaver County Fair** is held in August at the fairgrounds near Minersville to the west.

Recreation and Services

City parks offer picnic tables and playgrounds at Main and Center and at 400 East and 300 North. The second park also contains the indoor **Municipal Swimming Pool,** (435) 438-5066. **Tennis courts** are at the rodeo grounds on the east edge of town. Play golf at the nine-hole **Canyon Breeze Golf Course** on the east edge of town, (435) 438-2601. There's good **rockhounding** in the Mineral Mountains northwest of town and in other areas to the west; a brochure that describes collecting sites is available from many local businesses. The **post office** is at 20 S. Main, (435) 438-2321. **Beaver Valley Hospital** provides medical care at 85 N. 400 East, (435) 438-2531.

Information and Transportation

Foresters at the **Beaver Ranger District office,** 575 S. Main (P.O. Box E, Beaver, UT 84713), (435) 438-2436, provide information on camping, fishing, hiking, and road conditions in the forest lands of the Tushar Mountains to the east; open Mon.–Fri. 8 A.M.–5 P.M. The **Beaver County Visitor Information Center,** P.O. Box 272, Beaver, UT 84713, (435) 438-2975, can tell you more about sights and services in the area. The **public library** is at 55 W. Center, (435) 438-5274. The **Greyhound Bus** stops at El Bambi Cafe, 935 N. Main, (435) 438-2229.

THE TUSHAR MOUNTAINS

Although higher than the Wasatch Range, the Tushars remain relatively unknown and uncrowded. Travelers on surrounding highways get glimpses of their rocky summits, but people who hurry by rarely appreciate their size and height. Delano Peak (elev. 12,169 feet) crowns the Tushars and is the highest point in central Utah. From Beaver, UT 153 (200 North St.) winds into the alpine country of the Fishlake National Forest to a ski area, campgrounds, fishing spots, and hiking trails. (The first 19 miles are paved, followed by 21 miles of dirt.) The road takes you through meadows and forests before making a steep descent to the town of Junction on U.S. 89. Forest Route 137 branches off UT 153 10 miles from Beaver to Kents Lake, Anderson Meadow, and other pretty areas, then

returns to the highway to complete a scenic loop (54 miles round-trip from Beaver). Drivers with high-clearance vehicles can journey amidst the summits on the Kimberly/Big John Road Backway between UT 153 and the Kimberly Scenic Drive; much of this trip goes above timberline with spectacular views of peaks above and canyons below. For recreation information and road conditions, visit the Beaver Ranger District office at the corner of 200 North and 100 East in Beaver, (435) 438-2436.

Camping and Picnicking

Camping fees at the following campgrounds range from $8 to $11. From Beaver, the first campground and picnic area reached is **Little Cottonwood,** six miles east on UT 153. Sites are open with water from late May to early September; elevation is 6,500 feet. **Ponderosa Picnic Area** is 2.5 miles farther up Beaver Canyon on UT 153 in a grove of ponderosa pine; it has water in summer; its elevation is 7,000 feet. Little Cottonwood and Ponderosa lie along the rushing Beaver River, which has trout fishing. **Mahogany Cove Campground** overlooks Beaver Canyon 12 miles east of town on UT 153; open with water from late May to early Oct. Its name comes from the abundant curl-leaf mountain mahogany; other trees at the 7,500-foot elevation include ponderosa pine, Gambel oak, juniper, and cottonwood. **Puffer Lake,** 21 miles from town on UT 153, is set among forested hills of spruce, fir, and aspen at 9,700 feet. The lake, privately owned by **Puffer Lake Resort** on the other side of the highway, (435) 864-2751, has trout fishing, primitive camping, and a primitive boat ramp. The resort offers boat rentals, a small store, and cabins during warmer months.

To reach additional campgrounds or to drive the scenic loop, turn southeast on Forest Route 137 at a junction 10 miles east of town (near Milepost 10 on UT 153). The first eight miles are on a good gravel road (to Anderson Meadow), then there are seven miles of dirt road to UT 153; the last half is passable when dry by cars with good clearance, but it can be too rough for RVs. **Little Reservoir Campground** is less than a mile in on Forest Route 137; sites are in a ponderosa pine forest at 7,350 feet; open with water from late May to early Oct. The reservoir here covers only three acres but often has good trout fishing. **Kents Lake Campground** overlooks Kents Lake five miles in on Forest Route 137. Sites are in a forest of spruce, fir, and aspen at 8,800 feet; open with water from mid-June–early Oct. The 100-acre lake offers trout fishing. **Tushar Lakeside Campground** is a county-managed group area below Kents Lake, (435) 438-2975. **Anderson Meadow Campground** lies in high forests and meadows overlooking Anderson Meadow Reservoir at 9,500 feet, eight miles in on Forest Route 137. It's open with water from mid-June–early October. The reservoir has trout fishing. **La Baron Reservoir** is another popular fishing spot four miles farther (12 miles in on Forest Route 137), but it has only primitive camping; its elevation is 9,900 feet. Three miles farther you'll return to UT 153; turn right for City Creek Campground and the town of Junction, left for Puffer Lake, Elk Meadows Resort, and Beaver.

The gravel and dirt section of UT 153 from the town of Junction on U.S. 89 makes a relentless five-mile climb from the valley to the mountains—you'll need to use low gears going up and have good brakes coming down. This drive isn't recommended for trailers or RVs. The east side of UT 153 is open from late June until sometime in October. **City Creek Campground** is located near the bottom of the grade; from the turnoff five miles northwest of Junction, follow a side road in for one mile. Sites lie along City Creek in a diverse forest of cottonwood, aspen, ponderosa pine, piñon pine, Gambel oak, and juniper at an elevation of 7,600 feet. Open with water from Memorial Day to Labor Day weekends; free.

Hiking
Relatively few hikers have discovered this area, but good trails for hiking and horseback riding lead into the high country. Contact the Beaver Ranger District office in Beaver for details. Three peaks of the Tushars rise above 12,000 feet and make good climbing destinations—Delano Peak (elev. 12,169 feet), Mt. Belknap (12,139 feet), and Mt. Baldy (12,082 feet). Each involves an ascent of about 2,000 feet and can be reached on a day hike. (Strong hikers have climbed all three in one day!) Delano can be climbed by a route up its southwest slope, Mt. Belknap by a trail up its southeast side, and Mt. Baldy by a route from Blue Lake up its southeast side. (All three trails are reached from the Big John Flat Road, which turns north from UT 153 between Mileposts 16 and 17.) When dry, the dirt road is often okay for cars. Other climbing routes are possible, too. Hikers can reach the top of Delano Peak in just an hour via the southwest route; follow the Big John Flat Road past Big John Flat and park at the pullout between Griffith and Poison Creeks, 5.6 miles north of UT 153. The hike begins at an old jeep track marked by a sign saying it's closed to vehicles; follow the jeep tracks, then just head up the grassy slope to the summit. You're likely to see deer, hawks, and summer wildflowers on any hike in the area. Topo maps for the peaks are the 15-minute Delano Peak or the 7 1/2-minute Delano Peak, Mt. Brigham, Mt. Belknap, and Shelly Baldy Peak maps.

Elk Meadows Ski and Summer Resort
The resort offers skiing and year-round accommodations in the Tushars 18 miles east of Beaver. Ski season normally begins on Thanksgiving and lasts to mid-April. The ski area has a total of 36 runs up to 2.5 miles long and with a vertical drop of 1,400 feet; 20 percent of the runs are rated beginner, 50 percent intermediate, and 30 percent advanced. Three double chairs, one triple chair, a Poma, and a T-bar serve the slopes. Lift tickets cost $33 adults all day, $27 morning or afternoon, $18 seniors or children all day, $12 half day.

Free shuttle buses serve the ski area. The resort offers a ski school, rentals, races, several restaurants, and condominium-style accommodations. Lodging costs run $80–300 depending on room, day of week, and season. Contact Elk Meadows Resort at P.O. Box 511, Beaver, UT 84713, (435) 438-5433 or (888) 881-SNOW. The website is at www.elkmeadows.com.

SOUTH OF PROVO ALONG U.S. 89

SKYLINE DRIVE

This scenic back road, nearly all of which is unpaved, follows the crest of the Wasatch Plateau for about 100 miles between U.S. 6 in the north and I-70 in the south. Few people travel the entire length, however, preferring to do shorter sections reached from the many access roads. Much of the drive lies above 10,000 feet in vast meadows and alpine forests; above Ferron Reservoir, you'll reach the drive's summit at High Top (elev. 10,897 feet). Major attractions include sweeping vistas, fishing, hiking, horseback riding, and winter sports.

Probably the four most popular recreation areas on the plateau are **Scofield State Park, Huntington Canyon (UT 31), Joes Valley Reservoir,** and **Ferron Reservoir.** Cars can normally reach Skyline Drive from these places when the roads are dry. The easiest access to the drive is paved UT 31 between Fairview on the west and Huntington on the east; the road is kept clear in winter so that cross-country skiers, snowmobilers, and ice fishers can reach the plateau. Other roads may be too rough for low-clearance vehicles and even occasionally closed to all traffic; it's best to check with the Forest Service offices when planning a trip. A snowbank on Skyline Drive near Jet Fox Reservoir (east of Manti) often blocks traffic until middle or late July. The rest of the drive can usually be traveled from about mid-June to middle or late October. The drive may not be signed at either end; the north end is off U.S. 6 at a highway rest area near Tucker (between Mileposts 203 and 204); the south end is reached from I-70 Ranch Exit 71. You'll need the Manti–La Sal forest map (Sanpete, Ferron, and Price Ranger Districts) and, for the southern end, the Fishlake Forest map. Nearly the entire drive is in the Manti–La Sal National Forest. Get recreation information and road conditions from the **supervisor's office** at 599 W. Price River Dr., Price, UT 84502, (435) 637-2817. District offices are **Price Ranger District office** (same address and phone as the supervisor's office) for the northeastern part of the

Wasatch Plateau; **Ferron Ranger District office,** P.O. Box 310, Ferron, UT 84523, (435) 384-2372, for the southeastern part of the plateau; and **Sanpete Ranger District office,** 540 N. Main, Ephraim, UT 84627, (435) 283-4151, for the western half of the plateau.

FAIRVIEW

Mormon farmers settled on the grasslands of the upper San Pitch (or Sanpete) River Valley in 1859, giving their community its original name of North Bend. Many pioneer buildings can still be seen in town. The unusual Fairview Museum of History and Art is worth a visit. Fairview (pop. 1,635) lies 42 miles south of Provo on U.S. 89; turn east on UT 31 to reach the alpine lands of the Wasatch Plateau.

Fairview Museum of History and Art
Many of the varied exhibits show a sense of humor. You'll see stern-faced pioneer portraits, furniture, clothing, tools, telegraph and telephone equipment, mounted wildlife, Indian crafts, geology displays, and artwork. Noted Utah sculptor Dr. Avard Fairbanks donated much of the art including *Love and Devotion,* which depicts Peter and Celestia Peterson, Fairview residents who were married for 82 years. A large threshing machine and other antique farm equipment are outside. The museum is open from about mid-May–mid-October Monday–Saturday 10 A.M.–6 P.M. and Sunday 1–6 P.M.; free. It's located in a former elementary school (built in 1900) at 85 N. 100 East; from U.S. 89, turn east one block on 100 North, (435) 427-9216.

Accommodations
Under $50: Stay at the **Skyline Motel,** 236 N. State, (435) 427-3312, with basic and clean rooms. Across the street is the town's sole eatery.

San Pitch Mountains
This small range rises northwest of Ephraim. **Maple Canyon Campground** (elev. 6,800 feet) on the east side has pretty scenery but no water

(or fee). You can hike from the campground up **Maple Canyon Trail** along the middle fork or up **Left Fork Maple Canyon Trail.** The trails can be done as a loop using a section of forest road. Maple Canyon is 3.75 miles west of Freedom. **Chicken Creek Campground** (elev. 6,200 feet) is on the west side of the range; open early May to early Oct. with water and a $6 fee; head east four miles from Levan. A rougher forest road continues southeast past the campground and over to Wales, four miles south of Freedom. Although the San Pitch Mountains lie within the Uinta National Forest, they are administered by the Manti–La Sal National Forest; visit the Sanpete Ranger District office in Ephraim for information (see below). See the Fishlake National Forest map for ways to reach the campgrounds.

EPHRAIM

The first settlers arrived in 1854 and named this place after a tribe mentioned in the Book of Mormon. A fort guarded against Indian attacks during the first six years. Pioneer structures that date back more than a century can be seen on Ephraim's side streets. Turkey-raising is big business here and in nearby towns.

Ephraim (pop. 4,486) celebrates the **Scandinavian Festival** in May (Memorial Day weekend) with historic town tours, pioneer demonstrations, craft sales, and a fun run.

Snow College

One of the nation's leading junior colleges, Snow College began in 1888 as a Mormon academy. Today it's a state school with about 2,100 students and 75 faculty members. You're welcome to attend plays, concerts, and lecture series on campus; call (435) 283-4021, ext. 616 (public relations), for cultural events and general information. Many sports facilities at the Activity Center are open to the public, too, including an indoor pool, track, basketball, racquetball, tennis, and fitness center; 300 East and Center, (435) 283-7000. The Badgers football team won the junior college national championships in 1985; call the Activity Center for schedules of their games and other sporting events. Union Building has a snack bar and bookstore at 100 East and Center. The library is at 250 E. Center, (435) 283-4021,

ext. 364. For more information about Snow College, visit or write the Administration Building at 150 E. College Avenue, Ephraim, UT 84627.

Accommodations

Under $50: For inexpensive, no-fuss rooms, stay at **Iron Horse Motel,** 670 N. Main, (435) 283-4223, or **Travel Inn Motel,** 330 N. Main, (435) 283-4070, which has its own restaurant.

$50–75: Ephraim Homestead Bed & Breakfast has an 1860s log cabin and two cozy rooms with shared bath in an upstairs barn. This old homestead, which was a typical Mormon farm, sits on half an acre of gardens at 135 W. 100 North, (435) 283-6367. Another landmark pioneer home turned B&B is the **W. Pherson House B&B,** 244 S. Main St., (435) 283-4197 or (800) 944-4197. Built in 1895, it was the home of one of the town's early bankers.

Campgrounds: Turn east 8.5 miles on 4th South for **Lake Hill Campground** (open with water about mid-June–mid-Sept.; $9; elev. 8,400 feet) and farther for other areas of the Wasatch Plateau—the road continues to Skyline Drive.

Other Practicalities

The **post office** is at 45 E. 100 North, (435) 283-4189. **Ephraim Medical Clinic** is at 9 E. 100 North, (435) 283-4076. **Sanpete Ranger District office,** 540 N. Main, Ephraim, UT 84627, (435) 283-4151, has recreation and road information for the western half of the Wasatch Plateau and for the San Pitch Mountains; open Mon.–Fri. 8 A.M.–noon and 12:30–4:30 P.M.

MANTI

This town (pop. 2,643) dates from November 1849 and is one of the oldest in Utah. Brigham Young named it for a place mentioned in the Book of Mormon. An estimated 100 buildings built before 1880 can be seen on the side streets; Manti possesses some of the state's most splendid pioneer-era architecture. Manti is the Sanpete County seat.

The **Mormon Miracle Pageant** in July portrays the history of the Book of Mormon and of the pioneers and early church leaders. The very popular production takes place at night on Temple Hill; a large cast provides lots of action. **Sanpete**

County Fair is held in August. A **city park** at 300 W. 200 North, (435) 835-4961, has picnic tables, playground, and an outdoor pool.

Manti Temple
This temple, on a small hill, has a commanding position over the town. Brigham Young dedicated the site in April 1877, just three months before his death. Workers labored 11 years to complete construction, using locally quarried blocks of oolitic limestone. The temple architecture combines several 19th-century styles in a rectangular plan similar to the first Mormon temples in the Midwest.

Accommodations
Under $50: The town's best motel is **Manti Country Village,** 145 N. Main, (435) 835-9300 or (800) 452-0787, which has its own restaurant, a commodity in curiously short supply in the Sanpete Valley.

$50–75: Given the town's wealth of period architecture, it's no wonder that the best places to stay are historic B&Bs. **Manti House Inn,** 401 N. Main, (435) 835-0161 or (800) 284-4006, provides bed-and-breakfast accommodations in an 1880 pioneer house; workers who built the temple stayed here in the 1880s. The **Yardley Inn,** 190 W. 200 South, (435) 835-1861 or (800) 858-6634, is a turn-of the-century English-style home. All five rooms and one suite have private baths; two rooms have fireplaces. **Cedar Crest Inn** is located in a rural mountain setting on the left about one mile before Palisade State Park, south of town, (435) 835-6352, and offers seven bed-and-breakfast guest rooms and an elegant restaurant for guests (closed Sun.). If you prefer a modern B&B, try the **Legacy Inn,** 337 N. 100 East, (435) 835-8352, a new Victorian-style house. There are four guest rooms (two with private baths) and a family suite.

Campgrounds: In the Manti–La Sal National Forest, **Manti Community Campground**, seven miles east on 500 South/Manti Canyon Road, is open with water from early June to early Oct. and has a trout fishing pond. Fee is $8, elevation 7,400 feet. The road continues nine miles to Skyline Drive.

Other Practicalities
The **post office** is at 140 N. Main, (435) 835-5081. **Manti Medical Clinic** is at 159 N. Main,

(435) 835-3344. Manti's **public library** is downtown at 2 S. Main, (435) 835-2201.

VICINITY OF MANTI

Palisade State Park
People have been enjoying themselves at 70-acre Palisade Lake since 1873. A pleasure resort here once featured a dance hall and a steam excursion boat. Now a state park, the lake lies six miles south of Manti, then two miles east. Only nonmotorized craft may be used. Canoeing and sailboarding are popular here. Canoes can be rented at the park. Anglers catch rainbow and cutthroat trout. The swimming beach and fishing conditions are best early in the season, before the water level drops. Cottonwoods shade the picnic area and campground. The campground is open with showers from early April to late October. Restrooms close in winter, but self-contained campers can still stay here. Admission fees are $4 per vehicle for day use, $10 per vehicle for camping; P.O. Box H, Manti, UT 84642, (435) 835-7275 (ranger) or (800) 322-3770 (reservations). Campground reservations are a good idea on summer weekends.

The nine-hole **Palisade Golf Course,** just beyond the state park entrance, (435) 835-4653, has a clubhouse, pro shop, and driving range.

Gunnison Reservoir, three miles west of the state park, has good water-skiing and fishing for bass and perch; there are no developed facilities here, though people use the shore to launch boats (the west shore is best); ask directions in Manti. **Nine Mile Reservoir** has a fine reputation for rainbow and other trout; the small lake is west of U.S. 89 and two miles south of Sterling.

Gunnison
The name honors Captain John Gunnison, an Army surveyor killed by Indians in 1853 near Sevier Lake. Gunnison (pop. 2,101) is an agricultural center with two motels, a campground, and several places to eat. An information booth is open in summer in the park on North Main.

Accommodations
$50–75: The variety of lodging options offered at **Palisade Lodge,** 4.5 miles south of Manti,

(435) 835-5413, range from budget to deluxe. The lodge's recreation facilities include a pool, water slide, racquetball court, weight room, spas, and sauna.

SALINA

Salina (pronounced suh-LINE-uh by locals) is a Spanish word for "salt mine," one of which is found nearby. The first pioneers arrived in 1863, but Indian troubles forced them to evacuate the site from 1866 to 1872. Today, Salina is a handy travelers' stop, strategically located at the junction of U.S. 89 and I-70. You'll find more than half a dozen motels and places to eat downtown and near the I-70 interchange.

Accommodations

Under $50: Downtown, **Henry's Hideway,** 60 N. State St., (435) 529-7467 or (800) 354-6468, is a nicely maintained motor court with pool.

$50–75: The **Victorian Inn B&B,** 190 W. Main St., (435) 529-7342 or (800) 972-7183, is a refurbished Victorian mansion with wonderful moldings and stained glass. There are three guest rooms, all with private baths. Out by the freeway exit is **Shaheen's Best Western Motel,** 1225 S. State St., (435) 529-7455 or (800) 528-1234, with a small pool, guest laundry, and coffee shop. Another good stop is the **Scenic Hills Budget Host Inn,** 75 E. 1500 South, (435) 529-7483 or (800) 283-4678, with a 24-hour Denny's restaurant adjacent.

Campgrounds: Butch Cassidy Campground, 1100 S. State, between I-70 Exit 54 and downtown, (435) 529-7400, offers sites for tents ($9) and RVs ($16 without hookups, $22 with) with showers, store, and laundry. **Salina Creek R.V. Camp,** behind the Texaco Station at 1385 S. State (near I-70 Exit 54), (435) 529-3711, costs $18 with hookups; has showers, store, and laundry.

Food

There are a number of restaurants at the freeway exit, but for a more unique experience, drive downtown to **Moms Café,** 10 E. Main St., (435) 529-3921, with good home cooking in a vintage storefront.

Other Practicalities

Salina Medical Clinic is at 310 W. Main, (435) 529-7411. The **public library,** at 90 W. Main, (435) 529-7753, is open Monday–Friday 1:30–6 P.M. and Saturday noon–2 P.M. The **city pool** is behind the library.

Vicinity of Salina

The **Redmond Clay and Salt Company** operates an open-pit salt mine three miles north of Redmond; you're welcome to watch the operations from an overlook that is open Monday–Friday 8 A.M.–4:30 P.M. For more information, contact the mine office at 6005 N. 100 West, (435) 529-7402. Watch for the company's "Real Salt" brand salt in local gift shops and stores.

From I-70 east of Salina, you can turn north on back roads to Skyline Drive and the Wasatch Plateau or head south into the alpine country of the Fish Lake Mountains. The small **Gooseberry Campground** lies along Gooseberry Creek in an aspen forest of the Fish Lake Mountains; elevation is 7,800 feet. Open with water from late May to early Nov.; free. Take I-70 Gooseberry Road Exit 61 and go south 10 miles (six miles of pavement, then four miles of gravel). Snowmobiling is popular in this area during winter. The road continues south, climbing steadily through forests and meadows to **Niotche–Lost Creek Divide** (elev. 10,320 feet) in another 10 miles, then winds down to Johnson Valley Reservoir, where pavement continues to Fish Lake.

RICHFIELD

The seat of Sevier County and the center of a large agricultural region, Richfield (pop. 6,800) has a dozen motels, a good selection of restaurants, and other services for travelers; most are along the I-70 business route. This is by far the best-equipped town for travelers for some hundreds of miles.

See some local history in the museum exhibits inside the **Ralph Ramsey House** at 57 E. 200 North (behind the courthouse); hours vary, call (435) 896-6439 (city offices) to schedule a visit. The stuccoed-adobe structure dates from 1873–74. Before settling in Richfield, Ralph Ramsey carved the original eagle for the famous gate beside Brigham Young's residence in Salt Lake City.

Accommodations

$50–75: Almost all of Richfield's motels string along South Main Street. **Budget Host Knights Inn,** 69 S. Main, (435) 896-8228 or (800) 525-9024, has some kitchen units, and small pets are okay. **Best Western Appletree Inn,** 145 S. Main St., (435) 896-5481 or (800) 528-1234, offers large rooms including five two-bedroom units that can sleep up to eight. **Quality Inn,** 540 S. Main St., (435) 896-5465, has some kitchen units, an exercise room, and a free breakfast voucher for an adjoining restaurant. The **Days Inn,** 333 N. Main, (435) 896-6476 or (888) 275-8513, and the **Super 8,** 1575 N. Main, (435) 896-9204, are both new and north of town. Each of the above listings has a pool.

Campgrounds: Open year-round, **J.R. Munchies RV Park,** at 745 S. Main, (435) 896-9340, $11 RVs without hookups, $16 with, has a store, showers, and laundry. **Richfield KOA** is also open all year with spaces for tents and RVs at 600 S. 600 West, (435) 896-6674; $17 without hookups, $21 with; has pool, store, showers, and laundry.

Food

The steak house restaurant at the **Days Inn,** 333 N. Main, (435) 896-6476, is one of the best in town. The **Little Wonder Café,** 101 North Main St., (435) 896-8960, is the place to go for old-fashioned breakfasts and home-style meals. **Pepperbellys Restaurant,** 680 S. Main St., (435) 896-2097, is a lively Mexican-style restaurant with a '50s-theme dining room.

Events

Sevier County Fair in August presents entertainment, livestock shows, 4-H exhibits, and a demolition derby. September is a busy month with the **Rocky Mountain ATV Jamboree,** the **Fishlake Mountain Bike Festival,** the **Fall Festival of the Arts,** and the **Gathering of the Clans,** which features highland games and activities.

Services

The **city park** at Main and 300 North (where U.S. 89 makes a bend) has covered picnic tables, playground, and an information booth (open in summer). An indoor/outdoor **swimming pool** sits at 600 W. 500 North, (435) 896-8572. **K-C Waterslide,** 995 South 100 East, (435) 896-5334, offers another way to get wet in summer. **Cove View Municipal Golf Course** has nine holes on the southwest edge of town (take S. Airport Rd. from S. Main), (435) 896-9987. The **post office** is at 93 N. Main, (435) 896-6231. **Sevier Valley Hospital** is at 1100 N. Main, (435) 896-8271.

Information

For travel info, visit the **information booth** in an 1888 former hardware store moved to the city park at Main and 400 North (open Mon.–Sat. 10 A.M.–7 P.M. in summer) or contact the **Sevier County Travel Council** at 220 N. 600 West (Richfield, UT 84701), (435) 896-8898 or (800) 662-8898; open year-round Mon.–Fri. 9 A.M.–5 P.M. The **Richfield Ranger District office** of the Fishlake National Forest has recreation and road information for the mountain country south and east of town and sells maps and books; the **supervisor's office** has general information on the entire forest. Both offices are open Monday–Friday 8 A.M.–5 P.M. at 115 E. 900 North (Richfield, UT 84701), (435) 896-9233. The **BLM District office,** across the street from the USFS offices at 150 East 900 North (Richfield, UT 84701), can give you information about recreation areas controlled by the BLM for much of this part of Utah; open Mon.–Fri. 7:45 A.M.–4:30 P.M. The **public library** is open Monday–Saturday afternoons and evenings in a Carnegie building (built in 1913–1914) at 83 E. Center, (435) 896-5169.

VICINITY OF RICHFIELD

Paiute All-Terrain Vehicle Trail

ATVers enjoy this 200-mile scenic loop trail and its many side trips in the scenic Pahvant Range, the Tushar Mountains, and the Monroe Mountains surrounding Richfield. Trail users travel among cool mountains, rugged canyons, and desert country. The trail is multi-use and can be enjoyed by mountain bikers, hikers, horseback riders, and even those with four-wheel-drive automobiles. Not all of the trail is suitable for each mode of travel; some parts are rough, others are narrow. Obtain up-to-date information before starting. Access points include Beaver, Richfield, Fillmore, Fremont Indian State Park, Kanosh, Piute State Park, Marysvale, and Circleville—and more access points are planned. Information and a brochure are available from the Fishlake National Forest office (see Richfield information, above) and local tourist and state park offices. Information kiosks are also being built at the access points. **Millard County Tourism** also offers travel info on the entire trail; open Mon.–Fri. 9 A.M.–5 P.M. at 195 N. Main in Fillmore (P.O. Box 1082, Fillmore, UT 84631), (435) 743-7803 or (800) 441-4ATV.

Monrovian Park

A paved road leads southeast from Monroe into this park in a pretty canyon. Cottonwoods and Gambel oaks shade picnic areas along gurgling Monroe Creek. Drinking water is available in summer. Four trails from the park area wind up onto the high Sevier Plateau above. Most spectacular is the trail that goes up Monroe Creek from the picnic areas, then follows Third Left Hand Fork to Scrub Flat Trail (six miles one-way); you'll have to do some wading. A narrow unpaved road with steep grades also climbs into the mountains. The Richfield Ranger District office in Richfield has detailed information about exploring this area. To reach the park, head south on Main Street in Monroe and follow signs four miles.

FREMONT INDIAN STATE PARK

The prehistoric Fremont people had lived over much of Utah, but archaeologists weren't aware of this group's identity until 1931. Artifacts discovered along the Fremont River in central Utah indicated that the Fremont was a distinct culture. The largest excavated site was discovered in Clear Creek Canyon during construction of I-70 in 1983. The Five Finger Ridge Village site probably had more than 150 occupants at its peak, around A.D. 1100; more people lived nearby in the canyon. The Fremont farmed in the canyon bottom and sought game and wild plant foods. They lived in pit houses and stored surplus food in carefully constructed granaries. More than 500 rock-art panels in the canyon depict the religious and hunting aspects of Fremont

life in a cryptic form. Nothing remains at the village site, located across the canyon; workers constructing I-70 cut most of the ridge away to use as fill after the scientific excavations had been completed. Only an experienced eye can spot pit-house villages after nearly 1,000 years of weathering, so there was little to see at this village site anyway.

Visitors' Center

The park's visitors' center, dedicated in 1987, has excellent displays of artifacts found during excavations. Many aspects of Fremont life remain a mystery, but exhibits present ideas of how the Indians could have lived here. Children can use a Fremont mano and metate to grind corn. A 16-minute video program introduces the Fremont, their foods, events that may have caused their departure, and the excavation of Five Finger Ridge Village. The exhibit area also has short video programs on the Fremont. Models illustrate pit-house construction and how Five Finger Ridge Village may have looked. A full-size replica of a pit house includes audio explanations of the functions of the dwelling.

Three loop trails begin outside the visitors' center. Pick up a pamphlet inside for the Show Me Rock Art and Discovery Trails; keyed to numbered stops, the pamphlets provide more insight into Fremont life, partly on Hopi Indian legends. **Show Me Rock Art Trail** (200 yards) leads past fine petroglyphs; the trail is level and graded and can be used by people with strollers or wheelchairs. **Discovery Trail** (200 yards) goes to more rock art and climbs a short way above the visitors' center. **Canyon Overlook Trail** (1,000 feet) ascends about 500 feet above the visitors' center for fine views of the canyon and surrounding mountains; this starts as a nature trail but continues another mile. Park staff can tell you of 10 other trails and rock-art sites in the area, too. New trails are currently under construction and all park trails allow mountain-bike travel. Volunteers and rangers lead walks in summer.

You can purchase related books, maps, rock-art posters, petroglyph replicas, Indian crafts, T-shirts, and postcards in the center. Video programs are shown on request. Park staff will take groups to other sites in the canyon; call or write at least a week in advance; 15500 Clear Creek Canyon Rd., Sevier, UT 84766, (435) 527-4631.

Open daily 9 A.M.–6 p.m. in summer and daily 9 A.M.–5 P.M. the rest of the year; closed on winter holidays; $5 per vehicle. The park is near I-70 Exit 17 in Clear Creek Canyon, five miles west of U.S. 89 and 16 miles east of I-15. Two picnic areas are on the frontage road east of the visitors' center. You can camp at Castle Rock Campground (see below). A short scenic drive follows the old highway nine miles through Clear Creek Canyon between the visitors' center and I-70 Ranch Exit 8.

VICINITY OF FREMONT INDIAN STATE PARK

Castle Rock Campground

Clear Creek cut its canyon through tuff—a soft rock formed of hot volcanic ash from eruptions in the Tushar Mountains area. Erosion has carved towering buttresses and narrow canyons at Castle Rock, just off the main canyon. Campsites lie in a cottonwood and oak forest beside Joe Lott Creek; open with drinking water during the warmer months; $9. Register at the state park visitors' center. Take I-70 Fremont Indian State Park Exit 17, turn onto the south frontage road, and follow it 1.3 miles.

company housing at Upper Kimberly, ca. 1900

Kimberly Scenic Drive

This unpaved 16-mile road climbs to about 10,000 feet on the north slopes of the Tushar Mountains. You'll enjoy good views and cool forests of aspen and fir. Old Kimberly, a ghost-town site and once the center of the Gold Mountain Mining District, is reached about halfway. Miners started the town in 1888. Gold production peaked around the turn of the century, then dropped off after 1907; production has been only sporadic since. Little remains of the town, but you'll see mine shafts, tailings, mill ruins, and foundations. Prospectors haven't given up hope—more recent mining equipment can be seen along the road, too. Cars with good clearance can usually negotiate the road if it's dry; ask locally or check at the Beaver Ranger District office of the Fishlake National Forest, corner of 190 North and 100 East in Beaver, (435) 438-2436. Take I-70 Exit 17, turn west on the north frontage road and follow it under I-70; the drive ends at Marysvale on U.S. 89. Kimberly Scenic Drive connects with the Kimberly/Big John Road Backway (Forest Route 123) above Marysvale and winds through the alpine forests, rocky slopes, and meadows of the Tushar Mountains to UT 153 (high-clearance vehicles recommended). See the Fishlake National Forest map.

Big Rock Candy Mountain

This multicolored mountain, made famous in a song by Burl Ives, rises above the Sevier River. Cold mineral springs high on the mountainside are claimed to be very healthful and a cure for many ailments. The water, usually diluted before drinking, has a slight lemonade tang but no scent.

JUNCTION

This tiny village (pop. 138) near the confluence of the south and east forks of the Sevier River is the Piute County seat. The entire county contains only 1,329 inhabitants. It's one of the smallest and most mountainous in the state, but local people say that if all the mountains were ironed out, the county would be one of Utah's largest! The outlaw Butch Cassidy grew up in this country and learned his first lawless ways here by altering cattle brands. The rustic cabin the Cassidys once called home still stands 2.5 miles south of Circleville (between Mileposts 156 and 157 on U.S. 89). The bright red county courthouse dates from 1902–03; drop in on weekdays for tourist information.

Acccommodations

Under $50: This isn't a fancy place, but the **Junction Motel** is on the south edge of town, (435) 577-2629, with basic rooms. Two rooms have sitting rooms and fireplaces, and sleep up to six people; open Apr. 1-late Nov.

Campgrounds: Fat's Country Cafe and RV Park, (435) 577-2672, is one block west from the courthouse, open daily; $6 tents, $9 RVs without hookups, $14 RVs with; no showers. **City Creek Campground** is five miles northwest on UT 153, then right one mile; sites lie along wooded City Creek at an elevation of 7,600 feet; open with water from Memorial Day to Labor Day weekends; free.

Other Practicalities
The **"biggest little rodeo in the world"** is held in July in Marysvale. The **Piute County Fair** takes place in August. Vehicles with stout engines can follow UT 153 up a long grade into the Tushar Mountains to Puffer Lake (18 miles) and other scenic spots, then descend to Beaver (40 miles); pavement ends just outside Junction, then there's 25 miles of dirt road before pavement begins again. This road isn't recommended for trailers or RVs. (See The Tushar Mountains, above.)

VICINITY OF JUNCTION

Piute State Park
The 3,300-acre Piute Reservoir is one of the largest in central Utah. It's relatively undeveloped, however, with just an outhouse or two, a place to launch boats, and some docks. Anglers catch rainbow trout here. The lake also has plenty of room for water-skiers. The park has no drinking water, established sites, or fee. Contact Otter Creek State Park (see below) for more information. From the town of Junction, drive

north six miles on U.S. 89 and turn right 1.4 miles at the sign (near Milepost 172).

Otter Creek State Park
Otter Creek Reservoir has some of the best trout fishing in Utah; it's 6.5 miles long and one-half to three-quarters of a mile wide (2,500 acres). Birdwatching is often good—especially in winter for raptors and swans and in spring for waterfowl and songbirds. Shore fishing can be productive in spring and autumn, but in summer you really need a boat because of moss near the shore and because the fish move to deeper waters. The park stays open all year and offers ice fishing and ice-skating in winter. The campground area at the south end of the lake (elev. 6,400 feet) has showers, tables with windbreaks, boat ramp, dock, and a fish-cleaning station. Boats with motors can be rented just outside the park. You can make reservations for the developed sites, or you can nearly always find a slot in the adjacent overflow areas. People also camp and fish at Fisherman's Beach, Tamarisk Point, and South Point on the west shore; no water or charge (BLM land). Entrance fees at the state park are $4 per vehicle for day use, $11 per vehicle for camping, or $9 per vehicle for camping at overflow areas; P.O. Box 43, Antimony, UT 84712, (435) 624-3268 or (435) 322-3770 (reservations). From the town of Junction, go two miles south on U.S. 89, then turn east 13 miles on UT 62. **Otter Creek RV Park Marina,** across the highway, (435) 624-3292 or (800) 441-3292, offers RV sites ($9 without hookups, $15 with), a café (open daily for breakfast, lunch, and dinner), showers, boat rentals, and fishing supplies; open Mar. 1–Oct. 31.

FISH LAKE AND VICINITY

This large lake and the surrounding mountain country comprise an alpine setting of great beauty. You'll see expansive vistas, pristine meadows, sparkling streams, and dense forests on drives through the area. Hikers can reach more remote spots, such as the 11,633-foot summit of the Fish Lake Hightop Plateau. Part of what's intriguing about Fish Lake is the mix of ecosystems: sagebrush plateaus meet up with aspen forests at the water's edge.

Fish Lake formed when a block of the earth's crust collapsed. The water that filled the basin created one of Utah's largest natural lakes—six miles long and one mile wide. Anglers fish for lake (Mackinaw) and rainbow trout and splake (a hybrid of mackinaw and eastern brook trout). Swimming isn't recommended due to the cold (50° F) water temperatures. Summers are cool at this 8,800-foot elevation. Heavy winter snows provide recreation for snowmobilers and cross-country skiers.

The lake and surrounding country lie in the Loa Ranger District of the Fishlake National Forest. The **Forest Information Center** in Fish Lake Lodge, (435) 638-1033, is open daily in summer and sells or dispenses books, maps, and pamphlets. You can also contact the district office for the latest camping, fishing, hiking, and road conditions at 138 S. Main, Loa, UT 84747, (435) 836-2811; open all year Mon.–Fri. 8 A.M.–4:30 P.M. Paved UT 25 branches off UT 24 (31 miles southeast of Richfield, 14 miles northwest of Loa) and climbs seven miles over a pass to the lake; the road is usually kept open year-round.

FISH LAKE CAMPGROUNDS AND RESORTS

Most of the Forest Service campgrounds lie just off UT 25 along the lake's west shore. Dispersed camping isn't permitted near Fish Lake; you'll have to head farther into the backcountry if you'd like an undeveloped spot. The camping season runs from about late May to late October; all the campgrounds along the lake have water and charge an $10 fee. Picnic areas are free (groups can reserve for a charge). Half of the campsites and the group areas can be reserved by calling (800) 280-CAMP. Recreation sites, with distances from the junction of UT 25 and UT 24, are:

Doctor Creek (seven miles; in an aspen grove on the southwest shore; group areas can be reserved; has a dump station)

Twin Creek Picnic Area (8.8 miles; day use only; a ranger station is opposite the turnoff)

Mackinaw Campground (nine miles; in an aspen grove overlooking the lake)

Bowery Creek Campground and Picnic Area (10 miles; in an aspen grove overlooking the lake)

Joe Bush Fishermen Parking (10.7 miles)

Pelican Promontory (12 miles; turn left one mile for a panoramic view; not suitable for low-clearance vehicles)

Frying Pan Campground (14.5 miles; on the edge of an aspen grove near Johnson Valley Reservoir)

Tasha Equestrian Campground (14.7 miles, then one-half mile in; under construction; for people with horses)

Piute Parking Area (14.8 miles; access to the reservoir). At the junction just past the reservoir, you can turn north along Sevenmile Creek on Forest Route 640 to I-70 and Salina (36 miles) or south on Forest Route 036 to a boat ramp on Johnson Valley Reservoir (one mile), Fremont River (three miles), and Loa (20 miles). Both drives have exceptional scenery and go past many good spots for fishing and primitive camping; the roads are usually okay for cars.

Accommodations

$50–75: Fish Lake Resorts operate both the **Fish Lake Lodge** and **Lakeside Resort** and each offers accommodations, a store, and a marina on the lake's southwest shore. The marinas rent fishing and pontoon boats and provide boat ramps, slips, bait, tackle, and boat gas. However, the accommodations are quite different at each of the resorts. At **Lakeside Resort,** 7.3 miles in on UT 25, where the highway first meets the lake, (435) 638-1000, free-standing cabins cost $50 for double occupancy (slightly more on weekends and holidays); some are open all year; RV sites with hookups are open May 15–October 15 at $17 and $19. **Fish Lake Lodge,** 1.2 miles beyond Lakeside Resort, (435) 638-1000, is a huge, rambling log structure built in 1932; full of character, it has a dining area, dance hall, and a small store open Memorial Day–Labor Day weekends. "Rustic" (older) cabins open Memorial Day weekend to the end of hunting season start at $50. New cabins are available all year and cost $75 (both cabin styles are more on weekends and holidays). The rustic dining room in the lodge has lake views and is open daily for breakfast and dinner. Showers are available to the public for a small fee. Accommodations for Lakeside Resort and Fish Lake Lodge can be reserved year-round by contacting Fish Lake Resorts, 10 E. Center, Hwy. 25, Richfield, UT 84701, (435) 638-1000.

Bowery Haven Resort lies near Fish Lake about 10 miles in on UT 25, Fish Lake, UT 84701, (435) 638-1040 (in-season) or (435) 943-7885 (off-season). The resort's season lasts from late May to late October. Amenities include a marina (fishing boat rentals, ramp, slips, and supplies), cabins ($70 for a cabin with plumbing, and half that for a "rustic" cabin), motel rooms (starting at $70), RV park ($18 with hookups; has showers and laundry; no tents), café (open daily for breakfast, lunch, and dinner), and a small store.

Vehicles with high clearance (only) can drive up directly from Cathedral Valley via Forest Routes 020 and 022.

THOUSAND LAKE MOUNTAIN

This high plateau rises above the Fremont River to an elevation of 11,306 feet at Flat Top. Panoramas from the rim take in the wooded valleys surrounding Fish Lake to the west and the colorful rock formations and canyons of Cathedral Valley in Capitol Reef National Park to the east. Roads and trails provide access to viewpoints and fishing lakes on the plateau. Forest roads lead to the heights from UT 72 on the west and from the middle desert and Cathedral Valley on the east. Thousand Lake Mountain may have been misnamed—its lakes number far fewer than a thousand. Some people think that a mapmaker in the 1800s accidentally switched names between this and Boulder Mountain to the south, which has far more lakes. For more information, contact the Loa Ranger District office in Loa; maps are the 15-minute Torrey topo and the Fishlake National Forest.

Elkhorn Campground

This small campground makes a good base for hikes to lakes and the Flat Top summit; open with water from about mid-June–late Sept.; no charge. Meadows and a forest of aspen, fir, and spruce surround the sites; elevation is 9,300 feet. From the north edge of Loa, turn east and north 12 miles on UT 72 to Forest Route 206 and follow it eight miles to the campground. The winding mountain road is unpaved but passable by cars in dry weather. Desert View Overlook, three miles before the campground, has a fantastic view of Cathedral Valley and beyond. The road to Elkhorn Campground can also be approached from I-70 via UT 72; this paved road climbs over Hogan Pass (elev. 8,961 feet), past meadows, groves of aspen, and fine views of Cathedral Valley and the surrounding country.

LOA

Pioneers settled here in the mid-1870s. A former Mormon missionary who had served in Hawaii suggested the town's unusual name. A commemorative marker next to the 1897 Loa Tithing House, on Center Street one block west from Main, has a rock from Mauna Loa. The small town (pop. 487) is the Wayne County seat and a handy base for exploring the Fish Lake area to the north. The **Wayne County Fair** on the third weekend in August has a parade, rodeo, exhibits, barbecue, and games.

Loa's courthouse and **post office** are at the junction of Main and Center; step inside the courthouse to see a small rock and mineral collection in the lobby. The **Loa Ranger District office** has camping, fishing, hiking, and road condition information for the Fishlake National Forest lands north and east of town; there's also regional travel info. The office is at 138 S. Main, Loa, UT 84747, (435) 836-2811; open Mon.–Fri. 8 A.M.–4:30 P.M. You can visit the brook and rainbow trout at **Loa Fish Hatchery** 2.2 miles north of town; go north on Main and keep straight on the county road where UT 24 curves to the left; open daily 8 A.M.–4:30 P.M.; call (435) 836-2858 before coming out.

Accommodations

$75–100: The best place to stay in Loa is the **Road Creek Inn,** 90 S. Main, (435) 836-2485 or (800) 338-7688. Its restaurant features trout (from their own trout farm), steak, and sandwiches (open daily for dinner). The building was Loa's old hotel; its 12 guest rooms have been refurbished in period style and are now offered B&B style. The owners are part of a ranch family and can also provide horseback riding, cattle drives, and other guest ranch activities. There are also a couple of older motels in town.

NORTHEASTERN UTAH
INTRODUCTION

Northeastern Utah has an extremely diverse landscape comprising barren desert, deep canyons, high plateaus, and the lofty Uinta Mountains. Thousands of well-preserved bones unearthed in the region tell of a time about 140 million years ago when dinosaurs roamed the land in a relatively moist subtropical climate amid tree ferns, evergreens, and ginkgo trees. You can inspect the skeletons of these creatures in excellent museums in Vernal, Price, and Castle Dale, and visit bone excavations at Dinosaur National Monument and Cleveland-Lloyd Dinosaur Quarry.

The high country of the Uinta Mountains offers some of Utah's most scenic alpine scenery. Kings Peak tops the range at 13,528 feet—the highest point in the state. Anglers seek trout and arctic grayling in the countless lakes and streams of the Uintas. Trails provide access for hiking and pack trips into the High Uintas Wilderness at the heart of the range. Other popular recreation areas include Flaming Gorge National Recreation Area, Dinosaur National Monument, the Wasatch Plateau, and the San Rafael Swell. Anglers and boaters have a choice of many large reservoirs, seven of which are state parks. River-runners enjoy lively rides down the Green River through Red, Lodore, Whirlpool, Split Mountain, Desolation, and Gray Canyons.

You'll see two spellings in this region—Uinta and Uintah—both of which are pronounced "you-INT-ah." Geographical terms (Uinta Mountains, Uinta Basin) don't have an "h"; political divisions (Uintah County and Uintah and Ouray Indian Reservation) usually do.

Climate

In summer, the valleys have average highs of about 90° F, which drop to the low 50s at night. Valley temperatures plummet in winter to about 30° during the day and 5° at night. The Wasatch Plateau and Uinta Mountains experience cool weather year-round. Above 10,000 feet, summer highs rarely exceed 70° in the day and drop to the 30s and 40s at night; freezing weather may occur at any time of year. Winter in the mountains brings highs in the 20s and lows well below zero. Annual precipitation changes dramatically with elevation, from about eight inches in the desert to 40 inches in the high country. Snowfall is widespread in winter and very heavy in the mountains.

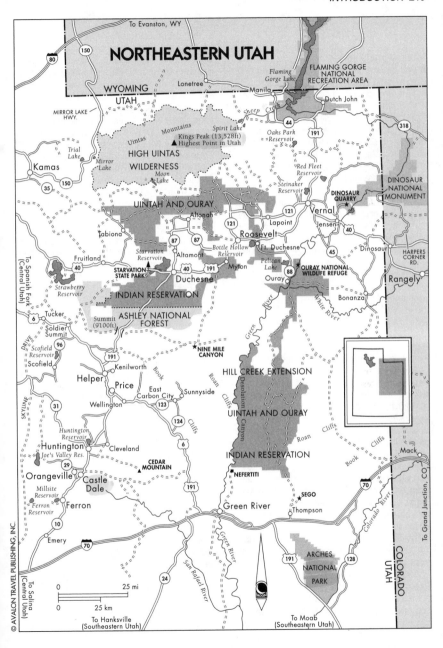

HISTORY

Native Americans

Paleo-Indians trekked across this land beginning at least 15,000 years ago. About A.D. 550, the Fremont culture emerged as a distinct group. The Fremont ranged widely in search of wild foods and places to grow their corn, beans, and squash. By 1300, however, the tribe had mysteriously disappeared, leaving behind village sites, artifacts, and intriguing rock art.

Nomadic Ute Indians moved in at about the same time that the Fremont culture faded away, but the Utes seemed to have no knowledge of their more sophisticated predecessors. Utes guided the Spanish Dominguez-Escalante Expedition through the Uinta Basin south of the Uinta Mountains in 1776 and were the first Indian group encountered by the Mormons in Utah. Mountain men traded with the tribe during the 1820s and 1830s on beaver-trapping expeditions. Neither the Utes nor the mountain men, however, made permanent homes in the Uinta Basin.

Early White Settlement

In the 1870s and early 1880s, the Mormon Church sent out calls for members to colonize lands east of the Wasatch Plateau. Though at first the land looked harsh and barren, crops and orchards eventually prospered with irrigation. Nevertheless, it was some time before the first families took a liking to this country. Mrs. Orange Seely of the Castle Dale area is credited with saying, "The first time I ever swore was when we arrived in Emery County and I said, 'Damn a man who would bring a woman to such a God-forsaken country!'" Individual families also came out on their own and started isolated farms and ranches in the Uinta Basin and along the eastern edge of the Wasatch Plateau to the south. Much of the land proved too dry or rugged for any use and remains in its natural state even today. Discoveries of coal in 1877 and oil in 1900 attracted waves of new people to the sleepy Mormon settlements east of the Wasatch Plateau. Immigrant miners fresh from Europe brought a new cultural diversity to the region.

UINTA MOUNTAINS

This outstanding wilderness area contains lofty peaks, lush grassy meadows, fragrant coniferous forests, crystal-clear streams, and thousands of tiny alpine lakes. The Uintas, unlike most other major ranges of the United States, run east-west. Underground forces pushed rock layers up into a massive dome 150 miles long and 35 miles wide. Ancient Precambrian rocks exposed in the center of the range consist largely of quartzite (metamorphosed sandstone). Outcrops of progressively younger rocks are found away from the center. Glaciers have carved steep ridges and broad basins and left great moraines. Barren rock lies exposed across much of the land, including the peaks and high ridges.

Trees, from 10,000 feet to timberline (about 11,000 feet), include limber pine, Engelmann spruce, and subalpine fir. Lower slopes (7,000–10,000 feet) support dense unbroken forests of lodgepole pine (the most common tree in the Uintas), aspen, Douglas fir, white fir, blue spruce, and scattered stands of ponderosa pine. Elk, moose, mule deer, and Rocky Mountain

goat (reintroduced) come here to graze in summer. Also foraging for food are black bear, mountain lion, coyote, bobcat, raccoon, porcupine, badger, pine marten, snowshoe hare, marmot, and pika. Anglers seek out arctic grayling and native cutthroat, Eastern brook, rainbow, German brown, and golden trout. Aerial stocking keeps even the most remote lakes swimming with fish. Your luck at a lake or stream can range from lousy to fantastic, depending on when it was last stocked and how many other anglers have discovered the spot.

The remote setting of the Uinta Mountains has protected much of the forests from the ravages of logging. The central part received protection in 1931 as a primitive area and designation in 1984 as the High Uintas Wilderness. Four of Utah's major rivers have their source in these mountains: the Bear and Weber Rivers on the north slope and the Provo and Duchesne on the south slope. Despite their great heights, the Uintas have a gentler terrain than the precipitous Wasatch Range. High plateaus and

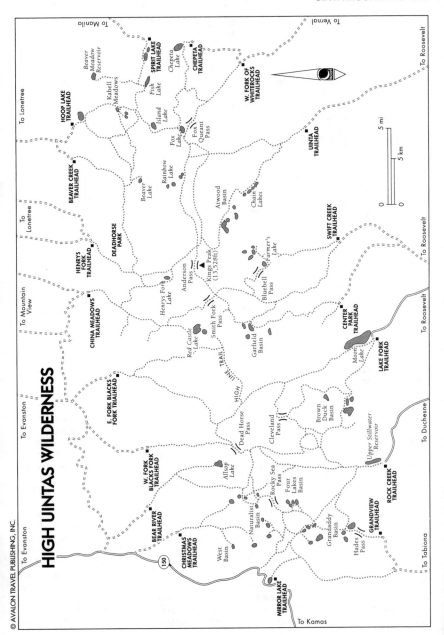

HIGH UINTAS WILDERNESS

© AVALON TRAVEL PUBLISHING, INC.

broad valleys among the peaks hold the abundant rain and snowfall in marshes and ponds, supporting large populations of wildlife and fish.

Visiting the Uintas

Winding over the western end of the range from the town of Kamas to the Wyoming border, UT 150 offers splendid panoramas and access to fishing lakes and hiking trails. On the east, U.S. 191 and UT 44 provide access to the Uintas and Flaming Gorge Reservoir from Vernal. Unpaved roads also lead to trailheads on all sides of the range. Developed and primitive campgrounds can be found along these highways and at other locations including many of the trailheads.

Most people prefer to visit the Uintas from mid-June to mid-September. Campers should be prepared for cold nights and freezing rain even in the warmest months. Afternoon showers are common in summer. Arm yourself with insect repellent to ward off the mosquitoes, especially in July. Snow stays on the ground until well into June, and the meltwater can make trails muddy until early July. The lakes and campgrounds along UT 150 become crowded on summer weekends and holidays, though you can usually get off by yourself on a short hike into the backcountry.

Uinta Chipmunk (Eutamias umbrinus)

An extensive trail system with about 20 trailheads goes deep into the wilderness and connects with many lakes. A great number of trips are possible, from easy day hikes to rigorous treks lasting weeks. Climbers headed for the summits can take trails to a nearby pass, then rock-scramble to the top. Kings Peak attracts the most attention because it's the highest point in Utah. The shortest approach is from Henrys Fork Trailhead on the north, which requires three days of hiking for the 32-mile round-trip; elevation gain is about 4,100 feet. Southern approaches from Swift Creek or Uinta Trailheads usually take an extra day. More than a dozen other peaks in the Uintas exceed 13,000 feet. No permits are needed for travel in the wilderness area, though it's recommended that you sign registers at the trailheads. Groups must not exceed 14 people. The High Uintas Wilderness, an area of about 450,000 acres, is closed

to mechanized vehicles (including bicycles). Horses can use nearly all trails in the wilderness area. An exception is Bluebell Pass, which is impassable for them; other passes may be rough going depending on recent storms and trail maintenance. Winter snows close UT 150 and the back roads, at which time snowmobilers and cross-country skiers come out to enjoy the snowy landscapes.

Information

The U.S. Forest Service manages the Uintas and surrounding forest lands. Northern and western parts are administered by the Wasatch National Forest, 8226 Federal Bldg., 125 S. State St., Salt Lake City, UT 84111, (435) 524-5030. Most of the southern and eastern areas are part of the Ashley National Forest, 355 N. Vernal Ave., Vernal, UT 84078, (435) 789-1181. For specific information, it's best to contact the district offices directly. In the Wasatch National Forest, contact the **Kamas Ranger District office,** P.O. Box 68, Kamas, UT 84036, (435) 783-4338; for the western end of the range, including the Provo River drainage, contact **Evanston Ranger District office,** P.O. Box 1880, Evanston, WY 82931-1880, (435) 642-6662 in summer or (307) 789-3194 year-round; for the northern side including Smiths Forks and Henrys Fork drainages, contact the **Mountain View Ranger District office,** P.O. Box 129, Mountain View, WY 82939, (307) 782-6555. In the Ashley National Forest, contact the **Flaming Gorge Ranger District office,** P.O. Box 278, Manila, UT 84046, (435) 784-3445, about the northeastern side including Spirit Lake and Sheep Creek; the **Vernal Ranger District office,** 355 N. Vernal Ave., Vernal, UT 84078, (435) 789-1181, for the southeastern end including Whiterocks River; the **Roosevelt Ranger District office,** 244 W. U.S. 40, P.O. Box 333-6, Roosevelt, UT 84066, (435) 722-5018, for the southern end including Lake Fork, Yellowstone, and Uinta drainages; and the **Duchesne Ranger District office,** 85 W. Main, P.O. Box I, Duchesne, UT 84021, (435) 738-2482, for the southwestern end including Rock Creek and the North Fork of Duchesne drainages. All these offices have the forest maps and the High Uintas Wilderness topo map (1:75,000 scale). Hikers will find good trail descriptions in the books *High Uinta Trails,* by Mel Davis, *Hiker's Guide to Utah,* by Dave Hall, and *Utah Mountaineering Guide,* by Michael Kelsey. If you plan to do some serious fishing, a set of 10 booklets, *Lakes of the High Uintas,* published by the Utah Division of Wildlife Resources, provides detailed descriptions of lakes, kinds of fish stocked, trail access, and camping. Each booklet covers different drainages; they're available from the main office at 1596 W. North Temple, Salt Lake City, UT 84116, (435) 538-4700, and from the Vernal office at 152 E. 100 North, Vernal, UT 84078, (435) 789-3103.

KAMAS AND THE MIRROR LAKE HIGHWAY (UT 150)

Kamas

Pioneers settled on this spot at the mouth of Beaver Creek Canyon in 1857. Today, Kamas is the start of what is probably Utah's most spectacular alpine drive. The Mirror Lake Highway (UT 150) begins here at an elevation of 6,500 feet and climbs to the crest of the western Uinta Mountains at Bald Mountain Pass (elev. 10,678 feet) before descending on the other side and continuing to Evanston, Wyoming.

Nearest motels are in Heber City (17 miles southwest) and Park City (19 miles west). The **Kamas Ranger District office** is at 50 E. Center (P.O. Box 68, Kamas, UT 84036), (435) 783-4338. Open Mon.–Sat. 8 A.M.–4:30 P.M. from June 1 to mid-Sept. and Mon.–Fri. 8 A.M.–4:30 P.M. the rest of the year. The office has forest maps and detailed recreation information; staff can advise on road conditions, campgrounds, hiking, cross-country skiing, and snowmobiling.

pika (Ochotona princeps)

Mirror Lake Highway

You can drive this scenic highway from about mid-June to mid-October. Campgrounds tend to fill on summer weekends, especially on holi-

days. Reservations can be made for some campsites by calling (800) 280-CAMP.

Snowplows keep the highway cleared in winter to Soapstone, 15.5 miles from Kamas, to provide access for cross-country skiing and snowmobiling. Five trails used by both skiers and snowmobilers begin along the highway and at Soapstone. Skiers using snowmobile trails will find the most solitude on weekdays. **Beaver Creek Cross-Country Trail** begins from Slate Creek (six miles east of Kamas) and parallels the highway to Pine Valley Campground, a distance of 5.5 miles one-way with an elevation gain of 440 feet. This trail is easy; branching off from it are other ski trails rated intermediate and advanced. Obtain information and brochures for these and other skiing areas from the Kamas Ranger District office. Mileages given below correspond to mileposts along the highway:

Mile 0.0: Heading east on UT 150 from the junction with U.S. 189 in Kamas.

Mile 0.1: Kamas Ranger District office on the right.

Mile 3.3: Kamas Fish Hatchery on the right; visitors welcome daily 8 A.M.–4 P.M.

Mile 3.7: Sign for Beaver Creek Nudist Ranch (someone's idea of a practical joke!).

Mile 6.1: Entering **Wasatch National Forest;** Slate Creek.

Mile 6.7: Yellow Pine Campground on the left. Sites are in a forest of ponderosa and lodgepole pine and juniper at an elevation of 7,200 feet; open late May–late Oct.; no water; $6 fee. **Yellow Pine Creek Trail** begins just north of the campground and goes up the creek to Lower Yellow Pine Lake (elev. 9,600 feet; four miles one-way) and beyond; this is a good hike early in the season.

Mile 8.2: Beaver Creek Campground on the right. Sites line both sides of Beaver Creek amid lodgepole pine and willow at 7,300 feet; open from early May to mid-Oct.; no water; $8 fee.

Mile 8.9: Taylor Fork ATV Campground on the right; **Taylor Fork-Cedar Hollow ATV Trail** begins here. Sites are along Beaver Creek in lodgepole pine and aspen at 7,400 feet; water from early June to mid-Sept.; $9 fee.

LOUISE FOOTE

Mile 9.3: Shingle Creek Campground and Picnic Area on the right. Sites are in a mixed forest of pine, spruce, and fir at 7,400 feet; water from early June to mid-Sept.; $10 fee (no charge for day use).

Mile 9.9: Shingle Creek Trail follows the creek upstream to East Shingle Lake (elev. 9,680 feet; 5.5 miles one-way) and Upper Setting Trail; this is a good early-season hike. Past the trailhead, the highway climbs over a small pass to the Provo River and follows it upstream.

Mile 10.5: Lower Provo River Campground is one mile south on Pine Valley Road. Sites are along the Provo River in a pine and spruce forest at 7,600 feet; water from early June to mid-Sept.; $10 fee. The nearby **Pine Valley Group Camping Area** is a group reservation area.

Mile 15.5: Soapstone Campground on the right. Sites are along the Provo River amid lodgepole pine at 8,200 feet; water from early June to mid-Sept.; $12 fee.

Mile 17.0: Shady Dell Campground on the right. Sites lie along the Provo River at 8,200 feet; water from early June to mid-Sept.; $10 fee.

Mile 17.7: West Portal of Duchesne Tunnel; a sign describes this six-mile conduit that brings water from the Duchesne River to the Provo River. **Duchesne Tunnel Camping Area** is a group reservation site; call (800) 280-CAMP.

Mile 18.8: Cobblerest Campground on the right. Sites are near the Provo River in a pine and spruce forest at 8,500 feet; water from mid-June to mid-Sept.; $10 fee.

Mile 22.3: Slate Gorge Overlook on the right.

Mile 23.1: Upper Provo Bridge Camping Area on the right at 9,200 feet; open early July to early September with tables and outhouses but no water; available by group reservation only.

Mile 23.9: Provo River Falls Overlook on the left.

Mile 25.4: Trial Lake Campground is a quarter mile to the left on Spring Canyon Road. Sites are on the southeast shore of the lake in a pine and spruce forest at 9,500 feet; water from early July to early Sept.; $10 fee. There's a parking area near the dam for anglers. Spring Canyon Road continues past the dam to Washington and Crystal Lakes and Crystal Lake Trailhead. **Notch Mountain Trail** begins at Crystal Lake Trailhead, goes north past Wall and Twin Lakes, through the Notch to Ibantik and Meadow Lakes,

to the Weber River (elev. 9,000 feet; 6.5 miles one-way), and to Bald Mountain Pass (elev. 10,678 feet; 10 miles one-way). The **Lakes Country Trail** starts at the Crystal Lake Trailhead and goes west past Island, Long, and other lakes before joining the Smith-Morehouse Trail after three miles.

Mile 26.4: Lilly Lake Campground to the left. Sites are in a spruce and fir forest at 9,800 feet; water from early July to early Sept.; $10 fee. Lilly, Teapot, and Lost Lakes lie within short walking distances.

Mile 26.7: Lost Creek Campground to the right. Sites are beside the creek in a spruce and pine forest at 9,800 feet; water from early July to early Sept.; $10 fee. Lost Lake is a short walk to the southwest.

Mile 29.1: Bald Mountain Pass (elev. 10,678 feet); **Bald Mountain Picnic Area and Trailhead** on the left. **Bald Mountain National Recreation Trail** climbs to the summit of Bald Mountain (elev. 11,947 feet) with great views all the way; the two-mile (one-way) trail climbs 1,269 feet, putting you in the midst of the Uinta Range's alpine grandeur. Expect a strenuous trip because of the high elevation and steep grades; carry rain gear to fend off the cold wind (even in summer) and possible storms. From the top, weather permitting, you'll enjoy panoramas of the High Uintas Wilderness, the Lakes Roadless Area, and the Wasatch Range. **Notch Lake Trail** also begins near the picnic area and connects with Trial Lake.

Mile 30.5: Moosehorn Campground on the left. Sites are on the east and north shores of Moosehorn Lake in a spruce and fir forest at 10,400 feet; water from early July to early Sept.; $10 fee. **Fehr Lake Trail** begins a quarter mile south and across the highway; it goes to Fehr Lake (one-half mile), Shepard Lake (1.5 miles), and Hoover Lake (1.5 miles).

Mile 31.2: Mirror Lake Campground and Picnic Area are a half mile to the right. This is the largest campground (91 sites) on the Mirror Lake Highway. Sites are near the lake in a forest of spruce, fir, and lodgepole pine at 10,200 feet; water from early July to early Sept.; $12 fee. Parking for picnicking and fishing costs $3. Anglers can park at the south end of the lake and at the Mirror Lake Trailhead. Boats can be hand-launched; no motors at all are permitted on the lake. **Highline and North Fork of the Duch-**

esne Trails lead from the trailhead to the High Uintas Wilderness.

Mile 32.1: Pass Lake Trailhead on the left, across the highway from Pass Lake. **Lofty Lake and Weber Canyon Trails** begin here and connect with other trails. Weber Canyon Trail goes to Holiday Park Trailhead (elev. 8,000 feet; seven miles one-way), reached by road from Oakley.

Mile 33.9: Butterfly Lake Campground on the left. Sites are on the south shore of the lake in a spruce, fir, and lodgepole pine forest at 10,300 feet; water from early July to early Sept.; $10 fee.

Mile 34.2: Hayden Pass (elev. 10,200 feet); **Highline Trailhead** on the right. This is the closest point on the highway to the **High Uintas Wilderness.** The Highline Trail tends to be muddy, rocky, and heavily used. It winds east from here across the Uintas nearly 100 miles to East Park Reservoir north of Vernal. The highway makes a gradual descent from the pass along Hayden Fork of the Bear River. Contact the Evanston Ranger District offices for camping, hiking, and back-road travel in this area.

Mile 35.0: Ruth Lake Trailhead on the left; the lake is an easy three-quarter-mile hike west. There are only a few parking spots available.

Mile 38.9: Sulphur Campground on the right. Sites lie near the Hayden Fork of Bear River in a forest of lodgepole pine, fir, and spruce at 9,000 feet; water from early June to mid-Sept.; $9 fee.

Mile 41.8: Beaver View Campground on the right. Sites overlook Hayden Fork of Bear River from a lodgepole pine and aspen forest at 8,900 feet; a beaver pond and lodge can be seen near the entrance station; water from early June to mid-Sept.; $9 fee.

Mile 42.4: Hayden Fork Campground on the right. Sites lie along Hayden Fork of Bear River in a lodgepole pine and aspen forest at 8,900 feet; water from early June to mid-Sept.; $9 fee.

Mile 45.6: Stillwater Campground on the right. Sites are in a lodgepole pine and aspen forest at 8,500 feet, near where Hayden Fork and Stillwater Fork meet the Bear River; water from early June to mid-Sept.; $9 fee.

Mile 45.8: Christmas Meadow Road goes right four miles to **Christmas Meadow Campground** and **Stillwater Trailhead.** Sites overlook a large meadow from a forest of lodgepole pine at 9,200 feet; water from early June to mid-Sept.; $9 fee. Stillwater Trailhead, near the camp-

ground, is the starting point for hikes to lakes in Amethyst, Middle, and West Basins to the south. **Wolverine ATV Trailhead Campground** is 1.5 miles in on Christmas Meadow Road, then one mile off; it offers sites for ATVers at 9,000 feet near a trailhead for a Lily Lake loop. Open mid-June–mid-Sept.; no water or fee.

Mile 46.5: Bear River Ranger Station on the right. Stop here for recreation information about the northwestern part of the Uinta Range. The office is open Monday–Thursday 8 A.M.–4:30 P.M., Friday and Saturday 8 A.M.–6 P.M., and Sunday and holidays 8 A.M.–5 P.M. In season, the campground is open weekends only mid-May–late May, daily late May–mid-October, then weekends only again in late October; (435) 642-6662. Off-season, you'll need to contact the office in Evanston, Wyoming, P.O. Box 1880, Evanston, WY 82931-1880, (307) 789-3194, one mile south of I-80 at 1565 UT 150, Suite A.

Mile 47.5: A road turns right two miles to **Lily Lake.** Most of the route is unmaintained dirt road.

Mile 48.2: Bear River Campground on the left. Sites are along the Bear River just upstream from the East Fork confluence in a lodgepole pine and aspen forest at 8,400 feet; water from early June to mid-Sept.; $9 fee.

Mile 48.3: East Fork Bear River Campground on the left. Sites are along the Bear River just below the East Fork confluence in a lodgepole pine and aspen forest at 8,400 feet; water from early June to mid-Sept.; $9 fee.

Mile 48.6: Forest Route 058 goes right about 17 miles to **Little Lyman Lake Campground.** Sites are near the east shore of the lake in a lodgepole pine forest at 9,200 feet; water from early June to mid-Sept.; $7 fee. Lyman Lake is just a short walk away. **Meeks Cabin Reservoir and Campground** are two miles farther on Forest Route 058, then left about five miles on Forest Route 073. Sites here are along the southwest shore of the reservoir in a lodgepole pine forest at 8,800 feet; water from early June to mid-Sept.; $9 fee.

Mile 48.7: Leaving Wasatch National Forest. This is approximately the end of the scenic drive. The valley opens up and supports sagebrush and scattered aspen groves.

Mile 54.6: Wyoming border; highway becomes WY 150. Evanston is 23 miles ahead with several motels and two large grocery stores.

VERNAL

One of the oldest and largest communities in northeastern Utah, Vernal makes a handy base for travels to the many sights of the region. The perennial waters of Ashley Creek—named for mountain man William H. Ashley, who passed by in 1825—attracted the first settlers to the valley during the early 1870s. The small community went through a succession of names—Hatchtown, Ashley Center, and Ashley—before residents decided on Vernal in 1893.

Rugged terrain and poor roads isolated the area from the rest of Utah for years. In 1916, when a local businessman wanted to order a shipment of bricks from Salt Lake City for the facade of a new bank, he solved the problem of expensive shipping costs by having the bricks sent by parcel post! Freight cost $2.50 per hundred pounds while the postal service charged only $1.05. Other Vernal residents caught on to the post office's bargain rates, and even started parcel-posting crops to market until the postal service changed its regulations. The Bank of Vernal, nicknamed the "Parcel Post Bank," still serves the town at the corner of Main and Vernal.

Growth of the oil industry in recent decades has been a mixed blessing because of its boom-and-bust cycles. Vernal is the Uintah County seat and has a population of 7,366.

SIGHTS

Utah Field House of Natural History State Park and Museum

This is a good place for both adults and children to learn about the dinosaurs that once roamed the Uinta Basin. Fifteen full-size models stalk or fly in the Dinosaur Gardens outside. The natural setting makes the strange creatures seem almost alive. Inside, the Geology and Fossil Hall has displays of 45-million-year-old skulls of ancient mammals, crocodiles, and alligators that once roamed across Utah. Other exhibits offer fossil specimens ranging in size from tiny insects to massive dinosaur bones. A geologic mural 36 feet across shows the structure of rock layers in northeastern Utah. Other exhibits trace Utah's Native Americans from the Desert Culture

through Anasazi and Fremont groups to the modern Ute. The Natural History Hall, located at 235 E. Main, (435) 789-3799, offers a close look at mounted wildlife of the state. It's open daily 8 A.M.–9 P.M. from Memorial Day to Labor Day weekends and 9 A.M.–5 P.M. daily in winter. Admission is $3 per person or $5 for a family of up to eight members; children five and under are free. The **Vernal Welcome Center** in the museum building has area travel information. A city park behind the museum contains a playground and offers a shady spot for a picnic.

Daughters of Utah Pioneers Museum

Get to know Vernal's pioneers here. The many historical photos and carefully labeled exhibits present a good idea of what life was like in the old days. The large collection includes a pioneer kitchen, spinning wheels, farm machinery, a buggy, old organs, clothing, guns, and a model of a Western town. You'll see Dr. Harvey Coe Hullinger's well-stocked medicine chest, last used in 1926 when he was 101 years old. One room of the museum is the stone tithing office, built in 1877. The Daughters of Utah Pioneers operate the museum located across the street from the Uintah Stake Temple at the corner of 200 South and 500 West; open Mon.–Sat. 1–7 P.M. June 1–Labor Day and at other times by request (ask at the Vernal Welcome Center).

Western Heritage Museum

This museum is located at the Western Park Complex, at 300 East and 200 South, (435) 789-7399, Vernal's new convention center, amphitheater, equestrian center, and race track. A pioneer museum and art gallery have a special emphasis on Utah's outlaw heritage (real or imaginary). Housed here is the gun used by Matt Dillon in the TV series *Gunsmoke*. Open in summer Mon.–Sat. 9 A.M.–6 P.M. and Mon.–Fri. 10 A.M.–5 P.M. in the off-season. Admission is included with the ticket to the Natural History Museum.

Ladies of the White House Doll Collection

Head for the Uintah County Library next door to the Utah Natural History Museum on Main Street to view a display of dolls fashioned after

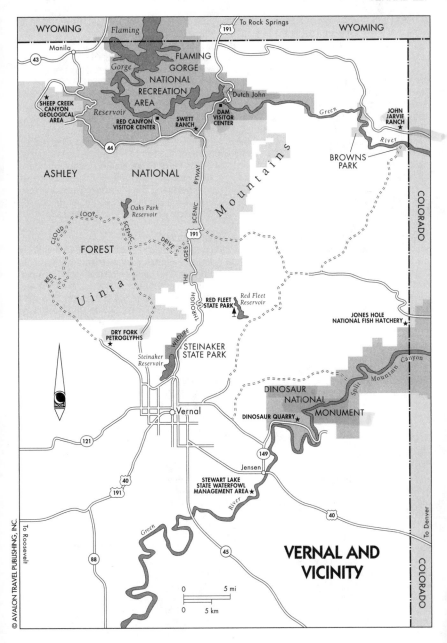

VERNAL AND VICINITY

each first lady. Each wears a handsewn reproduction of the dress she wore at the Inaugural Ball. Open Mon.–Thurs. 10 A.M.–8 P.M., Fri. and Sat. 10 A.M.–6 P.M.

Dry Fork Petroglyphs

Several panels of famous petroglyphs are located along a sharp sandstone bluff about 10 miles northeast of Vernal. Considered to be some of the best rock art in the United States, what makes these carvings so notable is the fact that they contain dozens of nearly life-sized human figures, many with elaborate headdresses and ornamentation. The significance of these murals is unknown, though they were probably carved by Fremont Indians and are reckoned to be between 1200 and 1600 years old.

To reach the Dry Fork Petroglyphs (also called the McConkie Petroglyphs), drive west from Vernal on Main and turn north on 500 West. Follow the main road when it turns to the left onto UT 121 and continue until the junction with 3500 West. Turn right (north) and follow this road for 6.8 miles. Watch for signs, and follow a private ranch access road to the marked parking area.

The petroglyphs are on private property, and a donation of $2 per vehicle is asked; there are no toilet facilities. Be sure to stay on the trails, and don't get immediately discouraged—the best of the carvings are about 15 minutes into the cliff-side hike. This area is very rich in petroglyphs, and you could easily spend hours wandering along the cliffs.

ACCOMMODATIONS

$50–75

Vernal offers high-quality lodgings; you can't go wrong at any of the following.

Well south of town along U.S. 191 is the **Weston Plaza Hotel,** 1684 W. U.S. 40, (435) 789-9550, with an indoor pool and hot tub. If you're coming in from the east on U.S. 40, watch for the **Split Mountain Motel,** 1015 E. U.S. 40, (435) 789-9020, a handy place to stay because it's close to good food at the Crack'd Pot Restaurant and to the water slide at Wildwaters. It's also one of the only places in town that allows pets.

The rest of Vernal's motels are closer to the center of things (such as they are in Vernal).

Rodeway Inn, 590 W. Main, (435) 789-8172 or (800) 228-2000, has kitchenettes and laundry facilities. **Best Western Antlers Motel,** 423 W. Main, (435) 789-1202 or (800) 528-1234, has a pool, hot tub, and fitness room. **Days Inn,** 260 W. Main, (435) 789-1011 or (800) 328-1011, has a pool, kitchenettes, and laundry; and **Sage Motel,** 54-56 W. Main St., (435) 789-1442 or (800) 760-1442, is pleasant and one of Vernal's least expensive lodgings.

The following downtown lodgings are within easy walking distance of the dinosaur displays at the Utah Field House. **Weston Lamplighter Inn,** 120 E. Main St., (435) 789-0312, has kitchenettes and a pool; and **Best Western Dinosaur Inn,** 251 E. Main St., (435) 789-2660 or (800) 528-1234, has a pool, hot tub, and exercise room.

Campgrounds

Vernal KOA is on the west side of town (turn in beside the Weston Plaza Hotel) at 1800 W. Sheraton, (435) 789-8935 or (800) KOA-7574. Facilities include a pool, store, showers, laundry, playground, and miniature golf; $14 tents or RVs without hookups, $17 with, $25 cabins. Open May 1–Sept. 30. **Campground Dina** is on the north side of town at 930 N. Vernal Ave., (435) 789-2148 or (800) 245-2148. It has showers, store, laundry, and miniature golf; grassy sites cost $12 for tents or RVs without hookups, $17 with; open May 1–Nov. 1. **Fossil Valley RV Park,** 999 W. U.S. 40, (435) 789-6450, has showers and laundry; $9 tents, $10 RVs without hookups, $18 full hookups. Open Apr.–Nov. Other campgrounds are at **Steinaker State Park,** eight miles north of Vernal on U.S. 191, and **Red Fleet State Park,** 12 miles north on U.S. 191. Open Apr.–Oct., these lakeside parks are popular places for fishing and water sports; call (435) 789-4432 for information. There's more camping 20 miles north in the Ashley National Forest and east at Dinosaur National Monument (23 miles).

OTHER PRACTICALITIES

Food

Many of the motels have their own restaurants, which serve up familiar American fare. Several other American restaurants are worth noting. Right downtown, the **Seven-Eleven Ranch**

Restaurant, 77 E. Main, (435) 789-1170, is open daily except Sunday for breakfast, lunch, and dinner and serves a Saturday chuck wagon dinner. For steaks and the area's fine dining, head to the **Crack'd Pot Restaurant,** 1089 E. U.S. 40, (435) 781-0133, with truly good steaks, sandwiches, and homemade pastries. This is a favorite of both the local mining executives and the motorboat crowd fresh from Flaming Gorge Reservoir, so it can be busy; Open breakfast, lunch, and dinner. **Stella's Kitchen,** north of town at 3340 N. Vernal, (435) 789-5657, offers made-from-scratch homecooking; open for three meals a day, seven days a week.

Two local Mexican restaurants are worth trying. **Casa Ríos,** a couple of miles south of town at 2015 W. U.S. 40, (435) 789-0103, specializes in south-of-the-border cuisine; open daily for lunch and dinner. **La Cabaña,** 56 W. Main, (435) 789-3151, also has good Mexican food; open Mon.–Sat. for lunch and dinner.

For the area's best Chinese food, go to **Mei Palace,** 2513 N. Vernal, (435) 789-8400.

Entertainment

See movies at **Tri Cinema,** 1400 W. U.S. 40, **Vernal Theatre,** 40 E. Main, or **Sunset Drive-In,** open in summer on W. U.S. 40. Call the Movie Information Line to find out what's playing at the theaters, (435) 789-6139.

Events

In **June,** the **Outlaw Trail Festival** brings in some wild characters for shooting events, a bank robbery, trail rides on old outlaw paths, musicals, Western art competition, oil-painting workshop, and a song-writing contest.

The **PRCA Dinosaur Roundup Rodeo** in **mid-July** pits man against beast. It's Vernal's biggest event of the year and includes a parade and country music showdown. A parade celebrates **Pioneer Day** on the 24th.

The **Uintah County Fair** comes to town in **August.**

River Tour Outfitters

River trips down the Green River's Split Mountain Gorge through the Dinosaur National Monument provide the excitement of big rapids and the beauty of remote canyons. Experienced rafters will enjoy the challenge of the class III–IV run down the Cross Mountain Gorge in the Yampa River. One-day and longer trips are offered by **Hatch River Expeditions,** P.O. Box 1150, Dept. S, Vernal, UT 84078, (435) 789-4316 or (800) 342-8243, www.hatchriver.com; **Adrift Adventures,** P.O. Box 192, Jensen, UT 84035, (435) 789-3600 or (800) 824-0150, www.adrift.com; and **Dinosaur River Expeditions,** 540 E. Main, Vernal, UT 84078, (435) 781-0717 or (800) 247-6197, www.dinoadv.com. Expect to pay about $60–80 for day trips and about $150 per day for longer excursions; children usually get discounts.

Recreation

Wildwaters has water-tube fun in summer at 1155 E. U.S. 40, (435) 789-5281. An outdoor **swimming pool** sits next to Independence Park at 170 S. 600 West, (435) 789-5775. Play **tennis** or **baseball** at the city park, corner of 400 North and 900 West. Golf at the 18-hole **Dinaland Municipal Golf Course,** 675 S. 2000 East, (435) 781-1428.

Services

In **emergencies** (police, medical, and fire), dial 911. The **post office** is near the corner of Main and 800 West, (435) 789-2393. **Ashley Valley Medical Center** provides hospital care at 151 W. 200 North, (435) 789-3342. Camping and fishing supplies are available at **Basin Sports,** 511 W. Main, (435) 789-2409.

Information

The staff at the **Vernal Welcome Center,** (435) 789-4002, next to the Utah Field House Museum at 235 E. Main, can fill you in on the many attractions of "Dinosaurland" and offers a short video program showing highlights of the region and other parts of Utah. A series of self-guided tour brochures has maps and mileages of suggested trips. The center is open daily 8 A.M.–9 P.M. in summer and daily 9 A.M.–5 P.M. the rest of the year. You can also contact the **Dinosaurland Travel Board** for tourist info and events at (800) 477-5558, 25 E. Main, Vernal, UT 84078.

Foresters at the **Vernal Ranger District office** of the Ashley National Forest, 355 N. Vernal Ave. (Vernal, UT 84078), (435) 789-1181, can tell you about scenic drives, camping, hiking, cross-country skiing, and snowmobiling in the eastern Uinta Mountains. Books and forest maps are sold there; travel plans showing vehicle restrictions are free. Open Mon.–Fri. 8 A.M.–5 P.M. The **Ashley National Forest supervisor's office** (at the same address and phone) has general information about the Flaming Gorge, Roosevelt, and Duchesne Districts. The **Bureau of Land Management Vernal District office,** 170 S. 500 East (Vernal, UT 84078), (435) 781-4400, offers information on the John Jarvie Historic Ranch in the northeast corner of the state and areas south of Vernal such as Pelican Lake and the White River; land-use maps and a variety of brochures on recreation areas are available. Open Mon.–Fri. 7:45 A.M.–4:30 P.M.

For detailed fishing and hunting information, stop at the **Utah Division of Wildlife Resources** on the second floor of the courthouse building, 152 E. 100 North (Vernal, UT 84078), (435) 789-3103. Books on fishing and wildlife are sold; open Mon.–Fri. 8 A.M.–5 P.M. The **U.S. Fish and Wildlife Service,** 266 W. 100 North

#2 (Vernal, UT 84078), (435) 789-0351, has information about the Ouray National Wildlife Refuge and the new Ouray National Fish Hatchery to the south and Jones Hole National Fish Hatchery to the northeast; open Mon.–Fri. 7 A.M.–4 P.M. The **Uintah County Library,** 155 E. Main, (435) 789-0091, has good reading; **Bitter Creek Books,** 684 W. Main, (435) 789-4742, offers a selection of regional and general titles and topo maps.

Transportation

Greyhound buses stop at 38 E. Main, (435) 789-0404 or (800) 231-2222, and travel each way between here and Salt Lake City and east to Denver via Vernal. Rent cars from **Avis** at the airport, (435) 789-7264, or **Showalter Ford,** 100 E. Main, (435) 789-3818. Catch a cab from **T-Rex Taxi,** (435) 790-7433. **Skywest Airlines,** (800) 453-9417, has scheduled flights between Vernal and Salt Lake City three times daily.

horned lark
(Eremophila alpestris)

LOUISE FOOTE

NORTH OF VERNAL

Wildlife Through the Ages Scenic Byway

This scenic interpreted route follows U.S. 191 and UT 44 north from Vernal to Flaming Gorge Reservoir. As the road climbs, you cross 19 geologic formations—an exceptionally thick geologic layer cake—revealing rock layers from the period of the creation of the Uinta Mountains and on through the periods of erosion that followed. The 30-mile drive begins four miles north of town on U.S. 191; a tour map at a pullout shows the formations to be seen ahead. *Wildlife through the Ages* brochures are available at the Vernal Welcome Center and Forest Service and BLM offices. Signs on the drive identify and briefly describe each formation from the Mancos (80 million years old) to the Uinta Mountain Group (one billion years old).

Steinaker State Park

Water sports, camping, and picnicking at the park's 750-acre Steinaker Reservoir make this a popular place in summer. Anglers catch largemouth bass, rainbow trout, and a few brown trout. Water-skiers have plenty of room on the lake's two-mile length. Warm weather brings bathers to a swimming beach near the picnic area. Scuba divers find the best conditions from midsummer to late autumn, when visibility is up to 30 feet. In winter, visitors come to ice fish or cross-country ski. The campground (elev. 5,500 feet) is open with drinking water all year; no showers or hookups. Other facilities include two covered pavilion areas and a paved boat ramp. The park charges $4 per vehicle for day use, $9 per vehicle for camping. From Vernal, go north six miles on U.S. 191, then turn left two miles; (435) 789-4432 or (800) 322-3770 (reservations).

Red Fleet State Park

Colorful cliffs and rock formations, including three large outcrops of red sandstone, inspired the name of Red Fleet Reservoir. You can hike three quarters of a mile or take a boat to see a dinosaur trackway. Anglers catch largemouth bass, rainbow trout, and some brown trout and bluegill. Like the larger Steinaker Reservoir, Red Fleet stores valuable water for irrigation and municipal use. A developed area offers covered picnic tables, water, restrooms, fish-cleaning station, and paved boat ramp; open year-round. Charges are $4 per vehicle for day use, $9 per vehicle for camping; call (435) 789-6614 or (800) 322-3770 (reservations) for more information. From Vernal, go north 10 miles on U.S. 191 to Milepost 211, then turn right two miles on a paved road to its end.

Jones Hole National Fish Hatchery

Canyon walls tower 2,000 feet above Jones Hole. Springs supply water for the young trout raised here that will later go to Flaming Gorge Reservoir and other areas. You can view the operation daily 7 A.M.–3:30 P.M. or see the outdoor raceways at any time during the day. The visitors' center has exhibits on the trout and the Jones Hole area. Tours can be arranged on weekdays with at least one day's notice. The fragile eggs usually aren't on display, but you can see the newly hatched fish swimming in tanks inside the buildings. Young trout spook easily, so they're kept indoors, where they eat better and grow faster. When the trout reach a length of three inches they go outside. At an age of 14 months, the trout are eight inches long and ready to be transplanted to the wild. The hatchery produces about three million rainbow, brown, brook, and cutthroat trout annually. Call (435) 789-4481 for information. Jones Hole is 38 miles northeast of Vernal via paved roads; head east on 500 North and follow the signs over Diamond Mountain Plateau.

Diamond Mountain is believed to be the site of a hoax played in the 1870s; two men salted the area with genuine diamonds, then sold out for a fortune; one culprit was caught, the other escaped. Unpaved roads connect Jones Hole Road with U.S. 191 and Browns Park. Hatchery staff discourage visits from mid-November to mid-March because ice and drifting snow can make driving hazardous; it's best not to come then unless you call ahead, have four-wheel drive, and are prepared for winter camping.

An easy hiking trail begins below the raceways and follows Jones Hole Creek four miles to the Green River in Dinosaur National Monument.

Hikers enjoy the spectacular canyon scenery, lush vegetation, a chance to see wildlife, and some Fremont Indian pictographs. The creek has good fishing; special regulations (posted) include use of artificial lures and flies only. You may camp midway on the trail near the confluence with Ely Creek by first obtaining a backcountry permit from Dinosaur National Monument. Ely Creek has good places to camp and explore. The trail begins at an elevation of 5,550 feet and descends 500 feet to the Green River in Whirlpool Canyon.

John Jarvie Ranch
Browns Park, along the Green River in Utah's northeast corner and adjacent to Colorado, has always been remote. The Wild Bunch and other outlaws often used the area as a hangout. John Jarvie settled here in 1880 and stayed until his death in 1909. He ran a store, post office, and ferry and still had time to take care of the ranch and do some prospecting. A guided tour of the restored ranch takes in the original 1880s corral, blacksmith shop and tools, farm implements, crude dugout, stone house, and other structures. Jarvie's store has been reconstructed and filled with shelves of canned goods, dried food, pots and pans, tools, harnesses, barbed wire, and other necessities of turn-of-the-century ranch life. Exhibits also show artifacts dug up from the original store site.

The John Jarvie Ranch is open daily 8 A.M.–5 P.M. from May to October; free, (435) 885-3307 (or call the BLM office in Vernal, 801-789-1362). Winter visits are possible, too; call first to find out road conditions. Boaters on the Green River can easily stop off to see the ranch; a sign marks where to pull in. You can camp at **Bridge Hollow Recreation Site** (water; $4 fee; one-quarter mile downstream from the ranch) and **Indian Crossing Recreation Site** (no water; $2 fee; one-quarter mile upstream from the ranch); the ranch also has drinking water.

Trucks or cars with good clearance can drive to the ranch on an unpaved road through scenic Crouse Canyon; this route branches off Jones Hole Road 26 miles from Vernal, goes north past Crouse Reservoir and into the canyon, winds west through hills and parallels the Green River (though the river is hard to see from the road), crosses a bridge over the swift-flowing Green, and turns left 0.3 mile; distance from Jones Hole Road is 28 miles. Another way in is to go north from Vernal on U.S. 191 to 0.7 mile past the Wyoming border and turn right 22 miles on a gravel road; a steep 14 percent grade into Browns Park makes climbing back out difficult for RVs and other underpowered vehicles. A third approach is from Maybell, Colorado, on CO 318 (paved until the Utah border); this is the best road, especially in winter. Colorado 318 also provides access to Browns Park National Wildlife Refuge, a stopover point for migratory waterfowl in spring and autumn and a nesting habitat for ducks and Great Basin Canada geese. A gravel tour road goes through the refuge.

Ashley National Forest (Vernal District)
The southeastern part of the Uinta Mountains has very pleasant mountain country with scenic drives, fishing, hiking, camping, picnicking, and winter sports. Contact the U.S. Forest Service office in Vernal for road conditions and recreation information. Roads at the higher elevations open about the beginning of June and are often passable through October. Most roads to the campgrounds and reservoirs are okay for cars. Some areas may be closed to vehicle use because of wet conditions, wildlife habitat, sheep ranges, or erosion problems. **Lodgepole Campground** offers sites with water from late May to early September at an elevation of 8,100 feet; it's 30 miles north of Vernal on U.S. 191 on the way to Flaming Gorge NRA; $12; some sites can be reserved by calling (800) 280-CAMP. **East Park Campground,** at East Park Reservoir, has water and a $8 fee; go 20 miles north of Vernal on U.S. 191, then 10 miles northwest on forest roads (all but the last mile is paved); elevation is 9,000 feet. **Iron Springs Campground and Picnic Area,** on the Red Cloud Loop Scenic Drive, is mainly a group area; individuals can also use the sites if there's room; a hand pump supplies water. Other campgrounds include **Red Springs** ($8 fee), **Oaks Park, Paradise Park, Kaler Hollow,** and **Whiterocks** ($8 fee).

Anglers will find rainbow trout in most of the lakes and streams. Brown trout and native cutthroat trout live in some areas. Most hiking trails are rocky with some steep sections; carry topo maps. Trails lead into the High Uintas Wilderness from Chepeta Lake and West Fork of Whiterocks trailheads; road distances to the trailheads are relatively long, then there's a hike of about six to seven miles to the wilderness boundary. In winter, three cross-country ski trails lead west from U.S. 191 into the Grizzly Ridge and Little Brush Creek areas; signed trailheads are about 25 miles north of Vernal. Most of these trails are rated intermediate to advanced, though some sections are good for beginners, too. Snowmobilers have an extensive network of trails that mostly follow forest roads.

Red Cloud Loop Scenic Drive

This 74-mile loop winds through scenic canyons and mountains northwest of Vernal. Allow about half a day for just the drive. Side roads go to East Park and Oaks Park Reservoirs, campgrounds, fishing streams, and hiking areas. Aspen trees put on a brilliant display in autumn. About half the drive follows unpaved forest roads, so it's a good idea to check road conditions first with the U.S. Forest Service office in Vernal. Cars with good clearance can usually make the trip if the roads are dry. Drive 20 miles north from Vernal on U.S. 191 (or 15 miles south from the junction of U.S. 191 and UT 44 in Flaming Gorge NRA) and turn west on the paved East Park Reservoir Road at the sign that says Red Cloud Loop. Signs then show the rest of the way. The Vernal Welcome Center's brochure *Red Cloud Loop* describes points of interest.

Flaming Gorge; view uplake from Red Canyon Overlook

FLAMING GORGE NATIONAL RECREATION AREA

Flaming Gorge Reservoir winds through 91 miles of gentle valleys and fiery red canyons. The rugged land displays spectacular scenery where the Green River cuts into the Uinta Mountains—cliffs rising as high as 1,500 feet, twisted rock formations, and sweeping panoramas. Although much of the lake lies in Wyoming, most of the campgrounds and other visitor facilities, as well as the best scenery, are in Utah. Boating on the clear blue waters of the lake or the river below is one of the best ways to enjoy the sights. Waterskiers have plenty of room on the lake's 66 square miles. Swimming is popular, too. Anglers regularly pull trophy trout and smallmouth bass from the lake and trout from the river. Rafting the lively Green River below the dam offers a thrilling ride that anyone with care and proper safety equipment can take—no special skills are needed. Be sure you're properly equipped before setting out. The U.S. Forest Service and private concessions offer boating facilities and about two dozen campgrounds in the recreation area.

Peace, quiet, and snow prevail in winter. Dedicated anglers still cast their lines into the Green River or fish through the lake ice. Cross-country skiers and snowmobilers make their trails through the woods. Campgrounds are closed, though snow campers and hardy RVers can stop for the night in parking areas.

Staff and volunteers at the **Flaming Gorge Ranger District/Manila Headquarters office** can answer your questions year-round at the junction of UT 44 and UT 43 in the center of Manila; open daily 8 A.M.–4:30 P.M. in summer and Mon.–Fri. 8 A.M.–4:30 P.M. the rest of the year; the office also sells forest and topo maps and some books; P.O. Box 279, Manila, UT 84046, (435) 784-3445.

W.C. McRAE

Information centers at Flaming Gorge Dam and Red Canyon Overlook have exhibits, video programs, maps, and literature. Flaming Gorge NRA can be easily reached by heading north 35 miles on U.S. 191 from Vernal. In Wyoming, head south on WY 530 from the town of Green River or U.S. 191 from near Rock Springs.

Look for groups of graceful pronghorn in the open country east of the lake at Antelope Flat (north of Dutch John) and in the Lucerne area on the west side. Other wildlife in the area includes deer, elk, moose, mountain lion, black bear, bighorn sheep, fox, bobcat, mink, and eagle.

Admission to the Flaming Gorge National Recreation Area is $2 per vehicle per day. The official website is at www.fs.fed.us/r4/ashley/fg_html_aw.html.

Flaming Gorge Dam and Visitor Center

Nearly a million cubic yards of concrete went into this dam, which was completed in 1964. The structure rises 502 feet above bedrock and is 1,285 feet long at the crest. The dam is open for self-guided tours daily from about the first weekend in April to the last weekend in September and for guided tours daily about early May to late September; tours last 20–30 minutes and are free; check hours at the visitors' center on the west end of the dam. You'll descend inside for a look at the three giant generators in the power-plant room, then go one floor below to where a shaft connects the turbine and generator of one of the units.

The visitors' center has a large 3-D map of the area, exhibits, and video programs; books and maps are on sale and staff will answer your questions. Open Thurs.–Mon. 9 A.M.–5 P.M. year-round, and daily with extended hours in summer. The dam and visitors' center are 6.5 miles northeast on U.S. 191 from the junction with UT 44, or 2.8 miles southwest of Dutch John.

Red Canyon Visitor Center

Sheer cliffs drop 1,360 feet to the lake below. The visitors' center and nearby viewpoints offer splendid panoramas up and down the canyon and to the lofty Uinta Mountains in the distance. A fully accessible nature trail connects the overlooks and has signs about the ecology. Exhibits inside describe local wildlife and flora, geology, Indian groups that once lived here, and early history and settlement of the area. Books and maps are for sale at an information desk; the staff answers visitor questions and offers video programs. Open daily 10 A.M.–5 P.M. from Memorial Day weekend to mid-Sept. Located 3.5 miles west on UT 44 from the junction with U.S. 191, then three miles in on a paved road.

Sheep Creek Canyon Geological Area

Canyon walls on this scenic loop drive reveal rock layers deformed and turned on end by immense geological forces. The earth's crust broke along the Uinta North Fault and the south side rose 15,000 feet relative to the north. Fossils of trilobites, corals, sea urchins, gastropods, and other marine animals show that the ocean once covered this spot before the uplifting and faulting. Rock layers of yet another time preserve fossilized wood and tracks of crocodile-like reptiles. Nongeologists can appreciate the drive, too. The road through Sheep Creek Canyon is paved but has some narrow and rough places; it's closed in winter. The 13-mile loop branches off UT 44 south of Manila between Mileposts 14 and 15 and rejoins UT 44 at Milepost 22; the loop can be done in either direction. The *Wheels of Time* geology brochure, available at visitors' centers and the Manila headquarters, describes geologic formations at marked stops. Three picnic areas line the drive—two in the lower part of the canyon and one in Palisades Memorial Park upstream where the road climbs out of the canyon. Camping in the canyon has been restricted ever since a flash flood in 1965 killed a family of seven; Palisades Memorial Park marks the site. Only dispersed camping is allowed along the drive and only from October 1 to May 15. Two primitive campgrounds (outhouses but no water or established sites) lie just off UT 44 along lower Sheep Creek a short way from the entrance to the scenic loop.

Swett Ranch

Oscar Swett homesteaded near Flaming Gorge in 1909, when he was just 16 years old, then built up a large cattle ranch in this isolated region. With the nearest store days away, Oscar ran his own blacksmith shop and sawmill and did much of the ranch work; his wife Emma tended the garden, made the family's clothing, raised nine children, and helped with the ranch chores. You can experience some of the early homestead life on a

visit to the ranch by joining Forest Service tours from Memorial Day to Labor Day Thursday–Monday 9 A.M.–5 P.M. (check hours at the visitors' centers). The house, cabins, spring house, root cellar, blacksmith shop, horse barn, cow shed, many other outbuildings, and farm machinery have been preserved. Drive north 0.3 mile on U.S. 191 from the UT 44 junction (or south 1.6 miles from Flaming Gorge Lodge), then turn west and follow signs 1.3 miles on a gravel road.

Boating on Flaming Gorge Reservoir

Watch for strong winds on the reservoir; they can whip up large waves without warning—even on a clear day. Rock reefs may appear and disappear as the lake level changes. Three marinas along the lake's length offer rentals, fuel docks, and supplies. Free paved boat ramps at these and several other locations are maintained by the Forest Service. **Cedar Springs Marina,** P.O. Box 337, Dutch John, UT 84023, (435) 889-3795, near the dam at the lower end of the lake, rents boats (fishing, ski, and pontoon) and fishing gear and has a fuel dock, slips, store, scenic tours, and guided fishing trips; open Apr.–Oct. Turnoff for the marina is 1.7 miles west of Flaming Gorge Dam on U.S. 191.

Lucerne Valley Marina, P.O. Box 10, Manila, UT 84046, (435) 784-3483, provides services on the broad central section of the lake near Manila; the marina has boat rentals (fishing, ski, pontoon, and houseboats), fishing gear rentals, a fuel dock, slips, store, and guided fishing trips;

open mid-Mar.–mid-Nov. The marina is eight miles east of Manila on paved roads.

Buckboard Marina is on the west shore in Wyoming, 22.5 miles northeast of Manila on UT 43/WY 530, or 23.5 miles south of Green River on WY 530. Services include boat rentals (fishing, ski, and pontoon), fishing gear rentals, a fuel dock, slips, store, scenic tours, and guided fishing trips; contact the marina at Star Route 1, Green River, WY 82935, (307) 875-6927 or (800) 824-8155.

The Green River Below Flaming Gorge Dam

The Green bounces back to life in the Little Hole Canyon below the dam and provides enjoyment for boaters, anglers, and hikers.

Float Trips: Anyone in good shape with a raft, life jacket (must be worn), a paddle (and a spare), bailing bucket, and common sense can put in at the launch area just below the dam and float downriver to Little Hole (2.5 hours for seven river miles) or to Indian Crossing just above the John Jarvie Historic Ranch (five–eight hours for 14.5 river miles). It's also possible to continue 11 miles beyond Indian Crossing to Swallow Canyon takeout or 35 miles to Gates of Lodore; these runs are mostly flat and have troublesome sandbars at low water. Gates of Lodore marks the beginning of some big rapids in Dinosaur National Monument; you'll need permits and white-water experience here—or you can make prior arrangements to join a commercial river trip.

Visitors with canoes, kayaks, and dories can float all sections of the Green between the dam and Gates of Lodore, though river experience is needed for these craft. Have proper equipment before you get in and go. Raft rentals and shuttle services are provided by Flaming Gorge Lodge, (435) 889-3773, Flaming Gorge Recreation Services at the Dutch John Store, (435) 885-3191, and Flaming Gorge Flying Service at the Dutch John Airport, (435) 885-3338. Rentals typically cost $45 per day for a six-person raft or $70 per day for one holding eight; shuttles cost about $25 to Little Hole, $70 to Indian Crossing, and $85 to Swallow Canyon. Drivers can also drop their vehicles off at Little Hole and take an early-morning shuttle back to the starting point.

Friday, Saturday, and holidays in summer often see large crowds on the river; you'll need reservations then for raft rentals and shuttles. For solitude, try to come Sunday to Wednesday. Guide services for boating and fishing trips can be contacted through the rental outfits. Life jackets (included with rentals) *must* be worn by all boaters—the water is too cold (57° F in summer, 40° in winter) to swim in for long. The 10 class-II rapids between the dam and Little Hole lend some excitement to the trip but aren't usually dangerous. Red Creek Rapid below Little Hole is a class-III rapid and can be difficult; scouting before running is recommended (many groups portage this one). Camping is permitted downstream from Little Hole at established primitive sites or dispersed sites. Bring drinking water or obtain some at Little Hole. No motors are allowed between the dam and Indian Crossing. Water flow varies according to power needs; allow more time if the flow is small. Call the Bureau of Reclamation for present conditions, (435) 885-3121.

The put-in is located at the end of a 1.4-mile paved road (may not be signed), which turns off U.S. 191 one-third mile east of the dam. The parking area at the river is small and for unloading boats and passengers only. The main parking areas are 0.7 mile back up the road. Drivers can take either of two foot trails which descend from the parking lots to the river. The shuttle to Little Hole is only eight miles (paved) via Dutch John. The drive to Indian Crossing is much longer, 38 miles (25 of them unpaved); go north on U.S. 191 0.7 mile beyond the Wyoming state line, then turn east on a gravel road to Browns

Park and follow signs; one section of this road has a 14 percent grade.

Fishing: Anglers can follow the **Little Hole National Recreation Trail** along the north bank of the Green River through Red Canyon for seven miles between the main parking area below the dam and Little Hole. Many good fishing spots can be found along the way. No camping, horses, ground fires, or motorized vehicles are allowed. The Green River downstream from the dam has a reputation for some of western America's best river fishing. Trophy catches have included 22-pound rainbow, 18-pound brown, and 14-pound cutthroat trout. Modifications to the dam allow the ideal temperature mix of warmer water near the lake's surface and cold water from the depths. Special regulations apply here to maintain the high-quality fishing (check for current regulations). Trout between 13 and 20 inches (the most prolific breeders) must be returned to the water; there's a three-fish limit (two under 13 inches, one over 20 inches), and only artificial lures and flies may be used. Anglers using waders should wear life jackets in case the river level rises unexpectedly; neoprene closed-cell foam waders are recommended for extra flotation and protection against hypothermia.

Hiking and Biking Trails

The **Canyon Rim Trail** is a popular 4.2 mile (one-way) hike or mountain-bike ride with trailheads at Red Canyon Visitor Center and the Greendale Overlook, a short distance from the junction of U.S. 191 and UT 44. **Browne Lake** is a popular starting point for hikes outside the recreation area: Trail #005 goes to the **Ute Mountain Fire Lookout Tower,** a national historic site (two miles one-way); Trail #016 goes to **Hacking Lake** (seven miles one-way); Trail #012 goes to **Tepee Lakes** (five miles one-way) and **Leidy Peak** (elev. 12,028 feet; eight miles one-way); and Trail #017 goes to **Spirit Lake** (15 miles one-way). Browne Lake is 4.5 miles west on unpaved Forest Route 221 from the Sheep Creek loop drive, then 1.5 miles southeast on the Browne Lake road; see the Ashley National Forest map. Visitors' centers and Forest Service offices have maps of hiking and mountain-bike trails and can suggest dirt roads suitable for either activity. The USGS topo maps are recommended, too.

Dutch John

Dutch John has always been a government town. It sprang up in 1957–58 to house workers during the construction of Flaming Gorge Dam and had a peak population of about 3,000. About 150 current residents work in various state and federal agencies.

Flaming Gorge Recreation/Dutch John Service, at the turnoff for Dutch John on U.S. 191, (435) 885-3191, has a snack bar (open daily Memorial Day–Labor Day weekends), store (open early Apr.–late Oct.), raft rental and shuttle services, hot showers, and a gas station (open all year). **Flaming Gorge Flying Service,** at Dutch John Airport, (435) 885-3338, offers raft rentals, river trips, guided fishing trips, shuttle service, hot showers, a Laundromat, and airplane fuel.

Manila

The tiny town of Manila, just west of the recreation area, is the seat of Daggett County, the smallest and least-populated county in Utah. Year-round population of Manila totals only 227. The name commemorates Admiral Dewey's capture of Manila in the Philippines, which occurred in 1898, while surveyors were laying out the Utah townsite. Manila is a handy base for travel in the Flaming Gorge area. The town is 63 miles northwest of Vernal and 46 miles south of Green River, Wyoming.

Food: Dine at **Flaming Gorge Cafe,** in the center of town, open daily for breakfast, lunch, and dinner; or **Niki's Inn,** W. UT 43, open daily for breakfast, lunch, and dinner. Both gas stations in the center of town have small stores and snack bars. The **3M Market** on E. UT 43 has groceries and fishing supplies.

Accommodations

Under $50: Stay at **Flaming Gorge Bunkhouse** in the center of town, (435) 784-3531; at **Niki's Inn,** W. UT 43, (435) 784-3117; or **Vacation Inn,** W. UT 43, (435) 784-3259, where all rooms have kitchenettes; open Apr. 1–Oct. 31.

$50–75: Flaming Gorge Lodge, seven miles southwest of Dutch John (Greendale, U.S. 191, Dutch John, UT 84023), (435) 889-3773, offers motel rooms and condos all year (with reduced winter rates) and a restaurant serving breakfast, lunch, and dinner daily all year. The lodge also

has a store, raft rentals, shuttles, and guided river fishing trips. **Red Canyon Lodge,** 790 Red Canyon Rd., (435) 889-3759, sits beside the privately operated Green's Lake a short distance from the Red Canyon Visitor Center. The resort is open early April–late October (and winter weekends) and has rustic cabins and luxury duplex cabins with kitchens (sleep up to six). A restaurant opens daily for breakfast, lunch, and dinner; a store with groceries and fishing supplies, bike rentals, horseback riding, and boat rentals on Green's Lake.

Campgrounds: The camping season begins with the opening of Lucerne Valley Campground (eight miles east of Manila), usually on Easter Sunday. By Memorial Day, everything should be open. Campgrounds begin closing after Labor Day, though at least one is left open through October for hunters. If you're here early or late in the season, stop by or call the Manila Forest Service office or the Flaming Gorge Dam Visitor Center to find out what's available. Most campgrounds have water and charge a $8 base fee. Group sites and single-family units in some areas can be reserved by calling (800) 280-CAMP. Two primitive campgrounds (outhouses but no water or established sites) lie just off UT 44 along lower Sheep Creek. Some primitive campgrounds on the lake can be reached only by boat or trail; these include Kingfisher, Island, Gooseneck, Hideout, and Jarvies Canyon. **Flaming Gorge KOA,** on W. UT 43, (435) 784-3184, has showers, laundry, pool, and playground; open May 1–Oct. 31; tent or RV spaces cost $18 without hookups, $25 with.

VICINITY OF FLAMING GORGE NRA

Spirit Lake has a beautiful setting in the high country of the Uintas. The lake (elev. 10,000 feet) offers fishing, boating, a campground, and a lodge. Hikers can take trails to nearby lakes (17 lie within three miles!) and to the High Uintas Wilderness. **Spirit Lake Campground** is in a fir, spruce, and lodgepole pine forest; open early June–late Oct.; $8; you may need to obtain water from the nearby Spirit Lake Lodge.

Browne Lake has a small campground (elev. 8,200 feet; no water or fee) and fishing for native cutthroat trout. Several trails start nearby (see

*loading up
for a pack trip at
Spirit Lake Lodge*

Hiking and Biking Trails, above). Browne Lake is 4.5 miles west on unpaved Forest Route 221 from the Sheep Creek loop drive, then 1.5 miles southeast on the Browne Lake road; see the Ashley National Forest map.

Ute Mountain Fire Lookout Tower (elev. 8,834 feet) has a good panorama of surrounding alpine lakes, Flaming Gorge Lake, and the Uintas. The tower has been restored as a historic site; ask at a visitors' center for days and hours (it is staffed by volunteers and has irregular hours). Turn west one mile on Forest Route 221 from the Sheep Creek loop drive, then 1.5 miles south on Forest Route 005.

EAST OF VERNAL

DINOSAUR NATIONAL MONUMENT

The monument owes its name and fame to one of the world's most productive sites for exhuming dinosaur bones. More than 1,600 bones of 11 different dinosaur species cover a rock face at the quarry. The spectacular canyons of the Green and Yampa Rivers form another aspect of the monument. Harpers Corner Scenic Drive winds onto high ridges and canyon viewpoints in the heart of Dinosaur Monument. River-running allows a close look at the geology and wildlife within the depths and provides the bonus of thrilling rapids. Dinosaur National Monument straddles the Utah-Colorado border, but only the quarry, in the western end of the monument, has dinosaur bones.

For supplementary information on Dinosaur National Monument, contact the Superintendent, 4545 U.S. 40, Dinosaur, CO 81610, (970) 374-2216, www.nps.gov/dino.

The Land

From the original 80 acres reserved at the quarry in 1915, Dinosaur National Monument has grown to more than 200,000 acres of rivers, canyons, valleys, plateaus, and mountains. Elevations range from 4,750 feet at the Green River near the quarry to 9,006 feet atop Zenobia Peak of Douglas Mountain. The high country is part of the east flank of the Uinta Mountains, whose geology is graphically revealed in the deep canyons of the Green and Yampa Rivers. Wildlife inhabiting this rugged terrain includes mule deer, elk, pronghorn, Rocky Mountain bighorn sheep, mountain lion, black bear, coyote, bobcat, red and gray fox, badger, striped and Western spotted skunks, ringtail cat, raccoon, beaver, bat, and many species of rats and mice. Streamside vegetation consists largely of cottonwood, box elder, willow, tamarisk, and some black birch. Desert plants such as sagebrush, greasewood, shadscale, saltbush, and rabbitbrush grow on the slopes at lower elevations.

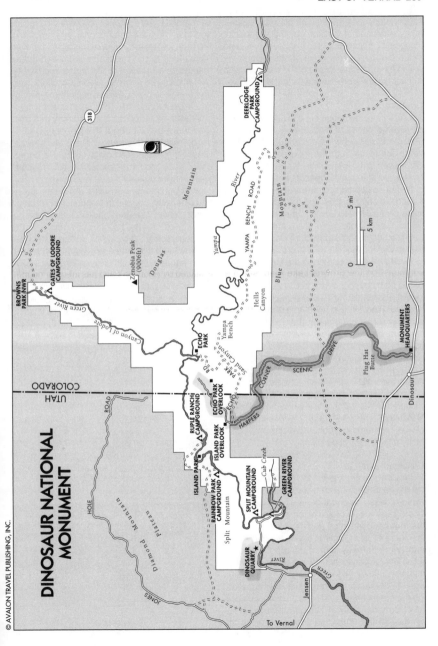

© AVALON TRAVEL PUBLISHING, INC.

DINOSAUR NATIONAL MONUMENT

Middle elevations have piñon pine and juniper trees, serviceberry, buckbrush, and sagebrush. Douglas fir, aspen, ponderosa pine, spruce, and mountain mahogany thrive on the mountains and in the protective shade of the canyon walls. Annual precipitation averages about nine inches.

Dinosaurs

A fortunate combination of sand and water preserved the bones of dinosaurs, turtles, crocodiles, and clam shells from about 145 million years ago at this spot. River floods washed the carcasses onto a sandbar, where they were buried and preserved. Pressure from thousands of feet of additional sediments above gradually turned the sand to rock, and the bones within it were partially mineralized. Later, uplift of the Rockies and Uintas tilted the sandstone layer nearly on edge and exposed the overlying rocks to erosion.

In 1909, Earl Douglass, of the Carnegie Museum in Pittsburgh, suspected that dinosaur bones might be found here because similar rock layers had yielded fine specimens in Colorado and Wyoming. He was right. A discovery of eight brontosaurus tail bones in their original positions the following year became the first of many rewarding finds at the site. Douglass and other workers continued excavations until 1924, removing 350 tons of bones and attached rock that included 22 complete skeletons and parts of hundreds of other specimens. (Some of the best mounted skeletons can be seen at the Carnegie Museum.) After 1924, quarry work shifted emphasis from removing bones to exposing them in relief in their natural positions.

Dinosaur Quarry

A large enclosure protects the quarry face from the elements and houses laboratories and visitor exhibits. Near the entrance, you'll pass a realistic stegosaurus before climbing a spiral ramp to the quarry observation deck. Exhibits illustrate the sandbar and Morrison scene and place the quarry in context within the span of geologic time. The rock layer is 8–12 feet thick and dates from the Jurassic period—about the middle of the Age of Dinosaurs. Workers have finished reliefing the quarry bones and have left them in place as a permanent exhibit. Roughly three quarters of the bones that you'll see come from

sauropods—giant plant eaters with long necks and tails. All the bones appear in a jumble in the rock, just as they were deposited in the river sands long ago. One skeleton has a number marked on each bone; a diagram lets you figure out which piece is which. Models, artwork, and specimens on the lower level depict the variety of dinosaurs found here. Exhibits also show how workers remove bones from the rock and how they learn details about the dinosaurs' size, shape, diet, and muscle structure. Peek through windows of the paleontology lab to see bones under study and the instruments used. In winter, you may see researchers at work here.

Staff will answer questions about the quarry and other places to see in the monument. Handouts available on request include information on backcountry roads, hiking, river-running, and Fremont rock art. A schedule posted during the main season lists times and places of ranger talks, nature walks, auto tours, children's programs, and campfire programs. A good selection of dinosaur and natural history books, posters, postcards, slides, topo and geologic maps, bird and mammal lists, and film is sold. The Dinosaur Quarry, (435) 789-2115, is open daily 8 A.M.–4:30 P.M. (extended to about 7 P.M. Memorial Day–Labor Day weekends) and closed

stegosaurus

Thanksgiving, Christmas, and New Year's Day. From Vernal, drive east 13 miles on U.S. 40 to Jensen, then turn north seven miles on UT 149. Admission to the quarry costs $10 per vehicle ($5 per bicyclist or bus passenger); free for children under 16. Parking space is in short supply during the busy summer season, so a free shuttle operates every 15 minutes between the quarry and a separate parking area during most of the day. The rest of the year you can drive all the way in, as can people with disabilities anytime. The privately owned **Dinosaur Quarry Gift Shop,** just outside the monument, has a snack bar; open summer only.

Quarry to Josie Morris Cabin Drive

Stop at the Dinosaur Quarry or a roadside pullout for the booklet *Tour of the Tilted Rocks,* which describes points of interest for an auto tour to the Cub Creek area. The drive goes 10 miles past the quarry turnoff to a historic ranch, passing sites of Fremont rock art and the Split Mountain and Green River Campgrounds on the way. A small overhang known as the **Swelter Shelter** contains some petroglyphs; the pullout is one mile beyond the quarry turnoff; a trail leads 200 feet to the cave. **Sound of Silence Nature Trail** begins on the left 1.9 miles past the quarry turnoff; this unusual nature trail makes a three-mile loop up Red Wash, enters an anfractuosity (a winding channel), crosses a bench and a ridge with fine panoramas, then descends through some slickrock back to Red Wash and the trailhead; you'll need the trail guide (best purchased at the quarry or headquarters) for this hike. Red Wash is also good for short strolls—just avoid it if thunderstorms threaten!

Continue on the drive to the Split Mountain Campground turnoff; the side road winds down one mile to the campground at the Green River. **Split Mountain Campground** is open only November–March while nearby Green River Campground is closed; no water or fee. The Green River emerges from Split Mountain Canyon here after some of the roughest rapids on the whole river. **Desert Voices Nature Trail** begins at the campground entrance and makes a two-mile loop; a trail brochure available at the quarry, headquarters, or near the start describes plants and geology seen along the way; allow 1.5–2 hours.

Back on the main road, a Green River overlook is on the left 1.2 miles past the Split Mountain Campground turnoff. The road to Green River Campground is a short way farther on the left; **Green River Campground** is open only in summer and has water; $12 fee. **Placer Point Picnic Area** is 1.1 miles beyond the junction, just before a bridge across the Green River. The main road continues past a private ranch, then pavement ends. A road fork on the right 2.7 miles past the bridge goes to Blue Mountain (high-clearance vehicles and good maps needed); keep left for the Josie Morris Cabin. A **petroglyph panel** is on the left beside the road 0.7 mile beyond the road fork. Continue past this panel 0.2 mile and park in a pullout on the right (may not be signed) for a look at no fewer than seven lizard petroglyphs on the cliffs above and to the left; a steep climb up the slope (no trail) allows a closer view of these and other figures. Large shade trees surround the **Josie Morris Cabin** at the end of the road, 0.9 mile farther. Josie grew up in Browns Park during the 1870s and 1880s and settled here about 1914. She spent much of the next 50 years alone at the ranch, tending the fields, garden, cows, pigs, and chickens. She was in her 90s when she died as a result of a hip broken in a riding accident. You can visit her cabin, outbuildings, orchards, and a nearby box canyon.

Monument Headquarters

A few exhibits and a 10-minute slide show (shown on request) introduce the monument's history, dinosaurs, and canyons. The staff offers handouts, books, and maps and will answer your questions. Open daily 8 A.M.–4:30 P.M. from Memorial Day to Labor Day weekends and Mon.–Fri. 8 A.M.–4:30 P.M. the rest of the year; 4545 U.S. 40, Dinosaur, CO 81610, (970) 374-2216. The River Office here handles permits for groups running the Green or Yampa River within the monument. A self-guided scenic drive to Harpers Corner begins at the headquarters. Admission to the exhibits and scenic drive is free. You won't see any dinosaur exhibits in this part of the monument—the bones are only at the quarry area. From Vernal, go 35 miles east on U.S. 40 to the Colorado town of Dinosaur, then continue another two miles east to the monument headquarters. Dinosaur has a couple of small motels and places to eat.

Harpers Corner Road

This scenic drive begins at monument headquarters in Colorado and winds north past many scenic overlooks. The road opens in about early May and closes after the first big snowstorm in November although it's kept clear to Plug Hat Butte overlook, 4.3 miles in. A booklet available at the quarry and headquarters has good background material on the area and describes the sights at numbered stops along the way. The paved road is 31 miles long (one-way); allow about two hours for the round-trip or half a day if you also plan to hike the two nature trails. You'll pass three picnic areas along the way, but no water or campgrounds are available. The road climbs a series of ridges with fine views of much of the monument, including Island Park, Echo Park, and the canyons of the Green and Yampa Rivers. You'll see spectacular faulted and folded rock layers and a complete range of vegetation, from the cottonwoods along the rivers far below to aspen and firs of the highlands.

Plug Hat Nature Trail is an easy half-mile loop in a piñon-juniper forest at a stop 4.3 miles from the beginning of the drive. At Island Park Overlook, about 26 miles along the drive, **Ruple Point Trail** heads west four miles (one-way) on an old jeep road to an overlook of the Green River in Split Mountain Canyon; carry water. The drive ends at Harpers Corner, a long and narrow peninsula. You can continue one mile on foot to the very tip by taking the **Harpers Corner Trail**; a brochure available at the start describes features visible from numbered stops. Cliffs on each side drop to a bend of the Green River at the beginning of Whirlpool Canyon, about 2,500 feet below. Echo Park, Steamboat Rock, and the sinuous curves of the Yampa River Canyon are visible, too. Allow 1.5–2 hours for the easy to moderately difficult walk. Binoculars come in handy for a better look at the geology and other features.

Echo Park

A rough dirt road branches off Harpers Corner Road 25 miles from monument headquarters and winds down more than 2,000 feet in 13 miles to Echo Park. The setting of Echo Park, near the confluence of the Green and Yampa Rivers, is one of the prettiest in the monument. The massive sandstone fin of Steamboat Rock looms

Echo Park, from Harpers Corner Trail

into the sky across the Green River. Echo Park offers a campground (water in summer; $6), river access for boaters (permit needed), and a ranger station (open summer only). Cars with good clearance can often make this side trip, though it's better to have a truck. Like all dirt roads in Dinosaur National Monument, when wet it shouldn't be attempted in any vehicle. The clay surface becomes extremely slick after rains but usually dries out in 2–3 hours. Hikers can follow an unmarked route from Echo Park along the banks of the Yampa River to the mouth of Sand Canyon; go up Sand Canyon until it opens out, cut across benchland to Echo Park Road in lower Pool Creek Canyon, and follow the road back to Echo Park. High water levels on the Yampa can block the route from about late May to late June; you'll need to do some rock-scrambling in Sand Canyon. The loop is 6–8 miles long, depending on the route taken.

Drivers with high-clearance trucks can also explore the backcountry on **Yampa Bench Road,** which turns off eight miles down the Echo

Park Road. Yampa Bench Road has views of the Yampa River Canyon and Douglas Mountain to the north and Blue Mountain to the south; allow 4–5 hours to drive the 38 miles between Echo Park Road and U.S. 40. It's always a good idea to get directions and the latest road conditions from a ranger before driving into the backcountry. Rains occasionally cut off travel, so it's recommended that you carry extra water, food, and camping gear.

Other Areas

Gates of Lodore, on the Green River, has a campground, a boat launching area for riverrunners, and a ranger station—all open yearround. **Gates of Lodore Campground** has water in summer and is $5. **Gates of Lodore Trail** follows the river downstream to the dramatic canyon entrance, an easy 1.5-mile roundtrip; get a trail leaflet at the ranger station or the trailhead. Gates of Lodore is 108 miles from monument headquarters via U.S. 40, CO 318, and 10 miles of gravel road.

Deerlodge Park Campground, at the east end of the monument, sits just upstream from the Yampa River Canyon. Camping is primitive, with no designated sites, water, or fee; closed in winter. River trips on the Yampa usually begin here. The site is 53 miles from monument headquarters by paved roads.

Rainbow Park and **Ruple Ranch** are on the west shore of the Green River at opposite ends of Island Park. Both offer primitive campgrounds (no water or fee) and places to launch or take out river boats. Easiest access is from the quarry area; distances are 26 miles to Rainbow Park and about another five miles to Ruple Ranch via the rough and unpaved Island Park Road. Cars with good clearance may be able to drive in, but the road is impassable during wet weather.

Hiking in the Monument

Any of the trails can easily be done on a day trip. The two longest—Jones Hole and Ruple Point—are each about eight miles round-trip and moderately difficult. The Echo Park-Sand Canyon route is a similar distance. Easier, selfguided nature walks are Red Rock (two miles round-trip), Plug Hat (half-mile round-trip), Harpers Corner (two miles round-trip), and Gates of Lodore (1.5 miles round-trip). Each trail is de-

scribed above (see North of Vernal for visiting Jones Hole). Overnight trips are possible on the longer trails or on cross-country routes. Off-trail hikers must be able to navigate with map and compass and find (or carry) water and should have experience in desert travel over rugged terrain. One possibility is the three- to five-day hike from Echo Park to Gates of Lodore; before starting, though, you'll need to find river-runners to take you across the Yampa. Obtain the required backcountry permit for overnight hikes from rangers at monument headquarters or at the Dinosaur Quarry.

River-running

Trips down the Green or Yampa River feature outstanding scenery and exciting rapids. All boaters in the monument must have permits or be with a licensed river-running company, even for day trips. A one-day trip on the Green gives a feeling for the river at a modest cost (see Tours under Practicalities in the Vernal section earlier in this chapter). The most popular one-day run begins at Rainbow Park or Ruple Park; you bounce through the rapids of Split Mountain Canyon to takeouts at Split Mountain Campground. Longer trips usually begin on the Green at Gates of Lodore in the north end of the monument. Names of rapids like Upper and Lower Disaster Falls, Harp Rapids, Triplet Falls, and Hells Half Mile in Canyon of Lodore suggest that this isn't a place for inexperienced boaters.

In 1869, John Wesley Powell lost one of his four boats and many supplies at Disaster Falls on his first expedition. As a result, the rest of the trip was too hurried to make all the scientific studies he had planned. Powell's second trip, in 1871, also had trouble when another boat was upset here.

Canyon depths reach 3,350 feet, the deepest in the monument. Echo Park marks the end of Canyon of Lodore 19 river miles later. The Yampa River joins the Green here and noticeably increases its size and power. Whirlpool Canyon begins downstream with modest rapids for the next 17 miles, followed by an interlude of slow water at Island Park. The river picks up speed again on entering the warped walls of Split Mountain Canyon and roars through Moonshine, S.O.B., Schoolboy, and Inglesby Rapids on the eight miles to Split Mountain Campground. From here, the Green flows placidly for the next 100 miles through open country.

The Yampa remains the last major undammed tributary of the Colorado River system. Snowmelt in the mountains of Colorado and Wyoming swells the Yampa to its highest and best levels from May to mid-July. Most boaters put in at Deerlodge Park at the east end of the monument. The next takeout point is 46 miles downriver at Echo Park. A series of rapids culminates in Warm Springs Rapids, the Yampa's wildest. Where the water is shallow, boaters may have difficulties with sandbars and rocks.

Guided river trips are often best for first-time visitors. Contact the monument for a list of river concessionaires. Private groups planning a trip on the Green or the Yampa should write far in advance to the River Unit at monument headquarters; the office will let you know about equipment regulations and how to obtain the required permits. One-day permits are the easiest to ob-

tain. Contact the River Unit at P.O. Box 210, Dinosaur, CO 81610, (970) 374-2468. The *Dinosaur River Guide,* by Laura Evans and Buzz Belknap, has maps and descriptions of both rivers in the monument.

VICINITY OF DINOSAUR NATIONAL MONUMENT

Stewart Lake State Waterfowl Management Area

Birders might want to make a short side trip south of Jensen to visit their feathered friends. Abundant vegetation in the water and on the shore of this shallow lake provides food and shelter for birdlife. Take the small paved road south 1.4 miles from Jensen, then, when the paved road curves right, keep going straight on the gravel road for 1.2 miles. The road is okay for cars but is too narrow for large rigs or trailers.

SOUTH OF VERNAL

Ouray National Wildlife Refuge

This desert oasis along the Green River provides a lush habitat for migratory and nesting waterfowl. Other birds and animals also find food and shelter in the brush, grass, marsh, and trees. A list compiled at the refuge names 206 bird species. More than 4,000 ducks nest in summer. Migratory populations peak in April and again in October. Some mallards and Canada geese winter along the Green River.

A self-guided auto tour loops through a variety of habitats on the 11,480-acre refuge. The tour begins at an information booth, which has a brochure and other literature, then follows gravel roads for nine miles past 12 numbered stops. Open daily all year during daylight hours; free; (435) 545-2522 or 789-0351 (Vernal office). An observation tower gives a bird's-eye view of the marshlands. Hiking is permitted (take insect repellent). Some roads may close during spring flooding and autumn hunting, and those in the east part of the refuge may require four-wheel drive in wet weather. From Vernal, head southwest 14 miles on U.S. 40, turn south 14 miles on UT 88, then turn into the refuge on a gravel road.

Ouray National Fish Hatchery

Ouray National Fish Hatchery was built to increase the numbers of four endangered fish species: the Colorado squawfish, the humpback chub, the razorback sucker, and the longtail chub. (For more information about these fish, see the special topic, Endangered Fish of the Colorado River, in the Southeastern Utah section.) The hatchery has 18 ponds and a number of buildings. The fish hatch in quantities much higher than the number that will survive. By collecting eggs and removing them from dangers in the stream, the hatchery insures that more of the fish will reach maturity and reproduce.

Pelican Lake

Birds also stop in large numbers at this lake west of Ouray National Wildlife Refuge. The BLM has a campground (no water or fee) and a boat ramp on the south shore. From a junction northwest of the lake, go south on a narrow road (partly paved) that swings around the lake's west side to the campground and boat ramp. The lake has fishing for largemouth bass and bluegill. There's no swimming because of schistosomes (parasitic flatworms) in the water.

White River

The White has some of the best canoeing in Utah and is good for kayaking and rafting, too. The river originates in Colorado's White Mountains and meanders west to meet the Green River near the town of Ouray, Utah. The scenic ride through White River Canyon has only a few rapids, and they're easy. Trips can be a day to a week long, depending on where you put in and take out. Boating provides good opportunities for viewing wildlife. Groves of cottonwoods make pleasant places to camp. The best time to go is during spring runoff, from mid-May to the end of June. No permits are needed—the BLM gives boaters the responsibility for proper boating safety and clean camping. Launch point is at the Bonanza Highway Bridge (40 miles south of Vernal) and takeout is at the Mountain Fuel Bridge, 40 river miles downstream. The shuttle between the two bridges is only 20 miles on graded dirt roads. The trip can be extended by putting in at Cowboy Canyon, nine miles upriver from Bonanza Highway Bridge on a very rough road, or by taking out at the confluence of the White and Green Rivers, 22 miles downriver from the Mountain Fuel Bridge. Both the confluence and Mountain Fuel Bridge takeouts are on Ute Indian land; the tribe requires a permit to park or boat on its land (below Mountain Fuel Bridge); contact the Ute Indians at P.O. Box 190, Fort Duchesne, UT 84026, (435) 722-5511. Bring life jackets, a spare paddle, insect repellent, and drinking water. Obtain information and a brochure on this trip from the BLM Vernal District office at 170 S. 500 East, Vernal, UT 84078, (435) 781-4400.

Other Places

The remote desert country south of Vernal has many sites of geologic or historic interest for those who enjoy exploring back roads. The BLM office in Vernal can suggest places to go. Fantasy Canyon contains eroded sandstone formations, but a high-clearance vehicle is needed to get in; contact the BLM for a map. The old Uinta Railway grade from Mack, Colorado, to the Utah ghost towns of Dragon, Watson, and Rainbow can be driven partway on a rough road. Gilsonite, a natural asphalt mined at these towns, provided the railway with most of its business. The narrow-gauge line operated 1904–39 and had some of the steepest slick track and sharpest curves in the world.

WEST OF VERNAL

UINTAH AND OURAY INDIAN RESERVATION

The nomadic Ute Indians moved into this part of Utah at about the same time that the older Fremont culture faded away, about 800 years ago, and practiced a hunting and gathering culture across much of the high-mountain basin country of Wyoming, Colorado, and Utah. The first white contact was with the Spanish missionary-explorer Dominguez-Escalante and his expedition in 1776, and the Utes were the first Indian group encountered by the Mormons in Utah.

Mountain men and trappers traded with the tribe during the 1820s and 1830s, though most whites figured that this land, seemingly short of water and most other resources, was worthless. Pressures of settlements elsewhere in Utah and Colorado gradually forced more and more Utes from their traditional lands into the Uinta Basin. In 1861, President Lincoln issued an executive order making nearly the entire Uinta Basin into the Uintah Indian Reservation—about 2,287,000 acres. By 1864, the U.S. Army had moved nearly all of the state's Utes onto the reservation. The Ouray Indian Reservation was established in 1881, then merged with the Uintah five years later.

Whites started having second thoughts, though, when they discovered coal and oil and realized the agricultural potential that irrigation held for the area. Much Indian land was taken back. Beginning in 1905, heavily promoted homesteading programs brought in floods of settlers. The Utes recovered some cash awards for their lost lands during the 1950s and obtained the Hill Creek Extension south of the Uinta Basin. The reservation now covers approximately one million acres in the Uinta Basin, in the foothills of the Uinta Range and Tavaputs Plateau, and in the remote East Tavaputs Plateau.

*Ute Indian Chief
Sevara and family,
ca. 1899*

CHURCH OF JESUS CHRIST OF LATTER-DAY SAINTS

The Ute Indian tribe today consists of three bands, the Uintah (of Utah), the Whiteriver (moved from Colorado in 1880), and the Uncampahgre (moved from Colorado in 1882). About half of the current 2,900 Utes living on the reservation and in nearby towns belong to the Uncampahgre band; the rest are equally divided between the Uintah and the Whiteriver. Each band elects two members to the Ute tribal government. Tribal headquarters are east of Roosevelt at Fort Duchesne (pronounced doo-SHAYN), site of a U.S. Army base from 1886 to 1912. A tribal museum at nearby Bottle Hollow Resort displays Ute artifacts and historic exhibits; you can also ask at the resort about Native American dances, powwows, and rodeos. In summer you might be able to see the Sun Dance, an important religious and social ceremony passed down from the Wind River Shoshone. Other ceremonies are the Bear Dance (performed in the spring) and the Turkey Dance (held on many social occasions).

Nontribal members must keep to the main roads on the reservation and purchase permits for most activities. Camping is allowed at the backcountry lakes open to fishing; you'll need either a fishing or a camping permit; boats need permits, too. Some lakes have boat ramps. A brochure with map and regulations also lists fishing areas and fees. Backcountry sites have outhouses and sometimes tables, but bring your own water.

Small-game hunting is permitted with a tribal license. You'll need special permission to explore outside the permitted areas. Obtain permits at the Ute Indian Tribe Fish & Game Department in Fort Duchesne, 1.5 miles south of U.S. 40, P.O. Box 190, Fort Duchesne, UT 84026, (435) 722-5511, or at sporting goods stores in Vernal, Price, Salt Lake City, and other towns.

Events
The July Fourth **Northern Ute Indian Pow Wow and Rodeo** is the main annual event here; Indian tribes from all over the West participate. Dances, rodeo action, craft displays, and food booths entertain the crowds. Other powwows, rodeos, and dances happen at different times of the year.

ROOSEVELT

President Theodore Roosevelt opened the way for settlement of whites on the Uintah and Ouray Indian Reservation by a proclamation in 1902. Three years later, grateful homesteaders named two of their new towns in his honor—Theodore (later renamed Duchesne) and Roosevelt. Today Roosevelt (pop. 4,314) is the largest town in Duchesne County and a supply center for surrounding agricultural and oil businesses and for the Ute Indians. Roosevelt offers a good selection of places to stay and eat along the main highway (200 East and 200 North Sts. downtown). The community is 30 miles west of Vernal and 146 miles east of Salt Lake City. Travelers can head north to Moon Lake and the High Uintas Wilderness. A scenic backcountry drive goes south to the many rock-art sites in Nine Mile Canyon (see Nine Mile Canyon Backcountry Byway under East of Price, below).

Accommodations
Under $50: The **Western Hills Motel,** 737 E. 200 North, (435) 722-5115, has a restaurant. The **Frontier Motel,** 75 S. 200 East, (435) 722-2201 or (800) 248-1014, has a swimming pool, hot tub, restaurant, and two kitchenettes.

$50–75: Best Western Inn, one mile east on U.S. 40, (435) 722-4644 or (800) 528-1234, has a hot tub, swimming pool, and restaurant.

Food
Besides the American-style restaurants at the above lodgings, there's **Sue's Diner,** 737 E. 200 North, (435) 722-4562, and **The Greenbriar,** just west of the Best Western Inn (one mile east of downtown), (435) 722-2236, a family-style place open daily for breakfast, lunch, and dinner. The **Cow Palace,** just east of the Best Western Inn (one mile east of downtown), (435) 722-2717, offers steaks in an informal Western setting; open Mon.–Sat. for lunch and dinner. **Pizza Hut** serves pizza daily for lunch and dinner on the east edge of town, (435) 722-4586. **Throckmorton's Pasta, Steaks, and BBQ,** 125 E. Lagoon, (435) 722-2604, has good steaks and ribs, plus salads and some Italian dishes.

Events
Festivities in the area on July 4 are the **Northern Ute Indian Pow Wow and Rodeo** at Fort Duchesne, **rodeos** in Neola and Tabiona, and a **Kid's Rodeo** in Altamont. **Altamont Longhorn Days & Rodeo** take place on July 24. The **U.B.I.C. (Uintah Basin In Celebration)** in early August is Roosevelt's biggest annual event with parades, craft shows, and entertainment.

Recreation and Services
The **city park** offers picnic tables, playground, and outdoor pool at 90 W. Lagoon, (435) 722-4851. **Roosevelt Golf Course** has nine holes about 1.5 miles west of downtown, (435) 722-9644. Catch movies at **Roosevelt Twin Theatre,** at 21 S. 200 East, or **Uinta Theatre,** at 41 N. 200 East; call (435) 722-2095 for both places. The **post office** is at 81 S. 300 East. **Duchesne County Hospital** is at 250 W. 300 North, (435) 722-4691.

Information
At the **Duchesne County Area Chamber of Commerce,** 48 S. 200 East (P.O. Box 1417, Roosevelt, UT 84066), (435) 722-4598, staff can tell you about points of interest in the area, events, and services. It's open Monday–Friday 8 A.M.–5 P.M. Foresters at the **Roosevelt Ranger District office** of the Ashley National Forest know about camping, fishing, hiking, and road conditions on the forest lands north of town including the High Uintas Wilderness; forest maps, topo maps, and books are offered for sale; open Mon.–Fri. 8 A.M.–noon and 1–5 P.M. (8 A.M.–5 P.M. in summer). The office is on the west edge of town at 244 W. U.S. 40 (P.O. Box 333-6, Roosevelt, UT 84066), (435) 722-5018. The **public library,** next to the city park at 70 W. Lagoon, (435) 722-4441, is open Monday–Saturday.

VICINITY OF ROOSEVELT

Guest Ranches and Resorts
A number of old-fashioned guest ranches operate in Ashley National Forest. The **U-Bar Wilderness Ranch,** P.O. Box 680846, Park City, UT 84068, (435) 645-7256 or (800) 303-7256, www.rockymtnrec.com, has been around since 1933, offering cabins, fly-fishing, horseback riding, and pack trips to those hankering to get away from it all. Lodging is in rustic one- or two-bedroom cabins ($75 double) or one cabin, which can sleep 10. Meals are extra; full board costs only $30 a day. The ranch is 26 miles north of Roosevelt, up UT 121 and Forest Route 118.

WELCOME TO **ROOSEVELT** A 'BULLY' GOOD TOWN! ELEVATION 5280 POPULATION 5000

Anglers will love the **LC Ranch,** located just north of Altamont. The ranch was established in 1901 by an enterprising homesteader who decided to develop his holdings into a series of streams and ponds. Now a private reserve, the ranch contains 28 lakes and ponds filled with brookies, rainbow, and brown trout. Accommodations are in the main lodge, a large seven-bed cabin, or a more intimate "honeymoon" cabin; rooms start at $75; meals are available. For information, contact LC Ranch/Western Rivers Flyfisher, 867 E. 900 South, Salt Lake City, UT 84105, (435) 454-3750 or 454-3090, www.lcranch.com.

The newest and most exclusive resort in the area is **Falcon's Ledge,** P.O. Box 67, Altamont, UT 84001, (435) 454-3737, www.utah.com/lodging/falcon. Falcon's Ledge was built originally to cater to fly fishers and upland game bird hunters, though the luxury-level rooms and fine restaurant attract an increasing number of people who simply want to enjoy solitude and soft recreation. Rooms are located in a central lodge and are extremely comfortable; basic accommodations (without recreational options, $165). Breakfast is included, but other meals are by reservation only and are served family style.

Ashley National Forest

Moon Lake is in the Uintas about 45 miles due north of Duchesne and 50 miles northwest of Roosevelt. Access roads are paved except for a seven-mile section crossing Indian lands. **Moon Lake Resort** offers cabins, boat rentals, store, mountain-bike rides, horseback rides, and guided pack trips from June 1 to Labor Day; write Mountain Home, UT 84051, (435) 454-3142 (in-season). **Moon Lake Campground** (elev. 8,100 feet) is open with water from Memorial Day weekend to one week after Labor Day; $10 fee.

Major access points to the High Uintas Wilderness near Roosevelt are (from west to east): Lake Fork at Moon Lake (three trails), Center Park at the head of Hells Canyon, Swift Creek on the Yellowstone River (two trails), Uinta Canyon on the Uinta River, and West Fork of Whiterocks River. In winter, snowmobilers use trails in the Snake John area north of Whiterocks.

Five campgrounds are located along the Yellowstone River on Forest Routes 119 and 124 northwest of Roosevelt; elevations range from 7,700 feet at **Yellowstone Campground** to 8,100 feet at **Swift Creek Campground;** all

have water and charge a $8 fee from late May to the week after Labor Day.

Uinta Canyon (no water; $8 fee Memorial Day weekend–week after Labor Day; also a group area) and **Wandin** (no water or fee) are along the Uinta River at an elevation of about 7,600 feet; take UT 121 and Forest Route 118 north of Roosevelt.

The **Pole Creek (Elkhorn) Scenic Loop** on Forest Route 117 winds through canyons and atop ridges east of the Uinta River; some sections may be rough, though the drive is usually passable by cars with good clearance. **Pole Creek Campground** (elev. 10,200 feet) is at the north end of the loop; no water or fee.

Big Sand Lake State Park

Good fishing attracts most of the visitors at this undeveloped park. The 390-acre reservoir has rainbow trout with some browns and cutthroats and lots of crayfish. People also come to waterski and swim; ice fishers try their luck in winter. A boat ramp is on the southeast shore. No water or other services are available; free. The park ranger is based at Starvation State Park, near Duchesne, (435) 738-2326. From Roosevelt, go southwest five miles on U.S. 40, turn west (then north) 10 miles to Upalco, continue straight (north) 0.7 mile where the main road curves left just past Upalco, then turn left 0.4 mile on a gravel road.

DUCHESNE

This small community (pop. 1,493), located at the confluence of the Duchesne and Strawberry Rivers, is the seat of thinly settled Duchesne (pronounced doo-SHAYN) County. The name is said to honor a French Catholic nun or a French fur trapper or to be a corruption of the name of an Indian chief. Ranching, farming, and the oil industry provide most of the employment. Main attractions for visitors are the High Uintas Wilderness and other sections of the Ashley National Forest, Starvation Lake, and fishing on the Duchesne and Strawberry Rivers.

Accommodations

Under $50: Not so long ago, there were three modest motels in this little town. All three are now operated by the **National 9 Inns of Duchesne** from its office at 23 W. Main, (435) 738-

2217. Just stop by the main office and they'll sort you out. Prices at all the motels include continental breakfast. The Río Damian also rents RV spaces; $16 with hookups.

Other Practicalities
Country Kitchen Cafe at 540 W. Main, (435) 738-2735, serves breakfast, lunch, and dinner daily except Sunday. **Cowan's Café,** 57 E. Main, (435) 738-5609, serves breakfast, lunch, and dinner daily.

The **city park** at Main and 100 West, (435) 738-2536, has picnic tables, playground, and an outdoor pool. **Footprints Through Duchesne** on July 4 celebrates the area's homesteading with historic displays, fireworks, and entertainment. The **Duchesne County Fair,** usually on the third weekend of August, features a rodeo, parade, horse show, demolition derby, and other entertainment. People at the **Duchesne Ranger District office** of the Ashley National Forest have information on campgrounds, trailheads, and road conditions of the forest and the High Uintas Wilderness to the north and the Tavaputs Plateau to the south; forest maps, topo maps, and some books are sold; open Mon.–Fri. 8 A.M.–5 P.M. (and Sat. 8 A.M.–4:30 P.M. from Memorial Day to Sept. 30). Offices are located at 85 W. Main (P.O. Box 981, Duchesne, UT 84021), (435) 738-2482.

VICINITY OF DUCHESNE

Guest Ranches
The **Rock Creek Guest Ranch** offers pack trips into the High Uintah Primitive Area—fishing, hunting, and trail rides in a remote mountain setting 32 miles northwest of Altamont. The ranch offers many family-oriented activities as well, including chuck wagon meals, horseshoes, baseball, and easy hikes. Accommodations are in cabins (one bed $40; two beds $50), and meals are available at the lodge or at special barbecue or Dutch oven picnics. For more information, write P.O. Box 510060, Mountain Home, UT, 84051, (435) 454-3332, www.stercon.com/rockcreek.

Uinta Mountains
Forest Route 144 turns north from Stockmore off UT 35, then follows the Duchesne River North Fork to **Aspen Grove Campground** (elev. 7,000

feet), **Hades Campground** (elev. 7,100 feet), and **Iron Mine Campground** (elev. 7,200 feet). All three campgrounds have water and charge a $9–10 fee from Memorial Day to one week after Labor Day; Iron Mine Campground also has a group reservation area. Forest Route 315 turns east from Defa's Ranch to **Grandview Trailhead,** an access point for the southwestern part of the High Uintas Wilderness; the grade is steep and rough, though cars with good clearance can make it in dry weather.

The **Rock Creek** area and **Upper Stillwater Reservoir** are reached by going north from Duchesne on UT 87, turning north to Mountain Home, then west on Forest Route 134. The road is paved to the reservoir. **Miner's Gulch Campground,** (435) 738-2482, is a group campground at an elevation 7,500 feet; no water. Parking for anglers is across the road. **Yellow Pine Campground** nearby (elev. 7,600 feet) has developed sites with water and a dump station from Memorial Day to one week after Labor Day. **Upper Stillwater Campground** (elev. 7,900 feet) lies just south of Upper Stillwater Reservoir; sites are open mid-May–mid-October. Rates for both are $10 (family), $18 (double), and $30 (group sites). **Rock Creek Visitor Center,** near Upper Stillwater Campground, has recreation and travel information in summer. **Rock Creek Trailhead** near the reservoir offers access into the High Uintas Wilderness.

Starvation State Park
The large Starvation Reservoir sits among rolling hills of high-desert country four miles west of Duchesne. Water-skiing is the biggest summer activity, followed by fishing, sailboarding, and sailing. Anglers catch walleye (a state record was taken here), smallmouth bass, and some largemouth bass and German brown trout. The marina is open mid-April–Labor Day with boat rentals (fishing, personal watercrafts, Wave Runners, and ski boats) and a store. A developed campground with pull-through and tent sites with showers overlooks the water. This exposed location can be windy. Continue past the campground turnoff for a picnic area near a sand beach. A second developed campground is just past the picnic area. There are four primitive camping areas around the reservoir; other facilities include a paved boat ramp, a fish-cleaning station, and a dump station. The park is open all year. The main

season, Memorial Day–Labor Day weekends, is sometimes extended up to a month earlier and later; $4 for day use, $7 for primitive camping, $11 for developed camping. The campground usually has vacancies except on major holiday weekends. Showers and restrooms close during the off-season, though outhouses are available. A paved four-mile road to the park turns off U.S. 40 just west of Duchesne. Address is P.O. Box 584, Duchesne, UT 84021, (435) 738-2326 or (800) 322-3770 (reservations).

Over the Mountains to Price
From Duchesne, U.S. 191 goes southwest 56 miles over the West Tavaputs Plateau to Price.

The route follows the Left Fork of Indian Canyon to a pass at an elevation of 9,100 feet, then descends through Willow Creek Canyon to the Price River. Snow may close the road in winter. **Avintaquin Campground** (elev. 8,800 feet) is reached by a short gravel road from just south of the pass; sites in a fir and aspen forest have water from Memorial Day to one week after Labor Day. Sites may have water and cost $8 (family), $10 (double), and $30 (group sites). The Bamberger Monument, between the pass and Price Canyon, commemorates construction of the highway by state prisoners in 1919; Governor Simon Bamberger gave the workers reduced sentences and other benefits for their efforts.

PRICE

In the beginning, Price was a typical Mormon community. Ranchers and farmers had settled on the fertile land surrounding the Price River in 1879. Four years later, everything changed when the railroad came through. A flood of immigrants from all over the world arrived to work in the coal mines and other rapidly growing enterprises. (An informal census taken in a pool hall at nearby Helper in the 1930s found 32 different nationalities in the room!) Coal mining has had its ups and downs in the last 100 years but continues to be the largest industry in the area. Price (pop. 8,834) is a modern city and a good base for exploring the surrounding mountains and desert.

The highly recommended Prehistoric Museum and the Price Mural are in town; the Western Mining and Railroad Museum is in Helper to the north. Other places to visit lie tucked into the surrounding backcountry and include Nine Mile Canyon (rock-art and historic sites), Cleveland-Lloyd Dinosaur Quarry, San Rafael Swell, and many ghost-town sites. Roads wind up canyons to the cool forests and lakes on the Wasatch Plateau. Obtain information and maps for Carbon and Emery Counties at the Castle Country travel office (see the Information section, below). A walking-tour leaflet available at the office describes historic buildings in Price.

The College of Eastern Utah's Prehistoric Museum is one of the state's best.

W.C. McRAE

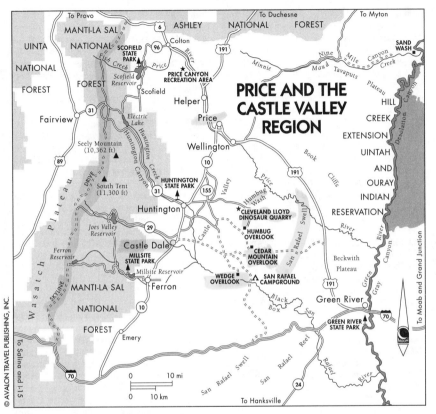

PRICE AND THE CASTLE VALLEY REGION

© AVALON TRAVEL PUBLISHING, INC.

SIGHTS

College of Eastern Utah Prehistoric Museum

An excellent museum of natural and human history, this is a must-stop for anyone interested in the prehistoric creatures and people that lived in Utah thousands of years ago. Dramatic dinosaur displays include the skeletons of a fierce flesh-eating allosaurus, a plant-eating camptosaurus (not to be fooled with, either), a camarasaurus, a chasmosaurus, a prosaurolophus, and a stegosaurus. See bones of the huge Huntington Canyon Mammoth recently discovered nearby, the colorful gemstones of the Mineralogy exhibits, and artifacts of the prehistoric Fremont and the modern Ute Indians in the outstanding Indian collection.

The power and mystery of prehistoric rock art is conveyed in a replica of the Barrier Canyon Mural. Contemporary art is on display in rotating exhibits. Kids can explore the hands-on displays in the Children's Room. The College of Eastern Utah operates the museum, at 155 E. Main, (435) 637-5060; open Mon.–Sat. (also Sun. in spring and summer) 10 A.M.–5 P.M.; summer hours may be extended; $2 suggested donation. A gift shop offers regional and natural history books, fossils, T-shirts, and postcards.

Price Mural

Artist Lynn Fausett captured the history of Price and Carbon County in a colorful mural four feet high and 200 feet long. It extends around all four walls in the foyer of the Price Municipal Building (enter from the east side). Look straight ahead for panels of the first settlers, Abram Powell and Caleb Rhodes. Follow the panels around to the right, past scenes of railroad workers, freight wagons, the first town hall in Price, religious leaders, the 1911 Fourth of July parade, and depictions of the coal-mining industry. A brochure available here gives details of each scene and identifies the self-portrait of the artist as a small boy. Fausett, a native of the area, used his own recollections and old photos for the project, which he worked on from 1938 to 1941. He also painted the Barrier Canyon Mural replica in the Prehistoric Museum and *The Pioneer Trek* at "This Is The Place" Monument near Salt Lake City. Open Mon.–Fri. 8 A.M.–5 P.M.; free; located at the corner of Main and 200 East.

College Of Eastern Utah (CEU)

The two-year community college began as Carbon Junior College in 1938 and took its present name in 1965. CEU's current enrollment of about 2,300 students meets on a four-quarter system. Most of the facilities, cultural activities, and sporting events are open to the public. Gallery East hosts state and national art exhibits during the school year in the main building; exhibits change monthly. You'll find the bookstore, snack bar, cafeteria, and formal dining room in the Student Activities Center. A variety of concerts, plays, choral performances, and ballets are presented on campus; call public relations at (435) 637-2120, ext. 288, for the schedule. The library, located in the middle of campus, has a good collection that includes a set of topo maps covering Utah. Outdoor expeditions organized by the college are often open to the public and include backpacking trips into wilderness areas and river runs on the Green, Colorado, and San Juan Rivers. Each outing emphasizes ecological education; contact Wilderness Studies Director Sara or Eric Ewert at (435) 637-2120, ext. 667 or ext. 609. The College of Eastern Utah is at 451 E. 400 North, Price, UT 84501.

ACCOMMODATIONS

Price has high-quality and inexpensive lodgings, which make it a great base for exploration of this part of Utah.

Under $50

Two motels sit on the east end of town near a clutch of fast-food restaurants and the local supermarket mall. The **Greenwell Inn,** 655 E. Main, (435) 637-3520 or (800) 666-3520, has a pool, exercise room, and restaurant. The **Best Western Carriage House Inn,** 590 E. Main, (435) 637-5660 or (800) 528-1234 in Utah, has an indoor pool and hot tub. At the other end of Main Street is a shopping center complex, which includes the **National 9 Price River Inn,** 641 W. Price River Dr. in Creekview Shopping Center, (435) 637-7000 or (800) 524-9999. Just to the north is the **Budget Host Inn,** 145 N. Carbonville Rd., (435) 637-2424 or (800) 283-4678; out at freeway Exit 240 is the **Holiday Inn and Suites,** 838 Westwood Blvd., (435) 637-8880 or (800) 325-7466, with an indoor pool, sauna, and spa. The local **Super 8,** is at 180 North Hospital Dr., (435) 637-8088, (800) 800-8000.

OTHER PRACTICALITIES

Food

A number of cafés and diners along Main Street serve standard American fare, though the **Golden Rock Cafe,** 838 Westwood Blvd. at the Days Inn just west of town, (435) 637-7637, is probably the best place in Price for straightforward American cuisine. The menu offers steak, prime rib, seafood, and pasta. Open daily for breakfast, lunch, and dinner; full liquor license. **Castle Rock Cafe & Pizza Deli,** on the west edge of town in the Creekview Shopping Center at 700 Price River Dr., (435) 637-8430, offers homestyle cooking and is open daily for breakfast, lunch, and dinner. **Grogg's Pinnacle Brewing Co.,** 1653 N. Carbonville Rd., (435) 637-2924, is the local brewpub, with burgers and sandwiches to accompany the hand-crafted beers.

The **Greek Streak,** 84 S. Carbon Ave., (435) 637-1930, specializes in Greek foods; open Mon.–Sat. for lunch and dinner. **Farlaino's Cafe,** 87 W. Main, (435) 637-9217, serves Italian and American cooking; open Mon.–Sat. for breakfast and lunch and Wed.–Sat. for dinner. **El Salto,** 19 S. Carbon Ave., (435) 637-6545, brings excellent south-of-the-border flavor to town; open Mon.–Sat. for lunch and dinner.

Entertainment and Events

Catch movies at the **King Coal Theaters 3,** 1171 E. Main, **Price Theatre,** 30 E. Main, or **Crown Theatre,** 30 W. Main; call (435) 637-2740 for recorded information. **Helper Outlaw Day** takes place in June at Helper with games, food, and a car show. **Black Diamond Stampede Rodeo** provides plenty of action in June. A **demolition derby** is also held in June. The **Greek Festival** in July features music, dancing, food, and tours of the Greek church. Wellington's **Pioneer Day** (July 24) festivities include a parade, rodeo, games, and food. **International Days and Carbon County Fair** in August celebrate the area's ethnic diversity with a parade, rodeo, agricultural exhibits, entertainment, contests, and food.

Services

For **emergencies** (police, fire, paramedic), call 911. The **post office** is at the corner of Carbon Avenue and 100 South, (435) 637-1638. **Castleview Hospital** is at 300 N. Hospital Drive on the west edge of town, (435) 637-4800. **Gart Bros. Sporting Goods** has camping and fishing gear in the Creekview Shopping Center on the west side of town, (435) 637-2077.

Recreation

Washington Park, 250 E. 500 North, (435) 637-7946, has picnic areas, playground, indoor swimming pool, outdoor Desert Wave Pool, tennis, volleyball, basketball, and horseshoes. Two historic cabins dating from the 1880s and a jogging track are across to the north in **Pioneer Park. South Price Park** offers a picnic area and tennis at 400 South and 100 East. **Carbon Country Club Golf Course** has 18 holes; located four miles north of town on U.S. 6/191, (435) 637-2388.

Information

Castle Country travel office offers literature and ideas for travel in Price and elsewhere in Carbon and Emery Counties; open Mon.–Fri. 9 A.M.–5 P.M. in the Prehistoric Museum at 155 E. Main (P.O. Box 1037, Price, UT 84501), (435) 637-3009 or (800) 464-3790 in Utah. The **Manti-La Sal National Forest** Supervisor's and Price District offices, across from the Creekview Shopping Center on the west edge of town (599 W. Price River Dr., Price, UT 84501), (435) 636-3600, have information about recreation in the beautiful alpine country of the Wasatch Plateau to the west; all the Utah forest maps and some regional books are sold; open Mon.–Fri. 8 A.M.–4:30 P.M. (till 5 P.M. in summer).

The **Bureau of Land Management** has the Price River Resource Area and San Rafael Resource Area offices in Price; both have the same address and phone number: 125 S. 600 West, (435) 636-3600. Staff can tell you about exploring the San Rafael Swell, Cleveland-Lloyd Dinosaur Quarry, and Nine Mile Canyon and about boating the Green River through Desolation, Gray, and Labyrinth Canyons; land-use maps are sold; open Mon.–Fri. 7:45 A.M.–4:30 P.M. **Price City Library** is next to the Price Municipal Building at 159 E. Main, (435) 637-0744; open Mon.–Fri. in summer and Mon.–Sat. the rest of the year.

Transportation

Greyhound buses travel west daily to Salt Lake City and east to Denver from the stop at Phillips 66, 277 N. Carbonville Rd., (435) 637-7153. **Amtrak** trains stop in nearby Helper on their runs between Denver and Salt Lake City, (800) 872-7245.

NORTH OF PRICE

HELPER

In 1883, the Denver & Rio Grande Western Railroad began building a depot, roundhouse, and other facilities here for its new line. Trains headed up the long grade to Soldier Summit needed extra locomotives, or "helpers," based at the little railroad community, so the place became known as Helper. Miners later joined the railworkers, and the two groups still make up most of the current population of 2,500. The fine examples of early 20th-century commercial and residential buildings in downtown Helper have earned designation as a national historic site. The local economy has suffered downturns from layoffs in the railroad and coal industries, and this is reflected in the many vacant structures awaiting new owners.

The vacated structures have begun to attract artists who need inexpensive studio space, and an arts community has begun to take hold. The **Helper Arts Festival,** held the second week of September, showcases the local arts scene.

Western Mining and Railroad Museum
A venerable red caboose and examples of coal-mining machinery sit outside next to the museum in downtown Helper at 296 S. Main, (435) 472-3009. Inside, you'll see two elaborate model railroad sets and photos of old steam locomotives in action. A mine room has models of coal mines (all are underground in this area) and equipment worn by the miners. Other exhibits illustrate Utah's two great mine disasters—the 1900 Scofield tragedy, in which 200 men and boys died, and the 1924 Castle Gate explosion, which killed 173. Other bits of history include ghost-town memorabilia, a Butch Cassidy exhibit, and a dentist's office. A company general store exhibit shows items that miners would buy with their company scrip. The new map room displays original maps showing hundreds of miles of tunnels. Video programs illustrate the area's mine and railroad history. The brick building housing the museum dates from about 1914, when it was the Hotel Helper; from 1942 to 1982 it served as a YMCA for railroad men. Open Tues.–Sat. 11 A.M.–4 P.M. from mid-May to the end of Sept.; donation. It may also be possible to visit on other days; call the phone number posted on the front door to reach the designated volunteer.

Ghost Towns
Many coal-mining communities have bloomed and died in surrounding canyons and hillsides. Most have fared poorly since they were abandoned, yet their picturesque ruins can be worth

the slumbering town of Helper

W.C. McRAE

seeking out. The mines and decaying buildings are dangerous and shouldn't be entered—security staff enforce no-trespassing rules. One former company town has survived intact. Kenilworth's residents bought their houses at low prices when the mines closed and have continued to live here; the large company store, however, now stands vacant; follow Helper's Main Street a short way south, then turn left (east) 3.8 miles on paved UT 157. A small *Driving Tour Guide* describes coal mines and town sites in Carbon and Emery Counties; it's sold at the museum in Helper. Also see the books *Utah Ghost Towns,* by Stephen Carr, and *Some Dreams Die: Utah's Ghost Towns and Lost Treasures,* by George Thompson, for histories and locations of the towns that have faded away.

Scenic **Spring Canyon** has some of the best and most easily visited ghost towns. The paved road begins as "Canyon Street" in east Helper (across U.S. 6/191 from downtown Helper). You'll see railroad grades, mines, and ruins along much of the road's 6.7 miles. Sagebrush hides most of the Peerless ghost-town site, 2.8 miles in. Only foundations and a few buildings survive from this community, which peaked in the 1920s and '30s with a population of about 300, then died in the '50s. A tramway brought coal down from the mine high on the hillside. Spring Canyon is a total ghost; only a loading platform remains of a community that had up to 1,000 people during the '20s, '30s, and '40s. The site is near a junction 3.8 miles in; keep straight at the junction (the road to the right is still used by mining companies and is gated).

A large concrete loading facility on the right greets you on arrival at Standardville, 4.9 miles in. The formerly attractive, well-planned community had a population of 550 during its best years and set a standard for other mining towns. Mines nearby operated from 1912 until 1950. A ghostly two-story stone building, once the Liberty Fuel Company offices, marks the site of Latuda, 5.9 miles in. Several hundred people lived here from about 1920 to 1950; Latuda died completely in the late 1960s. Extensive ruins of the mine can be seen on the slopes to the left. Only foundations remain from Rains, once a town of 500, located 6.5 miles from Helper. A large stone ruin, once a store, stands at the site of Mutual, just beyond Rains. Most of the 250 or so residents lived to the north along a fork of Spring Canyon. You may have to park at the gate and walk a short distance on the road to Mutual.

Price Canyon Recreation Area

This pleasant spot in the woods makes a good stopping place for a picnic or a camp. From the turnoff 8.2 miles north of Helper, follow a narrow paved road three miles to the picnic area (free day use), a canyon overlook, and the campground (elev. 8,000 feet), which is open with water and charges a $6 fee from Memorial Day to late October. **Bristlecone Ridge Trail** begins at the far end of the campground loop and winds through a forest of Gambel oak, ponderosa pine, and mountain mahogany to a ridgetop. Grand views from the top take in surrounding mountains and Price and Crandall Canyons below. The moderately difficult hike is about two miles round-trip with an elevation gain of 700 feet. Bristlecone pines and lots of chipmunks live on the ridge.

Scofield State Park

The 3,000-acre reservoir lies in a broad mountain valley at an elevation of 7,600 feet. Anglers go after rainbow and cutthroat trout and crayfish. Water-skiers and boaters have lots of room to roam. The main campground is on the east shore with a picnic area, showers, dump station, boat ramp, docks, and fish-cleaning station. Madsen Bay area at the north end, near the turnoff for Mountain View, has a campground, restrooms, fish-cleaning station, and dump station. The Mountain View area on the northwest side of the lake offers picnic and camping areas near a boat ramp and dock. The lake is accessible all year, though the park shuts down off-season; restrooms and showers are open from about early May to late October. In winter, Scofield Reservoir has excellent ice fishing. The State Division of Parks and Recreation grooms snowmobile trails nearby at Pond-Town Canyon (on the west side of the lake four miles north of the town of Scofield) and Left Fork of Whiteriver (near Soldier Summit). Cross-country skiing in the area is good, too, though no facilities or trails have been developed. Entrance fees are $5 for day use, $9–11 for camping; P.O. Box 166, Price, UT 84501, (435) 448-9449 during the season, (435) 637-8497 in winter. Call (800) 322-3770 for reservations. The park nearly always has room except during major summer holidays.

victims of the mine disaster, Scofield, 1900

UTAH STATE HISTORICAL SOCIETY

From Price, drive 23 miles north on U.S. 6, then turn left 13 miles on UT 96. Other approaches are from Provo (66 miles) via Soldier Summit or from UT 31 where it crosses the Wasatch Plateau to the south.

Scofield

Two coal mines operate near this tiny mining town south of Scofield Reservoir. Production began in 1879 and peaked about 1920, when the town had a population of nearly 2,000. Utah's worst mining disaster took place nearby on May 1, 1900, at the Winter Quarters Mine, where about 200 men and boys perished in an explosion of coal dust. Weathered tombstones in the cemetery on the hill east of town still give testimony to the tragedy. A paved road continues south and west from Scofield to UT 31 on the Wasatch Plateau. The **Lazy Anchor Campground,** with hot showers and a Laundromat, is open from snowmelt to first winter snows at the edge of town on the road from the lake. Cost is $10 for tents or RVs, (435) 448-9697.

Fish Creek

The forest lands surrounding Scofield have plenty of places for dispersed camping. The **Fish Creek Trailhead,** west of the lake, is suitable for primitive camping. This is also the start of the 10-mile **Fish Creek National Recreation Trail.** From Scofield, go northwest 3.7 miles on a partly paved road, then turn left 1.5 miles at a fork up Fish Creek Valley. This last section of road is slippery when wet and may be too rough for cars at any time. The easy trail follows the creek through meadows and forests of aspen and evergreens. This is a good area to look for wildlife including moose, elk, mule deer, black bear, mountain lion, bobcat, and beaver. Anglers will find many places to cast a line; special fishing regulations (posted) apply in upper Fish Creek. The trail is good for both day- and overnight hikes; Skyline Drive is 13 miles upstream.

EAST OF PRICE

Aside from a few ranches and coal mines, the rugged canyon country of the West Tavaputs Plateau remains largely a wilderness. Two especially good areas to visit here are Nine Mile Canyon (accessible by car) and Desolation and Gray Canyons of the Green River (accessible by raft or kayak). Adventurous drivers with high-clearance vehicles can explore other places, too; ask the BLM staff in Price about the backcountry roads.

Nine Mile Canyon Backcountry Byway

A drive through this scenic canyon takes you back in time to when Fremont Indians lived and farmed here, about 900 years ago. Although their pit-house dwellings can be difficult for a nonarchaeologist to spot, the granaries and striking rock art stand out clearly. The canyon is especially noted for its abundant petroglyphs and smaller numbers of pictographs. You'll also see several ranches and the ghost town of Harper. In the late 1800s and early 1900s; these roads through Nine Mile Canyon formed the main highway between Vernal and the rest of Utah.

Today the distances and dusty roads may discourage the more casual traveler. However, if you're interested in rock art or ancient Native America, then Nine Mile Canyon is an extremely scenic and compelling back road. Although the road is frequently rough and dusty, normal family cars should be able to make the trip with no problem as long as the road is dry.

Nine Mile Canyon is actually more than 40 miles long; the origin of its misleading name is unclear. The drive is about 120 miles round-trip from Price and takes most of a day. From Price, drive 10 miles southeast (three miles past Wellington) on U.S. 6/191 and turn north on 2200 East (Soldier Creek Road) at a sign for Nine Mile Canyon. The road passes Soldier Creek Coal Mine after 13 miles (pavement ends), continues climbing to an aspen-forested pass, then drops into the canyon.

Nine Mile Canyon can also be reached from the north, from near Myton (on U.S. 191) in the Uinta Basin, via Wells Draw and Gate Canyon. Gate Canyon is the roughest section and may be impassable after storms. Turnoff for the northern approach from U.S. 191 is 1.5 miles west of Myton; the turn is not well marked, so watch for signs to Pleasant Valley and turn south at 5500 Road. In about two miles, bear right at an unmarked intersection. You'll know you're on the right road if it soon turns into a graveled corduroy roadbed. It's 26 miles from U.S. 191 to the bottom of Nine Mile Canyon.

Obtain a brochure and road-log for Nine Mile Canyon in Price at the Castle Country tourist office, the Prehistoric Museum, or the BLM offices.

petroglyph panel in Nine Mile Canyon

W.C. McRAE

It describes the various rock-art sites, ancient villages, and historic relics.

Desolation and Gray Canyons of the Green River

The Green River leaves the Uinta Basin and slices deeply through the Tavaputs Plateau, emerging 95 miles downstream near the town of Green River. River-runners enjoy the canyon scenery, hikes up side canyons, a chance to see wildlife, and visits to Fremont rock-art sites. John Wesley Powell named the canyons in 1869, designating the lower 36 miles Gray Canyon. Boaters usually start at Sand Wash, the site of a ferry that operated here from the early 1920s to 1952; a 42-mile road (36 miles unpaved) south from Myton is the best way in. Another road turns east from Gate Canyon near Nine Mile Canyon. Some people save the long 200-mile car shuttle by fly-

ing from the town of Green River to an airstrip on a mesatop above Sand Wash. Swasey Rapids, north of the town of Green River, is the most common takeout point. The last part of Gray Canyon, between Nefertiti and Swasey Rapids, is a good day trip.

Although not as difficult as Cataract Canyon, Desolation and Gray Canyons do have about 60 rapids and riffles navigable by raft or kayak. Some are class III and require river-running experience. Contact the BLM Price River Resource Area office in Price, 125 S. 600 West, (435) 636-3600, for information and the required permits. Open Mon.–Fri. 7:45 A.M.–4:30 P.M.

Commercial trips through the canyons are available; the BLM can give you names of the companies. The *Desolation River Guide,* by Laura Evans and Buzz Belknap, has maps and descriptions.

THE CASTLE VALLEY AND NORTH SAN RAFAEL SWELL

High cliffs of the Wasatch Plateau rise fortresslike to the west above Castle Valley, which is traversed by UT 10 between Price and I-70 to the south. The wide band of the 10,000-foot-high uplands wrings all the moisture out of east-flowing storm systems, creating a rain shadow. However, perennial streams flow down the rugged canyons, enabling farmers to transform the desert into verdant orchards and fields of crops. To the east is the isolated and relatively unexplored canyon country of the San Rafael Swell.

Mormon pioneers didn't settle this side of the Wasatch Plateau until the 1870s, long after valleys on the other side of the plateau had been colonized. Water and good land began to run short by the time of the second generation of settlers, and many turned to jobs in nearby coal mines.

The barren mesas and badland formations, especially along the southern section of UT 10, make for fine scenery. However, the real attraction of this area is the backcountry routes that lead to wild and undeveloped destinations. Unpaved roads lead west into the Wasatch Plateau, up steep canyons to lakes and pretty alpine country, to link up with Skyline Drive, or to cross the range to the San Pete Valley and U.S. 89.

Backcountry explorers can follow unpaved roads east to the San Rafael Swell, an area of great dramatic beauty and unparalleled recreational opportunity that has somehow avoided the fame and throngs of the state's other canyon country. Destinations included in this near-wilderness are dinosaur fossil quarries and remote vista points and trailheads.

HUNTINGTON

This small town at the mouth of Huntington Canyon dates from 1878 and has a population of 2,800. While not exactly a tourist town, from Huntington travelers can head west on paved UT 31 and soon be in the cool forests and meadows of the Wasatch Plateau, or head east to the Cleveland-Lloyd Dinosaur Quarry and the San Rafael Swell.

Huntington State Park

The 250-acre Huntington Reservoir is a popular destination for picnicking, camping, swimming, fishing, and water-skiing. Lots of grass and shade trees and a swimming beach make the park especially enjoyable in summer. Boaters can use the boat ramp and docks. Anglers catch mostly largemouth bass and bluegill and some trout; crayfishing is good. The campground is open with showers from March to October. Reservations are a good idea for summer weekends. In winter, the park is open for ice-skating and ice fishing. Fees are $4 for day use, $11 for camping. Located one mile north of town on UT 10, P.O. Box 1343, Huntington, UT 84528, (435) 687-2491 (ranger) or (800) 322-3770 (reservations).

Huntington Canyon

Highway UT 31 turns west up the canyon from the north edge of town. The giant Huntington power plant looks out of place in the agrarian landscape of the lower canyon. Beyond the power plant, **Bear Creek Campground** offers sites shaded by cottonwoods on the left near Milepost 39 (8.8 miles in from UT 10). It has water and a small charge in summer; elevation is 6,900 feet. The canyon narrows as the road climbs higher and enters groves of spruce, fir,

Formations like this give Castle Valley its name.

W.C. McRAE

and aspen. **Forks of Huntington Canyon Campground** sits in a side canyon among fir and spruce trees and has water from early June to mid-September; fee is $10. The turnoff is on the left near Milepost 30 (18 miles in from UT 10); elevation is 7,600 feet. **Left Fork of Huntington Creek National Recreation Trail** begins at the end of the campground road and follows the creek up a pretty canyon. The trail offers easy walking and passes good trout-fishing spots; after four miles it comes to an open valley and connects with a jeep road.

Farther up the highway, **Old Folks Flat Campground** has sites in a spruce and aspen forest on the right; it has water from mid-June to mid-September; $10 fee. Group sites are available; located between Mileposts 28 and 27 (20.5 miles in from UT 10); elevation is 7,800 feet; reservations can be made by calling (800) 280-CAMP. **Electric Lake** offers rainbow and cutthroat trout fishing; a boat ramp is at the upper (north) end. The turnoff is on the right near Milepost 34 (34 miles in from UT 10), then eight miles in. **Skyline Drive** lies near the top of the plateau amidst expansive meadows and groves of fir and aspen. The junction for Skyline Drive to the south is on the left between Mileposts 14 and 13; the turnoff for Skyline Drive to the north is five miles farther west along the highway. Roads branch off the northern section of Skyline Drive to Gooseberry Campground (1.5 miles), Flat Campground (4.5 miles), Electric Lake (six miles), and Scofield (17 miles). **Gooseberry Campground** is near Lower Gooseberry Reservoir; take the north Skyline Drive turnoff and follow signs 1.5 miles; sites are open with water and a $6 fee from about mid-June to mid-September. Elevation is 8,400 feet. **Flat Canyon Campground** also provides a good base for fishing lakes of the high country; campsites are reached by a 5.5-mile paved road from the north Skyline Drive turnoff; open with water and a $10 fee from about mid-June to mid-September; elevation is 8,800 feet; reservations can be made by calling (800) 280-CAMP. From the campground, Boulger Reservoir is a quarter mile away, Electric Lake is two miles, and Beaver Dam Reservoir is two miles.

Other forest roads branch off the highway to more reservoirs and scenic spots; see the Manti-La Sal Forest map available from the Sanpete, Ferron, and Price Ranger District offices. Highway

allosaurus arm,
Cleveland-Lloyd
Dinosaur Quarry

UT 31 continues 10 miles down the other side of the plateau to Fairview on U.S. 89. Snowplows keep UT 31 open in winter, though drivers must have snow tires or carry chains from November 1 to March 31. Snowmobilers can use groomed trails on the plateau.

Accommodations
Under $50: In Huntington, the well-maintained **Village Inn Motel** is at 307 S. Main, (435) 687-9888. **Canyon Rim Café,** 505 North Main, (435) 687-9040, offers standard American fare on the north edge of town.

CLEVELAND-LLOYD DINOSAUR QUARRY

You can learn more about dinosaurs and see their bones in an excavation here in the desert 22 miles east of Huntington or 30 miles south of Price via U.S. 6. Dinosaurs stalked this land about 147 million years ago, when it had a wetter and warmer climate. Mud in a lake bottom trapped some of the animals and preserved their bones. The mud layer, which later became rock of the Morrison Formation, has yielded more than 12,000 bones of at least 14 different dinosaur species at this site. Local ranchers discovered the bones and then interested the University of Utah, which started digs in 1928. Princeton University and Brigham Young University (which currently does excavations) also have participated in the quarry work.

Visitor Center
The BLM has built a visitors' center, quarry exhibits, a nature trail, and picnic sites here. Inside the visitors' center, you'll see exhibits on the dinosaur family tree, techniques of excavating and assembling dinosaur skeletons, and local flora and fauna. A fierce allosaurus skeleton cast gazes down on you. Related books, postcards, and posters can be purchased. The enclosed dinosaur quarry, about 100 yards behind the visitors' center, contains excavation tools and exposed allosaurus, stegosaurus, camptosaurus, and camarasaurus bones. **Rock Walk Nature Trail** begins outside; a brochure available at the start outlines geology, dinosaurs, uranium mining, and ecology at numbered stops; allow 45 minutes.

Usually the quarry can be visited from 10 A.M. to 5 P.M. on weekends beginning at Easter, then daily from Memorial Day to Labor Day weekends; free; (435) 637-4584. The drive in is over graded dirt roads, though rains occasionally close them. From Price, drive south 13 miles on UT 10 and turn left 17 miles on UT 155 and follow the unpaved roads. From Huntington, go northeast two miles on UT 10 and turn right 20 miles on UT 155 and unpaved roads. Signs at the turnoffs from UT 10 indicate the days and hours the quarry is open. If it's closed, there's nothing to see. Visitors are not allowed to collect dinosaur bones at the quarry or on other public lands; bones are of greater scientific value when researchers can examine them in place.

Humbug Overlook Driving Tour

A brochure available at the visitors' center describes the plants and animals living in this desert country. The drive begins at the quarry and goes southeast seven miles to the rim of Humbug Canyon. Cars with good clearance can negotiate the road in dry weather. The **Jump Trail** winds from the viewpoint down to the canyon floor, about a half-mile one-way.

Look for hoodoos on the canyon walls. They are formed when water erodes rock material down to a hard cap rock. The resulting formation often resembles a mushroom or a human head on a thin neck.

Cedar Mountain Driving Tour

The overlook atop Cedar Mountain has a great panorama to the south across the gently curved dome of the San Rafael Swell and the many canyons cutting into it. Distant ranges include the Wasatch Plateau (west), the Thousand Lake Mountains (southwest), the Henry Mountains (south), and the Book Cliffs (east). A picnic area is at the second overlook at the end of the drive. **Fossil Ledge Nature Trail** makes a quarter-mile loop from the picnic area. Distances to the second overlook are 39 miles from Price, 27 miles from Huntington, or 25 miles from Cleveland-Lloyd Dinosaur Quarry. A graded dirt road climbs about 2,000 feet in elevation through woodlands of juniper and piñon and ponderosa pine. Cars can easily drive the road in dry weather. A brochure describing points of interest along the way is available from the quarry visitors' center or the BLM office in Price.

CASTLE DALE

The story goes that after founding the community in 1877, citizens applied for a post office for their town of Castle Vale, but the name was recorded wrong. Because they couldn't agree on which side of Cottonwood Creek to settle, two towns grew up here—Castle Dale (current pop. 1,788) on the north side and Orangeville (current pop. 1,513) on the south. Castle Dale has a good historical museum and is the seat of Emery County. A memorial in front of the courthouse honors the 27 miners who died nearby in the Wilberg Coal Mine fire on December 19, 1984.

Emery County Pioneer Museum

Period rooms depict life in the early days of Castle Valley settlements: a schoolroom, lawyer's office, country store, and kitchen. Pioneer rooms have farm and coal-mining tools and memorabilia of one-time outlaw Matt Warner. An art gallery exhibits local works. It's open Monday–Saturday 10 A.M.–4 P.M. weekdays and 1–4 P.M Saturday all year; donations requested. The museum is located at 93 E. 100 North in Castle Dale City Hall, one block north of the courthouse at 100 North and 100 East, (435) 381-5154.

Castle Valley Pageant

Museum of the San Rafael

This facility is located at 64 N. 100 East, diagonally across the street from the courthouse. Exhibits include a paleontology room with life-size skeletons of dinosaurs including a 22-foot allosaurus. The dinosaurs displayed include only those species that have been found in Emery County. There are also exhibits of the prehistoric Fremont and Anasazi Indians including a rabbit-fur robe, pottery, baskets, tools, jewelry, and the famous Sitterud Bundle (a bowmaker's kit). Admission is free, but donations are requested. Museum hours are 10 A.M.–4 P.M. weekdays and 1–4 P.M. Saturday; (435) 381-5252.

Accommodations

Under $50: The town's only lodging is the **Village Inn Motel,** 375 E. Main, (435) 381-2309.

Other Practicalities

Big Moma's Pizza and Deli, 340 E. Main, (435) 381-5080, offers pizza, spaghetti, and sandwiches Monday–Saturday for lunch and dinner.

Pioneer Day (July 24) is celebrated with a parade, rodeo, and games. **Castle Valley Pageant,** held in late July or early August, recounts the faith and trials of the pioneers who settled here; the pageant takes place on a hillside a short drive from town. The **Emery County Fair** is also in August; horse races are run in Ferron to the south, while the horse show, parade, and most exhibits are in Castle Dale.

The indoor **swimming pool** is open May–September; next to the city hall (one block north of the courthouse). The **city park,** between the courthouse and City Hall, has covered picnic tables. Castle Dale's **library** is open Monday–Friday 11 A.M.–6 P.M. next door to the city hall.

The High Country West of Castle Dale

Head northwest from town toward Joes Valley Reservoir on the paved road along Cottonwood Creek. After about 10 miles you'll reach a fork; an unpaved road turns right (north) along Cottonwood Creek to Upper Joes Valley (10 miles). The main road (UT 29) enters Straight Canyon. Seely Creek below the dam in Straight Canyon has good fishing for German brown trout. Joes Valley Reservoir covers 1,170 acres in a large valley at the upper end of Straight Canyon, 16 miles from Castle Dale. A road turns off the high-

way at the north end of the lake and goes north to **Indian Creek Campground** (nine miles) and UT 31 (21 miles). Indian Creek Campground is open with water from late June to mid-September and charges a $8 fee; sites should be reserved at the Ferron Ranger District office; elevation is 9,000 feet. This campground is designed for groups but individuals are allowed to stay at unoccupied sites.

Joes Valley Campground has two sections on the west shore of the reservoir; they have water from mid-May to mid-September and charge a $10 fee. One loop stays open all year (no water or charge off-season); elevation is 7,100 feet. Reservations can be made by calling (800) 280-CAMP. **Joes Valley Marina,** about 20 miles west of Castle Dale, (435) 381-2453, offers boat slips, rentals (fishing boats with motors, rowboats, and paddle boats), a café (breakfast, lunch, and dinner daily), a campground, and a small store; open mid-May–early Nov. Anglers catch rainbow and cutthroat trout in the lake. Lowry Fork to the north has good trout fishing in the spring. Water-skiing is popular on the lake, but winds are too erratic for reliable sailing. Pavement ends after the turnoff for Joes Valley Campground. A forest road continues west and climbs 13 miles to Skyline Drive (elev. 10,200 feet) at the top of the Wasatch Plateau. The clay road surface is usually fine for cars in dry weather but treacherously slippery when wet for *any* vehicle. The road from Castle Dale to the reservoir is kept open in winter for ice fishing and snowmobile access.

North Dragon Road turns south between the two sections of Joes Valley Campground and goes about 15 miles to a spectacular overlook above Castle Dale; the San Rafael Swell and the distant Henry, La Sal, and Abajo Mountains can be seen on a clear day; the road is unpaved (high-clearance vehicles recommended).

EXPLORING THE SAN RAFAEL SWELL (NORTHERN HALF)

About 65 million years ago, immense underground forces pushed rock layers into a dome about 80 miles long (north to south) and 30 miles wide. Erosion has exposed the colorful layers and cut deep canyons into this formation. I-70 divides the swell into roughly equal north and south halves. In the north, a 29-mile scenic drive passable by cars in dry weather branches off the road to Cedar Mountain and goes south past the Wedge Overlook, descends through Buckhorn Wash, crosses the San Rafael River, then winds across desert to I-70.

Much of the San Rafael Swell remains wild and remote. Seven sections of it are being considered for wilderness designation. The BLM San Rafael Resource Area office in Price has information about travel and wilderness status in this unique land; the office is at the corner of 900 North and 700 East (Price, UT 84501), (435) 637-4584. Good books for travel and historical background on this little-known region are *Canyoneering the San Rafael Swell,* by Steve Allen, *Hiking Utah's San Rafael Swell,* by Michael Kelsey, and *Utah's Scenic San Rafael,* by Owen McClenahan. Allen's guide has by far the most detailed coverage of drives, hikes, and some rock climbs; Kelsey's book emphasizes history and hiking; McClenahan's mostly describes driving tours (about half of which can be done by car).

Wedge Overlook

An inspiring panorama takes in surrounding mountains and canyons and the 1,000-foot sheer drop into the "Little Grand Canyon." Rain and snowmelt on the Wasatch Plateau feed tributaries of the San Rafael River, which has cut this deep canyon through the San Rafael Swell. Downstream from the Little Grand Canyon, the river plunges through narrow canyons of the Black Boxes and flows across the San Rafael Desert to join the Green River. The signed turnoff for Wedge Overlook is on the way to the San Rafael Bridge and Campground; see the Utah Travel Council's Northeastern Utah map for the different approaches from Price (23 miles), Huntington (15 miles), and Castle Dale (13 miles). Drive in 6.6 miles from the turnoff, keeping left at a fork near the beginning, to the first overlook, then continue to the left 0.9 mile for the best views at the end of the road. This area is fine for picnicking but be sure to drive only on designated roads and camp only in designated campgrounds. Walk along the rim for other views.

San Rafael Campground

Continue 12 miles past the Wedge Overlook turnoff to the bridge and campground at the San

San Rafael River, just above the campground

Rafael River. The road descends into the main canyon via pretty Buckhorn Wash and crosses the bridge to the camping area. The cottonwood trees at the campground mysteriously died, giving the area a bleak appearance. Tables and outhouses are provided, but there's no water. From here the road continues south 20 miles to I-70 at Ranch Exit 129.

Floating the Little Grand Canyon

The 15-mile trip through this canyon provides one of the best ways to enjoy the scenery. The swift waters have a few riffles and small sand waves, but no rapids. Canoes, kayaks, and rafts can do the excursion in 5–6 hours with higher spring flows. An overnight trip will allow more time to explore side canyons. Best boating conditions occur during the spring runoff in May and June. Some people float through with inner tubes later in the summer. Life jackets should always be worn. No permits are needed for boating; the BLM in Price can advise on river flows and road conditions. Put-in is at Fuller's Bottom; the turnoff is near the one for the Wedge Overlook, then it's 5.4 miles to the river. Takeout is at the San Rafael Campground. Extremely dangerous rapids and waterfalls lie downstream from the campground in the Black Boxes; *don't* attempt these sections unless you really know what you're doing! Hikers can explore the canyons above and below the campground on day and overnight trips; autumn has the best temperatures and lowest water levels; wear shoes suitable for wading.

FERRON

The town's name honors a surveyor who visited the valley in preparation for Mormon settlement. Millsite State Park and Ferron Reservoir are on a scenic road that connects Ferron with Skyline Drive. Ferron (pop. 1,703) celebrates its pioneer heritage in September during **Peach Days** with horse races, a demolition derby, games, craft exhibits, a dance, and fireworks. The **Ferron Ranger District office** on the main highway, P.O. Box 310, Ferron, UT 84523, (435) 384-2372, can help you plan a trip to the Wasatch Plateau. Open Mon.–Fri. 8 A.M.–noon and 12:30–4:30 P.M.

Canyon Road to Skyline Drive

Turn west on Canyon Road beside the Ferron Ranger District office for a trip to Millsite State Park and the high country of the Wasatch Plateau. **Millsite State Park** is four miles from town at an elevation of 6,200 feet. The 450-acre Millsite Reservoir is about twice the size of Huntington Reservoir and has the area's best sailing conditions and the most space for water-skiing. Anglers come to catch rainbow, cutthroat, and German brown trout. Ice fishing is done in winter. The park has picnic grounds, campground with showers (Mar.–Oct.), boat ramp, and dock. Facilities, except for showers, stay open all year. Day use of the park costs $4, camping $11; (435) 384-2552 (ranger), (435)

687-2491 (Huntington State Park) or (800) 322-3770 (reservations).

Millsite Golf Course, adjacent to the park, features nine challenging holes. Off-road vehicles are popular in the barren countryside near the reservoir; (435) 384-2887.

Pavement ends past the state park, but a fairly good gravel road (narrow and winding in places) continues high into the mountains. Stop at **Ferron Canyon Overlook** (14 miles from town) for a panorama of Millsite Reservoir, the surrounding mountains and valleys, and the San Rafael Swell. Signs point out features and geology; elevation here is 8,200 feet. The road continues climbing to alpine country with pretty lakes and groves of fir and aspen.

Ferron Reservoir (28 miles from town) is the largest of the high-country lakes (57 acres). The Forest Service Campground is open from mid-June to mid-September with water and a $8 fee; elevation is 9,400 feet. **Sky Haven Lodge** on the lake offers cabins, a small café (breakfast, lunch, and dinner daily), a small store, and boat rentals (with or without motors). Horseback rides and guided pack trips can be arranged. The road to Ferron Reservoir is open for vehicles only from about mid-June to late September, but the lodge plans to stay open in winter and organize snowmobile transportation. Skyline Drive is only two miles beyond Ferron Reservoir. Turn north on the drive to a fine view of the reservoir and canyon to the east and valleys near Manti to the west. The highest point on Skyline Drive, at 10,897 feet, is just 0.8 mile beyond the viewpoint. **Twelve Mile Flat Campground,** about 1.5 miles south of the Ferron road junction and the only campground actually on Skyline Drive, is open with water from about mid-June to late September; $6. Elevation is 9,800 feet.

For additional information about outdoor activities in the area, or to buy books and maps, consult the U.S. Forest Service office at 115 West Canyon Road (Ferron, UT 84523), (435) 384-2372 or (435) 384-2505.

SOUTHWESTERN UTAH

INTRODUCTION

Southwest Utah's climate and year-round recreation make this corner of the state seem more like an extension of Arizona—St. George is a major retirement mecca and golfing center—and its proximity to Nevada (the border is only nine miles away) lends a more worldly air to the region. The out-of-Utah feeling is enhanced by the local's habit of referring to the region as "Dixie." Whatever the name, the scenery in this corner of Utah is astonishing, with three of the nation's most popular national parks and an abundance of recreational opportunities. In the same day, you can hike through serpentine canyons or flower-filled meadows, hit the slopes at the Brian Head Ski Area, glide on cross-country skis across a high plateau, explore the desert, or play a leisurely round of golf.

Zion, Capitol Reef, and Bryce Canyon National Parks are part of the desert southwest's grand circle of natural wonders, and in all but the most severe depths of winter a steady stream of tourists explores the region. If you're looking for higher culture, Cedar City offers a well-respected summer Shakespeare festival; at Kanab, you can visit sets used for vintage movie and TV Westerns.

THE LAND

The Mojave Desert, the Great Basin, and the Colorado Plateau meet here to create a unique combination of climates and ecosystems. Plants and wildlife normally found only in Arizona and southern California live in the arid plains and rocky ranges of the desert. The lofty cliffs of the Colorado Plateau rise east of the desert country with some of the most spectacular scenery on earth—the grandeur and colors have to be seen to be believed. Great faults break the Colorado Plateau into a staircase of lesser plateaus across southern Utah and into northern Arizona. Angular features of cliffs and canyons dominate the landscape. Volcanic cones and lava flows have broken through the surface, some in geologically recent times. Elevations range from 2,350 feet at Beaver Dam Wash to 11,307 feet atop Brian Head Peak.

Climate

No matter what the season, you can nearly always find pleasant temperatures in some part of this region. Ever since Brigham Young built a

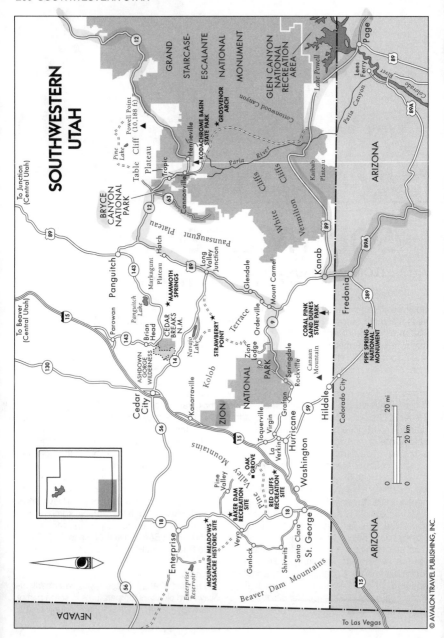

SOUTHWESTERN UTAH

© AVALON TRAVEL PUBLISHING, INC.

winter house at St. George to escape the cold and snow, people have been coming to take advantage of the mild climate. Midwinter temperatures at St. George (elev. 2,880 feet) may drop below freezing at night, but days are typically in the middle to upper 50s with bright sunshine. Spring and autumn bring ideal weather. Summer, when the highs often top 100° F at the lower elevations, is the time to head for the mountains and high plateaus. The alpine meadows and cool forests of the Beaver Dam Mountains, Cedar Breaks National Monument, and Bryce Canyon National Park provide a welcome refuge from summer heat. Precipitation ranges widely from place to place and from year to year, but most falls in winter/early spring and late summer. Annual precipitation averages 10.4 inches in St. George and more than 20 inches in the high country.

FLORA AND FAUNA

The land provides habitats for a great variety of plant and animal species. Sparse desert vegetation consists largely of big sagebrush, rabbitbrush, bitterbrush, blackbrush, yucca, cacti, and grasses. The distinctive Joshua tree, a member of the lily family, grows in the extreme south-western corner of the state. Perennial streams support cottonwood, willow, velvet and single-leaf ash, tamarisk, rushes, and sedges. Creatures of the desert include the chuckwalla, Gila monster (a poisonous lizard), California king snake, and roadrunner. Above about 4,000 feet, woodlands of piñon pine and Utah juniper take over from the desert; you'll often find cliffrose, Utah serviceberry, live oak, and Gambel oak here, too. At about 7,000–8,000 feet, ponderosa pine, Gambel oak, and Rocky Mountain juniper are common. Thriving in the cool mountain air above 8,000 feet are Douglas fir, subalpine fir, Engelmann spruce, aspen, and wildflowers. Larger wildlife, such as mule deer, elk, mountain lion, and coyote, migrate with the seasons between the high and low country. More than 200 bird species have been spotted in the region. Raptors include bald and golden eagles, red-tailed and Cooper's hawks, peregrine and prairie falcons, and the American kestrel.

HISTORY

Native Americans
Beginning about 15,000 years ago, groups of Paleo-Indians traveled across the region to hunt and gather wild plants. Only scant evidence remains of their long stay here. Nomadic bands of

CHURCH OF JESUS CHRIST OF LATTER-DAY SAINTS

William Carter behind his plow at St. George, January 19, 1893. Carter plowed the first furrows at Salt Lake City on July 23, 1847.

Southern Paiutes—possible descendants of the Paleo-Indians—inhabited the region when the first white settlers arrived. The Paiutes befriended and guided the early explorers and settlers, but troubles soon began when the Indians saw their lands taken over by farmers and ranchers. Unable to maintain their old lifestyle or defeat the newcomers, the Indians settled near the settlers' towns. They now have the Shivwits Reservation northwest of St. George and the Kaibab-Paiute Reservation in Arizona southwest of Kanab.

Explorers and Colonizers
In 1776, Spanish explorers of the Dominguez-Escalante Expedition were the first Europeans to visit and describe the region. They had given up partway through a proposed journey from Santa Fe to California and returned to Santa Fe along a route passing through the sites of present-day Cedar City and Hurricane.

In the first half of the 19th century, mountain men like Jedediah Smith and government surveyors such as John C. Frémont explored the land and learned about the Indians. In 1849–50, Mormon leaders in Salt Lake City took the first steps in colonizing the region when they sent an advance party led by Parley P. Pratt. Encouraging reports of rich iron ore west of Cedar Valley and of fertile land along the Virgin River convinced the Mormons to expand southward. Calls went out for members to establish missions, mine the iron ore, and supply iron products needed for the expanding Mormon empire. Parowan, now a sleepy community along I-15, became the

first settlement and Cedar City the second—both established in 1851. In 1855, a successful experiment in growing cotton along Santa Clara Creek near present-day St. George aroused considerable interest among the Mormons. New settlements soon arose in the Virgin River Valley. However, poor roads hindered development of the cotton and iron industries, most of which ended when cheaper products began arriving on the transcontinental railroad. Floods, droughts, disease, and hostile Indians discouraged some of Dixie's pioneers, but many of those who stayed prospered by raising food crops and livestock. The past 30 years have brought rapid growth to the region in the form of new industries, tourism, and retirement communities.

TOURS

Guided van tours of many of southwestern Utah's grandest sights are available from **Southern Utah Scenic Tours,** (435) 867-8690 or (888) 404-8687, www.utahscenictours.com. Tours depart from either Cedar City or St. George, and go to Zion and Bryce National Parks, the North Rim of the Grand Canyon, as well other beauty spots in the area. There are also a number of theme tours, including one that follows the legend of Butch Cassidy, one that visits the Western movie sets near Kanab, and another that visits a rural polygamist community! Custom tours are also available. Southern Utah Scenic Tours also offers a hotel reservation service.

ST. GEORGE

Southern Utah's largest town lies between lazy bends of the Virgin River on one side and rocky hills of red sandstone on the other. In 1861, more than 300 Mormon families in the Salt Lake City area answered the call to go south to start the Cotton Mission, of which St. George became the center (hence the frequently used term "Dixie" to describe the area). The settlers overcame great difficulties to farm and to build an attractive city in this remote desert. Brigham Young chose the city's name to honor George A. Smith, who had served as head of the Southern (Iron) Mission during the 1850s. (The title "Saint" means simply that he was a Mormon—a Latter-day Saint.) Visits to some of the historic sites will add to your appreciation of the city's past; ask for the brochure *St. George Historic Walking Tour* at the chamber of commerce. The warm climate, dramatic setting, and many year-round recreation opportunities have helped make St. George (pop. 46,186) the fastest-growing city in the state. Local boosters claim that this is where Utah's summer sun spends the winter.

SIGHTS

St. George Temple and Visitor Center

Visible for miles, the city's gleaming white temple rises from landscaped grounds in the center of St. George. In 1871, enthusiastic Mormons from all over the territory gathered to erect the temple. Dedicated on April 6, 1877, the structure was the church's first sacred house of worship in the West. The St. George Temple is the oldest active Mormon temple in the world. It's constructed of stuccoed stone in a castellated Gothic Revival style; a cupola with a weather vane caps the structure. Sacred ceremonies take place inside, so no tours are offered, but you're welcome to visit the grounds to admire the architecture. The temple is especially impressive at night when it's lit up against the black sky. A visitors' center on the northeast corner of the grounds has short films and videos introducing the Mormon religion; it's open daily 9 A.M.–9 P.M. (8 A.M.–10 P.M. in summer). The visitors' center and temple are

at 250 E. 400 S., at the corner of 200 South, (435) 673-5181.

St. George Tabernacle

When Brigham Young visited the Cotton Mission after its first year, he found the community afflicted with difficulties and low morale. Soon after, he ordered construction of a tabernacle to help rally the members. The task, paid for with tithes, took 13 years to complete. Builders used local red sandstone for the walls and placed a slender white steeple on the roof, reminiscent of a New England church. Tour guides explain some of the tabernacle's history and construction details. The 20-minute film *Windows of Heaven,* shown on request, dramatizes the revelation received here in 1899 by church President Lorenzo Snow. Guides offer free tours daily about 9 A.M.–6 P.M.; occasional concerts (free) and other presentations take place, too. Located downtown at Main and Tabernacle Sts., (435) 628-4072.

Daughters of Utah Pioneers Museum

Drop in to see hundreds of pioneer portraits and the tools and clothing used by early settlers. The spinning wheels and looms on display served in the mission's cotton and silk industries. Open Mon.–Sat. 10 A.M.–5 P.M.; donation requested. The museum, staffed by the Daughters of Utah Pioneers, is at 145 N. 100 East, behind the old county courthouse, (435) 628-7274.

Brigham Young Winter Home

Late in life, Brigham Young sought relief from rheumatism and other aches and pains by spending winters in Dixie's mild climate. This also gave him an opportunity to supervise more closely the affairs of the church here, especially construction of the temple. A telegraph line connected Young's house with Salt Lake City. He moved here late in 1873 and returned each winter until his death in 1877. The carefully restored adobe house contains furnishings of the era including some that belonged to Young. Fruit and mulberry trees grow in the yard; mulberry leaves once fed the silkworms of the short-lived pioneer industry. Free tours begin at

Young's office on the east side of the house. Open daily 9 A.M. (8 A.M. in summer) until sunset; 67 W. 200 North., (435) 673-2517.

Jacob Hamblin Home

No one did more to extend the Mormons' southern settlements and keep peace with the Indians than Jacob Hamblin. He came west in 1850 with four children (his first wife refused to come) and settled in the Tooele area with wife number two. At Brigham Young's request, Hamblin moved south in 1856 and helped build the Santa Clara Fort. He built the present sandstone house after floods washed away the fort in 1862. Almost always on the move serving on missions, Hamblin had little time for home life. He moved to Kanab in 1870, then to Arizona and New Mexico. Even so, he had four wives and managed to father 24 children. The kitchen, work areas, and living rooms provide a good idea of what pioneer life was like. Free tours offer a view of the house and tell of activities that once took place here. Located in the village of Santa Clara, four miles northwest of St. George, (435) 673-5181; open daily 9 A.M. until sunset.

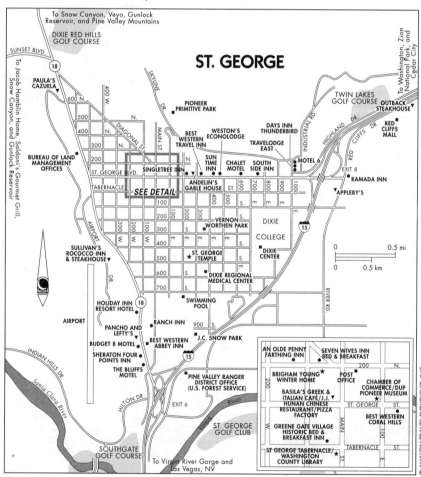

mural detail on the Fine Arts Building at Dixie State College

Dixie State College of Utah

A giant "D" on a hillside to the west watches over the "Home of the Rebels" and the surrounding town. The school began in 1911 as the St. George Stake Academy, founded by the Mormon Church. Dixie College is now a four-year college operated by the state. The approximately 5,000 students meet on a three-semester system.

Visitors are welcome to attend cultural and sporting events and to use many of the facilities. The Fine Arts Building (700 East and 100 South) has exhibits inside, but you'll find the biggest work outside on the south wall. A mosaic more than 15 feet high and 127 feet long depicts the region's history from the days of the Fremont Indians to Mormon settlement. To find out what's going on at Dixie College, visit the administration building (700 East and 200 South), call (435) 652-7800, or visit www.dixie.edu. The college's mailing address is St. George, UT 84770.

SPAS

St. George is now home to two major spa resorts and recreation centers. Both are outside of St. George, in gorgeous natural settings. **Green Valley Spa**, 1871 West Canyon View Dr., (435) 628-8060 or (800) 237-1068, www.greenvalleyspa.com, is a major fitness, sports, health, and beauty spa resort with all-inclusive rates. Facilities are numerous and of a very high quality, and include three pools, racquetball courts, fully equipped gym with an array of fitness classes, tennis instruction, golf club privileges, plus hiking and climbing in neighboring canyons. There's also a whole catalog of beauty and rejuvenation treatments, ranging from massage, wraps, and aromatherapy to Native American medicine ceremonies and Shamanic card divination. Lodging is in the Coyote Inn, a luxury condominium development that flanks a park-like pool and garden area. Three spa meals daily are included in the rates. Green Valley Spa requires a three-night minimum stay, with seven-day packages also available. Rates, which include all meals and most recreation and treatments, range from $1,200–1,350 for a three-night stay.

Slightly less grandiose, the **Red Mountain Spa**, 202 N. Snow Canyon Rd., (800) 407-3002, www.redmountainspa.com, focuses more exclusively on fitness, health, and weight loss programs. Facilities include numerous swimming and soaking pools, a fitness center and gym, tennis courts, salon, spa, conference rooms, plus access to lots of hiking and biking trails. Individualized coaching and fitness programs are designed for each guest; there is an abundance of exercise and aerobics classes each day. Three "health supportive meals" are offered daily. Treatments for relaxation and beauty include massage, facials, body polishing, and aromatherapy. Accommodations are in a series of lodge-like hotel structures, or in luxury casitas.

Four-, seven-, 10-, and 14-day programs are available. Prices, which include all meals, lodging, and use of most spa facilities and recreation, range from $685–1,360 for four days, depending on lodging type.

ACCOMMODATIONS

St. George offers a large number of places to stay and eat. Motel prices stay about the same year-round, though they may drop if business is slow in summer. Considering the popularity of this destination, prices are reasonable and quality is high. Golfers should ask about golf-and-lodging packages. You'll find most lodgings along the I-15 business route of St. George Boulevard (Exit 8) and Bluff Street (Exit 6). As for food, you'll find almost every fast-food place known to humanity just off the interstate on St. George Boulevard.

Under $50

Many of St. George's less expensive lodging choices operate at I-15's Exit 8 or on St. George Boulevard as it heads west to downtown. Right at the freeway exchange you'll find **Motel 6,** 205 N. 1000 E., (435) 628-7979 or (800) 466-8356, with a pool; pets okay. The **Travelodge East,** 175 N. 1000 East, (435) 673-4621 or (800) 578-7878, has some kitchenettes and a pool; small pets okay.

Heading toward downtown, the **South Side Inn,** 750 E. St. George Blvd., (435) 628-9000 or (888) 628-9081, offers a pool and a spa; pets okay in designated rooms. The **Chalet Motel,** 664 E. St. George Blvd., (435) 628-6272 or (888) 628-6272, offers some efficiency kitchens, two three-bed rooms, and a pool.

Weston's Econolodge, 460 E. St. George Blvd., (435) 673-4861, has a pool and a spa, and small pets are okay. The **Sun Time Inn,** 420 E. St. George Blvd., (435) 673-6181 or (800) 237-6253, has kitchenettes and a pool.

$50–75

East of the Exit 8 interchange is the **Ramada Inn,** 1440 E. St. George Blvd. (right beside the Factory Outlet Mall), (435) 628-2828 or (800) 713-9435; facilities include an outdoor pool and hot tub; a complimentary continental breakfast is included. The **Days Inn Thunderbird,** 150 N. 1000 East, (435) 673-6123 or (800) 527-6543, has a pool, hot tub, sauna, fitness center, free continental breakfast, and pets are okay.

The **Best Western Travel Inn,** 316 E. St. George Blvd., (435) 673-3541 or (800) 528-1234, has an outdoor pool and indoor spa; children under 12 stay free. The **Singletree Inn,** 260 E. St. George Blvd., (435) 673-6161 or (800) 528-8890, has a pool, hot tub, and free continental breakfast; pets okay with $5 fee. Special golf package rates.

Close to downtown is one of St. George's best, the **Best Western Coral Hills,** 125 E. St. George Blvd., (435) 673-4844 or (800) 542-7733, a very attractive property with indoor and outdoor pools and two spas, an exercise room, and a complimentary continental breakfast. Children under 12 stay free.

Leave the freeway at I-15 Exit 6 to find another selection of motels. Most rooms at **The Bluffs Motel,** 1140 S. Bluff St., (435) 628-6699 or (800) 832-5833, are suites with efficiency kitchens. Facilities include a pool and spa; pets okay. Two-night minimum for stays during Easter weekend and some special events. **Best Western Abbey Inn,** 1129 S. Bluff St., (435) 652-1234 or (888) 222-3946, is brand new, and all rooms have microwaves and refrigerators. There's an outdoor pool, indoor spa, recreation/fitness facilities, and a free hot breakfast. **Budget 8 Motel,** 1230 S. Bluff St., (435) 628-5234 or (800) 275-3494, offers a pool and spa.

The **Ranch Inn,** 1040 S. Main, (435) 628-8000 or (800) 332-0400, offers a number of suite-like rooms with efficiency kitchens; there's a guest laundry, pool, and indoor hot tub.

Just across from Brigham Young's winter home, the **Seven Wives Inn Bed & Breakfast,** 217 N. 100 West, (435) 628-3737 or (800) 600-3737, offers rooms in two historic homes. All 13 guest rooms have private baths and are decorated with antiques. Children are welcome, and guests share a swimming pool.

Also located in St. George's historic district is **An Olde Penny Farthing Inn,** 278 N. 100 West, (435) 673-7755. Built in the 1870s as a pioneer home, the handsome structure has been beautifully restored as an inn with five guest rooms, each individually decorated with period furnishings and fine art; all have private baths.

You'll find an entire compound of pioneer-era homes at the **Greene Gate Village Historic Bed & Breakfast Inn,** 76 W. Tabernacle, (435) 628-6999 or (800) 350-6999. Nine beautifully restored homes offer a variety of lodging options—groups or families can rent an entire home. Many rooms come with kitchens and private baths, some with private whirlpools; there's a pool for the enjoyment of all guests. Some pets are okay, children are welcome.

$75–100

The **Holiday Inn Resort Hotel & Convention Center,** 850 S. Bluff St., (435) 628-4235 or (800) 457-9800, is a large complex with a "Holidome" complete with indoor and outdoor pools, whirlpool, recreation/fitness facilities, tennis court, and putting green. Children under 18 stay free.

$100–125

The most prestigious address in St. George is the **Sheraton Four Points Inn,** 1450 S. Hilton Inn Dr., (435) 628-0463 or (800) 662-2525. Located on a golf course, the hotel has beautiful public areas and nicely appointed guest rooms. Facilities include a pool, sauna, and private tennis courts.

Campgrounds

Snow Canyon State Park, (435) 628-2255 or (800) 322-3770 (reservations), has a campground with showers open all year in a pretty canyon setting; go 12 miles north on UT 18, then left two miles; $12, $14 with hookups (see Vicinity of St. George, below). **McArthur's Temple View RV Resort,** 975 S. Main, (435) 673-6400 or (800) 776-6410, is located near the city center temple district and has a pool, laundry, and showers; $19 tents or RVs without hookups, $23 RVs with. East of town is **Settlers RV Park,** 1333 E. 100 South (near I-15 Exit 8), (435) 628-1624, with pool and showers; RVs only, $12 without hookups, $18 full hookups. Farther north, near I-15 Washington Exit 10, you'll find **St. George Campground & RV Park,** 2100 E. Middleton Dr., (435) 673-2970, with pool, laundry, and showers ($15 tents, $16 RVs with hookups); **Redlands RV Park,** 650 W. Telegraph, (435) 673-9700 or (800) 553-8269, with pool, store, laundry, and showers ($17 tents, $22 RVs with hookups).

OTHER PRACTICALITIES

Food

For a major recreation and retirement center, St. George is curiously lacking in unique places to eat. Most every chain restaurant can be found here, but don't expect a bevy of local fine dining houses. Some exceptions are listed below. You'll also find it bizarrely difficult to find restaurants open late; even in high season, most restaurants close up shop by 9 P.M.

Ancestor's Square, a boutique shopping development at the intersection of St. George Boulevard and Main Street, provides travelers with several ethnic food options. Eat Greek cuisine at highly regarded **Basila's Greek & Italian Cafe,** (435) 673-7671, which has a liquor license, or dine Chinese at **J.J. Hunan Chinese Restaurant,** (435) 628-7219. Pick up pizza at **Pizza Factory,** (435) 628-1234.

Unless noted, all the following serve wine and cocktails. **The Palms,** in the Holiday Inn, 850 S. Bluff St., (435) 628-4235, features steak, prime rib, and seafood dinners and a Sunday brunch. **Pancho & Lefty's,** 1050 S. Bluff St., (435) 628-4772, serves Mexican lunch and dinners in a semiformal atmosphere. For Mexican food with a view, try **Paula's Cazuela,** 745 W. Ridgeview Dr. on the northwest edge of town, (435) 673-6568; a hilltop restaurant serving fine Mexican fare for lunch and dinner. Recently opened chain restaurants include a new **Outback Steakhouse,** 250 Red Cliff Dr., (435) 674-7788, and an **Appleby's,** 150 S. River Rd., (435) 628-6600.

For formal dining and spectacular views, head west towards the airport for **Sullivan's Rococo Inn & Steak House,** 511 Airport Rd., (435) 628-3671; prime rib, steak, and seafood are the specialties. Locals go to **Andelin's Gable House,** 290 E. St. George Blvd., (435) 673-6796, for special multi-course fine dining with a seasonally changing menu; open for lunch and dinner (reservations advised; no alcohol). **Scaldoni's Gourmet Grill,** 929 W. Sunset Blvd., (435) 674-1300, offers Italian fine dining, along with good steaks. Dine in historic splendor at **Bentley House Restaurant,** at Greene Gate Village, 76 W. Tabernacle, (435) 656-3333, which offers fine dining in a restored pioneer home (no alcohol).

Entertainment and Events

The staff at the **St. George Visitors Center,** (435) 628-1658, and at the **Washington County Travel and Convention Bureau,** (800) 634-5747, will fill you in on upcoming events including concerts at Dixie Center and the tabernacle and the many small sporting events that take place in St. George.

Major annual events include the **Dixie Invitational Art Show,** which hosts regional artists in **February;** it begins President's Day weekend at the Fine Arts Building on Dixie College campus.

September brings the **Lions Dixie PRCA Round-Up Rodeo.** In **October,** the **Huntsman World Senior Games** presents a wide variety of Olympics-type competitions for seniors; you'll be amazed at the enthusiasm and abilities.

Golf

With one private and eight public golf courses in the area, St. George enjoys a reputation as Utah's winter golf capital. Red sandstone cliffs serve as the backdrop for **Dixie Red Hills,** 1250 N. 645 West, on the northwest edge of town, (435) 634-5852, a nine-hole, par-34 municipal course. **Green Spring Golf Course,** 588 N. Green Spring Dr. (just west of I-15 Washington Exit 10), (435) 673-7888, has 18 holes (par 71) and a reputation as one of the finest courses in Utah. The nine-hole **Twin Lakes Golf Course,** 660 N. Twin Lakes Dr. on the northeast edge of town (take the I-15 west frontage road, Highland Dr.), (435) 673-4441, is one of the area's most picturesque courses. Professionals favor the cleverly designed **Sunbrook Golf Course,** 2240 Sunbrook Dr. off Dixie Downs Rd., between Green Valley and Santa Clara, (435) 634-5866: 27 holes, par 72. **St. George Golf Club** has a popular 18-hole, par-73 course south of town in Bloomington Hills, (435) 634-5854. **Southgate Golf Course,** 1975 S. Tonaquint Dr. on the southwest edge of town, (435) 628-0000, has 18 holes and a 70 par. The adjacent Southgate Game Improvement Center, (435) 674-7728 can provide golfers with computerized golf swing analysis plus plenty of indoor practice space and lots of balls. **Entrada,** 2511 W. Entrada Trail, (435) 674-7500, is a new 18-hole course fast on its way to St. George's most respected. The Johnny Miller-designed course is

northwest of St. George, and incorporates natural lava flows, rolling dunes, and arroyos into its design. The 18-hole course, **Sky Mountain,** is located northeast of St. George in nearby Hurricane (see Vicinity of St. George, below).

Other Recreation

Vernon Worthen Park, 400 East and 200 South, offers shaded picnic tables, playground, and tennis courts. **J.C. Snow Park,** 400 East and 900 South, has picnic tables and playground (but little shade). **Pioneer Primitive Park** overlooks the city from the north; in desert country just off Skyline Drive, it has a few picnic tables. The outdoor public **swimming pool,** 250 E. 700 South, (435) 634-5867, features a hydro slide; open Memorial Day–Labor Day weekends. **Tennis** players may use the public courts at Dixie College and Vernon Worthen Park. The city's **Leisure Services Department,** (435) 634-5860, offers a wide range of activities for adults and youth, including classes (art, music, sports), field trips, and lectures.

Shopping

Red Cliffs Mall houses the big ZCMI, JCPenny, Wal-Mart, and other stores on Red Cliffs Drive, the east frontage road northeast of the I-15 St. George Boulevard Exit 8. **Zion Factory Stores** has many factory outlets nearby, just east of I-10 Exit 8. Purchase outdoor supplies at the **Outdoor Outlet,** 1062 E. Tabernacle, (435) 628-3611; **Hurst Sports Center,** 160 N. 500 West, (435) 673-6141; and **Wal-Mart,** Red Cliffs Mall, (435) 628-2802.

Services

The post office is at 180 N. Main, (435) 673-3312. Dixie Regional Medical Center provides hospital care at 544 S. 400 East, (435) 634-4000 (physician referral number is 801-628-6688). Elderhostel education and recreation programs (including activities as ambitious as raft trips and European tours) in St. George have been very popular with seniors; (435) 673-3704 or (800) 545-4653. Exchange foreign currency at First Security Bank, 410 E. Tabernacle, (435) 574-6600.

Information

The **St. George Chamber of Commerce** can tell you about the sights, events, and services of southwestern Utah; it has brochures of accommodations, restaurants, a historic walking tour, and area ghost towns; open Mon.–Fri. 9 A.M.–5 P.M. and Sat. 9 A.M.–1 P.M. The office is in the old county courthouse (built 1866–76) at 97 E. St. George Boulevard (St. George, UT 84770), (435) 628-1658.

For recreation information, see the **Pine Valley Ranger District office,** 196 E. Tabernacle, (St. George, UT 84770), (435) 652-3100, for information on fishing, hiking, and camping in the Dixie National Forest north of town; maps of the forest and Pine Valley Wilderness are available; open Mon.–Fri. 8 A.M.–5 P.M. The **Bureau of Land Management** oversees vast lands in Utah's southwest corner and the Arizona Strip; open Mon.–Fri. 7:45 A.M.–4:30 P.M.; the offices for Dixie Resource Area, (435) 688-3200, and the Shivwits and Vermilion Resource Areas of the Arizona Strip, (435) 628-4491, are at 345 E. Riverside.

Washington County Library, just south of the tabernacle at 50 S. Main, (435) 634-5737, offers a good selection of books, and a bulletin board lists community events and classes; open Mon.–Thurs. 9 A.M.–9 P.M., Fri. and Sat. 9 A.M.–6 P.M. **Dixie College's library** sits in the center of campus, (435) 673-4811, ext. 201; open Mon.–Thurs. 7:30 A.M.–11 P.M., Fri. 7:30 A.M.–5 P.M., Sat. 10 A.M.–5 P.M., and Sun. 1–8 P.M. during the main terms. **B. Dalton Bookseller,** in the Red Cliffs Mall, (435) 673-4224, offers a good assortment that includes regional and travel books. Other sources for Utah books include **R & K's Bookstore,** 116 E. City Center, (435) 673-5478, and **Deseret Book Co.,** 779 S. Bluff St., (435) 628-4495.

Tours

For van tours from St. George to the parks and sights of southeastern Utah, see information about Southern Utah Scenic Tours, (888) 404-8687, above.

Aerowest Aviation, (435) 674-1000, will show you spectacular scenery from the air on a variety of trips including a half-hour flight over St. George and Snow Canyon ($40), a one-hour trip across Zion National Park ($69), a two-hour flight over Zion and Bryce ($119), a two-hour tour of the Grand Canyon ($129), and a 3.5-hour loop to Zion, Grand Canyon, and Lake Powell ($339). (All prices are per person, with a minimum of two.)

Transportation

For a cab, call **Quality Cab,** (435) 656-5222, or **Dixie Cab Co.,** (435) 673-4068. Rent automobiles in town from **Budget Rent-A-Car,** 116 W. St. George Blvd., (435) 673-6825 or (800) 527-0700; **Dollar,** 1175 S. 150 East, (435) 628-6549. **National Car Rental,** (435) 673-5098 or (800) 227-7368, is at the airport. **Greyhound** buses depart from McDonald's Restaurant at 1235 S. Bluff Street for Salt Lake City, Denver, Las Vegas, and other destinations; (435) 673-2933. **St. George Shuttle** will take you to Las Vegas in a 15-passenger van for $20 from 850 S. Bluff Street (Holiday Inn); call (435) 628-8320 for schedule. **Skywest Airlines** has direct flights to Salt Lake City six times daily and to Las Vegas twice daily; (800) 453-9417.

VICINITY OF ST. GEORGE

Some good scenic drives begin at St. George. Whether you're short on time or have all day, a good choice is the 24-mile loop through Snow Canyon State Park via UT 18, the park road (UT 300), and Santa Clara. The old highway to Littlefield, Arizona, makes a 67-mile loop with I-15; this route follows former U.S. 91 through the pioneer settlement of Santa Clara and the sparsely settled Shivwits Reservation and over a 4,600-foot pass in the Beaver Dam Mountains to Littlefield; the I-15 section goes through the spectacular Virgin River Gorge upstream from Little-field. In summer, the cool forests of the Pine Valley Mountains, 37 miles northwest of town, are an especially attractive destination: you can make a 130-mile drive with many possible side trips by circling the mountains on UT 18, UT 56, and I-15. Zion National Park, with its grandeur and color, is about 40 miles northeast of St. George. Adventurous motorists may want to try some of the unpaved roads through the desert east and west of St. George; the back way to Hurricane via Fort Pearce can be driven by car in good weather.

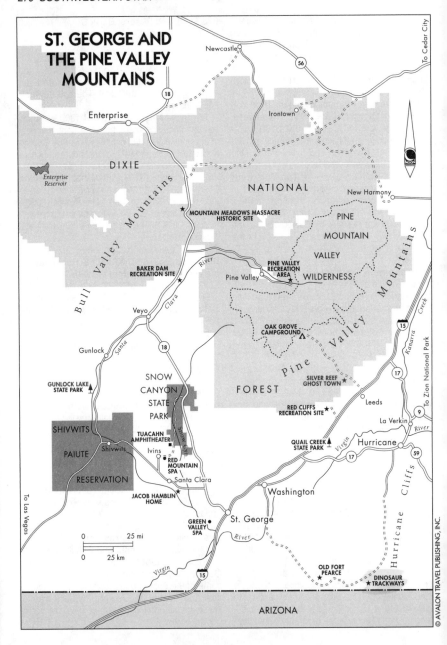

ST. GEORGE AND THE PINE VALLEY MOUNTAINS

To Cedar City

Newcastle

56

18

Enterprise

DIXIE

NATIONAL

Enterprise
Reservoir

New Harmony

Bull Valley Mountains

MOUNTAIN MEADOWS MASSACRE
HISTORIC SITE

PINE

MOUNTAIN

VALLEY

River

BAKER DAM
RECREATION SITE

PINE VALLEY
RECREATION
AREA

WILDERNESS

Pine Valley

Santa Clara

Veyo

Pine Valley Mountains

Gunlock

Santa

OAK GROVE
CAMPGROUND

15

Kanarra Creek

18

GUNLOCK LAKE
STATE PARK

SNOW
CANYON
STATE
PARK

Pine Valley

FOREST

SILVER REEF
GHOST TOWN

17

To Zion National Park

SHIVWITS

Leeds

La Verkin

9

PAIUTE

Shivwits

TUACAHN
AMPHITHEATER

Ivins

Snow Cyn.

RED
MOUNTAIN
SPA

RED CLIFFS
RECREATION SITE

River

RESERVATION

Santa Clara

QUAIL CREEK
STATE PARK

Virgin

Hurricane

59

JACOB HAMBLIN
HOME

Washington

17

To Las Vegas

GREEN
VALLEY
SPA

St. George

0   25 mi

0   25 km

River

Virgin

15

OLD FORT
PEARCE

Hurricane Cliffs

DINOSAUR
TRACKWAYS

ARIZONA

© AVALON TRAVEL PUBLISHING, INC.

MOON

SNOW CANYON STATE PARK

North of St. George, Snow Canyon State Park is a great place to explore and enjoy the desert scenery. Redrock canyons, sand dunes, volcanoes, and lava flows have formed an incredible landscape. Walls of Navajo Sandstone 50–750 feet high enclose five-mile-long Snow Canyon. Hiking trails lead into the backcountry for a closer look at the geology, flora, and fauna. Common plants are barrel, cholla, and prickly pear cacti, yucca, Mormon tea, shrub live oak, cliffrose, and cottonwood. Delicate wildflowers bloom mostly in the spring and autumn, following the wet seasons, but cactus and the sacred datura can flower in the heat of summer. Wildlife includes sidewinder and Great Basin rattlesnakes, Gila monster, desert tortoise, kangaroo rat, squirrel, cottontail, kit fox, coyote, and mule deer. You may find some Indian rock art, arrowheads, bits of pottery, and ruins. Many of the place names in the park honor Mormon pioneers. Snow Canyon was named for Lorenzo and Erastus Snow—not for the rare snowfalls. Cooler months have the best weather; summers are too hot for comfortable hiking except in early morning. Highway UT 18 leads past an overlook on the rim of Snow Canyon and to the paved park road (UT 300) that drops into the canyon and follows it to its mouth and the small town of Ivins. Snow Canyon is about 12 miles northwest of St. George. It's reached either by UT 18—the faster way—or via Santa Clara and Ivins. Each vehicle is charged a $4 day-use fee.

Hiking Trails

The park brochure contains an aerial photo of the area on which trails and other features have been drawn in. **Hidden Piñon Trail** (also signed as Nature Trail) begins across the road from the Shivwits Campground entrance, then weaves among sandstone hills and lava flows to the Varnish Mountain Overlook above Snow Canyon. At the overlook, desert varnish on sandstone has turned the rock jet black. The easy trail is 1.5 miles round-trip and has a small elevation gain; some sections cross rough rocks and deep sand. It's an easy scramble from the overlook area to the canyon floor below. **West Canyon Trail** is the longest in the park; it begins near the stables (0.7 mile south of the campground) and goes northwest along an old road up Snow Canyon to West Canyon. (You can also take cross-country hikes into other canyons passed on the way.) The trail is seven miles round-trip with a small elevation gain. **Lava Tubes Trail** winds across a lava field to an area of lava caves (one mile round-trip). The caves formed when molten lava broke out of the partly cooled flow and left rooms and tunnels behind. Artifacts indicate that Indians took shelter in the chambers. The trailhead is 1.5 miles north of the campground. The steep and strenuous **Volcano Trail** ascends a cinder cone northeast of Snow Canyon. The 1,000-year-old volcano is on the east side of UT 18 one mile north of the turnoff for Snow Canyon.

Practicalities

Set within the canyon, the **campground** at Snow Canyon State Park stays open all year with water, showers, and hookups. Sites cost $12; $14 with hookups. Camping reservations are especially recommended for spring and autumn weekends. Contact Snow Canyon State Park at P.O. Box 140, Santa Clara, UT 84765, (435) 628-2255 or (800) 322-3770 (reservations). **Snow Canyon Riding Stables,** (435) 628-6677, offers horseback riding, campfire breakfasts, and Western shows year-round; you can arrange overnight pack trips in the Pine Mountains in summer.

TUACAHN AMPHITHEATER

Tuacahn is an outdoor amphitheater that seats 1,900 set among 1,500-foot-high redrock cliffs northwest of St. George. Tuacahn offers a two-show summer theater season mostly featuring Broadway musicals. Recent performances have included *The Music Man* and *Fiddler on the Roof.* A new indoor performance space, the Haffen Theatre, features more intimate comedies and dramas. A Dutch-oven dinner is available before each production as well as free backstage tours. The show runs daily except Sunday mid-June–early-September, and ticket prices run $18–28 ages 12 and over, $12–18 for children under 12. Located northwest of St. George near the south entrance to Snow Canyon State Park. Call (800) 746-9882, or check out the website at www.showutah.com, for information and reservations.

VEYO AND VICINITY

Veyo Resort

Warm-water springs feed a swimming pool in this pretty spot. The family resort here has picnic tables and a snack bar; open from about the last weekend in March to Labor Day; (435) 574-2744. Take the Veyo Pool Resort Road from UT 18 southeast of town. The little village of Veyo lies along the Santa Clara River 19 miles northwest of St. George.

Gunlock Lake State Park

The 266-acre reservoir is set among red and gray hills 10 miles southwest of Veyo. A parking area, docks, and paved boat ramp lie just off the road near the dam. The red-sand beach across the lake can be reached by boat or by a short walk across the dam. Largemouth bass, channel catfish, bluegill, and the odd trout swim in the waters. Open all year; no water or charge; check with Snow Canyon State Park for current info at P.O. Box 140, Santa Clara, UT 84765, (435) 628-2255. Gunlock Lake can be reached from St. George via Veyo or by the slightly shorter route through Santa Clara.

Baker Dam Recreation Site

This 50-acre reservoir on BLM land is on the Santa Clara River upstream from Veyo. Anglers come for the rainbow and brown trout. An established campground is located just before the dam; drive across the dam to undeveloped camping areas and a boat ramp. Open all year; no water or charge. Go north four miles on UT 18 from Veyo, then turn right a half mile on a paved road (between Mileposts 24 and 25).

UTAH 18 NORTH TO ENTERPRISE

Mountain Meadows
Massacre Historic Site

A short trip from UT 18 west of the Pine Valley Mountains leads to the site of one of the darkest chapters of Mormon history. The pleasant valley had been a popular rest stop for pioneers about to cross the hot desert country to the west. In 1857, a California-bound wagon train whose members had already experienced trouble with Mormons of the region was attacked by an alliance of Mormons and local Indians. About 120 people in the wagon train died in the massacre. Only some small children too young to tell the story were spared. The closely knit Mormon community tried to cover up the incident and hindered federal attempts to apprehend the killers. Only John D. Lee, who was in charge of Indian affairs in southern Utah at the time, was ever brought to justice. After nearly 20 years and two trials, authorities took him back to this spot to be executed by firing squad. Many details of the massacre remain unknown. The major causes seem to have been a Mormon fear of invasion, aggressive Mormons and Indians, and poor communications between the Mormon leadership in Salt Lake City and southern Utah. A monument now marks the site of the tragedy; turn west one mile on a paved road from UT 18 between Mileposts 31 and 32.

Enterprise Reservoirs

Rainbow trout lurk in the lower and upper reservoirs. Larger Upper Enterprise Reservoir has a paved boat ramp and easier access. Nearby **Honeycomb Rocks Campground** (elev. 5,700 feet) has water ($8 fee) from about Memorial Day–October 31. Its name describes the outcrops of porous volcanic rock. The open country here supports mostly grass, sage, and some ponderosa pine and Gambel oak. Drive to the town of Enterprise, 41 miles northwest of St. George (47 miles west of Cedar City), then follow paved roads 11.5 miles west and south.

PINE VALLEY MOUNTAINS

A massive body of magma uncovered by erosion makes up the Pine Valley Mountains. Vegetation ranges from piñon pine and juniper woodlands on the lower slopes to ponderosa pine and aspen at the middle elevations to Douglas fir, subalpine fir, Engelmann spruce, and limber pine in the heights. Signal Peak (elev. 10,365 feet) tops the range, much of which has been designated the Pine Valley Mountain Wilderness Area.

Pine Valley

In 1856, pioneers arrived at Pine Valley (elev. 6,600 feet) to harvest the extensive forests and raise livestock. Lumber from Pine Valley helped build many southern Utah settlements and even went into Salt Lake City's great tabernacle organ. The town's picturesque white chapel was built in 1868 by Ebenezer Bryce, who later homesteaded at what's now Bryce Canyon National Park. The chapel is open for tours daily 11 A.M.–5 P.M. from Memorial Day to Labor Day weekends. Most of today's residents come up only in summer for the cool mountain air.

Pine Valley Recreation Area

Continue three miles on the paved road past Pine Valley to the picnic areas, campgrounds, and trails in Dixie National Forest. At Pine Valley Reservoir, 2.3 miles up on the right, you can fish for rainbow and some brook trout. There's also fair fishing in the Santa Clara River upstream and downstream. **Ponderosa Picnic Area** is 0.4 mile farther on the right; free for day use. Turn right just past the picnic area for **Pines Campground, Lower Pines Picnic Area,** and **Brown's Point Trailhead.** Continue straight for **Blue Springs** and **South and North Juniper Campgrounds** and for **Whipple Trailhead.** Each campground has water and a $8 single-unit fee during the May 20–October 31 season. Elevation is 6,800 feet. All campsites fill up most days in summer; try to arrive early or make reservations then. Reservations can be made by calling (800) 280-CAMP for individual sites at Blue Springs Campground, the group campground at Upper Pines, and group picnic areas. The **Pine Valley Ranger District office** in St. George (196 E. Tabernacle in St. George), (435) 652-3100, can advise on camping and other recreation here.

Pine Valley Wilderness

The 50,000-acre wilderness has the best scenery of the Pine Valley Mountains, but it can be seen only on foot or horseback. A network of trails from all directions leads into the wilderness. The road from Pine Valley provides access to the **Whipple Trailhead** and **Brown's Point Trailhead** on the east side of the wilderness area. Trails are usually open from about mid-June into October. **Summit Trail** is the longest (35 miles one-way) and connects with many other trails. Several loops are possible, though most are too long for day hikes. **Whipple National Recreation Trail** is one of the most popular for both day- and overnight trips; it ascends 2,100 feet in six miles to Summit Trail. **Brown's Point Trail** also climbs to Summit Trail, but in four miles. Strong hikers can use the Brown's Point and Summit Trails to reach the top of Signal Peak on a day hike; the last part of the climb is a rock-scramble. Generally, the trails from Pine Valley are signed and easy to follow; trails in other areas may not be maintained. Take topo maps and a compass if you're going for more than a short stroll. The Pine Valley Ranger District office has a recreation map that shows trails and trailheads. The Hiker's Guide to Utah, by Dave Hall, describes a 15-mile loop in the Pine Valley Mountains.

NORTH OF PINE VALLEY MOUNTAINS

Irontown

This is one of Utah's best-preserved 19th-century iron smelter sites. The original Iron Mission near Cedar City had poor success during its brief life in the 1850s. In 1870, though, more extensive ore deposits farther west at this site encouraged another attempt at iron-making. Daily production rose to nearly five tons, and a town of several hundred workers grew up around the smelter.

Profits began to decline in the 1880s when cheaper iron from the eastern states flooded in. The town soon died, though mining has since continued on and off in the vicinity. A brick chimney, stone foundations of the smelter, and a beehive-shaped charcoal kiln show the layout of the operation. Look around in the sagebrush for remnants of the town site and pieces of slag and iron. Drive 16 miles west from Cedar City or 30 miles east from Enterprise to the signed turnoff on UT 56 (just west of Milepost 41), then turn southwest 2.7 miles.

EAST OF PINE VALLEY MOUNTAINS

Leeds

This small community has two exits on I-15; southbound traffic on I-15 must use Exit 23 on the north side of town. Northbound traffic on I-15 must take Exit 22 south of town. **Leeds RV Park,** (435) 879-2450, has RV sites for $15 with hookups and showers (no tents); turn east on Center at the sign.

Silver Reef

This is probably Utah's most accessible ghost town. In about 1870, prospectors found rich silver deposits in the sandstone here, much to the surprise of mining experts who thought such a combination impossible. The town grew up several years later and boomed from 1878 to 1882.

The population peaked at 1,500 and included a sizable Chinese community. Then a combination of lower silver prices, declining yields, and water in the mines forced the operations to close one by one, the last in 1891. Other attempts at mining have since been made from time to time, including some uranium production in the 1950s and '60s, but the town had died.

The **Wells Fargo Building,** which once stood in the center of town, is now Silver Reef's main attraction. Built of stone in 1877, it looks as solid as ever. **Jerry Anderson Art Gallery** and the small **Silver Reef Museum** occupy the interior; open Mon.–Sat. 9 A.M.–5 P.M., (435) 879-2254. Encroaching modern houses detract a bit from the setting, but the ghosts are still here. Stone walls and foundations peek out of the sagebrush. A short walk on the road past the building takes you to the ruins and tailings of the mills that once shook the town with their racket. Take I-15 Leeds Exit 22 or 23 and follow signs 1.3 miles on a paved road.

Oak Grove Campground

On the east side of the Pine Valley Mountains, Oak Grove (elev. 6,800 feet) is in a forest of Gambel and shrub live oak, ponderosa pine, and some spruce. The small campground has water from about Memorial Day to October 31; $8. Leeds Creek has trout fishing, but dense shrubbery along the banks can make access difficult. **Oak Grove Trail** winds three miles from

Wells Fargo building at Silver Reef ghost town

the campground to Summit Trail in the Pine Valley Mountain Wilderness. Take I-15 Leeds Exit 22 or 23 and go northwest nine miles. The unpaved road may be rough, especially late in the season; it's usually passable by cars but isn't recommended for trailers.

Red Cliffs Recreation Site
Weather-sculptured cliffs of reddish-orange sandstone rise above this pretty spot. The seasonal Quail Creek emerges from a canyon, flows through the middle of the campground, then goes on to Quail Creek Reservoir two miles away. The campground and picnic area (elev. 3,240 feet) is open all year with water; there's a $7 camping fee. **Desert Trail** starts on the left near the beginning of the campground loop and follows the creek a half mile into the canyon. Idyllic pools and graceful rock formations line the way. You'll need to do some wading to continue upstream past trail's end. A shorter (quarter-mile round-trip) but more rugged trail begins near the end of the campground loop and crosses slickrock to Silver Reef Lookout Point. Here there's a good panorama of the area, though you can't actually see Silver Reef ghost town. Take I-15 Leeds Exit 22 or 23, go south three miles on the frontage road, then turn west 1.7 miles on a paved road. Long trailers may drag on dips at stream crossings.

Quail Creek State Park
Barren rock hills surround the 590-acre reservoir at this park. Most of the water comes from the Virgin River, but Quail Creek also contributes its share. Curiously, the reservoir has two dams to hold back the waters. The state park on the west shore offers a campground (water but no showers or hookups), swimming beach, paved boat ramp, and docks. Anglers come for the largemouth bass, rainbow trout, catfish, and bluegill. Other popular activities include water-skiing, personal watercrafting, and sailboarding. The park stays open all year; $4 per vehicle for day use, $9 per vehicle for camping. For information, contact the park at P.O. Box 1943, St. George, UT 84770, (435) 879-2378 or (800) 322-3770 (reservations). If coming from the north, take I-15 Leeds Exit 23 and follow the frontage road south 3.4 miles, then turn left 1.5 miles; from the south, take I-15 Hurricane Exit 16, go east 2.6 miles on UT 9, then north two miles on a paved road.

HURRICANE AND VICINITY

Legend has it that in the early 1860s a group of pioneers was descending the steep cliffs above the present town site when a strong wind came up; Erastus Snow compared it with a hurricane and named the place Hurricane Hill. (By the way, locals pronounce the town's name as HURaken.) A canal to bring water from the Virgin River to Hurricane Bench took 11 years of hard work to build, beginning in 1893, but it allowed farming in the area for the first time. Settlers founded the town in 1906. Many retirees and winter visitors live here now; and the area is quickly turning into a suburb of St. George complete with a lush golf course.

Enjoy the small but select collection of pioneer and Indian artifacts on display at the **Hurricane Valley Pioneer and Indian Museum** at 35 W. State Street; you can also obtain local and area information from the well-informed staff; open Mon.–Fri. 9:30 A.M.–5:30 P.M. and Sat. 10 A.M.–2 P.M.

Accommodations
Under $50: The **Dixie Hostel,** 73 S. Main St., (435) 635-9000, offers inexpensive dorm-style lodgings as well as private rooms; guests have access to a laundry and kitchen.

$50–75: The **Super 8,** 65 S. 700 West, (435) 635-0808 or (800) 800-8000, offers a pool and sauna. **Best Western Weston's Lamplighter Inn,** 280 W. State, (435) 635-4647 or (800) 528-1234, has a pool and spa. The **Days Inn,** 40 N. 2600 West, (435)-635-0500 or (800) 325-2525, has an indoor pool and complimentary continental breakfast. The new **Comfort Inn,** 43 N. Sky Mountain Rd., (435) 635-3500 or (800) 635-3577, has a pool and hot tub.

Campgrounds: Just west of town, **WilloWind RV** is at 1150 W. 80 South, (435) 635-4154; $12 tents, $19 RVs with hookups and has showers. **Brentwood RV Resort,** 4.5 miles west of town, (435) 635-2320 or (800) 447-2239, is open year-round with a nine-hole golf course, indoor pool, tennis courts, recreation room, and showers; $13 tents, $19 RVs with hookups. A restaurant, bowling alley, water slide, and mini golf course are across the street, (435) 635-2320. **Quail Lake RV Park,** (435) 635-9960, is open year-round with pool, spa, store, and showers; six miles west of town $18 with hookups. **Quail Creek State Park** (435) 879-2378, is 6.5 miles west, then two miles north.

Food

Grandma's Country Kitchen, 264 N. State St., (435) 635-2239, serves home-style American cooking; open for three meals a day Tues.–Sat. **New Garden Cafe,** 138 S. Main, (435) 635-9825, has an international menu with an emphasis on vegetarian sandwiches and entrées. Open Mon.–Sat. for breakfast, lunch, and dinner, and Sun. for brunch.

Golf

Sky Mountain Golf Course, 1000 N. 2600 West, (435) 635-7888, is one of the state's most highly regarded golf courses. The setting is spectacular, with the Hurricane Cliffs looming behind; volcanic outcrops jut up through the fairways, making for unique natural obstacles. This par-72 course has 18 holes; facilities include a clubhouse with full rental options.

Pah Tempe Hot Springs

Hot mineral water gushes from springs along the Virgin River and fills three sandy-bottomed soaking pools (about 106° F) and a swimming pool (high 90s). The Dominguez-Escalante Expedition passed by in 1776 and thought these hot springs characteristic of the entire river, which they named the Río Sulfureo. A small resort at the springs maintains the pools, a bed-and-breakfast ($65 double), and a campground. The resort is open daily 9 A.M.–10 P.M. Admission fees for the pools are $10 adults, $5 children 2–12, and free for infants; Wednesday and Saturday are half-price. The resort is on Enchanted Way just off UT 9 one mile north of Hurricane, (435) 635-2879 or (888) 726-8367.

With permission from the resort, you can take the old bridge across the river to see a group of undeveloped hot springs. Hikers can continue farther upstream to explore the canyon. Look for the Hurricane Canal in the cliffs high above the river.

The Dinosaur Trackways and Old Fort Pearce

Both of these sites illustrate periods of Utah's past. They're easily visited on a scenic back-road drive through the desert between Hurricane and St. George. Most of the road is unpaved and has some rough and sandy spots, but it should be okay for cautiously driven cars in dry weather. From Hurricane, drive south eight miles on 700 West, then turn west 8.5 miles to the dinosaur trackways turnoff and another two miles to the Fort Pearce turnoff. From St. George, head east on 700 South and follow the road as it turns south; turn left (east) 2.1 miles on a paved road immediately after crossing the Virgin River, turn left 3.5 miles on another paved road after a curve, then turn left (east) 5.6 miles on an unpaved road to the Fort Pearce turnoff (or another two miles to the dinosaur trackways turnoff). Signs for Warner Valley and Fort Pearce point the way at many, but not all, of the intersections.

A group of dinosaur trackways documents the passage of at least two different species more than 200 million years ago. The well-preserved tracks, in the Moenave Formation, may have been made by a 20-foot-long herbivore weighing an estimated 8–10 tons and by a carnivore half as long. No remains of the dinosaurs themselves have been found here.

The name of Old Fort Pearce honors Captain John Pearce, who led Mormon troops of the area during the Black Hawk War with Ute Indians from 1865 to 1869. In 1861, ranchers had arrived in Warner Valley to run cattle on the desert grasslands. Four years later, however, Indian troubles threatened to drive the settlers out. The Black Hawk War and periodic raids by Navajo Indians made life very precarious. Springs in Fort Pearce Wash—the only reliable water for many miles—proved the key to domination of the region. In December 1866, work began on a fort overlooking the springs. The stone walls stood about eight feet high and were more than 30 feet long. No roof was ever added. Much of the fort and the adjacent corral (built in 1869) have survived to the present. Local cattlemen still use the springs for their herds. Petroglyphs can be seen a quarter mile downstream from the fort along ledges on the north side of the wash.

ZION NATIONAL PARK

The sheer cliffs and great monoliths of Zion Canyon reach high into the heavens. Energetic streams and other forces of erosion created this land of finely sculptured rock. One can understand why the Mormon pioneers thought the name Zion appropriate for this spot. The large park spreads across 147,000 acres and contains eight geologic formations and four major vegetation zones. Elevations range from 3,666 feet, in lower Coalpits Wash, to 8,726 feet, atop Horse Ranch Mountain.

The highlight for most visitors is Zion Canyon—it's an approximate 2,400 feet deep. A scenic drive winds through it along the North Fork of the Virgin River past some of the most spectacular scenery in the park. Hiking trails branch off to lofty viewpoints and narrow side canyons. Adventurous souls can continue on foot past road's end into the eerie depths of the Virgin River Narrows in upper Zion Canyon. The spectacular Zion–Mt. Carmel Highway, with its switchbacks and tunnels, provides access to the canyons and high plateaus east of Zion Canyon. Two other roads enter the rugged Kolob section northwest of Zion Canyon. The Kolob, a Mormon name meaning "the brightest star, next to the seat of God," includes wilderness areas rarely visited by humans.

Zion's grandeur extends all through the year. Even rainy days can be memorable as countless waterfalls plunge from every crevice in the cliffs above. Spring and autumn are the choice seasons for the most pleasant temperatures and the best chances of seeing wildlife and wildflowers. From about mid-October to early November, cottonwoods and other trees and plants blaze with color. Summer temperatures in the canyons can be uncomfortably hot with highs hovering above 100° F. It's is also the busiest season. In winter, nighttime temperatures drop to near freezing and weather tends to be unpredictable, with bright sunshine one day and freezing rain the next. Snow-covered slopes contrast with colorful rocks. Snow may block some of the high-country trails and the road to Lava Point, but the rest of the park is open and accessible year-round.

The new Zion Canyon Visitor Center, at the mouth of Zion Canyon, is on UT 9 about midway between I-15 and U.S. 89. It's 43 miles northeast of St. George, 60 miles south of Cedar City, 41 miles northwest of Kanab, and 86 miles southwest of Bryce Canyon National Park. Large RVs and bicycles must heed special regulations for the long tunnel on the Zion–Mt. Carmel Highway (see East of Zion Canyon, below). Visitors short on time usually drop in at the visitors' center, travel the Zion Canyon Scenic Drive, and take short walks on Weeping Rock or Riverside Walk Trails. A stay of two days or longer is better to take in more of the grand scenery and hike other inviting trails.

Kolob Canyons Road, in the extreme northwestern section of the park, begins just off I-15 Exit 40 and climbs to an overlook for great views of the Finger Canyons of the Kolob; the drive is

relaxing beneath the cliffs of Zion National Park

W.C. McRAE

10 miles round-trip. Motorists with more time may also want to drive the Kolob Terrace Road to Lava Point for another perspective of the park; this drive is about 44 miles round-trip from Virgin (on UT 9) and has some unpaved sections. An entry fee of $20 ($10 for bus passengers and bicyclists)—good for seven days—is charged at the East and South Entrance Stations year-round. Entrance for Kolob Canyons or Lava Point drives only is $10.

For up-to-date information on the park, check out the website, www.nps.gov/zion, or call (435)

772-3256. The mailing address is Zion National Park, Springdale, UT 84767.

Geology

The rock layers at Zion began as sediments of oceans, rivers, lakes, or sand dunes deposited 65–240 million years ago. Navajo Sandstone laid down in about the middle of this period forms most of the cliffs and great temples of the park. Look for the slanting lines of desert sand dunes turned to stone in this formation, which is more than 2,000 feet thick in some places. A gradual

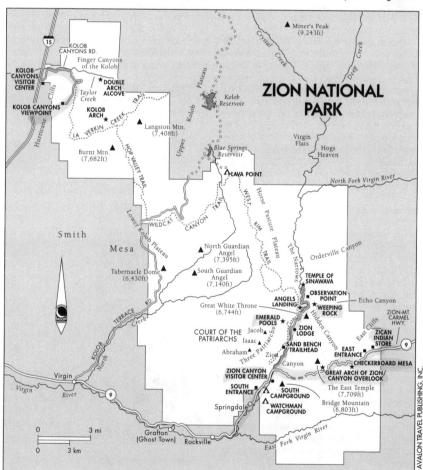

uplift of the Colorado Plateau, which continues today, has caused the formerly lazy rivers on its surface to pick up speed and knife through the rock layers. You can really appreciate these erosive powers during flash floods, when the North Fork of the Virgin River or other streams roar through their canyons. Erosion of some of the Virgin River's tributaries couldn't keep up with the main channel and were left as "hanging valleys" on the canyon walls. A good example is Hidden Canyon, reached by trail in Zion Canyon. Faulting has broken the Colorado Plateau into a series of smaller plateaus. At Zion you're on the Kolob Terrace of the Markagunt Plateau, whose rock layers are younger than those of the Kaibab Plateau at the Grand Canyon National Park and older than those exposed on the Paunsaugunt Plateau at Bryce Canyon National Park.

Flora and Fauna

Many different plant and animal communities live in the rugged terrain of deep canyons and high plateaus. Because the park lies near the meeting place of the Colorado Plateau, the Great Basin, and the Mojave Desert, species representative of all three regions can be found here. Only desert plants can endure the long dry spells and high temperatures found at lower elevations away from permanent water; they include cacti (prickly pear, cholla, and hedgehog), blackbrush, creosote bush, honey mesquite, and purple sage. Pygmy forests of piñon pine, Utah juniper, live oak, mountain mahogany, and cliffrose grow between about 3,900 and 5,600 feet. High plateaus and the cooler canyons have ponderosa pine, Douglas fir, white fir, and aspen. Permanent springs and streams support a profusion of greenery such as cottonwood, box elder, willow, red birch, horsetail, and ferns. Watch out for poison ivy in moist, shady areas. Colorful wildflowers pop out of the ground at all elevations from spring through autumn.

You're likely to see mule deer—they're common throughout the park. Other wildlife includes elk, mountain lion, bobcat, black bear, bighorn sheep (reintroduced), coyote, gray fox, porcupine, ringtail cat, black-tailed jackrabbit, rock squirrel, cliff chipmunk, beaver, and many species of mice and bats. Birders have spotted more than 270 species in and near the park, but most common are red-tailed hawk, turkey vulture, quail, mallard, great horned owl, hairy woodpecker, raven, scrub jay, black-headed grosbeak, bluegray gnatcatcher, canyon wren, Virginia's warbler, white-throated swift, and broad-tailed hummingbird. Hikers need to watch for Western rattlesnakes, though these relatively rare reptiles are unlikely to attack unless provoked.

History

As early as A.D. 285, the Kayenta-Virgin branch of the Anasazi built small villages of sunken pit houses in what's now the park. Their culture gradually developed over the centuries with improved agriculture and crafts until they left the region in about 1200. Next came the Kaibab Band of Southern Paiutes, who spent part of the year here on seasonal migrations. The Paiutes relied heavily on wild seeds for food, supplemented by hunting and some agriculture. Anglo settlers and their livestock depleted the range and wildlife so much that the Paiutes had to abandon this old lifestyle.

Mormon pioneers pushed up the Virgin River Valley in 1859 and founded Grafton, the first of a series of towns south of the present-day park. In 1863, the Isaac Behunin family began farming in Zion Canyon and built a one-room cabin near where Zion Lodge now stands. Other families settled and farmed the canyon until the area was established as a national monument. The canyon's naming is credited to Isaac Behunin, who believed this spot to be a refuge from religious persecution. When Brigham Young later visited the canyon, however, he found tobacco and wine in use and declared the place "not Zion"—which some dutiful followers then began calling it! A scientific expedition led by John Wesley Powell in 1872 helped make the wonders known to the outside world. Efforts by Stephen T. Mather, first director of the National Park Service, and others led to designation of Mukuntuweap (Straight Canyon) National Monument in 1909 and the establishment of Zion National Park in 1919.

ZION CANYON

In summer 2000, the National Park service instituted a **shuttle bus service** from Springdale, the new visitors' center, and sites along the Zion Canyon Scenic Drive. Private vehicles, without special authorization, are no longer allowed to drive up Zion Canyon. It's hoped that the shuttle buses will relieve the incredible congestion in the canyon; throughout much of the summer, the road was simply a parking lot for enormous RVs.

Riding the bus is free; cost of operation is included in the new fee structure. Buses run every 15 minutes or so from 6:30 A.M. to 9:30 P.M. There are two routes: one loops from the new visitors' center to stops in the town of Springdale, where there are a number of large visitor parking lots; the other travels from the visitors' center up the Zion Canyon and back. Confirmed guests of Zion Lodge can get a pass to drive their private vehicles as far as the lodge only.

Zion Canyon Scenic Drive is a six-mile road that follows the North Fork of the Virgin River upstream. Impressive natural formations along the way include the Three Patriarchs, Mountain of the Sun, Lady Mountain, Great White Throne, Angels Landing, and Weeping Rock. The bus stops at eight points of interest along the way; you can get on and off the bus as often as you wish at these stops. The road ends at Temple of Sinawava and the beginning of the Riverside Walk Trail.

Zion Canyon Visitor Center

In summer 2000, a new visitors' center opened near the Watchman Campground, across the road from the former visitors' center. Displays on the park's geology and natural and human history are featured. Staff can answer your questions about the park; they also have a variety of handouts and sales items on hiking, flora and fauna, history, and other aspects of the park. Many nature programs and hikes are offered from late March to November; check the posted schedule. Children's programs are held at Zion Nature Center near South Campground; ask at the visitors' center for details. An excellent selection of books in the visitors' center covers natural history, human history, and regional travel. Topo and geologic maps, posters, slides, postcards, and film are sold, too. A Backcountry Shuttle Board allows hikers to coordinate transportation between trailheads. The Zion Canyon Visitor Center is open daily 9 A.M.–5 P.M. in winter and 8 A.M.–8 P.M. in summer.

Zion Museum

The old visitors' center will reopen in 2002 as a museum of southern Utah natural and human history.

Zion Lodge

The rustic lodge, (435) 586-9476, sits in the heart of Zion Canyon, three miles up Zion Canyon Scenic Drive. Zion Lodge provides the only accommodations and dining places within the park. It's open year-round; reservations for rooms should be made as far in advance as possible. During high season, all rooms are booked months ahead. Double rooms begin at $95.

The moderately priced restaurant offers a varied American menu daily for breakfast, lunch, and dinner. Picnic lunches can be ordered in advance by calling (435) 772-3213, ext. 160. A snack bar serves fast food (closes in winter). Zion Lodge organizes horseback rides along the Virgin River (one hour) and Sand Bench Trail (three hours). Tours in open-air vehicles provide narrated sight-seeing trips in Zion Canyon; they run several times daily between Memorial Day and Labor Day weekends. The lodge also has evening programs, a post office counter (open Mon.–Sat.), and a gift shop. Make reservations for Zion Lodge by writing AMFAC Parks & Resorts, 1400 E. Iliff Ave., Ste. 600, Aurora, CO 80014, or call (303) 297-2757. Reserve on-line at www.amfac.com.

Zion Canyon Campgrounds

Campgrounds in the park often fill up on Easter and other major holidays and occasionally at other times. **South** and **Watchman** Campgrounds, just inside the South Entrance, have sites for $14 with water but no showers or hookups. Only group areas can be reserved. One of the campgrounds stays open in winter. Some of the pioneers' fruit trees in the campgrounds are still producing; you're free to pick your own. Additional campgrounds lie just outside the park in Springdale (see Vicinity of Zion National Park, below).

ZION CANYON HIKES

The trails in Zion Canyon provide perspectives of the park not available from the roads. Much of the hiking requires long ascents but isn't too difficult at a leisurely pace. Carry water on most hikes. Descriptions of the following trails are given in order from the mouth of Zion Canyon to the Virgin River Narrows.

Experienced hikers can do countless off-trail routes in the canyons and plateaus surrounding Zion Canyon; rangers can suggest areas. Rappelling and other climbing skills may be needed to negotiate drops in some of the more remote canyons. Groups cannot exceed 12 hikers per trail or drainage. Overnight hikers must obtain backcountry permits ($5) from either Zion Canyon or Kolob Canyons Visitor Center. Some areas of the park, mainly those near roads and major trails, are closed to overnight use. Zion Lodge offers shuttle services for hikers, or you can check the Backcountry Shuttle Board at the visitors' center.

Rock-climbers come to challenge the high cliffs, especially those of Navajo Sandstone. For route descriptions, see the climbing books available for reference at both visitors' centers. Check to make sure your climbing area is open—some are closed to protect wildlife. Climbing alone is discouraged.

Watchman Trail

From a trailhead north of Watchman Campground, the trail climbs 370 feet to a bench below Watchman Peak, the prominent mountain southeast of the visitors' center. You'll enjoy views of lower Zion Canyon and the town of Springdale. The well-graded trail follows a side canyon past some springs, then ascends to the overlook; distance is 2.4 miles round-trip and takes about two hours. A wide variety of trees and plants lines the way. In summer, it's best to get an early start. Rangers lead nature walks during the main season.

Court of the Patriarchs Viewpoint

A short trail from the parking area leads to the viewpoint. The Patriarchs, a trio of peaks to the west, overlook Birch Creek; they are (from left to right) Abraham, Isaac, and Jacob. Mount Moroni, the reddish peak on the far right, partly blocks the view of Jacob. Better views can be obtained by hiking a half mile or so up Sand Bench Trail.

Sand Bench Trail

This is an easy loop with good views of the three Patriarchs, the Streaked Wall, and other monuments of lower Zion Canyon. The trail is 1.7 miles long with a 500-foot elevation gain; allow about three hours. During the main season, Zion Lodge organizes three-hour horseback rides on

the trail. (The horses churn up dust and leave an uneven surface, though, so hikers usually prefer to go elsewhere.) The trail soon leaves the riparian forest along Birch Creek and climbs onto the dry benchland. Piñon pine, juniper, sand sage, yucca, prickly pear cactus, and other high-desert plants and animals live here. Hikers can park at Court of the Patriarchs Viewpoint, walk across the scenic drive, then follow a service road to the footbridge and trailhead. A 1.2-mile trail along the river connects the trailhead with Zion Lodge. In the warmer months, try to hike in early morning or late afternoon.

Emerald Pools Trails

Three spring-fed pools, small waterfalls, and views of Zion Canyon make this climb worthwhile. You have a choice of three trails. Easiest is the paved trail to the Lower Pool; cross the footbridge near Zion Lodge and turn right 0.6 mile. The Middle Pool can be reached by continuing 0.2 mile on a smaller trail or by taking a different trail from the footbridge at Zion Lodge (after crossing the bridge, turn left, then right up the trail). Together these trails make a 1.8-mile round-trip loop. The third trail begins at the Grotto Picnic Area, crosses a footbridge and turns left 0.7 mile; the trail forks left to the Lower Pool and right to the Middle Pool. A steep 0.4-mile trail leads from the Middle Pool to Upper Emerald Pool. This magical spot has a white-sand beach and towering cliffs rising above. Allow 1–3 hours to visit the pools. Photographers often get good pictures of rock reflections in the pools.

West Rim Trail

This strenuous trail leads to some of the best views of Zion Canyon. Backpackers can continue on the West Rim Trail to Lava Point and other destinations in the Kolob region. Start from Grotto Picnic Area (elev. 4,300 feet) and cross the footbridge, then turn right along the river. The trail climbs the slopes and enters the cool and shady depths of Refrigerator Canyon. Walter's Wiggles, a series of 21 closely spaced switchbacks, wind up to Scout Lookout and a trail junction—four miles round-trip and a 1,050-foot elevation gain. Scout Lookout has fine views of Zion Canyon. The trail is paved and well graded to this point. Turn right a half mile at the junction to reach the summit of Angels Landing.

Angels Landing rises as a sheer-walled monolith 1,500 feet above the North Fork of the Virgin River. Though the trail to the summit is rough, chains provide security in the more exposed places. The climb is safe with care and good weather. Anyone steady on his feet should be able to make it out, but don't go if the trail is covered with snow or ice or if thunderstorms threaten. Once on top, you'll see why Angels Landing got its name—the panorama makes all the effort worthwhile. Average hiking time for the round-trip between Grotto Picnic Area and Angels Landing is four hours.

Energetic hikers can continue 4.8 miles on the main trail from Scout Lookout to West Rim Viewpoint, which overlooks the Right Fork of North Creek. This strenuous 12.8-mile round-trip from Grotto Picnic Area has a 3,070-foot elevation gain. West Rim Trail continues through Zion's backcountry to Lava Point (elev. 7,890 feet), where there's a primitive campground. A car shuttle and one or more days are needed to hike the 13.3 miles (one-way) from Grotto Picnic Area. You'll have an easier hike by starting at Lava Point and hiking down to the picnic area; even so, be prepared for a *long* day hike. The trail has little or no water in some seasons.

Weeping Rock Trail

A favorite with visitors, this easy trail winds past lush vegetation and wildflowers to a series of cliffside springs above an overhang. Thousands of water droplets glisten in the afternoon sun. The springs emerge where water seeping through more than 2,000 feet of Navajo Sandstone meets a layer of impervious shale. The paved trail is a half-mile round-trip with a 100-foot elevation gain. Signs along the way identify some of the trees and plants.

Observation Point Trail

This strenuous trail climbs 2,150 feet in 3.6 highly scenic miles to Observation Point (elev. 6,507 feet) on the edge of Zion Canyon. Allow about six hours for the round-trip. Trails branch off along the way to Hidden Canyon, upper Echo Canyon, East Entrance, East Mesa, and other destinations. The first of many switchbacks begins a short way up from the trailhead at Weeping Rock parking area. You'll reach the junction for Hidden Canyon Trail (see Hidden Canyon, below)

after 0.8 mile. Several switchbacks later, the trail enters sinuous Echo Canyon. This incredibly narrow chasm can be explored for short distances upstream and downstream to deep pools and pour-offs. **Echo Canyon Trail** branches to the right at about the halfway point; this rough trail continues farther up the canyon and connects with trails to Cable Mountain, Deertrap Mountain, and the East Entrance Station (on Zion–Mt. Carmel Highway). The East Rim Trail then climbs slickrock slopes above Echo Canyon with many fine views. Parts of the trail are cut right into the cliffs. You'll reach the rim at last after three miles of steady climbing. Then it's an easy 0.6 mile through a forest of piñon pine, juniper, Gambel oak, manzanita, sage, and some ponderosa pine to Observation Point. Impressive views take in Zion Canyon below and mountains and mesas all around. **East Mesa Trail** turns right about 0.3 mile before Observation Point and follows the plateau northeast to a dirt road outside the park.

Hidden Canyon

See if you can spot the entrance to Hidden Canyon from below! Inside the narrow canyon are small sandstone caves, a little natural arch, and diverse plantlife. The high walls, rarely more than 65 feet apart, block sunlight except for a short time at midday. Hiking distance on the moderately difficult trail is about three miles round-trip between Weeping Rock parking area and the lower canyon; follow East Rim Trail 0.8 mile, then turn right 0.7 mile on Hidden Canyon Trail to the canyon entrance. Footing can be a bit difficult in places due to loose sand, but chains provide handholds on the more exposed sections. Steps chopped into the rock just inside Hidden Canyon help to bypass some deep pools. Allow 3–4 hours for the round-trip; elevation change is about 1,000 feet. After heavy rains and spring runoff, the creek forms a small waterfall at the canyon entrance. The canyon is about one mile long and mostly easy walking, though the trail fades away. Look for the arch on the right about a half mile up the canyon.

Riverside Walk

This is one of the most popular hikes in the park. The nearly level paved trail begins at the end of Zion Canyon Scenic Drive and winds one mile upstream along the river to the Virgin River Narrows. Allow about two hours to take in the scenery. Countless springs and seeps on the canyon walls support luxuriant plant growth and swamps. Most of the springs occur at the contact between the Navajo Sandstone and the less permeable Kayenta Formation below. The water and vegetation attract abundant wildlife; keep an eye out for birds and animals and their tracks. At trail's end, the canyon is wide enough for only the river. Hikers continuing upstream must wade and sometimes even swim (see The Narrows, below). Late morning is the best time for photography. In autumn, cottonwoods and maples display bright splashes of color.

The Narrows

Upper Zion Canyon is probably the most famous backcountry area in the park, yet it's also one of the most strenuous. There's no trail and you'll be wading much of the time in the river, which is usually knee- to chest-deep. In places, the high fluted walls of upper North Fork of the Virgin River are only 20 feet apart, and very little sunlight penetrates the depths. Mysterious side canyons beckon. Hikers should be well prepared and in good condition—river hiking is more tiring than that over dry land. The major hazards are flash floods and hypothermia. Finding the right time to go through can be tricky: spring runoff is too high, summer thunderstorms bring hazardous flash floods, and winter is too cold. That leaves just part of early summer (mid-June–mid-July) and early autumn (mid-Sept.–mid-Oct.) as the best bets. You can get through the entire 16-mile (one-way) Narrows in about 12 hours, though two days is best to enjoy the beauty of the place. Children under 12 shouldn't attempt hiking the entire canyon. Talk with rangers at Zion Canyon Visitor Center before starting a trip; they also have a handout with useful information on planning a Narrows hike. You'll need a permit for hikes all the way through the Narrows—even on a day trip. No permit is needed if you're just going partway and back in one day, though you must first check conditions and the weather forecast with rangers. The limited number of Narrows permits, for both day and overnight trips, become available after 5 P.M. on the day preceding the hike. A one-night limit applies. No camping is permitted below Big Springs. Group size for hiking and camping is limited to 12 (of the same affiliation, family, etc.) on the *entire* route.

A hike downstream saves not only climbing but also the work of fighting the river currents. In fact, the length of the Narrows should only be hiked downstream. The upper trailhead is near Chamberlain's Ranch, reached by an 18-mile dirt road that turns north from UT 9 east of the park. The lower trailhead is at the end of the Zion Canyon Scenic Drive. Elevation change is 1,280 feet. A good half-day trip begins at the end of Gateway to the Narrows Trail and follows the Narrows 1.5 miles upstream to Orderville Canyon, then back the same way. Orderville Canyon makes a good destination in itself; you can hike quite a way up from Zion Canyon.

EAST OF ZION CANYON

The east section of the park is a land of sandstone slickrock, hoodoos, and narrow canyons. You can see much of the pretty scenery along the Zion–Mt. Carmel Highway (UT 9) between the East Entrance Station and Zion Canyon. Most of this region invites exploration on your own. Try hiking a canyon or heading up a slickrock slope (the pass between Crazy Quilt and Checkerboard Mesas is one possibility). Highlights on the plateau include views of the White Cliffs and Checkerboard Mesa (both near the East Entrance Station) and a hike on the Canyon Overlook Trail (it begins just east of the long tunnel). Checkerboard Mesa's distinctive pattern is due to a combination of vertical fractures and horizontal bedding planes, both accentuated by weathering. The highway's spectacular descent into Zion Canyon goes first through a 530-foot tunnel, then a 5,600-foot tunnel, followed by a series of six switchbacks to the canyon floor. Because the tunnel (completed in 1930) is narrow, any vehicle over 7 feet 10 inches wide, 11 feet 4 inches high, or 40 feet long (50 feet with trailer) must go through in one-way traffic; a $10 fee (good for two passages) is charged at the tunnel to do this. Bicycles must be carried through the long tunnel (it's too dangerous to ride).

Canyon Overlook Trail

This popular hike features great views from the heights without the stiff climbs found on most other Zion trails. Allow about an hour for the

a short hike on the Canyon Overlook Trail

one-mile round-trip; elevation gain is 163 feet. A booklet available at the start or at the Zion Canyon Visitor Center describes the geology, plantlife, and clues to the presence of wildlife. The trail winds in and out along ledges of Pine Creek Canyon, which opens into a great valley. Panoramas at trail's end take in lower Zion Canyon in the distance. A sign at the viewpoint identifies Bridge Mountain, Streaked Wall, East Temple, and other features. The Great Arch of Zion—termed a "blind arch" because it's open on only one side—lies below; the arch is 580 feet high, 720 feet long, and 90 feet deep. Canyon Overlook Trail begins across from the parking area just east of the longer (west) tunnel on the Zion–Mt. Carmel Highway.

Guest Ranches
Zion Ponderosa Resort, five miles north of the east entrance to the park on U.S. 89, (435) 581-9817 or (800) 293-5444, is a new all-inclusive resort development that offers high-quality accommodations and access to swimming pool, tennis courts, horseback riding, and other recreation. Lodging is in freestanding fully modern log cabins. The central lodge has a restaurant open for three meals a day. All-inclusive (meals and recreation included) rates begin at $250 per couple per day. For information, write P.O. Box 521436, Salt Lake City, UT 84152-1436.

Zican Indian Store, just outside the East Entrance Station, is open all year with a café, gas station, groceries, and souvenirs. A campground is across the highway with hot showers, restrooms, tent sites ($12), and RV sites ($18 without hookups, $20 with; (435) 648-2154.

THE KOLOB

North and west of Zion Canyon lies the remote backcountry of the Kolob. This area became a second Zion National Monument in 1937, then was added to Zion National Park in 1956. You'll see all but one of the rock formations present in the park and evidence of past volcanic eruptions. Two roads lead into the Kolob. The paved five-mile Kolob Canyons Road begins at the Kolob Canyons Visitor Center just off I-15 and ends at an overlook and picnic area; it's open all year. Kolob Terrace Road is paved from the town of Virgin (15 miles west on UT 9 from the South Entrance Station) to the turnoff for Lava Point; snow usually blocks the way in winter.

Kolob Canyons Visitor Center
Though small and with just a handful of exhibits, the visitors' center is a good place to stop for information on exploring the Kolob region. Hikers can learn current trail conditions and obtain the permits required for overnight trips and Zion Narrows day trips. Books, topo and geologic maps, posters, postcards, slides, and film are sold. Open daily 8 A.M.–4:30 P.M. (to 5 P.M. in summer); (435) 586-9548. The visitors' center and the start of the Kolob Canyons Road lie just off I-15 Exit 40.

Campgrounds

The Kolob section of the park doesn't have a campground. The nearest one within the park is Lava Point Campground (see Lava Point, below). **Redledge Campground,** in Kanarraville, is the closest commercial campground to the Kolob Canyons area; go two miles north on I-15, take Exit 42, and continue 4.5 miles into downtown Kanarraville, (435) 586-9150. The campground is open year-round with store, showers, and laundry; $14 tents or RVs without hookups, $17.50 RVs with, and campers cabins or a tepee for $12. The tiny agricultural community was named after a local Paiute chief. A low ridge south of town marks the southern limit of prehistoric Lake Bonneville. Hikers can explore trails in Spring and Kanarra Canyons within the **Spring Canyon Wilderness Study Area** just east of town.

Kolob Canyons Road

This five-mile scenic drive winds past the dramatic Finger Canyons of the Kolob to Kolob Canyons Viewpoint and a picnic area at the end of the road. The road is paved and has many pullouts where you can stop to admire the scenery. The first part of the drive follows the 200-mile-long Hurricane Fault that forms the west edge of the Markagunt Plateau. Look for the tilted rock layers deformed by friction as the plateau rose nearly one mile. **Taylor Creek Trail,** which begins two miles past the visitors' center, provides a close look at the canyons (see Taylor Creek Trail, below). Lee Pass, four miles beyond the visitors' center, was named after John D. Lee of the infamous Mountain Meadows Massacre; he's believed to have lived nearby for a short time after the massacre. **La Verkin Creek Trail** begins at Lee Pass Trailhead for trips to Kolob Arch and beyond. Signs at the end of the road identify the points, buttes, mesa, and mountains. The salmon-colored Navajo Sandstone cliffs glow a deep red at sunset. **Timber Creek Overlook Trail** begins from the picnic area at road's end and climbs a half mile to the overlook (elev. 6,369 feet); views encompass the Pine Valley Mountains, Zion Canyons, and distant Mt. Trumbull.

Taylor Creek Trail

This is an excellent day hike from Kolob Canyons Road. The easy to moderate trail begins on the left two miles from Kolob Canyons Visitor Center

Taylor Creek, Zion National Park

and heads upstream into the canyon of Middle Fork of Taylor Creek. Double Arch Alcove is 2.7 miles from the trailhead; a dry fall 0.2 mile farther blocks the way (water flows over it during spring runoff and after rains). A giant rockfall occurred here in June 1990. Other nearby canyons, such as North and South Forks of Taylor Creek, can be explored, too. **South Fork of Taylor Creek Trail** leaves the drive at a bend 3.1 miles from the visitors' center, then goes in 1.2 miles.

Hiking to Kolob Arch

Kolob Arch vies with Landscape Arch in Arches National Park as the world's longest natural rock span. Differences in measurement techniques have resulted in a controversy as to which is longer: Kolob Arch's span has been measured variously at 292–310 feet, Landscape Arch's at 291–306 feet. Kolob probably takes the prize because its 310-foot measurement was done with an accurate electronic method. Kolob's height is 330 feet and its vertical thickness is 80 feet. The arch makes a fine destination for a backpack trip. Spring and autumn are the best seasons to go; summer temperatures rise into the 90s and winter snows make the trails hard to follow. You have a choice of two moderately difficult trails. **La Verkin Creek Trail** begins at Lee Pass (elev. 6,080 feet) on Kolob Canyons Scenic Drive, four miles beyond the visitors' center. The trail drops into Timber Creek (intermittent flow), crosses over hills to La Verkin Creek (flows year-round; some springs, too), then turns up side canyons to the arch. The 14-mile round-trip can be done as a long day trip, but you'll enjoy the best lighting for photos at the arch if you camp in the area and see it the following morning. Carry plenty of water for the return trip; the 800-foot climb to the trailhead can be hot and tiring.

You can also hike to Kolob Arch on the **Hop Valley Trail,** reached from Kolob Terrace Road. Hop Valley Trail is seven miles one-way to Kolob Arch with an elevation drop of 1,050 feet; water is available in Hop Valley and La Verkin Creek. You may have to do some wading in the creek, and the trail crosses some private land (don't camp there).

Lava Point

The panorama from Lava Point (elev. 7,890 feet) takes in the Cedar Breaks area to the north, the Pink Cliffs to the northeast, Zion Canyon Narrows and tributaries to the east, the Sentinel and other monoliths of Zion Canyon to the southeast, and Mt. Trumbull on the Arizona Strip to the south. Signs help identify features. Lava Point, which sits atop a lava flow, is a good place to cool off in summer—temperatures are about 20° F cooler than in Zion Canyon. Aspen, ponderosa pine, Gambel oak, and white fir grow here. A small

primitive **campground** near the point offers sites during the warmer months; no water or charge.

Two trails begin from West Rim Trailhead; either drive here or walk the one-mile **Barney's Trail** from Site 2 in the campground. **West Rim Trail** goes southeast to Zion Canyon, 13.3 miles one-way with an elevation drop of 3,600 feet (3,000 of them in the last six miles). Water can normally be found along the way at Sawmill, Potato Hollow, and Cabin Springs. **Wildcat Canyon Trail** heads southwest five miles to a trailhead on Kolob Terrace Road (16 miles north of Virgin); elevation drop is 450 feet. This trail lacks a reliable water source. You can continue east toward Kolob Arch by taking the four-mile **Connector Trail** to **Hop Valley Trail.** Snow blocks the road to Lava Point for much of the year; the usual season is May or June–early November. Check road conditions with the Zion Canyon or Kolob Canyon Visitor Center. From the South Entrance Station in Zion Canyon, drive west 15 miles on UT 9 to Virgin, turn north 21 miles on Kolob Terrace Road (signed Kolob Reservoir), then turn right 1.8 miles to Lava Point.

Kolob Reservoir

This high-country lake north of Lava Point has good fishing for rainbow trout. An unpaved boat ramp is at the south end near the dam. People sometimes camp along the shore, although there are no facilities. Most of the surrounding land is private. To reach the reservoir, continue north 3.5 miles on Kolob Terrace Road from the Lava Point turnoff. The fair-weather road can also be followed past the reservoir to the Cedar City area. Blue Springs Reservoir, near the turnoff for Lava Point, is closed to the public.

VICINITY OF ZION NATIONAL PARK

SPRINGDALE AND VICINITY

This small Mormon settlement (pop. 333) dates from 1862. Springdale lies just outside the park's south entrance and offers many services for travelers including high-quality motels and some excellent B&Bs. Farther down the road toward Hurricane are the little towns of Rockville and Virgin, both quickly becoming B&B suburbs of Springdale.

Zion Canyon Giant Screen Theatre

Meet Anasazi Indians, watch Spanish explorers seek golden treasure, witness the hardships of pioneer settlers, enter remote slot canyons, and join rock-climbers hundreds of feet up vertical cliff faces in this facility with a screen six stories tall and 80 feet wide. The feature program is *Treasure of the Gods,* shot on large film for high-resolution viewing. Shows start on the hour 9 A.M.–9 P.M. from April 1 to October 31 and 11 A.M.–7 P.M. the rest of the year; $7.50

adults, $4.50 children under 12. Call (435) 772-2400 or (888) 256-FILM for more information.

O.C. Tanner Amphitheater

The summer highlight at this open-air theater is a series of musical concerts held on Saturday evenings throughout the summer. The amphitheater is located just outside the park entrance; call (435) 652-7994 for information.

Accommodations

$50–75: The most reasonably priced lodging in Springdale is the **Zion Park Motel**, 865 Zion Park Blvd., (435) 772-3251, with clean basic rooms and a small pool. **Flanigan's Inn**, 428 Zion Park Blvd., (435) 772-3244 or (800) 765-7787, is an attractive option, with a good restaurant, pool, and a complimentary breakfast buffet. **Canyon Ranch Motel**, 668 Zion Park Blvd., (435) 772-3357, offers individual cottages—some with kitchenettes—scattered around a grassy shaded courtyard.

Pioneer Lodge Motel, 838 Zion Park Blvd., (435) 772-3233, has a restaurant, pool, and spa. There are a variety of room styles available including a three-bed unit and a deluxe suite. **El Río Lodge**, at 995 Zion Park Blvd., (435) 772-3205, or (888) 772-3205, offers rooms in a green, shady location with a sundeck.

There are quite a number of good B&Bs springing up around Zion. Most ask for two-night minimums on holiday weekends.

In Springdale, **O'Toole's Under the Eaves B&B**, 980 Zion Park Blvd., (435) 772-3457, features six homey guest rooms, two with shared bath, in a vintage home. Children over 10 welcome. **Red Rock Inn**, 998 Zion Park Blvd., (435) 772-3139, $74–79 (single or double), offers lodgings in newly constructed individual cabins, all with canyon views. Full-breakfast baskets are delivered to your door. **The Blue House Bed & Breakfast Inn** sits in a pretty country setting in the small community of Rockville, five miles from the park entrance, 125 E. Main, (435) 772-3912 or (800) 869-3912.

$75–100: Best Western Driftwood Lodge, 1515 Zion Park Blvd., (435) 772-3262 or (800) 528-1234, has a pool and spa. The new **Best Western Zion Park Inn**, 1215 Zion Park Blvd., (435) 772-3200 or (800) 934-7275, is an attractive complex with a good restaurant, swimming pool, gift shop, and some of the nicest rooms in Spring-

dale. In addition to regular rooms, there are also various suites and kitchen units available.

Harvest House B&B, 29 Canyonview Dr., (435) 772-3880, is an expertly run B&B in the center of Springdale with an old-fashioned porch and a hot tub. The four guest rooms, all with private baths, are nicely decorated.

Novel House Inn at Zion, 73 Paradise Rd., (435) 772-3650 or (800) 711-8400, is a newly constructed B&B with 10 guest rooms, each decorated with a literary theme and named after an author (including Mark Twain, Rudyard Kipling, and Louis L'Amour). All rooms have private baths and great views.

In Rockville is the **Handcart House Bed & Breakfast**, 244 W. Main, (435) 772-3867, a handsome modern home that looks like a pioneer landmark but offers all modern comforts. All guest rooms have private baths.

For a B&B with a Western difference, try the **Snow Family Guest Ranch**, 633 E. UT 9, in Virgin. Located on 12 acres, the ranch raises horses and offers nine guest rooms to travelers. Children are accepted with prior arrangement only; no pets.

$100–125: Probably the nicest place to stay in Springdale is the new **Desert Pearl Inn**, 707 Zion Park Blvd., (435) 772-8888 or (888) 828-0898, a very handsome lodgelike hotel perched above the Virgin River. Much of the wood used for the beams and the finish moldings was salvaged from a railroad trestle made of century-old Oregon fir and redwood that once spanned the north end of the Great Salt Lake. The rooms are all large and beautifully furnished. Just outside the south gates to Zion, the **Cliffrose Lodge**, 281 Zion Park Blvd., (435) 772-3234 or (800) 243-8824, sits in five acres of lovely, well-landscaped gardens with riverfront access. The rooms are equally nice, and there's a pool and a guest laundry.

Campgrounds: The **Zion Canyon Campground**, 479 Zion Park Blvd., (435) 772-3237, offers cabins, new motel rooms, tent sites, and RV sites; facilities include a store, pizza parlor, game room, laundry, and showers.

Food

Oscar's Deli, 61 Zion Park Blvd., (435) 772-3232, offers food to eat in or take out with picnic meals or day-pack fare prepared to order; open daily. **Electric Jim's**, 198 Zion Park Blvd., (435) 772-3838, offers '50's-style burgers and shakes;

open daily for all three meals; closed Dec. and Jan. **Panda Garden Chinese Restaurant,** 805 Zion Park Blvd., (435) 772-3535, serves multi-region Chinese cuisine daily for lunch and dinner. **Zion Pizza and Noodle,** 868 Zion Park Blvd., (435) 772-3815, dishes up pizza and pasta daily for breakfast, lunch, and dinner. The American-style menu at the **Bumbleberry Inn,** 897 Zion Park Blvd., (435) 772-3224, includes bumbleberry pies and pancakes; open Mon.–Sat. for breakfast, lunch, and dinner.

The following restaurants all offer full liquor service. **Flanigan's Inn,** 428 Zion Park Blvd., (435) 772-3244, has varied Southwestern and traditional American offerings; open daily for breakfast, lunch, and dinner. The **Pioneer Restaurant,** 828 Zion Park Blvd., (435) 772-3009, serves American food, with vegetarian specialties, daily for breakfast, lunch, and dinner.

The **Bit & Spur Restaurant,** 1212 Zion Park Blvd., (435) 772-3498, is usually mentioned when people discuss Utah's best Mexican, Latin American, and Southwestern restaurants. The menu goes far beyond the usual south-of-the-border concoctions, and even offers some Native American dishes. Open for dinner only. The **Switchback Grille,** 1149 Zion Park Blvd., (435) 772-3777, is new and offers wood-fired pizza, rotisserie chicken, and steaks and seafood in a pleasantly trendy atmosphere. There's patio seating in good weather; open for three meals a day.

Other Practicalities and Events

The **Zion Canyon Field Institute,** (435) 772-3072, offers free nature walks from the Old Church as well as other activities (children's stories, hikes, tours, and guided rock-climbing) at nominal charge. Old Church also houses **Zion Canyon Cycling Co.,** (435) 772-3929, where you may buy bicycling equipment, parts, maps, and books or rent bicycles. Also in Old Church is an art gallery, the **Zion Canyon Collection,** (435) 772-3620, where paintings, sculptures, and photographs by local artists are available.

You may also want to check out the many art galleries, rock shops, and gift shops along Zion Park Boulevard. The **Southern Utah Folklife Festival** remembers pioneer days with demonstrations, food, and entertainment in September.

Services

Tourist Information is available in summer at Town Center Old Church, 868 Zion Park Blvd., (435) 772-3072, or check out the website at www.zionpark.com. **Zion Canyon Medical Clinic,** (435) 772-3226, provides emergency services from about May to October; take the turnoff for the O.C. Tanner Amphitheater. The **post office** is in the center of town on Zion Park Boulevard, (435) 772-3950.

GRAFTON

Grafton is one of the best-preserved and most picturesque ghost towns in Utah. Photos of the deserted site grace the covers of no fewer than three books on ghost towns of Utah. Mormon families founded Grafton in 1859 near the Virgin River at a spot one mile downstream from the present site, but a big flood two years later convinced them to move here. Hostilities with the native Paiutes during the Black Hawk War forced residents to depart again for safer areas from 1866 to 1868. Floods and irrigation difficulties made life hard even in the best of times, and the population declined in the early 1900s until only ghosts remained.

Moviemakers discovered Grafton and used it for *Butch Cassidy and the Sundance Kid,* among other films. You may notice a few fiberglass chimneys and other "improvements." A schoolhouse, store, houses, cabins, and a variety of outbuildings still stand. One story goes that the Mormon bishop lived in the large two-story house with wife number one while wife number two had to settle for the rough cabin across the road—probably not an amicable situation! Grafton's cemetery is worth a visit, too; it's on the left at a turn 0.3 mile before the town site. A monument commemorates three settlers killed by Indians in 1866. Many of Grafton's families now live in nearby Rockville; they tend the cemetery and look after the old buildings. From Springdale, follow UT 9 southwest two miles to Rockville and turn south 3.5 miles on Bridge Road (200 East). The last 2.6 miles are unpaved but should be okay for cars in dry weather; keep right at a road junction 1.6 miles past Rockville.

THE VERMILION CLIFFS AND CANAAN MOUNTAIN

The rocky hills south of Springdale and Rockville offer fine scenery for back-road drives or hikes. The **Smithsonian Butte National Back Country Byway,** a 7.6-mile dirt road from the Grafton road, climbs into the scenic high country south of the Virgin River and continues to UT 59 (near Milepost 8) between Hurricane and Hildale on the other side; follow the directions to Grafton but turn left at the road junction 1.6 miles past Rockville. Panoramas take in Zion National Park, Smithsonian Butte, Canaan Mountain, and the rugged countryside all around. You can also find good places to hike or camp along the way. Cars with good clearance can usually make this trip if the road is dry.

Canaan Mountain (elev. 7,200 feet), a wilderness study area south of Springdale, rises more than 2,000 feet above the surrounding land. The summit is a plateau of rolling slickrock, pinnacles, balanced rocks, and deep fractures similar to the plateaus of Zion National Park. High cliffs on three sides give you the feeling of being on an island in the sky. Eagle Crags Trailhead (elev. 4,400 feet) near Rockville provides access from the north past the Eagle Crags, a group of towering sandstone monoliths. Squirrel Canyon Trailhead (elev. 5,100 feet) near Hildale is the starting point for hikes from the south via Water or Squirrel Canyon. See the USGS 7 1/2-minute topo maps Springdale West, Springdale East, Smithsonian Butte, and Hildale. Contact the BLM office in St. George, (435) 688-3200, and use *The Hiker's Guide to Utah,* by Dave Hall, for hiking information.

CEDAR CITY

A cultural, tourist, and trade center, Cedar City (pop. 18,953) is a popular stop for travelers. The excellent Utah Shakespearean Festival in summer presents several of the master's plays and a whole array of Elizabethan dances, concerts, sideshows, seminars, and backstage tours. The presence of Southern Utah University also lends the town a pleasantly youthful buzz.

With a large selection of good hotels and restaurants, Cedar City is also a good hub for exploring the other major sites of southwestern Utah. Just east of town rise the high cliffs of the Markagunt Plateau—a land of panoramic views, colorful rock formations, desolate lava flows, extensive forests, and flower-filled meadows. Also on the Markagunt Plateau is the Cedar Breaks National Monument, an immense amphitheater eroded into the vividly hued underlying rock. Within an easy day's drive are Zion National Park to the south, Bryce Canyon National Park to the east, the Pine Valley Mountains to the southwest, and the remote desert country to the west and north. Cedar City is just east of I-15, 52 miles northeast of St. George and 253 miles southwest of Salt Lake City; take I-15 Exit 57, 59, or 62.

History
Cedar City began as a mission in 1851 to supply the Mormon settlements with much-needed iron products. Church leaders, upon hearing of promising iron ore and coal deposits, decided to launch the first major colonizing effort since the settlement of the Salt Lake area. The first wagon loads of families and supplies left Provo in December 1850 for Parowan, 18 miles northeast of present-day Cedar City. Other settlers arrived at Cedar City late the following year. All had to start from scratch. Farmers planted crops to feed the new communities while miners and engineers laid plans for iron-manufacturing industries. Hard winters, crop failures, floods, and shortages of skilled workmen nearly doomed the whole project. The final blow came when Johnston's Army and others brought cheaper iron from the East. Only a small amount of iron was produced, and operations ceased in 1858.

Sizable quantities of iron ore did exist, though; large-scale mining west of Cedar City began in the 1920s, peaked in 1957, and has tapered off in recent years.

Paiute Indians have lived here since before pioneer days. Sponsorship by the Mormon community allowed them to remain when the federal government forced most other Indians in the state to move onto reservations. There's a Paiute village in the northeastern part of Cedar City. The tribe puts on the Paiute Restoration Gathering in mid-June.

SIGHTS

Utah Shakespearean Festival
The enthusiasm of the actors and the community makes this summer festival come alive. The festival has a good reputation and provides a good learning experience; visitors soon find themselves caught up in the spirit. The festival presents three Shakespearean plays each season, choosing from both well-known and rarely performed works. The management's long-term goal is to produce every play from the Shakespeare canon. Most of the action centers on the Adams Shakespeare Theatre, an open-air theatre in the round, which is closely designed after the original Globe Theatre from Elizabethan London. The new indoor Randall Jones Theatre presents the "Best of the Rest"—works by other great playwrights such as Chekhov, Molière, and Arthur Miller. A total of eight plays are staged each from late June through mid-October.

Days at the festival are filled with entertaining and educational activities. Costumed actors stage the popular Greenshow each day before the performances with a variety of Elizabethan comedy skits, Punch and Judy shows, period dances, music, juggling, and other good natured 16th-century fun. Another activity, the Royal Feaste, presents a pre-performance Elizabethan-style dinner (a feast with no silverware!) and entertainment from Tudor times ($30 per person, reservations required). Backstage tours of the costume shop, makeup room, and stage

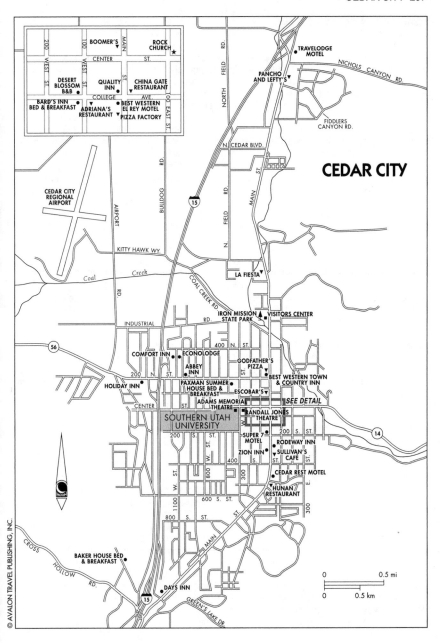

show you how the festival works. At literary seminars each morning, actors and Shakespearean scholars discuss the previous night's play. The actors like to meet the audience, and you'll have plenty of opportunities to talk with them. Production seminars, held daily except Sunday, take a close look at acting, costumes, stage props, special effects, and other details of play production.

The season begins in late June and lasts through mid-October. The Greenshow and seminars are free; you'll have to pay for most other events. Tickets for the evening's Shakespeare performances cost $15–40, and $22–40 for the season's non-Shakespeare shows; matinees are $15–34. It's wise to purchase tickets well in advance. However, 40 tickets are kept back for sale on the day of performance, and unused tickets returned to the courtesy booth are almost always available to last-minute theater-goers; call (435) 586-7790 for more information. There are also a few non-reservable bench seats available the day of performance for $10–12. Both matinee and evening plays are scheduled so you can plan a visit to see all six of the summer plays in just three days. Detailed brochures listing activities and dates of performances are available at many tourist offices in Utah or by mail from the Utah Shakespearean Festival, Cedar City, UT 84720, (435) 586-7878 or (800) PLAYTIX (box office). Or check the website at www.bard.org.

The theaters are on the Southern Utah University campus near the corner of Center and 300 West. Rain occasionally dampens the performances (the Elizabethan theater is open to the sky), and plays may move to a conventional theater next door, where the box office is located.

Southern Utah University

The towns of southern Utah eagerly sought a branch of the state's teacher training school after it had been authorized in 1897 by the Utah legislature. A committee awarded the school to Cedar City, and classes began the same year in a borrowed church building. Some people say that Cedar City was chosen because it was the only one of the candidate towns without a saloon or pool hall! This satellite school inevitably became a four-year university with 6,000 students and today offers major fields of study in education, arts and letters, science, and business.

The attractively landscaped campus occupies 104 acres just west of downtown.

Braithwaite Fine Arts Gallery presents changing exhibits in the Braithwaite Fine Arts Center; open during the Shakespearean Festival Monday–Friday 10 A.M.–7:30 P.M., Saturday and Sunday 1–5 P.M.; open the rest of the year Monday–Thursday and Saturday 10 A.M.–7:30 P.M., Friday 10 A.M.–5 P.M.; it's located about one block north of the intersection of 200 South and 400 West; (435) 586-5432. The Utah Shakespearean Festival is the main summer event on campus. The scheduling office can tell you of upcoming convocations and other cultural happenings; (435) 586-1989. Sports facilities open to the public include an indoor swimming pool, tennis and racquetball courts, and gym at the Physical Education Building, 600 W. 200 South, (435) 586-7815. Contact the college through campus information, Southern Utah University, Cedar City, UT 84720, (435) 586-7700.

Iron Mission State Park Museum

This large museum dedicates itself to the history of the cultures that have lived in and developed Iron County. Exhibits illustrate the Iron Mission's early hardships and the first iron production on September 30, 1852. Past members of the Iron Mission cast the old community bell on display. A diverse array of carriages is the museum's main attraction. You'll see everything from a bullet-scarred Overland stagecoach to an elegant clarence carriage. All the sleighs, utility wagons, hearses, and many other forms of 19th-century transport have been meticulously restored. Also displayed are artifacts of prehistoric and modern Indian tribes. Pioneer memorabilia include clothing, furniture, saddles, and a bathtub. A large collection of horse-drawn farm machinery sits out back. The museum is open daily 9 A.M.–6 P.M. from mid-May to mid-September, then daily 9 A.M.–5 P.M. the rest of the year; closed major holidays. Park admission is $2 per person or $5 per carload. Located at 589 N. Main, (435) 586-9290.

Rock Church

Depression-era residents needed a new LDS Church building but lacked the money to build one. Undaunted, they set to work using local materials and came up with this beautiful structure composed of many different types of rocks. Skilled craftspeople made the metal lamps, carpets, Western red cedar pews, and most other furnishings. Open for tours daily in summer; free admission; located at the corner of Center and 100 East.

ACCOMMODATIONS

With so much to see in the area and so many things going on in town, Cedar City is popular with visitors, and room reservations at least a day or two ahead is a good idea in summer. The quality of lodging is high. Generally speaking, there are two major concentrations of motels. A half dozen large chain hotels cluster around I-15 exit, together with lots of fast-food restaurants and strip malls. Downtown, along Main Street are even more motels, ranging from classy new resort-like hotels to well-maintained budget motels. You can easily walk from most of the downtown motels to the Shakespearean Festival. Most of Cedar City's B&Bs are also within a stroll of the festival grounds.

Note that the following prices are for the high summer festival season. Outside of high season, expect rates to drop about a third.

Under $50

At I-15 exit 52 is a brand new **Econolodge,** 333 N 1100 West, (435) 867-4700 or (888) 326-6613, with an outdoor pool and hot tub. Downtown along Main Street are more budget choices. The **Zion Inn,** 222 S. Main, (435) 586-9487, offers kitchenettes and accepts pets. The **Travelodge Motel,** 2555 N. Main, (435) 586-7435 or (800) 348-8216, is a real deal with a pool and spa; pets okay.

$50–75

The following motels string along Main Street in downtown Cedar City. The **Cedar Rest Motel,** 479 S. Main, (435) 586-9471, offers basic rooms with a free continental breakfast, and the **Super 7 Motel,** 190 S. Main, (435) 586-6566, has standard motel rooms and accepts pets. The **Rodeway Inn,** 281 S. Main, (435) 586-9916 or (800) 424-4777, has a pool, sauna, and spa; pets okay.

Best Western El Rey Inn, 80 S. Main, (435) 586-6518 or (800) 528-1234, offers suites, a restaurant, a pool, sauna, and spa. The **Quality Inn,** 18 S. Main, (435) 586-2433 or (800) 228-5151, has an outdoor pool and a complimentary continental breakfast.

Out at I-15 Exit 59, the **Comfort Inn,** 250 N. 1100 West, (435) 586-2082 or (800) 627-0374, has a pool, spa, some kitchenettes, and a complimentary continental breakfast.

Out at 1-15 exit 57 is Cedar City's newest hotel. The **Days Inn,** 1204 S Main, (435) 867-8877 or (888) 556-5637, has an indoor pool and complimentary continental breakfast.

$75–100

One of the best places to stay in Cedar City is the **Best Western Town & Country Inn,** 200 N. Main, (435) 586-9911. It is a large lodging complex with nicely furnished rooms and suites, indoor and outdoor pools, and spas. Rooms have microwaves and refrigerators; several restaurants are adjacent.

The **Abbey Inn,** 940 W. 200 North, (435) 586-9966 or (800) 325-5411, offers a pool and kitchenettes. The **Holiday Inn,** 1575 W. 200 North (I-15 Exit 59), (435) 586-8888 or (800) HOLIDAY, also offers a pool, a good restaurant, spa, and sauna; pets are okay.

Bed-and-breakfast inns and Shakespeare seem to go hand-in-hand. The **Bard's Inn Bed & Breakfast,** 150 S. 100 West, (435) 586-6612, is two blocks from the Shakespearean Festival. There are seven guest rooms, all with private bath, plus there's a two-bedroom cottage. Open during the festival season only. **Paxman Summer House Bed & Breakfast,** 170 N. 400 West, (435) 586-3755 or (888) 586-3755, is an antique-furnished Victorian home with four guest rooms, all with private baths. Two-night minimum on summer weekends in July and August. Located two blocks from the Shakespearean Festival. For a more rural touch, the **Willow Glen Inn Bed & Breakfast,** 3308 N. Bulldog Rd., (435) 586-3275, offers a three-bedroom inn plus two cottages (with a total of six guest rooms); located on a 10-acre farm five miles north of downtown Cedar City, I-15 Exit 62; some shared baths. **Desert Blossom Bed and Breakfast Inn,** 140 S. 100 West, (435) 867-4691, has four rooms all with private bathrooms in a restored early 20th-century cottage. The inn is just around the corner from the festival grounds.

$100–125

The **Baker House Bed & Breakfast,** 1800 Royal Hunte Dr., (435) 867-5695 or (888) 611-8181, www.bbhost.com/bakerhouse, is a few minutes drive from the festival, but the rooms here are some of the most luxurious in Cedar City and most have great views. There are five guest rooms in this modern Queen Anne mansion, all with private baths, fireplaces, and TVs.

Campgrounds

Cedar City KOA, 1121 N. Main, (435) 586-9872, is open all year with showers, playground, and a pool; $16 tents or RVs without hookups, $19 RVs with. **Country Aire RV Park,** 1700 N. Main, (435) 586-2550, is open all year with showers and a pool; $19 RVs with hookups, no tent sites. The **Town and Country RV Park,** 50 W 200 North, (435) 586-9900, is close to downtown, but has not tent sites.

OTHER PRACTICALITIES

Food

Family restaurants dominate Cedar City's cuisine. **Sullivan's Cafe,** 301 S. Main, (435) 586-6761, is a favorite for casual family dining. **Boomer's,** 5 N. Main St., (435) 865-9665, serves burgers, shakes, fries, and American standards. Upstairs is **Boomer's Pasta Garden,** a sister restaurant with a selection of pasta dishes.

For Cantonese-style food, there's **Hunan Restaurant,** 501 S. Main, (435) 586-8952, and **China Garden Restaurant,** 64 N. Main, (435) 586-6042, whose giant sign you surely won't miss in downtown Cedar City. Good places for Mexican include **Escobar's,** 155 N. Main, (435) 865-0155, open for late breakfast, lunch, and dinner. You can have a drink with your meal at **Pancho and Lefty's,** 2107 N. Main, (435) 586-7501, and **La Fiesta,** 900 N. Main, (435) 586-4646. For pizza, try the **Pizza Factory,** 124 S. Main, (435) 586-3900; open Mon.–Sat., or **Godfather's Pizza,** 241 N. Main. (435) 586-1111, located in the old train station.

The following fine dining restaurants each serve wine and cocktails. **Adriana's Restaurant,** 161 S. 100 West, (435) 865-1234, has an English atmosphere with fine dining, and is open in summer Monday–Saturday for lunch and dinner; call for hours off-season. East of Cedar City on Highway 14 is a dramatic desert canyon with two of the area's finest restaurants; both are open for dinner only. Five miles east of town is Western-style **Milt's Stage Stop,** (435) 586-9344, serving steak, prime rib, and seafood. The steak house atmosphere is more formal at **Rusty's Ranch House,** two miles east on Highway 14, (435) 586-3839, a new restaurant in a dramatic canyon setting.

Events

The community's largest event is the **Utah Shakespearean Festival,** running from late June through mid-October. Other events and festivals include the **Canyon Country Western Arts Festival** in **March.** The highlights are the readings by cowboy poets; there's also a display of Western art and music events.

In **June,** the local Indian community sponsors the **Paiute Restoration Gathering** with a parade, dances, traditional games, native food, and a beauty pageant on the second weekend in June. Utah athletes compete in the **Utah Summer Games** during late June; events, patterned after the Olympic games, begin with a torch relay and include track and field, 10-K and marathon runs, cycling, boxing, wrestling, basketball, tennis, soccer, karate, and swimming.

Everyone dresses up in period clothing in **July** for the **Utah Midsummer Renaissance Faire** of 16th-century entertainment, crafts, and food. **Pioneer Day** honors Utah's early settlers with a parade and games in town on July 24. Dances by the **American Folk Ballet** portray America's southern and Western folk history.

In **August,** mountain men and Indians set up camp for black-powder shoots and games in the **Jedediah Smith High Mountain Rendezvous** in the mountains above Cedar City.

The season ends in **November,** when Cedar City celebrates its birthday on the 11th with games and pioneer crafts in **Iron Mission Days.**

Recreation

The main **city park** has picnic tables, playground, and horseshoe courts at Main and 200 North. The **municipal swimming pools** at 400 Harding Avenue (400 W. 100 North), (435) 586-2869, have indoor and outdoor areas and a hydrotube. Look for **tennis courts** at Canyon Park (on UT 14, three blocks east of Main). From this park the new, paved Coal Creek walking and biking trail leads four miles up the desert canyon.

Shopping and Services

The **Renaissance Square** and **South Main Mall** shopping centers are on South Main at the south edge of town. Camping and other outdoor supplies are sold at **Ron's Sporting Goods,** 138 S. Main, (435) 586-9901, and **Gart Bros. Sporting Goods,** 606 S. Main, (435) 586-0687. **Valley View Medical Center,** 595 S. 75 East, (435) 586-6587, provides hospital care. The **post office** is at 333 N. Main, (435) 586-6701.

Information

Iron County Travel Council has literature and advice on travel in the area; open Mon.–Fri. 8 A.M.–7 P.M. and Sat. 9 A.M.–1 P.M. in summer, then Mon.–Fri. 8 A.M.–5 P.M. the rest of the year; located at 581 N Main, (P.O. Box 1007, Cedar City, UT 84720), (435) 586-5124. **Cedar City Ranger District office** of the Dixie National Forest has information on recreation and travel on the Markagunt Plateau; at 82 N. 100 East (P.O. Box 627, Cedar City, UT 84721-0627), (435) 865-3200. The Dixie National Forest **supervisor's office,** in the same building, provides general information for the entire forest; P.O. Box 580, Cedar City, UT 84721-0580, (435) 865-3700 (supervisor's office). The **BLM's Cedar City District office** can tell you about the BLM lands in southwestern Utah, including Beaver River, Dixie, Kanab, and Escalante Resource Areas; open Mon.–Fri. 7:45 A.M.–4:30 P.M.; located just off Main at 176 E. DL Sargeant Drive on the north edge of town (Cedar City, UT 84720), (435) 586-2401. For more specific info on the southern Wah Wah Mountains and other desert areas around town, visit the **BLM's Beaver River Resource Area office;** open Mon.–Fri. 7:45 A.M.–4:30 P.M.; at 365 S. Main (Cedar City, UT 84720), (435) 586-2458. **Cedar City Public Library,** 136 W. Center, (435) 586-6661, has good reading material; open Mon.–Thurs. 9 A.M.–9 P.M., Fri. and Sat. 9 A.M.–6 P.M. **Mountain West Bookstore,** 77 N. Main, (435) 586-3828, offers a selection of Utah history, travel, general reading, and LDS titles.

Transport

Rent a car from **National Car Rental,** at the airport, (435) 586-4004, or at National's office at the Town and Country Inn, 200 N Main, (435) 586-9900. **Speedy Rentals,** 650 N. Main, (435) 586-7368, rents vans, cars, pick-ups and motorhomes. **Greyhound Bus,** 1355 S. Main (near the south I-15 interchange), (435) 586-1204, offers service twice daily to Salt Lake City, Denver, St. George, Las Vegas, and other destinations from the C-Mart Texaco. **Skywest Airlines** has flights between the Cedar City Municipal Airport and Salt Lake City, (800) 453-9417.

PAROWAN

Although just a small town, Parowan (pop. 1,800) is southern Utah's oldest community and the seat of Iron County. Highway UT 143 turns south from downtown to the Brian Head Ski Area, Cedar Breaks National Monument, and other scenic areas on the Markagunt Plateau. To the west lies Utah's desert country. Accommodations in town offer a less expensive alternative to those in Brian Head. **Iron County Fair** presents a parade, rodeos, horse races, exhibits, and entertainment during the Labor Day holiday. In April, cowboys come to Parowan for the **Iron County Cowboy Days & Poetry Gathering.**

The **Parowan Chamber of Commerce** will answer your questions about the area; open Mon.–Fri. 9 A.M.–4 P.M. at 73 N. Main (P.O. Box 664, Parowan, UT 84761), (435) 477-1033 or (888) PAROWAN. Parowan is 18 miles northeast of Cedar City and 14 miles north of Brian Head; take I-15 Exits 75 or 78. The **public library** is across the street at 16 S. Main, (435) 477-3391.

Parowan Gap Petroglyphs

Indians have pecked many designs into the rocks at this pass 10.5 miles northwest of Parowan. The common route for Indians and wildlife hunting the Red Hills crossed this gap, and it may have served as an important site for hunting rituals. The rock art's meaning hasn't been deciphered but it probably represents the thoughts of many different Indian tribes over the past 1,000 or more years. Geometric designs, snakes, lizards, mountain sheep, bear claws, and human figures are all still recognizable. You can get here on a good gravel road from Parowan by going north on Main and turning left 10.5 miles on the last street (400 North).

Or, from Cedar City, go north on Main (or take I-15 Exit 62), follow signs for UT 130 north 13.5 miles, then turn right 2.5 miles on a good gravel road (near Milepost 19). You'll find an interpretive brochure and map at the BLM offices in Cedar City (see Information, above).

Accommodations
Under $50: The **Ace Motel,** 72 N. Main, (435) 477-3384, is a basic motel and allows pets.

$50–75: Grandma Bess' Cottage Bed & Breakfast, 291 W. 200 South, (435) 477-8224, has rooms starting at $50. The **Days Inn,** 200 S. 600 W. Holyoak Lane (I-15 business route), (435) 477-3326 or (888) 530-3138, has new rooms and an on-site restaurant. **Best Western Swiss Village Inn,** 580 N. Main, (435) 477-3391 or (800) 528-1234, has a pool, spa, and restaurant.

Campgrounds: For both RVs and tents, there is **Sportsmen's Country RV Park,** 492 N Main, (435) 477-3714.

Food
Parowan Cafe, 33 N. Main, is open Monday–Saturday for breakfast, lunch, and dinner. **Pizza Barn,** 595 W. 200 South, (435) 477-8240, serves pizza and pasta daily for dinner. For great ribs, go to **Partner's Getaway Restaurant,** 215 S. 600 West, (435) 477-8646. **La Villa** 13 S. Main St., serves Mexican food.

THE MARKAGUNT PLATEAU

Markagunt is an Indian name for "Highland of Trees." The large, high plateau—much of the land is between 9,000 and 11,000 feet in elevation—consists mostly of gently rolling country, forests, and lakes. Black tongues of barren lava extend across some parts of the landscape. Cliffs at Cedar Breaks National Monument are the best-known feature of the plateau, but the land also drops away in the colorful pink cliffs farther southeast.

Two Scenic Byways cross this highly scenic area. Highway 14 climbs up a very dramatic cliff-lined canyon from Cedar City, reaching vista points over Zion National Park before dropping onto Long Valley Junction on Highway 89. Highway 143 departs from Parowan climbing steeply up to lofty Brian Head with its ski and recreation area, passed Panguitch Lake and down to Panguitch in the Sevrier Valley. Brian Head is southern Utah's most popular ski area, and in summer the lifts carry mountain bikes up to elevations of nearly two miles, allowing gear heads to explore high mountain glades and meadows.

Popular activities on the Markagunt include fishing, hiking, mountain biking, downhill and cross-country skiing, and snowmobiling. Contact the Cedar City Ranger District of the Dixie National Forest at 82 N. 100 East (P.O. Box 627, Cedar City, UT 84721-0627), (435) 865-3200, for a forest map and information on exploring the area. In summer, you can find volunteers or foresters at the visitors' center on UT 14 opposite the Duck Creek Campground turnoff. Picnickers may stop at Duck Creek, Panguitch Lake, and Vermilion Castle Campgrounds free of charge for up to two hours.

MARKAGUNT SCENIC BYWAY (HWY 14)

Starting at Cedar City's eastern boundary, Highway 14 plunges into a narrow canyon flanked by steep rock walls before climbing up to the top of the Markagunt Plateau. This is a very scenic route, passing dramatic rock cliffs and pink rock hoodoos that echo the formations at Zion and Bryce Canon National Parks. This isn't a quick drive, especially if you get caught behind a lumbering RV. But the scenic qualities of the canyon and the incredible vistas—which extend across Zion and down into Arizona—will amply repay your patience. The route also passes a number of wooded campgrounds and small mountain resorts. Due to their elevations—mostly 8,000–9,000 feet—these high mountain getaways are popular when the temperatures in the desert basin towns begin to bake. The route ends at the Long Valley Junction, at Highway 89, a distance of 41 miles from Cedar City.

Zion Overlook
A sweeping panorama takes in the deep canyons and monuments of Zion National Park

to the south. Located 16.5 miles east of Cedar City on the south side of the road.

Bristlecone Pine Trail

This easy half-mile loop, graded for wheelchair access, leads to the rim of the Markagunt Plateau and excellent views. A dense spruce and fir forest opens up near the rim, where storm-battered limber and bristlecone pines cling precariously near the edge. You can identify the bristlecone pines by their short-needled, "bottle-brush" branches. The trailhead is 17 miles east of Cedar City on the south side of UT 14.

Cedar Breaks National Monument

Eighteen miles east of Cedar City is the junction with Utah 148, which leads north to Cedar

Breaks National Monument (see below). The route climbs up to elevations well over 10,000 feet, and is usually open from late-May through mid-October.

Navajo Lake

Lava flows dammed this unusual 3.5-mile-long lake, which has no surface outlet. Instead, water drains through sinkholes in the limestone underneath and emerges as Cascade Falls (in the Pacific Ocean drainage) and Duck Creek (Great Basin drainage). From a pullout along the highway 24 miles east of Cedar City, you can sometimes see three of the sinkholes at the east end; a dam prevents the lake from draining into them. Anglers catch rainbow trout and occasionally some eastern brook and brown trout; ice fishing

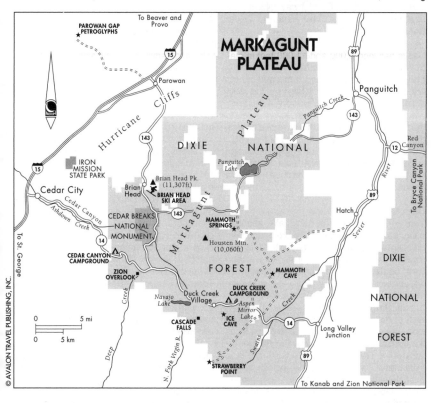

is possible in winter. You can hand-launch small boats at Navajo Campground or from boat ramps at Navajo Lake Lodge and Behmer Lodge & Landing. Take the Navajo Lake turnoff, 25.5 miles east of Cedar City, for the campgrounds, marina, and lodge along the south shore.

Virgin River Rim Trailhead

This trail stretches about 38 miles along the rim between Deer Haven Group Campground and Strawberry Point. Beautiful panoramas of Zion National Park and the headwaters of the Virgin River reward trail users. You can also reach it at Te-Ah Campground, from Navajo Lake via short (one-half to three-quarter mile) spur trails and at the start of the Cascade Falls National Recreation Trail. The entire length is open to hikers and mountain bikers. Off-highway vehicles can use the section from Deer Haven to Te-Ah Campgrounds.

Cascade Falls National Recreation Trail

Splendid views and a waterfall make this an exciting trip. The easy trail is 1.1 miles round-trip with some ups and downs. It begins at the south rim of the Markagunt Plateau, drops a short way down the Pink Cliffs, then winds along the cliffs to the falls. The falls gush from a cave and bounce their way down to the North Fork of the Virgin River and Zion Canyon. The flow peaks during spring runoff. Take the Navajo Lake turnoff from UT 14, go 0.3 mile, then turn left three miles on a gravel road to its end.

Duck Creek Campground

Turn north from UT 14 at Duck Lake, about 28 miles east of Cedar City. The creek and lake adjacent to the campground offer trout fishing. You'll see why Duck Lake got its name. A **visitors' center,** staffed by the Dixie Interpretive Association, is open daily 10 A.M.–5 P.M. in summer across the highway from the campground turnoff. **Singing Pines Interpretive Trail,** just east of the visitors' center, makes a half-mile loop—an amusing information sheet introduces the forest trees through songs. **Old Ranger Interpretive Trail** makes a one-third-mile loop from Duck Creek Campground; look for a large pullout on the left where the main campground road makes a curve to the right (near the amphitheater); the information sheet explains the

forest through the eyes of an old-time forest ranger. Pick up information sheets for both trails from the visitors' center. The **Lost Hunter Trail** makes a three-mile loop from the same trailhead in Duck Creek Campground to the top of Duck Creek Bench; elevation gain is about 600 feet with many fine views.

Ice Cave

Cool off inside this small cave, where the lava rock insulates ice throughout the summer. The road may be too rough for cars—ask conditions at the visitors' center. Turn south on the dirt road beside the visitors' center, keep left at the fork 0.2 mile in, keep right at another fork 0.8 mile farther, and continue 0.4 mile to the cave at the end of the road; signs mark the way.

Aspen Mirror Lake

Trout and scenic beauty attract visitors to this pretty reservoir. The turnoff is on the north side of UT 14 about midway between Duck Creek Campground and Duck Creek Village. Park, then walk the level trail about one-quarter mile.

Duck Creek Village

Hollywood has used this area since the 1940s to film such productions as *How the West Was Won, My Friend Flicka,* and the *Daniel Boone* TV series. This handsome village—a collection of lodges, cabins, and log-built homes—lies at the edge of a large meadow (elev. 8,400 feet) about 30 miles east of Cedar City. The surrounding countryside is excellent for snowmobiling, a popular winter sport here. A big snowmobile race takes place on the weekend closest to Valentine's Day. Cross-country skiing is good, too, on a variety of meadow, forest and bowl terrain. The snow season lasts from about late November to late March. Blue Pine Tours, at Pinewoods Resort (see below), (800) 848-2525, offers snowmobile tours and rentals, as well as cross-country ski and snowshoe rentals. In summer, Blue Pine Tours has mountain bike rentals.

Food: The **Pinewoods Restaurant,** (435) 682-2512, prepares prime rib, steak, seafood, and other fare all year; open for breakfast, lunch, and dinner Friday–Monday. The **Duck Creek Village Inn,** (435) 682-2565, offers American fare three meals a day year-round.

Strawberry Point

A magnificent panorama takes in countless ridges, canyons, and mountains south of the Markagunt Plateau. You can spot Zion National Park and even the Arizona Strip from this lofty perch (elev. 9,016 feet). Erosion has cut delicate pinnacles and narrow canyons into the Pink Cliffs on either side below the viewpoint. Turn south from UT 14 between Mileposts 32 and 33 (32.5 miles east of Cedar City) onto a gravel road and go nine miles to its end. A 500-foot path continues to Strawberry Point. Take care near the edge—the rock is crumbly and there are no guardrails.

Accommodations

Under each category, the accommodations are listed from west to east along UT 14.

$50–75: Navajo Lake Lodge, at the west end of the lake, (702) 646-4197, has cabins, a small café, store, boat rentals, and boat ramp. Open Memorial Day weekend–late Oct.

In Duck Creek Village, **Meadeau View Lodge** on UT 14, (435) 682-2495, operates bed-and-breakfast rooms all year.

Falcon's Nest, 60 Movie Ranch Rd., (435) 682-2556 or (800) 240-4930, offers A-frame cabins with kitchens; adjacent is the Duck Quick Cafe. Two-night minimum on weekends (three nights on holidays). Open year-round.

$75–100: To reach the rest of Duck Creek Village, drive one mile east, then a half-mile south. The **Inn at Cedar Mountain,** (435) 682-2378 or (800) 897-4995), has condo-style rooms for up to eight people, open all year. Rates include a continental breakfast. **Pinewoods Resort,** 121 Duck Creek Ridge Rd., (435) 682-2512 or (800) 848-2525, offers two-bedroom condominiums in a log lodge; open year-round. All units have fireplaces and kitchens, and pets are okay.

Campgrounds: Sites in the **Cedar Canyon Campground** lie along Crow Creek among aspen, fir, and spruce in a pretty canyon setting; elevation is 8,100 feet. Open with water from early June to mid-Sept.; $5; located 12 miles east of Cedar City on UT 14.

The U.S. Forest Service maintains **Spruces** and **Navajo Campgrounds** along the lake and **Te-Ah Campground** 1.5 miles west; all have water and charge a $10 fee from mid-June to mid-Sept.; expect cool nights at the 9,200-foot elevation. Aspen, spruce, and fir trees grow along the lake.

Duck Creek Campground (see above), north from UT 14 at Duck Lake, has sites (elev. 8,600 feet) that are open early June–mid-September with water and a $10 fee.

BRIAN HEAD–PANGUITCH LAKE SCENIC BYWAY 143 (HWY 143)

Beginning in Parowan, Highway 143 very quickly climbs up to nearly 10,000 feet, ascending some of the steepest paved roads in Utah in the process (some of the grades here are 13 percent). The terrain changes from arid desert, to pine forests, and to alpine aspen forests in a distance of just 14 miles.

At an elevation of 9,850 feet, Brian Head is the highest municipality in Utah, with a year-round population of 95. The town takes its name from the flat-topped peak towering above to the east. Originally called Monument Peak, it got its present (misspelled) name in 1890 when its founders decided to honor the famed orator and politician William Jennings Bryan. Winter skiers like Brian Head for its abundant snow, challenging terrain, and good accommodations. Summer visitors come to enjoy the high country and to plunge down the slopes on mountain bikes. The beautiful colors of Cedar Breaks National Monument lie just a few miles south. Panguitch Lake, to the east, receives high ratings for its excellent trout fishing.

bobcat (Lynx rufus)

Brian Head Peak

You can drive all the way to Brian Head's 11,307-foot summit by car when the road is dry, usually from July to October. Panoramas from the top take in much of southwestern Utah and beyond into Nevada and Arizona. Sheep graze the grassy slopes below. From Brian Head, follow the highway about two miles south, then turn left (northeast) three miles on a gravel road to the summit. The stone shelter here was built by the Civilian Conservation Corps in the 1930s.

Brian Head Resort
Brian Head comes alive during the skiing season, from about mid-November to mid-April. There are two ski areas at Brian Head: Navajo Peak, good for beginners and families, and Giant Steps, with more advanced runs. In addition, snow cats transport more daring skiers to thrilling chutes and bowls on Brian Head Peak. A total of five triple and one double lift carry skiers up to elevations of 10,920 feet; the resort has 53 runs and 500 skiable acres, with a vertical drop of 1,707 feet. Thirty percent of the terrain is rated beginner, 40 percent intermediate, and 30 percent advanced. The resort also features two snowboard parks and night-skiing to 10 P.M. on weekends and holidays. Lift tickets cost $35 adults full day, $30 half day; children 12 and under and seniors ski for $22 full day, $20 half day. Rentals, lessons, shops, and children's day care are available. For more ski information contact Brian Head Resort, Brian Head, UT 84719, (435) 677-2035 or (800) 272-7426, www.brianhead.com.

Cross-Country Skiing
Brian Head Cross-Country Center (in the Cedar Breaks Lodge) grooms about 42 kilometers of trails in the area; ask for its map, (435) 677-2012. The short **North Rim Trail** goes to overlooks in Cedar Breaks National Monument. Experienced skiers with maps and compasses can head out on backcountry routes to the summit of Brian Head Peak and many other areas. There is no fee for use of the trails; rentals available at the lodge.

Mountain Biking
Brian Head's second season is during the summer and fall, roughly June–October, when the area comes alive with mountain bikers taking advantage of great terrain and discounted accommodation. Brian Head Resort opens itself to bikers as a mountain-bike park, complete with chairlift and trailhead shuttle services, bike wash,

rentals, and repair services. Thrifty bikers can come away with some really good deals by shopping area hotels for mountain-bike lodging packages, which combine a few days of lodging with lift tickets, shuttle service, and sometimes even food and bike rentals. Be sure to pick up a copy of the free *Brian Head Hiking and Bicycling Guide,* which details 19 popular biking trails around Brian Head, Panguitch and Panguitch Lake, Parowan, Duck Creek Village, and Cedar City. The guide is available from Bicycle Utah Vacation Guides, P.O. Box 738, Park City, UT 84060, (435) 649-5806. Bike-oriented summertime events in Brian Head include a late-July bike festival and mountain-bike races in August, September, and March. Mountain bike rentals are available from Brian Head Resort, (435) 677-2035.

Food
At the Brian Head Mall, the **Black Diamond Deli & Grill,** (435) 677-3111, serves breakfasts and lunchtime sandwiches (and dinner during the summer). Next door, **Bump & Grind** serves gourmet coffee and pastries, (435) 677-3111.

At Cedar Breaks Lodge, there are three dining rooms. The **Columbine Café** is open for breakfast and lunch, the **Summit Dining Room** offers Western-style fine dining in the evening only, and **Pinnacle Breaks Private Club** offers drinks and casual dining. The Lodge at Brian Head, (435) 677-3222, houses **Big One Pizza** and the **Club Royale,** a private club with drinks and fine dining.

For food on the slopes, the **Brian Head Station** serves breakfast and lunch daily during the ski season next to chairs #4 and 6, (435) 677-2035. At the base of Brian Head Peak, nonmembers are permitted to lunch or dine on sandwiches, steak, seafood, and pasta dishes at the restaurant in **Club Edge,** near Giant Step Lodge, (435) 677-3343; alcohol available; closed part of spring and autumn.

Information
You can reach **Brian Head Chamber of Commerce** at P.O. Box 190325, Brian Head, UT 84719, (435) 677-2810 or (888) 667-2810. Or check out the website at www.brianheadutah.com. The **post office** is in Brian Head Mall, near the center of town.

Cedar Breaks National Monument

The northern entrance to this showcase of spectacular erosion (see below) is two miles south of Brian Head on Highway 143.

Panguitch Lake and Vicinity

This 1,250-acre reservoir sits in a volcanic basin surrounded by forests and barren lava flows. The cool waters have a reputation for outstanding trout fishing, especially for rainbow. Some German browns can also be caught in the lake and downstream in Panguitch Creek. Recently, the lake has gained popularity for ice fishing. A number of resorts line the lakeshore; many are venerable older fishing lodges with basic lodging in free-standing cabins; a couple are more upscale. Panguitch Lake is increasingly popular as a site for resort homes, as a glance at the dirt moving equipment and piles of building supplies make apparent.

Panguitch Lake lies along UT 143 about 16 miles southwest of Panguitch and 14 miles northeast of Cedar Breaks National Monument. The lake has public boat ramps on the south and north shores.

Mammoth Springs

Moss and luxuriant streamside vegetation surround the crystal-clear spring waters at this beautiful spot. Mammoth Springs is about 5.5 miles south of Panguitch Lake. The last two miles are on gravel Forest Route 068. See the Dixie National Forest map (available at the Pine Valley and Cedar City Ranger District offices). A foot bridge leads across the stream to the springs.

Mammoth Cave

Step a few feet underground to explore the inside of a lava flow. When this mass of lava began to cool, the molten interior burst through the surface and drained out through a network of tunnels. A cave-in revealed this section of tunnel, which has two levels. One of them you can follow through to another opening. The lower tunnel (with the large entrance) goes back about a quarter mile. To explore beyond that or to check out other sections, you'll have to stoop or crawl. Bring at least two reliable, powerful flashlights; the caves are very dark. Mammoth Cave is about 14 miles south of Panguitch Lake. Roads also lead in from Duck Creek on UT 14 and Hatch on U.S. 89. You'll need the forest map to navigate the back roads, though there are some signs for Mammoth Cave.

Accommodations

Lodgings and campgrounds along UT 143 are concentrated around Panguitch Lake, and a number of accommodations serve Brian Head.

$50–75: On the west shore of Panguitch Lake, the **Rustic Lodge,** 186 S. West Shore Rd., (435) 676-2627 or (800) 427-8345, offers a number of handsome kitchen-equipped cabins in a forested glen. Unfortunately, the resort is not directly on the lake (the lodge and cabins face onto a pasture) but this is otherwise a very pleasant place to stay. Campsites available also. Additional amenities include a boat moorage and boat rentals, a restaurant and pub, and laundry facilities. Two-night minimum on summer weekends. **Deer Trail Lodge Resort,** northwest of the lake on Clearcreek Canyon Rd., (435) 676-2211, offers new creek-side cabins in a steep canyon; again unfortunately, these pleasant cabins are some distance from the lake itself. The resort also offers a restaurant (serving breakfast, lunch, and dinner daily) and campsites. Take West or North Shore Road to Clear Creek Canyon Road, then turn west a half mile.

Bear Paw Lakeview Resort is on the east shore of Panguitch Lake at 905 S. UT 143, (435) 676-2650 or (888) 553-8439, and has lakeview cabins and an RV park. There's also a small store, on-site restaurant, post office, and boat and bike rentals. Open early May–mid-Nov.

$75–100: A few resorts are actually on Panguitch lake. The nicest is **Beaver Dam Lodge** on the north shore, (435) 676-8339 or (800) 262-9181, a handsome, newly built log lodge right on the lake, overlooking a small marina. Also in the lodge is a good restaurant (open daily for breakfast, lunch, and dinner), small store, and a boat rental office.

Blue Springs Lodge is the Panguitch area's newest resort, near the general store at 225 N. Shore Rd., (435) 676-2277 or (800) YUR-LODGE. Also a ways from the lake, this resort is comprised of a number of modern log cabins with kitchens. Most can sleep six adults. The location—right on Highway 143—is about the only downside.

$100–125: Rates at Brian Head are steep during the ski season, though most places offer skiers vacation-package discounts. The easiest way to book a room or a complete holiday is to use **Brian Head Resort Central Reservations,** (435) 677-3000 or (800) 272-7426, www.destinationbrianhead.com, which provides information and bookings for the resort, plus several hotels and several resort-affiliated **condominium** projects in town.

In the center of town, **The Lodge at Brian Head,** 314 Hunter Ridge Rd., (435) 677-3222 or (800) 386-5634, has a pool and hot tub. You have a choice of deluxe hotel rooms, studios, and one-bedroom suites. The most upscale lodging choice in Brian Head is the **Cedar Breaks Lodge,** 223 Hunter Ridge Rd., (435) 667-3000 or (888) ATCEDAR, www.cedarbreakslodge.com, at the base of Navajo Peak on the north (lower) side of town. All rooms come with jetted tubs, refrigerator, in-room coffee, and cable TV; kitchens are available in some rooms. There's also an indoor pool, two hot tubs, a steam room, sauna, and fitness center. Lodging choices range from hotel rooms to three-bedroom suites.

There are a number of new condo developments at Brian Head. **Brian Head Condo Reservations,** (435) 677-2045 or (800) 722-4742, offers units near both the Giant Steps and Navajo Mountain lifts in a total of five large condo developments. Most units come with two bedrooms and two baths, full kitchen, plus a wood-burning fireplace. Prices for one-bedroom condos start at about $100 (double) in summer; during the ski season expect to pay at least $125.

Campgrounds: The U.S. Forest Service has three campgrounds nearby Panguitch Lake; all are open with water from early June to mid-September. **Panguitch Lake North Campground,** on the southwest side of the lake, has developed sites in a ponderosa pine forest at an elevation of 8,400 feet; a basic site costs $10. **Panguitch Lake South Campground,** across the highway, is more suited for small rigs and tents; $8. **White Bridge Campground** (elev. 7,900 feet) lies among cottonwoods and junipers along Panguitch Creek four miles northeast of the lake; $10 fee.

Located three miles down West Shore Road off UT 143, **Panguitch Lake General Store and RV Park,** near the turnoff for West Shore Road, (435) 676-2464, has an RV park with hookup sites for self-contained RVs at $16. The store is open all year and sells groceries, gas, gifts, and fishing supplies.

CEDAR BREAKS NATIONAL MONUMENT

Erosion on the west edge of the Markagunt Plateau has carved a giant amphitheater 2,500 feet deep and more than three miles across. A fairyland of forms and colors appears below the rim. Ridges and pinnacles extend like buttresses from the steep cliffs. Cottony patches of clouds often drift through the craggy landscape. Traces of iron, manganese, and other minerals have tinted the normally white limestone a rainbow of warm hues. The intense colors blaze during sunsets and glow even on a cloudy day. Rock layers look much like those at Bryce Canyon National Park and, in fact, are the same Claron Formation, but here they're 2,000 feet higher. Elevations range from 10,662 feet at the rim's highest point to 8,100 feet at Ashdown Creek below. In the distance beyond the amphitheater, you can see Cedar City and the desert's valleys and ranges. Dense forests broken by large alpine meadows cover the rolling plateau country away from the rim. More than 150 species of wildflowers brighten the meadows during summer; the colorful display peaks during the last two weeks in July.

A five-mile scenic drive leads past four spectacular overlooks, each with a different perspective. Avoid overlooks and other exposed areas during thunderstorms, which are common on summer afternoons. Heavy snows close the road most of the year. You can drive in only from about late May until the first big snowstorm of autumn, usually sometime in October. Winter visitors can come in on snowmobiles (unplowed roads only), skis, or snowshoes from Brian Head (two miles north of the monument) or from UT 14 (2.5 miles south). Cedar Breaks National Monument is 24 miles east of Cedar City, 17 miles south of Parowan, 30 miles southwest of Panguitch, and 27 miles northwest of Long Valley Junction. Nearest accommodations and restaurants are two miles north in Brian Head.

Visitor Center and Campground
A log cabin contains exhibits and an information desk. The exhibits provide a good introduction to the Markagunt Plateau and identify local rocks, wildflowers, trees, animals, and birds. Related

books, topo and forest maps, posters, slides, and film are sold. Staff offer nature walks, geology talks, and campfire programs; see the schedules posted in the visitors' center and at the campground. Open daily 8 A.M.–6 P.M. from about June 1 to mid-Oct. A $4 per-vehicle entrance fee is collected near the visitors' center; there's no charge if you're just driving through the monument without stopping. The small campground to the east has water and a $9 fee; camping is first-come, first-served. The campground is open from about June 1 to mid-September. A picnic area is near. Contact the monument at 2390 West Highway 56, Suite #11, Cedar City, UT 84720-4151, (435) 586-9451, www.nps.gov/cebr.

Hiking Trails

Two easy trails near the rim give an added appreciation of the geology and forests here. Allow extra time while on foot—it's easy to get out of breath at these high elevations! Regulations prohibit pets on the trails. **Spectra Point/Wasatch Rampart Trail** begins at the visitors' center, then follows the rim along the south edge of the amphitheater to an overlook. The hike is four miles round-trip with some ups and downs. Weather-beaten bristlecone pines grow at Spectra Point, about halfway down the trail.

Alpine Pond Trail forms a two-mile loop that drops below the rim into one of the few densely wooded areas of the amphitheater. The trail winds through enchanting forests of aspen, subalpine fir, and Engelmann spruce. You can cut the hiking distance in half with a car shuttle between the two trailheads or by taking a connector trail that joins the upper and lower parts of the loop near Alpine Pond. Begin from either Chessmen Ridge Overlook or the trailhead pullout 1.1 miles farther north. A trail guide is available at the start or at the visitors' center.

ASHDOWN GORGE WILDERNESS

Experienced hikers can explore this wilderness in the Dixie National Forest and enter the Cedar Break National Monument's lower valleys. Although no trails within the monument itself wind from the rim down to the bottom, you can take **Rattlesnake Creek Trail** from a trailhead on the rim just outside the monument's north boundary. The rugged trail drops 3,400 feet in nine miles, following Rattlesnake and Ashdown Creeks to the lower trailhead on UT 14 about seven miles east of Cedar City. Upon reaching Ashdown Creek, you have a choice of heading several miles upstream into the monument or entering the depths of Ashdown Gorge downstream. Check the weather forecast beforehand to avoid getting caught in a flash flood within the gorge. Hikers must be good at map reading and keeping an eye out for the next cairn or tree blaze. Rattlesnake and Ashdown Creeks usually have water, though it can be silty or polluted by livestock. You may have to do some wading in the gorge. Topo map is the 7½-minute Flanigan Arch or 15-minute Cedar Breaks. Check with staff at Cedar Breaks National Monument or Cedar City Ranger District for current trail conditions.

BRYCE CANYON NATIONAL PARK

A geologic fairyland of rock spires rises beneath the high cliffs of the Paunsaugunt Plateau. This intricate maze, eroded from a soft limestone, now glows with warm shades of reds, oranges, pinks, yellows, and creams. The rocks provide a continuous show of changing color through the day as the sun's rays and cloud shadows move across the landscape.

Visitors perceive a multitude of wondrous forms. Some see the natural rock sculptures as Gothic castles, others as Egyptian temples, subterranean worlds inhabited by dragons, or vast armies of a lost empire. The Paiute Indian tale of the Legend People relates how various animals and birds once lived in a beautiful city built for them by Coyote; when the Legend People began behaving badly toward Coyote, he transformed them all into stone.

Bryce Canyon National Park contains some of the best scenery, though what's popularly called Bryce Canyon isn't a canyon at all, but the largest of a series of massive amphitheaters cut into the Pink Cliffs. You can gaze into the depths from viewpoints and trails on the plateau rim or descend moderate grades winding among the spires. More of the park can be seen along a 17-

mile scenic drive south past Bryce Canyon to other overlooks and trailheads. The nearly 36,000 acres of Bryce Canyon National Park offers many opportunities to explore spectacular rock features, dense forests, and expansive meadows. Many wildlife and plant communities make their homes in the park.

Cool temperatures prevail most of the year at the park's 6,600- to 9,100-foot elevations. Expect pleasantly warm days in summer, frosty nights in spring and autumn, and snow in winter. The visitors' center, scenic drive, and a campground stay open through the year. Allow a full day to see the visitors' center exhibits, enjoy the viewpoints along the scenic drive, and take a few short walks. Photographers usually obtain best results early and late in the day when shadows set off the brightly colored rocks. Memorable sunsets and sunrises reward visitors who stay overnight. Moonlit nights reveal yet another spectacle.

From Bryce Junction (on U.S. 89, seven miles south of Panguitch), turn east 14 miles on UT 12, then south three miles on UT 63. Or, from Torrey (near Capitol Reef National Park), head west 103 miles on UT 12, then turn south three miles (winter snows occasionally close this section).

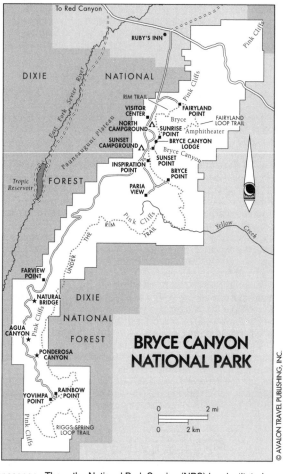

Both approaches have spectacular scenery. The park entrance fee of $20 per vehicle ($5 bicyclists) is charged May 15–September 30; the rest of the year the entrance fee is $10 per vehicle. Admission is good for seven days. Admission on foot or bicycle is $5. A brochure available at the entrance station and visitors' center has a map of major scenic features, drives, and trails.

Park Shuttle Bus

In response to increased traffic congestion, decreased federal funding for infrastructure repair, and concern about environmental degradation,

the National Park Service (NPS) has instituted a shuttle service through Bryce Canyon Park. These tour buses depart from a parking area just off Highway 12 at the park entrance every 15 minutes or so, and stop at the major viewpoints along the main amphitheater, as well as at the campgrounds, the visitors' center, and Bryce Canyon Lodge. Service is less frequent to Rainbow Point at the end of the park's 18-mile scenic drive. Passengers can take as long as they like at any viewpoint, and catch a later bus. The shuttle bus service also makes it easier for hikers, who don't need car shuttles between trailheads.

Use of the shuttle bus system is not mandatory; you can still bring in your own vehicle. However, park visitors who use the shuttle system to visit the park are charged only $15-per-vehicle admission (instead of $20). The shuttle operates May 15–September 30, 7 A.M.–dark.

The Hoodoos

The park's landscape originated about 60 million years ago as sediments in a large body of water—named Lake Flagstaff by geologists. Silt and calcium carbonate and other minerals settled on the lake bottom. These sediments consolidated and became the Claron Formation; a soft, silty limestone with some shale and sandstone. Lake Flagstaff had long since disappeared when the land began to rise as part of the Colorado Plateau uplift about 16 million years ago. Uneven pressures beneath the plateau caused it to break along fault lines into a series of smaller plateaus at different levels known as the Grand Staircase. Bryce Canyon National Park occupies part of one of these plateaus—the Paunsaugunt. The spectacular Pink Cliffs on the east edge contain the famous erosional features known as the hoodoos, carved in the Claron Formation. Variations in hardness of the rock layers result in these strange features, which seem almost alive. Water flows through cracks, wearing away softer rock around hard, erosion-resistant caps. Finally, a cap becomes so undercut that the overhang allows water to drip down, leaving a "neck" of rock below the harder cap. Traces of iron and manganese provide the distinctive coloring. The hoodoos continue to change—new ones form and old ones fade away. Despite appearances, wind plays little role in creation of the landscape; it's the freezing and thawing, snowmelt, and rainwater that dissolve weak layers, pry open cracks, and carve out the forms. The plateau cliffs, meanwhile, recede at a rate of about one foot every 50–65 years; look for trees on the rim that now overhang the abyss. Listen, and you might hear the sounds of pebbles falling away and rolling down the steep slopes.

Flora and Fauna

Vegetation in the park changes considerably with elevation. Piñon pine, Utah juniper, and Gambel oak dominate the warmer and drier slopes below about 7,000 feet. Ponderosa pines rise majestically over greenleaf manzanita and other shrubs between elevations of 7,000 and 8,500 feet. Blue spruce, white fir, Douglas fir, limber pine, bristlecone pine, and aspen thrive in the cool moist conditions above 8,500 feet. Wildflowers put on a showy display from spring to early autumn. Springs and seeps below the rim support water birch, bigtooth maple, willows, and narrow-leaf cottonwood.

Larger wildlife visit the higher elevations in summer, then move down out of the park as winter snows arrive. You can often spot mule deer grazing in meadows, especially in morning and evening. Other residents include mountain lion, black bear, coyote, bobcat, gray fox, striped skunk, badger, porcupine, Utah prairie dog, yellow belly marmot, Uinta chipmunk, and golden-mantled ground squirrel. Beaver live near the park on the East Fork of Sevier River. (Paunsaugunt is Paiute for "Home of the Beaver.") Despite the cool climate, you can find a few reptiles; look for the short-horned lizard, skink, and Great Basin rattlesnake. Birds appear in greatest numbers from May to October. Violet-green swallows and white-throated swifts dive and careen among the hoodoos in hot pursuit of flying insects. Other summer visitors are the golden eagle, red-tailed hawk, Western tanager, and mountain bluebird. Year-round residents include woodpeckers, owls, raven, Steller's jay, Clark's

hoodoo at Agua Canyon Overlook

nutcracker, and blue grouse. Although some wild creatures may seem quite tame, they must not be fed or handled—rodents may have diseases, and young deer contaminated with human scent might be abandoned by their mothers. Also, animals who become dependent on humans may die in winter when left to forage for themselves after the summer crowds have left.

History

Prehistoric Anasazi lived in the lower country surrounding Bryce and probably made frequent trips into what is now the park area to hunt game and gather piñon nuts and other wild foods. Nomadic groups of Paiute Indians later wandered into the area on seasonal migrations. Mormon pioneer Ebenezer Bryce homesteaded near the town site of Tropic in 1875, but the work of scratching a living from the rugged land became too hard. He left five years later for more promising areas in Arizona. The name of the park commemorates his efforts. He is remembered as saying, "Well, it's a hell of a place to lose a cow."

A later settler, Ruben "Ruby" Syrett, recognized the tourist potential of the area and opened the first small lodge near Sunset Point in 1919, then Ruby's Inn in 1924. Enthusiasm for the scenic beauty led to creation of Bryce Canyon National Monument in 1923. The name changed to Utah National Park in the following year, then took its current name in 1928. Tours organized by the Union Pacific Railroad, beginning in the late 1920s, made Bryce well known and easily visited.

Visitor Center

From the turnoff on UT 12, follow signs past Ruby's Inn to the park entrance; the visitors' center is a short distance farther on the right. A brief slide show, screened on request, introduces the park. Geologic exhibits illustrate how the land was formed and how it has changed. Historic displays interpret the Paiute Indians, early explorers, and the first settlers. Trees, flowers, and wildlife are identified. Rangers present a variety of naturalist programs, including short hikes, from mid-May to early September; see the posted schedule. Staff sell travel and natural history books, maps of the park and adjacent Dixie National Forest, posters, postcards, slides, and film. Open daily all year (except Christmas) 8 A.M.–4:30 P.M., with extended hours during the warmer months. Contact the park at Bryce Canyon, UT 84717, (435) 834-5322.

Special hazards you should be aware of include crumbly ledges and lightning strikes. People who have wandered off trails or gotten too close to the drop-offs have had to be pulled out by rope. Avoid cliffs and other exposed areas during electrical storms, which are most common in late summer.

Winter Visits

Try a visit during the winter, too. Snow on the rocks appears like frosting on a cake. The deep blue sky and crystal-clear air between storms make panoramas particularly inspiring. Roads and most viewpoints are plowed. Snowshoes (loaned free at the visitors' center) or cross-country skis (rented at Ruby's Inn) allow excursions into the backcountry. **Paria Ski Trail** (five-mile loop) and **Fairyland Ski Trail** (2.5-mile loop) are marked for snowshoers and cross-country skiers. A $5 backcountry permit is needed for overnight excursions.

SCENIC DRIVE

From elevations of about 8,000 feet near the visitors' center, the scenic drive gradually winds 1,100 feet higher to Rainbow Point. About midway you'll notice a change in the trees from largely ponderosa pine to spruce, fir, and aspen. On a clear day, you can enjoy vistas of more than 100 miles from many of the viewpoints. Because of parking shortages on the drive, trailers must be left at the visitors' center or campsite. Visitors wishing to see the rest of the viewpoints may choose to walk on the Rim Trail.

Fairyland Point

To reach the turnoff (just inside the park boundary), go north 0.8 mile from the visitors' center, then east one mile. Whimsical forms line Fairyland Canyon a short distance below. You can descend into the "fairyland" on the **Fairyland Loop Trail** or follow the **Rim Trail** for other panoramas.

Sunrise and Sunset Points

These overlooks are off to the left about one mile past the visitors' center; they're connected by a

a misty morning at Sunrise Point

half-mile paved section of the **Rim Trail.** Panoramas from each point take in large areas of Bryce Amphitheater and beyond. The lofty Aquarius and Table Cliff Plateaus rise along the skyline to the northeast; you can recognize the same colorful Claron Formation in cliffs that faulting has raised about 2,000 feet higher. **Queen's Garden Trail** from Sunrise Point and **Navajo Loop Trail** from Sunset Point provide different experiences within the amphitheater. **Sunrise Nature Center,** near the parking area for Sunrise Point, has book sales, a few exhibits, and ranger information.

Inspiration Point

Walk south three-quarters of a mile along the **Rim Trail** from Sunset Point or drive a bit more than a mile to see a fantastic maze of hoodoos in the "Silent City." Weathering along vertical joints has cut many rows of narrow gullies, some more than 200 feet deep.

Bryce Point

This overlook at the south end of Bryce Amphitheater has memorable views to the north and east. It's also the start for the **Rim, Peekaboo Loop,** and **Under-the-Rim Trails.** From the turnoff two miles south of the visitors' center, follow signs 2.1 miles in.

Paria View

Cliffs drop precipitously into the headwaters of Yellow Creek, a tributary of the Paria River. You can see a section of Under-the-Rim Trail winding up a hillside near the mouth of the amphitheater below. Distant views take in the Paria River Canyon, White Cliffs (of Navajo Sandstone), and Navajo Mountain. The plateau rim in the park forms a drainage divide. Precipitation falling west of the rim flows gently into the East Fork of Sevier River and the Great Basin; precipitation landing east of the rim rushes through deep canyons in the Pink Cliffs to the Paria River and on to the Colorado River and the Grand Canyon. Take the turnoff for Bryce Point, then keep right at the fork.

Farview Point

The sweeping panorama takes in a lot of geology. You can see levels of the Grand Staircase that include the Aquarius and Table Cliff Plateaus to the northeast, Kaiparowits Plateau to the east, and White Cliffs to the southeast. Look beyond the White Cliffs to see a section of the Kaibab Plateau that forms the north rim of the Grand Canyon in Arizona. The overlook is on the left nine miles south of the visitors' center.

Natural Bridge

This large feature lies just off the road on the left, 1.7 miles past Farview Point. The span is 54 feet wide and 95 feet high. Most likely it was formed by weathering from rain and freezing, rather than by stream erosion like a true natural bridge. Once the opening reached ground level, runoff began to enlarge the hole and to dig a gully through it.

Agua and Ponderosa Canyons

You can admire sheer cliffs and hoodoos from the Agua Canyon overlook on the left, 1.4 miles past Natural Bridge. With a little imagination, you might be able to pick out the Hunter and the Rabbit below. Ponderosa Canyon overlook, on the left 1.8 miles farther, offers a panorama similar to that at Farview Point.

Yovimpa Point and Rainbow Point

The land drops away in rugged canyons and fine views at the end of the scenic drive, 17 miles south of the visitors' center. At an elevation of 9,105 feet, this is the highest area of the park. Yovimpa and Rainbow Points lie only a short walk apart yet offer different vistas. **Bristlecone Loop Trail** is an easy one-mile loop from Rainbow Point to ancient bristlecone pines along the rim. **Riggs Spring Loop Trail** makes a good day hike; you can begin from either Yovimpa Point or Rainbow Point and descend into canyons in the southern area of the park. **Under-the-Rim Trail** starts from Rainbow Point and winds 22.5 miles to Bryce Point; day-hikers could make a 7.5-mile trip by using the Agua Canyon Connecting Trail and a car shuttle.

HIKING

Hikers enjoy close-up views of the wondrous erosional features. The approximately 61 miles of trails also add to an appreciation of the geology at Bryce. Most of the hiking is moderately difficult, with many ups and downs, but the paths are well graded and signed. Hikers not accustomed to the 7,000- to 9,000-foot elevations will find the going relatively strenuous and should allow extra time. A hat and sunscreen protect against sunburn, which can be a problem at these elevations. Don't forget rain gear because storms can come up suddenly. Always carry water for day trips as only a few natural sources exist. Ask at the visitors' center for current trail conditions and water sources; you can also pick up a free hiking map at the visitors' center. Snow may block some trail sections in winter and early spring. Overnight hikers can obtain the required backcountry permits at the visitors' center (camping is allowed only on the Under-the-Rim and Riggs Spring Loop Trails). Backpack stoves must be used for cooking, because open fires and wood gathering damage the natural environment. Horses are permitted only on Peekaboo Loop. Pets must stay above the rim; they're allowed on the Rim Trail only between Sunset and Sunrise Points. Don't expect much solitude during the summer on the popular Rim, Queen's Garden, Navajo, and Peekaboo Loop Trails. Fairyland Loop Trail is less used and the back-country trails are almost never crowded. September and October are the choice hiking months—the weather is best and the crowds smallest, though nighttime temperatures in late October can dip well below freezing.

Rim Trail

This easy trail follows the edge of Bryce Amphitheater for 5.5 miles between Fairyland Point and Bryce Point; elevation change is 540 feet. Most people walk just sections in leisurely strolls or use the trail to connect with five others. The half-mile section near the lodge between Sunrise and Sunset Points is paved and nearly level; other parts are gently rolling.

Fairyland Loop Trail

The trail winds in and out of colorful rock spires in the northern part of Bryce Amphitheater. Though it's well graded, remember the 900-foot climb you'll make when you exit. You can take a loop hike of eight miles from either Fairyland Point or Sunrise Point by using a section of the **Rim Trail;** a car shuttle saves three hiking miles. The whole loop is too long for many visitors, who enjoy short trips down and back to see this "fairyland."

Queen's Garden Trail

A favorite of many people, this trail drops from Sunrise Point through impressive features in the middle of Bryce Amphitheater to a hoodoo resembling a portly Queen Victoria. The hike is 1.5 miles round-trip and has an elevation change of 320 feet, which you'll have to climb on the way back. This is the easiest excursion below the rim and takes about 1.5 hours. Queen's Garden Trail also makes a good loop hike with **Navajo** and **Rim** Trails; most people who do the loop prefer to descend the steeper Navajo and climb out on Queen's Garden Trail for a 3.5-mile hike. Trails also connect with the **Peekaboo Loop Trail** and go to the town of Tropic.

Navajo Loop Trail

From Sunset Point, you'll drop 520 feet in three quarters of a mile through a narrow canyon. At the bottom, the loop leads into deep, dark **Wall Street**—an even narrower canyon a half-mile long—then returns to the rim; total distance is about 1.5 miles. Other destinations from the bottom of Navajo Trail are **Twin Bridges, Queen's**

Garden Trail, Peekaboo Loop Trail, and the town of Tropic. The 1.5-mile trail to Tropic isn't as scenic as the other trails, but it does provide another way to enter or leave the park; ask at the visitors' center or in Tropic for directions to the trailhead.

Peekaboo Loop Trail

An enchanting walk full of surprises at every turn—and there are lots of turns! The trail is in the southern part of Bryce Amphitheater, which has some of the most striking rock features. You can start from Bryce Point (6.5 miles round-trip), from Sunset Point (5.5 miles round-trip via Navajo Trail), or from Sunrise Point (seven miles round-trip via Queen's Garden Trail). The loop itself is 3.5 miles long with many ups and downs and a few tunnels. Elevation change is 500–800 feet, depending on the trailhead you choose.

Under-the-Rim Trail

The longest trail in the park winds 22.5 miles below the Pink Cliffs between Bryce Point in the north and Rainbow Point in the south. Allow at least two days to hike the entire trail; elevation change is about 1,500 feet with many ups and downs. Four connecting trails from the scenic drive allow you to travel Under-the-Rim Trail as a series of day hikes, too. Another option is to combine Under-the-Rim and **Riggs Spring Loop** Trails for a total of 31.5 miles.

The **Hat Shop** of delicate spires capped by erosion-resistant rock makes a good day-hiking destination; begin at Bryce Point and follow Under-the-Rim Trail for about two miles. Most of this section is downhill (elevation change of 900 feet), which you'll have to climb on the way out.

Bristlecone Loop Trail

The easy one-mile loop begins from either Rainbow or Yovimpa Point and goes to viewpoints and ancient bristlecone pines along the rim. These hardy trees survive fierce storms and extremes of hot and cold that no other tree can. Some of the bristlecone pines here are 1,700 years old.

Riggs Spring Loop

One of the park's more challenging day hikes or a leisurely overnighter, this trail begins from either Yovimpa Point or Rainbow Point and descends into canyons in the southern area of the park.

The loop is about nine miles long with an elevation change of 1,625 feet. A shortcut bypassing Riggs Spring saves three quarters of a mile.

Mossy Cave Trail

This easy trail near the east edge of the park goes up Water Canyon to a cool alcove of dripping water and moss. Sheets of ice and icicles add beauty to the scene in winter. The hike is only one mile round-trip with a small elevation gain. A side trail, just before the cave, branches right a short distance to a little waterfall; look for several small arches in the colorful canyon walls above. Although the park lacks perennial natural streams, the stream in Water Canyon flows even during dry spells. Mormon pioneers labored three years to channel water from the East Fork of the Sevier River through a canal and down this wash to the town of Tropic. Without this irrigation, the town might not even exist. From the visitors' center, return to UT 12 and turn east 3.7 miles toward Escalante; the parking area is on the right just after a bridge (between Mileposts 17 and 18). Rangers schedule guided walks to the cave and the waterfall during the main season.

ACCOMMODATIONS

Travelers can have a hard time finding accommodations and campsites from April to October in both the park and nearby areas. Advance reservations at lodges and motels are a good idea; otherwise, plan to arrive by late morning. Bryce Canyon Lodge is the only lodging in the park itself—you'll need to make reservations months in advance to get a room in this historic landmark. Fortunately, the NPS also runs two campgrounds in the park. Park campgrounds operate on a first-come, first-served basis; arrive by noon in the main season to be assured of a spot.

Reach the **Bryce Canyon Information Line,** an area motel reservation service, at (800) 444-6689.

Under $50

There aren't many inexpensive places to stay around the gates of the park. However, there are a few hostel-type rooms available for under $20 at the **Bryce Canyon Resort,** near the turnoff for the park, (435) 834-5351 or (800) 834-0043. (Linens and towel provided.)

Bryce Canyon Lodge

W.C. McRAE

$75–100

Bryce Canyon Lodge: Set among ponderosa pines a short walk from the rim, **Bryce Canyon Lodge** was built in 1923 by a division of the Union Pacific Railway; a spur line once terminated at the front entrance. The lodge has lots of charm and is listed on the National Historic Registry. It also has by far the best location of any Bryce-area accommodation.

You have a choice of motel rooms and Western cabins starting at $88, or a lodge suite ($108); open Apr. 1–Nov. 1. The lodge organizes horseback rides, park tours, evening entertainment, and ranger talks; a gift shop sells souvenirs.

Try to make reservations for accommodations as far in advance as possible (eight months advised) with AMFAC Parks & Resorts, 14001 E. Iliff Ave., Ste. 600, Aurora, CO 80014, (650) 372-1705 or (435) 834-5351 (Bryce Canyon Lodge), in-season. You can also make reservations at the website, www.amfac.com.

Ruby's Inn: The large, resort-like **Best Western Ruby's Inn** offers many year-round services on UT 63 just north of the park boundary (Bryce, UT 84764), (435) 834-5341 or (800) 468-8660. The hotel features two indoor pools and a spa; rooms start just under $100. Kitchenettes and family rooms are also available; pets are okay. Ruby's Inn is more than just a place to stay, however. This is one of the area's major centers for all manner of recreational outfitters, dining, entertainment, and shopping.

The **general store** has a large stock of groceries, camping and fishing supplies, film and processing, Indian crafts, books, and other souvenirs. The **Bryce post office** is at the store, too. Horseback rides, helicopter tours, and airplane rides are arranged in the lobby (see Recreation, below). In winter, cross-country skiers can rent gear and use trails located near the inn as well as in the park. Snowmobile trails are available (snowmobiles may not be used within the park). Western-fronted shops across from Ruby's Inn offer trail rides, chuck wagon dinners, mountain-bike rentals, souvenirs, and a petting farm. **Rodeos** take place in the nearby arena nightly Monday–Saturday in-season.

Red Canyon Area: Other hotels are clustered on UT 12, right outside the park boundary. Many of these are have seen a lot of use over the years, usually without a lot of attendant upkeep. Prices will range between $80–100 per night. One of the newest lodgings is the **Bryce View Lodge,** near the park turnoff, (435) 834-5180 or (888) 279-2304, with rooms in handsome lodge-like structures. At **Bryce Canyon Resort,** near the turnoff for the park, (435) 834-5351 or (800) 834-0043, rooms in the main wing start at just under $100 a night. Rooms in the old building start are about $20 cheaper, with cabins cheaper still. Six miles west of the park turnoff, **Bryce Canyon Pines Motel,** (435) 834-5441 or (800) 892-7923, has mid-priced rooms, a seasonal covered pool, and a restaurant open daily for breakfast, lunch, and dinner from early April to late October.

Farther west of the park, at U.S. 89 and UT 12 junction, the **Bryce Junction Inn,** (435) 676-2221 or (800) 437-4361, is a standard motel open March 15–October 30.

Tropic, just 11 miles east of the park entrance, is a good spot to seek out lodgings if the best options at Bryce are taken and what's available isn't to your taste. See Vicinity of Bryce National Park, below.

Campgrounds

The park's two **campgrounds** both have water, some pull-through spaces, and cost $10. Try to arrive early for a space during the busy summer season, as both campgrounds usually fill by 1 or 2 P.M. and only group areas may be reserved. **North Campground** is on the left just past the visitors' center. **Sunset Campground** is about 2.5 miles farther on the right, across the road from Sunset Point. Sunset has campsites accessible to people with disabilities.

Groceries, camping supplies, and coin-operated showers and laundry are available mid-May–late September at the **General Store,** between North Campground and Sunrise Point. During the rest of the year, you can go outside the park to Ruby's Inn for these services.

The Dixie National Forest has three Forest Service **campgrounds** located in scenic settings among ponderosa pines. Often they'll have room when campgrounds in the park itself have filled. Group sites can be reserved, but the rest are available on a first-come, first-served basis. All sites have water and cost $7–9. **Pine Lake Campground** lies at 7,700 feet just east of Pine Lake in a forest of ponderosa pine, spruce, and juniper. Sites are open mid-June–mid-September. From the highway junction north of the park, head northeast 11 miles on UT 63 (gravel), then turn southeast six miles. **King Creek Campground** is located on the west shore of Tropic Reservoir, which has a boat ramp and fair trout fishing. Sites are at 8,000 feet and are usually open May–late September. Head seven miles south of UT 12 down the gravel East Fork Sevier River Road, located 2.8 miles west of the park turnoff. To reach **Red Canyon Campground,** turn off UT 12 four miles east of U.S. 89. It's located at 7,400 feet, below brilliantly colored cliffs, and stays open from late May to late September. Contact the Powell Ranger District office in Pan-

guitch, (435) 676-8815, for more information on Kings and Red Canyon Campgrounds and at the Escalante Ranger District office in Escalante, (435) 826-5400, for Pine Lake.

Private campgrounds in the area are $20 and above a night. The **Ruby's Inn Campground,** at the park junction, (435) 834-5301, is open from early April to late October with spaces for tents and RVs; showers and laundry are open all year. All the considerable facilities at Ruby's are available to camping patrons. The **Bryce Canyon Pines Campground,** four miles west of the park entrance, (435) 834-5441 or (800) 892-7923, has an indoor pool, game room, groceries, and shady sites.

OTHER PRACTICALITIES

Food

The dining room at the **Bryce Canyon Lodge,** (435) 586-9476 offers a varied menu with moderate prices; open daily in season for breakfast, lunch, and dinner (reservations advised for dinner). With 12 hours advance notice, you can order a box lunch.

The Ruby's Inn's **Canyon Diner,** (435) 834-5341, is one of Bryce Canyon's better restaurants; open for breakfast, lunch, and dinner daily. Casual lunch and dinner fare is served in the inn's snack bar April–October. Also check at Ruby's for seasonal chuck wagon meals, accompanied by singers and Western entertainment. **Bryce Canyon Resort,** near the turnoff for the park, (435) 834-5351 or (800) 834-0043, has an on-site restaurant that features steak and barbecue and is open daily for breakfast, lunch, and dinner. Two miles west of the park turnoff is **Foster's,** (435) 834-5227, a long-standing institution with old-fashioned diner food.

Recreation and Sight-Seeing

Ruby's Inn is a good place to take measure of the opportunities for organized recreation and sight-seeing excursions in and around Bryce Canyon. The lobby is filled with outfitters anxious to take you out on the trail; you'll find each of the following there, along with other vendors who organize hayrides, barn dances, and chuck wagon dinners. **Red Canyon Horseback Rides,** (800) 468-8660, has horseback riding near Bryce

Canyon from May to October. There's a choice of half ($40) and whole ($75 including lunch) day trips. Shorter rides (as well as half- and full-day trips) are offered by **Scenic Rim Trail Rides,** (435) 834-5341 ext. 217, which also operates out of Ruby's. An hour long ride is $19. Ruby's also sponsors a rodeo nightly Monday–Saturday at 7 P.M. across from the inn.

You can also explore the area around Bryce Canyon on a more up-to-date kind of steed. Guided ATV tours of Red Canyon are offered by **Great Western ATV,** (345) 834-5200 or (800) 432-5383. A one-hour trip is $28, a three-hour trip is $69.

If you'd like to get a look at Bryce and the surrounding area from the air, you can choose to take a scenic flight-seeing tour from **Bryce Canyon Airlines,** (435) 834-5341, which offers both plane and helicopter tours. There's quite a range of options, ranging from a 15-minute trip to a nearby mesa ($35) to a 2.5-hour trip that takes in the Grand Canyon ($295).

In winter, snow carpets the high elevations and Bryce Canyon becomes a haven for cross-country skiers. **Ruby's Inn Nordic Center,** (435) 843-5341, grooms more than 30 kilometers of trails beside the park, and trails within the park itself remain open, though they are not groomed.

VICINITY OF BRYCE CANYON NATIONAL PARK

RED CANYON

The drive on UT 12 between U.S. 89 and the turnoff for Bryce Canyon National Park passes through this well-named canyon. You may think that it should have been included in the national park, as the brightly colored rocks belong to the same Claron Formation that's exposed at Bryce. However, because its not part of the park, the trails at Red Canyon are open to kinds of recreation that is prohibited in the park, principally mountain biking and ATV riding. In fact, this canyon is becoming very popular as other Utah mountain-biking destinations become over-popularized. However, many trails are restricted to foot traffic.

Staff at **Red Canyon Visitor Center** can tell you about the trails, as well as scenic backcountry roads, that wind through the area; books and maps are sold; open daily about 8 A.M.–6 P.M. during the warmer months; located between Mileposts 3 and 4 on UT 12, a quarter mile west of Red Canyon Campground. You can contact the Powell Ranger District office in Panguitch for information year-round, (435) 676-8815. (For details about Red Canyon Campground, see the Accommodations section under Bryce Canyon National Park, above.)

Hiking

The U.S. Forest Service has many scenic hiking trails that wind back from the highway to give you a closer look at the geology. The following are open to hikers only. **Pink Ledges Trail,** the easiest and most popular, loops a half-mile past intriguing erosional features from Red Canyon Visitor Center. Signs identify some of the trees and plants; elevation gain is 100 feet. **Birdseye Trail** winds through formations and connects the visitors' center with a parking area on UT 12 just inside the forest boundary, 0.8 mile away. **Buckhorn Trail** begins from Site #23 in Red Canyon Campground and climbs one mile for views of erosional forms and Red Canyon; the

campground is on the south side of UT 12 between Mileposts 3 and 4. **Tunnel Trail** ascends 300 feet in 0.7 mile for fine views of the canyon. The trail begins from a pullout on the south side of UT 12 just west of a pair of tunnels, crosses the streambed, then climbs a ridge to viewpoints on the top. Ask at the visitors' center for other good area trails worth exploring.

Mountain Biking

The primary allure in Red Canyon for gear heads is the **Casto Canyon Trail,** a 17-mile one-way trail that winds through a variety of unique red rock formations and forest. The route starts and ends along Highway 12; If you don't have a shuttle vehicle at each of the trailheads, you'll need to peddle back another eight miles along the highway to retrieve your vehicle. Start at Tom Best Road, just east of Red Canyon. You'll climb up through forest turning onto Berry Spring Creek Road and then Cabin Hollow Road. When the trail starts heading into Casto Canyon, you'll have five downhill miles of wonderful red rock scenery. When you reach the Casto Canyon Trailhead, you can choose to return to Highway 12, or you can pedal out to Highway 89 and Panguitch. Much of the trail is quite strenuous, and you'll need to take water along; there's no source along the way. There are several sidetrails along the way to make this into a shorter ride; see the Forest Service brochure on Red Canyon trails.

POWELL POINT

Even in a state with many superb viewpoints, Powell Point (elev. 10,188 feet) is outstanding. Yet surprisingly few people know about this lofty perch at the southern tip of the Table Cliff Plateau, a southwestern extension of the Aquarius Plateau. Its light-colored cliffs stand about 15 air miles northeast of Sunset Point in Bryce Canyon National Park. Getting to Powell Point involves a bit of adventure. You can drive a car with good clearance within 4.3 miles of the point;

high-clearance vehicles can go to within 0.6 mile. From the highway junction north of the national park, drive northeast 11 miles on UT 63 (gravel), turn southeast six miles to Pine Lake, continue east six miles on Forest Route 132 up onto the plateau, then look for the one-lane dirt road on the right to Powell Point; high-clearance vehicles can turn in 3.7 miles to the Powell Point trailhead. If you're not equipped for driving this rough road, you'll still find it good for hiking or mountain biking. The road ends where the ridge becomes too narrow for it; a clearing here is fine for camping (no facilities).

A foot trail continues 0.6 mile to the very end of Powell Point. On the way you'll pass through an extremely weather-beaten and picturesque forest of bristlecone and limber pine. Panoramic views begin well before trail's end; at the point itself you'll feel as though you're at the end of the world. Much of southern Utah and northern Arizona stretches out below to the far horizon. The colorful cliffs of the Claron Formation lie directly underfoot; take care near the crumbly cliff edges. Avoid Powell Point if thunderstorms threaten. (Note the many lightning scars on trees here!) The **Escalante Ranger District office** may have current road conditions to Powell Point, (435) 826-5400.

TROPIC

Mormon pioneers settled six villages near the upper Paria River between 1876 and 1891. The towns of Tropic, Cannonville, and Henrieville still survive. Tropic lies just 11 miles east of Bryce Canyon National Park, visible from many of the park's viewpoints. Travelers think of Tropic primarily for its cache of motels lining Main Street (UT 12); a number of pleasant B&Bs also grace the town. A **log cabin** built by Ebenezer Bryce has been moved to a site beside the Bryce Pioneer Village Motel; ask to see the cabin's small collection of pioneer and Indian artifacts. A **tourist booth** in the center of town is open daily about 11 A.M.–7 P.M. from early May to late October.

Accommodations
$50–75: For a place to stay, **Doug's Place Country Inn,** (435) 679-8600 or (800) 993-6847, has basic motel rooms, a restaurant, and a store.

Bryce Valley Inn, (435) 679-8811 or (800) 442-1890, has rooms in an attractive wood-fronted, Western-look motel, restaurant, and a gift shop. Pets okay with fee. On the south end of town, **Bryce Pioneer Village Motel,** (435) 679-8546 or (800) 222-0381, has motel rooms plus a number of brand new cabins (one with kitchen); there's also a campground. Also new are the **Bryce Country Cabins,** 80 S. Main St., (435) 679-8643 or (888) 679-8643. The cabins overlook a meadow, and each has a private bath. Open Mar. 1–Oct. 31. A half-mile south of town is the log-cabin style **Francisco's Farm Bed & Breakfast,** 51 Francisco Ln., (435) 679-8721 or (800) 642-4136, which offers rooms in a farmhouse, all with private baths.

$75–100: There are also a number of very nice B&Bs in Tropic. Located a few blocks from the highway, **Bryce Point Bed & Breakfast,** 61 N. 400 West, (435) 679-8629, is a large modern home with very nice rooms, all with private baths, TVs and VCRs, and views out every window. All rooms have private entrances. There's also a guest cabin. The **Bullberry Inn B&B,** (435) 679-8820, is a very attractive B&B with wrap-around porches, and guest rooms with private baths and rustic-style furniture. At **Canyon Livery B&B,** 660 W. 50 S., (435) 679-8780 or (888) 889-8910, every room has a private bath, balcony, and views of Bryce Canyon.

Food
Hoo-Doos Restaurant is part of Doug's Place Country Inn, (435) 679-8632, and serves Mexican food, Texas-style barbecue, and steaks. It's open for breakfast, lunch, and dinner daily. Licensed for liquor. The **Hungry Coyote Restaurant,** at the Bryce Valley Inn, (435) 679-8811, has a liquor-licensed restaurant with an outdoor mesquite barbecue. Open for three meals daily.

KODACHROME BASIN STATE PARK

Visitors come to this basin southeast of Bryce Canyon National Park to see not only colorful cliffs but also strange-looking rock pillars that occur nowhere else in the world. Sixty-seven rock pillars (here called sand pipes) found in and near the park range in height from six to nearly 170 feet. One theory of their origin is that earthquakes caused sediments deep underground to be churned up by water under high pressure. The particles of calcite, quartz, feldspar, and clay in the sand pipes came from underlying rock formations, and the pipes appeared when the surrounding rock eroded away. Most of the other rocks visible in the park are Entrada Sandstone: the lower orange layer is the Gunsight Butte Member and the white layer with orange bands is the Cannonville Member. Signs name some of the rock features. "Big Stoney," the phallus-shaped sand pipe overlooking the campground, is so explicit that it doesn't need a sign! An article, "Motoring into Escalante Land," by Jack Breed in the September 1949 issue of *National Geographic,* brought attention to the scenery and renamed the area "Kodachrome Flat." The state park makes a worthwhile stop, both as a day trip to see the geology and as a pleasant spot to camp. A $4 per-vehicle day-use fee is charged.

To reach the park, drive to Cannonville (on UT 12, 12 miles southeast of the Bryce Canyon National Park turnoff and 36 miles southwest of Escalante) and follow signs south and east for nine miles on paved roads. Adventurous drivers can also approach the park from U.S. 89 to the south via the Cottonwood Canyon road (39 miles) or the Skutumpah road through Bull Valley Gorge and Johnson Canyon (48 miles). These routes may be impassable in wet weather but may be okay for cars with good clearance in dry weather; ask about current conditions at Kanab, Paria Ranger Station (on U.S. 89 near Milepost 21), or the visitors' center at Glen Canyon Dam.

Campground
The state park's campground sits in a natural amphitheater at an elevation of 5,800 feet. It's open all year, has restrooms, showers, a dump station, and sites for $12. During the winter restrooms and showers may close but pit toilets are available. The campground usually has room except on summer holidays. For information or reservations, contact the park at P.O. Box 238, Cannonville, UT 84718, (435) 679-8562 or (800) 322-3770 (reservations).

Hiking Trails
The short **Nature Trail** introduces the park's ecology. **Panorama Trail** loops through a highly scenic valley with sand pipes and colorful rocks; the easy trail is three miles round-trip and takes about two hours. **Angel's Palace Trail** begins just east of the group campground and makes a three-quarter-mile loop with fine views; elevation gain is about 300 feet. **Grand Parade Trail** makes a 1.5-mile loop with good views of rock pinnacles; begin from the concession stand or group campground. **Eagles View Trail,** a historic cattle trail, climbs nearly 1,000 feet up steep cliffs above the campground, then drops into Henrieville, two miles away; the highest overlook is a steep half-mile ascent from the campground. **Arch Trail** is a half-mile round-trip hike to a natural arch; access the trailhead by a signed dirt road or a two-mile (round-trip) trail; a brochure and numbered stops identify local plants.

Horseback Riding
Scenic Safaris operates guided horseback and horse-drawn coach rides in the park. You can arrange rides at **Trailhead Station,** a small store in the park that sells groceries and camping supplies from about early April to late October, or contact P.O. Box 278, Cannonville, UT 84718, (435) 679-8536 or (435) 679-8787.

SOUTH OF KODACHROME BASIN STATE PARK

Several highly scenic canyon systems cut deep into the plateaus south of Kodachrome Basin. The book *Hiking and Exploring the Paria River,* by Michael Kelsey, outlines some of the hiking possibilities in the region. The area between Kodachrome Basin and Highway 89 is now all part of the **Grand Staircase–Escalante National Monument,** and while the land will remain open to hikers, mountain bikers, and back road explorers, there may soon be restrictions on ATVs and dirt bikes. Check road conditions and current restrictions with the monument offices at Escalante, (435) 826-5499 or at the Kanab headquarters, (435) 644-2672. Spring and autumn are the best hiking seasons, when you'll avoid the desert extremes found in winter and summer. Gnats and biting flies can be troublesome from late May into July; bring repellent and long pants.

Cottonwood Canyon and Grosvenor Arch

The road from Cannonville continues past the turnoff to Kodachrome Basin State Park and drops into the upper reaches of Cottonwood Creek (a tributary of the Paria River) and follows it for about 15 miles. Total distance on this scenic drive between Cannonville and U.S. 89 is 46 miles one-way, nearly all of which is dirt. If coming from the south, look for the turnoff on U.S. 89 between Mileposts 17 and 18. Cars with good clearance can do the trip any time of year if the road is dry. Be especially cautious if any of the washes contain water—cars sometimes get stuck in them. When wet, the road is slippery and hazardous even with four-wheel-drive vehicles. Check current conditions at Kodachrome Basin State Park, Paria Ranger Station (on U.S. 89 near Milepost 21), Kanab, or the visitors' center at Glen Canyon Dam. A one-mile side road leads to the magnificent Grosvenor Arch; the largest of the two openings is 99 feet across. The 1949 National Geographic Society Expedition named the double arch in honor of the society's president. The turnoff is 10 miles from the state park turnoff and 29 miles from U.S. 89.

Hackberry Canyon

Hikers can travel the 18-mile length of this scenic canyon in two to three days. The headwaters lie just south of the Cottonwood Canyon road between Kodachrome Basin State Park and Grosvenor Arch at an elevation of about 6,000 feet. The lower canyon meets Cottonwood Canyon at an elevation of 4,700 feet. The Cottonwood Canyon road provides access to both ends. A small spring-fed stream flows down the lower half of Hackberry. Many side canyons invite exploration. One of them, Sam Pollock Canyon, is on the west about 4.5 miles upstream from the junction of Hackberry and Cottonwood Canyons; follow it 1.75 miles up to **Sam Pollock Arch** (60 feet high and 70 feet wide). Available topo maps include the metric 1:100,000 Smoky Mountain or the 7½-minute Slickrock Bench and Calico Peak. Michael Kelsey's *Hiking and Exploring the Paria River* contains trail and trailhead information and a history of the Watson homestead, located a short way below Sam Pollock Canyon.

Upper Paria River Canyon

Although not as well known as the lower canyon, the upper section has some beautiful scenery and offers many side canyons to explore, too. The Paria lies west of both Hackberry and Cottonwood Canyons. Access to the upper end is from the Skutumpah or Cottonwood Canyon Road near Kodachrome Basin State Park (elev. about 5,900 feet). The usual lower entry is from near Pahreah ghost town (elev. 4,720 feet); turn north six miles from U.S. 89 between Mileposts 30 and 31 and continue past the Pahreah movie set to road's end. (The clay road surface is very slippery when wet but is okay for cars when dry.) The upper canyon is about 25 miles long, and the hike takes 3–4 days (allowing some time to explore side canyons). You can find water at springs along the main canyon and in many side canyons (purify first); try not to use water from the river itself as it may contain chemical pollution. Topo maps are the metric 1:100,000 Kanab and Smoky Mountain or the 7½-minute Cannonville, Bull Valley Gorge, Deer Range Point, and Calico Peak. Again, Michael Kelsey's *Hiking and Exploring the Paria River* is a good source of history and hiking information for this area.

ALONG U.S. 89: PANGUITCH TO KANAB

PANGUITCH

Pioneers arrived in 1864, but hostile Ute Indians forced evacuation just two years later. A second attempt by settlers in 1871 succeeded, and Panguitch (Big Fish) is now the largest town in the area.

Panguitch is one of the more pleasant towns in this part of Utah, and there are an abundance of reasonably priced motels, and a couple good places to eat. It's also a good hub for exploring the many scenic highlights of south-central Utah.

The early 20th-century commercial buildings downtown have some of their original facades. On side streets you can see sturdy brick houses built by the early settlers. Stop by the **Daughters of Utah Pioneers Museum** in the old bishop's storehouse at 100 East and Center to see historic exhibits of Panguitch; open Mon.–Sat. about

wooden Indian in front of a Panguitch store

4–8 P.M. in summer and by appointment the rest of the year; phone numbers to volunteers are on the door.

The **Paunsagaunt Wildlife Museum,** 250 East Center St., (435) 676-2500, in the old Panguitch public school, is a taxidermy collection of more than 400 animals from western North America displayed in dioramas resembling their natural habitats. There are also displays of stuffed animals from Africa, India, and Europe. It's actually quite well done, and kids seem to love it. There's also a good collection of Native American artifacts. Admission is $4 adult, $2.50 children 6–12.

Accommodations
$50–75: Pets are okay at both the **Blue Pine Motel,** 130 N. Main St., (435) 676-8197 or (800) 299-6115, and the **Bryce Way Motel,** 429 N. Main St., (435) 676-2400 or (800) 225-6534; the latter has a heated indoor pool. The **Color Country Motel,** 526 N. Main St., (435) 676-2386 or (800) 225-6518, has an outdoor pool and very

clean and well-maintained rooms. The **Panguitch Inn Motel,** 50 N. Main St., (435) 676-8871 or (800) 331-7407, is open seasonally May–October. The **Adobe Sands,** (435) 676-8874 or (800) 497-9261, has both regular guest rooms with all the usual touches, plus a dozen economy rooms if you're traveling on a budget.

$75–100: Along U.S. 89, the **New West Best Western,** 180 E. Center St., (435) 676-8876 or (800) 528-1234, has a swimming pool and hot tub, plus laundry facilities. Another well-maintained motor inn is the **Canyon Lodge,** 210 North Main, (435) 676-8292 or (800) 440-8292.

Seven miles south of Panguitch, at the junction of Highways 89 and 12 is a large new development called the **Western Town Resort,** (435) 676-8770 or (888) 687-4339. The resort looks like a vintage frontier town, with trading posts, country stores, and stables, but most of the buildings, in fact, offer motel accommodations. The resort is in the process of becoming a full-service resort, with an emphasis on recreation and the lore of the Old West. Guided mountain bike and horseback rides are offered, as well as pack trips. Western culture events are common, including country and Western musical entertainment and cowboy and Indian poetry evenings. The resort also offers a saloon and dance hall, swimming pool, and a restaurant.

Campgrounds: Open year-round, **Hitch-N-Post Campground,** 420 N. Main, (435) 676-2436, offers spaces for tents ($10) and RVs ($17 with hookups) and has showers and laundry. **Big Fish KOA Campground,** 555 S. Main, (435) 676-2225, on the road to Panguitch Lake is open April 1–October 31 with a pool, recreation room, laundry, and showers; $20 tents and RVs without hookups, $21.50 for RVs with hookups.

Food
Buffalo Java, 47 N. Main St., (435) 767-8900, serves pastries, bagels, and real espresso drinks. The **Flying M Restaurant,** 580 N Main, (435) 676-8008, is a favorite for hearty breakfast and standard American fare. For more hearty steaks and burgers, try **Cowboy's Smokehouse Bar-B-Q,** 95 N. Main St., (435) 676-8030. Traditional Italian favorites, with a number of vegetarian options, are dished up at **Grandma Tina's Spaghetti House,** 523 N. Main St., (435) 676-2377. The specialty at the **Wild Bunch Restaurant,** at

Western Town Resort seven miles south of Panguitch is Dutch-oven cooking.

Events and Recreation

Major annual events include **Fourth of July** celebrations (parade, fireworks, and FFA junior rodeo in town; fireworks at Panguitch Lake), **Pioneer Day** on July 24 (parade and rodeo), and **Garfield County Livestock Show and Fair** in mid-August. The **city park** on the north edge of town has picnic tables, a playground, tennis courts, and a tourist information cabin. A **swimming pool** is at 250 E. Center by the high school, (435) 676-2259.

Services and Information

The **post office** is at 65 N. 100 West, (435) 676-8853. **Garfield Memorial Hospital** provides medical services at 224 N. 400 East, (435) 676-8811 (hospital), (435) 676-8842 (clinic). The **information center** in the city park, (435) 676-8131 or (800) 444-6689 (Bryce Canyon Information Line), offers brochures and suggestions for services in Panguitch and travel to Bryce Canyon National Park and other scenic destinations nearby; open daily 9 A.M.–5 P.M. from early May to late Oct.; closed in winter. Contact the **Garfield County Travel Council** year-round at P.O. Box 200, Panguitch, UT 84759, (435) 676-8421. The **Powell Ranger District office** of the U.S. Forest Service has information on campgrounds, hiking trails, fishing, and scenic drives in the forest and canyons surrounding Bryce Canyon National Park; open Mon.–Fri. 8 A.M.–4:30 P.M. at 225 E. Center (U.S. 89) or write P.O. Box 80, Panguitch, UT 84759, (435) 676-8815. The **public library** is at 25 S. 200 East (across the street from the Forest Service office), (435) 676-2431.

HATCH

The Hatch family started a ranch in the upper Sevier River Valley during the early 1870s. Colorful cliffs of the Paunsaugunt Plateau contrast with the blue sky to the east. Stop in at the **Daughters of Utah Pioneers Museum** to learn about the pioneers and see their artifacts; it's usually open summer afternoons (except Sun.), or you can call the telephone numbers posted on the front door to reach a volunteer; turn west one block at the sign in the center of town. **Garfield Information Center,** just south of town, is open daily 9 A.M.–5 P.M. from early May to late October with literature and advice for travel in Garfield County.

Accommodations

Under $50: None of the following places is fancy by any stretch of the imagination, but they are a good value. **New Bryce Motel,** 227 North Main, (435) 735-4265, has an on-site restaurant. It's open about mid-March–late November. **Dream Catcher Motel,** 216 N Main, (435) 735-4098, also has a café (open daily for breakfast, lunch, and dinner) and basic rooms; open late Mar.–Sept. **Riverside Motel and Campground** is just north of town, (435) 735-4223 or (800) 824-5651, and has sites for tents and RVs year-round; it also offers a store, laundry, showers and trout fishing in the Sevier River.

Mammoth Creek Hatchery

This is one of about 11 state hatcheries producing trout and other game fish. You're welcome to visit during daylight hours. Indoor areas house the eggs and fry; larger fish swim in the outdoor raceways. Go one mile south of Hatch on U.S. 89 and turn west two miles on a paved road at the sign. An unpaved road continues to Mammoth Cave and other attractions on the Markagunt Plateau.

LONG VALLEY

Highway U.S. 89 follows the East Fork of the Virgin River past a series of small Mormon towns north of Kanab. Nearly all travelers visiting the national parks of the region will pass through this forested valley. Most of the towns in Long Valley offer a handful of motels, campgrounds, and restaurants.

Long Valley Junction

The junction (elev. 7,200 feet) marks the divide between the East Fork of the Virgin River to the south and the Sevier River to the north. Turn west on UT 14 to visit Cedar Breaks National Monument and the alpine country of the Markagunt Plateau. Continue south 13 miles for Glendale or north 13 miles on U.S. 89 for Hatch.

Glendale

The original settlers named their community Berryville in 1864. A small fort helped protect against Navajo raids, but continued Indian troubles forced all the valley's inhabitants to leave by 1866. A new group arrived in 1871 and renamed the site Glendale after the town in Scotland.

Orderville

Orderville began as an experiment in communal life in 1875 as part of the Mormon United Order.

Everyone worked on cooperative farms and industries, divided income according to need, shared meals at a common table, and met twice daily for worship. The experiment succeeded admirably for about 10 years, longer than in any other Mormon town. A combination of internal disagreements and external pressures eventually convinced community leaders to end the United Order and to return its property to private ownership. The **Orderville DUP Museum** contains pioneer artifacts; open on request (call

THE UNITED ORDER OF ENOCH

The United Order of Enoch was an attempt by Brigham Young to remedy several ills caused by an economic boom in the church community. The arrival of the railroad had brought some forms of prosperity to the Mormons, especially in allowing the development of mining. But the railroad also brought in a rougher class of folk who had no intention of emulating the quiet, industrious lifestyle of the Mormons, and it allowed the import of commercially produced goods at cheaper prices than could be had locally. Both factors spelled trouble for a church seeking self-sufficiency.

As Joseph Smith had envisioned in his Law of Consecration, the United Order was proposed as a policy of communal living in which members would commit all their privately owned goods toward a common end. Many members had surrendered their property in the early days of the church, but the troubled times the church found in the east had thwarted the success of true communal villages. In the 1870s, church leaders felt the time had come.

When Brigham Young reactivated the United Order, it took life in several forms. The earliest and one of the most successful was the Brigham City Cooperative (BCC), started by Lorenzo Snow in 1864. BCC was a cooperative general store that met with great success, expanding over the years to 40 departments. The store was run on investments by voluntary members who received dividends based on their contributions. So successful was this venture that its business was barely touched by the Panic of 1873.

Branches of the order offered full communal living in which members ate in a communal dining hall, wore uniform clothing, and worked in community-owned facilities. In such a commune, all private possessions were surrendered upon membership. The most successful commune of this type may have been Or-

derville, where travel-weary settlers went about living the United Order in its most idealistic form.

Orderville's effort was largely a success, but citizens from surrounding communities openly scoffed at the spartan life of the commune. Mormon children were gradually swayed by the taunts of their peers, which led to a "trouser rebellion." One story tells of a Mormon youth who sought permission and money to buy pants more fashionable than the standard communal issue. When he was denied on the grounds that his present pair was still serviceable, he took to work, earned the money himself, and promptly purchased a pair in the fashionable store-bought style. He was taken before the commune's elected board, which lauded his enterprise but decreed that every youth had to have the new pants or no one would. It was considered wasteful to replace pants that were still wearable, so youngsters were soon busy at the community grindstone wearing out the seats of their britches.

Younger members of the Orderville commune also suffered in that, unlike their elders, they didn't receive shares in the community when relinquishing their property. They were paid only a wage with no dividends—$.75 a day until they reached 18, $1.50 thereafter. Eventually, the younger population trickled away, seeking higher-paying jobs in the surrounding area.

Most communal attempts, though, lasted less than a year, crippled primarily by human nature. Wealthy residents didn't wish to relinquish their property, dissatisfaction with the distribution of goods was common, and residents were often lured away by employment and business opportunities outside the commune. The Orderville community lasted 11 years, during which time its communal property nearly quadrupled in value. In that, it can be considered something of a success.

telephone numbers posted on door to reach a designated volunteer).

Mt. Carmel

This agricultural community, a few miles north of Mt. Carmel Junction, was first settled in 1865 as Winsor. Threats by Navajo and Paiute Indians forced its abandonment a year later and it wasn't reestablished until 1871, when it was named Mt. Carmel for a mountain in Israel. The Elkhart Cliffs of white Navajo Sandstone rise to the east.

Mt. Carmel Junction

Highway UT 9 turns west here from U.S. 89 to Zion National Park.

Accommodations

The following accommodations along U.S. 89 from Long Valley Junction to Mt. Carmel Junction are listed north to south under each price category.

Under $50: Inexpensive accommodations in Orderville are offered by the **Parkway Motel,** (435) 648-2380, and the **Hummingbird Bed & Breakfast,** 102 Frost Ln., at the south end of town, (435) 648-2415.

$50–75: The historic **Smith Hotel** (1927), on Main St. north of Glendale, (435) 648-2156, has been restored as a bed-and-breakfast; all rooms have baths.

The **Arrowhead B&B** in Mt. Carmel, at White Cliffs Ranch, 2155 S. State St., (435) 648-2569 or (888) 821-1670, has four attractive rooms in a ranch home surrounded by meadows and grassland. You'll enjoy the swimming pool, hot tub, and exercise equipment. Each room has a TV and VCR.

Clean basic rooms in Mt. Carmel Junction are available at the **Golden Hills Motel,** (435) 648-2268 or (800) 648-2268. The on-site **Golden Hills Restaurant** serves breakfast, lunch, and dinner daily.

$75–100: In Glendale, **The Eagle's Nest B&B,** 500 West Lydia's Canyon Rd., (435) 648-2200 or (800) 293-6378, is a very attractive modern home with four guest rooms; all rooms have private baths and two have fireplaces. The proprietors are world travelers, and the home is filled with folk art from every continent.

In Mt. Carmel Junction, **Best Western Thunderbird Motel,** (435) 648-2203, features a good restaurant, nine-hole golf course, a pool, and large attractive rooms with balconies. Their **Thunderbird Restaurant** serves breakfast, lunch, and dinner daily.

Guest Ranch: Coral Canyons Ranch, three miles south of Mt. Carmel Junction, (800) 469-3789, www.gowildwest.com, is a working ranch that takes in guests. You're free to tag along with the hands as they do ranch work, or you can simply relax and enjoy the surroundings. Organized activities like cattle drives and backcountry tours are also available. B&B rates are $99 per night, working ranch stays, which include three meals plus horseback riding, are $149 per day.

Campgrounds: Bauer's Canyon Ranch RV Camp, one block east of the highway on Center St., (435) 648-2564, offers hot showers and a Laundromat; open early Mar.–early Nov. Sites cost $17. **Bryce-Zion KOA Kampground,** five miles north of Glendale, (435) 648-2490, has a pool, store, horseback rides, laundry, and showers; open May 1–Oct. 15; $16 tents or RVs without hookups, $18–20 with, $28 for "kamping kabins."

Tortoise and the Hare Campground, one mile north of Orderville, (435) 648-2312, has sites for tents ($9) and RVs ($11 with hookups) with showers and laundry; open early Apr.–late Oct.

KANAB AND VICINITY

Striking scenery surrounds this small town in Utah's far south. The Vermilion Cliffs to the west and east glow with a fiery intensity at sunrise and sunset. Streams have cut splendid canyons into surrounding plateaus. The Paiute Indians knew the spot as Kanab (Place of the Willows), which still grow along Kanab Creek. Mormon pioneers arrived in the mid-1860s and tried to farm along the unpredictable creek. Irrigation difficulties culminated in the massive floods of 1883, which in just two days gouged a section of creekbed 40 feet below its previous level. Ranching proved better suited to this rugged and arid land.

Hollywood discovered the dramatic scenery in the 1920s and has filmed more than 150 movies and TV series here since. Famous films shot hereabouts include movies as different as *My Friend Flicka, The Lone Ranger,* and *The Greatest Story Ever Told.* The TV series *Gunsmoke* and *F Troop* were shot locally. Film crews have constructed several Western sets near Kanab, but most lie on private land and are difficult to visit. The Paria set east of town, however, is on BLM land and open to the public. Ask at the visitors' center for advice on visiting sets, as enterprising ranchers sometimes decide to make a buck by opening up their land to visitors.

Travelers find Kanab (pop. 5,500) a handy stopover on trips to Bryce, Zion, and Grand Canyon National Parks and to the Glen Canyon National Recreation Area. A good selection of motels and restaurants lines U.S. 89, which zigzags through town. Short detours on many of the side streets reveal 19th-century houses of Kanab's pioneer days.

SIGHTS

Kanab Heritage House

This 1895 Queen Anne–style Victorian house reflects the prosperity of two of Kanab's early Mormon residents. Henry Bowman built it, but he lived here only two years before going on a mission. He sold the property to Thomas Chamberlain, who led a busy life serving as a leader in the Mormons' United Order and caring for his six wives and 55 children. (There's a family photo in the sitting room.) A guide will show you around the house and explain its architectural details. Photos, furnishings, and artifacts give an idea of what life was like in early Kanab. The town had no stores when the house was built, so each family grew its own vegetables and fruit. The grape arbor, berry bushes, and trees here represent those grown during pioneer times; fruit is free for the picking to visitors. The house is usually open for tours in summer Monday–Friday

near Kanab, a set for the Gunsmoke TV series

W.C. McRAE

9 A.M.–noon and 1–5 P.M.; free admission. You might be able to visit at other times by appointment; call the number posted on the front of the house to reach a volunteer. Located one block off U.S. 89 at the corner of Main and 100 South.

Frontier Movie Town

The owners assembled this movie-set replica in Kanab to show tourists a bit of Hollywood's Old West. Some of the buildings have seen actual use in past movies and TV shows. Many small exhibits display Western and movie memorabilia; there's a selection of Western costumes available if you feel like getting gussied up as a cowboy or showgirl. Shops sell handicrafts and snacks. Local tour information is available too.

On most nights there's a Dutch-oven cookout at Frontier Movie Town, along with light entertainment and a shootout; $20 for everything. Open Apr. 1–Oct. 31 about 10 A.M.–9 P.M. Turn in off W. Center between Brandon Motel and Gift City, (435) 644-5337; free.

Best Friends Animal Sanctuary

Located in Angel Canyon just north of Kanab, this is one of the more unusual destinations in Utah. The scenic canyon was formerly the set for several Western movies and TV shows (including *The Outlaw Josie Wales* and *Rin Tin Tin*), and several of the sets are still standing. However, the canyon is now home to Best Friends Animal Sanctuary, the largest no-kill animal shelter in the country. Best Friends takes in unwanted or abused "companion animals"—pets, farm animals, or other abandoned or neglected creatures—and gives them a permanent home on the preserve's 350 acres. Most animals are rehabilitated and are given new homes. Around 1,800 animals live at the sanctuary at any given time.

Ninety minute tours of the facility are offered, normally at 10 A.M. and 1:30 P.M. Call (435) 644-2001 for reservations. Donations gladly accepted. The tour also visits some of the movie sets and features a short talk on the natural history of the canyon.

Squaw Trail

This well-graded trail provides a close look at the geology, plantlife, and animals of the Vermilion Cliffs just north of town. Allow about an hour on the moderately difficult trail to reach the first overlook (two miles round-trip with a 400-foot elevation gain) or 1.5 hours to go all the way up (three miles round-trip with an 800-foot elevation gain). Views to the south take in Kanab, Fredonia, Kanab Canyon, and the vast Kaibab Plateau. At the top, look north to see the White, Gray, and Pink Cliffs of the Grand Staircase. The trailhead is at the north end of 100 East near the city park. Pick up a trail guide at the information center (brochures may also be available at the trailhead or BLM office). Bring water. Try to get a very early start in summer.

Moqui Cave

This is a natural cave that's been turned into a tourist attraction with a large collection of Indian artifacts. Most of the arrowheads, pottery, sandals, and burial items on display have been excavated locally. A diorama re-creates an Anasazi ruin located five miles away in Cottonwood Wash. Fossils, rocks, and minerals are exhibited, too, including what's claimed to be one of the largest fluorescent mineral displays in the country. The collections and a gift shop lie within a spacious cave that stays pleasantly cool even in the hottest weather. Open daily except Sunday from early March to mid-November; summer hours are 9 A.M.–7 P.M., with shorter hours in spring and autumn; $4 adults, $3.50 seniors, $3 children 13–17, and $2 ages 6–12. The cave is five miles north of Kanab on U.S. 89, (435) 644-2987.

ACCOMMODATIONS

Lodging reservations are a good idea during the busy summer months. All of the motels and campgrounds lie along U.S. 89, which follows 300 West, Center, 100 East, and 300 South through town.

Under $50

Canyonlands International Youth Hostel is a great place to meet other travelers, many from foreign countries. Guests stay in simple dorm-style accommodations. Facilities include kitchen, laundry, TV room, patio, lawn, locked storage, and a reference library of regional maps and books. Open year-round; check-in is 9 A.M.–11 P.M. No hostel card required. Centrally located a half-block off U.S. 89 at 143 E. 100 South, (435) 644-5554.

Treasure Trail Motel, 150 W. Center, has basic, clean rooms and a pool, (435) 644-2687 or (800) 603-2687. **Aiken's Lodge National 9 Inn** is at 79 W. Center, (435) 644-2625 or (800) 524-9999, and has a pool; closed Jan. and Feb. **Sun-N-Sand Motel** at 347 S. 100 East, (435) 644-5050 or (800) 654-1868, has a pool, spa, and kitchenettes. **Brandon Motel,** 223 W. Center, (435) 644-2631 or (800) 839-2631, has a pool, kitchenettes, and accepts pets. **Riding's Quail Park Lodge,** 125 U.S. 89 N., (435) 644-5094 or (800) 644-5094, has a pool and accepts pets.

$50–75

The one lodging in Kanab that varies from the usual motor-court formula is the **Parry Lodge,** 89 East Center, (435) 644-2601 or (800) 748-4104. Built during Kanab's heyday as a movie-making center, the Parry Lodge was where the stars stayed; 60 years later, this is still a pleasant place to spend the night. At the very least, you'll want to stroll through the lobby, where there are lots of photos of the celebrities that once stayed here. There are a number of two-bedroom units, a pool, and a good restaurant.

Four Seasons Motel, 36 N. 300 West, (435) 644-2635, has a pool and accepts pets. The **Super 8,** 70 S. 200 West, (435) 644-5500, has a heated pool. The **Shilo Inn,** 296 W. 100 North, (435) 644-2562 or (800) 222-2244, has a number of room types, all nicely decorated and all with microwave, refrigerator and iron/board. There's also a pool and complimentary continental breakfast.

$75–100

Best Western Red Hills Motel, at 125 W. Center, has a pool, (435) 644-2675 or (800) 830-2675. **Holiday Inn Express** is a mile east of downtown at 815 E. U.S. 89 and offers a nine-hole golf course, free breakfast bar, pool, and hot tub; (435) 644-8888 or (800) HOLIDAY.

Campgrounds

Kanab RV Corral has sites with hot showers, pool, and Laundromat open all year at 483 South 100 East, (435) 644-5330; $17 tents, $20 RVs with hookups. **Hitch'n Post RV Park** has sites with showers open all year at 196 E. 300 South,

(435) 644-2681 or (800) 458-3516; $12 tents or RVs without hookups, $16 with. **Crazy Horse Campark,** 625 E. 300 South, (435) 644-2782, has sites with pool, store, game room, and showers; open mid-Apr.– late Oct.; $13.50 tents or RVs without hookups, $15 RVs with.

OTHER PRACTICALITIES

Food

The **Vermillion Café,** 4 E. Center, (435) 644-3886, is the place for espresso drinks, pastries, and deli sandwiches. You can find a good selection of organic and natural foods, including deli items, at **Wildflower Health Foods,** 18 E. Center, (435) 644-3200.

Parry Lodge has a lovely dining room featuring steak, seafood, and some international dishes at 89 E. Center, (435) 644-2601; open daily for breakfast, lunch, and dinner (closed 2–6 P.M.). Photos of former movie-star guests decorate the walls. **Chef's Palace Restaurant,** 176 W. Center, (435) 644-5052, offers steak, prime rib, and seafood; open daily for breakfast, lunch, and dinner.

For a choice of Mexican and American cooking, try **Nedra's Too,** 300 S. 100 East in Heritage Center, (435) 644-2030, with its homey atmosphere; open daily for breakfast, lunch, and dinner; or **Houston's Trail's End Restaurant,** 32 E. Center, (435) 644-2488; open daily for breakfast, lunch, and dinner. The **Wok Inn,** 86 S. 200 West, (435) 644-5400, has Hunan and Szechuan cuisine; open weekdays for lunch and dinner and weekends for dinner only; closed in winter. The best place for Mexican food is **Escobar's,** 373 E. 300 South, (435) 644-3739. Beer is served; closed Sat.

Entertainment and Events

In summer, there are free musical concerts at the city park gazebo, at the center of town. Wednesdays bring an on-going local talent show. One of summer's largest events is the **Southern Utah Fiddle Championship,** held annually in mid-July. An even more unique Kanab event is the **Greyhound Gathering** in mid-May, when hundreds of greyhound owners converge on the town. Events include a parade, a race and a howl-in. The Greyhound

Gang, a nonprofit organization dedicated to the rescue, rehabilitation, and adoption of ex-racing greyhounds, hosts this unlikely festival. Contact the visitors' center for more information.

Kanab Theatre has movies at 29 W. Center, (435) 644-2334. The **Kanab 10-K** run is in May. **Kanab West Fest** features a rodeo, Western art, and festivities in October.

Services and Shopping
The **city park** has picnic tables, playground, tennis courts, and a ball field at the north end of 100 West; the trailhead for Squaw Trail starts here (see Squaw Trail under Sights, above). An outdoor **swimming pool** opens in summer at 44 N. 100 West (behind the State Bank), (435) 644-5870. **Coral Cliffs Golf Course** has nine holes and a driving range on the east edge of town, (435) 644-5005. You can arrange **trail rides** from an hour to 10 days in length and stagecoach rides through Frontier Movie Town, (435) 644-5337. The **post office** is at 34 S. Main, (435) 644-2760. **Kane County Hospital** provides emergency care at 221 W. 300 North, (435) 644-5811.

Alderman & Son Photo, 19 W. Center, (435) 644-5981, supplies film and camera needs (including repairs) beyond what you would expect in a town this size. The shop almost qualifies as an antique camera museum.

Denny's Wigwam, 78 E. Center, (435) 644-2452, is a landmark Old West trading post with lots of quality Western jewelry, cowboy hats and boots, and souvenirs. Denny's also hosts elaborate chuck wagon meals and entertainment, but usually only for bus tours. If a shindig is already scheduled, you can sometimes join the festivities by paying for an individual ticket.

Information
Staff at the **information center** offers literature and advice for services in Kanab and travel in Kane County; they're in the center of town at 70 S. 100 East (Kanab, UT 84741), (435) 644-5033; open Mon.–Sat. 8 A.M.–8 P.M. all year. The new **Grand Staircase–Escalante National Monument** headquarters is in Kanab at 41 S. 100 East, (800) 733-5263, though visitor information is dispensed out of the current **BLM office** at 318 N. 100 East (Kanab, UT 84741), (435) 644-2672;

open Mon.–Fri. 7:45 A.M.–4:30 P.M. The **public library** is at 13 S. 100 East, (435) 644-2394.

CORAL PINK SAND DUNES STATE PARK

Churning air currents funneled by surrounding mountains have deposited huge sand dunes in this valley west of Kanab. The ever-changing dunes reach heights of several hundred feet and cover about 2,000 of the park's 3,700 acres. Moviemakers have used the location for filming. Tiny particles of quartz make up the sand; the "coral pink" refers only to the color. Average summer temperatures at the 6,000-foot elevation range from about 55° F at night to 95° during the day; winter days have highs of about 55°, lows below freezing at night. Most wildlife is difficult to spot, though you may see tracks in the sand. Coyotes are often heard at night. Wildflowers put on a fine show in June and July. Different areas in the park have been set aside for hiking, off-road vehicles, and a campground with hot showers. If you see what looks like a family reunion, it might be just a man and his wives from the nearby polygamist settlements of Colorado City or Hildale!

From Kanab, the shortest drive is to go north eight miles on U.S. 89 (to between Mileposts 72 and 73), turn left 9.3 miles on the paved Hancock Road to its end, then turn left (south) one mile on a paved road into the park. From the north, you can follow U.S. 89 3.5 miles south of Mt. Carmel Junction, then turn right (south) 11 miles on a paved road. The back road from Cane Beds in Arizona has about 16 miles of gravel and dirt with some sandy spots; ask a park ranger for current conditions. Entrance fees are $4 per vehicle for day use, $12 per vehicle for camping. Contact the park at P.O. Box 95, Kanab, UT 84741, (435) 648-2800 or (800) 322-3770 (reservations).

Day-Use Area
On the left just past the contact station, a short boardwalk leads into a protected section of the dunes; signs explain the geology and illustrate some animals and plants that live in this semiarid desert. Photographers and families can explore on foot and use the sheltered picnic area.

Riding the Dunes
Drivers of off-road vehicles can head for the sands from a trailhead between the day-use area and the campground. The thrills of traveling across the Sahara-like landscape attract motorcyclists, ATVers, and dune-buggy enthusiasts. Paddle-type tires work best on the soft sand. Park regulations ask drivers to attach an eight-foot whip with a flag to their vehicles, to observe quiet hours from 10 P.M.–9 A.M., and to avoid riding across vegetation. All vehicles must be registered for off- or on-highway use. It's a good idea to ride where other drivers can see you. Rangers have a complete list of regulations.

Campground
The pleasant campground sits in a piñon pine, juniper, and oak woodland. Facilities include restrooms with showers, paved pull-through sites, and a dump station. Ice, firewood, and off-road vehicle whips may be sold by park staff. Open all year, but the water is shut off from late October until Easter; winter campers need to bring their own. Reservations are recommended for the busy Memorial Day–Labor Day season.

Other Areas
The canyon country surrounding the park has good opportunities for hiking and off-road vehicle travel; the BLM office in Kanab can supply maps and information. The BLM maintains **Ponderosa Grove Campground** on the north edge of the dunes; no water or fee; it's on the paved Hancock Road that turns off one mile north of the park or eight miles north of Kanab from U.S. 89 (between Mileposts 72 and 73). The campground is two miles in from the road to the park and 7.3 miles in from U.S. 89. Drivers with four-wheel-drive vehicles can turn south on Sand Springs Road (1.5 miles east of Ponderosa Grove Campground) and go one mile to Sand Springs and another four miles to South Fork Indian Canyon Pictograph Site in a pretty canyon. Visitors may not enter the Kaibab-Paiute Indian Reservation, which is south across the Arizona state line, from this side.

THE ARIZONA STRIP

Lonely and vast, the "Strip" lies north and west of the Colorado River and south of Utah. Phoenix and the rest of Arizona seem a world away. The Arizona Strip's history and geography actually tie it more closely to Utah. Some beautiful desert and mountain country await the adventurous traveler. In addition to Grand Canyon National Park, nine designated wilderness areas totaling nearly 400,000 acres protect the most scenic and unique sections. See the *Arizona Handbook* for places to visit in the backcountry. Several tiny communities in the Arizona Strip offer food and accommodations for travelers. More-extensive facilities lie just outside the region: Kanab and St. George across the Utah border to the north and Page across the river to the east.

PIPE SPRING NATIONAL MONUMENT

Step back to the days when cowboys and pioneers first settled this land. Excellent exhibits in Winsor Castle, an early Mormon ranch southwest of Kanab, provide a look into frontier life.

Abundant spring water attracted prehistoric Indians, who settled nearby more than 1,000 years ago, then departed. Nomadic Paiute Indians came more recently and now live on the surrounding Kaibab-Paiute Indian Reservation. Mormons discovered the springs in 1858 and began ranching five years later, but swift Navajo raiding parties stole some stock and killed two men who pursued the Indians. A treaty signed in 1870 between the Mormons and Navajo ended the raids and opened the land to development.

Brigham Young, the Mormon president, then decided to locate the church's southern Utah tithing herd at Pipe Spring. A pair of two-story stone houses went up, with walls connecting the ends to form a protected courtyard. Workmen added gun ports "just in case," but the settlement was never attacked. The structure became known as Winsor Castle because the ranch's superintendent, Anson P. Winsor, possessed a regal bearing and was thought to be related to the English royal family. Winsor built up a sizable herd of cattle and horses and oversaw dairying and farming at the ranch. A telegraph office (Arizona's first) opened in 1871, bringing Utah closer to the rest of the world. So many newlyweds passed through the area, after having been married in the St. George Temple, that their route became known as the Honeymoon Trail. In the 1880s, the Mormon Church entered a period of turmoil and feared that the federal government would seize church property in the dispute over polygamous marriages. Winsor Castle, whose importance to the church had been declining, was sold to a non-Mormon.

President Harding proclaimed Pipe Spring a national monument in 1923 "as a memorial of Western pioneer life." National Park Service staff keeps the frontier spirit alive by maintaining the ranch as it was in the 1870s. Activities such as cattle branding, gardening, weaving, spinning, quilt-making, and baking still take place on a small scale. You can take a short tour of Winsor Castle or explore the restored rooms and out-buildings on your own. A half-mile loop trail climbs the small ridge behind the ranch to a viewpoint; signs tell of local history and geology.

Visitor Center

Historic exhibits are open daily 8 A.M.–4:30 P.M. year-round; $2 per-person admission; (435) 643-7105, www.nps.gov/pisp. A short video introduces the monument. Demonstrations of ranch skills and Paiute crafts and lifeways take place in the summer months. Produce from the garden and goodies from the kitchen may be sold or given away. A shop offers regional books and Southwestern Indian arts and crafts. The Paiute tribe operates **Heart Canyon Campground** a half-mile northeast of the monument; sites have showers and stay open all year: $5, $10 with hookups. Nearest restaurants, and motels are in Fredonia. Pipe Spring National Monument is just off AZ 389, 21 miles southwest of Kanab.

PARIA CANYON

The wild and twisting canyons of the Paria River and its tributaries offer a memorable experience for experienced hikers. Silt-laden waters have sculpted the colorful canyon walls, revealing 200 million years of geologic history. Paria means

"Muddy Water" in the Paiute language. You enter the 2,000-foot-deep gorge of the Paria in southern Utah, then hike 37 miles downstream to Lees Ferry in Arizona, where the Paria empties into the Colorado River.

Ancient petroglyphs and campsites show that Pueblo Indians traveled the Paria more than 700 years ago. They hunted mule deer and bighorn sheep while using the broad, lower end of the canyon to grow corn, beans, and squash. The Dominguez-Escalante Expedition stopped at the mouth of the Paria in 1776 and were the first white men to see the river. John D. Lee and three companions traveled through the canyon in 1871 to bring a herd of cattle from the Pahreah settlement to Lees Ferry. After Lee began a Colorado River ferry service in 1872, he and others farmed the lower Paria Canyon. Prospectors came here to search for gold, uranium, and other minerals, but much of the canyon remained unexplored. In the late 1960s, the Bureau of Land Management organized a small expedition whose research led to protection of the canyon as a primitive area. The Arizona Wilderness Act of 1984

the Narrows

designated Paria Canyon a wilderness, along with parts of the Paria Plateau and Vermilion Cliffs. The area is now under consideration for national monument status. For up-to-date information on recreation in the wilderness, be sure to check the website at www.paria.az.blm.gov.

Hiking Paria Canyon

Allow 4–6 days to hike Paria Canyon because of the many river crossings and because you'll want to make side trips up some of the tributary canyons. The hike is considered moderately difficult. Hikers should have enough backpacking experience to be self-sufficient, as help may be days away. Flash floods can race through the canyon, especially July–September. Because the upper end has the narrowest passages (between miles 4.2 and 9.0), rangers require that all hikers start here in order to have up-to-date weather information.

The BLM Paria Canyon Ranger Station is in Utah, 43 miles east of Kanab on U.S. 89 near Milepost 21. It's on the south side of the highway, just east of the Paria River. The actual trailhead is two miles south on a dirt road near an old homestead site called White House Ruins. Exit trailhead is in Arizona at Lonely Dell Ranch of Lees Ferry, 44 miles southwest of Page via U.S. 89 and 89A (or 98 miles southeast of Kanab on U.S. 89A).

You must register at a trailhead or the visitors' center, or the Kanab BLM office at 318 N. 100 East in Kanab, UT 84741, (435) 644-2672; open Mon.–Fri. 7:45 A.M.–4:30 P.M. year-round. You can also register online at the website www.paria.az.blm.gov. Permits to hike the canyon are $5 per day per person and per dog. The visitors' center and the office both provide weather forecasts and brochures with map and hiking information. The visitors' center always has the weather forecast posted at an outdoor information kiosk.

All visitors need to take special care to minimize impact on this beautiful canyon. Check the BLM "Visitor Use Regulations" for the Paria before you go. Regulations include: no campfires in the Paria and its tributaries, a pack-in/pack-out policy, and latrines be made at least 100 feet away from river and campsite locations. Also, remember to take some plastic bags to carry out toilet paper; the stuff lasts years and years in this desert climate. You don't want to haunt future hikers with TP flowers!

The Paria ranger recommends a group size of six maximum; regulations specify a 10-person limit. No more than 20 people a day can enter the canyon for overnight trips. The best times to travel along the Paria are from about mid-March to June and October to November. May, especially Memorial Day weekend, tends to be crowded. Winter hikers often complain of painfully cold feet. Wear shoes suitable for frequent wading; canvas shoes are better than heavy leather hiking boots.

You can get good drinking water from springs along the way (see the BLM hiking brochure for locations); it's best not to use the river water because of possible chemical pollution from farms and ranches upstream. Normally the river's only ankle deep, but in spring or after rainy spells, it can become waist deep. During thunderstorms, levels can rise to over 20 feet deep in the Paria Narrows, so heed weather warnings! Quicksand, most prevalent after flooding, is more a nuisance than a danger—usually it's just knee deep. Many hikers carry a walking stick to probe the opaque waters for good crossing places.

Wrather Canyon Arch

One of Arizona's largest natural arches lies about one mile up this side canyon. The massive structure has a 200-foot span. Turn right (southwest) at Mile 20.6 on the Paria hike. (The mouth of Wrather Canyon and other points along the Paria are unsigned; you need to follow your map.)

Shuttle Services

You'll need to make a 150-mile round-trip car shuttle for this hike or make arrangements for someone else to do it for you, using either your car (about $60) or theirs ($125–150). Authorized shuttle operators include Betty Price, (520) 355-2252 and Barry Warren, (520) 640-0191.

Buckskin Gulch

This amazing tributary of the Paria has convoluted walls hundreds of feet high, yet it narrows to as little as four feet in width. In places the walls block out so much light that it's like walking in a cave. Be *very* careful to avoid times of flash-flood danger. Hiking can be strenuous with rough terrain, deep pools of water, and log and rock

Jacob Hamblin

the best place for up-to-date information is the website at www.paria.az.blm.gov.

The BLM has divided the area into Coyote North and Coyote South, with a limit of 10 people per day in each. The Wave—the most photographed of the buttes—is in the north, so this region is the most popular (and easiest to reach from Utah). Coyote North is reached from Wirepass Trailhead (8.3 miles south of Hwy. 89 on Rock House Valley Rd.); BLM staff will give you a map and directions when you get your permit. After the trailhead, you're on your own, as the wilderness lacks signs. Permits are more difficult to obtain in spring and autumn—the best times to visit—and on weekends. The fragile sandstone can break if climbed on, so it's important to stay on existing hiking routes and wear soft-soled footwear.

LEES FERRY

The deeply entrenched Colorado River cuts one gorge after another as it crosses the high plateaus of southern Utah and northern Arizona. Settlers

John Doyle Lee

jams that may require the use of ropes. Conditions vary considerably from one year to the next. You can descend into Buckskin from two trailheads, Buckskin and Wire Pass, both reached by a dirt road, not always passable by cars. The hike from Buckskin Trailhead to the Paria River is 16.3 miles long (one-way) and takes 12 or more hours. From Wire Pass Trailhead it's 1.7 miles to Buckskin Gulch, then 11.8 miles to the Paria. You can climb out on a route to a safe camping place about halfway down Buckskin Gulch. Carry water to last until the mouth of Buckskin Gulch.

Coyote Buttes
You've probably seen photos of these dramatic rock formations: towering sand dunes frozen into rock. These much-photographed buttes are located on the Paria Plateau, just south of Paria Canyon. Access is strictly controlled and you can only enter the area with advanced reservation and by permit. The number of people allowed into the area is also strictly limited. However, the permit process, fees, and restrictions are exactly the same as for Paria Canyon; again,

and travelers found the river a dangerous and difficult barrier until well into this century. A break in the cliffs above Marble Canyon provided one of the few places to build a road to the water's edge. Until 1929, when Navajo Bridge spanned the canyon, vehicles and passengers had to cross by ferry. Zane Grey expressed his thoughts about Lees Ferry in *The Last of the Plainsmen* (1908): "I saw the constricted rapids, where the Colorado took its plunge into the box-like head of the Grand Canyon of Arizona; and the deep, reverberating boom of the river, at flood height, was a fearful thing to hear. I could not repress a shudder at the thought of crossing above that rapid."

In 1776 the Dominguez-Escalante Expedition tried without success to cross at what's now known as Lees Ferry. The river proved too cold and wide to swim safely, and winds frustrated the attempts to raft across. The Spaniards had to go 40 miles upstream into present-day Utah before finding a safe ford. About 100 years later, Mormon leaders began eyeing the Lees Ferry crossing as the best route for expanding Mormon settlements from Utah into Arizona. Jacob Hamblin led a failed attempt at rafting the river in 1860; he returned in 1864 and made it across safely. Mormons built a guard post in 1869 to prevent others from taking over the strategic spot.

Although Hamblin was the first to recognize the value of this crossing, it now bears the name of John D. Lee. This colorful character gained notoriety in the 1857 Mountain Meadows Massacre. To get Lee out of sight, the Mormon Church leaders asked him to start a regular ferry service on the Colorado River, which he began in 1872. One of Lee's wives remarked on seeing the isolated spot, "Oh, what a lonely dell!" which became the name of their place. Lee managed to establish the ferry service despite boat accidents and sometimes hostile Navajo, but his past caught up with him. In 1877, authorities took Lee back to Mountain Meadows where a firing squad and casket awaited.

Miners and farmers came to try their luck along the Colorado River and its tributaries. The ferry service continued, too, though it suffered fatal accidents from time to time. The last run took place in June 1928 while the bridge was being constructed six miles downstream. The ferry operator on that trip lost control in strong currents and the boat capsized; all three persons aboard and a Model-T Ford were lost. Fifty-five years of ferryboating had come to an end. Navajo Bridge opened in January 1929, an event hailed by the Flagstaff *Coconino Sun* as the "Biggest News in Southwest History."

Navajo Bridge—The Old and the New

A new, wider bridge for traffic has replaced the old Navajo Bridge across Marble Canyon. The old bridge, admired for its design and beauty, has been preserved as a pedestrian path just upstream from the new one. Now you can enjoy a walk 470 feet above the water on the old bridge's 909-foot length. Do not throw anything off the bridge as even a small object can pick up lethal velocity from such a height and hurt boaters below. A 1930s stone shelter built by the Civilian Conservation Corps and a new visitor center stand just west of the bridges. Indoor and outdoor exhibits illustrate the history and construction details of both structures. You'll find local travel information for the Grand Canyon and Glen Canyon National Recreation Area and a large selection of books, maps, videos, music (Indian and Southwest), and posters in the Navajo Bridge Interpretive Center; it's open daily 9 A.M.–5 P.M. Navajo Indians sell crafts on the old bridge's east end. Both ends of the old bridge have parking.

SOUTHEASTERN UTAH

INTRODUCTION

The Colorado River and its tributaries have carved extraordinary landscapes in southeastern Utah. Intricate mazes of canyons, delicate arches, and massive rock monoliths make this a region like no other. First-time visitors often need a while to appreciate this strange land before they're won over by the infinite colors and beauties of the sculptured rock. The thousands of canyons invite exploration—they offer solitude, ruins of prehistoric villages, wildlife, and dramatic records of geologic history.

THE LAND

About 300 million years ago, this land was at times a great Sahara-like desert and at others covered by water. Thick layers of sediment built up one on top of the other. During the last 50 million years, powerful forces within the earth slowly pushed the entire region a mile upward. The ancestral Colorado River and other streams appeared and began to carve the deep gorges seen today. Some of the younger rock layers of the uplifted Colorado Plateau have been eroded, yet the deposits that remain represent more than 150 million years. Ancient dunes, turned to stone, make up many of the sheer canyon cliffs, arches, and spires of the region. Delicate crossbedded lines of the former dunes add grace to these features. Forces within the restless plateau have also buckled and folded rock layers into great reefs as long as 100 miles. Weathering then carved them into rainbow-hued rock monuments. Volcanic pressures deep in the earth also shaped the land. Thick sediments above, however, prevented most of the molten rock from reaching the surface. Massive intrusions of magma bowed up overlying rock layers before cooling and solidifying. Erosion has since uncovered four of these dome-shaped ranges in southeastern Utah—the Henrys, the La Sals, the Abajos, and Navajo Mountain. Rain and snowmelt captured by these high peaks nourish the plants and wildlife of the region.

Climate

The high-desert country of southeastern Utah lies mostly between 3,500 and 6,500 feet in elevation. Annual precipitation ranges from an extremely dry three inches in some areas to about 10 inches over much of the land. Mountainous regions between 10,000 and 13,000 feet receive abundant rainfall in summer and heavy snows in winter. The rugged character of the canyon country causes many local variations in climate. Sunny skies prevail through all four seasons. Spring comes early to the canyon country with weather that's often windy and rapidly changing. Summer can make its presence known in April, though the real desert heat doesn't set in until late May or early June. Temperatures then soar into the 90s and 100s at midday, though the dry air makes the heat more bearable. Early morning is the choice time for travel in summer. A canyon seep surrounded by hanging gardens or a mountain meadow filled with wildflowers provides a refreshing contrast to the parched desert; other ways to beat the heat include hiking in the mountains and river-rafting. Huge billowing thunderstorm clouds in late summer bring refreshing rains and coolness. Autumn begins after the rains and lasts into November or even December; days are bright and sunny with ideal temperatures, but nights become cold. Winter lasts only about two months at the lower elevations. Light snows on the canyon walls add new beauty to the rock layers. Nighttime temperatures commonly dip into the teens—too cold for most campers. Otherwise winter can be a fine time for travel. Heavy snows rarely occur below 8,000 feet.

Flash Floods

The bare rock and loose soils so common in the canyon country do little to hold back the flow of water. A summer thunderstorm or a rapid late-winter snowmelt can send torrents of mud and boulders rumbling down dry washes and canyons. Backcountry drivers, horseback riders, and hikers need to avoid hazardous locations when storms threaten or unseasonably warm winds blow on the winter snowpack. Logs and other debris wedged high on canyon walls give proof enough of past floods.

and other plants often adapt by growing in rock cracks that concentrate moisture and nutrients. Small mammals such as mice, wood rats, rock squirrels, and chipmunks find food and shelter in these outposts of vegetation. Even meager soils permit growth of hardy shrubs like blackbrush, greasewood, sagebrush, rabbitbrush, and Mormon tea. Prickly pear and other types of cacti do well in the desert, too.

Perhaps the most unusual plant communities are the cryptobiotic crusts found on sandy soils. Mosses, lichens, fungi, algae, and diatoms live together in a gray-green to black layer up to several inches thick. Microclimates surrounding canyon seeps and springs provide a haven for hanging gardens of grasses, ferns, orchids, columbines, mosses, and other water-loving plants. River and stream banks have their own vegetation including river willows, cattails, tamarisks, and cottonwoods. Wildlife you might see in the semiarid desert are mule deer, desert bighorn sheep, pronghorns, coyotes, bobcats, foxes, skunks, porcupines, and many species of rodents. Ravens, eagles, hawks, owls, falcons, magpies, and smaller birds fly overhead. Watch out for the poisonous rattlesnakes and scorpions, though these shy creatures won't attack unless provoked.

At elevations between 7,000 and 8,500 feet, the desert gives way to forests of aspen, Gambel oak, ponderosa pine, and mountain mahogany. Conifers dominate up to the treeline, at about 12,000 feet. Alpine flowering plants, grasses, sedges, and mosses cling to the windy summits of the La Sal Mountains. Wildlife of the forests includes many of the desert dwellers, as well as elk, bear, mountain lion, marmot, and pika. A herd of bison roams freely in the Henry Mountains; the surrounding desert keeps them from going elsewhere.

FLORA AND FAUNA

The region's elevation range—from 3,700 feet at Lake Powell to 12,721 feet atop the La Sal Mountains—provides a wide variety of habitats. Yet the dry conditions and thin or nonexistent soils limit both plant- and wildlife. Annuals simply wait for a wet year before quickly flowering and spreading their seeds. Piñon pines, junipers,

HISTORY

Prehistoric Indians

Nomadic bands of hunter-gatherers roamed the canyon country for at least 5,000 years. The climate was probably cooler and wetter when the first Indians arrived; food plants and game animals would have been more abundant than today. Agriculture introduced from the south about 2,000 years ago brought about a slow transition to a settled village life. The Fremont culture emerged in the northern part of the region and the Anasazi in the southern part. Thousands of stone dwellings, ceremonial kivas, and towers built by the Anasazi still stand. Both groups also left behind intriguing rock art, either pecked in (petroglyphs) or painted (pictographs). The Anasazi and Fremont departed from this region about 800 years ago, perhaps because of drought, warfare, or disease. Some of the Anasazi moved south and joined the Pueblo tribes of present-day Arizona and New Mexico. The fate of the Fremont Indians remains a mystery.

After the mid-1200s and until white settlers arrived in the late 1800s, small bands of nomadic Ute and Paiute moved through southeastern Utah. The Navajo began to enter Utah in the early 1800s. None of the three Indian groups established firm control of the region north of the San Juan River. A remnant of the Ute and Paiute Indian tribes now lives on the small White Mesa Reservation south of Blanding.

The Navajo

Relatives of the Athapascans of western Canada, the seminomadic Navajo wandered into New Mexico and Arizona between A.D. 1300 and 1500. This adaptable tribe learned agriculture, weaving, pottery, and other skills from their Pueblo neighbors, and they became expert horsemen and sheepherders with livestock obtained from the Spanish. Later, though, the old Navajo habits of raiding neighboring tribes and white settlements almost brought their downfall. In 1863–1864 the U.S. Army rounded up all the Navajo they could find and forced the survivors on "The Long Walk" from Fort Defiance in northeastern Arizona to a bleak camp in eastern New Mexico. This internment was a dismal failure, and the Navajo were released four years later.

In 1868 the federal government "awarded" land to the Navajo that has since grown to a giant reservation spreading from northeastern Arizona into adjacent Utah and New Mexico. The Navajo Nation, with 172,000 members, now ranks as the largest Indian tribe in the country. Their Utah land lies mostly south of Lake Powell and the San Juan River in the extreme southeastern corner of the state but includes some acreage north of the San Juan near Montezuma

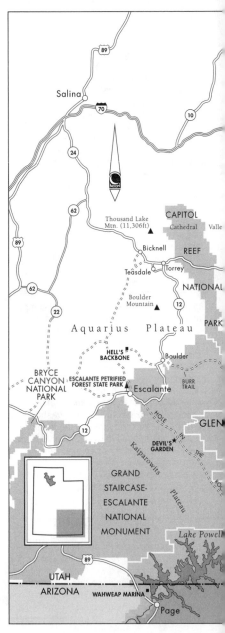

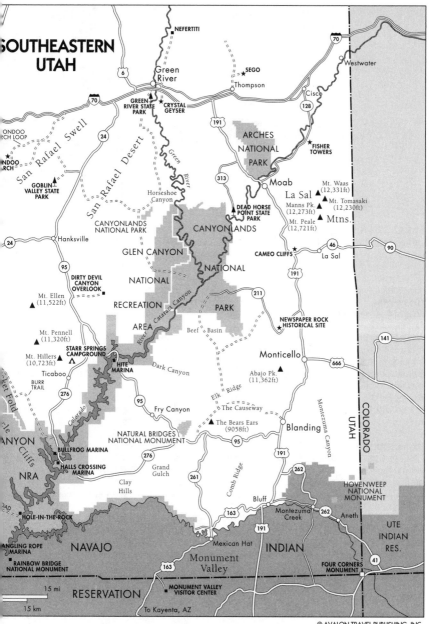

SOUTHEASTERN UTAH

NEFERTITI

Green River

SEGO

Thompson

Westwater

GREEN RIVER STATE PARK

CRYSTAL GEYSER

Cisco

ONDOO RCH LOOP

San Rafael Swell

San Rafael Desert

Green River

ARCHES NATIONAL PARK

FISHER TOWERS

NDOO RCH

GOBLIN VALLEY STATE PARK

Horseshoe Canyon

Moab

La Sal

Mt. Waas (12,331ft)

CANYONLANDS NATIONAL PARK

DEAD HORSE POINT STATE PARK

Manns Pk. (12,273ft)

Mt. Tomasaki (12,230ft)

Hanksville

CANYONLANDS

Mt. Peale (12,721ft)

Mtns.

GLEN CANYON

NATIONAL

CAMEO CLIFFS

La Sal

DIRTY DEVIL CANYON OVERLOOK

NATIONAL

RECREATION

PARK

Mt. Ellen (11,522ft)

NEWSPAPER ROCK HISTORICAL SITE

Green River

Cataract Canyon

Beef Basin

AREA

Mt. Pennell (11,320ft)

STARR SPRINGS CAMPGROUND

Monticello

Mt. Hillers (10,723ft)

HITE MARINA

Dark Canyon

Abajo Pk. (11,362ft)

Ticaboo

BURR TRAIL

Colorado

Fry Canyon

Elk Ridge

The Causeway

NATURAL BRIDGES NATIONAL MONUMENT

The Bears Ears (9058ft)

Blanding

Montezuma Canyon

BULLFROG MARINA

ANYON

CANYON

Cliffs

HALLS CROSSING MARINA

Grand Gulch

Clay Hills

Comb Ridge

COLORADO

UTAH

NRA

HOLE-IN-THE-ROCK

Bluff

HOVENWEEP NATIONAL MONUMENT

ANGLING ROPE MARINA

RAINBOW BRIDGE NATIONAL MONUMENT

NAVAJO

Montezuma Creek

Aneth

UTE INDIAN RES.

Mexican Hat

INDIAN

FOUR CORNERS MONUMENT

15 mi

15 km

Monument Valley

RESERVATION

MONUMENT VALLEY VISITOR CENTER

To Kayenta, AZ

© AVALON TRAVEL PUBLISHING, INC.

Navajo medicine man with his ceremonial sand painting

Creek. Oil, gas, and ranching are important sources of income. The Navajo own the spectacular Monument Valley Tribal Park on the Utah-Arizona border.

Religion is a vital part of Navajo culture. Most ceremonies involve healing and often take place late at night. If someone is sick, his or her family calls in a medicine man or woman who uses sandpaintings, chants, and dancing to effect a cure. The Navajo make beautiful silver jewelry and woven rugs. You'll see these in trading posts on and off the reservation. Colorful velveteen blouses and long flowing skirts like those worn by Navajo women are sometimes available for purchase; the Navajo women adopted the style during the tribe's 1860's New Mexico internment. It's what the U.S. Army wives were wearing!

Exploration and Settlement

The Spanish Dominguez-Escalante Expedition skirted the east edge of the region in 1776 in an unsuccessful attempt to find a route west to California. Retreating back to New Mexico, the explorers encountered great difficulties in the canyons of southern Utah before finding a safe ford across the Colorado River. This spot, known as the "Crossing of the Fathers," now lies under Lake Powell. Later explorers established the Old Spanish Trail through Utah to connect New Mexico with California. The route crossed the Colorado River near present-day Moab and was used from 1829 to 1848, when the United States acquired the western territories. Fur trappers

also traveled the canyons in search of beaver and other animals during the early 1800s; inscriptions carved into the sandstone record their passage. The U.S. Army's Macomb Expedition visited southeastern Utah in 1859 and made the first documented description of what's now Canyonlands National Park. Major John Wesley Powell's pioneering river expeditions down the Green and Colorado in 1869 and 1871–1872 filled in many blank areas on the maps.

Hostile Indians discouraged early attempts by the Mormons to start settlements in southeastern Utah. The Elk Ridge Mission, founded in 1855 near present-day Moab, lasted only a few months before Ute Indians killed three Mormons and sent the rest fleeing for their lives. Church members had better success during the 1870s in the Escalante area (1876) and Moab (1877).

For sheer effort and endurance, no group of pioneers is cited as much as the Hole-in-the-Rock Expedition of 1879–1880. Sixty families with 83 wagons and more than 1,000 head of livestock crossed some of the West's most rugged canyon country in an attempt to settle at Montezuma Creek on the San Juan River. They almost didn't make it: a journey expected to take six weeks turned into a six-*month* ordeal. The exhausted company arrived on the banks of the San Juan River on April 5, 1880. Too tired to continue just 20 easy miles to Montezuma Creek, they stayed and founded the town of Bluff. The Mormons established other towns in southeastern Utah, too, relying on ranching, farming, and mining for their livelihoods. None of the communities in the region ever reached a large size; Moab is the biggest with a population of 4,500. More and more people have come to realize that the scenery and wilderness qualities of this unique land are its most valuable resources.

HIGHWAY 12 SCENIC BYWAY

It's well worth emphasizing that Highway 12, which begins near Bryce Canyon National Park and continues along the wild canyon and slickrock country of the new Grand Staircase–Escalante National Monument, is commonly regarded as one of the most scenic roads in Utah. In fact, *Car and Driver* magazine rates this route as one of the 10 most scenic in all of the U.S. In addition to Red Rock Canyon and Bryce Canyon National Park (see Southwestern Utah chapter), and the sites detailed below, there are innumerable other swallow-your-gum vistas and geologic curiosities that will keep you on the edge of your car seat.

GRAND STAIRCASE–ESCALANTE NATIONAL MONUMENT

In September 1996, President Bill Clinton declared 1.8 million acres of Utah a national monument, ending a decades-old debate about the preservation of the wilderness canyons in south central Utah. The monument is the largest land grouping designated as a national monument in the lower 48 states. The federal government's move sought to prevent the establishment of coal mines in the area, which had been planned by a Dutch resource-extraction consortium.

The monument is a cobbled-together unit of land formerly supervised by the BLM, the Forest Service, and the state of Utah. The responsibility for administering the monument was assigned to the BLM, which built new offices in Kanab—at the southwestern edge of the monument—for overseeing the preserve.

Preservation of the canyons as a national monument angered the Republican Utah legislative delegation and many others in this deeply conservative state. They argued that the federal government should not interfere with business and the local community. However, the move pleased environmentalists and backcountry recreationalists, who feared the existence of a mining operation, no matter how environmentally sound, would destroy the area's unique scenic splendor and ancient Anasazi art and ruins.

In the years since the establishment of the monument, local anger has only intensified; due in part to disinformed individuals seeking to make political hay and in part to early ham-fisted moves by federal policy makers. Also, the national attention President Clinton's announcement brought increased the number of outsiders wanting to visit this wide swathe of federal land; and this isn't always what traditional-minded ranchers and townspeople want. To make the situation even more murky is the fact that administrative employees at the federal offices in charge of the monument are apt to give contradictory information. For example, you can be told at the monument's visitors' center in Escalante that certain trails are now closed to mountain bikes, while the next day you can be told by officials at the headquarters in Kanab that there are no restrictions on mountain bikes in the monument.

At the very least, before planning a trip to the Grand Staircase–Escalante area, realize that the situation is quite fluid and getting straightforward information can be difficult. You also need to realize the tempers of local citizens can run very high. You won't be in southern Utah many hours before encountering vociferous anger about the establishment of the monument. Seemingly polite inquiries even at visitors' centers can lead to unpleasant confrontations with the local staff. In the Escalante area, there are especially hard feelings, with the local paper filled with stories of environmental-minded citizens being shot at and their pets being killed.

However, most of this hostility is directed at the distant and high-handed federal government. The irony in all of this is that so far, in terms of land usage, very little has changed for either the farmers and ranchers who have leased these federal lands for generations, or for the hikers and bikers who want to explore the wilds of this canyon country. The BLM has moved very slowly to reassess access to the land and is trying to preserve the land's tradition as a multi-use area (with ranchers retaining grazing leases on federal land). However, because of local anger and intransigence, bureaucratic wrangling, and the slow-moving nature of the federal government, most recreationalists will find very little has changed in terms of access or amenities in the Grand Staircase–Escalante area. Certain restrictions are in place, but these mostly affect the use of ATVs and non-street legal vehicles (OHVs, dune buggies, and certain kinds of dirt bikes). Certain primitive roads will not receive regular maintenance. You'll hear rumors aplenty about other restrictions being considered, but drastic changes don't seem imminent. As has always been the case, the major considerations in planning a trip to this area remain the weather and the condition of the roads, not the federal government.

For information on the monument contact the Kanab BLM field office, 318 N 100 East, Kanab, UT 84741, (435) 644-2672, or the Escalante Interagency office, 755 W. Main, Escalante, UT 84726, (435) 826-5499. For up-to-date information, another good spot to do research is the website, www.ut.blm.gov/monument.

Currently, there is no fee to visit the monument, though a fee structure is being developed. Two campgrounds have fees: Calf Creek campground, along Hwy 12 between Escalante and Boulder ($7), and Deer Creek Campground, six miles east of Boulder along the Burr Trail ($4); campfires are restricted. Be mindful of cultural and historical sites (many vestiges of Fremont and Anasazi villages remain), and of the natural treasures of the area. Specific restrictions or considerations follow in discussions of individual destinations within the monument.

ESCALANTE

The outstanding scenery of the countryside surrounding the town of Escalante has been discovered, and the town is being dragged, kicking and screaming, into a new reality: as a major center for eco-tourism. Escalante is a natural hub for exploration of the new Grand Staircase–Escalante National Monument. Even if you don't have time or the inclination to explore the rugged canyon country that the monument protects, you'll discover incredible scenery just by traveling Highway 12 through the Escalante country.

Highlights of a visit include seeing the Escalante River system's magnificent canyons, driving the historic Hole-in-the-Rock Road across a landscape little changed from pioneer days, fishing the trout lakes on the high Aquarius Plateau, and enjoying the area's splendid panoramas. Escalante also has some good, completely serviceable motels and a decent restaurant—relatively rare in rural Utah.

History

Anasazi and Fremont Indians lived here from about A.D. 1050 to 1200. You can spot their petroglyphs, pictographs, artifacts, storage rooms, and village sites while you're hiking in the canyons of the Escalante River and its tributaries. High alcoves in canyon walls protect small stone granaries; check the floors of sandstone caves for things left behind—pieces of pottery, arrowheads, mats, sandals, and corncobs. (Federal laws prohibit removal of artifacts; please leave *everything* for the next person to enjoy.) You can visit an excavated Anasazi village, along with a modern replica of the original, 27 miles east in Boulder.

Southern Paiute arrived in the 1500s and stayed until white settlers took over. The nomadic Paiute had few possessions and left little behind despite their long stay. Mormon colonists didn't learn about the Escalante region until 1866, when Captain James Andrus led his cavalry east from Kanab in pursuit of Paiute Indians. Reports of the expedition described the upper Escalante, which was named Potato Valley after the wild tubers growing there.

Major John Wesley Powell's expedition down the Green and Colorado Rivers in 1869 had failed to recognize the mouth of the Escalante River; it seemed too shallow and narrow for a major tributary. In 1872, a detachment of Powell's second expedition led by Almon H. Thompson and Frederick S. Dellenbaugh stumbled across the Escalante on an overland journey. After some confusion they realized that an entire new river had been found, and they named it for Spanish explorer and priest Silvestre Valez de Escalante. The elusive river was the last to be discovered in the contiguous United States. Mormon ranchers and farmers arrived in the upper valleys of the Escalante in 1876 from Panguitch and other towns to the west, not as part of a church-directed mission but simply in search of new and better lands.

At first glance Escalante looks like a town that time has passed by. Only 950 people live here, in addition to the resident cows, horses, and chickens that you'll meet just a block off Main Street. Yet this little community is the biggest place for more than 60 miles around and a center for ranchers and travelers. Escalante (elev. 5,813 feet) has the neatly laid-out streets and trim little houses typical of Mormon settlements. The former LDS Tithing office (behind the Griffin grocery store) dates from 1884. Pioneers had little cash then and paid their tithes in potatoes, fruit, and other produce. The building now has historic exhibits of the Daughters of Utah Pioneers; open by appointment (phone numbers to volunteers are listed on the door).

ESCALANTE PETRIFIED FOREST STATE PARK

This pleasant park just northwest of town offers camping, boating, fishing, picnicking, hiking, a visitors' center with displays of petrified wood and dinosaur bones, and a chance to see petrified wood along trails. Rivers of 140 million years ago carried trees to the site of present-day Escalante and buried them in sand and gravel. Burial prevented decay as crystals of silicon dioxide gradually replaced the wood cells. Mineral impurities added a rainbow of colors to the trees as they turned to stone. Weathering has exposed this petrified wood and the water-worn pebbles and sand of the Morrison Formation. For a look at some colorful petrified wood, follow the **Petrified Forest Trail** from the campground up a hill-side wooded with piñon pine and juniper. At the top of the 240-foot-high ridge, continue on a loop trail to the petrified wood; allow 45–60 minutes for the one-mile round-trip. **Rainbow Loop Trail** (three quarters of a mile) branches off the Petrified Forest Trail to more areas of petrified wood.

The campground stays open all year, offering drinking water and showers but no hookups. The adjacent 139-acre Wide Hollow Reservoir offers fishing, boating, and bird-watching. The park is 1.5 miles west of town on UT 12, then 0.7 mile north on a gravel road; $4 per vehicle for day use, $16 per vehicle to camp. Contact P.O. Box 350, Escalante, UT 84726, (435) 826-4466 (ranger) or (800) 322-3770 (reservations).

ACCOMMODATIONS

Under $50
The following are pretty basic, but perfectly acceptable. **Moqui Motel,** 480 W. Main, (435) 826-4210, has rooms and some kitchenettes and an RV park ($15 with hookups; no tents). **Circle D Motel,** 475 W. Main, (435) 826-4297, has a restaurant, and pets are welcome in some rooms. In addition to regular rooms, there's one two-bedroom unit ($70) and one four-bedroom ($95).

The following close in winter and generally open March–October. The **Padre Motel,** 20 E. Main, (435) 826-4276, (800) 462-7923, (800) 733-8824, has regular motel rooms and five mini-suites with two bedrooms each. Bunkhouse-style cabins sleeping two are available at **Escalante Outfitters,** 310 W. Main, (435) 826-4266.

$50–75
You can enjoy staying at the pleasant and modern **Rainbow Country B&B,** 586 E. 300 South, (435) 826-4567 or (800) 252-UTAH, and also avail yourself of their custom tours. The B&B's four guest rooms share two and one-half baths; guests have the use of a hot tub, pool table, and TV lounge. The hosts offer several tour itineraries featuring your choice of hiking, back-road four-wheel-drive exploring, or even camping trips. You can also arrange personalized tours to suit your interests. **Prospector Inn,** 380 W. Main, (435) 826-GOLD, is Escalante's newest motel; there's a restaurant and lounge on premises. Open year-round; children 12 and under stay free.

Campgrounds

Besides the state park described above, you can stay at **Broken Bow RV Camp,** 495 W. Main St., (435) 826-4959 or (888) 241-8785, which has cabins (starting at $20), sites for tents ($12) and RVs ($17 with hookups), plus showers and a laundromat; closed in winter.

Calf Creek Recreation Area lies in a pretty canyon 15.5 miles east of Escalante on UT 12; sites run $7 and are open early April–late October; you can reserve group sites through the BLM office. **Calf Creek Falls Trail** (5.5 miles round-trip) begins at the campground and follows the creek upstream to the 126-foot-high falls.

Campgrounds at **Posey Lake** (16 miles north) and **Blue Spruce** (19 miles north) sit atop the Aquarius Plateau in Dixie National Forest. Sites ($7) open around Memorial Day weekend and close in mid-September. Take the dirt Hell's Backbone Road from the east edge of town.

OTHER PRACTICALITIES

Food

The **Ponderosa Restaurant,** 45 N. 400 W., (435) 826-4658, offers Escalante's best food, in a large log lodge in the center of town. Besides the steaks and burgers you'd expect, you'll find a selection of German dishes as well. Alcohol served. **Cowboy Blues Diner and Bakery,** 530 W. Main, (435) 826-4251, serves Western-style food and bakery goods. The **Circle D Restaurant,** 425 W. Main, (435) 826-4251, serves American and Mexican food. **Golden Loop Cafe,** 39 W. Main, (435) 826-4433, has standard American fare. All are open daily for breakfast, lunch, and dinner.

Services

Kazan-Ivan Memorial Clinic, on Center St. behind Bob Munson's Grocery, (435) 826-4374, offers medical care Monday and Thursday. The **Municipal Park** on the west edge of town has covered picnic tables, restrooms with water (except in winter), grills, and a small playground. **Escalante Outfitters,** 310 W. Main, (435) 826-4266, probably has that camping item you forgot as well as topo maps and books.

Information

You can obtain travel advice and literature from the **information booth,** near the Padre Motel; open daily about 10 A.M.–6 P.M. from mid-May to mid-Sept. The new Escalante Interagency office at 755 W. Main on the west edge of town has an **information center** for visitors to Forest Service, Bureau of Land Management, and National Park Service areas around Escalante; this is also one of the best places for gathering information on the Grand Staircase–Escalante National Monument; open Mon.–Fri. (daily from early March to late October) 8 A.M.–5 .P.M. Write P.O. Box 246, Escalante, UT 84726, (435) 826-5499. Normally it's thought best to contact the information center first, but you can also communicate directly with the **Dixie National Forest office,** P.O. Box 246, Escalante, UT 84726, (435) 826-5400; the **Bureau of Land Management office,** P.O. Box 225, Escalante, UT 84726, (435) 826-4291; or the **National Park Service (NPS) office,** P.O. Box 511, Escalante, UT 84726, (435) 826-4315. Hikers headed for overnight trips on the Escalante River system can obtain permits at the information center or at trailheads.

VICINITY OF ESCALANTE

Hell's Backbone Road

This scenic 38-mile drive climbs high into the forests north of Escalante with excellent views of Death Hollow and Sand Creek Canyons and the distant Navajo, Fiftymile, and Henry Mountains. **Posey Lake Campground** (elev. 8,700 feet) offers sites amid aspen and ponderosa pines; open with drinking water from Memorial Day weekend to mid-September ($7). Rainbow and brook trout swim in the adjacent lake. A hiking trail (two miles round-trip) begins near space number 14 and climbs 400 feet to an old fire lookout tower with good views of the lake and surrounding country. Posey Lake is 14 miles north of Escalante, then two miles west on a side road.

Blue Spruce Campground (elev. 7,860 feet) is another pretty spot but has only six sites. Anglers can try for pan-sized trout in a nearby stream. The campground, surrounded by blue spruce, aspen, and ponderosa pine, has drinking water from Memorial Day weekend to mid-September ($7); go north 19 miles from town, then turn left and drive a half mile. Hell's Backbone Road reaches an elevation of 9,200 feet on the slopes of Roger Peak before descending to Hell's Backbone, 25 miles from town. Mule teams used this narrow ridge, with precipitous canyons on either side, as a route to Boulder until the 1930s. At that time a bridge built by the Civilian Conservation Corps allowed the first vehicles to make the trip. You can still see the old mule path below the bridge. After 38 miles the road ends at UT 12; turn right 24 miles to return to Escalante or turn left three miles to Boulder. Cars can usually manage the gravel and dirt Hell's Backbone Road when it's dry. Snows and snowmelt, however, block the way until about late May. Check with the Interagency office in Escalante for current conditions. Trails and rough dirt roads lead deeper into the backcountry to more vistas and fishing lakes.

Calf Creek Recreation Area

Calf Creek Campground lies in a pretty canyon 15.5 miles east of Escalante on UT 12; sites are open with drinking water from early April to late October ($7). Reserve group sites through the In-teragency office. The hike to Calf Creek Falls offers a good introduction to the pleasures of hiking in the Escalante River system. Walking between high cliffs of Navajo Sandstone streaked with desert varnish, you'll see beaver ponds, Indian ruins and pictographs, and the misty 126-foot-high Lower Calf Creek Falls. A brochure available at the trailhead next to the campground identifies many of the desert and riparian plant species along the way. Round-trip is 5.5 miles with only a slight gain in elevation; bring water and perhaps a lunch. Summer temperatures can soar but the falls and the crystal-clear pool beneath stay cool. Sheer cliffs block travel farther upstream.

The Calf Creek area is now part of the Grand Staircase–Escalante National Monument.

HOLE-IN-THE-ROCK ROAD

The building of this road by determined Mormons was one of the great epics in the colonization of the West. Church leaders organized the Hole-in-the-Rock Expedition to settle the wild lands around the San Juan River of southeastern Utah, feeling a Mormon presence would aid in ministering to the Indians there and prevent non-Mormons from moving in. In 1878, the Parowan Stake issued the first call for a colonizing mission to the San Juan, even before a site had been selected. Preparations and surveys took place the following year as the 236 men, women, and children received their calls. Food, seed, farming and building tools, 200 horses, and more than 1,000 head of cattle would be taken along. Planners ruled out lengthy routes through northern Arizona or eastern Utah in favor of a straight shot via Escalante that would cut the distance in half. The expedition set off in the autumn of 1879, convinced that they were part of a divine mission. Yet hints of trouble to come filtered back from the group as they discovered the Colorado River crossing to be far more difficult than first believed. Lack of springs along the way added to their worries. From their start at Escalante, road builders progressed rapidly for the first 50 miles, then slowly over

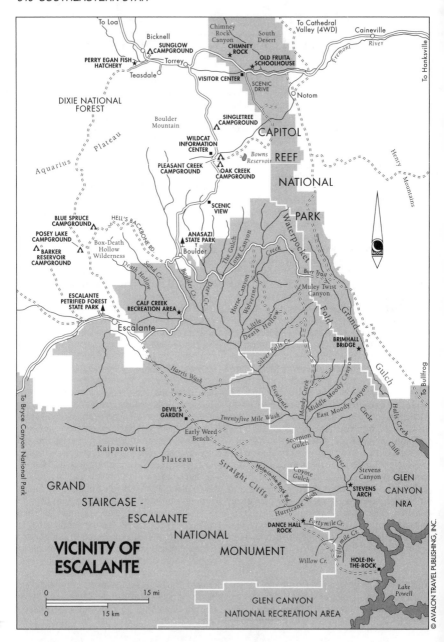

VICINITY OF ESCALANTE

© AVALON TRAVEL PUBLISHING, INC.

rugged slickrock for the final six miles to Hole-in-the-Rock. A 45-foot sheer drop below this narrow notch was followed by three quarters of a mile of extremely steep slickrock to the Colorado River. The route looked impossible, but three crews of workers armed with picks and blasting powder worked simultaneously to widen the notch and to construct a precarious wagon road down to the river and up cliffs on the other side. The job took six weeks. Miraculously, all the people, animals, and wagons made it down and were ferried across the Colorado River without a serious accident. Canyons and other obstacles continued to block the way as the weary group pressed on. Only after six months of exhausting travel did they stop at the present-day site of Bluff on the San Juan River.

Today, on a journey from Escalante, you can experience a bit of the same adventure the pioneers knew. Except for scattered signs of ranching, the land remains unchanged. Hole-in-the-Rock Road is also one of the main access routes for the new Grand Staircase–Escalante National Monument, which now contains the majority of this road. If the road's dry, vehicles with good clearance can drive to within a short distance of Hole-in-the-Rock. The rough conditions encountered past Dance Hall Rock require more clearance than most cars. Bring sufficient gas, food, and water for the entire 126-mile round-trip from Escalante. The turnoff from UT 12 is five miles east of town. In addition to rewarding you with scenic views, Hole-in-the-Rock Road passes many side drainages of the Escalante River to the east and some very remote country of the Kaiparowits Plateau high above to the west. Staff at the information center just west of Escalante can give current road conditions and suggest hikes.

Metate Arch and other rock sculptures decorate **Devil's Garden,** 12.5 miles down Hole-in-the-Rock Road. Turn west 0.3 mile at the sign to the parking area, as you can't really see the "garden" from the road. Red- and cream-colored sandstone formations sit atop pedestals or tilt at crazy angles. Delicate bedding lines run through the rocks. There are no trails or markers—just wander about at your whim. The BLM has provided picnic tables, grills, and outhouses for day use. No overnight camping is permitted at Devil's Garden.

Dance Hall Rock (38 miles down Hole-in-the-Rock Road) jumped to the fiddle music and lively steps of the expedition members in 1879. Its natural amphitheater has a relatively smooth floor and made a perfect gathering spot when the Hole-in-the-Rock group had to wait three weeks at nearby Fortymile Spring for road work to be completed ahead. Dance Hall Rock is an enjoyable place to explore and only a short walk from the parking area. Solution holes, left from water dissolving in the rock, pockmark the Entrada Sandstone structure.

At road's end (57 miles from UT 12), continue on foot across slickrock to the notch and views of the blue waters of Lake Powell below. Rockslides have made the descent impossible for vehicles, but hikers can scramble down to the lake and back in about an hour. Elevation change is 600 feet. The half-mile round-trip is strenuous. After a steep descent over boulders, look for steps of Uncle Ben's Dugway at the base of the notch. Below here the grade is gentler. Drill holes in the rock once held oak stakes against which logs, brush, and earth supported the outer wagon wheels. The inner wheels followed a narrow rut 4–6 inches deep. About two-thirds of the route down is now under water, though the most impressive road work can still be seen.

Elizabeth Morris Decker described the descent in a letter to her parents on February 22, 1880:

If you ever come this way it will scare you to death to look down it. It is about a mile from the top down to the river and it is almost strait down, the cliffs on each side are five hundred feet high and there is just room enough for a wagon to go down. It nearly scared me to death. The first wagon I saw go down they put the brake on and rough locked the hind wheels and had a big rope fastened to the wagon and about ten men holding back on it and then they went down like they would smash everything. I'll never forget that day. When we was walking down Willie looked back and cried and asked me how we would get back home.

HIKING THE ESCALANTE RIVER AND ITS TRIBUTARIES

The maze of canyons presents exceptional hiking opportunities. You'll find everything from easy day hikes to challenging backpacking treks. The Escalante's canyon begins just downstream from the town of Escalante and ends at Lake Powell about 85 miles beyond. In all this distance only one road (UT 12) bridges the river. Many side canyons provide additional access to the Escalante and most are as beautiful as the main gorge. The river system covers such a large area that you can find solitude even in spring, the busiest hiking season. The many eastern canyons remain virtually untouched. The Escalante canyons preserve some of the quiet beauty once found in Glen Canyon, now lost under the waters of Lake Powell. Prehistoric Anasazi and Fremont Indians have left ruins, petroglyphs, pictographs, and artifacts in many locations. These archaeological resources are protected by federal law. Please don't collect or disturb them.

Practicalities

Visit the people at the information center on the west edge of Escalante for the required free permit to backpack in the Grand Staircase–Excalate National Monument, and the latest trail and road conditions before setting out. Be sure to check on restrictions on group size, which are in force on some of the more popular trails. You can also obtain topo maps and literature that show trailheads, mileages, and other info useful in planning trips. Some of the more popular trailheads have self-registration stations for permits. A useful book, *Hiking the Grand Staircase-Escalante and the Glen Canyon Region,* by Ron Adkison, introduces the region and describes 59 trips with comments on the geology, flora and fauna, and history. Best times for a visit are early March to early June and mid-September to early November. Summertime trips are possible, too—just be prepared for higher temperatures and greater flash-flood danger in narrow canyons. Travel along the Escalante River involves frequent crossings, and there's always water in the main canyon, usually ankle- to knee-deep. Pools in the "Narrows" section between Scorpion Gulch and Stevens Canyon can

be up to chest deep in spots (which you can bypass), but that's the exception. All this wading can destroy leather boots, so it's best to wear canvas shoes or boots. High-topped "Vietnam boots," available at surplus stores, work well and prevent gravel from getting inside. Occasional springs, some tributaries, and the river itself provide drinking water. Always purify it first; the NPS and BLM warn of the unpleasant disease giardiasis, caused by an invisible protozoan. Don't forget insect repellent—mosquitos and deer flies seek out hikers in late spring and summer. Long-sleeved shirts and long pants also discourage biting insects and protect against the brush.

Walking Softly

Only great care and awareness can preserve the pristine canyons. You can help if you pack out all trash, avoid trampling on the fragile cryptobiotic soils (dark areas of symbiotic algae and fungus on the sand), travel in groups of 12 or fewer, don't disturb Indian artifacts, and protect wildlife by leaving your dogs at home. (Dogs must be leashed within Glen Canyon NRA) Most important, bury human waste well away from water sources, trails, and camping areas; unless there's a fire hazard, burn toilet paper to aid decomposition. Campfires in developed or designated campgrounds are allowed only in fire grates, fire pits, or fire pans. Wood collection in these areas is not permitted. The use of backpacker stoves is recommended by the NPS and the BLM. Visitors are encouraged to maximize efforts to leave no trace of their passage in the area.

Floating the Escalante

Most of the year, shallow water and rocks make boat travel impossible, but for 2–3 weeks during spring runoff, river levels rise high enough, peaking between early April and late May. (In some years there may not be enough water in any season.) Keep in touch with the information center in Escalante to hit the river at its highest. Shallow draft and maneuverability are essential, so inflatable canoes or kayaks work best (also because they are easier to carry out at trip's end or if water levels drop too low for floating). Not recommended are rafts (too wide and bulky) and hard-shelled kayaks and canoes (get banged up on the many rocks). The usual launch is the UT 12 bridge; Coyote Gulch—a 13-mile hike—is a good spot to get out, as are the Crack in Wall route (a 2.75-mile hike on steep sand from the junction of Coyote and Escalante Canyons to Forty-Mile Ridge Trailhead; four-wheel drive needed; a rope is required to negotiate the vessel over the canyon rim), and Hole-in-the-Rock (a 600-foot ascent over boulders; rope suggested). You could also arrange for a friend to pick you up by boat from the Halls Crossing or Bullfrog Marina. River boaters need a free backcountry permit from either the BLM or the National Park Service.

Trailheads

The many approaches to the area allow all sorts of trips. Besides the road access at Escalante and the UT 12 bridge, hikers can reach the Escalante River through western side canyons from Hole-in-the-Rock Road or eastern side canyons from Burr Trail Road. The western-canyon trailheads on Hole-in-the-Rock Road can be more easily reached by car, thus facilitating vehicle shuttles. To reach eastern-canyon trailheads, with the exceptions of Deer Creek and the Gulch on Burr Trail Road, you'll need lots of time and, if the road is wet, a four-wheel-drive vehicle. You'll also need to carry water for these more remote canyons. With the exception of Deer Creek, they're usually dry.

Town of Escalante to UT 12 Bridge

(15 miles)
This first section of canyon offers easy walking and stunning canyon scenery. Tributaries and sandstone caves invite exploration. You'll find good camping areas all along. Usually the river here is only ankle deep. Either enter Escalante River at the bridge next to the sawmill, or go one mile east of town on UT 12 and turn north past the cemetery (visible from highway) and town dump. Almost immediately the river knifes its way through the massive cliffs of the Escalante Monocline, leaving the broad valley of the upper river behind. Although there is no maintained trail along this stretch of the east-flowing river, it's relatively easy to pick your way along the river bank.

Death Hollow, far prettier than the name suggests, comes in to the Escalante from the north after 7.5 miles. Several good swimming holes carved in rock lie a short hike upstream from the Escalante; watch for poison ivy among the greenery. Continue farther up Death Hollow to see

Parts of Escalante Canyon are now protected as a national monument.

more pools, little waterfalls, and outstanding canyon scenery. You can bypass some pools, but some you'll have to swim—bring a little inflatable boat, air mattress, or waterproof bag to ferry packs. Hikers looking for a real challenge can start from a trailhead 24 miles north of town on Hell's Backbone Road, scramble and swim their way to the Escalante River (22.5 extremely strenuous miles one-way), then walk the Escalante 7.5 miles to town or the UT 12 bridge. The first 11 miles of this route are dry—then you're swimming! Allow 4–5 days. The average hiker would most enjoy exploring Death Hollow up from its confluence with the Escalante River.

Sand Creek, on the Escalante's north side 4.5 miles downstream from Death Hollow, is also worth exploring; deep pools begin a short way up from the mouth. After another half mile down the Escalante, a natural arch appears high on the canyon wall. Then the Escalante Natural Bridge comes into view about a half mile farther, just two miles from the UT 12 bridge. In

W.C. McRAE

fact, Escalante Natural Bridge makes a good day-hike destination from the highway.

UT 12 Bridge to Harris Wash
(26.5 miles)

In this section, the Escalante Canyon offers a varied show: in places the walls close in to make constricted narrows, at other places they step back to form great valleys. Side canyons filled with lush greenery and sparkling streams contrast with dry washes of desert, yet all can be fun to explore. A good hike of 4–6 days begins at the highway bridge, goes down the Escalante to Harris Wash, then up Harris to a trailhead off Hole-in-the-Rock Road (37 miles total).

From the UT 12 bridge parking area, a trail leads to the river. Canyon access goes through private property; cross the river at the posted signs to avoid barking dogs at the ranch just downstream. **Phipps Wash** comes in from the south (right side) after 1.5 miles and several more river crossings. Turn up its wide mouth a half mile to see Maverick Bridge in a drainage to the right. To reach Phipps Arch, continue another three quarters of a mile up the main wash, turn left into a box canyon, and scramble up the left side (see 7 1/2-minute Calf Creek topo map).

Bowington (Boynton) Arch is an attraction of a north side canyon known locally as Deer Creek. Look for this small canyon on the left one mile beyond Phipps Wash; turn up it one mile past three deep pools and then turn left a short way into a tributary canyon. In 1878, gunfire resolved a quarrel between local ranchers John Boynton and Washington Phipps. Phipps was killed, but both their names live on.

Waters of **Boulder Creek** come rushing into the Escalante from the north in the next major side canyon, 5.75 miles below the UT 12 bridge. The creek, along with its Dry Hollow and Deer Creek tributaries, provides good canyon walking; deep areas may require swimming or climbing up on the plateau. (You could also start down Deer Creek from the Burr Trail Road where they meet, 6.5 miles southeast of Boulder at a primitive BLM campground; starting at the campground, follow Deer Creek 7.5 miles to Boulder Creek, then 3.5 miles down Boulder to the Escalante.) Deer and Boulder Creeks have water year-round.

High sheer walls of Navajo Sandstone constrict the Escalante River in a narrow channel below Boulder Creek, but the canyon widens again above **the Gulch** tributary, 14 miles below the highway bridge. Hikers can head up the Gulch on a day hike or start from Burr Trail Road (the trailhead is 10.8 miles southeast of Boulder). The hike from the road down to the Escalante is 12.5 miles, but there's one difficult spot: a 12-foot waterfall in a section of narrows about halfway down has to be bypassed. When Rudi Lambrechtse, author of *Hiking the Escalante,* tried friction climbing around the falls and the pool at their base, he fell 12 feet and broke his foot. That meant a painful three-day hobble out. Instead of taking the risk, Rudi recommends backtracking about 300 feet from the falls and friction climbing out from a small alcove in the west wall (look for a cairn on the ledge above). Climb up Brigham Tea Bench, walk south, then look for cairns leading back east to the narrows, and descend to the streambed (a rope helps to lower packs in a small chimney section).

Most springs along the Escalante are difficult to spot. One that's easy to find is in the first south bend after the Gulch; water comes straight out of the rock a few feet above the river. The Escalante Canyon becomes wider as the river lazily meanders along. Hikers can cut off some of the bends by walking in the open desert between canyon walls and riverside willow thickets. A bend cut off by the river itself loops to the north just before Horse Canyon, three miles below the Gulch. Along with its tributaries **Death Hollow** and **Wolverine Creek, Horse Canyon** drains the Circle Cliffs to the northeast. Floods in these mostly dry streambeds wash down pieces of black petrified wood. (Vehicles with good clearance can reach the upper sections of all three canyons from a loop road off Burr Trail Road.) Horse and Wolverine Creek Canyons offer good easy-to-moderate hiking, but if you really want a challenge, try Death Hollow (sometimes called "Little Death Hollow" to distinguish it from the larger one near Hell's Backbone Road). Starting from the Escalante River, go about two miles up Horse Canyon and turn right into Death Hollow; rugged scrambling over boulders takes you back into a long section of twisting narrows. Carry water for Upper Horse Canyon and its tributaries; Lower Horse Canyon usually has water.

About 3.5 miles down the Escalante from Horse Canyon, you'll enter Glen Canyon NRA and come to Sheffield Bend, a large grassy field on the right. Only a chimney remains from Sam Sheffield's old homestead. Two grand amphitheaters lie beyond the clearing and up a stiff climb in loose sand. Over the next 5.5 river miles to Silver Falls Creek you'll pass long bends, dry side canyons, and a huge slope of sand on the right canyon wall. Don't look for any silver waterfalls in **Silver Falls Creek**—the name comes from streaks of shiny desert varnish on the cliffs. You can approach Upper Silver Falls Creek by a rough road from Burr Trail Road, but a car shuttle between here and any of the trailheads on the west side of the Escalante River would take all day. Most hikers visit this drainage on a day hike from the river. Carry water.

When the Hole-in-the-Rock route proved so difficult, pioneers figured there had to be a better way to the San Juan Mission. Their new wagon road descended Harris Wash to the Escalante River, climbed part of Silver Falls Creek, crossed the Circle Cliffs, descended Muley Twist Canyon in the Waterpocket Fold, then followed Hall's Creek to Hall's Crossing on the Colorado River. Charles Hall operated a ferry there from 1881 to 1884. Old maps show a jeep road through Harris Wash and Silver Falls Creek Canyons, used before the National Park Service closed off the Glen Canyon NRA section. Harris Wash lies just a half mile downstream and across the Escalante from Silver Falls Creek.

Harris Wash

(10.25 miles one-way from trailhead to river)
Clear shallow water glides down this gem of a canyon. High cliffs streaked with desert varnish are deeply undercut and support lush hanging gardens. Harris Wash provides a beautiful route to the Escalante River, but it can also be a destination in itself; tributaries and caves invite exploration along the way. The sand and gravel streambed makes for easy walking. Reach the trailhead from UT 12 by turning south 10.8 miles on Hole-in-the-Rock Road, then left 6.3 miles on a dirt road (keep left at the fork near the end). Don't be dismayed by the drab appearance of upper Harris Wash. The canyon and creek appear a few miles downstream. The Harris Wash Trailhead now has a restriction of 12 persons per group.

Harris Wash to Lake Powell

(42.75 miles)
The Escalante continues its spectacular show of wide and narrow reaches, side canyons to explore, and intriguing rock formations. A trip all the way from Harris Wash Trailhead to the Escalante, down the Escalante to near Lake Powell, then out to the Hurricane Wash Trailhead is 66.25 miles, taking 8–10 days. Many shorter hikes using other side canyons are possible, too.

Still in a broad canyon, the Escalante flows past **Fence Canyon** (on the west) 5.5 miles from Harris Wash. Fence Canyon has water and is a strenuous 3.5-mile cross-country route out to the end of Egypt Road. Get trail directions from a ranger and bring a topo map. (Adventurous hikers could do a three-day, 20-mile loop via Fence Canyon, the Escalante River, and the northern arm of Twentyfive Mile Wash.) To reach the trailheads, take Hole-in-the-Rock Road 17.2 miles south of UT 12, then turn left (east) 3.7 miles on the Egypt Road for Twentyfive Mile Wash Trailhead or 9.1 miles for Egypt Trailhead.

Twentyfive Mile Wash, on the west side 11.5 miles below Harris Wash, is a good route for entering or leaving the Escalante River. The moderately difficult hike is 13 miles one-way from trailhead to river. Scenery transforms from that of an uninteresting dry wash in the upper part to a beautiful canyon with water and greenery in the lower reaches. To get to the trailhead, take Hole-in-the-Rock Road 17.2 miles south of UT 12, then turn left 3.7 miles on Egypt Road.

Moody Creek enters the Escalante six meandering river miles below Twentyfive Mile Wash (or just 2.25 miles as the crow flies). A rough road off Burr Trail Road gives access to Moody Creek, Purple Hills, and other eroded features. Distance from trailhead to river is seven miles one-way (moderately strenuous), though most hikers find it more convenient to hike up from the Escalante. **Middle Moody Creek** enters Moody Creek three miles above the Escalante. Moody and Middle Moody Canyons feature colorful rock layers, petrified wood, a narrows, and solitude. Carry water, as springs and waterpockets cannot be counted on. Canyons on the east side of the Escalante tend to be much drier than those on the west side.

East Moody Canyon enters the Escalante 1.5 miles downstream from Moody Canyon, and it, too, makes a good side trip. There's often water about one-half mile upstream. Continuing down the Escalante, look on the left for a rincon, a meander cut off by the river. **Scorpion Gulch** enters through a narrow opening on the right, 6.5 miles below Moody Canyon. A strenuous eight-mile climb up Scorpion Gulch over rockfalls and around deep pools brings you to a trailhead on Early Weed Bench Road. Experience, directions from a ranger, and a topo map are needed. A challenging four-day, 30-mile loop hike uses Fox Canyon, Twentyfive Mile Wash, the Escalante River, and Scorpion Gulch. Water is found only in lower Twentyfive Mile Wash, the river, and lower Scorpion Gulch. The Early Weed Bench turnoff is 24.2 miles south on Hole-in-the-Rock Road from UT 12; head in 5.8 miles to Scorpion Gulch Trailhead.

In the next 12 miles below Scorpion Gulch, Escalante Canyon is alternately wide and narrow. Then the river plunges into the **Narrows**, a five-mile-long section choked with boulders; plan on spending a day picking a route through. Watch out for chest-deep water here! Remote and little-visited, **Stevens Canyon** enters from the east near the end of the Narrows. Stevens Arch stands guard 580 feet above the confluence; the opening measures 225 feet wide and 160 feet high. The upper and lower parts of Stevens Canyon usually have some water.

Coyote Gulch, on the right 1.5 miles below Stevens Canyon, marks the end of the Escalante for most hikers. In some seasons Lake Powell comes within one mile of Coyote Gulch and occasionally floods the canyon mouth. Coyote can stay flooded for several weeks, depending on the release flow of Glen Canyon Dam and water volume coming in. The river and lake don't have a pretty meeting place—quicksand and dead trees are found here. Logjams make it difficult to travel in from the lake by boat.

Coyote Gulch has received more publicity than other areas of the Escalante, and you're more likely to meet other hikers here. Two arches, a natural bridge, graceful sculpturing of the streambed and canyon walls, deep undercuts, and a cascading creek make a visit worthwhile. The best route in starts where Hole-in-the-Rock Road crosses Hurricane Wash, 34.7 miles south of UT 12. It's 12.5 miles one-way from the trailhead to the river and the hike is

moderately strenuous. For the first mile you follow the dry, sandy wash without even a hint of being in a canyon. Water doesn't appear for three more miles. You'll reach Coyote Gulch, which has water, at 5.25 miles from the trailhead. Another way into Coyote Gulch begins at the Red Well Trailhead; it's 31.5 miles south on Hole-in-the-Rock Road, then 1.5 miles east (keep left at the fork). A start from Red Well adds three-quarters of a mile more to the hike than the Hurricane Wash route, but it is also less crowded.

Other Adventures

Dry Fork of Coyote Gulch contains three enchanting canyons named Peek-a-boo, Spooky, and Brimstone. Enjoy the narrows, natural bridges, and deep pools. See *Hiking the Escalante,* by Rudi Lambrechtse, for directions.

Three canyons near the end of Hole-in-the-Rock Road lead down to Lake Powell: Fortymile Gulch (strenuous, 12 miles round-trip), Willow Gulch (moderately difficult, six miles round-trip), and Fiftymile Creek (easy to moderately difficult, eight miles round-trip). As none are signed, you'll need a topo map, directions from a ranger, or *Hiking the Escalante* to find them.

BOULDER

About 150 people live in this farming community at the base of Boulder Mountain. Ranchers began drifting in during the late 1870s, though not with the idea of forming a town. By the mid-1890s Boulder had established itself as a ranching and dairy center. Remote and hemmed in by canyons and mountains, Boulder remained one of the last communities in the country to rely on pack trains for transportation. Motor vehicles couldn't drive in until the 1930s. Today Boulder is worth a visit to see an excavated Anasazi village and the spectacular scenery along the way. Take paved UT 12 either through the canyon and slickrock country from Escalante or over the Aquarius Plateau from Torrey (near Capitol Reef National Park). Burr Trail Road connects Boulder with Capitol Reef National Park's southern district via Waterpocket Fold and Circle Cliffs. A fourth way in is from Escalante on the dirt Hell's Backbone Road, which comes out three miles west of Boulder at UT 12.

Anasazi State Park

Museum exhibits, an excavated village site, and a pueblo replica provide a look into the life of these ancient people. The Anasazi stayed here for 50–75 years sometime between A.D. 1050 and 1200. They grew corn, beans, and squash in fields nearby. Village population peaked at about 200, with an estimated 40–50 dwellings. Why the Anasazi left or where they went isn't known for sure, but a fire swept through much of the village before the Anasazi abandoned it. Perhaps they burned the village on purpose, knowing they would move on. University of Utah students and faculty excavated the village, known as the Coombs Site, in 1958 and 1959. You can view pottery, ax heads, arrow points, and other tools found at the site in the museum, along with more perishable items like sandals and basketry that came from more protected sites elsewhere. A diorama shows how the village might have appeared in its heyday. You can see video programs on the Anasazi and modern tribes upon request.

The self-guided tour of the ruins begins behind the museum. You'll see a whole range of Anasazi building styles—a pit house, masonry walls, jacal walls (mud reinforced by sticks), and combinations of masonry and jacal. Replicas of habitation and storage rooms behind the museum show complete construction details. The park is open daily 8 A.M.–6 P.M. from mid-May to mid-September, then 9 A.M.–5 P.M. the rest of the year. Admission is $2 per person, or $5 per vehicle (whichever is the least). Books, videos, T-shirts, and postcards are sold. Located on UT 12, 28 miles northeast of Escalante and 38 miles south of Torrey, (435) 335-7308.

Accommodations

$50–75: You wouldn't expect to find one of Utah's nicest places to stay in tiny Boulder, but the **Boulder Mountain Lodge,** along UT 12 right in town, (435) 355-7460 or (800) 556-3446, offers the kinds of facilities and setting that make this one of the few destination lodgings in the state. The lodge's buildings are grouped around the edge of a private, 15-acre pond that serves as an ad hoc wildlife refuge. You can sit on the deck or wander paths along the pond, watching and listening to the amazing variety of birds that make this their home. The guest rooms and suites are in a handsome and modern Western-style lodge facing the pond; rooms are nicely decorated with quality furniture and beddings, and there's a central Great Room with a fireplace and library.

Poole's Place (closed in winter), across the road from the state park, (435) 335-7422 or (800) 730-7422, has a well-maintained motel, café, and gift shop.

Campgrounds: Hall's Store, next to Anasazi State Park, (435) 335-7304, runs a small RV park ($13; self-contained; no tents). Otherwise, there are several Forest Service campgrounds on nearby Boulder Mountain (follow Hwy 12 north from town).

Boulder Mountain Lodge adjoins a small wetlands.

W.C. McRAE

Food

The Boulder Mountain Lodge restaurant, the **Hell's Backbone Grill,** (435) 355-7460 or (800) 556-3446, offers just about the only fine dining in all of southern Utah. You'll find fresh fish and seafood, adventurous game and meat preparations, and excellent deserts; open for three meals a day. For simpler fare, the **Burr Trail Cafe** (open Memorial Day weekend–autumn) is at the intersection of UT 12 and Burr Trail Road, (435) 335-7432.

Guest Ranch

Cowboy up at the **Boulder Mountain Ranch,** seven miles from Boulder on the Hell's Backbone Rd., (435) 355-7480, www.boulderutah.com/bmr. Guests have a choice of simple B&B accommodations in the lodge or freestanding cabins ($55 to $65), horseback riding, or multi-day pack trips along the Great Western Trail. There are also two- to five-day riding and lodging packages based out of the ranch. Contact the ranch at P.O. Box 1373, Boulder, UT 84716.

Tours and Excursions

Red Rock 'n Llamas, P.O. Box 1304, Boulder, UT 84716, (435) 559-7325, offers a variety of fully outfitted hiking adventures in the Escalante Canyon area. Llamas will carry most of the gear, leaving you to explore in comfort. Most trips are four days and cost between $500–650. Write for a schedule.

If llamas don't strike you as Western enough for your backcountry adventure, **Escalante Canyon Outfitters,** P.O. Box 1330, Boulder, UT 84716, (435) 335-7311 or (888) 326-4453, www.ecohike.com, offers a selection of full-service guided tours of the Escalante country with pack horses.

Information and Services

Look for a **visitor information** booth in town; usually it's in front of Burr Trail Cafe. Open daily May–Oct. about 9 A.M.–6 P.M. The two gas stations in Boulder sell groceries and snacks.

BURR TRAIL ROAD

The Burr Trail Road, originally a cattle trail blazed by stockman John Atlantic Burr, extends from the town of Boulder on Utah Highway 12 to the Notom-Bullfrog Road, which runs between Highway 24 near the eastern entrance to Capitol Reef National Park and Bullfrog Marina on Lake Powell, off Highway 276. Starting at Boulder, roughly the first third of this 67.4-mile road is now paved. Pavement ends at the boundary of Capitol Reef National Park, where the route traverses the Circle Cliffs, as well as spectacular canyon areas such as Long Canyon and The Gulch. Included in this section is a breathtaking set of switchbacks rising some 800 feet in only one-half mile. These switchbacks are not considered suitable for RVs or vehicles towing trailers. The unpaved sections of the road are subject to change due to weather conditions. Visitors should inquire about road and weather conditions before traveling.

The Burr Trail Road joins the Notom-Bullfrog Road just before exiting the park. For information on the Notom-Bullfrog Road, turn to Capitol Reef National Park, below.

BOULDER MOUNTAIN SCENIC DRIVE

Utah 12 climbs high into forests of ponderosa pine, aspen, and fir on Boulder Mountain between the towns of Boulder and Torrey. The modern highway replaces what used to be a rough dirt road. Travel in winter is usually possible now, though heavy snows can close the road. Viewpoints along the drive offer sweeping panoramas of the Escalante canyon country, Circle Cliffs, Waterpocket Fold, and the Henry Mountains. Hikers and anglers can explore the alpine country of Boulder Mountain and seek out the 90 or so trout-filled lakes. The Dixie National Forest map (Escalante and Teasdale Ranger District offices) shows the back roads, trails, and lakes. The U.S. Forest Service has three developed campgrounds about midway along this scenic drive: **Oak Creek** (18 miles from Boulder, elev. 8,800 feet), **Pleasant Creek** (19 miles from Boulder, elev. 8,700 feet), and **Singletree** (24 miles from Boulder, elev. 8,600 feet). The season with water lasts from about late May to mid-September; sites cost $8. Campgrounds may also be open in spring and autumn without water for $3. **Lower Bowns Reservoir** (elev. 7,400 feet) has primitive camping (no water or

Chriss Lake, one of many pretty spots on Boulder Mountain

fee) and fishing for rainbow and some cutthroat trout; turn east five miles on a rough dirt road (not recommended for cars) just south of Pleasant Creek Campground. Contact the **Teasdale Ranger District office,** near Torrey, (435) 425-3702, for recreation information in the northern and eastern parts of Boulder Mountain; contact the **Escalante Ranger District office,** Escalante, (435) 826-5499/5400, for the southern and western areas. **Wildcat Information Center,** near Pleasant Creek Campground, has forest information; open in the summer with irregular hours.

TORREY AND VICINITY

Torrey (pop. 135) is a highly attractive little town, with a real Western feel. Only 11 miles west of the Capitol Reef National Park Visitor Center, it's a friendly and convenient place to stay, with several excellent lodgings and a good restaurant. As Torrey is at the junction of Highways 12 and 24, it's a great hub for exploring the wild country of the Grand Staircase–Escalante National Monument area just to the south.

Other little towns lie along the Fremont River, which drains this steep-sided valley. Teasdale is a small community just four miles east, in a grove of piñon pines. Bicknell, a small farm and ranch town, is eight miles east of Torrey.

The **J. Perry Egan Fish Hatchery,** near Bicknell, produces 25–30 million trout eggs a year. It's the largest in Utah and supplies eggs for most of the state's other hatcheries. The raceways have fish divided according to species, strain, and age. Trout spawn when three years old and are kept to produce here for another three years, after which they're released into high-pressure fishing areas. You'll see cutthroat, German brown, brook, and 4–6 strains of rainbow trout (including albinos). Visitors are welcome to see the operation; open during daylight hours. Turn south 2.5 miles on a paved road off UT 24 between Mileposts 63 and 64 (southeast of Bicknell).

Accommodations
Under $50: The cabins at the center of town, at the **Torrey Trading Post,** 75 W. Main St., (435) 425-3716, are just $35 a night. **Capitol Reef Inn and Cafe,** (435) 425-3271 (closed in winter), has standard motel rooms, a small café serving breakfast and dinner, and a gift shop.

$50–75: The main business in Torrey is its old trading post and country store. Immediately behind it in a grove of trees is the **Chuck Wagon Lodge,** (435) 425-3335 or (800) 863-3288, with rooms in an older motel (under $50) or in a brand-new and attractive lodgelike building. There's a pool, hot tub, and some campsites; open mid-Apr.–mid-Nov.

The **Wonderland Inn,** just east of town near the UT 12 turnoff for Boulder, (435) 425-3775 or (800) 458-0216, has clean rooms, and a restaurant serving breakfast, lunch, and dinner daily. The local **Super 8 Motel** is also just east of town on Highway 24, (435) 425-3688. In Teasdale, four miles west of Torrey, **Pine Shadows,** 125 S. 200 West, (435) 425-3939 or (800) 708-1223, offers new pine bungalows in a piñon forest. Or stay in a historic pioneer-era home in nearby Teasdale. The historic **Cockscomb Inn B&B,** 97 S. State St., (435) 425-3511 or (800) 530-1038, has three guest rooms with queen beds, plus a garden cottage. All rooms have private bathrooms.

In Bicknell, the **Aquarius Motel,** (435) 425-3835 or (800) 833-5379, offers rooms, some with kitchens. There's also a café open daily for breakfast, lunch, and dinner.

$75–100: The lovely **SkyRidge Bed and Breakfast** is one mile east of downtown, (435) 425-3222. The modern inn has been decorated with high-quality Southwestern art and artifacts; all five guest rooms have private baths. SkyRidge sits on a bluff amid 75 acres; guests are invited to explore the land on foot or on bike.

The **Lodge at Red River Ranch,** between Bicknell and Torrey, (435) 425-3322 or (800) 20-LODGE, is located beneath towering cliffs of red sandstone on the banks of the Fremont River. This wonderful wood-beamed lodge sits on a working ranch, but there's nothing rustic or unsophisticated about the accommodations here. The three-story structure is newly built, though in the same grand architectural style of old-fashioned mountain lodges. The great room has a massive stone fireplace, cozy chairs and couches, and a splendid Old West atmosphere. There are 15 guest rooms, most decorated according to a theme, and all have private baths. Guests are welcome to wander ranch paths, fish for trout, or tinker in the gardens and orchards. For information, write P.O. Box 280, Bicknell, UT 84715.

The **Days Inn,** at the junction of UT 12 and UT 24, (435) 425-3111 or (888) 425-3113, has a pool. Just east of Torrey, toward the park, is **Best Western Capitol Reef Resort,** (435) 425-3761 or (800) 528-1234, which features luxury accommodations, a pool, and an attractive restaurant (open daily for breakfast, lunch, and dinner). There's also a brand new **Holiday Inn Express,** east of town toward Capital Reef, (435) 425-3866 or (888) 232-4082.

Campgrounds: For campers **Thousand Lakes RV Park,** one mile west of town on UT 24, (435) 425-3500, has sites with showers, laundry, and store; open Apr. 1–Oct. 31; $14 tents or RVs without hookups, $17 RVs with. Thousand Lakes also has a nightly Western-style cookout in an outdoor pavilion. **Wonderland Resort and RV Park,** a half block south on UT 12 from UT 24 junction, (800) 458-0216, both tenting and RV sites ($13.50), phone and modem hook-ups, and laundry facilities. U.S. Forest Service's **Sunglow Campground** is just east of Bicknell; sites are open mid-May–late October with water and a $8 charge; elevation is 7,200 feet; the surrounding red cliffs really light up at sunset.

Food

Several of the motels in town offer American-style food, though it's probably **Cafe Diablo,** 599 W. Main, (435) 425-3070, that you'll remember long after you've left Utah. Their specialty is zesty Southwestern cuisine, with excellent dishes like chipotle ribs, shrimp with habañero peppers, and pumpkin seed trout. Worth a detour, as there aren't many restaurants this good in rural Utah; open for lunch and dinner.

Information and Services

Teasdale Ranger Station of the Dixie National Forest has info about hiking, horseback riding, and road conditions in the northern and eastern parts of Boulder Mountain and the Aquarius Plateau; books and forest maps are available. The office is two miles west of Torrey on UT 24, then 1.5 miles south to Main and 138 East (P.O. Box 99, Teasdale, UT 84773), (435) 425-3702; open Mon.–Fri. 8 A.M.–4:30 P.M. **Hondoo Trails,** P.O. Box 98, Torrey, UT 84775, (435) 425-3519, leads horseback and driving tours of 1–8 days in the scenic backcountry of southern Utah.

CAPITOL REEF NATIONAL PARK

Wonderfully sculptured rock layers in a rainbow of colors put on a fine show here. Though you'll find these same rocks through much of the Four Corners region, their artistic variety has no equal outside Capitol Reef National Park. About 70 million years ago, gigantic forces within the earth began to uplift, squeeze, and fold more than a dozen rock formations into the central feature of the park today—Waterpocket Fold, so named for the many small pools of water trapped by the tilted strata. Erosion has since carved spires, graceful curves, canyons, and arches. Waterpocket Fold extends 1,100 miles between Thousand Lake Mountain in the north and Lake Powell in the south. The most spectacular cliffs and rock formations of Waterpocket Fold form Capitol Reef, located north of Pleasant Creek and curving northwest across the Fremont River toward Thousand Lake Mountain. The reef was named by explorers who found Waterpocket Fold a barrier to travel and likened it to a reef blocking passage on the ocean. The rounded sandstone hills reminded them of the Capitol Dome in Washington, D.C., hence the name Capitol Reef.

Roads and hiking trails in the park provide access to the colorful rock layers and to the plants and wildlife that live here. You'll also see remnants of the area's long human history—petroglyphs and storage bins of the prehistoric Fremont Indians, a schoolhouse and other structures built by Mormon pioneers, and several small uranium mines of the 20th century. Legends tell of Butch Cassidy and other outlaw members of the "Wild Bunch" who hid out in these remote canyons in the 1890s.

NATURAL HISTORY

The Geologic Story

Exposed rocks reveal windswept deserts, rivers, mud flats, and inland seas of long ago. Nearly all the layers date from the Mesozoic era (65–230 million years ago), when dinosaurs ruled the earth. Later uplift and twisting of the land—which continues to this day—built up the Colorado Plateau of southern Utah and the Rocky Moun-

tains to the east. Immense forces squeezed the rocks until they bent up and over from east to west in the massive crease of Waterpocket Fold.

Climate

Expect hot summer days (highs in the upper 80s and low 90s) and cool nights. Winter brings cool days (highs in the 40s) and night temperatures dropping into the low 20s and teens. Snow accents the colored rocks while rarely hindering traffic on the main highway. Winter travel on the back roads and trails may be halted by snow, but it soon melts when the sun comes out. Annual precipitation averages only seven inches, peaking in the late summer thunderstorm season.

Flora and Fauna

Ponderosa pine and other cool-climate vegetation grow on the flanks of Thousand Lake Mountain (7,000–9,000 feet high) in the northwest corner of the park. Most of Waterpocket Fold, however, is at 5,000–7,000 feet, covered with sparse juniper and piñon pine that cling precariously in cracks and thin soils of the slickrock. The soil from each rock type generally determines what will grow. Mancos Shale forms a poor clay soil supporting only saltbush, shadscale, and galleta grass. On Dakota Sandstone you'll see mostly sage and rabbitbrush. Clays of the Morrison Formation repel nearly all plants, while its sandstone nurtures mostly juniper, piñon pine, and cliffrose; uranium prospectors discovered that *astragalus* and prince's plume commonly grow near ore deposits. Sands of the Summerville Formation nourish grasses and four-wing saltbush. The Fremont River and several creeks provide a lush

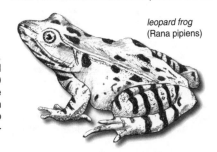

leopard frog
(Rana pipiens)

LOUISE FOOTE

habitat of cottonwood, tamarisk, willow, and other water-loving plants.

Streamside residents include beaver, muskrat, mink, tree lizard, Great Basin spadefoot toad, Rocky Mountain toad, and leopard frog. Spadefoot toads, fairy shrimp, and insects have adapted to the temporary water pockets by completing the aquatic phase of their short life cycles in a hurry. Near water or out in the drier country, you might see mule deer, coyote, gray fox, porcupine, spotted and striped skunks, badger, blacktailed jackrabbit, desert cottontail, yellow belly marmot, rock squirrel, Colorado chipmunk, Ord's kangaroo rat, canyon mouse, and five known species of bats. With luck, you may sight a relatively rare mountain lion or black bear. While you can't miss seeing the many small lizards along the trails, snakes tend to be more secretive; those in the park include the striped whipsnake, Great Basin gopher snake, wandering garter snake, and the rarely seen desert faded pygmy rattlesnake. Some common birds are the sharp-shinned hawk, American kestrel, chukar, mourning dove, white-throated swift, blackchinned and broad-tailed hummingbirds, violetgreen swallow, common raven, piñon and scrub jays, canyon and rock wrens, and rufous-sided towhee. Most wildlife, except birds, wait until evening to come out, and they disappear again the following morning.

HUMAN HISTORY

Prehistoric Peoples

By A.D. 700, Fremont Indians had found good farming land in some of the valleys. They grew corn, beans, and other crops to supplement hunting and the gathering of wild plants. They protected food from rodents and insects by carefully constructing stone or wooden storage rooms. Many of these have survived in sheltered cliff overhangs, but the pit house dwellings have nearly vanished. Intriguing pictographs and petroglyphs portray the Fremont adorned with headdresses, shields, sashes, and jewelry. Figures of desert bighorn sheep are seen, too. Was this artwork casual doodlings? Or did it have religious importance? The meaning hasn't been deciphered. Archaeologists first described and named the Fremont culture from sites along

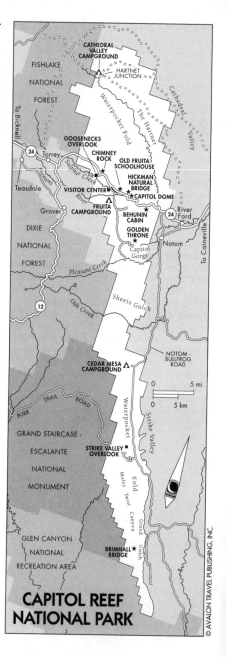

CAPITOL REEF NATIONAL PARK

© AVALON TRAVEL PUBLISHING, INC.

the Fremont River at Capitol Reef in 1929. Droughts and possible conflict with other tribes may have been factors in the disappearance of the Fremont from the area about 1250. Until the white settlers arrived, small groups of Ute and Paiute spent winters hunting here, then moved to the high country in summer.

Mormon Settlement

You can see why early explorers detoured around this natural barrier, though some trappers may have entered its canyons. Capitol Reef remained one of the last places in the West to be discovered. First reports came in 1866 from a detachment of Mormon militia pursuing renegade Indians. In 1872, Professor Almon H. Thompson of the Powell Expedition led the first scientific exploration in the fold country and named several park features along the group's Pleasant Creek route. Mormons, expanding their network of settlements, arrived in the upper Fremont Valley in the late 1870s and spread downriver to Hanksville. Junction (renamed Fruita in 1902) and nearby Pleasant Creek (Sleeping Rainbow/Floral Ranch) were settled about 1880. Floods, isolation, and transport difficulties forced many families to move on, especially downstream from Capitol Reef. Irrigation and hard work paid off in Fruita with prosperous fruit orchards and the sobriquet "the Eden of Wayne County." Fruita averaged about 10 families who grew alfalfa, sorghum (for syrup), vegetables, and a wide variety of fruit. Getting the produce to market required long and difficult journeys by wagon. The region remained one of the most isolated in Utah until after World War II.

Creation of the Park

In the 1920s local residents began to extol the wonders of Capitol Reef to the outside world. Impressed visitors lobbied for a national monument, which President Franklin D. Roosevelt granted in 1937. The original 37,060-acre Capitol Reef National Monument included the highly scenic areas around the Fremont River canyon and Capitol Gorge. Expansions to the north and south in 1969, followed by more additions and national park status in 1971, brought the park to its current 241,904 acres. Fruita residents moved out in the 1960s as the National Park Service purchased the old homesteads. The schoolhouse, Behunin Cabin, Merin Smith's blacksmith shop, and other buildings survive to commemorate Fruita's pioneer settlers. And the orchards still produce fruit that visitors may pick.

VISITING THE PARK

The visitors' center and main highway (UT 24) through Capitol Reef stay open all year. Even travelers short on time will enjoy a quick look at visitor-center exhibits and a drive on UT 24 through an impressive cross section of Capitol Reef cut by the Fremont River. You can see more of the park on the Scenic Drive, a narrow paved road that heads south from the visitors' center. The drive passes beneath spectacular cliffs of the reef and enters scenic Grand Wash and Capitol Gorge Canyons; allow at least 1.5 hours for the 21-mile round-trip (plus side trips). The fair-weather Notom/Bullfrog Road (paved as far as Notom) heads south along the other side of the reef for almost 80 miles with fine views of Waterpocket Fold. Burr Trail Road (dirt inside the park) in the south actually climbs over the fold in a steep set of switchbacks, connecting Notom Road with Boulder. Only drivers with high-clearance vehicles can explore Cathedral Valley in the park's northern district. All these roads provide access to viewpoints and hiking trails. A $4 per-vehicle park entrance fee is collected on the Scenic Drive.

Visitor Center

Start with a 10-minute slide show, shown on request, introducing Capitol Reef's natural wonders and history. A giant relief map gives you a bird's-eye view of the entire park. Rock samples and diagrams illustrate seven of the geologic formations you'll be seeing. Photos identify plants and birds found here. Prehistoric Fremont Indian artifacts on display include petroglyph replicas, sheepskin moccasins, pottery, basketry, stone knives, spear and arrow points, and bone jewelry. Other historic exhibits outline exploration and early Mormon settlement. Visitors headed for the back roads should ask at the desk about conditions and the weather forecast. Hikers planning overnight trips can get the required backcountry permit free. Besides answering questions, rangers will give out or sell info sheets for special interests. Hikers can pick up a map of trails that are near the visitors' center and of longer routes in the southern park areas; naturalists will want the checklists of plants, birds, mammals, and other wildlife; and history buffs can learn more about the area's settlement and the founding of the park. You can also choose from a good selection of pamphlets and books about the park, natural history, archaeology, pioneer history, and regional travel. Topo maps, posters, postcards, film, petroglyph and pottery replicas, and other souvenirs are here, too. Rangers offer nature walks, campfire programs, and other special events from Easter to mid-October; the bulletin board outside the visitors' center lists what's on. Hours at the visitors' center are daily 8 A.M.–7 P.M. June–September, and daily 8 A.M.–4:30 P.M. the rest of the year. The visitors' center is on UT 24 at the turnoff for Fruita Campground and the Scenic Drive. For more information, contact Capitol Reef National Park, Torrey, UT 84775, (435) 425-3791, www.nps.gov/care.

Hiking and Rock-Climbing

Fifteen day-hiking trails begin within a short drive of the visitors' center. Of these, only Grand Wash, Capitol Gorge, Sunset Point, and Goosenecks are easy. The others involve moderately strenuous climbs and travel over irregular slickrock. Signs and rock cairns mark the way, but it's all too easy to wander off if you don't pay attention to the route. Rewards of hiking in the park include superb views, a chance to see wildlife and flora, and a deeper appreciation of the area's geologic history. Innumerable canyon and cross-country possibilities exist all over the park; talk to the rangers for ideas. To avoid intimidating the wildlife, pets may not be taken on trails or into the backcountry. Be cautious on slickrock: although it's not really slippery unless wet, hikers have gotten into trouble by attempting too steep a slope. You'll need a canteen on most hikes because few of the canyons and natural waterpockets are reliable water sources. Spring and autumn offer the most comfortable temperatures and less chance of bothersome insects (worst from mid-May–late June). Though most trails can easily be done in a day, backpackers might want to try longer trips in Chimney Rock/Spring Canyons in the north or Muley Twist Canyon and Halls Creek in the south. Obtain the required backcountry permit (free) from a ranger and camp at least a half mile from the nearest maintained road or trail. (Cairned routes like Chimney Rock Canyon, Muley Twist Canyon, and Halls Creek don't count as trails but are backcountry routes.) Bring a stove for cooking, as backcountry users may not build fires. Avoid camping or parking in washes at any time—torrents of mud and boulders can carry away everything! Technical rock-climbers should check with rangers to learn about restricted areas; registration is voluntary. Climbers must use "clean" techniques (no pitons or bolts) and keep at least 25 feet from rock-art panels.

Fruit Picking

Though Fruita's citizens have departed, the National Park Service still maintains the old orchards. Visitors are welcome to pick and carry away the cherries, apricots, peaches, pears, and apples during the harvest seasons. Harvest times begin in late June or early July and end in October. You'll be charged about the same as in commercial pick-your-own orchards. You may also wander through any orchard and eat all you want on the spot before and during the designated picking season (no charge).

PRACTICALITIES

In The Park

Fruita Campground stays open all year and has drinking water but no showers or hookups ($10); Nov.–Apr. you have to get water from the visitors' center. The surrounding orchards and lush grass make this an attractive spot, one mile from the visitors' center on the Scenic Drive. Sites often fill by early afternoon in the busy May–October season. One group campground (by reservation only) and a picnic area are nearby. If you're just looking for a place to park for the night, check out the public land east of the park boundary off UT 24. Areas on both sides of the highway (about nine miles east of the visitors' center) may be used for primitive camping; no facilities or charge. The five-site **Cedar Mesa Campground** is in the park's southern district just off Notom-Bullfrog Road (dirt); campers enjoy fine views of Waterpocket Fold and the Henry Mountains. Open all year; no water or charge; from the visitors' center, go east 9.2 miles on UT 24, then turn right 22 miles on Notom-Bullfrog Road (avoid if wet). **Cathedral**

Valley Campground serves the park's northern district; it has five sites (no water or charge) near the Hartnet Junction, about 30 miles north of UT 24; take either the Caineville Wash or Hartnet (has a river ford) roads; both are dirt and should be avoided if wet.

Other Areas

Accommodations, campgrounds, and restaurants are at Capitol Reef Resort and Rim Rock Ranch (eight miles west of the visitors' center), Torrey (11 miles west of the visitors' center), and Bicknell (19 miles west of the visitors' center); see Torrey and Vicinity under Vicinity of Escalante earlier in this chapter. Caineville has a campground 15 miles east of the visitors' center and a restaurant 21.5 miles east of the visitors' center. The U.S. Forest Service has three developed campgrounds (open with water late May–mid-Sept.) on UT 12 between Torrey and Boulder. With distances from the park and elevations, they are: **Singletree** (22 miles, 8,200 feet); **Pleasant Creek** (27 miles, 8,600 feet); and **Oak Creek** (28 miles, 8,800 feet). **Lower Bowns Reservoir** has primitive camping (no water or fee) and fishing for rainbow trout and some cutthroat (elev. 7,400 feet); turn east five miles on a dirt road just south of Pleasant Creek Campground. **Hondoo Trails** offers four-wheel-drive and horseback tours of the park and nearby areas; P.O. Box 98, Torrey, UT 84775, (435) 425-3519. Horseback trips are also offered by **Pleasant Creek Trail Rides** at Rim Rock Rustic Inn, (435) 425-3315 or (800) 892-4597, and by **Best Western Capitol Reef Resort** three miles east of Torrey, (435) 425-3761 or (888) 610-9600.

SIGHTS AND DAY HIKES ALONG UTAH 24

These are listed from west to east.

Chimney Rock Trail

The trailhead is three miles west of the visitors' center on the north side of the highway. Towering 660 feet above the highway, Chimney Rock is a fluted spire of dark red rock (Moenkopi Formation) capped by a block of hard sandstone (Shinarump Member of the Chinle Formation). A 3.5-mile loop trail ascends 540 feet from the parking lot (elev. 6,100 feet) to a ridge overlooking Chimney Rock; allow 2.5 hours. Panoramic views take in the face of Capitol Reef. Petrified wood along the trail has been eroded from the Chinle Formation (the same rock layer found in Petrified Forest National Park in Arizona). It is not legal to take any of the petrified wood.

Spring Canyon Route

This moderately difficult hike begins at the top of the Chimney Rock Trail. The wonderfully eroded forms of Navajo Sandstone present a continually changing exhibition. The riverbed is normally dry; allow about six hours for the 10-mile (one-way) trip from Chimney Rock parking area to the Fremont River and UT 24. (Some maps show all or part of this as "Chimney Rock Canyon.") Check with rangers for the weather forecast before setting off—flash floods can be dangerous, and the Fremont River (which you must wade across) can rise quite high. Normally the river runs less than knee deep to UT 24 (3.7 miles east of the visitors' center). With luck you'll have a car waiting for you. Summer hikers can beat the heat with a crack-of-dawn departure. Carry water, as this section of canyon lacks a reliable source. From the Chimney Rock parking area, hike Chimney Rock Trail to the top of the ridge and follow signs for Chimney Rock Canyon. Enter the unnamed lead-in canyon and follow it downstream. A sign marks Chimney Rock Canyon, which is 2.5 miles from the start. Turn right 6.5 miles (downstream) to reach the Fremont River. A section of narrows requires some rock-scrambling (bring a cord to lower backpacks), or the area can be bypassed on a narrow trail to the left above the narrows. Farther down, a natural arch high on the left marks the halfway point.

Upper Chimney Rock Canyon could be explored on an overnight trip. A spring (purify before drinking) is located in an alcove on the right side about one mile up Chimney Rock Canyon from the lead-in canyon. Wildlife use this water source, so camp at least a quarter mile away. Chimney Rock Canyon, the longest in the park, begins high on the slopes of Thousand Lake Mountain and descends nearly 15 miles southeast to join the Fremont River.

Sulphur Creek Route

This moderately difficult hike begins by following a wash across the highway from the Chimney

Rock parking area, descending to Sulphur Creek, then heads down the narrow canyon to the visitors' center. The trip is about five miles long (one-way) and takes 3–5 hours. Park rangers sometime schedule guided hikes on this route. Warm weather is the best time because you'll be wading in the normally shallow creek. Three small waterfalls can be bypassed fairly easily; two falls are just below the goosenecks and the third is about a half mile before coming out at the visitors' center. Carry water. The creek's name may be a mistake as there's no sulphur along it; perhaps outcrops of yellow limonite caused the confusion. You can make an all-day eight-mile hike in Sulphur Creek by starting where it crosses the highway between Mileposts 72 and 73, five miles west of the visitors' center.

Panorama Point, the Goosenecks, and Sunset Point

The turnoff is 2.5 miles west of the visitors' center on the south side of the highway. Follow signs south for 0.15 mile to Panorama Point and views of Capitol Reef to the east and Boulder Mountain to the west. A sign explains how glacial meltwaters carried basalt boulders from Boulder Mountain to the reef 8,000–200,000 years ago. Goosenecks of Sulphur Creek are 0.9 mile farther on a gravel road. A short trail leads to the Goosenecks Overlook on the rim (elev. 6,400 feet) for dizzying views to the creek below. Canyon walls display shades of yellow, green, brown, and red. Another easy trail leads a third mile to Sunset Point and panoramic views of the Capitol Reef cliffs and the distant Henry Mountains.

Fruita Schoolhouse

Located 0.8 mile east of the visitors' center on the north side of the highway, early settlers completed the one-room log structure in 1896. Teachers struggled at times with rowdy students, but the kids learned their three R's in grades one through eight. Mormon Church meetings, dances, town meetings, elections, and other community gatherings took place here. Lack of students caused the school's closing in 1941. Rangers are on duty some days in summer (ask at the visitors' center). At other times you can peer inside the windows and listen to a recording of a former teacher recalling what school life was like.

Indian artifacts illustrate a talk at the petroglyphs.

Petroglyphs

Located 1.2 miles east of the visitors' center on the north side of the highway, Fremont petroglyphs of several human figures with headdresses and mountain sheep decorate the cliff. You can see more petroglyphs by walking to the left and right along the cliff face. Stay on the trail and do not climb the talus slope.

Hickman Natural Bridge, Rim Overlook, and Navajo Knobs Trails

The trailhead is two miles east of the visitors' center on the north side of the highway. The graceful Hickman Natural Bridge spans 133 feet across a small streambed. Numbered stops along the self-guiding trail correspond to descriptions in a pamphlet available at the trailhead or visitors' center. Starting from the parking area (elev. 5,320 feet), the trail follows the Fremont River's green banks a short distance before gaining 380 feet in the climb to the bridge. The last section of trail follows a dry wash shaded by cottonwood, juniper, and piñon pine trees. You'll pass under the bridge (eroded from the Kayenta Formation) at trail's end. Capitol Dome and other sculptured features of the Navajo Sandstone surround the site. The two-mile round-trip hike takes about 1.5 hours. Joseph Hickman served as principal of Wayne County High School and later in the state legislature during the 1920s; he and another local man, Ephraim Pectol, led efforts to promote Capitol Reef.

A splendid overlook 1,000 feet above Fruita beckons hikers up the Rim Overlook Trail. Take the Hickman Natural Bridge Trail a quarter mile from the parking area, then turn right two miles at the signed fork. Allow 3.5 hours from the fork for this hike. Panoramic views take in the Fremont River valley below, the great cliffs of Capitol Reef above, the Henry Mountains to the southeast, and Boulder Mountain to the southwest.

Continue another 2.2 miles and more than 500 feet higher from the Rim Overlook to reach Navajo Knobs. Rock cairns lead the way over slickrock along the rim of Waterpocket Fold. A magnificent panorama at trail's end takes in much of southeastern Utah.

Cohab Canyon and Frying Pan Trails

Park at Hickman Natural Bridge Trailhead, then walk across the highway bridge. This trail climbs Capitol Reef for fine views in all directions and a close look at the swirling lines in the Navajo Sandstone. After three quarters of a mile and a 400-foot climb, you'll reach a trail fork: keep right one mile to stay on Cohab Canyon Trail and descend to Fruita Campground or turn left onto Frying Pan Trail to Cassidy Arch (3.5 miles away) and Grand Wash (four miles away). The trail from Cassidy Arch to Grand Wash is very steep. All these interconnecting trails offer many hiking possibilities, especially if you can arrange a car shuttle. For example, you could start up Cohab Canyon Trail from UT 24, cross over the reef on Frying Pan Trail, make a side trip to Cassidy Arch, descend Cassidy Arch Trail to Grand Wash, walk down Grand Wash to UT 24, then walk (or car shuttle) 2.7 miles along the highway back to the start (10.5 miles total).

Cohab is a pretty little canyon in the Wingate Sandstone overlooking the campground. Mormon polygamists supposedly used the canyon to escape federal marshals during the 1880s. Hiking the Frying Pan Trail involves an additional 600 feet of climbing from either Cohab Canyon or Cassidy Arch Trails. Once atop Capitol Reef, the trail follows the gently rolling slickrock terrain.

Grand Wash

The trailhead is 4.7 miles east of the visitors' center on the south side of the highway. One of only five canyons cutting completely through the reef, Grand Wash offers easy hiking and great scenery. There's no trail—just follow the dry gravel riverbed. Flash floods can occur during storms. Canyon walls of Navajo Sandstone rise 800 feet above the floor and close in to as little as 20 feet in width. Cassidy Arch Trailhead (see Grand Wash Road, below) is two miles away, and parking for Grand Wash from the Scenic Drive is a quarter mile farther.

Behunin Cabin

Located 6.2 miles east of the visitors' center on the south side of the highway. Elijah Cutlar Behunin used blocks of sandstone to build this cabin in about 1882. He moved on, though, when floods made life too difficult. Small openings allow a look inside the dirt-floored structure, but no furnishings remain.

Small Waterfall in the Fremont River

Parking is 6.9 miles east of the visitors' center on the north side of the highway. The river twists through a narrow human-made crack in the rock before making its final plunge into a pool below. A sign warns of hazardous footing above the falls, which are dangerous for children. Instead, take the sandy path from the parking area to where you can safely view the falls from below. Use extreme caution if you intend to cool off in the pool at the base of the waterfall, as there is a very strong and dangerous undertow.

SIGHTS AND DAY HIKES ALONG THE SCENIC DRIVE

Turn south from UT 24 at the visitors' center to experience some of the reef's best scenery and to learn more about its geology. An illustrated pamphlet, available on the drive or in the visitors' center, has keyed references to numbered stops along the 25-mile (round-trip) drive. Descriptions identify rock layers and explain how they were formed. Just a quick tour takes 1.5 hours, but several hiking trails may tempt you to extend your stay. The scenic drive is paved, though side roads have gravel surfaces. You'll first pass orchards and several of Fruita's buildings. A **blacksmith shop** (0.7 miles from the visitors' center on the right) displays tools, harnesses, farm machinery, and Fruita's first tractor. The tractor didn't arrive until 1940—long after the rest of the country had modernized. In a recording, a rancher tells about living and working in Fruita.

Fremont Gorge Overlook Trail

From the start at the blacksmith shop, the trail crosses Johnson Mesa and climbs steeply to the overlook about 1,000 feet above the Fremont River; round-trip distance is 4.5 miles.

Picnic Area

Located 0.8 mile from the visitors' center on the left, fruit trees and grass make this a pretty spot for lunch. A short trail crosses orchards and the Fremont River to the Fruita Schoolhouse.

Cohab Canyon Trail

The trailhead is across the road from Fruita Campground, 1.3 miles from the visitors' center. The trail follows steep switchbacks during the first quarter mile, then more gentle grades to the top, 400 feet higher and a mile from the campground. You can take a short trail to viewpoints or continue three quarters of a mile down the other side of the ridge to UT 24. (See description under Sights and Day Hikes Along Utah 24, above.) Another option is to turn right at the top on Frying Pan Trail to Cassidy Arch (3.5 miles one-way) and Grand Wash (four miles one-way).

Fremont River Trail

From the trailhead near the amphitheater at Fruita Campground, 1.3 miles from the visitors' cen-

ter, the trail passes orchards along the Fremont River (elev. 5,350 feet), then begins the climb up sloping rock strata to a viewpoint on Miner's Mountain. Sweeping views take in Fruita, Boulder Mountain, and the reef. The round-trip distance of 2.5 miles takes about 1.5 hours; elevation gain is 770 feet.

Grand Wash Road

Turn left off the Scenic Drive 3.6 miles from the visitors' center. This side trip follows the twisting Grand Wash for one mile. At road's end you can continue on foot 2.25 miles (one-way) through the canyon to its end at the Fremont River (see Grand Wash under Sights and Day Hikes Along Utah 24, above).

Cassidy Arch Trail begins near the end of Grand Wash Road. Energetic hikers will enjoy good views of Grand Wash, the great domes of Navajo Sandstone, and the arch itself. The 3.5-mile round-trip trail ascends the north wall of Grand Wash (Wingate and Kayenta Formations), then winds across slickrock of the Kayenta Formation to a vantage point close to the arch, also of Kayenta. Allow about three hours, as the elevation gain is nearly 1,000 feet. The notorious outlaw Butch Cassidy may have traveled through Capitol Reef and seen this arch. Frying Pan Trail branches off Cassidy Arch Trail at the one-mile mark, then wends its way across three miles of slickrock to Cohab Canyon (see Cohab Canyon and Frying Pan Trails under Sights and Day Hikes Along Utah 24, above).

The "Castle" stands near the visitor center.

Old Wagon Trail

Wagon drivers once used this route as a shortcut between Grover and Capitol Gorge. Look for the trailhead 0.7 mile south of Slickrock Divide, between Grand Wash and Capitol Gorge. The old trail crosses a wash to the west, then ascends steadily through piñon and juniper woodland on Miners Mountain. After 1.5 miles, the trail leaves the wagon road and goes north a half mile to a high knoll for the best views of the Capitol Reef area. The four-mile (round-trip) hike climbs 1,000 feet.

Pleasant Creek Road

Turn right 8.3 miles from the visitors' center where the Scenic Drive curves east toward Capitol Gorge. Pleasant Creek Road turns south and continues below the face of the reef. After three miles the sometimes rough dirt road passes Sleeping Rainbow/Floral Ranch (closed to public) and ends at Pleasant Creek. A rugged four-wheel-drive road continues on the other side but is much too rough for cars. Floral Ranch dates back to Capitol Reef's early years of settlement. In 1939 it became the Sleeping Rainbow Guest Ranch, from the Indian name for Waterpocket Fold. Now the ranch belongs to the park, but the former owners still live here. Pleasant Creek's perennial waters begin high on Boulder Mountain to the west and cut a scenic canyon completely through Capitol Reef. Hikers can head downstream through the three-mile-long canyon and return, or continue another three miles cross-country to Notom Road.

Capitol Gorge

This is the end of the Scenic Drive, 10.7 miles from the visitors' center. Capitol Gorge is a dry canyon through Capitol Reef much like Grand Wash, though with a somewhat different character. Believe it or not, the narrow, twisting Capitol Gorge was the route of the main state highway through south-central Utah for 80 years! Mormon pioneers laboriously cleared a path so wagons could go through, a task repeated every time flash floods rolled in a new set of boulders. Cars bounced their way down the canyon until 1962, when the present UT 24 opened, but few traces of the old road remain today. Walking is easy along the gravel riverbed, but don't enter if storms threaten. The first mile downstream is the most scenic: Fremont Indian petroglyphs (in poor condition) appear on the left after 0.1 mile; narrows of Capitol Gorge close in at 0.3 mile; a "pioneer register" on the left at one-half mile consists of names and dates of early travelers and ranchers scratched in the canyon wall; natural water tanks on the left at three quarters of a mile are typical of those in Waterpocket Fold. Hikers can continue another three miles downstream to Notom Road.

Golden Throne Trail also begins at the end of the scenic drive. Instead of heading down Capitol Gorge from the parking area, turn left up this trail for dramatic views of the reef and surrounding area. Golden Throne is a massive monolith of yellow-hued Navajo Sandstone capped by a thin layer of red Carmel Formation. The four-mile round-trip trail climbs 1,100 feet in a steady grade to a viewpoint near the base of Golden Throne; allow four hours.

THE NORTH DISTRICT

Only the most adventurous travelers get into the remote canyons and desert country of the north. The few roads *cannot* be negotiated by ordinary cars. In good weather, high-clearance vehicles can enter the region from the east, north, and west. The roads lead through stately sandstone monoliths of Cathedral Valley, volcanic remnants, badlands country, many low mesas, and vast sand flats. Foot travel allows closer inspection of these features or lengthy excursions into the canyons of Polk, Deep, and Spring Creeks, which cut deeply into the flanks of Thousand Lake Mountain. Much of the north district is good for horseback riding, too. **Cathedral Valley Campground's** five sites provide a place to stop for the night; rangers won't permit car camping elsewhere in the district. The **Upper Cathedral Valley Trail,** just below the campground, is an enjoyable one-mile walk offering excellent views of the Cathedrals. Hikers with a backcountry permit must camp at least a half mile from the nearest road. You can purchase a small guide to this area at the visitors' center.

THE SOUTH DISTRICT

Notom-Bullfrog Road

Capitol Reef is only a small part of Waterpocket Fold. By taking the Notom-Bullfrog Road, you'll see nearly 80 miles of the fold's eastern side. This route crosses some of the younger geologic layers, such as those of the Morrison Formation that form colorful hills. In other places, eroded layers of the Waterpocket Fold jut up at 70-degree angles. The Henry Mountains to the east and the many canyons on both sides of the road add to the memorable panoramas. The road has been paved as far as Notom (more will be paved in the future) but is still dirt and gravel to Bullfrog. Keep an eye on the weather before setting out—the dirt and gravel surface is usually okay for cars when dry but can be too slippery and gooey for *any* vehicle when wet. Sandy spots and washouts may present a problem for low-clearance vehicles; contact the visitors' center to check current conditions. Have a full gas tank and carry extra water and food because no services are available between UT 24 and Bullfrog Marina. Purchase a small guide to this area at the visitors' center. Features and mileage along the drive from north to south include:

Mile 0.0: The turnoff from UT 24 is 9.2 miles east of the visitors' center and 30.2 miles west of Hanksville (another turnoff from UT 24 is three miles east).

Mile 2.2: Pleasant Creek; the mouth of the canyon is 5–6 miles upstream, though it's only about three miles by heading cross-country from south of Notom. Hikers can follow the canyon three miles upstream through Capitol Reef to Pleasant Creek Road (off the Scenic Drive).

Mile 4.1: Notom Ranch is to the west; once a small town, Notom is now a private ranch.

Mile 8.1: Burrow Wash; hikers can explore the narrow canyon upstream.

Mile 9.3: Cottonwood Wash; another canyon hike just upstream.

Mile 10.4: Five Mile Wash; yet another canyon hike.

Mile 13.3: Sheets Gulch; a scenic canyon lies upstream here, too.

Mile 14.1: Sandy Ranch Junction; high-clearance vehicles can turn east 16 miles to the Henry Mountains.

Mile 14.2: Oak Creek Access Road to the west; turn here for Oak Creek. The creek cuts a two-mile-long canyon through Capitol Reef that's a good day hike. Backpackers sometimes start upstream at Lower Bowns Reservoir (off UT 12) and hike the 15 miles to Oak Creek Access

Road. The clear waters of Oak Creek flow all year but must be treated for drinking.

Mile 14.4: Oak Creek crossing.

Mile 20.0: Entering Capitol Reef National Park; a small box has info sheets.

Mile 22.3: Cedar Mesa Campground to the west; the small five-site campground is surrounded by junipers and has fine views of Waterpocket Fold and the Henry Mountains. Sites have tables and grills; there's an outhouse but no drinking water; free. **Red Canyon Trail** begins here and heads west into a huge box canyon in Waterpocket Fold; four miles round-trip.

Mile 26.0: Bitter Creek Divide; streams to the north flow to the Fremont River; Halls Creek on the south side runs through Strike Valley to Lake Powell, 40 miles away.

Mile 34.1: Burr Trail Road Junction; turn west up the steep switchbacks to ascend Waterpocket Fold and continue to Boulder and UT 12 (36 miles). Burr Trail is the only road that actually crosses the top of the fold and it's one of the most scenic in the park. Driving conditions are similar to the Notom-Bullfrog Road—okay for cars when dry. Pavement begins at the park boundary and continues to Boulder. Although paved, the Burr Trail still needs to be driven slowly because of its curves and potholes. The section of road through Long Canyon has especially pretty scenery.

Mile 36.0: Surprise Canyon Trailhead; a hike into this narrow, usually shaded canyon takes 1–2 hours.

Mile 36.6: The Post; a small trading post here once served sheepherders and some cattlemen, but today this spot is just a reference point. Park here to hike to Headquarters Canyon. A trailhead for Lower Muley Twist Canyon via Halls Creek lies at the end of a half-mile-long road to the south.

Mile 37.5: Leaving Capitol Reef National Park; a small box has info sheets. Much of the road between here and Glen Canyon National Recreation Area has been paved.

Mile 45.5: Road junction; turn right (south) to continue to Bullfrog Marina (25 miles) or go straight (east) for Starr Springs Campground (23 miles) in the Henry Mountains.

Mile 46.4: The road to the right (west) goes to Halls Creek Overlook. This turnoff is poorly signed and easy to miss; look for it 0.9 mile south of the previous junction. Turn in and follow the road three miles, then turn right at a fork 0.4 mile to the viewpoint. The last 0.3 mile may be too rough for low-clearance cars. A picnic table is the only "facility" here. Far below in Grand Gulch, Halls Creek flows south to Lake Powell. Look across the valley for the double Brimhall Bridge in the red sandstone of Waterpocket Fold. A steep trail descends to Halls Creek (1.2 miles one-way) and it's possible to continue another 1.1 miles up Brimhall Canyon to the bridge. A register box at the overlook has info sheets on this route. Note, however, that the last part of the hike to the bridge requires difficult rock-scrambling and wading or swimming through pools! Hikers looking for another adventure might want to follow Halls Creek 10 miles downstream to the narrows. Here, convoluted walls as high as 700 feet narrow to little more than arms' length apart. This beautiful area of water-sculpted rock sometimes has deep pools that require swimming.

Mile 49.0: Colorful clay hills of deep reds, creams, and grays rise beside the road. This clay turns to goo when wet, providing all the traction of axle grease.

Mile 54.0: Beautiful panorama of countless mesas, mountains, and canyons. Lake Powell and Navajo Mountain can be seen to the south.

Mile 65.3: Junction with paved UT 276; turn left (north) for Hanksville (59 miles) or right (south) to Bullfrog Marina (5.2 miles).

Mile 70.5: Bullfrog Marina (see Glen Canyon National Recreation Area, later in this chapter).

Lower Muley Twist Canyon

"So winding that it would twist a mule pulling a wagon," said an early visitor. This canyon has some of the best hiking in the southern district of the park. In the 1880s, Mormon pioneers used the canyon as part of a wagon route between Escalante and new settlements in southeastern Utah, replacing the even more difficult Hole-in-the-Rock route. Unlike most canyons of Waterpocket Fold, Muley Twist runs lengthwise along the crest for about 18 miles before finally turning east and leaving the fold. Hikers starting from Burr Trail Road can easily follow the twisting bends down to Halls Creek, 12 miles away. Two trailheads and the Halls Creek route allow a variety of trips. You could start from Burr Trail Road near the top of the switchbacks (2.2 miles

west of Notom-Bullfrog Road) and hike down the dry gravel streambed. After four miles you have the options of returning the same way, taking the Cut Off route east 2.5 miles to the Post Trailhead (off Notom-Bullfrog Road), or continuing eight miles down Lower Muley Twist Canyon to its end at Halls Creek. Upon reaching Halls Creek, turn left (north) five miles up the creekbed or the old jeep road beside it to the Post. This section of creek lies in an open dry valley. With a car shuttle, the Post would be the end of a good two-day, 17-mile hike, or you could loop back to Lower Muley Twist Canyon via the Cut Off route and hike back to Burr Trail Road for a 23.5-mile trip. It's a good idea to check the weather beforehand and avoid the canyon if storms threaten.

Cream-colored cliffs of Navajo Sandstone lie atop the red Kayenta and Wingate Formations. Impressively deep undercuts have been carved in the lower canyon. Spring and autumn offer the best conditions (summer temperatures can exceed 100° F). Elevations range from 5,640 feet at Burr Trail Road to 4,540 feet at the confluence with Halls Creek to 4,894 feet at the Post. An info sheet available at the visitors' center and trailheads has a small map and route details. Topo maps of Wagon Box Mesa, Mt. Pennell, and Hall Mesa, and the 1:100,000-scale Escalante and Hite Crossing maps are sold at the visitors' center. You'll also find this hike described in Dave Hall's *Hiker's Guide to Utah* and in Michael Kelsey's *Canyon Hiking Guide to the Colorado Plateau* and *Utah Mountaineering Guide*. Carry all water for the trip, as natural sources are often dry or polluted.

Upper Muley Twist Canyon

This part of the canyon has plenty of scenery. Large and small natural arches along the way add to its beauty. Upper Muley Twist Road turns north off Burr Trail Road about one mile west from the top of a set of switchbacks. Cars can usually go in a half mile to a trailhead parking area, while high-clearance four-wheel-drive vehicles can head another 2.5 miles up a wash to the end of the primitive road. Look for natural arches on the left along this last section. **Strike Valley Overlook Trail** (three quarters of a mile round-trip) begins at the end of the road and leads to a magnificent panorama of Waterpocket Fold and beyond. Return to the canyon, where you can hike as far as 6.5 miles (one-way) to the head of Upper Muley Twist Canyon.

Two large arches lie a short hike upstream; Saddle Arch, the second one on the left, is one and three quarters miles away. The **Rim Route** begins across from Saddle Arch, climbs the canyon wall, follows the rim (good views of Strike Valley and the Henry Mountains), and descends back into the canyon at a point just above the narrows, 4.75 miles from the end of the road. (The Rim Route is most easily followed in this direction.) Proceed upcanyon to see several more arches. A very narrow section of canyon beginning about four miles from the end of the road must be bypassed to continue; look for rock cairns showing the way around to the right. Continuing up the canyon past the Rim Route sign will take you to several small drainages marking the upper end of Muley Twist Canyon. Climb a high tree-covered point on the west rim for great views; experienced hikers with a map can follow the rim back to Upper Muley Road (no trail or markers on this route). Bring all the water you'll need, as there are no reliable sources in Upper Muley Twist Canyon.

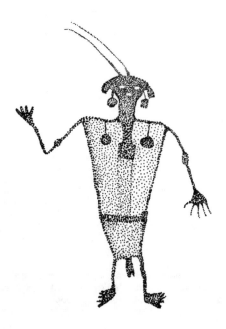

EAST OF CAPITOL REEF NATIONAL PARK

HANKSVILLE

Ebenezer Hanks and other Mormon settlers founded this out-of-the-way community in 1882 along the Fremont River, then known as the Dirty Devil River. The isolation attracted polygamists like Hanks and other fugitives from the law. Butch Cassidy and his gang found refuge in the rugged canyon country of "Robbers' Roost" east of town.

Even by Utah standards, Hanksville is still pretty remote. The population is only about 400, but it has outlasted several other farm communities upstream. Today most people work at ranching, farming (hay, corn feed, and watermelons), mining, or tourism. Several houses and the old stone church on Center, one block south of the highway, survive from the 19th century.

Travelers exploring this scenic region find Hanksville a handy if desultory stopover; Capitol Reef National Park lies to the west, Lake Powell and the Henry Mountains to the south, the remote Maze District of Canyonlands National Park to the east, and Goblin Valley State Park to the north. The book *Hiking and Exploring Utah's Henry Mountains and Robbers Roost,* by Michael Kelsey, has a wealth of history and travel information about the Hanksville area.

Wolverton Mill

E.T. Wolverton built this ingenious mill during the 1920s at his gold-mining claims in the Henry Mountains. A 20-foot waterwheel, still perfectly balanced, powered ore-crushing machinery and a sawmill. Owners of claims at the mill's original site didn't like a steady stream of tourists coming through to see the mill, so it was moved to the BLM office at Hanksville. Drive south a half mile on 100 West to see the mill and some of its original interior mechanism.

Accommodations

$50–75: You'll want to drive by the **Desert Inn Motel,** 197 E. 100 North, (435) 542-3241, just to see ingenious "found-metal" dinosaur sculptures and if you want to stay the night, it offers

clean, basic rooms. The new **Whispering Sands Motel,** 68 E. 100 North, (435) 542-3238, has spacious rooms with cable TV and phones.

Campgrounds: In the center of town, **Redrock Campground,** (435) 542-3235 or (800) 894-3242 (reservations), offers sites for tents ($11) and RVs ($15 with hookups); has showers and laundry; open Mar. 15–Oct. 31.

Food

The **Redrock Restaurant,** adjacent to the campground, (435) 542-3235, serves American food daily for breakfast, lunch, and dinner; closed in winter. **Blondie's Eatery,** (435) 542-3255, and **Stan's Burger Shack,** (435) 542-3441, on the south edge of town are open daily with fast food.

Other Practicalities

The **post office** is at 118 E. 100 North, (435) 542-3422. The **Bureau of Land Management**

whimsical dinosaurs at Hanksville

W. C. McRAE

staff has regional travel literature and can tell you about road conditions, hiking, camping, and the buffalo herd in the Henry Mountains. A recreation map and USGS topo maps are available; open Mon.–Fri. 7:45 A.M.–noon and 12:45–4:30 P.M.; turn south a half mile on 100 West from UT 24 or write P.O. Box 99, Hanksville, UT 84734, (435) 542-3461.

Caineville

Mormons founded this village on the Fremont River midway between the present-day Capitol Reef Visitor Center and Hanksville. **Sleepy Hollow Campground,** at Milepost 95 on UT 24, (435) 456-9130, has a store, showers, and sites for tents and RVs; $11 without hookups, $15 with electric hookup. Facilities are shut down in winter but primitive camping is permitted with reduced fees.

HENRY MOUNTAINS AND VICINITY

Great domes of intrusive igneous rock pushed into and deformed surrounding sedimentary layers about 70 million years ago. Erosion later uncovered the domes, revealing mountains towering 5,000 feet above the surrounding plateau. Mount Ellen's North Summit Ridge (elev. 11,522 feet) and Mt. Pennell (elev. 11,320 feet) top the range. Scenic views and striking geologic features abound in and around the Henrys. Rock layers tilt dramatically in Waterpocket Fold to the west and in the Pink Cliffs on the south side of Mt. Hillers. Sheer cliffs of the Horn, between Mt. Ellen and Mt. Pennell, attract rock climbers.

The arid land and rugged canyons surrounding the Henry Mountains so discouraged early explorers and potential settlers that the range wasn't even named or described until 1869, when members of the Powell River Expedition sighted it. Indian tales of a lost Spanish gold mine have long enticed prospectors, yet only modest amounts of the yellow metal have been found, mostly in the Bromide Basin. A brief gold boom here in the early 1890s gave rise to Eagle City mining camp along Crescent Creek. Other minerals occur in the area, too; a uranium mine is just south of the Henrys in Shootaring Canyon, near Ticaboo.

Vegetation ranges from sparse desert plants such as galleta grass and blackbrush on the lower slopes to piñon pine and juniper woodlands higher up, then to forests of ponderosa pine, aspen, Douglas fir, spruce, and bristlecone pine. Alpine plants and grasslands cover the highest summits. Buffalo, brought to the Henrys from Yellowstone National Park in 1941, form one of the few free-roaming herds in the United States. They winter in the southwestern part of the mountains, then move higher as the snow melts. Mule deer keep mostly to the higher elevations, while pronghorn stay in the desert country to the east. Most of the bighorn sheep are found in the Little Rockies, a southeastern extension of the Henry Mountains. Mountain lions live near the Henrys, too, but they're more likely to see you than you are to see them!

Exploring the Henry Mountains

Roads with panoramic views cross the range between the high peaks at Bull Creek, Pennellen, and Stanton Passes. Most driving routes are best suited for high-clearance vehicles. The road through Bull Creek Pass (elev. 10,485 feet) is snow-free only from about early July to late October. Rains, which peak in August, occasionally make travel difficult in late summer. Roads tend to be at their best after grading in autumn, just before the deer-hunting season. Travel at the lower elevations is possible all year, though spring and autumn have the most pleasant temperatures. Check in first with the BLM office in Hanksville before exploring the backcountry. Staff members can advise you about water sources, road and trail conditions, and, in case of trouble, they will have an idea of where to look for you. Take precautions for desert travel, and have water, food, and extra clothing with you. The Henry Mountains remain a remote and little-traveled region.

Campgrounds

You'll find the only easily accessible campsites in the Henry Mountains at **Starr Springs Campground,** off UT 276 north of Ticaboo. The campground sits in an oak forest at the base of Mt. Hillers. Sites (elev. 6,300 feet) stay open all year and usually have water for a $6 fee from early May to early October. **Panorama Knoll Trail** begins from the campground and makes a half-mile loop to an overlook. A good gravel road to Starr Springs Campground turns off UT

276 near Milepost 17 (23 miles north of Bull-frog and 43 miles south of Hanksville) and goes in four miles.

The handful of campgrounds along the Notom Road–Bull Creek Road route described above operate May–October only; most with water. These campgrounds are upwards of 30 miles off the pavement on often-marginal roads. Check with the Hanksville BLM office for road conditions and details on campgrounds.

Hiking

Countless mountain and canyon hiking possibilities exist in the range; Michael Kelsey's book on the Henry Mountains has trip suggestions and practical advice. Most routes go cross-country or follow old mining roads. The **Mt. Ellen Summit Route** is a good day hike and probably attracts the greatest number of hikers. Easiest way is to follow the North Summit Ridge north from the road at Bull Creek Pass; there's an unsigned trail the first mile and on the final climb up Mt. Ellen; elevation gain is 1,030 feet. Nearly all of this route lies above timberline with spectacular panoramas. Another popular approach begins from Dandelion Flat Picnic Area; a trail follows an old road that climbs the slopes part of the way, then it's cross-country; elevation gain is 3,400 feet. Either route is about four miles round-trip and takes half a day. Interestingly, Mt. Ellen Peak shown on the maps isn't the true high point; the North Summit Ridge of Mt. Ellen, just to the south, is 16 feet higher at 11,522 feet. You can also hike the South Summit Ridge south of Bull Creek Pass. See the 7¹/₂-minute Mount Ellen and Dry Lakes Peak or the 15-minute Mt. Ellen topo maps.

Little Egypt

Eerie rock formations similar to those in Goblin Valley, but covering a smaller area, lie east of the Henrys. Kids will enjoy exploring the area, and it's a fine place for a picnic. Turn southwest 1.5 miles from UT 95 between Mileposts 20 and 21; when dry, the gravel road is usually okay for cars. No facilities or even a sign mark the site, so note mileage from UT 95.

Dirty Devil Canyon Overlook

The muddy waters of the Dirty Devil River have carved a deep canyon southeast of Hanksville. Views from the overlook at Burr Point take in some impressive scenery. Desperadoes around the turn of the century hid out in the rugged canyonlands of "Robbers' Roost" across the river. In 1869, when one of Powell's expedition members was asked if the waters had trout, he replied with disgust that the smelly and muddy river was "a dirty devil." An unpaved road winds east for 11 miles from UT 95 (between Mileposts 15 and 16). Cars with good clearance should be okay in dry weather. Park near where the road makes a sharp right just before the edge, or follow the road south for other views. Walking along the rim also affords different perspectives.

GOBLIN VALLEY STATE PARK

Thousands of spooky rock formations inhabit this valley. Little eyelike holes in the "goblins" make you wonder who's watching whom. All of the goblins have weathered out of the Entrada Formation, here a soft red sandstone and even softer siltstone. **Carmel Canyon Trail** (1.5-mile loop) begins at the northeast side of the parking lot at road's end, then leads into a strange landscape of goblins, spires, and balanced rocks. Just wander about at your whim; this is a great place for the imagination!

Curtis Bench Trail begins on the road between the parking lot and the campground and goes south to a viewpoint of the Henry Mountains; cairns mark the 1.5-mile (one-way) route. The state park provides a campground with showers on the drive in and a covered picnic area and an overlook at the end of the road. The park stays open all year; $4 per vehicle for day use or $11 per vehicle for camping; P.O. Box 637, Green River, UT 84525, (435) 564-8110 or (800) 322-3770 (reservations). The turnoff from UT 24 is at Milepost 137, 21 miles north of Hanksville and 24 miles south of I-70; follow signs west five miles on a paved road, then south seven miles on a gravel road.

Temple Mountain Bike Trail traverses old mining roads, ridges, and wash bottoms about 12 miles north of the state park. Popular hikes near the state park include the Little Wild Horse and Bell Canyons Loop, Chute and Crack Canyons Loop, and Wild Horse Canyon. The park is also a good base for exploring the **San Rafael Swell** area to the northwest.

SOUTHERN SAN RAFAEL SWELL

The massive fold and uplift of the earth's crust called the San Rafael Swell is crossed by I-70 about 19 miles west of Green River. The east face and "flat irons" of the Swell, known as the San Rafael Reef, rise dramatically 2,100 feet above the desert. Several view areas allow stopping for a look at the colorful rock layers. San Rafael Swell is 80 miles long (north to south) and 30 miles wide (for a more complete discussion of the region's history and geology, see The Castle Valley and Northern San Rafael Swell, above). For information, contact the BLM San Rafael Resource Area, 900 North and 700 East, Price, UT 84501, (435) 637-4584.

Black Dragon Canyon
Don't worry about the dragon; he doesn't bite. This narrow canyon in the San Rafael Swell is just off I-70, 15 miles east of Green River. A quarter-mile walk up the streambed leads to a pair of pictograph panels of the dragon (he's actually red), human figures, a dog, and geometric designs. Continue farther upcanyon for more good scenery. To reach the trailhead, turn north on a dirt road from the I-70 westbound lane just past Milepost 145; this isn't a regular exit and is not signed. If coming from the west, you'll have to turn around at the Hanksville Exit 147 and backtrack two miles. The dirt road crosses a wash (best to walk from here if it's filled with water), goes through a second gate, and crosses the streambed from Black Dragon Wash, 1.1 miles from I-70. Turn left 0.4 mile up the streambed (normally dry) to the canyon entrance. High-clearance vehicles can drive a short way up the canyon.

Hondoo Arch Loop
Dirt roads south of I-70 provide a scenic drive into some of the San Rafael's prettiest country. Either turn south and west 15 miles from I-70 Ranch Exit 129 or take the Goblin Valley State Park turnoff from UT 24 and head west 20 miles to the beginning of the loop. The 29-mile loop drops into Reds Canyon with fine panoramas on the descent. Look for Hondoo Arch high in the cliffs across the Muddy River. Side roads off the loop go to Muddy River (beside Tomsich Butte), Hid-den Splendor Mine, and other old mining areas. The Tomsich Butte area contains old cabins and uranium mines, which are dangerous to enter. Hikers can find many adventurous trips along the Muddy River, washes, and canyons of the area; check *Canyoneering the San Rafael Swell,* by Steve Allen, for hiking details. The San Rafael Desert 1:100,000 topo map covers the loop area. Roads can become impassable after rain or snow; drivers of cars need to be especially careful in this remote area.

GREEN RIVER

The small town began in 1878 as a mail station on the long run between Salina in central Utah and the Colorado border. Today Green River is still the only sizable settlement (nearly 2,1000 people) on this route, now I-70, with a number of quality places to stay. Travelers can stop for a rest or meal here, take a day trip on the river, or use the town as a base for exploring the scenic San Rafael Swell country nearby.

Green River is known for its melons. In summer, stop at roadside stands and partake of wondrous cantaloupe and watermelons. The blazing summer heat and ample irrigation water make such delicacies possible. **Melon Days** celebrates the harvest on the third weekend of September with a parade, city fair, music, canoe race, games, and free melons.

A pleasant **city park** offers shaded tables, playground, and tennis courts at the corner of Main and 100 East.

The town of Green River rests midway between two popular river-rafting areas. The Green River's Desolation and Gray Canyons are upstream, while Labyrinth and Stillwater Canyons lie downstream. Several river companies organize day and multi-day trips through these areas.

John Wesley Powell River History Museum
Stop by this fine museum to learn about Powell's daring expeditions down the Green and Colorado Rivers in 1869 and 1871–1872. An excellent multimedia presentation about both rivers uses narratives from Powell's trips; 21 minutes; free. Historic river boats on display include a replica of Powell's *Emma Dean.* Other exhibits show places to visit in the area.

The Green River flows placidly below Gray Canyon.

The **Grand County Travel Council office,** in the museum, (435) 564-3526, has local travel information (P.O. Box 335, Green River, UT 84525). A gift shop sells books, maps, Indian crafts, T-shirts, and other souvenirs.

The Powell Museum, on the east bank of the Green River, is at 885 E. Main (the I-70 business route through town), (435) 564-3427/3428. Both the museum and the tourist office are open daily 9 A.M.–8 P.M. in summer and daily 9 A.M.–5 P.M. the rest of the year.

Floating Desolation and Gray Canyons

These canyons of the Green River cut through the Tavaputs Plateau, the vast and mostly untracked region between Roosevelt in the north and the town of Green River. Outfitters normally fly rafting parties into a remote airstrip at Sand Wash, south of Myton, and take 4–7 days to complete the 85-mile trip. Prices vary between outfitters. The river has a few Class III rapids, interspersed with flat water, making for a good family adventure. Expect to pay $800 for four days on the river, or up to $920 for a full week. Outfitters also offer day trips through the lower sections of the Gray Canyon, usually for around $50. Experienced kayakers or rafters can make the trip on their own; see Green River Scenic Drive, below, for details.

For information on guided day or multi-day Desolation and Gray Canyon trips, contact one of the following local companies, **Adventure River Expeditions,** 185 S. Broadway, (435) 564-34545 or (800) 564-3648, or **Moki-Mac River Expeditions,** 100 Silliman Ln., (435) 564-3361. A number of Moab, Salt Lake City, and Grand Junction, Colorado, outfitters also offer multi-day trips down the Desolation Canyon; contact the Green River tourist office or the BLM Price River Resource Area office, at 600 Price River Dr., Price, UT 84501, (435) 637-4591, for a complete list of licensed outfitters. You'll need both a permit and river-running experience to float the canyons on your own.

Canoeing Labyrinth and Stillwater Canyons

Labyrinth and Stillwater Canyons lie downstream from Green River, between the town of Green River and the river's confluence with the Colorado River in Canyonlands National Park. Primarily a canoeing or kayaking river, the Green at this point is calm and wide as it passes into increasingly deep, rust-colored canyons. This isn't a wilderness river, however, as regular power boats can also follow the river below town to the confluence with the Colorado River and head up the Colorado to Moab, 2–3 days and 186 river miles away. In fact, the town of Green River sponsors an annual **Friendship Cruise** on this route on Memorial Day weekend.

Guided canoe trips leave from Mineral Canyon and paddle 52 miles to the river's confluence; the remainder of the trip through the Colorado's Cataract Canyon is on raft (around $1,000 for a six-day trip). You'll find both guided and self-guided canoe trips available between Green River State Park just south of town and the Mineral Canyon boat launch. Depending on how fast you paddle it will be a three- or four-day trip. Prices for a guided trip run between $400 and $525; canoe rentals are $15 to $20 a day, though the shuttle from Mineral Canyon back to Green River will cost you around $200 (for up to four people). For information on canoe trips on the Green River, contact **Moki-Mac,** 100 Silliman Ln., (435) 564-3361; **Tex's Riverways,** P.O. Box 67, Moab, UT 84532, (435) 259-5101; or **Red River Canoe Company,** 497 North Main St., Moab, UT 84532, (435) 259-7722. Each company also offers shuttle and full rental service.

Accommodations

Green River has over a dozen well-kept older motels as well as new chain motels to choose from; each of the following has a pool—a major consideration in this often sweltering desert valley.

Under $50: The **Bookcliff Lodge,** 395 E. Main, (435) 564-3406, is part of a large motel and restaurant complex. **Sleepy Hollow Motel,** 94 E. Main, (435) 564-8189, is an attractive well-maintained brick motel.

$50–75: The **Super 8,** 1248 E. Main, (435) 564-8888 or (800) 888-8888, is out by I-70 Exit 162. The **Comfort Inn,** 1065 E. Main, (435) 564-3300, operates a bit closer to town. The **Motel 6,** 946 E. Main, (435) 564-3436 or (800) 466-8356, is just two blocks from the river.

$75–100: The nicest place to stay in town is the **Best Western River Terrace Motel,** 880 E. Main, (435) 564-3401 or (800) 528-1234, with very large, nicely furnished rooms, some of which overlook the Green River.

Campgrounds: Four campgrounds, all with showers, offer sites for tents and RVs. **Shady Acres RV Park,** 360 E. Main, (435) 564-8290, costs $19 without hookups, $22 with; open all year with store, showers, and laundry. **United Campground,** 910 E. Main, (435) 564-8195, is $13.50 without hookups, $18.50 with; open Apr. 1–Oct. 15 with a pool, store, showers, and laundry. **Green River State Park,** 150 S. Green River Blvd., (435) 564-3633 or (800) 322-3770 (reservations), offers pleasant sites shaded by

large cottonwoods and a boat ramp for $4 day use, $11 camping; open all year. **Green River KOA,** 550 S. Green River Blvd., (435) 564-3651, runs $15.50 tents or RVs without hookups, $20 with, and $29 for "kamping kabins." Open Apr. 1–Oct. 15 with a pool, store, and laundry.

Food

Directly adjacent to the Best Western River Terrace Motel is a good restaurant, **The Tamarisk,** also with riverfront views and open for three meals a day; (435) 564-8109.

Other than motel restaurants and fast food, the one really notable place to eat in Green River is **Ray's Tavern,** 25 S. Broadway, (435) 564-3511. Ray's doesn't look like much from the outside, but inside you'll find a friendly welcome, tables made from tree trunks, and some of the best steaks, chops, and burgers in this part of the state. Don't expect cuisine, but the food is good and the atmosphere is truly Western; beer drinkers will be glad for the selection of regional microbrews after a long day navigating the river or driving desert roads.

Services

The **post office** is on E. Main. **Green River Medical Center,** 250 E. Main, (435) 564-3434, offers services Monday–Friday 9 A.M.–5 P.M. The **emergency number** is 911.

VICINITY OF GREEN RIVER

Crystal Geyser

With some luck, you'll catch the spectacle of this cold-water geyser on the bank of the Green River. The gusher shoots as high as 60 feet but only three or four times daily, so you may have to spend a half day here in order to see it. Though the area offers no facilities, camping is possible nearby, so you might be able to see the geyser by moonlight. Staff at the Grand County Travel Council often know the latest eruption schedule. An eruption typically lasts seven minutes and discharges 4,350 cubic feet of salt water. Carbon dioxide and other gases power the gushing fountain. A 2,267-foot-deep petroleum test well drilled in 1935–1936 concentrated the geyser flow, but thick layers of old travertine deposits attest that mineral-laden springs have long been active at this site. Colorful newer travertine forms delicate terraces around the opening and down to the river. The orange and dark red of the minerals and algae make this a pretty spot, even if the geyser is only quietly gurgling.

Crystal Geyser is 10 miles south of town by road (boaters should look for the geyser deposits on the left about 4.5 river miles downstream from Green River). From downtown, drive east one mile on Main, turn left three miles on signed Frontage Road (near Milepost 4), then turn right six miles on a narrow paved road just after going under a railroad overpass. The road goes under I-70, then is unpaved for the last 4.5 miles; keep right at a fork near some power lines. Some washes have to be crossed, so the drive isn't recommended after rains. When the weather's fair, cars shouldn't have a problem. Buildings and antennas passed on the way belong to the Utah Launch Complex of White Sands Missile Range. From 1963 to 1979 several hundred Pershing and Athena rockets blasted off here for targets at White Sands, New Mexico, 400 miles away.

Green River Scenic Drive

Splendid cliffs of Gray Canyon enclose the Green River 10 miles north of town. An unpaved road winding 8.5 miles into the canyon allows drivers easy access to the scenery. Cars with good clearance can travel through the canyon in dry weather; when the clay road surface gets wet, don't attempt it in any vehicle.

From downtown Green River, head east on Main Street and turn north on Hastings Road (1200 East); it's the first paved road to the north past the bridge. After two miles the road follows the banks of the Green River a short way with views north to the castlelike cliffs of the Beckwith Plateau, through which the Green River has carved Gray Canyon. At 6.3 miles after turning off Main, make a right turn onto an unpaved road just before the paved road enters a ranch. The turn may have a small sign for Nefertiti. Follow the unpaved road 3.8 miles across a wash, then along the river to Swasey Beach and Rapids near the mouth of Gray Canyon. A primitive camping area under the cottonwoods is an inviting place to spend the night. The camping area has an outhouse; no drinking water or charge. A large sandy beach stretches along the shore just below the rapids.

The road becomes a bit rougher and narrows to a single lane in spots past Swasey Beach for the remaining 8.5 spectacular miles to Nefertiti. You'll see Price River Canyon entering Gray Canyon on the other side of the river two miles before Nefertiti. Look for petroglyphs near the end of the road. Hikers can explore many rugged side canyons or follow cattle trails a long distance upstream. Cowboys on horseback still work the range on the plateaus to the north much as they've always done. Cattle are driven on these trails to the high country in spring and brought back down in autumn. Michael Kelsey's book *Canyon Hiking Guide to the Colorado Plateau* details hiking possibilities through Gray and Desolation Canyons and their side canyons.

Commercial **raft day trips** provide a more relaxed way of enjoying this extremely remote part of Utah. River-runners enjoy half a dozen lively rapids on the section of river from the boat launch just above Nefertiti Rapid to the take-out at Swasey Beach. You can also do it yourself. This makes a good day trip with rafts or kayaks; canoeists will find the white water very challenging. All boaters must wear life jackets and carry proper equipment (spare oar or paddle, extra life jacket, and bail bucket or pump). You will also need a portable toilet and, if planning a campfire, a firepan to contain the ashes. You won't need a permit, though the BLM has a register at the put-in.

SEGO CANYON AND GHOST TOWN

Prehistoric rock art and ruins of a coal-mining town lie within scenic canyons of the Book Cliffs just a short drive north from Thompson and I-70. In the early 1900s, a local rancher discovered thick seams of high-quality coal here. A mining camp, served by the Ballard and Thompson Railroad, sprang to life at the site. Residents named their little town after Utah's state flower, the sego lily, which grew profusely in the canyons. Population peaked at about 500; families lived in fine houses or in rustic dugouts, while the bachelors stayed in a two-story boardinghouse. Production continued through water shortages, fires, and management troubles until the early 1950s, when the railroads switched to diesel locomotives and no longer needed Sego's coal. The town folded and was sold for salvage. Plenty of good coal remains; if steam locomotives ever come back into style, perhaps Sego will, too!

Visitors to the town can see the company store's stone walls, the frame boardinghouse, dugout houses, railroad grades, and foundations of coal-handling structures. Cars with good clearance can travel the road in dry weather; don't enter the canyons after recent rains or if storms threaten.

To reach Sego Canyon, take I-70 Thompson Exit 185 (25 miles east of Green River or five miles east of the U.S. 191 turnoff to Moab) and drive one mile north to Thompson. The small railroad community has a café and convenience store near I-70. Continue north across the tracks on a paved road, which becomes dirt after half a mile, into Thompson Canyon. At the first creek ford, 3.5 miles from town, look for petroglyphs and pictographs on cliffs to the left. Recently, a pit toilet and picnic tables have been added. You'll see more rock art, though in poorer condition, to the right at the second ford, just past the first. Look for a road fork on the right leading through a notch into Sego Canyon 0.3 mile after the second ford. This turnoff is easily missed. The ghost town lies one mile up Sego Canyon. Both the Sego and Thompson Canyon Roads lead deeper into the rugged Book Cliffs. Drivers with four-wheel drive and hikers can explore more of this land, seldom visited except in deer season.

MOAB

By far the largest town in southeastern Utah, Moab (pop. 5,500) makes an excellent base for exploring Arches and Canyonland National Parks and the surrounding canyon country. Moab lies near the Colorado River in a green valley enclosed by high sandstone cliffs. The biblical Moab was a kingdom at the edge of Zion, and early settlers must have felt themselves at the edge of their world, too, being so isolated from Salt Lake City—the Mormon city of Zion. Moab's existence on the fringe of Mormon culture and the sizable gentile population gave the town a unique character.

In recent years, Moab has become nearly synonymous with mountain biking. The slickrock canyon country seems made for exploration by bike, and people come from all over the world to pedal the backcountry. River trips on the Colorado River are nearly as popular, and a host of other outdoor recreational diversions—from horseback riding to four-wheel jeep exploring to hot-air ballooning—combine to make Moab one of the most popular destinations in Utah.

Moab is also one of the most youthful and vibrant communities in the state; thousands of young people travel to Moab for the recreation, while hundreds of others work here as guides and outfitters. Call them "recreationals," funpigs, gearheads, or even "yummies" (for Young Urban Macho Men Into Extreme Sports)—the fact is that tanned, fit and Lycra-ed bodies are the norm here, and the town's brewpubs, bike shops, and cafés do a booming trade.

As Moab's popularity has grown, so have concerns that the town and the surrounding countryside is simply getting loved to death. The landscape has always been a staple in car ads (remember those Chevy pickups balanced on a redrock pinnacle?); now the landscape sells the "Just Do It" lifestyle for MTV, Nike, and other merchandisers of youth culture. On a busy day, hundreds of mountain bikers form queues to negotiate the trickier sections of the famed Slick Rock Trail and upwards of 20,000 people crowd into town on busy weekends to bike, hike, float, and party. As noted in an article in *Details* magazine, "Moab is pretty much the Fort Lauderdale of the intermountain West." Whether this old Mormon town and the delicate desert environment can endure such an onslaught of popularity is a question of increasing concern.

History

Prehistoric Fremont and Anasazi Indians once lived and farmed in the bottoms of the canyons around Moab. Their rock art, granaries, and dwellings can still be seen. Nomadic Ute Indians had replaced the earlier groups by the time the first white settlers arrived. The Old Spanish Trail, opened in 1829 between New Mexico and California, passed through Spanish Valley and crossed the Colorado River near present-day Moab.

Mormon missionaries tried to establish the Elk Mountain Mission here in 1855. They managed to plant some fields, build a stone fort, and convert some of the Utes before a series of attacks killed three missionaries and sent the others fleeing back to civilization. The valley reverted to the Indians and small numbers of explorers, outlaws, ranchers, and trappers for the next 20 years. Settlers with better success founded Moab in the 1870s. Indian troubles ceased after 1881 and the community became a quiet farming and ranching center.

Oil exploration in the 1920s caused some excitement, but nothing like that of the uranium boom that began in 1952. Moab's population tripled in just three years as eager prospectors swarmed into the canyons. One of these hopefuls, Charlie Steen, did hit it big. Experts had laughed at Charlie's efforts until he discovered the Mi Vida uranium bonanza about 30 miles south of town. An instant multimillionaire, he built a large mansion overlooking Moab and hosted lavish parties attended by Hollywood celebrities. Charlie Steen and most of

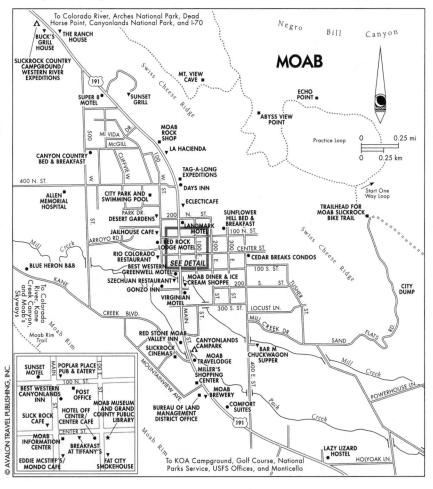

the prospectors have moved on, but Moab has never been the same since.

SIGHTS

Dan O'Laurie Museum

This regional museum tells the story of Moab's and Grand County's past, from prehistoric and Ute Indian artifacts to the explorations of Spanish missionaries. Photos and tools show pioneer Moab life, much of which centered around ranching or mining; here, too, you'll find displays of rocks and minerals, as well as bones of huge dinosaurs that once tracked across this land. Ask for a *Moab Area Historic Walking Tour* leaflet to learn about historic buildings in town. Located at 118 E. Center, (435) 259-7985; open in summer Mon.–Sat. 1–5 P.M. and 7–9 P.M., then the rest of the year Mon.–Thurs. 3–5 P.M. and 7–9 P.M. and Fri.–Sat. 1–5 P.M. and 7–9 P.M.; free.

Hole 'N The Rock

Albert Christensen worked 12 years to excavate his dream home within a sandstone monolith south of town. When he died in 1957, his wife Gladys worked another eight years to complete the project. The interior has notable touches like a 65-foot chimney drilled through the rock ceiling, paintings, taxidermy exhibits, and a lapidary room. The 14-room home is open for tours daily 9 A.M.–6 P.M. in summer and daily 9 A.M.–5 P.M. the rest of the year; $2.50 adults, $1.50 ages 6–12. It also has a gift shop, (435) 686-2250. A picnic area and snack bar are outside. Located 15 miles south of Moab on U.S. 191.

Moab's Skyway

One of Moab's newest tourist attractions is this 12-minute tramway, which lifts you up 1,000 feet to the top of the redrock rims that flank the city to the southwest. Once on top of the rims, you can relax with refreshments, or hike along trails. An easy one-mile trail follows the rims; more adventurous hikers can use the Skyway as a shortcut to Hidden Canyon (see Hiking, below). Bicycles are carried free on the skyway; from on top, you'll have nowhere to go but down on a number of biking trails. Adult tickets are $9, seniors $8, and children 12 and under $7. Open daily, 9 A.M.–late evening (lighted night rides available in warm weather). The Skyway is one mile west of Moab off Kane Creek Boulevard (turn west at the McDonalds), (435) 259-7799.

Expect another tram ride attraction to the top of the rims on the north end of town, to open in 2001.

ACCOMMODATIONS

Moab has been a tourist destination for generations and offers a wide variety of lodging choices, ranging from older motels to new upscale resorts. Luckily, lodgings are relatively inexpensive. The only time when Moab isn't busy is in the dead of winter, from November through February. At all other times, be sure to make reservations well in advance.

If you're having trouble finding a room, **Moab/Canyonlands Central Reservations,** (435) 259-5125, (800) 748-4386, or (800) 505-5343, can make bookings at 85 percent of Moab's accommodations, which include area bed-and-breakfasts, motels, condos, cabins, private houses, and luxury vacation homes. Summer rates are shown; those in winter typically drop 40 percent.

Under $50

The **Lazy Lizard Hostel,** 1213 S. U.S. 191, (435) 259-6057, costs just $8 a night for simple dorm-style accommodations. You won't need a hostel card, and all guests share access to a hot tub, kitchen, barbecue, coin-op laundry, and common room with cable TV. Camping ($6 per person), showers for nonguests ($2), and private rooms ($22 double occupancy) are offered, too. New log cabins here can sleep two ($27) to four ($36) people. The Lazy Lizard sits one mile south behind A-1 Storage; the turnoff is about 200 yards south of Moab Lanes.

For just a few more dollars, you can stay at the vintage **Hotel Off Center,** 96 E. Center, (435) 259-4244 or (800) 237-4685, which has basic rooms (bath down the hall) or bunks in a dorm.

$50–75

The **Sunset Motel,** 41 W. 100 North, (435) 259-5191 or (800) 421-5614, offers kitchenettes, a pool and hot tub, and pets are okay. The motel also offers a fully furnished apartment and a

12-sleeper with two bathrooms, four bedrooms, and a kitchen ($250 a night). The **Red Rock Lodge Motel,** 51 N. 100 West, (435) 259-5431, has rooms with refrigerators and coffee makers; there's a hot tub and locked bicycle storage facilities. At the **Virginian Motel,** 70 E. 200 South, (435) 259-5951 or (800) 261-2063, over half the rooms have kitchenettes; pets okay. **Red Stone Moab Valley Inn,** 535 S. Main St., (435) 259-3500 or (800) 772-1972, is a newer, one-story motel; most rooms have efficiency kitchens. Other amenities include a bicycle maintenance area, covered patio with gas barbecue grill, and guest laundry. Pets okay in smoking rooms only with $5 per night fee. The **Days Inn,** 426 N. Main, (435) 259-4468 or (800) 325-2525, has a pool. The **Moab Travelodge,** 550 S. Main, (435) 259-6171 or (800) 325-6171, has a pool and a restaurant.

$75–100

The local **Super 8 Motel,** 889 N. Main, (435) 259-8868 or (800) 800-8000, has a pool and hot tub. For a bit more luxury, try the **Landmark Motel,** located right in the center of Moab at 168 N. Main, (435) 259-6147 or (800) 441-6147. The Landmark is nicely maintained, with a pool and small waterslide, hot tub, guest laundry, and three family units. The **Best Western Canyonlands Inn,** 16 S. Main, (435) 259-2300 or (800) 528-1234, is also in the heart of Moab, with suites, a pool, fitness room and spa, restaurant, and bike storage area. The **Comfort Suites,** 800 S. Main, (435) 259-5252 or (800) 228-5150, is south of town with some kitchen units and a pool.

One of the newest and most unique looking accommodations in Moab is the **Gonzo Inn,** 100 W. 200 S., (435) 259-2515 or (800) 791-4044. With a look somewhere between an adobe inn and a postmodern warehouse, the Gonzo doesn't try to appear anything but young and hip. Expect large rooms with Day-Glo colors, a pool, and a friendly welcome.

Located in an old residential area, the **Sunflower Hill Bed & Breakfast,** 185 N. 300 East, (435) 259-2974, offers high-quality lodgings in one of Moab's original farmhouses and in a newly built garden cottage with patios and balconies. All 11 rooms have private baths, air conditioning, and queen beds; there are also two suites. Guests share access to an outdoor hot tub, bike storage, patios, and large gardens. Children are welcome from age eight; open year-round.

Blue Heron B&B, 900 W. Kane Creek Blvd., (435) 259-4921 or (800) 870-6537, is a large home on four acres between downtown and the Colorado River. The four guest rooms are nicely decorated; two have private baths. Facilities include bike storage and hot tub. **Canyon Country Bed & Breakfast,** 590 N. 500 West, (435) 259-5262 or (800) 635-0284, is a large Southwestern-style ranch home just north of downtown. The five guest rooms have both private and shared baths; guests share a hot tub and can rent kayaks and mountain bikes. No pets or children under six.

If you want seclusion and a wilderness setting, stay at the **Castle Valley Inn B&B,** located in Castle Valley, 18 miles east of Moab, (435) 259-6012. The inn adjoins a wildlife refuge in a stunning landscape of redrock mesas and needle-pointed buttes. You can stay in one of the main house's five guest rooms or in one of the three bungalows with kitchens. For an additional fee and with advance notice, dinner is available for guests. Facilities include a hot tub; no children or pets; two-night minimum on weekends. To reach Castle Valley Inn, follow UT 128 east from Moab for 16 miles and turn south 2.3 miles toward Castle Valley. Open Feb. 15–Dec. 15.

If you're looking for a bit more room or a longer-term stay, consider the **Cedar Breaks Condos,** 10 S. 400 East, (435) 259-7830, with six two-bedroom units with living rooms and full kitchens. Daily maid service is provided and breakfast food is stocked daily in the refrigerator. Rates are $85 for two people, $12.50 each additional.

The three two-bedroom cottages which compose **Desert Gardens,** 123–127 W. 200 North, (435) 259-5125 or (800) 505-5343, each contains a full kitchen, bath, and living room. The cottages sit in a large shaded yard with access to a hot tub, barbecue, and nicely maintained gardens. Rates are $75 for two, $10 for each additional person. Two-night minimum stay.

$100–125

The **Best Western Greenwell Motel,** 105 S. Main, (435) 259-6151 or (800) 528-1234, has a pool, an on-premises restaurant, and some kitchenettes. The **Ramada Inn,** 182 S. Main, (435) 259-7141 or (888) 989-1988, has nicely appointed rooms (some with balconies) and a pool, spa, and facilities for small meetings. South of downtown is the **Comfort Suites,** 800 S. Main, (435) 259-5252 or (800) 228-5150, an all-suites motel with large, nicely furnished rooms complete with microwaves and refrigerators. Facilities include an indoor pool, spa, exercise room, locked bike storage, and a guest laundry.

Guest Ranch

If you want to experience a bit of the Wild West during your Moab visit, stay at the **Pack Creek Ranch,** on La Sal Pass Rd., 15 miles southeast of Moab in the La Sal Mountains foothills, (435) 259-5505. Accommodations are in cabins, and facilities include a swimming pool and hot tub; massage therapy is available; pets okay. Rates start at $135 per person. Trail rides start at $25 for 1.5 hours. Adventure packages also available. For more information, write P.O. Box 1270, Moab, UT 84532, or visit the website at www.packcreekranch.com. The dining room at the ranch serves excellent steaks, with wondrous views over the canyon country.

Campgrounds

Spanish Trail RV Park, 2980 S. U.S. 191, (435) 259-2411 or (800) 787-2751, has showers, laundry, and restrooms and is open year-round. Sites range from $18 for tents to $22 for hookups. **Canyonlands Campground,** 555 S. Main St., (435) 259-6848 or (800) 522-6848, is open all year; it has showers, laundry, store, and pool; sites run $15–20. **Slickrock Campground,** one mile north of Moab at 1301½ N. U.S. 191, (435) 259-7660 or (800) 448-8873, remains open year-round; it has showers, store, outdoor café, a pool, and cabins with air conditioning and heat; $17 tents or RVs without hookups, $21 with basic hookup, and $31 for cabins. **Moab Valley RV & Campark,** two miles north of Moab at 1773 N. U.S. 191 (opposite the turnoff for UT 128), (435) 259-4469, is also open all year; it has showers; sites for tents or RVs start at $20. **Moab KOA,** four miles south of Moab at 3225 S. U.S. 191, (435) 259-6682 or (800) 562-0372, is open March–November; it has showers, laundry, store, mini golf, and a pool; $24.50 tents or RVs without hookups, $26 with; "kamping kabins" go for $34–38.

The Bureau of Land Management now requires that all camping along the Colorado River (accessible by road above and below Moab), Kane Creek, and near the Moab Slickrock Bike Trail *must* be in developed designated sites (with toilets) or undeveloped designated sites (your own porta-potty required; no restrooms or fee). The following four camping areas along UT 128, $10 fee. From the U.S. 191/UT 128 junction, you'll find Jay Cee Park at 4.2 miles, Hal Canyon at 6.6 miles, Oak Grove at 6.9 miles, and Big Bend Recreation Site at 7.4 miles. Contact the Moab Information Center for locations of additional campgrounds. You'll also find campgrounds farther out at Arches and Canyonlands National Parks, Dead Horse Point State Park, La Sal Mountains, and Canyon Rims Recreation Area.

FOOD

Moab has the best restaurants in all of southern Utah; no matter what else the recreational craze has produced, it has certainly improved the food.

Breakfast and Light Meals

Start the day at **Breakfast at Tiffany's,** 90 E. Center, (435) 259-2553, a happening coffee shop with fresh pastries and a deli. For a traditional breakfast, try the **Jailhouse Cafe,** 101 N. Main St., (435) 259-3900. Another favorite is **Mondo Café,** 59 S. Main St., in the McStiff's Plaza, (435) 259-5551; fresh baked goods, espresso drinks, and sandwiches for lunch. **Moab Diner & Ice Cream Shoppe,** 189 S. Main St., (435) 259-4006, is a good place to know about—you'll find the breakfasts old-fashioned and abundant, a Southwestern green chili edge to the food, and the best ice cream in town; open for breakfast, lunch, and dinner. **EclectiCafe,** 352 N. Main, (435) 259-6896 has a good selection of organic and vegetarian dishes, mostly with ethnic roots. Open for three meals daily.

Casual Dining

Unless otherwise noted, each of the following has a full liquor license. Entrées range $8–$15.

For light meals and snacks, try the **Poplar Place Pub & Eatery,** Main and 100 North, (435) 259-6018, which serves pizza, pasta, and deli sandwiches in a pub atmosphere; open daily for lunch and dinner. **Slick Rock Cafe,** 5 N. Main, (435) 259-8004, is another versatile restaurant. Open for breakfast, lunch, and dinner in a historic building downtown, the Slick Rock serves up-to-date food at reasonable prices, all with a spicy Southwestern or Caribbean kick.

The **Rio Colorado Restaurant,** 100 W. Center St., (435) 259-6666, can fill the bill for most any appetite—sandwiches, Mexican food, steak, seafood, chicken, pasta, and salads; open Sat. and Sun. for breakfast and daily for lunch and dinner. Moab's only true Mexican restaurant is **La Hacienda,** 574 N. Main, (435) 259-6319, with a large selection of excellent house specialties.

Only one restaurant in town serves Asian food: the **Szechuan Restaurant,** 105 S. Main, (435) 259-8984. Fortunately, the food is good, spicy, and inexpensive. **Fat City Smokehouse,** 36 S. 100 West, (435) 259-4302, specializes in Texas-style pit barbecue for lunch and dinner; open Mon.–Sat. Beer only.

For a Western night out, consider **Bar M Chuckwagon Supper,** located on the banks of Mill Creek at 541 S. Mulberry Ln., just southeast of town, (435) 259-2276. Tasty cowboy-style cooking is served up from chuck wagons, followed by a variety of live Western entertainment; open for dinner only (call to check on times) Mon.–Sat. Apr.–Oct.; beer only. The meal plus entertainment costs $20 for everyone 11 years and older, $10 for younger children.

Brewpubs

After a hot day out on the trail, who can blame you for thinking about a cold brew and a good meal at a brewpub? Luckily, Moab has two excellent pubs to fill the bill. **Eddie McStiff's,** 57 S. Main in Western Plaza, (435) 259-BEER, was the first brewpub in Moab and is an extremely popular place to sip a cool one or eat a hearty meal of pasta, pizza, steaks, salads, chicken, and Mexican food. The pub is a convivial place to meet like-minded travelers; in good weather there's seating in a nice courtyard. You'll have to try hard not to have fun here; open daily for lunch and dinner.

There's more good beer and maybe better food at **Moab Brewery,** 686 S. Main St., (435) 259-6333, though this more recent restaurant has yet to attract the kind of scene you'll find at Eddie McStiffs. The atmosphere is light and airy, and the food is good—steaks, sandwiches, burgers, and a wide selection of salads. There's deck seating when weather permits.

Fine Dining

The **Ranch House** serves elegant meals in an 1896 pioneer house at 1266 N. U.S. 191 on the north edge of town, (435) 259-5753; specialties are regional Mountain West cuisine. Expect to pay $20–27 for entrées. Open daily for dinner; reservations recommended. **Sunset Grill,** 900 N. U.S. 191, (435) 259-7146, is located in the uranium king Charlie Steen's mansion high above Moab, with "million dollar" sweeping views of the valley. Chefs offer steaks, fresh seafood, and a selection of modern pasta dishes ($17–25). Sunday brunch is a popular institution; open Mon.–Fri. for lunch and daily for dinner.

Buck's Grill House, 1393 N. U.S. 191, (435) 259-5201, is a steak house with a difference. The restaurant features a pleasant Western atmosphere, and the food seems familiar enough—steaks, prime rib, roast chicken, seafood, grilled pork loin—but the quality of the preparation and the side dishes makes the difference. The butter spice rub on the cowboy steaks or prime rib is excellent. Entrées range between $11 and $19. Moab's most up-to-date restaurant is the **Center Cafe,** downtown at 92 E. Center St., (435) 259-4295. The menu is eclectic, with a wide selection of pasta dishes (including several vegetarian choices) and a selection of steaks and seafood that feature continental influences ($17–28); open Mon.–Sat. for dinner.

OTHER PRACTICALITIES

Nightlife and Entertainment

A lot of Moab's nightlife focuses on the two brewpubs, the rowdy and well-loved **Eddie McStiff's,** 57 S. Main in Western Plaza, (435) 259-BEER, and the newer and posher **Moab Brewery,** 686 S. Main St., (435) 259-6333. For live music, try the **Outlaw Saloon,** 44 W. 200 North, (435) 259-2654, the **Club Río,** 100 W. Center St., (435) 259-6666, or the **Sportsman's Lounge,** 1991 S. Hwy 191, (435) 259-9972.

For a selection of movies, head for **Slickrock Cinemas,** at 580 Kane Creek Blvd., (435) 259-4441.

Events

To find out about local happenings, contact the Moab Information Center, (435) 259-8825. Major annual events include the **Moab Half Marathon** in late **March** (third Sat.). **April** brings the **Cannondale Cup Bicycle Race.**

Over Memorial Day weekend in **May** is the **Green River to Moab Friendship Cruise** on the Green and Colorado Rivers.

June kicks up dust at the fair grounds with two rodeos, the professional **P.R.C.A. Rodeo** early in the month and the **Canyonlands Rodeo,** with rodeo, parade, dance, horse racing, and 4-H gymkhana towards the end of the month.

August means it's time for the **Grand County Fair,** with agricultural displays, crafts, and arts judging.

The **Moab Music Festival** keeps getting larger, with several weekends of music by jazz, bluegrass, and other groups, plus outdoor chamber music.

Shopping and Services

Hogan Trading Co. Gallery, at 100 S. Main, (435) 259-8118, offers an upscale selection of Indian art; other shops lie scattered around town.

Back of Beyond Books, 83 N. Main, (435) 259-5154, features an excellent selection of regional books and maps. A good selection of books and maps is sold at **Times Independent Maps** at 5 E. Center St., (435) 259-7525.

The **Grand County Public Library,** 25 S. 100 East (next to the Dan O'Laurie Museum), (435) 259-5421, is a good place for local history and general reading; open Mon.–Thurs. 1–9 P.M., Fri. 1–5 P.M., and Sat. 10 A.M.–2 P.M.

The **post office** is downtown at 50 E. 100 North, (435) 259-7427. **Allen Memorial Hospital** provides medical care at 719 W. 400 North, (435) 259-7191. For **emergencies** (ambulance, sheriff, police, or fire), dial 911.

Parks and Recreation

The **city park,** 181 W. 400 North, (435) 259-8226, has shaded picnic tables, a playground, and an outdoor swimming pool. **Lions Park** offers picnicking along the Colorado River two miles north of town. **Rotary Park,** on Mill Creek Dr., is family-oriented and has lots of activities for kids. **Moab Arts and Recreation,** 111 East 100 North, (435) 259-6272, sponsors year-round activities for kids; you don't need to be a resident to take part.

Moab Golf Club, 2705 S. East Bench Rd., (435) 259-6488, features an 18-hole course, driving range, and pro shop. Go south five miles on U.S. 191, turn left two miles on Spanish Trails Road, then right a quarter mile on Murphy Lane.

Information

The **Moab Information Center,** Main and Center, (435) 259-8825 or (800) 635-MOAB, is the place to start for nearly all local and area information. The National Park Service, the Bureau of Land Management, the U. S. Forest Service, the Grand County Travel Council, and the Canyonlands Natural History Association all are represented in this multi-agency facility. Visitors needing help from any of these agencies should start at the information center rather than at the agency of-

Moab loves a parade.

W.C. McRAE

fices. Free literature is available and a large selection of books and maps are sold. Especially useful is the free *Southeastern Utah Travel Guide,* which describes features of and opportunities for recreation in the Arches and Canyonlands National Parks. Included are comprehensive lists of tour operators, places to rent and purchase recreation equipment, and campgrounds. The office is open daily from 8 A.M.–9 P.M. in the summer (reduced hours the rest of the year). There are a number of Moab-related travel websites; probably the best is at www.canyonlands-utah.com.

The **National Park Service office** in Moab, 2282 Southwest Resource Blvd., Moab, UT 84532 (three miles south of downtown), (435) 259-7164/7164, is headquarters for Canyonlands and Arches National Parks and Natural Bridges National Monument. Open Mon.–Fri. 8 A.M.–4:30 P.M. **Manti–La Sal National Forest office** is also at 2282 Southwest Resource Blvd., (435) 259-7155; open Mon.–Fri. 8 A.M.–noon and 12:30–4:30 P.M. The **BLM District office** is at 82 E. Dogwood on the south side of town behind Comfort Suites; mailing address is P.O. Box 970, Moab, UT 84532; (435) 259-8193 (general info); open Mon.–Fri. 7:45 A.M.–4:30 P.M. Some land-use maps are sold; this is where you pick up your river-running permits.

Transportation
Sunrise Airlines, (800) 842-8211 or (435) 259-3422, flies twice daily round-trip to/from Salt Lake City (from Nov.1 to Mar. 31, there are no flights on the weekends). The only other public transport option to Moab is the ARK Shuttle run by Bighorn Express, (888) 655-7433, website: www.bighornexpress.com, which makes one minibus run daily between Moab and Salt Lake City. Advance reservations are required.

For rental cars, contact **Certified Ford,** 500 S. Main, (435) 529-6107, or and **Thrifty,** 400 N. Main, (435) 259-7317. **Taxi** service includes shuttles for bicyclists and river runners, (435) 259-TAXI.

MOAB-AREA RECREATION

Moab sits at the center of some of the most picturesque landscapes in North America. Even the most casual visitor will want to get outdoors and explore the river canyons, natural arches, and mesas. Mountain biking and river tours are the recreational activities that get the most attention in the Moab area, though hikers, climbers, and horseback riders will find plenty to do. If you're less physically adventurous, you can explore the landscape on scenic flights or on hot-air balloon trips, or follow old mining roads in four-wheel drives to remote backcountry destinations.

Contact the Moab Information Center, (435) 259-8825 or (800) 635-6622, for full information about the area's recreational options; the center, located at Main and Central Streets in the center of town, has representatives of the National Park Service, the BLM, and the U.S. Forest Service on staff, and they can direct you to the adventure of your liking. The offices also have literature, books, and maps. BLM people can also give locations of the developed and undeveloped designated campsites near the Moab Slickrock Bike Trail, Kane Creek, and along the Colorado River; you must use the designated sites in these areas.

Sports and Equipment Rentals
Global Expeditions, 711 N. 500 West, (435) 259-6604, rents camping, mountaineering, and cross-country ski equipment and offers instruction in climbing and cross-country ski touring. **Rim Cyclery,** 94 W. 100 North, (435) 259-5333, offers mountain bikes and cross-country skis; mountain-bike tours are offered, too. Mountain-bike rentals and tours are also available at **Moab Cyclery,** 391 S. Main, (435) 259-7423; **Poison Spider Bicycles,** 497 N. Main, (435) 259-7882; and **Western Spirit Cycling,** 38 S. 100 West, (435) 259-8969. Expect to pay about $35 a day to rent a mountain bike.

Canyon Voyages, 401 N. Main St., (435) 259-6007, and **Tag-A-Long Expeditions,** 452 N. Main St., (435) 259-8946, are two local rafting companies that rent rafts and kayaks for those who would rather organize their own river adventure. Canoe rental from **Red River Canoe Company,** 497 N. Main St., (435) 259-7722, costs $18–25 per person and includes necessary equipment and transportation.

Rent jeeps and other four-wheel-drive vehicles at **Farabee 4X4 Adventures,** 83 S. Main, (435)

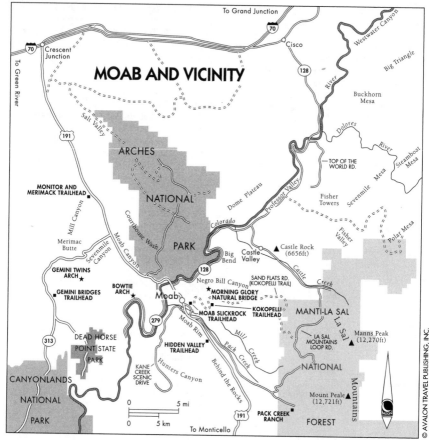

MOAB AND VICINITY

259-7494, or **Slickrock Jeep Rentals,** 284 N. Main, (435) 259-5678.

MOUNTAIN BIKING

Moab is the West's most noted mountain-bike destination. In addition to the famed and challenging slickrock trails (slickrock is the exposed sandstone that composes much of the land's surface here) that wind through astonishing desert landscapes, cyclists can pedal through alpine meadows in the La Sal Mountains, while near-abandoned four-wheel-drive tracks open

up the backcountry to the adventurous. Be aware that the most famous trails, like the Slickrock Bike Trail, are not for beginning mountain bikers. You'll need to be fit, as well as expert in fat-tire technique to enjoy and, in some cases, make it all the way through these trails. Other trails are better matched to the skills of novices.

It's a good idea to read up on Moab-area trails before planning a trip here (heaps of books and pamphlets are available; see the booklist). You can also hire an outfitter to teach you about the special skills needed to mountain-bike in slickrock country, or join a guided tour. A good place to start is the Trails Illustrated *Bike Map #501* of the Moab area, which has mountain-bike routes color-coded according to difficulty. Or pick up a *Moab Area Mountain Bike Trails* map at the Moab Information Center.

Most people come to Moab to mountain-bike between mid-March and late May, and then again in fall, from mid-September to the end of October. Unless you are an early riser, summer is simply too hot for extended bike touring in these desert canyons. Be prepared for crowds, especially in mid-March, during university's spring break. In 1999, the Slickrock Trail alone attracted over 150,000 people.

If you've never biked on slickrock or in the desert, here are a few basic guidelines. Take care if venturing off a trail—it's a long way down some of the sheer cliff faces! A trail's steep slopes and sharp turns themselves can be tricky—a helmet is a must. Knee pads and riding gloves also protect from scrapes and bruises. Fat bald tires work best on the rock; partially deflated knobby tires do almost as well. Carry plenty of water—one gallon in summer, half a gallon in cooler months. Tiny plant associations, which live in fragile cryptobiotic soil, don't want you tearing through their homes; stay on the rock and avoid sand areas.

MOUNTAIN-BIKE ETIQUETTE

When mountain biking in the Moab area, don't expect an instant wilderness experience. Because of the popularity of the routes, the fragile desert environment is under quite a bit of stress, and you'll need to be considerate of the thousands of other people who share the trails. By keeping these rules in mind, you'll help keep Moab from being loved to death.

Ride only on open roads and trails. Much of the desert is made up of extremely fragile plant and animal ecosystems, and riding recklessly through cryptobiotic soils can destroy desert life and lead to erosion. If you pioneer a trail, chances are someone else will follow the tracks, leading to ever more destruction.

Protect and conserve scarce water sources. Don't wash, swim, walk, or bike through potholes, and camp well away from isolated streams and waterholes. The addition of your insect repellant, body oils, suntan lotion, or lubrication from your bike can destroy the thronging life of a pothole. Camping right next to a remote stream can deprive shy desert wildlife of life-giving water access.

Leave all Native American sites and artifacts as you find them. First, it's against the law to disturb antiquities; second, it's stupid. Enjoy looking at rock art, but don't touch the images—body oils hasten their deterioration. Don't even think about taking pot shards, arrowheads, or artifacts from where you find them. Leave them for others to enjoy or for archaeologists to decipher.

Dispose of human solid waste thoughtfully. The desert can't easily absorb human fecal matter. Desert soils have few microorganisms to break down organic material, and, simply put, mummified turds can last for years. Be sure to bury human solid waste at least 6–12 inches deep in sand and at least 200 feet away from streams and water sources. Pack out toilet paper in resealable bags.

On the Moab Slickrock Bike Trail; La Sals stand in the distance.

Dozens of trails thread the Moab area; some of the best and most noted follow.

Slickrock Bike Trail

Undulating slickrock just east of Moab challenges even the best mountain-bike riders; this is not an area to learn mountain-bike skills. Originally, motorcyclists laid out this route, though now about 99 percent of riders rely on leg and lung power. The practice loop near the beginning allows first-time visitors a chance to get a feel for the slickrock. The "trail" consists only of painted white lines. Riders following it have less chance of getting lost or finding themselves in hazardous areas. Plan on about five hours to do the 9.6-mile main loop and expect to do some walking.

Side trails lead to viewpoints overlooking Moab, the Colorado River, and arms of Negro Bill Canyon. Panoramas of surrounding canyon country and the La Sals add to the pleasure of biking.

To reach the trailhead from Main Street in Moab, turn east 0.4 mile on 300 South, turn right 0.1 mile on 400 East, turn left (east) a half mile on Mill Creek Drive, then left 2.5 miles on Sand Flats Road.

The practice loop also makes an enjoyable 2.5-mile hike. Steep drop-offs into tributaries of Negro Bill Canyon offer breathtaking views. It's best to walk off to the side of the white lines marking the route. You'll reach the practice loop a quarter mile from the trailhead.

Kokopelli's Trail

Mountain bikers have linked together a series of back roads through the magical canyons of eastern Utah and western Colorado. You can start on Sand Flats Road in Moab and ride east to Castle Valley (21.1 miles), Fisher Valley (44.9 miles), Dewey Bridge (62.9 miles), Cisco Boat Landing (83.5 miles), Rabbit Valley (108 miles), and Loma (140 miles). Lots of optional routes and access points allow for many possibilities. Campsites along the trail have tables, grills, and outhouses. See the book *The Utah-Colorado Mountain Bike Trail System, Route 1— Moab to Loma*, by Peggy Utesch, for detailed descriptions. An excel-

lent brochure, *Kokapelli's Trail Map,* is available free at the Moab Information Center.

Gimini Bridges (Bull Canyon) Trail

This 14-mile trail passes through tremendous natural rock arches and the slickrock fins of the Wingate Formation, making this one of the most scenic of Moab-area trails; it's also one of the more moderate trails in terms of necessary skill and fitness. The trail begins 12.5 miles up UT 313 (the access road to Dead Horse Point State Park), a total of 21 miles—all uphill—from Moab, so a shuttle or drop-off is a good idea.

Monitor and Merimack Trail

A good introduction to the varied terrains in the Moab area, the 13.2-mile Monitor and Merimack Trail also includes a trip to a dinosaur fossil bed. The trail climbs through open desert and up Tusher Canyon, then explores red sandstone towers and buttes across slickrock before dropping down Mill Canyon. At the base of the canyon, you can leave your bike and hike the Mill Canyon Dinosaur Trail before completing the loop to the parking area. Reach the trailhead by traveling 15 miles north of Moab on U.S. 191.

Guided Tours

Guided mountain-bike tours through local areas of Canyonlands National Park start at around $35 for a half day, $50 for a full day. Bring your own bike or be prepared to face extra rental charges. Longer multi-day trips to places like the Maze District, White Rim Canyon, or even the North Rim of the Grand Canyon typically cost around $600–700 for 4–5 days of adventuring. **Dreamrides Custom Mountainbike Tours**, (435) 259-6419, www.dreamride.com, focuses on leading personally tailored half- or full-day mountain-biking adventures; though they offer a substantial discount to people who show up ready to share someone else's dream tour. **Rim Tours**, 1233 S. U.S. 191, Moab, UT 84532, (435) 259-5223 or (800) 626-7335, www.rim-tours.com, and **Kaibab Mountain Bike Tours**, operated out of Moab Cyclery at 391 S. Main, Moab, UT 84532, (435) 259-7423 or (800) 451-1133, www.kaibabtours.com, lead

bear petroglyph

LOUISE FOOTE

half-day, full-day, and multi-day trips on mountain bikes; some of their tours combine cycling with rafting and/or hiking.

Western Spirit Cycling, P.O. Box 411, Moab, UT 84532, (435) 259-8969 or (800) 845-BIKE, www.westernspirit.com, specializes in multi-day tours of the Moab area during spring and autumn and the high country of Colorado, Idaho, and Montana in summer. Utah trips include the White Rim and Abajos. You can arrange custom trips to such places as Lockhart Basin and Kokopelli's Trail; rentals, day trips (on request, with a four-person minimum), and instructional clinics are offered, too.

Nichols Expeditions, 497 N. Main, (435) 259-7882 or (800) 635-1792, www.nicholsexpeditions.com, goes to all three districts of Canyonlands National Park, while other bike trips go to Grand Canyon North Rim and Idaho. Utah rides go in spring or autumn.

Shuttle Services
Many mountain-bike trails are essentially one-way, and unless you want to cycle back the way you came, you'll need to arrange a shuttle service to pick you up and return you to Moab or to your vehicle. Also, if you don't have a vehicle or a bike rack, you will need to use a shuttle service to get to more distant trailheads. **Roadrunner Shuttle,** (435) 259-9402 and **Acme Bike Shuttle,** (435) 260-2534, both operate shuttle services; the usual fare is $10 per person. Both companies will also shuttle hikers to trailheads, or pick up rafters. Roadrunner also serves as a taxi service for groups.

RIVER TOURS

Even a visitor with a tight schedule can get out and enjoy the canyon country on rafts and other watercraft. Outfitters offer both laid-back and exhilarating day trips, which usually require little advance planning. Longer, multi-day trips include gentle canoe paddles along the placid Green River and thrilling expeditions down the Colorado River.

Moab is full of river-trip companies, and most offer a variety of day and multi-day trips; in addition, many will combine raft trips with biking, hiking, or four-wheel-drive excursions. Call for brochures or check out the many websites—listed below are major outfitters and some of their offerings.

You'll need to reserve well in advance for most of the longer trips, as the BLM and the National Park Service limit the numbers of trips through the backcountry, and space, especially in high season, is at a premium. Experienced rafters can also plan their own unguided trips, though you'll need a permit for all areas except for the day-long Fisher Towers float upstream from Moab.

The rafting season runs April–September, and jetboat tours run February–November. Contact the Moab Information Center and the National Park Service office for lists or brochures of tour operators; independent river-runners can also visit the center for Colorado River info, though you need to pick up permits from the BLM or National Parks offices. Most river-runners obtain their permits by applying in January and February for a March drawing; the Moab Information Center BLM Ranger can advise on this process and provide the latest information about available cancellations.

Day Trips
The most popular day-run near Moab starts upstream on the Colorado River near Fisher Towers and bounces through several moderate rapids on the way back to town. Full-day raft trips from Fisher Towers to near Moab generally cost $45–50 per person. **Western River Expeditions,** (801) 942-6669 or (800) 453-7450, www.westernriver.com, has several half-day and full-day excursion options, as do **Tag-A-Long Expeditions,** 452 N. Main, (435) 259-8946 or (800) 453-3292, www.tagalong.com; **Navtec Expeditions,** 321 N. Main (P.O. Box 1267, Moab, UT 84532), (435) 259-7983 or (800) 833-1278, www.navtec.com; and **Canyon Voyages,** (435) 259-6007 or (800) 733-6007, www.canyonvoyages.com. In addition to half- and full-day trips, **Adrift Adventures,** 378 N. Main, (435) 259-8594 or (800) 874-4483, www.adrift.net, also gives adventurers the option of exploring canyonland petroglyphs and rock formations on a combination raft and jeep trip ($72) or a raft/horseback trip ($77). **Moki-Mac,** (435) 564-3361 or (800) 284-7280, www.mokimac.com, offers full-day trips down the tamer Gray Canyon section of the Green River.

a peaceful morning on the Colorado River, below Moab

The Fisher Towers section of the Colorado is gentle enough for amateur rafters to negotiate on their own. Rent a raft or kayak from one of the equipment rental outfits listed above. A popular one-day raft trip with mild rapids begins from the Hittle Bottom Recreation Site, 23.5 miles up UT 128 near Fisher Towers and ends 14 river miles downstream at Take-Out Beach, 10.3 miles up UT 128 from U.S. 191. You can rent rafts and the mandatory life jackets in Moab, and you won't need a permit on this section of river. Daily raft rentals begin at $65 or so, kayaks rent for $25.

For a more adventurous rafting day trip, the Colorado's rugged Westwater Canyon offers lots of white water and several class III–IV rapids near the Utah/Colorado border. These trips are more expensive, typically $120–135 a day (longer trips are also available; see below). Contact **Canyon Voyages, Tag-A-Long Expeditions, Moki-Mac** (for details, see above), or **Sheri Griffith Expeditions,** (503) 259-8229 or (800) 332-2439, www.griffithexp.com.

Jetboat Tours: Guided jetboat excursions through Canyonlands National Park start at around $50 for a half-day trip. **Tex's Riverways,** (435) 259-5101, offers trips of various lengths; **Tag-A-Long Expeditions,** (435) 259-8946 or (800) 453-3292, and **Adrift Adventures,** (435) 259-8594 or (800) 874-4483, both offer half-day trips and full-day combination jetboat/jeep excursions.

Motorboat Tours: Canyonlands by Night tours leave at sunset in an open motorboat and go several miles upstream on the Colorado River; a guide points out canyon features. The sound and light show begins on the way back; music and historic narration accompany the play of lights on canyon walls. Cost is $25 adults, $15 ages 4–12; boats run May–mid-October. Dinner cruises available. **Canyonlands by Day** trips go downriver into the Colorado River Canyon near Dead Horse Point. Of the two trips offered, one goes 60 miles downstream ($55 adults, $40 ages 4–12) and the other travels 30 miles ($35 adults, $25 ages 4–12). Tours operate March–October; reservations are a good idea as the boat fills up fast. Trips depart from the Spanish mission-style office just across the Colorado River from Moab, (435) 259-5261, www.moab-utah.com/bynight.

Multi-Day Trips

Multi-day excursions are the best way to experience the most serious Canyonlands white water, which is found in the Colorado River's Westwater and Cataract Canyons. Adventure trips on these class III–IV rapids cost $150–200 per person per day; usually, no previous white-water experience is necessary. All of the following operators offer trips down these popular runs plus special side offerings of their own. For details on most of these outfitters, see Day Trips, above. **Canyon Voyages** also offers trips on the Delores River and the Green River's Labyrinth Canyon. **Sheri Griffith Expeditions,** has gained a positive reputation for their women-only excursions. In addition to white-water rafting trips, **Moki Mac,** also offers fully outfitted canoe trips on the Labyrinth Canyons of the Green River. Contact **Adrift Adventures,** for combination jeep/raft or horseback/raft expeditions. **Adventure Bound River Expeditions,** 2392 H Rd., Grand Junction, CO 81505, (970) 245-5428 or (800) 423-4668, www.raft-colorado.com, generally start in Colorado and end in Utah.

Experienced white-water rafters with permits can put in at the BLM's Westwater Ranger Station in Utah or at the Loma boat launch in Colorado. A start at Loma adds a day or two to the trip and the sights of Horsethief and Ruby Canyons. Normal take-out is at Cisco, though it's possible to continue 16 miles on slow-moving water through open country to Dewey Bridge. The **Dolores River,** also enjoyed by river-runners, joins the Colorado about two miles upstream from Dewey Bridge. The season lasts mid-May–June—none at all in dry years. Boaters need experience and a permit for both rivers; kayakers should have their rolls down well. The BLM office in Moab handles permits and provides information for these rivers.

Canoeists can also sample the calm waters of the Labyrinth section of the Green River on multi-day excursions. **Red River Canoe Company,** 497 N. Main St., Moab, UT 84532, (435) 259-7722, leads expeditions here as well as into the Colorado River's Ruby and Horsethief Canyons. The company also conducts whitewater canoe workshops on the Colorado's Professor Valley and combination canoe and mountain-bike trips. Cost ranges $110–$140 per person per day.

HIKING

To reach most of Moab's prime hiking trails will require a short drive to trailheads; these routes are all very picturesque and are fully described below. For more options, pick up the brochure "Moab Area Hiking Trails" at the visitors' center, and turn the chapters on Arches and Canyonlands National Parks.

Hiking Trails from Kane Creek Scenic Drive

The high cliffs just southwest of town provide fine views of the Moab Valley, highlands of Arches National Park, and the La Sal Mountains. The

Moab Rim Trail turns off Kane Creek Boulevard 1.5 miles downriver from Moab. The total driving distance from the junction of Main Street and Kane Creek Boulevard is 2.6 miles; look for the trailhead on the left 0.1 mile after a cattle guard.

You can see the sky through Little Arch across the river from the trailhead. Four-wheel-drive vehicles can also ascend the Moab Rim Trail, though the rough terrain is considered difficult for them; the first 200 yards will give drivers a feel for the difficulty. The trail climbs northeast 1.5 miles along tilted rock strata of the Kayenta Formation to the top of the plateau. This is a moderately difficult hike, a gain of 940 feet, with good views nearly all the way. Once on top, hikers can follow jeep roads southeast to Hidden Valley Trail and descend on a hiking trail to U.S. 191 south of Moab—a 5.5-mile trip one-way. Experienced hikers can also head south from the rim to **Behind the Rocks,** a fantastic maze of sandstone fins.

You'll see not only a "hidden valley" from the **Hidden Valley Trail** but also panoramas of the Moab area and Behind the Rocks. The moderately difficult trail ascends 500 feet in a series of switchbacks to a broad shelf below the Moab Rim, then follows the shelf ("hidden valley") to the northwest. It then crosses a low pass and follows a second shelf in the same direction. Near the end of the second shelf, the trail turns left to a divide, where you can see a portion of the remarkable fins of Behind the Rocks. This divide is one mile from the start and 680 feet higher in elevation. The trail continues a third of a mile from the divide down to the end of the Moab Rim Trail, a jeep road and hiking trail. Or, instead of turning left to the divide, you can make a short side trip (no trail) to the right for views of Moab.

To reach the Hidden Valley Trailhead, drive south three miles on U.S. 191 from Moab, turn right 0.4 mile on Angel Rock Road to its end (the turnoff is just south of Milepost 122), then right 0.3 mile on Rimrock Lane.

A look at the topo map will show that something strange is going on at the area called **Behind The Rocks.** Massive fins of Navajo Sandstone 100–500 feet high, 50–200 feet thick, and up to a half-mile long cover a large area. Narrow vertical cracks, sometimes only a few feet wide, separate the fins. Archaeological sites and several arches are in the area. No maintained trails exist here, and some routes require technical climbing skills. The maze offers endless exploration routes. If you get lost (very easy to do), remember that the fins are oriented east-west; the rim of the Colorado River Canyon is reached by going west, and Spanish Valley is reached by going east. Bring plenty of water, a topo map (Moab 7½-minute), and a compass. Access routes are Moab Rim and Hidden Valley Trails (from the north and east) and Pritchett Canyon (from the west and south). Though only a couple of miles from Moab, Behind the Rocks seems a world away. The BLM is studying a possible wilderness designation to protect the solitude and character of this strange country.

Hikers along **Hunters Canyon** enjoy seeing a rock arch and other rock formations in the canyon walls and the lush vegetation along the creek. Off-road vehicles have made tracks a short way up, then you'll be walking, mostly along the creekbed. Short sections of trail lead around thickets of tamarisk and other water-loving plants. Look for Hunters Arch on the right about a half-mile up. Most of the water in Hunters Canyon comes from a deep pool surrounded by hanging gardens of maidenhair fern. A dry fall and a small natural bridge lie above the pool. This pretty spot marks the hike's three-mile point and an elevation gain of 240 feet. At this point the canyon becomes very brushy. To reach the trailhead from Moab, drive eight miles on Kane Creek Boulevard along the Colorado River and up Kane Creek Canyon. The road is asphalted where it fords Hunter Creek but the asphalt is usually covered with dirt washed over it by the creek.

You can make a longer hike by going up Hunters Canyon and descending on Pritchett Canyon Road. The road crosses the normally dry creekbed just upstream from the deep pool. To bypass the dry fall above the pool, backtrack 300 feet down the canyon and rock-scramble up a short, steep slope—on your right heading upstream. At a junction just east of there, a jeep road along the north rim of Hunters Canyon meets Pritchett Canyon Road. Walk northeast a half mile on Pritchett Canyon Road to a spur trail on the left leading to Pritchett Arch. Then continue 4.5 miles on Pritchett Canyon Road to Kane Creek Boulevard. This country is more open and desertlike than Hunters Canyon. A 3.2-mile car shuttle or hike is needed to return to Hunters Canyon Trailhead.

Hiking Trails from UT 279

The **Portal Overlook Trail** switchbacks up a slope, then follows a sloping sandstone ledge of the Kayenta Formation to an overlook. A panorama takes in the Colorado River, Moab Valley, Arches National Park, and the La Sals. The hike is 1.5 miles (one-way) with an elevation gain of 980 feet. This trail is a twin of the Moab Rim Trail (described above) across the river. Begin from the Jaycee Park Campground on the right, 3.8 miles from the turnoff at U.S. 191; mulberry trees shade the attractive spot. Expect to share this trail with many mountain bikers.

The 1.5-mile (one-way) **Corona Arch and Bowtie Arch Trail** leads across slickrock country to these impressive arches. You can't see them from the road, though a third arch—Pinto—is visible. Signed trailhead is on the right 10 miles from U.S. 191 (midway between Mileposts 5 and 6); you'll see railroad tracks just beyond the trailhead. The trail climbs up from the parking area, crosses the tracks, and follows a bit of a jeep road and a small wash to an ancient gravel bar. Pinto (or Gold Bar) Arch stands to the left, though there's no trail to it. Follow cairns to Corona and Bowtie. Handrails and a ladder help in the few steep spots.

Despite being only a few hundred yards apart, each arch has a completely different character and history. Bowtie formed when a pothole in the cliffs above met a cave underneath. It used to be called Paul Bunyan's Potty before that name was appropriated for an arch in Canyonlands National Park. The hole is about 30 feet in diameter. Corona Arch, reminiscent of the larger Rainbow Bridge, eroded out of a sandstone fin. The graceful span is 140 feet long and 105 feet high. Both arches are composed of Navajo Sandstone. If you have time for only one hike in the Moab area, this one is especially recommended.

Hiking Trails off UT 128

Negro Bill Canyon is one of the most popular hiking destinations in the Moab Area. The route follows a lively stream pooled by beavers and surrounded by abundant greenery and sheer canyon cliffs. The high point of the hike is Morning Glory Natural Bridge, the sixth-longest natural rock span in the country at 243 feet. The trailhead is on the right just after crossing a concrete bridge three miles from U.S. 191. A trail leads upcanyon, along the creek in some places, high on the banks in others.

To see Morning Glory Natural Bridge, head two miles up the main canyon to the second side canyon on the right, then follow a good side trail a half mile up to the long slender bridge. The spring and small pool underneath keep the air cool even in summer; ferns, columbines, and poison ivy grow here. Elevation gain is 330 feet. William ("Nigger Bill") Granstaff was a mulatto who lived in the area from about 1877 to 1881. Modern sensibilities have changed his nickname to "Negro Bill."

Experienced hikers can continue up the main canyon about eight miles and rock-scramble (no trail) up the right side, then drop into Rill Creek, which leads to the North Fork of Mill Creek and into Moab. Total distance is about 16 miles one-way; you'll have to find your own way between canyons. The upper Negro Bill and Rill Canyons can also be reached from Sand Flats Road. The Moab and Castle Valley 15-minute and Moab 1:100,000 topo maps cover the route. This would be a good overnight trip, though fast hikers have done it in a day. Expect to do some wading and rock-scrambling. Water from the creeks and springs is available in both canyon systems; purify first.

A car shuttle is necessary between the Negro Bill and Mill Creek Trailheads. You can reach Mill Creek from the end of Powerhouse Lane on the east edge of Moab (see the Moab map), but *don't park here.* Vehicle break-ins are a serious problem. Either have someone meet or drop you off here or park closer to town near houses. A hike up the North Fork offers very pretty scenery. A deep pool and waterfall lie three quarters of a mile upstream; follow Mill Creek upstream and take the left (north) fork. Negro Bill and Mill Creek Canyons are BLM wilderness study areas.

You can't miss the **Fisher Towers** as you drive UT 128. These spires of dark red sandstone rise 900 feet above Professor Valley. You can hike around the base of these needle

Fisher Towers

rocks on a trail accessed from the BLM picnic area. Titan, the third and highest rock tower, stands one mile from the picnic area; you'll find a viewpoint overlooking Onion Creek 1.1 miles farther along. Carry water for this moderately difficult hike.

Hiking Trails North of Moab, off U.S. 191

The short **Mill Creek Dinosaur Trail** with numbered stops identifies the bones of dinosaurs who lived here 150 million years ago. You'll see fossilized wood, too. Pick up the brochure from the Moab Information Center or at the trailhead. From Moab, go 14 miles north on U.S. 191 (or four miles north of the Dead Horse Point turnoff) and turn left two miles on a dirt road, keeping right at a fork 1.1 miles in.

You'll find many other points of interest nearby. A copper mill and tailings dating from the late 1800s lie across the canyon. Halfway Stage Station ruins, where travelers once stopped on the Thompson to Moab run, are a short distance down the other road fork. Jeepers and mountain bikers can do a 13- to 14-mile loop to Monitor and Merimac Buttes (an information sign just in from U.S. 191 has a map and details).

FOUR-WHEEL TOURING

Road tours offer visitors a special opportunity to view unique canyonland arches and spires, indigenous rock art, and wildlife. An interpretive brochure at the Moab Information Center outlines the Moab Area Rock Art Auto Tour, which routes motorists to petroglyphs tucked away behind golf courses and ranches. You might also pick up a map of Moab Area four-wheel-drive trails—four rugged, 15- to 54-mile loop routes through the desert, which take from 2.5 to four hours to drive. Those who left their trusty 4X4 and off-road driving skills at home can take an off-road jeep tour through a private operator. Both **Tag-A-Long Tours,** 452 N. Main, Moab, UT 84532, (435) 259-8946 or (800) 453-3292, www.tagalong.com, and **Adrift Adventures,** 378 N. Main (P.O. Box 577, Moab, UT 84532), (435) 259-8594 or (800) 874-4483, www.adrift.net, have half-day (around $50) and full-day jeep tours (around $90) with combination jetboat or hiking options. Full-day tours include lunch.

Moab Rock Shop/Lin Ottinger's Tours, 600 N. Main, Moab, UT 84532, (435) 259-7312, offers backcountry driving trips from mid-April to mid-October. Lin has been poking around the canyons of this area since the uranium boom of the 1950s, and he knows the best places; frequent stops allow plenty of time to walk around for a look at Indian art and scenic and geologic features. Half-day trips are $65, full-day $80.

You can also rent 4X4s from **Canyonlands 4X4,** 550 N. Main St., (435) 259-4567, **Farabee 4X4 Adventures,** 234 N. Main, (435) 259-7494, or **Slick Rock 4X4 Rental,** 284 N. Main, (435) 259-5678.

HORSEBACK RIDING

Pack Creek Ranch, (435) 259-5505, offers two-hour horseback rides in Arches National Park and the La Sal Mountains ($35). Pack trips tour the La Sals and canyon country. **Cowboy Trails,** 2231 S. Hwy. 191, (435) 259-8053, leads short

2.5-hour evening and morning rides ($35), half- or full-day rides ($90), and overnight pack trips.

AIR TOURS

You'll have a bird's-eye view of southeastern Utah's incredible landscape from Moab or Green River Airport with **Redtail Aviation,** P.O. Box 515, Moab, UT 84532, (435) 259-7421 (Moab), (435) 564-3412 (Green River), or (800) 842-9251. Flights feature Canyonlands National Park (Needles, Island in the Sky, and Maze Districts; one hour, $75). Longer tours are available, too. Rates are based on two or more persons. Flights operate all year. **Slickrock Air Guides,** 2231 S. U.S. 191, Moab, UT 84532, (435) 259-6216 or (800) 332-2439, www.slickrockairguides.com, offers an hour over the Canyonlands area for $80 per person, and $255 for 3.5 hours over Canyonlands, Natural Bridges, Lake Powell, and the Capitol Reef area with a stop for lunch at the Marble Canyon Lodge. **Mountain Flying Service,** (888) 653-7365, offers three narrated flight tours through the canyonlands. Cost is $75 for one hour, $149 for 2.5 hours, and $125 for four hours. Meet your flights at the airport, 18 miles north of Moab on U.S. 191, or arrange to have the company pick you up, usually at no extra cost.

SCENIC DRIVES AND EXCURSIONS

Each of the following routes is accessible at least in part to standard low-clearance highway vehicles. If you have a four-wheel drive, you'll have the option of additional, off-road exploring.

You'll find detailed travel information on these and other places in the books and separate maps by F.A. Barnes, *Canyon Country Off-Road Vehicle Trails: Island Area* (north of Canyonlands National Park) and *Canyon Country Off-Road Vehicle Trails: Arches & La Sals Areas* (around Arches National Park). The BLM takes care of nearly all this land; staff in the Moab offices may know current road and trail conditions.

Utah Scenic Byway 279

Utah 279 goes downstream through the Colorado River Canyon on the other side of the river from Moab. Pavement extends 16 miles past fine views, prehistoric rock art, arches, and hiking trails. A potash plant marks the end of the highway; a rough dirt road continues to Canyonlands National Park. From Moab, head north 3.5 miles on U.S. 191, then turn left on UT 279. The highway enters the canyon at the Portal, 2.7 miles from the turnoff. Towering sandstone cliffs rise on the right and the Colorado River drifts along just below on the left.

Stop at a signed pullout on the left 0.6 mile past the canyon entrance to see **Indian Ruins Viewpoint,** a small prehistoric Indian ruin tucked under a ledge across the river. The stone structure was probably used for food storage.

Groups of **petroglyphs** cover cliffs along the highway 5.2 miles from U.S. 191. These may not be signed; they are 0.7 mile beyond Milepost 11. Look across the river to see The Fickle Finger of Fate among the sandstone fins of Behind the Rocks. A petroglyph of a bear is 0.2 mile farther down the highway. Archaeologists think that Fremonts and the later Ute Indians did most of the artwork in this area.

A signed pullout on the right 6.2 miles from U.S. 191 points out **dinosaur tracks** and petroglyphs visible on rocks above. Sighting tubes help locate the features. It's possible to hike up the steep hillside for a closer look.

The aptly named **Jug Handle Arch,** with an opening 46 feet high and three feet wide, is close to the road on the right, 13.6 miles from U.S. 191. Ahead the canyon opens up. Underground pressures of salt and potash have folded the rock layers into an anticline.

At the **Moab Salt Plant,** mining operations inject water underground to dissolve the potash and other chemicals, then pump the solution to evaporation ponds. The ponds are dyed blue to hasten evaporation, which takes about a year. You can see these colorful solutions from Dead Horse Point and Anticline Overlook on the canyon rims.

High-clearance vehicles can continue on the unpaved road beyond the plant. The road passes through varied canyon country with views overlooking the Colorado River. At a road junction in Canyonlands National Park (Island in the Sky District), you have a choice of turning left for the 100-mile White Rim Trail (four-wheel drive only past Musselman Arch), continuing up the steep switchbacks of the Shafer Trail Road (four-wheel drive recommended) to the paved park road, or returning the way you came.

Utah Scenic Byway 128

Utah 128 turns northeast from U.S. 191 just south of the Colorado River Bridge, two miles north of Moab. This exceptionally scenic canyon route follows the Colorado for 30 miles upstream before crossing at Dewey Bridge and turning north to I-70. The entire highway is paved. In 1986, a new bridge replaced the narrow Dewey suspension bridge that once caused white knuckles on drivers of large vehicles. Lions Park picnic area at the turnoff from U.S. 191 is a pleasant stopping place. Big Bend Recreation Site is another good spot 7.5 miles up UT 128.

A network of highly scenic jeep roads branches off Castle Valley and Onion Creek Roads into side canyons and the **La Sal Mountains Loop Road,** described in the book and separate map *Canyon Country Off-Road Vehicle Trails: Arches & La Sals Areas,* by F.A. Barnes. This paved scenic road goes through Castle Valley, climbs high into the La Sals, then loops back to Moab. Allow at least three hours to drive the 62-mile loop. Turnoff from UT 128 is 15.5 miles up from U.S. 191.

A graded county road, the **Onion Creek Road,** turns southeast off the highway 20 miles from U.S. 191 and heads up Onion Creek, crossing it many times. Avoid this route if storms threaten. The unpleasant-smelling creek contains poisonous arsenic and selenium. Colorful rock formations of dark red sandstone line the creek, and you'll cross an upthrusted block of crystalline gypsum. After about eight miles the road climbs steeply out of Onion Creek to upper Fisher Valley and a junction with Kokopelli's Trail, which follows a jeep road over this part of its route.

The Gothic spires of **Fisher Towers** soar as high as 900 feet above Professor Valley. The BLM has a picnic area nearby and a hiking trail that skirts the base of the three main towers; Titan, the tallest, is the third one.

In 1962, three climbers from Colorado made the first ascent of Titan Tower. The almost vertical rock faces, overhanging bulges, and sections of rotten rock made for an exhausting 3.5 days of climbing (the party descended to the base for two of the nights). Their final descent from the summit took only six hours. See the November 1962 issue of *National Geographic* magazine for the story and photos. Supposedly, the name "Fisher" is not that of a pioneer, but a corruption of the geologic term "fissure" (a narrow crack). An unpaved road turns southeast off UT 128 near Milepost 21 (21 miles from U.S. 191) and continues in two miles to the picnic area.

The modern two-lane concrete **Dewey Bridge** has replaced the picturesque wood and steel suspension bridge built in 1916. Here, the BLM has built the Dewey Bridge Recreation Site with a picnic area, trailhead, boat launch, and a small campground. Bicyclists and hikers can still use the old bridge; an interpretive sign explains its history. Drivers can continue on the highway to I-70 through rolling hills nearly devoid of vegetation.

Upstream from Dewey Bridge are the wild rapids of **Westwater Canyon.** The Colorado River cut this narrow gorge into dark metamorphic rock. You can raft or kayak down the river in one day or a more leisurely two days. Camping is limited to a single night. Unlike most desert rivers, this section of the Colorado also offers good river-running at low water levels in late summer and autumn. Westwater Canyon's inner gorge, where boaters face their greatest challenge, is only about 3.5 miles long. However, you can enjoy scenic sandstone canyons both upstream and downstream.

The bumpy four-wheel-drive route, the **Top-of-the-World Road,** climbs to an overlook with outstanding views of Fisher Towers, Fisher Valley, Onion Creek, and beyond. Turn right (east) on the Entrada Bluffs Road (just before crossing Dewey Bridge). After 5.5 miles, keep straight on a dirt road when the main road curves left, then immediately turn right (south) and go uphill 100 yards through a gate (gateposts are railroad ties) and continue about 4.5 miles on the Top-of-the-World Road to the rim. Elevation here is 6,800 feet, nearly 3,000 feet higher than the Colorado River.

Kane Creek Scenic Drive

This road heads downstream along the Colorado River on the same side as Moab. The four miles through the Colorado River Canyon are paved, followed by six miles of good dirt road through Kane Springs Canyon. This route also leads to several hiking trails (see above). People with high-clearance vehicles or mountain bikes can continue across a ford of Kane Springs Creek to Hurrah Pass and an extensive network of four-wheel-drive trails. The book and separate map *Canyon Country Off-Road Vehicle Trails: Canyon Rims & Needles Areas,* by F.A. Barnes, has detailed back-road information.

LA SAL MOUNTAINS

The forests and lakes in Utah's second-highest mountain range provide a dramatic contrast to the barren slickrock and sands of the surrounding desert. Mount Peale (elev. 12,721 feet) crowns the range at a height nearly 9,000 feet above the Colorado River. Volcanic intrusions formed the La Sals about 30 million years ago, twisting and upturning surrounding rock layers at the same time. Streams and glaciers later carved knifelike ridges in the peaks and deep canyons in the foothills. The range comprises three distinct mountain groups in an area about 15 miles long from north to south and six miles wide. Major peaks in the northern part are Mt. Waas (12,331 feet), Manns Peak (12,273 feet), and Mt. Tomasaki (12,230 feet). The middle group contains Mt. Mellenthin (12,646 feet), Mt. Peale (12,721 feet), and Mt. Tukuhnikivatz (12,483 feet). The Indian name of this last mountain is reputed to mean "Land Where the Sun Shines Longest." South Mountain (11,798 feet) dominates the southern group.

Wildlife you might see include black bear (one of the state's largest populations lives here), Rocky Mountain elk, mule deer, mountain lion, badger, ringtail cat, porcupine, pika, Merriam's turkey, and golden eagle. Native cutthroat and some brook and brown trout swim in streams at the middle to higher elevations. Reservoirs and Mill Creek contain rainbow trout. Early Spanish explorers, seeing the range when it was covered with snow, named it La Sal ("salt"). Other names include Salt Mountains and Elk Mountains. Gold fever peaked here at the turn of the century with activity concentrated in Miners and Gold Basins. Old mines and ruins of former mining camps can still be found in these areas.

Hiking in the La Sals

Miners traveling through the mountains during the boom years built many of the trails in use today. The current network of about 18 trails totals about 65 miles. Trails cross the range from north to south and branch off to scenic lakes, basins, and canyons. Hiking conditions range from easy to difficult. Horseback riders can use the trails, too. Signs mark most trailheads and junctions, but backcountry users should still have topo maps and a compass. Nearly all the canyons and valleys have springs or streams (purify first). Climbers can choose from half a dozen peaks exceeding 12,000 feet. All summit routes require rock-scrambling and routefinding skills. Hazards include loose rock, lightning, and altitude sickness. You can climb Mt. Peale from the south off La Sal Pass Road from about three quarters of a mile east of La Sal Pass; follow a jeep track here up a valley to either Mt. Peale or Mt. Tukuhnikivatz. Look for the most gradual slope; you'll find the best footing near the trees where roots have stabilized the dirt and rocks. The pass itself also makes a good starting point for Mt. Tukuhnikivatz. See the 7½-minute topo maps or the 1:100,000 La Sal map. Road conditions may be good enough for cars on the east side via UT 46, but the west side from Pack Creek has much steeper and rougher conditions—don't try this road without a high-clearance vehicle! The Moab Information Center is the place to start your search for trail and climbing information.

Winter Sports

Cross-country skiers often head to Miners Basin, Beaver Basin, Geyser Pass, Gold Basin, La Sal Pass, and Dark Canyon. The La Sal Mountains Loop Road (southern section) and 4.5 miles of the Geyser Pass Road are plowed. Snowmobilers may also use the roads and trails in the mountains. Travelers here need proper experience, equipment, and knowledge of avalanche hazards and means of rescue. Always go with a companion. The Moab Information Center has information on groomed trails and marked routes for skiers and snowmobilers; you can also call (435) 259-SNOW for information.

LA SAL MOUNTAINS LOOP ROAD

This paved road on the west side of the range provides a good introduction to the high country. Side roads and trails lead to lakes, alpine meadows, and old mining areas. Viewpoints overlook Castle Valley, Arches and Canyonlands National Parks, Moab Rim, and other scenic features. Vegetation along the drive runs the whole range from cottonwoods, sage, and rabbitbrush of the desert to forests of aspen, fir, and spruce. The 62-mile loop road can easily take a full day with stops for scenic overlooks, a picnic, and a bit of hiking or fishing. Because of the high elevations, the loop's season usually lasts May–October. Stock up on supplies in Moab—you won't find any stores or gas stations after leaving town. Before venturing off the Loop Road, it's a good idea to check current back-road conditions with the U.S. Forest Service office in Moab, where you should ask for a road log of sights and side roads.

ARCHES NATIONAL PARK

A concentration of arches of marvelous variety has formed within the maze of sandstone fins at this park, one of the most popular in the U.S. Balanced rocks and tall spires add to the splendor. Paved roads and short hiking trails provide easy access to some of the more than 1,500 arches in the park. If you're short on time, a drive to the Windows Section (23.5 miles round-trip) allows a look at some of the largest and most spectacular arches. To visit all the stops and hike a few short trails would take all day. The entrance fee of $10 per vehicle ($5 bicyclists) is good for seven days at Arches only. The park brochure available at the entrance station or visitors' center has a map of major scenic features, drives, trails, and back roads.

How the Arches Got Here

An unusual combination of geologic forces created the arches. About 300 million years ago, evaporation of inland seas left behind a salt layer more than 3,000 feet thick in the Paradox Basin of this region. Sediments, including those that later became the arches, then covered the salt. Unequal pressures caused the salt to gradually flow upward in places, bending the overlying sediments as well. These upfolds, or anticlines, later collapsed when ground water dissolved the underlying salt. The faults and joints caused by the uplift and collapse opened the way for erosion to carve hundreds of freestanding fins. Alternate freezing and thawing action and exfoliation (flaking caused by expansion when water or frost penetrates the rock) continued to peel away more rock until holes formed in some of the fins. Rockfalls within the holes helped to enlarge the arches. Nearly all arches in the park eroded out of Entrada Sandstone.

Eventually all the present arches will collapse, but we should have plenty of new ones by the time that happens! The fins' uniform strength and hard upper surfaces have proved ideal for arch formation. Not every hole in the rock is an arch. The opening must be at least three feet in one direction and light must be able to pass through. Although the term "windows" often refers to openings in large walls of rock, windows and arches are really the same. Water seeping through the sandstone from above has created a second type of arch—the pothole arch. You may also come across a few natural bridges cut from the rock by perennial water runoff.

Desert Life

Elevation at the park ranges from 3,960 feet along the Colorado River to 5,653 feet in the Windows area. Annual precipitation averages only 10–11 inches. Even so, plants and wildlife have found niches in this rugged high-desert country. Shrubs and grasslands cover most of the land not occupied by barren rock. Cottonwood trees grow along some of the washes while piñon pine and juniper form pygmy forests at the higher elevations. Specially adapted plant communities thrive in the dark cryptobiotic crusts on the soil. Hanging gardens surround springs and seeps. Tracks across the sands show the presence of shy or nocturnal wildlife. Animals include mule deer, coyote, gray fox, porcupine, bobcat, ringtail cat, kangaroo rat, antelope ground squirrel, collared lizard, and midget faded rattlesnake.

History

Prehistoric Anasazi and Fremont Indians hunted in the area and collected wild plant foods. The modern Utes hunted here, too. Chert, a hard rock from Salt Valley, provided material for toolmaking. Rock art and artifacts mark the former presence of these tribes. Most of the early settlers and cowboys of the region paid little attention to the scenery. However, in 1923 a prospector by the name of Alexander Ringhoffer interested officials of the Rio Grande Railroad in the scenic attractions at what he called Devils Garden (now known as Klondike Bluffs). The railroad men liked the area and contacted Stephen Mather, first director of the National Park Service. Mather started the political process that led to designation of two small areas as a national monument in 1929, but Ringhoffer's Devils Garden wasn't included until later. Early visitors had to endure travel over nonexistent or barely passable roads; see the August 1947 issue of *National Geographic* magazine for a well-written account of the monument as it once was. It grew in size over the years and became Arches National Park in 1971. The park now comprises 76,519 acres—it's small enough to be appreciated in one day, yet large enough to warrant extensive exploration.

Visitor Center

Located just past the entrance booth, the visitors' center provides a good introduction to what to expect ahead. Exhibits identify the rock layers, describe the geologic and human history, and illustrate some of the wildlife and plants of the park. Staff members present a short slide program upon request and answer your questions. Look for the posted list of special activities; rangers host campfire programs and lead a wide variety of guided walks from April through September. You'll also find checklists, pamphlets, books, maps, posters, postcards, and film here for purchase. See the ranger for advice and the free backcountry permit required for overnight trips. The easy 0.2-mile **Desert Nature Trail** begins in front of the visitors' center and identifies some of the native plants. Picnic areas lie outside the visitors' center and at Balanced Rock and Devils Garden. The park is open all year; visitors' center hours are daily 8 A.M.–4:30 P.M. and with extended hours in summer. Arches National Park is five miles north of downtown Moab on U.S. 191, P.O. Box 907, Moab, UT 84532, (435) 719-2299, www.nps.gov/arch.

Devils Garden Campground

The park's campground is located near the end of the 18-mile scenic drive, though in summer you must pre-register at the visitors' center. The campground is open all year with water; $10. Try to arrive early during the busy Easter–October season; only groups can reserve spaces. Elevation here is 5,355 feet. During summer evenings, rangers at the Campfire Circle tell about the park's geology, history, wildlife, flora, and environment.

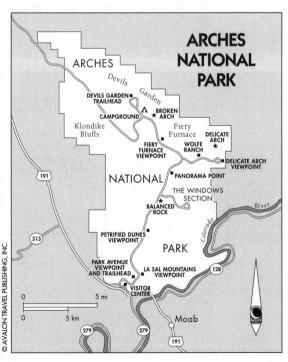

Hiking, Biking, and Climbing

Established trails lead to many fine arches and overlooks that can't be seen from the road. You're free to wander cross-country, too, but please stay on rock or in washes to avoid damaging the fragile cryptobiotic soils. Wear good walking shoes with rubber soles for travel across slickrock. The summer sun can be especially harsh on the unprepared hiker—don't forget water, hat, and sunscreen. The desert rule is to carry at least one gallon of water per person for an all-day hike. Take a map and compass for off-trail hiking. Be cautious on the slickrock; the soft sandstone can crumble easily. Also, remember that it's easier to go up a steep slickrock slope than to come back down! You can reach almost any spot in the park on a day hike, though you'll also find some good overnight possibilities. Areas for longer trips include Courthouse Wash in the southern part of the park and Salt Wash in the eastern part. All backpacking is done off-trail. A backcountry permit must be obtained from a ranger before camping in the backcountry. Hiking regulations include no fires, no pets, camping out of sight of any road (at least one mile away) or trail (at least a half mile away) and at least 300 feet from a recognizable archaeological site or nonflowing water source. Bicycles *must* stick to established roads in the park; cyclists have to contend with heavy traffic on the narrow paved roads and dusty, washboarded surfaces on the dirt roads. Beware of the deep sand on the four-wheel-drive roads. Nearby, BLM and Canyon-lands National Park areas offer much better mountain biking. Rock-climbers don't need a permit, though they should first discuss their plans with a ranger. Most features named on USGS maps are *closed* to climbing.

SIGHTS AND HIKES ALONG THE PARK ROAD

A road guide to Arches National Park, available at the visitors' center, has detailed descriptions that correspond to place names along the main road. Be sure to stop only in parking lots and designated pullouts. Watch out for others who are sight-seeing in this popular park. The following are major points of interest.

Moab Fault

The park road begins a long but well-graded climb from the visitors' center up the cliffs to the northeast. A pullout on the right after 1.1 miles gives a good view of Moab Canyon and its geology. The rock layers on this side of the canyon have slipped down more than 2,600 feet in relation to the other side. Movement took place about six million years ago along the Moab Fault, which follows the canyon floor. Rock layers at the top of the far cliffs are nearly the same age as those at the *bottom* on this side! If you could stack the rocks of this side on top of rocks on the other side, you'd have a complete stratigraphic column of the Moab area—more than 150 million years' worth.

Park Avenue

South Park Avenue Overlook and Trailhead are on the left 2.1 miles from the visitors' center.

The Windows in Arches National Park

Great sandstone slabs form a "skyline" on each side of this dry wash. A trail goes north one mile down the wash to North Park Avenue Trailhead (1.3 miles ahead by road). Arrange to be picked up there or backtrack to your starting point. The large rock monoliths of Courthouse Towers rise north of Park Avenue. Only a few small arches exist now, though major arches may have formed in the past.

Balanced Rock

This gravity-defying formation is on the right 8.5 miles from the visitors' center. A boulder more than 55 feet high rests precariously atop a 73-foot pedestal. Chip Off the Old Block, a much smaller version of Balanced Rock, stood nearby until it collapsed in the winter of 1975–1976. For a closer look at Balanced Rock, take the 0.3-mile trail encircling it. There's a picnic area across the road. Author Edward Abbey lived in a trailer near Balanced Rock during a season as a park ranger in the 1950s; his journal became the basis for the classic *Desert Solitaire*.

Windows Section

Turn right 2.5 miles on a paved road past Balanced Rock. Short trails (one-quarter to one mile long one-way) lead from the road's end to some massive arches. Windows Trailhead is the start for North Window (an opening 51 feet high and 93 feet wide), South Window (66 feet high and 105 feet wide), and Turret Arch (64 feet high and 39 feet wide). Double Arch, a short walk from a second trailhead, is an unusual pair of arches; the larger opening—105 feet high and 163 feet wide—is best appreciated by walking inside. The smaller opening is 61 feet high and 60 feet wide. Together, the two arches frame a large opening overhead, but this isn't considered a true arch.

Garden of Eden Viewpoint, on the way back to the main road, has a good panorama of Salt Valley to the north. Under the valley, the massive body of salt and gypsum that's responsible for the arches comes close to the surface. Tiny Delicate Arch can be seen across the valley on a sandstone ridge. Early visitors to the Garden of Eden saw rock formations resembling Adam (with an apple) and Eve. Two other viewpoints of the Salt Valley area lie farther north on the main road.

Delicate Arch

Drive north 2.5 miles on the main road from the Windows junction and turn right 1.8 miles to the Wolfe Ranch, where a bit of pioneer history survives. John Wesley Wolfe came to this spot in 1888, hoping the desert climate would provide relief for health problems related to a Civil War injury. He found a good spring high in the rocks, grass for cattle, and water in Salt Wash to irrigate a garden. The ranch that he built provided a home for him and some of his family for more than 20 years, and cattlemen later used it as a line ranch. Then sheepherders brought in their animals, which so overgrazed the range that the grass has yet to recover. A trail guide available at the entrance tells about the Wolfe family and features of their ranch. The weather-beaten cabin built in 1906 still survives. A short trail leads to petroglyphs above Wolfe Ranch; figures of horses indicate that Ute Indians did the artwork. Park staff can give directions to other rock-art sites; great care should be taken not to touch the fragile artwork.

Delicate Arch stands in a magnificent setting atop gracefully curving slickrock. Distant canyons and the La Sal Mountains lie beyond. The span is 45 feet high and 33 feet wide. A moderately strenuous hike to the arch begins at Wolfe Ranch and crosses the swinging bridge, climbs a slickrock slope, follows a gully, then contours across steep slickrock to the main overlook. Round-trip distance is three miles with an elevation gain of 500 feet; carry water. This is one of the most scenic hikes in the park. Just before the end of the trail, walk up to a small arch for a framed view of the final destination. The classic photo of Delicate Arch is taken late in the afternoon when the sandstone glows with golden hues.

Another perspective on Delicate Arch can be obtained by driving 1.2 miles beyond Wolfe Ranch. Look for the small arch high above. A steep trail (a half-mile round-trip) climbs a hill for the best panorama.

Fiery Furnace

Return to the main road and continue three miles to the Fiery Furnace Viewpoint and Trailhead on the right. Closely packed sandstone fins form a maze of deep slots, with many arches and at least

deep within the Fiery Furnace on a ranger-led hike

one natural bridge inside. The Fiery Furnace can be fun to explore (with the required free permit, obtainable at the visitors' center), though route-finding is tricky. What look like obvious paths often lead to dead ends. Drop-offs and ridges make straight-line travel impossible. It's easy to get lost! Ranger-led hikes of about 1.5 hours during the summer season provide the best way to see the wonders within. You'll need a reservation for this trip, obtainable in person only from the visitors' center up to 48 hours in advance. The Fiery Furnace gets its name from sandstone fins that turn flaming red on occasions when thin cloud cover at the horizon reflects the warm light of sunrise or sunset. Actually, the shady recesses provide a cool respite from the hot summer sun.

Broken Arches

Trailhead is on the right 2.4 miles past the Fiery Furnace turnoff. A short trail leads to small Sand Dune Arch (opening is eight feet high and 30 feet wide) tucked within fins. A longer trail (one mile round-trip) crosses a field to Broken Arch, which you can also see from the road. The opening is 43 feet high and 59 feet wide. Up close, you'll see that the arch isn't really broken. These arches can also be reached by trail from near comfort station #3 at Devils Garden Campground. Low-growing Canyonlands biscuitroot, found only in areas of Entrada Sandstone, colonizes sand dunes. Hikers can protect the habitat of the biscuitroot and other fragile plants by keeping to washes or rock surfaces.

Skyline Arch

Located on the right one mile past Sand Dune/Broken Arch Trailhead. In desert climates, erosion may proceed imperceptibly for centuries until a cataclysmic event happens. In 1940, a giant boulder fell from the opening of Skyline Arch, doubling the size of the arch in just seconds. The hole is now 45 feet high and 69 feet wide. A short trail leads to the base of the arch.

Devils Garden Trail

The trailhead, Devils Garden Picnic Area, and the campground all lie near the end of the main park road. Devils Garden offers fine scenery and more arches than any other section of the park. The trail leads past large sandstone fins to Landscape and six other named arches. Carry water if the weather is hot or if you might want to

continue past the one-mile point at Landscape Arch. Adventurous hikers could spend days exploring the maze of canyons among the fins.

The first two arches lie off a short side trail to the right. Tunnel Arch has a relatively symmetrical opening 22 feet high and 27 feet wide. The nearby Pine Tree Arch is named for a piñon pine that once grew inside; the arch has an opening 48 feet high and 46 feet wide. Continue on the main trail to Landscape Arch, which has an incredible 306-foot span (six feet longer than a football field!). This is one of the longest unsupported rock spans in the world. The thin arch looks ready to collapse at any moment. A rockfall from the arch on September 1, 1991, worries some people who fear the end may be near. Height is 106 feet. Distance from the trailhead is two miles round-trip, an easy one-hour walk.

The trail narrows past Landscape Arch and continues a quarter mile to Wall Arch, in a long wall-like fin. The opening is 41 feet high and 68 feet wide. A short side trail branches off to the left beyond Wall to Partition Arch (26 feet high and 28 feet wide) and Navajo Arch (13 feet high and 41 feet wide). Partition was named because a piece of rock divides the main opening from a smaller hole eight feet high and 8.5 feet wide. Navajo Arch is a rock-shelter type; perhaps prehistoric Indians camped here. The main trail continues northwest and ends at Double O Arch (four miles round-trip from the trailhead). Double O has a large oval-shaped opening (45 feet high and 71 feet wide) and a smaller hole (nine feet high and 21 feet wide) underneath. Dark Angel is a distinctive rock pinnacle a quarter mile northwest; cairns mark the way. Another primitive trail loops back to Landscape Arch via Fin Canyon. This route goes through a different area of Devils Garden, adding about a mile to your trip (three miles back to the trailhead instead of two). Pay careful attention to the trail markers to keep on the correct route.

Klondike Bluffs and Tower Arch

Relatively few visitors come to the spires, high bluffs, and fine arch in this northwestern section of the park. A fair-weather dirt road turns off the main drive 1.3 miles before Devils Garden Trailhead, winds down into Salt Valley, and heads northwest. After 7.5 miles, turn left one mile on the road signed Klondike Bluffs to the Tower Arch Trailhead. These roads may be washboarded but are usually okay in dry weather for cars; don't drive on them if storms threaten. The trail to Tower Arch winds past the Marching Men and other rock formations; the distance is three miles round-trip. Alexander Ringhoffer, who discovered the arch in 1922, carved an inscription on the south column. The area can also be fun to explore off-trail (map and compass needed). Those with four-wheel-drive vehicles can drive close to the arch on a separate jeep road. Tower Arch has an opening 34 feet high by 92 feet wide. A tall monolith nearby gave the arch its name.

Four-Wheel-Drive Road
A rough road near Tower Arch in the Klondike Bluffs turns southeast past **Eye of the Whale Arch** in Herdina Park to Balanced Rock on the main park road, 10.8 miles away. The road isn't particularly difficult for four-wheel-drive enthusiasts, though normal backcountry precautions should be taken. A steep sand hill north of Eye of the Whale Arch is very difficult to climb for vehicles coming from Balanced Rock; it's better to drive from the Tower Arch area instead.

DEAD HORSE POINT STATE PARK

The land drops away in sheer cliffs from this lofty perch west of Moab. Nearly 5,000 square miles of rugged canyon country lie in the distance. Two thousand feet below, the Colorado River twists through a gooseneck on its long journey to the sea. The river and its tributaries have carved canyons that reveal a geologic layer cake of colorful rock formations. Even in a region of impressive views around nearly every corner, Dead Horse Point stands out for its breathtaking panorama. You'll also see below you, along the Colorado River, the result of powerful underground forces:

salt, under pressure, has pushed up overlying rock layers into an anticline. This formation, the Shafer Dome, contains potash that is being processed by the Moab Salt Plant. You can see the mine buildings, processing plant, and evaporation ponds (tinted blue to hasten evaporation).

A narrow neck of land only 30 yards wide connects the point with the rest of the plateau. Cowboys once herded wild horses onto the point, then placed a fence across the neck to make a 40-acre corral. They chose the desirable animals from the herd and let the rest go. According

Colorado Gooseneck and canyon country from Dead Horse Point

to one tale, a group of horses left behind after such a roundup became confused by the geography of the point. They couldn't find their way off and circled repeatedly until they died of thirst within sight of the river below. You may hear other stories of how the point got its name.

Besides the awe-inspiring views, the park also offers a visitors' center (with displays), campground, picnic area, group area, nature trail, and hiking trails. The point has become popular with hang gliders. If you are lucky in timing your visit, you may see one or more crafts gliding back and forth above or below the viewpoint. Dead Horse Point is easily reached by paved road, either as a destination itself or as a side trip on the way to the Island in the Sky District of Canyonlands National Park. From Moab, head northwest 10 miles on U.S. 191, then turn left 22 miles on UT 313. The drive along UT 313 climbs through a scenic canyon and tops out on a ridge with panoramas of distant mesas, buttes, mountains, and canyons. Several rest areas are along the road.

Visitor Center and Campground
Stop here for registration ($5 per vehicle for day use) and exhibits about the park. Staff will answer questions and provide checklists of local flora and fauna. A short slide presentation is given on request. In summer, rangers give talks at the amphitheater behind the visitors' center. Books, maps, posters, postcards, film, T-shirts, charcoal, ice, and soft drinks can be purchased. Open daily 8 A.M.–6 P.M. in summer (May 16–Sept. 15) and 9 A.M.–5 P.M. the rest of the year. Contact the park at P.O. Box 609, Moab, UT 84532, (435) 259-2614 or (800) 322-3770 (reservations). A short nature trail that begins outside introduces the high-desert country and its plants. Continue 1.5 miles on the main road to viewpoints and picnic areas on the point itself. Primitive trails connect the point with several other overlooks, the visitors' center, and the campground. Ask for a map at the visitors' center.

Kayenta Campground, just past the visitors' center, offers sites with electric hookups but no showers; open with water from about mid-March to late October; $11. The campground nearly always fills up during the main season. Either make reservations or try to arrive by early afternoon to ensure a space. Winter visitors may camp on the point; no hookups are available, but the restrooms have water.

CANYONLANDS NATIONAL PARK

The canyon country of southeastern Utah puts on its supreme performance in this vast park, which spreads across 527 square miles. The deeply entrenched Colorado and Green Rivers meet in its heart, then continue south as the mighty Colorado through tumultuous Cataract Canyon Rapids. These two rivers form the **River District** and divide Canyonlands National Park into three other districts. **Island in the Sky** lies north between the rivers, the **Maze** is to the west, and **Needles** is to the east. Each has its own distinct character. No bridges connect the three land districts, so most visitors have to leave the park to go from one region to another. The huge park can be seen in many ways and on many levels. Paved roads reach a few areas, four-wheel-drive roads go to more places, and hiking trails reach still more, yet much of the land shows no trace of human passage. To get the big picture, fly over this incredible complex of canyons (see Air Tours in the Moab section earlier in this chapter). However, only a river trip or a hike lets you experience the solitude and detail of the land. The park can be visited in any season of the year, with spring and autumn the best choices. Summer temperatures can get into the 100s; carrying (and drinking) water becomes critical then; carry at least one gallon per person per day. Arm yourself with insect repellent from late spring to midsummer. Winter days tend to be bright and sunny, though nighttime temperatures can dip into the teens or subzeros. Visitors coming in winter should inquire about travel conditions, as snow and ice occasionally close roads and trails at the higher elevations.

Visiting the Park
There are four districts to the park, each affording great views, spectacular geology, a chance to see wildlife, and endless opportunities to ex-

plore. You won't find crowds or elaborate park facilities—most of Canyonlands remains a primitive backcountry park.

Island in the Sky District has paved roads on its top to impressive overlooks and to Upheaval Dome, a strange geologic feature. If you're short on time or don't want to make a rigorous backcountry trip, you'll find this district the best choice. The "Island," actually a large mesa, is much like Dead Horse Point on a giant scale; a narrow neck of land connects the north side with the "mainland." Hikers and those with suitable vehi-

cles can drop off the Island in the Sky and descend about 1,300 feet to the White Rim 4WD Road, which follows cliffs of the White Rim around most of the island.

Few visitors make it over to the **Maze District,** some of the wildest country in the United States. Only the rivers and a handful of four-wheel-drive roads and hiking trails provide access. Experienced hikers can explore the "maze" of canyons on unmarked routes. **Horseshoe Canyon Unit,** a detached section of Canyonlands National Park northwest of the Maze District, protects the Great

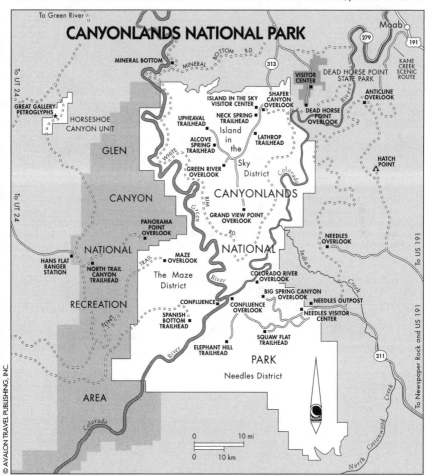

© AVALON TRAVEL PUBLISHING, INC.

ENDANGERED FISH OF THE COLORADO RIVER

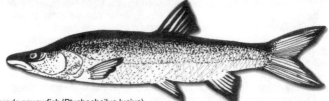

Colorado squawfish (Ptychocheilus lucius)
Native only to the Colorado and its tributaries, this species is the largest minnow in North America. It has been reported as weighing up to 100 pounds and measuring six feet long. Loss of habitat due to dam construction has greatly curtailed its size and range. Fisherman often confuse the smaller more common roundtail chub (Gila robusta) with the Colorado squawfish; the chub is distinguished by a smaller mouth extending back only to the front of the eye.

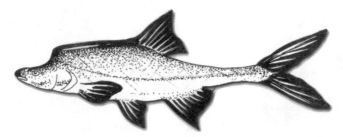

humpback chub (Gila cypha)
Scientists first described this fish only in 1946 and know little about its life. The small fish usually weighs in under two pounds and under 13 inches. Today the humpback chub hangs on the verge of extinction; it has retreated to a few small areas of the Colorado River where the water still runs warm, muddy, and swift. The bonytail chub (Gila robusta elegans) has a similar size and shape, but without a hump; its numbers are also rapidly declining.

humpback or razorback sucker (Xyrauchen texanus)
This large sucker grows to weights of 10–16 pounds and lengths of about three feet. Its numbers have been slowly decreasing, especially above the Grand Canyon. They require warm, fast-flowing water to reproduce. Mating is done as a bizarre ritual in the spring. When the female has selected a suitable spawning site, two male fish press against the sides of her body. The female begins shake her body until the eggs and spermatozoa are expelled simultaneously. One female can spawn three times, but she uses a different pair of males each time.

Gallery, a group of pictographs left by prehistoric Indians.

Colorful rock spires prompted the name of the **Needles District.** Splendid canyons contain many arches, strange rock formations, and archaeological sites. Hikers enjoy day hikes and backpack treks on the network of trails and routes within the district. Drivers with four-wheel-drive vehicles have their own challenging roads through canyons and other highly scenic areas. Overlooks and short nature trails can be enjoyed from the paved scenic drive in the park. South of Moab, UT 211 branches off U.S. 191, providing easy access to the Needles District.

The **River District** includes long stretches of the Green and the Colorado. River-running provides one of the best ways to experience the inner depths of the park. Boaters can obtain helpful literature and advice from park rangers. Groups planning their own trip through Cataract Canyon need a river-running permit. Flat-water permits are also required, and payment of a fee is necessary.

Admission to the park is $10 per vehicle, or $5 per bicyclist or pedestrian. In addition, fees are charged for backcountry camping, 4X4 exploration and river-rafting, detailed below. For information on the park, contact Canyonlands National Park, 2282 S. West Resource Blvd., Moab, UT 84532, (435) 259-7164 or 259-3911, or the website at www.nps.gov/cany.

Geology

Deep canyons of the Green and the Colorado have sliced through rocks representing 150 million years of deposition. The Paradox Formation, exposed in Cataract Canyon, contains salt and other minerals responsible for some of the folded and faulted rock layers in the region. Under the immense pressure of overlying rocks, the Paradox flows like plastic, forming domes where the rock layers are thinnest and causing cracks or faults as pressures rise and fall. Each of the overlying formations has a different color and texture; they're the products of ancient deserts, rivers, and seas that once covered this land. Views from any of the overlooks reveal that an immense quantity of rock has already been washed downriver toward California. Not so evident, however, is the 10,000 vertical feet of rock that geologists say once lay across the high mesas. The

dry climate and sparse vegetation allow clear views of the remaining rock layers and the effects of erosion and deformation. You can read the geologic story at Canyonlands National Park in the 3,500 feet of strata that remain, from the bottom of Cataract Canyon to the upper reaches of Salt Creek in the Needles District.

Desert Life

Extremes of flash flood and drought, hot summers, and cold winters discourage all but the most hardy and adaptable life. Desert grasses, small flowering plants, cacti, and shrubs like blackbrush and saltbush survive on the mostly thin soils and meager 8–9 inches of annual precipitation. Trees either grow in cracks that concentrate rainfall and nutrients or rely on springs or canyon streams for moisture. Piñon pine and juniper prefer the higher elevations of the park, while cottonwoods live in the canyon bottoms that have permanent subsurface water. Tamarisk, an exotic streamside plant, and willows often form dense thickets on sandbars along the Green and Colorado Rivers. The hanging gardens of lush vegetation that surround cliffside springs or seeps seem oblivious to the surrounding desert. Fragile desert ecology can easily be upset. Cattle, especially in the Needles District, once overgrazed the grasslands and trampled cryptobiotic crusts and other vegetation. Increased erosion and growth of undesirable exotic plants like cheatgrass have been the result. Scars left by roads and mines during the uranium frenzy of the 1950s can still be seen, most commonly in the Island in the Sky District.

Fewer than 10 species of fish evolved in the canyons of the Colorado and the Green. These fish developed streamlined bodies and strange features, such as humped backs, to cope with the muddy and varying river waters. Species include Colorado squawfish, humpback chub, bonytail chub, and humpback sucker; most of these live nowhere else. All have suffered greatly reduced populations and restricted ranges due to recent dam-building.

Of the approximately 65 mammal species living in the park, about one-third are rodents and another third are bats. You're most likely to see chipmunk, antelope ground squirrel, and rock squirrel, which are often active during the day. Most other animals wait until evening to come out and feed; in the morning, look for tracks of mule deer, bighorn sheep, coyote, gray fox, badger, porcupine, spotted skunk, beaver, black-tailed jackrabbit, wood rat, kangaroo rat, and many species of mice.

History

Prehistoric Anasazi Indians once settled throughout this area, while the Fremont lived mostly west of the Green and Colorado Rivers. Both groups departed from the region in the middle to late 1200s. They left behind hundreds of archaeological sites with rock art, granaries, dwellings, and stone tools. Nomadic Ute Indians later roamed through the canyons and drew rock art of their own. The Navajo may have made trips into the park area from the south during the 1800s.

At least one mountain man, Denis Julien, visited the Colorado and Green Canyons in 1836, leaving his signatures but little else to tell of his travels. Julien may have been the first person to raft the rivers here. In 1859, Capt. John Macomb and his party noted the beautiful rock sculptures in Needles on an overland trip, but they judged the country worthless. Major John Wesley Powell led the first scientific expedition by boat through the Green and lower Colorado River Canyons in 1869, then repeated most of the journey in 1871–72. Cowboys brought in cattle during the 1870s. Some of their camps, corrals, and inscriptions still survive, though grazing no longer takes place in the park. The Powell Expedition and the later cowboys named many of the park's features. Uranium prospectors swarmed through the area with Geiger counters during the 1950s, staking thousands of claims and opening some mines. Most of the jeep roads in use today date from that time.

Serious interest in establishing a park didn't begin until the early 1960s. Stewart Udall, Secretary of the Interior under President Kennedy, realized the area's potential as a national park while flying over the Colorado River to examine a possible dam site. The superintendent of Arches National Monument, Bates Wilson, also worked hard for creation of a new park here. Canyonlands National Park became a reality in 1964 and enlarged to its present size in 1971.

Visitor Centers and Information

Each of the three land districts has a visitors' center near the park entrance, but you may find it convenient to stop at the Moab Information Center, at the corner of Main and Center, (435) 259-8825 or (800) 635-MOAB. Any of the offices has brochures, maps, and books, as well as someone to answer your questions.

Vehicle camping is allowed only in established campgrounds and designated backcountry campsites. Except for the main campgrounds at Willow Flat (Island in the Sky) and Squaw Flat (Needles), you'll need a backcountry permit for overnight stays. There is a $15 fee for a backpacking permit and a $30 fee for a vehicle site permit. Each of the three districts has a different policy for backcountry vehicle camping, so it's a good idea to make sure that you understand the details. Backcountry permits will also be needed for any technical climbing and trips with stock; check with a ranger for details. Pets aren't allowed on trails and must always be leashed. No firewood collecting is permitted in the park; backpackers need stoves for cooking. Vehicle and boat campers can bring in firewood but must use grills or fire pans. The best maps for the park are a series of expensive topos printed on waterproof paper by Trails Illustrated; these have the latest trail and road information. A giant USGS topo map, Canyonlands National Park and Vicinity, has the same 1:62,500 scale at a lower cost, but without the updated information and fancy paper. Handouts from the ranger offices describe natural history, travel, and other aspects of the park.

Back-Road Travel

Canyonlands National Park offers hundreds of miles of exceptionally scenic jeep roads. Normally you must have a vehicle with both four-wheel drive and high clearance. Park regulations require all motorized vehicles to have proper registration and licensing for highway use (ATVs are prohibited); drivers must be licensed. It's essential for both motor vehicles and bicycles to stay on existing roads to prevent damage to the delicate desert vegetation. Carry tools, extra fuel, water, and food in case of breakdown in a remote area. Mountain bikers enjoy travel on many of the back-country roads, too. Before making a trip, drivers and cyclists should talk with a ranger to register and to learn of current road conditions, which can change drastically from one day to the next. Also, the rangers will be more knowledgeable about where to seek help in case you become stuck. Primitive campgrounds are provided on most of the roads, but you'll need a backcountry permit from a ranger. Books on backcountry exploration include local author F.A. Barnes's *Canyon Country Off-Road Vehicle Trails: Island Area* and *Canyon Country Off-Road Vehicle Trails: Canyon Rims & Needles Areas* and Jack Bikers's *Canyon Country Off-Road Vehicle Trails: Maze Area* (see booklist for all titles).

RIVER DISTRICT

River-running above the Confluence
The Green and Colorado Rivers flow smoothly through their canyons above the confluence of the two rivers. Almost any shallow-draft boat can navigate these waters: canoes, kayaks, rafts, and power boats are commonly used. Any travel requires advance planning because of the remoteness of the canyons and the scarcity of river access points. No campgrounds, supplies, or other facilities exist past Moab on the Colorado River or the town of Green River on the Green. All river-runners must follow park regulations, which include the carrying of life jackets, use of a fire pan for fires, and packing out all garbage and solid human waste. The river flow on both the Colorado and the Green averages a gentle 2–4 mph (7–10 mph at high water). Boaters typically do 20 miles a day in canoes and 15 miles a day in rafts.

The Colorado has one modest rapid called the Slide, 1.5 miles above the confluence, where rocks constrict the river to one-third of its normal width; the rapid is roughest during high water levels in May and June. This is the only difficulty on the 64 river miles from Moab. Inexperienced canoeists and rafters may wish to portage around it. The most popular launch points on the Colorado are the Moab Dock (just upstream from the U.S. 191 bridge near town) and the Potash Dock (17 miles downriver on the Potash Road, UT 279).

On the Green, boaters at low water need to watch for rocky areas at the mouth of Millard Canyon (33.5 miles above the confluence, where a rock bar extends across the river) and at the mouth of Horse Canyon (14.5 miles above the confluence, where a rock and gravel bar on the right leaves only a narrow channel on the left side). The trip from the town of Green River through Labyrinth and Stillwater Canyons is 120 miles. Launch places include Green River State Park (in Green River) and Mineral Canyon (52 miles above the confluence; reached on a fair-weather road from UT 313).

No roads go to the confluence. Easiest return to civilization for nonmotorized craft is a pick-up by jetboat from Moab by Tex's Riverways or Tag-A-Long Tours (see River Tours under Practicalities in the Moab section earlier in this chapter). A far more difficult way out is hiking either of two trails just above the Cataract Canyon Rapids to four-wheel-drive roads on the rim. Park rangers require that boaters above the confluence obtain a backcountry permit either in person from the Moab office or by mail (two weeks in advance). River notes on boating the

Cataract Canyon (Colorado River) by Navtec sportboat

Green and Colorado are available on request from the Moab office, (435) 259-3911. Bill and Buzz Belknap's *Canyonlands River Guide* has river logs and maps pointing out items of interest on the Green River below the town of Green River and all of the Colorado from the upper end of Westwater Canyon to Lake Powell. Don Baar's *A River Runner's Guide to Cataract Canyon* also has good coverage.

River-running through Cataract Canyon

The Colorado River enters Cataract Canyon at the confluence and picks up speed. The rapids begin four miles downstream and extend for the next 14 miles to Lake Powell. Especially in spring, the 26 or more rapids give a wild ride equal to the best in the Grand Canyon. The current zips along (up to 16 mph) and forms waves more than seven feet high! When the excitement dies down, boaters have a 34-mile trip across Lake Powell to Hite Marina; most people either carry a motor or arrange for a power boat to pick them up. Because of the real hazards of running the rapids, the National Park Service requires boaters to have proper equipment and a permit ($30). Many people go on a commercial trip in which everything has been taken care of (write the park for a list of boat companies). Private groups need to contact the Canyonlands River Unit far in advance for permit details at 2282 W. Resource Blvd., Moab, UT 84532, (435) 259-3911.

ISLAND IN THE SKY DISTRICT

Panoramic views from the "Island" can be enjoyed from any point along the rim; you'll see much of the park and southeastern Utah. Short hiking trails lead to overlooks, Mesa Arch, Aztec Butte, Whale Rock, Upheaval Dome, and other features. Longer trails make steep, strenuous descents from the island to the White Rim 4WD Road below. Elevations on the island average about 6,000 feet. *Bring water for all hiking, camping, and travel on Island in the Sky*. No services are available, except at the visitors' center in emergencies (bottled water is sold).

Visitor Center

Stop here for information about Island in the Sky and to see some exhibits; books and maps can

the vertiginous Shafer Trail in Canyonlands National Park

be purchased. A $10 per-vehicle charge is made unless you have a receipt issued within the last seven days from the Needles District of Canyonlands. Obtain a backcountry permit ($15 for backpack camping, $30 for a vehicle campsite) if making an overnight hike or planning to stay at campgrounds along the White Rim 4WD Road (reservations by mail, phone, or in person are required for sites; $25 reservation fee). The visitors' center is open daily 8 A.M.–4:30 P.M. with reservations made from 12:30–4:30 P.M. Mon.–Sat. (may close from noon–1 P.M. in winter), (435) 259-4351. A bulletin board outside has park information. The visitors' center is located just before crossing "the neck" to Island in the Sky. From Moab, go northwest 10 miles on U.S. 191, turn left 15 miles on UT 313 to the junction for Dead Horse Point State Park, then continue straight seven miles.

Shafer Canyon Overlook

Continue a half mile past the visitors' center to this overlook on the left (just before crossing the neck). Shafer Trail Viewpoint, across the neck, provides another perspective a half mile farther. The neck is a narrow land bridge just wide enough for the road, and it's the only vehicle access to the 40-square-mile Island in the Sky. The overlooks have good views east down the canyon and the incredibly twisting **Shafer Trail Road.** Cattlemen Frank and John Schafer built the trail in the early 1900s to move stock to additional pastures (the "c" in their name was later dropped by mapmakers). Uranium prospectors upgraded the trail to a four-wheel-drive road during the 1950s so that they could reach their claims at the base of the cliffs. Today the Shafer Trail Road connects the mesa top with the White Rim 4WD Road and the Potash Road 1,200 feet and four miles below. High-clearance vehicles should be used on the Shafer, preferably with four-wheel drive if you plan to climb up. Road conditions can vary considerably, so it's a good idea to contact a ranger before starting.

Neck Spring Trail

The trail begins near the Shafer Canyon Overlook. A brochure should be available at the trailhead. This moderately difficult hike follows a five-mile loop down Taylor Canyon to Neck and Cabin Springs, formerly used by ranchers, then climbs back to the Island in the Sky Road at a second trailhead a half-mile south of the start. Elevation change is 300 feet. Water at the springs supports maidenhair fern and other water-loving plants. Also watch for birds and wildlife attracted to this spot. Bring water with you, as the springs aren't suitable for drinking.

Lathrop Trail

This is the only marked hiking route going all the way from Island in the Sky to the Colorado River. The trailhead is on the left 1.3 miles past the neck. The first 2.5 miles cross Gray's Pasture to the rim, then the trail descends steeply, dropping 1,600 feet over the next 2.5 miles to the White Rim 4WD Road. Part of this section follows an old mining road past several abandoned mines, all relics of the uranium boom; don't enter the shafts, as they're in danger of collapse and may contain poisonous gases. From the mining area, the route descends through a wash to the White Rim 4WD Road, follows the road a short distance south, then goes down Lathrop

Canyon Road to the Colorado River, another four miles with a descent of 500 feet. Total distance for the strenuous hike is nine miles one-way, with an elevation change of 2,100 feet. The trail has little shade and can be very hot.

Mesa Arch Trail

This easy trail leads to an arch on the rim. The trailhead is on the left 5.5 miles from the neck. On the way, the road crosses the grasslands and scattered juniper trees of Gray's Pasture. A trail brochure available at the start describes the ecology of the mesa. Hiking distance is only a half-mile round-trip with an 80-foot elevation change. The arch, eroded from Navajo Sandstone, frames views of rock formations below and the La Sal Mountains in the distance.

Murphy Point and Grand View Point

Go straight at the road junction just past the Mesa Arch Trailhead for these and other spectacular viewpoints. After 2.5 miles, a rough dirt road turns right 1.7 miles to Murphy Point. Hikers can take **Murphy Trail,** which begins off the road to the point, to the White Rim 4WD Road. This strenuous route forks partway down; one branch follows Murphy Hogback (a ridge) to Murphy Campground on the four-wheel-drive road, and the other branch follows a wash to the road one mile south of the campground. A loop hike along both branches is nine miles round-trip with an elevation change of 1,100 feet.

Continue 2.5 miles on the main road past the Murphy Point turnoff to **Grand View Picnic Area,** a handy lunch stop. Two trails start here. **White Rim Overlook Trail** is an easy 1.5-mile hike (round-trip) east along a peninsula to an overlook of Monument Basin and beyond. **Gooseberry Trail** drops off the mesa and descends some extremely steep grades to the White Rim 4WD Road just north of Gooseberry Campground; the strenuous trip is 2.5 miles one-way with an elevation change of 1,400 feet.

Continue one mile on the main road past the picnic area to **Grand View Point,** perhaps the most spectacular panorama from Island in the Sky. Monument Basin lies directly below, and countless canyons, the Colorado River, the Needles, and mountain ranges are in the distance. **Grand View Trail** continues past the end of the road for other vistas from the point, which is the southernmost tip of Island in the Sky. The easy hike is 1.5 miles round-trip.

Green River Overlook
and Willow Flat Campground

Return to the road junction, turn west a quarter mile, then turn south 1.5 miles on an unpaved road to the overlook. Soda Springs Basin and a section of the Green River (deeply entrenched in Stillwater Canyon) can be seen below. Small Willow Flat campground is passed on the way to the overlook; it's open all year (no water or charge). Rangers present campfire programs here spring through autumn. Sites often fill except in winter; a sign near the visitors' center indicates when they're full.

Aztec Butte Trail

The trailhead is on the right one mile northwest of the road junction. Aztec Butte is one of the few areas at Island in the Sky with Indian ruins; shortage of water prevented permanent settlement. An easy trail climbs 200 feet in half a mile to the top of the butte for a good panorama of the Island.

Whale Rock

The trailhead is on the right 4.4 miles northwest of the road junction. An easy trail climbs this sandstone hump near the outer rim of Upheaval Dome. Distance is a half-mile round-trip with an ascent of 100 feet.

Upheaval Dome

Continue to the end of the road, 5.3 miles northwest of the road junction, for a look at this geological curiosity. There's also a small **picnic area** here. The easy **Crater View Trail** leads to overlooks on the rim of Upheaval Dome; the first viewpoint is a half-mile round-trip, the second is one mile round-trip. A fantastically deformed pile of rock lies below within a crater about three miles across and 1,200 feet deep. For many years, Upheaval Dome has kept geologists busy trying to figure out its origin. They once assumed that salt of the Paradox Formation pushed the rock layers upward to form the dome. Now, however, there is strong evidence that a meteorite impact caused the structure. The surrounding ring depression (caused by collapse) and the convergence of rock layers upward toward the

center correspond precisely to known impact structures. Shatter cones and microscopic analysis also indicate an impact origin. When the meteorite struck, sometime in the last 150 million years, it formed a crater up to five miles across. Erosion removed some of the overlying rock, perhaps as much as a vertical mile. The underlying salt may have played a role in uplifting the central section.

Energetic hikers can reach Upheaval Dome from the parking area at the overlook or from White Rim 4WD Road below. **Syncline Loop Trail** makes a strenuous eight-mile circuit completely around Upheaval Dome; elevation change is 1,200 feet. The trail crosses Upheaval Dome Canyon about halfway around from the overlook; walk east 1.5 miles up the canyon to enter the crater itself. This is the only nontechnical route into the center of the dome. A hike around Upheaval Dome with a side trip to the crater totals 11 miles, best done as an overnight trip. Carry plenty of water for the entire trip; this dry country can be very hot in summer. The Green River is the only reliable source of water. From near Upheaval Campsite on White Rim 4WD Road, you can hike four miles on **Upheaval Trail** through Upheaval Canyon to a junction with the Syncline Loop Trail, then another 1.5 miles into the crater; elevation gain is about 600 feet.

Alcove Spring Trail

Another hiking possibility in the area, the Alcove Spring Trail leaves the road 1.5 miles before the Upheaval Dome parking area and connects with the White Rim 4WD Road in Taylor Canyon. Total distance is 10 miles one-way (five miles on the trail in Trail Canyon and five miles on a jeep road in Taylor Canyon); elevation change is about 1,500 feet. Carry plenty of water—the strenuous trail is hot and dry.

White Rim 4WD Road

This driving adventure follows the White Rim below the sheer cliffs of Island in the Sky. Travel along the winding road presents a constantly changing panorama of rock, canyons, river, and sky. Keep an eye out for desert bighorn sheep. You'll see all three levels of Island in the Sky District, from the high plateaus to the White Rim to the rivers. Only four-wheel-drive vehicles with high clearance can make the trip. With the proper vehicle, driving is mostly easy but slow and winding; a few steep or rough sections have to be negotiated. The 100-mile trip takes 2–3 days. Allow an extra day to travel all the road spurs. Mountain bikers find this a great trip, too; most cyclists arrange an accompanying vehicle to carry water and camping gear. Primitive campgrounds along the way provide convenient stopping places. You'll need to obtain reservations and a backcountry permit for the White Rim campsites from the Island in the Sky Visitor Center; this can be done in person, by mail, or by phone, (435) 259-4351; open Mon.–Sat. 12:30–4:30 P.M. Demand exceeds supply during the popular spring and autumn seasons, when you should make reservations as far in advance as possible. A $25 fee per reservation applies for White Rim trips. No services or developed water sources exist anywhere on the drive, so be sure to have plenty of fuel and water with some to spare. Access points are Shafer Trail Road (from near Island in the Sky) and Potash Road (UT 279 from Moab) on the east and Mineral Bottom Road on the west. White Rim Sandstone forms the distinctive plateau crossed on the drive. A close look at the rock reveals ripple marks and crossbeds laid down near an ancient coastline. The plateau's east side is about 800 feet above the Colorado River. On the west side, the plateau meets the bank of the Green River.

MAZE DISTRICT

Only adventurous and experienced travelers will want to visit this rugged land west of the Green and Colorado Rivers. Vehicle access wasn't even possible until 1957, when mineral exploration roads first entered what later became Canyonlands National Park. Today, you'll need a high-clearance four-wheel-drive vehicle, a horse, or your own two feet to get around. The National Park Service plans to keep this district in its remote and primitive condition. An airplane flight, recommended if you can't come overland, provides the only easy way to see the scenic features here. However, the National Park Service is currently studying the future of such flights and they may be curtailed or discontinued. The names of erosional forms describe the landscape—Orange Cliffs, Golden Stairs, the Fins,

Land of Standing Rocks, Lizard Rock, the Doll House, Chocolate Bars, the Maze, and Jasper Canyon. The many-fingered canyons of the Maze gave the district its name. Although not a true maze, these canyons give that impression.

Ranger Station and Information

Glen Canyon National Recreation Area borders the Maze District on the west with scenic canyons, cliffs, rock monuments, and overlooks of its own. The Hans Flat Ranger Station for the Maze District lies inside Glen Canyon NRA; the station is open daily 8 A.M.–4:30 P.M., (435) 259-2652. (In winter the station may close, but a ranger is usually available.) *There are no developed sources of water in the Maze District.* Hikers can obtain water from springs in some canyons (check with a ranger to find which are flowing) or from the rivers; purify all water before drinking. The Maze District has nine camping areas (two at Maze Overlook, seven at Land of Standing Rocks) with a 15-person, three-vehicle limit. A backcountry permit is needed for these or for backpacking. Note that a backcountry permit in this district is *not* a reservation—you may have to share a site with someone else, especially in the popular spring months. Also, as in the rest of the park, only designated sites can be used for vehicle camping. You don't need a permit to camp in the Glen Canyon NRA or on BLM land. The Trails Illustrated topo map of the Maze District describes and shows the few roads and trails here; some routes and springs are marked on it, too. Agile hikers experienced in desert and canyon travel may want to take off on cross-country routes, which are either unmarked or lightly cairned. Extra care must be taken for preparation and travel in both Glen Canyon NRA and the Maze. Always talk with the rangers beforehand to find out current conditions. Be sure to leave an itinerary with someone reliable who can contact the rangers if you're overdue. Unless the rangers know where to look for you in case of breakdown or accident, a rescue could take weeks!

Dirt roads to the Hans Flat Ranger Station and Maze District branch off from UT 24 (a half-mile south of the Goblin Valley State Park turnoff) and UT 95 (take Hite/Orange Cliffs Road between the Dirty Devil and Hite Bridges at Lake Powell). The easiest way in is the graded 46-mile road from UT 24; it's fast, though sometimes badly corrugated. The Hite Road (also called Orange Cliffs Road) is longer, bumpier, and, for some drivers, tedious; it's 54 miles from the turnoff at UT 95 to the Hans Flat Ranger Station via the Flint Trail. In winter or other times when the Flint Trail is closed, drivers must take the Hite Road to reach the Maze Overlook, Land of Standing Rocks, and the Doll House areas. All roads to the Maze District cross Glen Canyon National Recreation Area. From UT 24, two-wheel-drive vehicles with good clearance can travel to Hans Flat Ranger Station and other areas near, but not actually in, the Maze District. (All the mileages given here come from the author's vehicle— they're not always the same as signs.)

North Point

Hans Flat Ranger Station, and this peninsula that reaches out to the east and north, lie at an elevation of about 6,400 feet. Panoramas from North Point take in the vastness of Canyonlands, including all three districts. From **Millard Canyon Overlook**, just 0.9 mile past the ranger station, you can see arches, Cleopatra's Chair, and features as distant as the La Sals and Book Cliffs. For the best views, drive out to Panorama Point, about 10.5 miles one-way from the ranger station. A spur road goes left two miles to Cleopatra's Chair, a massive sandstone monolith and area landmark. The trailhead for **North Trail Canyon** begins just down the North Point Road (or 2.4 miles from the ranger station). Two-wheel-drive vehicles can usually reach this spot, where hikers can follow the trail down seven miles (1,000-foot elevation change) through the Orange Cliffs, follow four-wheel-drive roads six miles to the Maze Overlook Trail, then one more mile into a canyon of the Maze. Because North Point belongs to the Glen Canyon NRA, you can camp on it without a permit.

Flint Trail

This narrow, rough, four-wheel-drive road connects the Hans Flat area with the Maze Overlook, Doll House, and other areas below. The road, driver, and vehicle should all be in good condition before driving it! Winter snow and mud close the road from late December into March, as can rainstorms anytime. Check conditions

first with a ranger. If you're starting from the top, stop at the signed overlook just before the descent to scout for vehicles headed up (the Flint Trail has very few places to pass). The top of the Flint Trail is 14 miles south of Hans Flat Ranger Station; at the bottom, 2.8 nervous miles later, you can turn left two miles to the Golden Stairs Trailhead or 12.7 miles to the Maze Overlook; keep straight 28 miles to the Doll House or 39 miles to UT 95.

The Golden Stairs

Hikers can descend this steep two-mile (one-way) foot trail to the Land of Standing Rocks Road in a fraction of the time it takes for drivers to follow roads! The trail offers good views of Ernies Country and the Fins but lacks shade or water. The upper trailhead is east two miles from the road junction at the bottom of the Flint Trail.

Maze Overlook

Now you're actually in Canyonlands National Park and at the edge of the sinuous canyons of the Maze. You can stay at primitive camping areas (backcountry permit needed) and enjoy the views. **Maze Overlook Trail** drops one mile into the South Fork of Horse Canyon; a rope helps to lower packs in a difficult section. Once in the canyon you can walk around to the Harvest Scene, a group of prehistoric pictographs, or do a variety of day hikes or backpacks. These canyons have water in some places; check with the ranger when getting your permits. At least four routes connect with the four-wheel-drive road in Land of Standing Rocks (see the Trails Illustrated map). Hikers can also climb Petes Mesa from the canyons or head downstream to explore Horse Canyon (a dry fall blocks access to the Green River, however).

Land of Standing Rocks

Here, in the heart of the Maze District, strange-shaped rock spires stand guard over myriad canyons. Six camping areas offer scenic places to stay (permit needed). Hikers have a choice of many ridge and canyon routes from the four-wheel-drive road, a trail to a confluence overlook, and a trail that descends to the Colorado River near Cataract Canyon. The well-named Chocolate Bars can be reached by a hiking route from the

Wall near the beginning of the Land of Standing Rocks. A good day hike makes a loop from Chimney Rock to the Harvest Scene pictographs; take the ridge route (toward Pete's Mesa) one direction and the canyon fork northwest of Chimney Rock the other. Follow your topo map through the canyons and the cairns between the canyons and ridge. Other routes from Chimney Rock lead to lower Jasper Canyon (no river access) or into Shot and Water Canyons and on to the Green River. Tall, rounded rock spires near the end of the road reminded early visitors of dolls, hence the name Doll House. The Doll House makes a delightful place to explore in itself, or you can head out on routes and trails. **Spanish Bottom Trail** begins here, then drops steeply to Spanish Bottom beside the Colorado River in 1.2 miles (one-way); a thin trail leads downstream into Cataract Canyon and the first of a long series of rapids. **Surprise Valley Overlook Trail** branches right off the Spanish Bottom Trail after about 300 feet and winds south past some dolls to a T-junction (turn right for views of Surprise Valley, Cataract Canyon, and beyond); the trail ends at some well-preserved granaries; 1.5 one-way. The **Colorado/Green River Overlook Trail** heads north five miles (one-way) from the Doll House to a viewpoint of the confluence. See the area's Trails Illustrated map for routes, trails, and roads.

Getting to the Land of Standing Rocks takes some careful driving, especially on a three-mile stretch above Teapot Canyon. The many washes and small canyon crossings here make for slow going. Short-wheelbase vehicles have the easiest time, as usual. The turnoff for Land of Standing Rocks Road is 6.6 miles from the junction at the bottom of the Flint Trail via a wash shortcut (add about three miles if driving via the four-way intersection). The lower end of the Golden Stairs foot trail is 7.8 miles in, the western end of Ernies Country route trailhead is 8.6 miles in, the Wall is 12.7 miles in, Chimney Rock is 15.7 miles in, and the Doll House is 19 miles in at the end of the road. If you drive from the south on the Hite/Orange Cliffs Road, stop at the self-registration stand at the four-way intersection, about 31 miles in from UT 95; you can write your own permit for overnights in the park here. This may change, however, so check with a ranger for current information.

HORSESHOE CANYON UNIT

This canyon contains exceptional prehistoric rock art in a separate section of Canyonlands National Park. Ghostly life-size pictographs in the Great Gallery provide an intriguing look into the past. Archaeologists think that the images had religious importance, although the meaning of the figures remains unknown. The Barrier Canyon style of these drawings has been credited to an archaic Indian culture beginning at least 8,000 years ago and lasting until about A.D. 450. Horseshoe Canyon also contains rock art left by the subsequent Fremont and Anasazi. The relation between the earlier and later prehistoric groups hasn't been determined.

Great Gallery
Horseshoe Canyon lies northwest of the Maze District. Two moderately difficult trails and a very rough jeep road lead down the canyon walls. In dry weather, cars with good clearance can be driven to a trailhead on the west rim. To reach this trailhead from UT 24, drive to a junction a half-mile south of Goblin Valley State Park turnoff, then turn east 30 miles on a dirt road (keep left at

mysterious figures from the past . . .
Great Gallery detail

the Hans Flat Ranger Station/Horseshoe Canyon turnoff 25 miles in). From the rim, the trail descends 800 feet in one mile on an old jeep road, now closed to vehicles. At the canyon bottom, turn right two miles upstream to the Great Gallery. The sandy canyon floor is mostly level; trees provide shade in some areas.

A four-wheel-drive road goes north 21 miles from Hans Flat Ranger Station and drops steeply into the canyon from the east side. The descent on this road is so rough that most people prefer to park on the rim and hike the last mile of road. A vehicle barricade prevents driving right up to the rock-art panel, but the 1.5-mile walk is easy. A branch off the jeep road goes to the start of **Deadman's Trail** (1.5 miles one-way), which is less easy and more difficult.

Look for other rock art along the canyon walls on the way to the Great Gallery. Take care not to touch any of the drawings; they're very fragile as well as irreplaceable. (The oil from your hands will remove the paints.) Horseshoe Canyon also offers pleasant scenery and spring wildflowers. Carry plenty of water. Neither camping nor pets are allowed in the canyon, but you can stay on the rim. Contact the Hans Flat Ranger Station or the Moab office for road and trail conditions.

NEEDLES DISTRICT

The Needles District showcases some of the finest rock sculptures in Canyonlands National Park. Spires, arches, or monoliths appear in almost any direction you look. Prehistoric ruins and rock art exist in greater variety and quantity than elsewhere in the park. Year-round springs and streams bring greenery to the desert. A paved road, several four-wheel-drive roads, and many hiking trails offer a variety of ways to explore the Needles.

Needles Outpost
A general store just outside the park boundary offers a campground ($12 tent or RV without hookups), groceries, ice, gas, propane, snack bar, showers, jeep rentals and tours, and scenic flights. Call or write ahead, if possible, to arrange for jeep tours and scenic flights: P.O. Box 1107, Monticello, UT 84535, (435) 979-4007. The season at Needles Outpost is mid-March–late Oc-

tober. Turnoff from UT 211 is one mile before the Needles Visitor Center.

Visitor Center
Stop here to find out about hiking, back roads, and other aspects of travel in the Needles. The staff has backcountry permits (required for all overnight stays in the backcountry), maps, brochures, and books. Open daily 8 A.M.–5 P.M., (435) 259-4711. A $10 per vehicle charge is made unless you have a receipt issued within the last seven days from Island in the Sky of Canyonlands. Outside of office hours, get information at the bulletin board. To reach the Needles District, go 40 miles south from Moab (or 14 miles north of Monticello), turn west on UT 211, and continue 38 miles.

Scenic Drive
The main road continues 6.5 miles past the visitors' center to Big Spring Canyon Overlook. On the way, you can stop at several nature trails, turn off on four-wheel-drive roads, or take short spur roads to trailheads and Squaw Flat Campground.

Roadside Ruin is on the left 0.4 mile past the visitors' center. A one-third-mile loop trail goes near a well-preserved granary left by Anasazi Indians. A trail guide available at the start tells about the Anasazi and the local plants.

Cave Spring Trail introduces the geology and ecology of the park and goes to an old cowboy line camp. Turn left 0.7 mile past the visitors' center and follow signs about one mile to the trailhead. Pick up the brochure at the beginning. The 0.6-mile loop goes clockwise, crossing some slickrock; two ladders assist on the steep sections. Cowboys used the cave as a line camp from the late 1800s until establishment of the park in 1964; the line camp is just 50 yards in from the trailhead.

A road to **Squaw Flat Campground** and **Elephant Hill** turns left 2.7 miles past the ranger station. The campground, about a half mile in from the main road, has water and charges a $10 fee from mid-March to September; it's open the rest of the year with no water or charge (water can be obtained year-round at the visitors' center). Rangers present evening programs at the campfire circle on Loop A from spring through autumn. A **picnic area** is at the base of Elephant Hill, three miles past the campground turnoff and on the scenic drive. Hiking trails lead into wonderful rock forms and canyons from both the campground and picnic areas. Only experienced drivers in four-wheel-drive vehicles should continue past the picnic area up Elephant Hill.

Pothole Point Nature Trail is on the left of the main road 5.0 miles past the visitors' center. Highlights of this 0.6-mile loop hike are the many potholes dissolved in the Cedar Mesa Sandstone. A brochure illustrates the fairy shrimp, tadpole shrimp, horsehair worm, snail, and other adaptable creatures that spring to life when rains fill the potholes. You'll also enjoy fine views of distant buttes from the trail.

Slickrock Trail begins on the right 6.2 miles past the visitors' center. The trail makes a loop of 2.4 miles round-trip and takes you north to an overlook of the confluence of Big Spring and Little Spring Canyons. Hiking is easy and offers good panoramas.

Big Spring Canyon Overlook, 6.5 miles past the visitors' center, marks the end of the scenic drive but not the scenery. The **Confluence Overlook Trail** begins here and winds west to an overlook of the Green and Colorado Rivers (see Confluence Overlook Trail, below).

Hiking

The Needles District has about 55 miles of backcountry trails. Many interconnect to provide all sorts of day and overnight trips. Cairns mark the trails; signs point the way at junctions. You can normally find water in upper Elephant Canyon and canyons to the east in spring and early summer, though the remaining water often becomes stagnant by midsummer. Always ask the rangers about sources of water—don't depend on its availability. Treat water from all sources, including springs, before drinking. Chesler Park and other areas west of Elephant Canyon are very dry; you'll need to bring all water. Mosquitoes, gnats, and deer flies can be very pesky from late spring to midsummer, especially in the wetter places—bring insect repellent. To plan your trip, obtain the small hiking map available from the visitors' center, Trails Illustrated's Needles District map, or USGS topo maps.

Confluence Overlook Trail

This trail goes west 5.5 miles from Big Spring Canyon Overlook (at the end of the scenic drive) to a fine viewpoint overlooking the Green and Colorado Rivers 1,000 feet below. You might see rafts in the water or bighorn sheep on the cliffs. The trail crosses Big Spring and Elephant Canyons and follows a jeep road for a short distance. Higher points have good views of the Needles to the south. Except for a few short steep sections, this trail is level and fairly easy. A very early start is recommended in summer, as there's little shade. Carry water even if you don't plan to go all the way. This enchanting country has lured many a hiker beyond his or her original goal!

Hiking Trails from Squaw Flat Trailhead

The main trailhead sits a short distance south of the campground and is reached by a separate signed road. You can also begin from a trailhead in the campground itself.

Peekaboo Trail winds southeast five miles (one-way) over rugged terrain, including some steep sections of slickrock (best avoided when wet, icy, or covered with snow). There's little shade; carry water. The trail follows Squaw Canyon, climbs over a pass to Lost Canyon, then crosses more slickrock before descending to Peekaboo Campground on Salt Creek 4WD Road. Look for Anasazi ruins on the way and rock art at the campground. A rockslide took out Peekaboo Spring, shown on some maps. Options on this trail include a turnoff south through Squaw Canyon or Lost Canyon to make a loop of 8.75 miles or more.

Squaw Canyon Trail follows the canyon south for 3.75 miles one-way. Intermittent water can often be found until late spring. You can take a connecting trail (Peekaboo, Lost Canyon, and Big Spring Canyon) or cross a slickrock pass to Elephant Canyon.

Lost Canyon Trail, 3.25 miles long one-way, is reached via Peekaboo or Squaw Canyon Trails and makes a loop with them. Water supports abundant vegetation; you may need to wade. Most of the way is in the wash bottom, except for a section of slickrock to Squaw Canyon.

Big Spring Canyon Trail crosses an outcrop of slickrock from the trailhead, then follows the canyon bottom to the head of the canyon, 3.75 miles one-way. You can usually find intermittent water along the way except in summer. At canyon's end, a climb up steep slickrock (hazardous if covered by snow or ice) takes you to

Squaw Canyon Trail and back to the trailhead for a good 7.5-mile loop. Another possibility is to turn southwest to the head of Squaw Canyon, then hike over a slickrock saddle to Elephant Canyon for a 10.5-mile loop.

Hiking Trails from Elephant Hill Trailhead

Drive west three miles past the campground turnoff to the picnic area and trailhead at the base of Elephant Hill. Sounds of racing engines and burning rubber can often be heard from above as vehicles attempt the difficult four-wheel-drive road that begins just past the picnic area. All of the following destinations can also be reached by trails from the Squaw Flat Trailhead, though distances will be slightly greater.

Chesler Park is a favorite hiking destination. A lovely desert meadow contrasts with the red and white spires that gave the Needles District its name. An old cowboy line camp is on the west side of the rock island in the center of the park. Distance on **Chesler Park Trail** is about six miles round-trip. The trail winds through sand and slickrock before ascending a small pass through the Needles to Chesler Park. Once inside, you can take **Chesler Park Loop Trail** (five miles) completely around the park. The loop includes the unusual half-mile **Joint Trail** which follows the bottom of a very narrow crack. Camping in Chesler Park is restricted to certain areas; check with a ranger.

Druid Arch reminds many people of the massive stone slabs at Stonehenge, popularly associated with the druids, in southern England. The arch is an 11-mile round-trip (15 miles if you start at Squaw Flat Trailhead). Follow the Chesler Park Trail two miles to Elephant Canyon, turn up the canyon 3.5 miles, then make a quarter-mile climb to the arch. Upper Elephant Canyon has seasonal water but the narrow canyon is closed to camping.

Lower Red Lake Canyon Trail provides access to Cataract Canyon of the Colorado River. This is a long, strenuous trip best suited for experienced hikers and completed in two days. Distance from the Elephant Hill Trailhead is 19 miles round-trip; you'll be walking on four-wheel-drive roads and trails. If you can drive Elephant Hill 4WD Road to the trail junction in Cyclone Canyon, the hike is only eight miles round-trip. The most difficult trail section is a steep talus slope that drops 700 feet in a half mile into the lower canyon. Total elevation change is 1,000 feet. The canyon has little shade and lacks any water source above the river. Summer heat can make the trip grueling; temperatures tend to be 5–10° hotter than on other Needles trails. The river level drops between midsummer and autumn, allowing hikers to go along the shore both downstream to see the rapids and upstream to the confluence. Undertows and strong currents make the river dangerous to cross.

Upper Salt Creek Trail

Several impressive arches and many inviting side canyons attract adventurous hikers to the

Chesler Park from its southern edge (near the Joint Trail)

extreme southeast corner of the park. The trail begins at the end of the 13.5-mile four-wheel-drive road up Salt Creek, then goes south 12 miles upcanyon to Cottonwood Canyon/Beef Basin Road near Cathedral Butte, just outside the park boundary. The trail is nearly level except for a steep climb at the end. Water can usually be found. Some wading and bushwhacking may be necessary. The famous "All-American Man" pictograph, shown on some topo maps (or ask a ranger), is in a cave a short way off to the east at about the midpoint of the trail; follow your map and unsigned paths to the cave but don't climb in—it's dangerous to both you and the ruins and pictograph inside. Many more archaeological sites can be discovered near the trail; they're all fragile and need great care when visited.

Four-Wheel-Drive Roads

A back-road tour allows you to see beautiful canyon scenery, arches, and Indian rock-art sites in the Needles District. Check with a ranger about special hazards before setting out. Also obtain a backcountry permit ($30 per vehicle) if you plan to use one of the campgrounds available along Salt Creek or in the area past Elephant Hill. Mountain bikers enjoy the challenge of going up Elephant Hill Road and the roads beyond. Colorado Overlook 4WD Road is good riding, too, but Salt Creek and the other eastern canyons have too much loose sand.

Salt Creek Canyon 4WD Road begins near Cave Spring Trail, crosses sage flats for the next 2.5 miles, then heads deep into this spectacular canyon. Round-trip distance, including a side trip to 150-foot-high Angel Arch, is 26 miles. Agile hikers can follow a steep slickrock route into the window of Angel Arch. You can also explore side canyons of Salt Creek or take the Upper Salt Creek Trail (the "All American Man" pictograph makes a good day-hike destination of 12 miles round-trip). **Horse Canyon 4WD Road** turns off to the left shortly before the mouth of Salt Canyon. Round-trip distance, including a side trip to Tower Ruin, is about 13 miles; other attractions include Paul Bunyan's Potty, Castle Arch, Fortress Arch, and side-canyon hiking. Salt and Horse Canyons can easily be driven in four-wheel-drive vehicles. Usually Salt Canyon is closed due to quicksand after flash floods in summer and shelf ice in winter.

Four-wheel-drive roads enter **Davis Canyon** and **Lavender Canyon** from UT 211 east of the park boundary. Both canyons are accessed through Davis Canyon Road off UT 211 and contain great scenery, arches, and Indian sites, and both are easily visited. Davis is about 20 miles round-trip and Lavender is about 26 miles round-trip. Try to allow plenty of time in either canyon, as there is much to see and many inviting side canyons to hike. You can camp on BLM land just outside the park boundaries—but not in the park itself.

Colorado Overlook 4WD Road begins beside the visitors' center and follows Salt Creek to Lower Jump Overlook. Then it bounces across slickrock to a view of the Colorado River (upstream from the confluence). Driving is easy to moderate, though very rough the last 1.5 miles. Round-trip distance is 14 miles.

Elephant Hill 4WD Loop Road begins three miles past the Squaw Flat Campground turnoff. Only experienced drivers with stout vehicles should attempt the extremely rough and steep climb up Elephant Hill (coming up the back side of Elephant Hill is even rougher!). The loop is about 10 miles round-trip. Connecting roads go to the Confluence Overlook Trailhead (the viewpoint is one mile round-trip on foot), the Joint Trailhead (Chesler Park is two miles round-trip on foot), and several canyons. Some road sections on the loop are one-way. The parallel canyons in this area are grabens caused by faulting where a layer of salt has shifted deep underground. In addition to Elephant Hill, a few other difficult spots must be negotiated. This area can also be reached by a long route south of the park using Cottonwood Canyon/Beef Basin Road from UT 211, about 60 miles one-way. You'll enjoy spectacular vistas from the Abajo Highlands. Two *very* steep descents from Pappys Pasture into Bobbys Hole effectively make this section one-way; travel from Elephant Hill up Bobbys Hole is possible but much more difficult than going the other way and may require hours of roadbuilding. The Bobbys Hole route may be impassable at times—ask about conditions at the BLM office in Monticello or at the Needles Visitor Center.

UTAH'S SOUTHEASTERN CORNER

BLM NEWSPAPER ROCK HISTORICAL MONUMENT

At Newspaper Rock a profusion of petroglyphs depicts human figures, animals, birds, and abstract designs. These represent 2,000 years of human history during which archaic tribes and Anasazi, Fremont, Paiute, Navajo, and Anglo travelers have passed through Indian Creek Canyon. The patterns on the smooth sandstone rock face stand out clearly, thanks to a coating of dark desert varnish. Newspaper Rock lies just 150 feet off UT 211 on the way to the Needles District of Canyonlands National Park. A quarter-mile nature trail introduces you to the area's desert and riparian vegetation. Picnic areas lie along Indian Creek across the highway. The park is relatively undeveloped; no drinking water or charge. From U.S. 191 between Moab and Monticello, turn west 12 miles on UT 211.

CANYON RIMS RECREATION AREA

Viewpoints atop the high mesa east of Canyonlands National Park offer magnificent panoramas of the surrounding area. The BLM has provided two fenced overlooks, two campgrounds, and good access roads. Other overlooks and scenic spots can be reached on jeep roads or by hiking. The 20-mile-long mesa, shown on maps as Hatch Point, features rock monoliths, canyons, slickrock, and rolling hills. You have a good chance of seeing the graceful antelope-like pronghorn that thrive in this high-desert country. The turnoff for Hatch Point of Canyon Rims is at Milepost 93 on U.S. 191, 32 miles south of Moab and seven miles north of the UT 211 junction for the Needles District. Canyon Rims Recreation Area has been greatly expanded recently to include surrounding BLM lands and the Beef Basin and Dark Canyon areas. Author and BLM volunteer Fran Barnes has written and published the large book *Canyon Country's Canyon Rims Recreation Area,* about exploring these areas. The book includes a 235-mile long "Canyon Rims Recreation Area Mountain Bike Challenge Route." For back-road travel in this area, you'll find Fran Barnes' book and separate map *Canyon Country Off-Road Vehicle Trails: Canyon Rims Recreation Area* very helpful. Cyclists will also find good info in Peggy and Bob Utesch's *Mountain Biking in Canyon Rims Recreation Area.* Also check out the website: www.blm.gov/utah/ moab/canyon_rims.html.

Newspaper Rock

W.C. McRAE

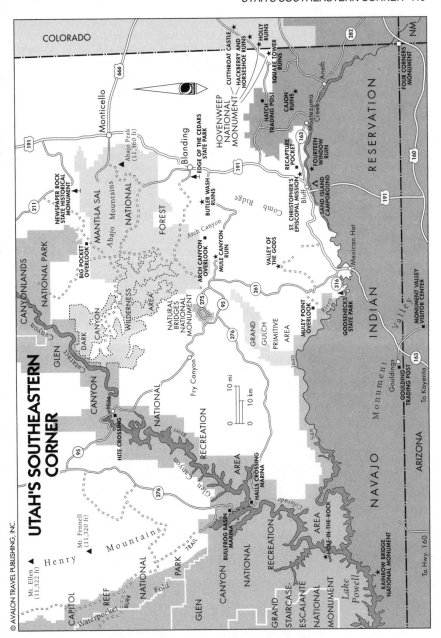

© AVALON TRAVEL PUBLISHING, INC.

UTAH'S SOUTHEASTERN CORNER

Needles Overlook

Follow the paved road 22 miles west to its end (turn left at the junction 15 miles in). The BLM has a picnic area and interpretive exhibits here. A fence protects visitors from the sheer cliffs that drop off more than 1,000 feet. You can see much of Canyonlands National Park and southeastern Utah. Look south for Six-Shooter Peaks and the high country of the Abajo Mountains; southwest for the Needles (thousands of spires reaching for the heavens); west for the confluence area of the Green and Colorado Rivers, the Maze District, the Orange Cliffs, and the Henry Mountains; northwest for the lazy bends of the Colorado River Canyon and the sheer-walled mesas of Island in the Sky and Dead Horse Point; north for the Book Cliffs; and northeast for the La Sal Mountains. The changing shadows and colors of the canyon country make for a continuous show throughout the day.

Anticline Overlook

Head west 15 miles on the paved road, then go straight (north) 17 miles on a good gravel road to the fenced overlook at road's end. Here you're standing 1,600 feet above the Colorado River. The sweeping panorama over the canyons, the river, and the twisted rocks of the Kane Creek Anticline is nearly as spectacular as that from Dead Horse Point, only 5.5 miles west as the crow flies. Salt and other minerals of the Paradox Formation pushed up overlying rocks into the dome visible below. Downcutting by the Colorado River has revealed the twisted rock layers. The Moab

Salt Mine across the river to the north uses a solution technique to bring up potash from the Paradox Formation several thousand feet underground. Pumps then transfer the solution to the blue-tinted evaporation ponds. Look carefully on the northeast horizon to see an arch in the Windows Section of Arches National Park, 16 miles away.

You can reach **Pyramid Butte Overlook** by a gravel road that turns west off the main drive two miles before Anticline Overlook; the road goes around a rock monolith to viewpoints on the other side (1.3 miles round-trip). Vehicles with four-wheel drive can go west out to **Canyonlands Overlook** (17 miles round-trip) on rough unmarked roads. The turnoff, which may not be signed, is about 0.3 mile south of the Hatch Point Campground turnoff.

Campgrounds

Each camping area has water (mid-Apr.–mid-Oct.), tables, grills, and outhouses and charges a $10 fee. **Windwhistle Campground,** backed by cliffs to the south, has fine views to the north and a nature trail; follow the main road from U.S. 191 for six miles and turn left. At **Hatch Point Campground,** in a piñon-juniper woodland, you can enjoy views to the north; water available Apr.–mid-Oct. Go 24 miles in on the paved and gravel roads toward Anticline Overlook, then turn right one mile.

Trough Springs Trail

Hikers can follow this old livestock trail on the east side of Hatch Point. To reach the trailhead,

*view into Canyonlands
National Park*

W.C. McRAE

descent into Bobbys Hole; Canyon Rims Recreation Area

turn east 0.6 mile on a dirt road five miles north of the Hatch Point Campground turnoff (or four miles south of Anticline Overlook). The trail begins from an abandoned well pad and follows the canyon to its mouth at Kane Creek Road. The first one-third mile follows a jeep road, then cairns mark the way. Carry water. The moderately difficult hike is five miles round-trip and has an elevation change of 1,200 feet.

Beef Basin

The rugged canyon country south of Canyonlands National Park's Needles District contains beautiful scenery, knock-out panoramas, and Anasazi pueblo ruins. You'll need a four-wheel-drive, high-clearance vehicle, maps, camping gear, and emergency supplies to explore this remote region. Drive in from the east via County Road 104, or from the south over the Abajo Highlands of the Manti–La Sal National Forest. Although these approach roads are graded, high-clearance vehicles are still recommended. Snow and mud close the roads in winter and spring, especially from the Abajo Highlands. The Beef Basin Road drops from the forests into a series of grassy parks. Spur roads branch out to other canyons and parks and make a loop in Beef Basin.

Many Anasazi pueblos stand out in the open in Middle and Ruin Parks; others lie tucked into canyon alcoves. One road runs northwest past Ruin Park, makes two *very* steep and rough descents into Bobbys Hole, then continues to Elephant Hill in Canyonlands National Park. Only hard-core jeepers should consider this route into Canyonlands National Park! The road may be impassable in the reverse (uphill) direction or totally impassable altogether; ask at the BLM office in Monticello or the Needles Visitor Center in the park.

Big Pocket Overlook

A rough jeep road branches north 2.5 miles from the Cottonwood Canyon/Beef Basin Road to spectacular panoramas of upper Salt and Lavender Canyons. Binoculars help to pick out natural arches and other details. The road, also good for hiking or mountain biking, makes a loop along the east side of this narrow peninsula. Although on BLM land, you'll be surrounded by some of the best views in the Needles District of Canyonlands National Park. A hiking trail into upper Salt Creek Canyon begins about one mile west of the Big Pocket Overlook turnoff.

Cameo Cliffs

Canyons, arches, and panoramas attract visitors to this little-known area east of U.S. 191. Author Fran Barnes called it Cameo Cliffs because the pink cliffs reminded him of an old-fashioned pink-and-white cameo locket. You're not likely to see this unofficial name on maps, however. Barnes describes the area, divided by UT 46 into Cameo Cliffs North and South, in a small guidebook and separate map, *Cameo Cliffs: Biking-Hiking-Four-Wheeling*.

MONTICELLO

The Mormon settlers who arrived in 1888 found the cool climate more suited to raising sheep and cattle than crops. Monticello (pronounced mon-ti-

SELL-o) lies at an elevation of 7,050 feet just east of the Abajo (uh-BAH-hoe) Mountains. The small town (pop. 1,904) is the seat of San Juan County (Utah's largest, at five million acres) and serves as a base for travelers to visit surrounding mountains and canyons, including the Needles District of Canyonlands National Park. Monticello is 54 miles south of Moab and 21 miles north of Blanding. Highway U.S. 666 (Central) goes east from downtown to the Colorado border (17 miles) and Mesa Verde National Park (89 miles).

The **Monticello Museum,** in the library building at the city park, 80 N. Main, has exhibits of Anasazi artifacts, pioneer memorabilia, historic documents, and mineral specimens; open Mon.–Thurs. 2–9 P.M., Fri. 2–6 P.M., and Sat. 10 A.M.–2 P.M. from June 1 to August 31. The librarian next door at the county library can let you in outside official hours.

Accommodations

$50–75: The unique offerings at **The Grist Mill Inn,** 64 S. 300 East, (435) 587-2597 or (800) 645-3762, include bed-and-breakfast accommodations in a turn-of-the-century flour mill, a granary, and a 1924 caboose. The inn is a showcase of sensitive architectural restoration. All rooms have private baths.

Navajo Trail National 9 Inn is a well maintained older motel at 248 N. Main, (435) 587-2251 or (888) 449-NINE. The **Days Inn** is at 549 N. Main, (435) 587-2458 or (800) 329-7466, has an indoor pool and spa. **Triangle H Motel,** 164 E. Central, (435) 587-2274 or (800) 657-6622, has well-maintained rooms. **Best Western Wayside Motor Inn,** 195 E. Central, (435) 587-2261 or (800) 633-9700, has a pool. The new **Super 8,** (435) 587-2489 or (877) 2-GO-WEST, is on the north edge of town.

Campgrounds: With showers and laundry, **Mountain View RV Park,** 632 N. Main, (435) 587-2974, is open May 1–October 31; $12 tents, $15.75 RVs with hookups. **Westerner Trailer Park,** 516 S. Main, near the golf course, (435) 587-2762, costs $13 tents or RVs without hookups, $17 with; it has showers; closed in winter. **Monticello/Canyonlands KOA,** (435) 587-2884, is on a ranch with buffalo, cows, horses, and other farm animals; go east five miles on Central/U.S. 666, then north a half mile; open May 1–Sept. 30, $16 tents or RVs without

hookups, $21 with, $30 for "kamping kabins"; has showers, store, pool.

The U.S. Forest Service has two campgrounds located nearby on paved roads in the Abajos. **Dalton Springs** (elev. 8,400 feet) has water early June–early October; $10. Go west 5.3 miles on 200 South. **Buckboard** (elev. 8,700 feet) has water mid-June–early October; $10. Go west 6.5 miles on 200 South. Campgrounds may also be open off-season without water or fee.

Food

Houston's of Monticello, 296 N. Main, (435) 587-2531, serves homemade American food daily (except Tues.) for breakfast and lunch. **Wagon Wheel Pizza,** 164A S. Main, (435) 587-2766, spins out pizza, sandwiches, and salads daily for lunch and dinner. **MD Ranch Cookhouse,** 380 S. Main, (435) 587-3299, dishes up cowboy food including steaks and buffalo in a Western atmosphere with genuine ranching artifacts; open daily for breakfast, lunch, and dinner (closed Dec.–Feb.). **Juniper Tree Restaurant,** 133 E. Central, (435) 587-2870, features steak, prime rib, roast beef, and other items daily for dinner. **Lamplight Restaurant,** 655 E. Central, (435) 587-2170, is the best restaurant in the region, offering steaks, fish, prime rib, and a salad bar; open Tues.–Sat. for dinner. **La Casita,** 280 E. Central, (435) 587-2959, has Mexican and American food; open Mon.–Sat. for lunch and dinner.

Entertainment and Events

Watch movies at **The Movies,** 696 E. Central, (435) 587-2535. Annual events include **Monticello/Canyonlands Triathlon** in mid-March, **Pioneer Day** (parade, softball, games, and food) on July 24, **San Juan Golf Tourney and Mountain Cookout** in early August, and **San Juan County Fair** (rodeo, exhibits, and dance) on the third weekend in August.

Services and Recreation

The **post office** is at 197 S. Main, (435) 587-2294. **San Juan Hospital** provides medical care at 364 W. 100 North, (435) 587-2116. The **city park** has picnic areas and a playground at Main and Central. A covered **swimming pool** (open in summer, 801-587-2907), **tennis courts,** and **ball fields** are three blocks west of Main on Central. **Blue Mountain Meadows Public Golf**

Course, 549 S. Main (south edge of town), (435) 587-2468, has nine holes, pro shop, and snack bar. **Four Corners School of Outdoor Education** offers programs on the wildlife, geology, and archaeology of the Southwest. Write for a brochure at P.O. Box 1029, Monticello, UT 84535, (435) 587-2156.

Ranch Vacations and Trail Rides

Live the life of a cowboy on a working ranch run by third- and fourth-generation cowboys. Operations cover 200,000 acres near Monticello. Depending on the season, you'll be involved in trailing, moving pastures, and gathering and working cattle. **Dalton Gang Adventures** provides the horse, cattle, and range at $125 per person per day. This isn't your standard guest ranch—you'll be taken on as a working cowboy. Contact the ranch for a brochure that gives the activities of the different seasons: P.O. Box 8, Monticello, UT 84534, (435) 587-2416.

Information

Visit the **San Juan County Multi-Agency Visitor Center,** on the side of the county courthouse at 117 S. Main (P.O. Box 490, Monticello, UT 84535), (435) 587-3235 or (800) 574-4386, for information about San Juan County towns and backcountry; staff and literature represent the San Juan County Travel Council, National Park Service, U.S. Forest Service, Bureau of Land Management, Canyonlands Natural History Association, and Utah Travel Council; regional books and maps are sold. Open Apr. 1–Oct. 31 Mon.–Fri. 8 A.M.–5 P.M. and Sat. and Sun. 10 A.M.–5 P.M., then Mon.–Fri. 9 A.M.–5 P.M. the rest of the year. The **Bureau of Land Management** San Juan Resource Area office, 435 N. Main (P.O. Box 7, Monticello, UT 84535), (435) 587-1500, knows about Grand Gulch, Fish and Owl Canyons, Dark Canyon, Arch Canyon, and many other scenic hiking areas; they can also advise on back-road travel in San Juan County. Open Mon.–Fri. 7:45 A.M.–4:30 P.M. The **Manti–La Sal National Forest office,** 496 E. Central (P.O. Box 820, Monticello, UT 84535), (435) 587-2041, has information about roads, camping, and hiking in the Abajos and surrounding high country; its Monticello district includes the upper reaches of Dark Canyon. Open Mon.–Fri. 8 A.M.–noon and 12:30–4:30 P.M. The **public library** at 80 N. Main in the city park, (435) 587-2281, has general reading and an extensive collection of southeastern Utah history; open Mon.–Thurs. 2–9 P.M., Fri. 2–6 P.M., and Sat. 10 A.M.–2 P.M.

VICINITY OF MONTICELLO

Abajo Peak

The rounded Abajos (or Blues, as they're sometimes called) actually rise higher than they seem to. Early Spanish explorers climbed the La Sals to the northeast and named these mountains Abajo (below). Intrusive volcanic rocks created the range in much the same way as they formed the Henry and La Sal Mountains. Abajo Peak tops the range at 11,362 feet. You can easily reach the summit by road (high-clearance vehicles work best); head west 0.9 mile on 200 South from U.S. 191, then turn left 13 miles on South Creek Road (pavement ends one mile in at Loyd's Lake). You'll likely see deer and raptors, as well as summer wildflowers, on the drive up. Panoramas on a clear day at the top take in the Four Corners region including mountain ranges in Colorado, Shiprock in New Mexico, the Chuska Mountains in Arizona, Monument Valley, Cedar Mesa, the Henry Mountains, the Needles District of Canyonlands National Park, the La Sal Mountains, and the forests and meadows of the Abajos. Other peaks and canyons of the Abajos have good hiking trails; see the foresters in Monticello and the Manti-La Sal Forest map and the more detailed Trails Illustrated topo map for the back roads and trails of the area. The metric 1:100,000 Blanding topo map covers nearly all the range.

You can enjoy several scenic drives in the Abajos. Cars with good clearance can often do these trips in dry weather; ask at the U.S. Forest Service office in Monticello. The range can be crossed to Blanding by heading west on 200 South, turning southwest on Forest Route 079 up North Canyon, then descending along Johnson Creek (about 37 miles total one-way). A longer drive continues west from the junction of Forest Routes 079 and 095 to Elk Ridge and through the Bears Ears to UT 95 near Natural Bridges National Monument. The drive has great views of rugged canyons and forested hills. You'll cross a knife-edge ridge on the Causeway at about the middle of Forest Route 095; at the west end, turn south around the upper drainages of Dark Canyon to the Bears Ears on Forest Route 088 or turn north to Beef Basin and Big Pocket Overlook Roads (see Canyon Rims Recreation Area, above). Winter visitors come to the mountains for cross-country skiing and snowmobiling, though no trails or ski areas exist (Blue Mountain Ski Area has closed). The road from Monticello to Dalton Springs is plowed for winter access. A good scenic loop saves about 16 miles from the highway route between Monticello and Canyonlands National Park; take Forest Route 105 about nine miles to Forest Route 174, perhaps stopping to enjoy a beautiful scenic overlook of Canyonlands from a high point before descending to Route 174, which brings you, in another six miles, to UT 211 near Newspaper Rock.

BLANDING

The largest town in San Juan County, Blanding (pop. 3,516) is also a handy travelers' stop. The state park on the northwest edge of town provides an excellent introduction to the Anasazi Indians, who left behind many ruins in the Four Corners area. Pioneers began work on an irrigation system in 1897 to bring water from the Abajo Mountains to the rich soil of White Mesa. The first families arrived at the town site, then known as Sidon, in 1905. Many of the Mormon farmers who followed had been driven from Mexico by political and religious intolerance or had lost their farms to floods at nearby Bluff. Residents apparently liked changing the name of their community. Originally known as Sidon, the town became Grayson, then Blanding. The story goes that in 1915 townsfolk jumped at the offer of a free library by Thomas W. Bicknell on the condition that they name their town after him. The town of Thurber in central Utah also wanted the library, so it was divided between the two communities; Thurber became Bicknell and Grayson became Blanding, the maiden name of Mrs. Bicknell.

Anasazi cup

Edge of the Cedars State Park

Prehistoric Anasazi built at least six groups of pueblo structures between A.D. 700 and 1220 just outside present-day Blanding. The state museum features an excellent array of pottery, baskets, sandals, jewelry, and stone tools. The pottery collection on the second floor stands out for its rich variety of styles and decorative designs. Other displays illustrate Anasazi life and how archaeologists have learned about these ancient peoples through studies of stratigraphy, dendrochronology, and village layouts. The Special Exhibits room has changing shows related to the region and inhabitants. An observation tower in the museum provides panoramic views of the ruins outside and of mountains in four states; signs identify the features.

A short trail behind the museum leads past six clusters of ruins, each of which contains both rectangular rooms on the surface and circular depressions of underground kivas and pit houses. Only Complex 4 has been excavated and partly restored to give an idea of the village's appearance when the Anasazi lived here. You may enter the kiva by descending a ladder through the restored roof; the walls and interior features are original. The other five ruin groups haven't been restored and require some imagination. A large pit near Complex 4 is all that remains of a great kiva, a structure rarely seen this far north. Edge of the Cedars likely served as an important community center in its day.

The museum also has exhibits and artifacts of the people who followed the Anasazi—the Ute and Navajo Indians and the early Anglo pioneers. You may enter a Navajo hogan outside. Videos and slide presentations, shown on request in the auditorium, illustrate Anasazi, Navajo, and pioneer cultures. There's often an art or photo exhibition in the auditorium as well as in the art gallery. **Archaeology Week,** held in spring, has demonstrations and talks. A gift shop sells books on the region's Indians and pioneer history. Picnic tables outside provide a spot for having lunch. Edge of the Cedars is open daily 9 A.M.–6 P.M. from May 16 to September 15, then daily 9 A.M.–5 P.M. the rest of the year; closed Thanksgiving Day, Christmas Day, New Year's Day, Civil Rights Day and Presidents Day; $2 adults, $1 ages 6–16, or $5 per vehicle, (435) 678-2238. Head north on Main from downtown and follow signs one mile.

The Dinosaur Museum

This museum, 754 S. 200 West, (435) 678-3454, showcases the prehistoric plant and animal life of this corner of Utah. Exhibits include life-size models of dinosaurs, fossils, and skeletons. Don't miss the History Hall of Hollywood Dinosaurs, which recounts the evolution of film's depictions of the thunder lizard. Open Mon.–Sat. 9 A.M.–5 P.M. Apr. 15–Oct. 15; adults $2, children and seniors $1.

Accommodations

Under $50: The **Cliff Palace Motel** offers basic accommodation at 132 S. Main, (435) 678-2264 or (800) 553-8093. The **Sunset Inn** is at 88 W. Center, (435) 678-3323, is a good deal with all queen beds, remote-control cable TVs, and a hot tub; pets allowed.

$50–75: The hospitality is gracious and the facilities are top-notch at **The Grayson Country Inn B&B,** 118 E. 300 South (turn east one block at Cedar Mesa Pottery), (435) 678-2388 or (800) 365-0868. It features rooms in a 1908 Victorian home, plus an additional cottage with three bedrooms for a family or group. All rooms have private baths. **Rogers House B&B,** 412 S. Main, (435) 678-3932 or (800) 355-3932, is a renovated 1915 home with private baths, whirlpool tubs, and queen-size beds.

The **Four Corners Inn,** 131 E. Center, (435) 678-3257 or (800) 574-3150, has a restaurant, free continental breakfast, and children under 12 stay free. The **Comfort Inn,** at 711 S. U.S. 191, (435) 678-3271 or (800) 622-3250, has suites, guest laundry, indoor pool, hot tub, and exercise room. A new **Super 8,** 591 S. Main, (435)678-3880 or (800) 800-8000, is on the south edge of town. The **Best Western Gateway Inn,** 88 E. Center, (435) 678-2278 or (800) 257-4780, has a pool and restaurant.

Campgrounds: At the south edge of town, **KamPark** has a store and showers on S. U.S.

191, (435) 678-2770; $11 tents, $11 RVs without hookups, $14 with. **Devil's Canyon Campground** (elev. 7,100 feet) in the Manti–La Sal National Forest has sites with water from early May to late October; $10 (no water or fee off-season). A quarter-mile nature trail begins at the far end of the campground loop. Go north eight miles on U.S. 191, then west 1.3 miles on a paved road (turnoff is between Mileposts 60 and 61). **Nizhoni Campground** (elev. 7,760 feet), also in the Manti–La Sal National Forest, has sites with water from early June to late September; $10. Turn north 14 miles on 100 East in Blanding (last part is a gravel road). You can also reach Nizhoni on backways from Monticello via the Abajo Peaks or from Natural Bridges National Monument via the Bears Ears, Elk Ridge, and the Causeway.

Food

Elk Ridge Restaurant, 120 E. Center, (435) 678-3390, offers a varied American menu with a few Mexican items; open daily (except Sun.) for breakfast, lunch, and dinner. The best place for a full meal is the **Old Tymer Restaurant,** 733 S. Main, (435) 678-2122, with sandwiches, steak, prime rib, and chicken; open for three meals a day.

Events, Shopping, and Services

A three-day **Fourth of July Celebration** has fireworks, a parade, horse events, "meller-dramas," and a mudbog competition. Navajo and Ute Indians produce handpainted ceramics at **Cedar Mesa Pottery,** Main and 300 South, (435) 678-2241. You can step into the adjacent factory on weekdays to watch the craftspeople at work. **Blue Mountain Trading Post,** one mile south of town, has a large selection of high-quality Indian art and crafts; the adaptable Navajo produce much of the work—even the kachina dolls (borrowed from Hopi traditions). **White Mesa Institute,** 639 W. 100 South (50-1), Blanding, UT 84511, sponsored by the College of Eastern Utah, offers educational programs for youth and adults on the archaeology, modern Indian tribes, pioneer history, wildlife, and geology of the Southwest. The **post office** is at the corner of Main and 100 North, (435) 678-2627. The **Blanding Clinic** provides medical services at 930 N. 400 West, (435) 678-2254. Contact the county hospital in Monticello at (435) 678-2830.

Recreation

Blanding Pool and a **tennis court** are at 50 West and 200 South, (435) 678-2157. **Reservoir Park** (picnic area and playground) and the nine-hole **Blanding Golf Course** are three miles north on 300 West; the small reservoir has trout fishing. **Recapture Reservoir** offers boating and trout fishing three miles northeast of town; head northeast 1.3 miles on U.S. 191, turn left (north) on a paved road between Mileposts 53 and 54 (just before the highway enters a road cut), then go 1.7 miles to the lake's southern shore; this road is the old highway and makes a good boat ramp where submerged. For access to the north and west sides of the reservoir, follow U.S. 191 across the dam, continue a half mile, then turn west onto a gravel road. Anglers can also turn in at either end of the dam to fish from the shore. No facilities are at the reservoir, though people sometimes camp (the west end is best).

Information and Tours

The staff at the state park knows about Blanding and can tell you of other Anasazi ruins in the area. The **public library** is at Main and 300 South, (435) 678-2335; open Mon.–Sat.

Flights by **Scenic Aviation** fly over spectacular canyon country. Destinations include Canyonlands National Park, Lake Powell, and Monument Valley. Half-hour flights start at $40. Call (435) 678-3222 for more information; the airport is three miles south of town.

HOVENWEEP NATIONAL MONUMENT

The Anasazi Indians built many impressive masonry buildings during the early to mid-1200s, near the end of their 1,300-year stay in the area. A drought beginning in A.D. 1274 and lasting 25 years probably hastened their migration from this area. Several centuries of intensive farming, hunting, and woodcutting had already taken their toll on the land. Archaeologists believe the inhabitants retreated south in the late 1200s to sites in northwestern New Mexico and northeastern Arizona. The Ute Indian word Hovenweep means "Deserted Valley," an appropriate name for the lonely high-desert country left behind. The Anasazi at Hovenweep had much in common with the Mesa Verde culture, though the Dakota Sandstone here doesn't form large alcoves suitable for cliff-dweller villages. Ruins at Hovenweep remain essentially unexcavated, awaiting some future archaeologist's trowel.

The Anasazi farmers had a keen interest in the seasons because of their need to know the best time for planting crops. Astronomical stations (alignments of walls, doorways, and tiny openings) allowed the sun priests to determine the equinoxes and solstices with an accuracy of one or two days. This precision also may have been necessary for a complex ceremonial calendar. Astronomical stations at Hovenweep have been discovered at Hovenweep Castle and Unit-Type House of Square Tower Ruins and at Cajon Ruins.

Admission to the monument is $6 per vehicle, or $3 per person.

Visitor Center

Hovenweep National Monument protects six groups of villages left behind by the Anasazi.

Hovenweep National Monument

W.C. McRAE

The sites lie near the Colorado border southeast of Blanding. Square Tower Ruins Unit, where the visitors' center is located, has the greatest number of ruins and the most varied architecture. In fact, you can find all of the Hovenweep architectural styles here. The visitors' center has a few exhibits on the Anasazi and photos of local wildlife. A ranger will answer your questions, provide brochures and handouts about various aspects of the monument, and give directions for visiting the other ruin groups. Related books can be purchased. Hours at the visitors' center are 8 A.M.–4:30 P.M. year-round; (970) 749-0510; the ruins stay open all the time. There's also a small campground at the monument, $10 a site, no reservations. Mesa Verde National Park administers Hovenweep from Mesa Verde National Park, CO 81330, (970) 529-4465. Nearest places for groceries and fuel are Aneth (20 miles south in Utah; has a telephone), Hatch Trading Post (16 miles west in Utah; groceries only) and Ismay Trading Post (14 miles southeast in Colorado). Gnats can be very pesky in May and June; be sure to bring insect repellent.

One approach from U.S. 191 between Blanding and Bluff is to head east nine miles on UT 262, continue straight six miles on a small paved road to Hatch Trading Post, then follow signs 16 miles. A good way in from Bluff is to go east 21 miles on the paved road to Montezuma Creek and Aneth, then follow signs north 20 miles. A scenic 58-mile route through Montezuma Canyon begins five miles south of Monticello and follows unpaved roads to Hatch and on to Hovenweep; you can stop at the BLM's Three Turkey Ruin on the way. From Colorado, take a partly paved road west and north 41 miles from U.S. 666 (the turnoff is four miles south of Cortez).

Square Tower Ruins

This extensive group of Anasazi towers and dwellings lines the rim and slopes of Little Ruin Canyon, a short walk from the visitors' center. Obtain a trail guide booklet from the ranger station; the booklet's map shows the several loop trails. You can take easy walks of less than a half mile on the rim or combine all the trails for a loop of about two miles with only one up-and-down section in the canyon. The booklet has good descriptions of Anasazi life and architecture

Tower at Cajon Ruins. Archaeologists removed the small ring of stones at upper left (reconstructed earlier this century) because the ring wasn't authentic.

and of the plants growing along the trail. You'll see towers (D-shaped, square, oval, and round), cliff dwellings, surface dwellings, storehouses, kivas, and rock art. Take care not to disturb the fragile ruins. Keep an eye out for the prairie rattlesnake (a subspecies of the Western rattlesnake), which is active at night in summer and during the day in spring and autumn. Please stay on the trail—don't climb ruin walls or walk on rubble mounds.

Other Ruins

These are good to visit if you'd like to spend more time in the area. You'll need a map and directions from a ranger to find them, as they aren't signed. One group, the Goodman Point, near Cortez, Colorado, has relatively little to see except unexcavated mounds.

Holly Ruins group is noted for its Great House, Holly Tower, and Tilted Tower. Most of Tilted Tower fell away after the boulder on which it sat shifted. Great piles of rubble mark the sites of structures built on loose ground. Look for remnants of farming terraces in the canyon below the Great House. A hiking trail connects the campground at Square Tower Ruins with Holly Ruins; the route follows canyon bottoms and is about eight miles round-trip. Ask a ranger for a map and directions. Hikers could also continue to Horseshoe Ruins (one mile farther) and Hackberry Ruins (one-third mile beyond Horseshoe). All of these lie just across the Colorado border and about six miles (one-way) by road from the visitors' center.

Horseshoe Ruins and **Hackberry Ruins** are best reached by an easy trail (one mile round-trip) off the road to Holly Ruins. Horseshoe House, built in a horseshoe shape similar to Sun Temple at Mesa Verde, has exceptionally good masonry work. Archaeologists haven't determined the purpose of the structure. An alcove in the canyon below contains a spring and small shelter. A round tower nearby on the rim has a strategic view. Hackberry House has only one room still intact. Rubble piles and wall remnants abound in the area. The spring under an alcove here still has a good flow and supports lush growths of hackberry and cottonwood trees along with smaller plants.

Cutthroat Castle Ruins were remote even in Anasazi times. The ruins lie along an intermittent stream rather than at the head of a canyon like most other Hovenweep sites. Cutthroat Castle is a large multistory structure with both straight and curved walls. Three round towers stand nearby. Look for wall fragments and the circular depressions of kivas. High-clearance vehicles can go close to the ruins, about 11.5 miles (one-way) from the visitors' center. Visitors with cars can drive to a trailhead and then walk to the ruins (1.5 miles round-trip on foot).

Cajon Ruins are at the head of a little canyon on Cajon Mesa in the Navajo Reservation in Utah, about nine miles southwest of the visitors' center. The site has a commanding view across the San Juan Valley as far as Monument Valley. Buildings include a large multiroom structure, a round tower, and a tall square tower. An alcove just below has a spring and some rooms. Look for pictographs, petroglyphs, and grooves in rock (used for tool grinding). Farming terraces were located on the canyon's south side.

BLUFF

The 1880 Hole-in-the-Rock Expedition arrived here after an epic journey by wagon train from Escalante. Too tired to go any farther, they chose this section of the San Juan River Canyon in which to plant their fields and build new homes. They hoped that their presence here would secure the region for Mormon settlement and lead to conversion of the Indians. The settlers tried repeatedly to farm the fertile canyon soils, only to have the river wash their fields away. Most residents gave up and moved to more promising areas, but many of those who stayed prospered with large cattle herds.

Today Bluff is a sleepy community of about 300 inhabitants, nestled in a very striking physical location. Take the signed Bluff City Historic Loop to see pioneer houses along the back streets. Many visitors also drive to the cemetery atop a small hill to read inscriptions and enjoy views of the valley (turn in beside Turquoise RV Park, turn

the Twin Rocks tower above the town of Bluff

left just past the Decker Pioneer House, and follow the paved road to the top). Indians from the Navajo Reservation across the river occasionally have dance performances, horse races, rodeos, and other get-togethers in Bluff.

In the past few years, Bluff has become a rather unlikely mecca for recreationalists and escapees from urban congestion. The quality of lodging is better than almost any other town of this size in the state, and a growing number of outfitters make it easy to get out and enjoy the remarkable scenery hereabouts.

Floating the San Juan River

From the high San Juan Mountains in southern Colorado, this intriguing river winds its way into New Mexico, enters Utah near Four Corners, and twists through spectacular canyons before ending at Lake Powell. Sand waves spring up during flooding, usually in May and June. The waves can pop up out of flat water to heights of three feet and occasionally as much as seven or eight feet! Swift currents on the sandy bottom cause these harmless waves, which can migrate up or downstream before disappearing.

Below the town of Bluff, the muddy river picks up speed and dives deep within its canyon walls. Most boaters put in at Sand Island Campground near Bluff and take out at the town of Mexican Hat, 30 river miles downstream. This trip combines ancient Native American ruins, rock art, and a trip through Monument Upwarp and the Upper Canyon, with fast water for thrills (class III rapids) and weirdly buckled geology to ponder. Longer trips continue on through the famous Goosenecks, the "entrenched meanders" carved thousands of feet below the desert surface, and through more class III rapids on the way to Clay Hills Crossing or Paiute Farms (not always accessible) on Lake Powell. Allow at least four days for the full trip, though more time will allow exploration of side canyons and visits to Anasazi sites. Rafts, kayaks, and canoes can be used. The season now usually lasts all year, due to the Navajo Reservoir upstream.

Many commercial river-running companies offer San Juan trips. If you go on your own, you should have river-running experience or be with someone who has. Private groups need to obtain permits from the BLM San Juan Resource Area office well in advance: P.O. Box 7, Monticello, UT 84535,

(435) 587-2141. The book *San Juan Canyons, A River Runner's Guide,* by Don Baars and Gene Stevenson, has a river log with detailed maps, practical advice, and background. Some people also like to run the river between Montezuma Creek and Sand Island, a leisurely trip of 20 river miles. The solitude often makes up for the lack of scenery. It's easy to get a river permit for this section because no use limits or fees apply.

If you're looking for a multi-day trip on the San Juan, contact some of the larger Moab-based outfitters, who often offer a San Juan trip when interest allows. Or contact local **Wild Rivers Expeditions,** P.O. Box 118, Bluff, UT 84512, (435) 672-2244 or (800) 422-7654 out of state, www.riversandruins.com, which offers both day and multi-day trips out of Bluff; trips run daily in summer and only a day's notice is usually needed to join a float. Day excursions to Mexican Hat cost $94 (motors may be used if water level is low). The office is on the main highway through town.

Accommodations

$50–75: New and attractive, the **Desert Rose Inn,** 701 W. Main St., (435) 672-2303 or (888) 475-7673, www.desertroseinn.com, is one of the nicest lodgings in all of southern Utah. The large, lodgelike log structure has two-story wrap-around porches and rooms furnished with pine furniture, quilts, and Southwestern art. At the edge of the property are a number of handsome one-bedroom log cabins. Definitely a class act.

The other great place to stay is **Recapture Lodge,** P.O. Box 309, Bluff, UT 84512, (435) 672-2281. For many years the heart and soul of Bluff, the lodge is operated by long-time outfitters and the lodge has an easy nonchalance that is immediately welcoming. Besides rooms and kitchenettes, Recapture Lodge has a swimming pool, hot tub, Laundromat, tours, and llama pack trips. Groups can reserve rooms in the 1898 Decker Pioneer House. The owners know of Indian ruins and scenic places in the backcountry. They offer free slide shows in the evenings during the season and can suggest places to go. Or you can take one of their organized full-day naturalist tours to Monument Valley, Comb Ridge, Recapture Pocket, and other locations. Guided camping trips can also be arranged in the canyon country of southeastern

Utah. They also can provide a shuttle service for rafting trips. **Kokopelli Inn Motel,** (435) 672-2322 or (800) 541-8854, just next door, is a pleasant place to stay, though it pales in comparison to Bluff's unique lodges.

Campgrounds: Near the center of Bluff, **Cadillac Ranch RV Park,** (435) 672-2262 or (800) 538-6195, has RV hook-ups ($16) and tenting sites ($12). **Cottonwood RV Park,** on the west end of Bluff, (435) 672-2287, has both tent ($14) and RV ($16-20) sites. **Sand Island Recreation Area** is a primitive camping area along the San Juan River three miles south of town; large cottonwood trees shade this pretty spot. No drinking water or charge; tenters need to watch for thorns in the grass. River runners often put in at the campground. You can see a panel of pictographs along the cliff one-third mile downstream from the camping area along a gravel road.

Food, Shopping, and Information

Cow Canyon Trading Post, (435) 672-2208, is a café that serves homemade dinners in an old trading post on the northeast edge of town; open Thurs.–Mon. Apr.–Oct. The trading post is open all year with Indian crafts. **Twin Rocks Trading Post,** also on the Bluff City Historic Loop, (435) 672-2341, has a café and a selection of high-quality Indian crafts, much of it produced locally by Navajo Indians. The **post office** is on the main highway. A small **library/travel information center,** open irregular hours, sits on the Historic Loop behind the post office.

VICINITY OF BLUFF

The canyon country of Cedar Mesa, Comb Ridge, and other nearby areas has beautiful scenery, Anasazi ruins, and abundant wildlife. Recapture Pocket has unusual rock formations (it's *west* of Recapture Creek—not east, as some maps show). Local information should be obtained for backcountry trips.

St. Christopher's Episcopal Mission

Father Harold Lieber came to the Bluff area in 1943 and established this mission for the Navajo Indians. Relying on donations and volunteer help, he built a school, chapel, and other build-

ings. Visitors are welcome to the pleasant tree-shaded grounds; go east two miles on the paved road from the northeast edge of Bluff.

San Juan Footbridge and 14-Window Ruin

An easy walk of about two miles round-trip crosses a suspension bridge over the San Juan River and follows roads to this Anasazi cliff dwelling. From Bluff, drive east two miles on the paved road to St. Christopher's Episcopal Mission, continue straight 1.3 miles, and turn right a half mile on a dirt road (it may not be signed; keep right at a fork 0.1 mile in) to the footbridge. Walk across the bridge, follow dirt roads winding southeast about a half mile to a road running beneath the cliffs, turn right (west) a half mile, and look for the ruins in an alcove on the left. You can scramble up for a closer look, but don't enter the rooms—the ruins can easily be damaged. The walk passes farm lands on the Navajo Reservation; please resist the temptation to take shortcuts across the fields.

WEST OF BLANDING TO NATURAL BRIDGES NATIONAL MONUMENT

Utah 95 turns west from U.S. 191 four miles south of Blanding and crosses Comb Ridge, Cedar Mesa, and many canyons. Follow UT 95 to Natural Bridges National Monument or continue on to Hite Marina at Lake Powell. UT 261 turns south along Cedar Mesa before twisting down the hairpin curves of the Moki Dugway north of Mexican Hat (this section of the road is not paved). Utah 276 turns off for Halls Crossing Marina and the ferry across Lake Powell to Bullfrog Marina. Fill up with gas before venturing out on UT 95; you won't find any gas stations on the highway until Hanksville, which is 122 miles away. Hite and the other Lake Powell marinas do have gas and supplies, however.

Cedar Mesa and its canyons have an exceptionally large number of prehistoric Anasazi Indian sites. Several groups of ruins lie just off the highway. Hikers will discover many more. If you would like to explore the Cedar Mesa area, be sure to drop in at the **Kane Gulch Ranger Station,** located four miles south on UT 261 from UT 95. Bureau of Land Management staff issues the permits required to explore the Cedar Mesa backcountry at $8 per person for overnight stays in

Grand Gulch, Fish Creek Canyon, and Owl Creek Canyon. The number of people permitted to camp at a given time is limited, so you may wish to call ahead; (435) 587-1532. BLM people will also tell you about archaeological sites and their values, current hiking conditions, and locations of water. Day hikers will pay a $2 fee to hike certain sections of the monument. Check out the website at www.blm.gov/utah/monticello for current information.

Butler Wash Ruins

Well-preserved pueblo ruins left by the Anasazi lie tucked under an overhang across the wash 11 miles west on UT 95 (between Mileposts 111 and 112) from U.S. 191. At the trailhead on the north side of the highway, follow cairns a half mile through juniper and piñon pine woodlands and across slickrock to the overlook.

Comb Ridge

Geologic forces have squeezed up the earth's crust in a long ridge running 80 miles south from the Abajo Peaks into Arizona. Sheer cliff faces plunge 800 feet into Comb Wash on the west side. Engineering the highway down these cliffs took considerable effort. A parking area near the top of the grade offers expansive panoramas across Comb Wash. The overlook is between Mileposts 108 and 109, 2.5 miles west of Butler Wash Ruins. Scenic **jeep roads** between UT 95 and U.S. 163 follow the west side of Comb Ridge through Comb Wash and the east side of Comb Ridge through Butler Wash. Another jeep road traces the route of the 1880 Mormon Hole-in-the-Rock Expedition between UT 261 on Cedar Mesa and Comb Wash (a high-clearance vehicle is needed to go down, a four-wheel drive to go up).

In 1923, the West's last shoot-out between Indians and settlers took place in the Comb Ridge area. Conflicts between Ute Indians and ranchers had simmered for 57 years, with Anglos taking the Indians' land and the Utes taking the Anglos' livestock. A group of renegade Utes under Chief Posey fled to this rugged area, knowing that the Blanding posse would have great difficulty in finding the few trails that existed then. The posse, however, caught up with the Indians, killing one of them. The disheartened Utes then surrendered. Old Chief Posey, who had been shot earlier in Blanding, evaded capture only to die of his wounds about a week later, alone in a cave. The event drew national attention to the plight of the tribe, which was later given the White Mesa Indian Reservation 12 miles south of Blanding.

Arch Canyon

This tributary canyon of Comb Wash has spectacular scenery and many Indian ruins. Much of the canyon can be seen on a day hike, but 2–3 days are needed to explore the upper reaches. The main streambeds usually have water (purify before drinking). To reach the trailhead, turn north 2.5 miles on a dirt road in Comb Wash (between Mileposts 107 and 108 of UT 95), go past a house and water tank, then park in a grove of cottonwood trees before a stream ford. This is also a good place to camp. The mouth of Arch Canyon lies just to the northwest (it's easy to miss!). Sign in at the register here. Look for an Indian ruin just up Arch Canyon on the right. More ruins lie tucked under alcoves farther upcanyon.

From the trailhead (elev. 5,200 feet), the canyon extends about 13 miles upstream into Elk Ridge and has several tributary canyons worth exploring. The first one is 2.5 miles up on the right; it goes in 1.5 miles to a ruin and a spring. A second canyon on the right, six miles up the main canyon, also has a ruin and springs 1.5 miles up. You'll reach Texas Canyon on the left 7.5 miles up (elev. 5,600 feet) in a grove of ponderosa pines; look across Arch Canyon from this junction to see a large arch. Texas Canyon goes back about five miles and has one fork. Continuing up Arch Canyon, you'll see a second arch on the right, then Butts Canyon on the right nine miles from the trailhead. From this point, Arch and Butts Canyons both extend about four miles to their heads (elev. 7,500 feet). Spring and autumn are the best times for hiking, though the upper reaches can be fine in summer, too. In late spring and early summer, arm yourself with long pants and insect repellent against the deer flies. Most of the route follows the canyon bottoms; sometimes off-road vehicles travel the lower few miles. See the $7^{1}/_{2}$-minute topos, the 1:100,000 Blanding map, or Trails Illustrated's Grand Gulch Plateau map. The BLM offices at Kane Gulch or Monticello can advise on hiking.

Arch Canyon Overlook

A road and short trail to the rim of Arch Canyon provide a beautiful view into the depths. Turn north four miles on Texas Flat Road (County 263) from UT 95 between Mileposts 102 and 103, park just before the road begins a steep climb, and walk east on an old jeep road about a quarter mile to the rim. This is a fine place for a picnic, although it has no facilities or guardrails. Texas Flat Road is dirt but okay when dry for cars with good clearance. Trucks can continue up the steep hill to other viewpoints of Arch and Texas Canyons.

Mule Canyon Ruin

Archaeologists have excavated and stabilized this Anasazi village on the gentle slope of Mule Canyon's South Fork. A stone kiva, circular tower, and 12-room structure can be seen, all originally connected by tunnels. Cave Towers, two miles to the southeast, would have been visible from the top of the tower here. Signs describe the ruin and periods of Anasazi development. Turn north 0.3 mile on a paved road from UT 95 between Mileposts 101 and 102. Hikers can explore other Indian ruins in North and South Forks of Mule Canyon; check with the Kane Gulch Ranger Station for advice and directions. You might see pieces of pottery and other artifacts in this area. Please leave *every* piece in place so that future visitors can enjoy the discovery, too. Federal laws also prohibit removal of artifacts.

NATURAL BRIDGES NATIONAL MONUMENT

Streams in White Canyon and its tributaries cut deep canyons, then formed three impressive bridges. Silt-laden floodwaters sculpted the bridges by gouging tunnels between closely spaced loops in the meandering canyons. You can distinguish a natural bridge from an arch because the bridge spans a streambed and was initially carved out of the rock by flowing water. In the monument, these bridges illustrate three different stages of development, from the massive, newly formed Kachina Bridge to the middle-aged Sipapu Bridge, to the delicate and fragile span of Owachomo. All three natural bridges will continue to widen and eventually collapse

under their own weight. A nine-mile scenic drive has overlooks of the picturesque bridges, Anasazi ruins, and the twisting canyons. You can follow short trails down from the rim to the base of each bridge or hike through all three bridges on an 8.6-mile trail loop. Paved highways allow easy access to the monument: from Blanding, drive 42 miles west on UT 95; from Hite Marina, drive 50 miles southeast on UT 95; from Halls Crossing Marina, drive 59 miles northeast on UT 276; from Mexican Hat, drive 44 miles north via UT 261 (there's a three-mile section of steep unpaved switchbacks). The National Park Service has a visitors' center and a small campground.

History

Ruins, artifacts, and rock art indicate a long Indian occupation by tribes ranging from archaic groups to the Anasazi. Many fine cliff dwellings built by the Anasazi still stand. In 1883, prospector Cass Hite passed on tales of the huge stone bridges that he had discovered on a trip up White Canyon. Adventurous travelers, including a 1904 *National Geographic* magazine expedition, visited this isolated region to marvel at the bridges. The public's desire for their protection led President Theodore Roosevelt to proclaim the area a national monument in 1908. Federal administrators then changed the original bridge names from Edwin, Augusta, and Caroline to the Hopi names used today. Although the Hopi never lived here, the Anasazi of White Canyon very likely have descendants in the modern Hopi villages in Arizona.

Visitor Center

From the signed junction on UT 95, drive in 4.5 miles on UT 275 to the visitors' center (elev. 6,505 feet). Monument Valley Overlook, two miles in, has a panorama south across a vast expanse of piñon pine and juniper trees to Monument Valley and distant mountains. A slide show in the visitors' center illustrates how geologic forces and erosion created the canyons and natural bridges. Exhibits introduce the Indians who once lived here, as well as the area's geology, wildlife, and plants. Outside in front, labels identify common plants of the monument. Rangers will answer your questions about the monument and surrounding area. If asked, staff will provide details on locations of ruins and rock-art sites. You can purchase regional books, topo and geologic maps, postcards, slides, and film. Checklists of birds, other wildlife, and plants are available, too. Hours at the visitors' center are daily 8 A.M.–5 P.M. March 1–May 1 and October 1–October 31, 8 A.M.–6 P.M. May 1–October 1, and 9 A.M.–4:30 P.M. the rest of the year; closed holidays Oct–Apr. Admission is $6 per vehicle, or $3 per person or bicyclist. The Bridge View Drive is always open during daylight hours except after heavy snowstorms. A winter visit can be very enjoyable; ice or mud often close the steep Sipapu and Kachina Trails, but the short trail to Owachomo Bridge usually stays open. Pets aren't allowed on the trails or in the backcountry at any time. Address is P.O. Box 1, Natural Bridges, Lake Powell, UT 84533, (435) 692-1234. The nearest accommodations and café are at Fry Canyon, 26 miles northwest of the visitors' center on UT 95; the closest gas is 40 miles east near Blanding or 50 west miles at Hite.

Photovoltaic Array
A large solar electric-power station sits across the road from the visitors' center. This demonstration system, the largest in the world when constructed in 1980, has a quarter-million solar cells spread over nearly an acre and produces up to 100 kilowatts. Batteries, located elsewhere, store a two-day supply of power. The monument lies far from the nearest power lines, so the solar cells provide an alternative to continuous running of diesel-powered generators.

Natural Bridges Campground
Drive 0.3 mile past the visitors' center and turn right into the campground, set in a forest of piñon pine and juniper. Sites stay open all year; $10. Obtain water from a faucet in front of the visitors' center. Rangers give talks several evenings each week during the summer season. The campground is often full, but there is a designated overflow area near the intersection of UT 95 and UT 261. RVs or trailers more than 21 feet long will also have to use this parking area.

Bridge View Drive
The nine-mile drive begins its one-way loop just past the campground. You can stop for lunch at a picnic area. Allow about 1.5 hours for a quick trip around. To make all the stops and do a bit of leisurely hiking will take most of a day. The

Owachomo Bridge (from Armstrong Canyon)

crossbedded sandstone of the bridges and canyons is the 265-million-year-old Cedar Mesa Formation.

Sipapu Bridge viewpoint is two miles from the visitors' center. The Hopi name refers to the gateway from which their ancestors entered this world from another world below. Sipapu Bridge has reached its mature or middle-aged stage of development. The bridge is the largest in the monument and has a span of 268 feet and a height of 220 feet. Many people think Sipapu the most magnificent of the bridges. Another view and a trail to the base of Sipapu are 0.8 mile farther. The viewpoint is about halfway down on an easy trail; allow a half hour. A steeper and rougher trail branches off the viewpoint trail and winds down to the bottom of White Canyon, probably the best place to fully appreciate the bridge's size. Total round-trip distance is 1.2 miles with an elevation change of 600 feet.

Horse Collar Ruin, built by the Anasazi, looks as though it has been abandoned only a few decades, not 800 years. At 3.1 miles from the visitors' center, a short trail leads to an overlook. The name comes from the shape of the doorway openings in two storage rooms. Hikers walking in the canyon between Sipapu and Kachina Bridges can scramble up a steep rock slope to the site. Like all ancient ruins, these are very fragile and must not be touched or entered. Only with such care will future generations of visitors be able to admire the well-preserved structures. Other groups of Anasazi dwellings can be seen in or near the monument too; ask a ranger for directions.

Kachina Bridge viewpoint and trailhead are 5.1 miles from the visitors' center. The massive bridge has a span of 204 feet and a height of 210 feet. A trail, 1.5 miles round-trip, leads to the canyon bottom next to the bridge; elevation change is 650 feet. Look for pictographs near the base of the trail. Some of the figures resemble Hopi kachinas (spirits) and inspired the bridge's name. Armstrong Canyon joins White Canyon just downstream from the bridge; floods in each canyon abraded opposite sides of the rock fin that later became Kachina Bridge.

Owachomo Bridge viewpoint and trailhead are 7.1 miles from the visitors' center. An easy walk leads to Owachomo's base—a half-mile round-trip with an elevation change of 180 feet. Graceful Owachomo spans 180 feet and is 106 feet high. Erosive forces have worn the venerable bridge to a thickness of only nine feet. Unlike the other two bridges, Owachomo spans a smaller tributary stream instead of a major canyon. Two streams played a role in the bridge's formation. Floods coming down the larger Armstrong Canyon surged against a sandstone fin on one side while floods in a small side canyon wore away the rock on the other side. Eventually a hole formed, and waters flowing down the side canyon took the shorter route through the bridge. The name Owachomo means "flat-rock mound" in the Hopi language; a large rock outcrop nearby inspired the name. Before construction of the present road, a trail winding down the opposite side of Armstrong Canyon provided the only access for monument visitors. The trail, little used now, connects with UT 95.

Hiking

A canyon hike through all three bridges can be the highlight of a visit to the monument. Unmaintained trails make an 8.6-mile loop in White and Armstrong Canyons and cross a wooded plateau. The trip is easier if you start from Sipapu and come out the relatively gentle grades at Owachomo. Most people take 5–6 hours for this moderately difficult hike. You can save 2.5 miles by arranging a car shuttle between Sipapu and Owachomo Trailheads. Another option is to go in or out on the Kachina Bridge Trail midway, cutting the hiking distance about in half. On nearing Owachomo Bridge from below, a small sign points out the trail that bypasses a deep pool. The canyons remain in their wild state; you'll need some hiking experience, water, proper footwear, compass, and map (the handout available at the visitors' center is adequate). The USGS 7½-minute topo maps also cover this area. When hiking in the canyons, keep an eye out for natural arches and Indian writings. Please don't step on midget faded rattlesnakes or other living entities (such as the fragile cryptobiotic soil). Be aware of flash-flood dangers, especially if you see big clouds billowing in the sky in an upstream direction. You don't need a hiking permit, though it's a good idea to talk beforehand with a ranger to find out current conditions. Overnight camping within the monument is permitted only in the campground. Backpackers, however, can go up or down the canyons and camp outside the monument boundaries. Just be careful to choose high ground in case a flood comes rumbling through! Note that vehicles can't be parked overnight on the loop drive.

VICINITY OF NATURAL BRIDGES NATIONAL MONUMENT

Fry Canyon Lodge

The store here originally served uranium mining camps during the 1950s. Today this venerable café and motel, (435) 259-5334, www.frycanyon.com, offer the only services on UT 95 between Blanding and Hite Marina. Rooms cost $89 (double). In winter, the café may be closed, but accommodations are usually still available. Two Anasazi ruins can be viewed nearby; a road goes to an overlook of one ruin and a short trail goes to the other. Ask for directions. Fry Canyon is 19 miles northwest of the Natural Bridges National Monument turnoff and 24 miles southeast of the Hite Marina turnoff.

Dark Canyon

This magnificent canyon system lies about 15 air miles north of Natural Bridges National Monument. Dark Canyon, with its many tributaries, begins in the high country of Elk Ridge and extends west to Lake Powell in lower Cataract Canyon. Steep cliffs and the isolated location have protected the relatively pristine environment. The upper canyons tend to be wide with open areas and groves of Douglas fir and ponderosa pine. Creeks dry up after spring snowmelt, leaving only widely scattered springs as water sources for most of the year. Farther downstream, the canyon walls close in and the desert trees of piñon pine, juniper, and cottonwood take over. At its lower end, Dark Canyon has a year-round stream and deep plunge pools; cliffs tower more than 1,400 feet above the canyon floor. Springs and running water attract wildlife, including bighorn sheep, black bear, deer, mountain lion, coyote, bobcat, ringtail cat, raccoon, fox, and spotted skunk.

Experienced hikers enjoy the solitude, wildlife, Anasazi ruins, and varied canyon scenery. Although it's possible to visit Dark Canyon on a day hike, you'll need several days to get a feel for this area. To explore the entire canyon and its major tributaries would take weeks! Hiking through the canyons is mostly easy, though strenuous scrambles are needed to bypass a few pour-offs and other obstacles. Elevations of Dark Canyon range from 8,200 feet at its upper end to 3,700 feet at Lake Powell. Hikers must be extra cautious and self-sufficient, because outside help can be days away. Check with people at the BLM or U.S. Forest Service offices before a trip. Horses can do the trails in the upper (National Forest) section but not in the constricted lower canyon. Maps available are the 7¹/₂-minute topos, the 1:100,000 Hite Crossing and Blanding maps, and Trails Illustrated's map of the Abajos and Dark Canyon. Or look for the *Dark Canyon Trail Guide* published by Canyonlands Natural History Association.

The upper half of the canyon system lies within Dark Canyon Wilderness, administered by the Manti-La Sal National Forest, P.O. Box 820, Monticello, UT 84535, (435) 587-2041. The Monticello office has information sheets on the 10 access trails to Dark Canyon and can advise on road conditions to the trailheads. A variety of loop hikes can be made in the tributary canyons. Woodenshoe Canyon is used by more than 50 percent of visitors to the area. Snow and mud usually block roads, all of which are unpaved, until mid-May or early June. When the roads are closed, hikers sometimes drive to Bears Ears Pass and hike to their trailhead. Spring through autumn are good hiking seasons in the higher country, though snowmelt sometimes causes spring flooding.

The lower half of Dark Canyon, currently designated a primitive area, lies mostly within BLM land; the area is a candidate for wilderness status. Trail notes describing hiking conditions, water sources, trailheads, and wilderness etiquette are available from the BLM offices at Kane Gulch Ranger Station (trailhead for Grand Gulch) or Monticello (435 N. Main, Monticello, UT 84535, 435-587-1500). Obtain a $2 day trip, $8 overnight permit from the BLM before visiting its lands.

The **Sundance Trail** is the most popular entry to lower Dark Canyon. The start of the trail can be reached on dirt roads that branch off UT 95 southeast of the Hite Marina turnoff; this approach can be used year-round in dry weather. Cairns mark the trail, which drops 1,200 feet in less than one mile on a steep talus slope. Boaters can reach the lower end of Dark Canyon in Glen Canyon National Recreation Area by going 14 miles up Lake Powell from Hite Marina. The lower canyon can be hiked year-round, with spring and autumn the best choices.

Grand Gulch Primitive Area

Within this twisting canyon system lies some of the most captivating scenery and largest concentrations of Anasazi ruins in all of southeastern Utah. The main canyon begins only about six miles southeast of Natural Bridges National Monument. From an elevation of 6,400 feet, Grand Gulch cuts deeply into Cedar Mesa on a tortuous path southwest to the San Juan River, dropping 2,700 feet in about 53 miles. Sheer cliffs, alcoves, pinnacles, Anasazi cliff dwellings, rock-art sites, arches, and a few natural bridges line Grand Gulch and its many tributaries. Canyon depths reach 600 feet. Nearly all of Grand Gulch has been cut out of Cedar Mesa Sandstone. The lower 1.5 miles of canyon also reveal exposures of the older Cutler Formation (Halgaito Shale Member) and the Honaker Trail Formation. Wildlife to look for include mule deer, mountain lion, black bear, coyote, bobcat, fox, ringtail cat, spotted skunk, cottontail, white-tailed antelope squirrel, white-throated wood rat, Ord kangaroo rat, piñon mouse, Great Basin gopher snake, Hopi rattlesnake, and midget faded rattlesnake. Some birds in the area are red-tailed hawk, great horned owl, peregrine falcon, mourning dove, titmouse, rock wren, and piñon jay. Vegetation includes piñon pine, juniper, cottonwood, Gambel oak, singleleaf ash, willow, sagebrush, blackbrush, rabbitbrush, prickly pear cactus, and flowering annuals.

The Anasazi left behind hundreds of dwellings and thousands of pictographs and petroglyphs. They lived in Grand Gulch from A.D. 200–400 (Basketmaker II), 650–725 (late Basketmaker III), and 1060–1270 (Pueblo II–III); droughts may have caused all three departures. Mormon pioneers of the Hole-in-the-Rock Expedition named the canyon in 1880, but the exhausted group was in no mood to enjoy the scenery.

Kane Gulch and Bullet Canyon provide access to the upper end of Grand Gulch from the east side. A popular loop hike using these canyons is 23 miles long (3–4 days); you'll need a 7.5-mile car shuttle or you can hitch. Ask at the ranger station if a shuttle service is available. Collins Canyon, reached from Collins Spring Trailhead, leads into lower Grand Gulch from the west side. Hiking distance between Kane Gulch and Collins Spring Trailheads is 38 miles one-way (5–7 days). A car shuttle of about 29 miles (including eight miles of dirt road) is needed. River runners can travel up the mouth from the San Juan River. The San Juan is 53 miles from Kane Gulch Trailhead and 19 miles from Collins Spring Trailhead. The lower third of Grand Gulch (below Collins Canyon) lacks the abundant Anasazi sites found in the middle and upper reaches and has few water sources.

The book *Wind in the Rock,* by Ann Zwinger, presents a personal account of the wonders of travel in Grand Gulch and nearby canyons. Spring and autumn are the choice times for hiking; it is also possible in summer, though you'll want to sit out the midday heat. Winter snow makes some of the slickrock sections hazardous. Be sure to visit the BLM's Kane Gulch Ranger Station or

mountain lion (Felis concolor)

ANNE LONG LARSEN

Monticello office for a permit and information. You'll need to have a day-use ($2) or overnight camping permit ($8) to enter the area. The BLM map of Grand Gulch Primitive Area shows the topography, mileages for each section of canyon, and major points of interest; it's good for both planning a trip and using while hiking. Other maps include the 7½-minute, 1:100,000 metric, and Trails Illustrated's Grand Gulch Plateau topos. Springs provide water in most parts of Grand Gulch but aren't always reliable, especially in summer; the BLM staff can give you an idea of what to expect. "Innocent vandalism" caused by visitors touching and climbing on the ruins and middens has caused serious damage. BLM staff will offer advice and literature on how to safely visit the ancient sites. Pot hunting has been another problem; report any suspicious behavior to the BLM. Grand Gulch receives heavy use, so respecting the ruins and camping without leaving any traces are extra important.

Kane Gulch Ranger Station

The BLM provides permits, archaeological information, current hiking conditions, literature, and sales of maps and books at this bare-bones facility. (Try to get maps in advance as rangers are sometimes out on patrol.) The station is at Kane Gulch Trailhead, four miles south on UT 261 from UT 95; open daily, dependably from 8 A.M.–noon early Mar.–late Nov. No telephone, water, or trash collection is available. Normally this is the best place for firsthand information.

You can also visit the BLM office at 435 N. Main in Monticello (P.O. Box 7, Monticello, UT 84535), (435) 587-1500. Open year-round Mon.–Fri. 7:45 A.M.–4:30 P.M. Everyone visiting the Cedar Mesa backcountry should drop in for the required permit and to get the latest information. Permits run $5 per person for overnight camping and are limited to 12 persons. Note that groups of eight or more people with pack animals need to obtain permits at least three weeks beforehand from the ranger station or office. Help protect fragile desert soils by keeping all vehicles— including mountain bikes—on established roads. Campfires are not permitted in the canyons.

Fish Creek and Owl Creek Loop Hike

Varied canyon scenery, year-round pools, Anasazi ruins, and a magnificent natural arch make this an excellent hike. Fish Creek and its tributary Owl Creek lie east of Grand Gulch on the other side of UT 261. A 1.5-mile trail atop Cedar Mesa connects upper arms of the two creeks to make a 15.5-mile loop. From the trailhead (elev. 6,160 feet), you'll descend 1,400 feet to the junction of the two creeks. Opinions differ as to which direction to begin the loop, but either way is fine. Owl Creek might be the better choice for a day hike because it's closer to the trailhead and has the added attractions of easily accessible ruins just a half mile away and Nevill's Arch 3.5 miles farther (one-way). Contact the Kane Gulch or Monticello BLM offices for trail notes and current trail and water conditions. You'll also need to buy permits, $2 for day trips, $8 for overnight trips. Maps are essential for navigation, because it's easy to get off the route in some places. The BLM trail notes have a topo map. Camping places are easy to locate; just avoid washes. You can always find at least intermittent water in the upper parts of both creeks.

The canyons have been carved in Cedar Mesa Sandstone, which forms many overhangs where the Anasazi Indians built cliff dwellings. Unfortunately, nearly all ruins sit high in the cliffs and can be hard to spot from the canyon bottoms (canyon depths average 500 feet). Binoculars come in handy for seeing the ruins, some of which are marked on the topo maps. Climbing equipment may not be used to reach the ruins.

The turnoff for the trailhead is between Mileposts 27 and 28 of UT 261, one mile south of Kane Gulch Ranger Station. Head east 5.2 miles on San Juan County 253, passable by cars when dry, to a parking area at the site of an old drill hole. A sign points the way north 1.5 miles to Fish Creek and southeast a quarter mile to Owl Creek. Cairns show the way into the canyons, then you just follow the creekbeds. The route into Fish Creek goes north 1.5 miles across the mesa from the trailhead (watch closely for cairns—it's easy to miss the trail where it climbs out of a wash), makes a steep descent into an arm of Fish Creek, and follows Fish Creek downstream to the confluence with Owl Creek; total distance from the trailhead to this point is nine miles one-way. Turn right 2.5 miles up Owl Creek, normally dry in this section, to Nevill's Arch. It's possible to rock-scramble up the slope to the window of the arch, where you'll enjoy fine views of the canyons and beyond. Owl Creek has water and becomes prettier and prettier as you head upstream. On the four miles from the arch to the trailhead, you'll need to circumvent three pour-offs—the first and second by going around to the right, the third by going to the left (look for the cairned routes). The first and second pour-offs have small waterfalls and idyllic pools. Above the third pour-off, you'll pass a well-preserved group of Anasazi ruins on the left. From here there's only a short but steep scramble to the rim, then a quarter mile across slickrock back to the trailhead.

Slickhorn Canyon

Adventurous hikers enjoy the Indian ruins and impressive scenery in this rugged canyon south of Grand Gulch. Canyon depths along Slickhorn's 12-mile length range from about 300 feet in the northern reaches to 800 feet near the confluence with the San Juan River. Boulders, talus slopes, and pour-offs in the streambed hamper travel and discourage casual visitors. Allow about four days to explore Slickhorn Canyon and some of its tributaries. A more ambitious trip is to go down Slickhorn to the San Juan River, hike downstream along a high, narrow ledge to the mouth of Grand Gulch, then travel up to one of the Grand Gulch trailheads in a week or more of hiking. The BLM offices at Kane Gulch and Monticello have information sheets, trailhead information, and a map; overnight permits are $8. The BLM's Grand Gulch hiking map covers this area. Several trailheads can be reached by turning west on an unpaved road from UT 261 opposite the signed Cigarette Springs Road, 9.4 miles south of the Kane Gulch Ranger Station.

John's Canyon

This varied canyon lies southeast of Grand Gulch and Slickhorn Canyons. A fingerlike network of deep narrow canyons in the upper drainages contrasts with a broad alluvial bottom downstream that's up to a mile wide. The main canyon is about 13 miles long and empties into the San Juan River. Canyon depths average about 1,000 feet. Experienced hikers will find the going relatively easy, as there are only a few boulder falls and small pour-offs in the upper canyons. High pour-offs in the lower canyon, however, effectively block access to the San Juan River. A map and information sheet available from the BLM offices have trailhead and spring information and a brief description of hiking in the canyon. Cliffs and overhangs on the rim in the north restrict access to only a few points; the BLM map shows one entry point, reached by a short dirt road off UT 261. In the south, a jeep road branches off UT 316 (the road to Goosenecks State Park), follows the rim of the San Juan River west, and then turns up into middle John's Canyon.

MEXICAN HAT

Spectacular geology surrounds this tiny community perched on the north bank of the San Juan River. Folded layers of red and gray rock stand out dramatically. Alhambra Rock, a jagged remnant of a volcano, marks the southern approach to Mexican Hat. Another rock, which looks just like an upside-down sombrero, gave Mexican Hat its name; you'll see this formation two miles north of town. The land has never proved good for much except its scenery; farmers and ranchers thought it next to worthless. Stories of gold in the San Juan River brought a frenzy of prospecting in 1892–93, but the mining proved mostly a bust. Oil, first struck by drillers in 1908, has brought mostly modest profits. The uranium mill across the river at Halchita gave a boost to the economy from 1956 until it closed in 1965. Mexican Hat now serves as a modest

trade and tourism center. Monument Valley, Valley of the Gods Scenic Drive, Goosenecks State Park, and Grand Gulch Primitive Area lie only short drives away. The shore near town can be a busy place in summer as river runners on the San Juan put in, take out, or just stop for ice and beer.

Accommodations

$50–75: The **San Juan Inn & Trading Post,** at a dramatic location above the river just west of town, (435) 683-2220 or (800) 447-2022, offers rooms, Indian trade goods, and a restaurant, the **Olde Bridge Bar and Grill,** (435) 683-2220, serving American, Mexican, and Navajo food daily for breakfast, lunch, and dinner. **Canyonlands Motel,** (435) 683-2230, offers recently remodeled rooms; closed in winter. **Mexican Hat Lodge,** (435) 683-2222, offers rooms, a pool, and a restaurant (American food daily for lunch and dinner). **Burch's Motel,** (435) 683-2221, has motel rooms and a café with American, Mexican, and Navajo food (open daily for breakfast, lunch, and dinner), Indian crafts, groceries, and car shuttles.

Campgrounds: In addition to rooms, **Burch's Motel,** above, has tent camping for $12, and RV sites for $18 with hookups. **Valle's Trading Post and RV Park,** (435) 683-2226, open all year, has tent and RV sites with hookups for $12. The trading post offers Indian crafts, groceries, showers, vehicle storage, and car shuttles. **Burch's Cattle Co.** offers horseback riding, (435) 683-2221.

VICINITY OF MEXICAN HAT

Valley of the Gods

Great sandstone monoliths, delicate spires, and long rock fins rise from the broad valley. This strange redrock landscape resembles better-known Monument Valley but on a smaller scale. A 17-mile dirt road winds through the spectacular scenery. Cars can usually travel the road at low speeds if the weather is dry (washes are crossed). Allow 1–1.5 hours for the drive. The east end of the road connects with U.S. 163 at Milepost 29 (7.5 miles northeast of Mexican Hat or 15 miles southwest of Bluff); the west end connects with UT 261 just below the Moki Dugway switchbacks (four miles north of Mexican Hat on U.S. 163, then 6.6 miles northwest on UT 261).

Goosenecks State Park

The San Juan River winds through a series of incredibly tight bends 1,000 feet below. So closely spaced are the bends that the river takes six miles to cover an air distance of only 1.5 miles! The bends and exposed rock layers form exquisitely graceful curves. Geologists know the site as a classic example of entrenched meanders, caused by gradual uplift of a formerly level plain. Signs at the overlook explain the geologic history and identify the rock formations. Goosenecks State Park is an undeveloped area with a few tables and vault toilets the only facilities. Camping is available; no water or charge. From the junction of U.S. 163 and UT 261, four miles north of Mexican Hat, go one mile northwest on UT 261, then turn left three miles on UT 316 to its end.

Muley Point Overlook

One of the great views in the Southwest lies just a short drive from Goosenecks State Park and more than 1,000 feet higher. Although the view of the Goosenecks below is less dramatic than at the state park, the 6,200-foot elevation provides

Muley Point

W.C. McRAE

a magnificent panorama across the Navajo Indian Reservation to Monument Valley and countless canyons and mountains. To get here, travel northwest nine miles on UT 261 from the Goosenecks turnoff. At the top of the Moki Dugway switchbacks (an 1,100-foot climb on gravel roads with sharp curves and 5–10 percent grades), turn left (southwest) 5.3 miles on gravel County Road 241 (the turnoff may not be signed) and follow it toward the point. This road is not suitable for wet-weather travel.

MONUMENT VALLEY

Towering buttes, jagged pinnacles, and rippled sand dunes make this an otherworldly landscape. Changing colors and shifting shadows during the day add to the enchantment. Most of the natural monuments are remnants of sandstone eroded by wind and water. Agathla Peak and some lesser summits are roots of ancient volcanoes, whose dark rock contrasts with the pale yellow sandstone of the other formations. The valley lies at an elevation of 5,564 feet in the Upper Sonoran Life Zone; annual rainfall averages about 8.5 inches.

In 1863–64, when Kit Carson was ravaging Canyon de Chelly in Arizona to round up the Navajo, Chief Hoskinini led his people to the safety and freedom of Monument Valley. Merrick Butte and Mitchell Mesa commemorate two miners who discovered rich silver deposits on their first trip to the valley in 1880. On their second trip both were killed, reportedly shot by Paiute Indians. Hollywood movies made the splendor of Monument Valley known to the outside world. *Stagecoach,* filmed here in 1938 and directed by John Ford, became the first in a series of Westerns that has continued to the present. John Wayne and many other movie greats rode across these sands.

The Navajo have preserved the valley as a tribal park with a scenic drive, visitors' center, and campground. From Mexican Hat, drive 22 miles southwest on U.S. 163 and turn left 3.5 miles to the visitors' center. From Kayenta, go 24 miles north on U.S. 163 and turn right 3.5 miles. At the junction of U.S. 163 are a village-worth of outdoor market stalls, where you can stop to buy Navajo art and crafts.

Visitor Center

An information desk, exhibits, a restaurant, and an Indian crafts shop are open daily about 7 A.M.–8 P.M. May–September, then daily 8 A.M.–5 P.M. the rest of the year; (435) 727-3287. Visitors pay a $3 fee ($1 ages 60 and over, free for six and under), collected on the entrance road. Navaho entrepreneurs offer a variety of driving, horseback, and hiking tours from their booths located near the visitor center.

Monument Valley Drive

A 17-mile, self-guided scenic drive begins at the visitors' center and loops through the heart of the valley. Overlooks provide sweeping views from different vantage points. The dirt road is normally okay for cautiously driven cars. Avoid stopping and becoming stuck in the loose sand that sometimes blows across the road. Allow 1.5 hours for the drive; open 7 A.M.–7 P.M. in summer and 8 A.M.–5 P.M. the rest of the year. No hiking or driving is allowed off the signed route. Water and restrooms are available only at the visitors' center.

Monument Valley

Valley Tours

Take one of the guided tours leaving daily year-round from the visitors' center to visit a hogan, a cliff dwelling, and petroglyphs in areas beyond the self-guided drive. The trips last 2.5–3 hours and cost $17–22 per person. Guided horseback rides from near the visitors' center cost around $20 for an hour; longer day and overnight trips can be arranged too. If you'd like to hike in Monument Valley, you must hire a guide; hiking tours of two hours to a day or more can be arranged at the visitors' center.

Campgrounds

Sites at **Mitten View Campground** near the visitors' center cost $12; coin-operated hot showers are available. The season is mid-March–mid-October. Tenters should be prepared for winds in this exposed location. Goulding's Lodge has the nearest motel and store. Motels are also found at Kayenta in Arizona and Mexican Hat and Bluff in Utah.

Goulding's Lodge and Trading Post

This is by far the nicest place to stay in the Monument Valley area, though it's not cheap. Harry Goulding and his wife Mike opened this dramatically located trading post in 1924. It's tucked under the rimrocks two miles west of the U.S. 163 Monument Valley turnoff, just north of the Arizona-Utah border.

Goulding's Museum, in the old trading post building, displays prehistoric and modern Indian artifacts, movie photos, and memorabilia of the Goulding family. Open daily, but may close in winter; admission by donation. Modern motel rooms, most with incredible views of Monument Valley, start at $148 in summer, less off-season; guests can use a small indoor pool; meals are available in the dining room. A gift shop sells souvenirs, books, and high-quality Indian crafts. The nearby store has groceries and gas pumps. Monument Valley tours operate year-round; $30 half day, $60 full day, with a six-person minimum (children under 12 go at half-price). Horseback riding is also available. The lodge stays open all year. For accommodation and tour info, write P.O. Box 360001, Monument Valley, UT 84536, (435) 727-3231 or (800) 874-0902.

W.C. McRAE

Monument Valley Campground, (435) 727-3235, offers tent and RV sites a short drive west; rates are $14 tents, $22 RVs with hookups. Open Apr. 1–Nov. 1. The Seventh-Day Adventist Church runs a hospital and mission nearby.

FOUR CORNERS MONUMENT

A concrete slab marks the point where Utah, Colorado, New Mexico, and Arizona meet. It's the only spot in the United States where you can put your finger on four states at once. Over 2,000 people a day are said to stop at the marker in the summer season. Average stay?—7–10 minutes. On the other hand, five national parks and 18 national monuments are within a radius of 150 miles from this point! Indians, mostly Navajo with perhaps some Ute and Pueblo, set up dozens of craft and refreshment booths in summer. Navajo Parks and Recreation collects a $2 per vehicle ($1 motorcycle) fee during the tourist season.

KAYENTA

The "Gateway to Monument Valley" is a town of 5,200 in a bleak, windswept valley (elev. 5,660 feet) in Arizona. Its name is loosely derived from the Navajo word Teehindeeh, meaning "bog hole," as there were once shallow lakes here. Kayenta, a handy stop for travelers, has several good motels and restaurants.

Accommodations
$75–100: One mile north of U.S. 160, **Best Western Wetherill Inn** is in the center of town on U.S. 163, (520) 697-3231. Its name honors John Wetherill, an early trader and rancher of the region who discovered Betatakin, Mesa Verde, and other major Anasazi sites. The new adobe-style **Hampton Inn,** on U.S. 160, (520) 697-3170 or (800) 426-7866, has a pool and very nicely furnished rooms.

$100–125: The **Holiday Inn,** on U.S. 160 at the turnoff for Kayenta, (520) 697-3221 or (800) HOLIDAY, has expansive rooms, a restaurant, and pool.

Food
The **Holiday Inn's** restaurant, 520) 697-3221, has good Navajo tacos and standard American fare; open daily for breakfast, lunch, and dinner. The **Blue Coffee Pot,** (520) 697-3396, is on the other side of the highway; open daily for breakfast, lunch, and dinner. **Golden Sands Cafe,** near the Wetherill Inn, (520) 697-3684, offers American food daily for breakfast, lunch, and dinner.

Shopping and Services
Look for **Native American crafts** at the motels, Lee's Trading Co. (in the Kayenta shopping center), and Burch's Indian Room (near Wetherill Inn). The motels can recommend local agencies that offer tours in four-wheel-drive vehicles to Monument Valley and surrounding country; costs start at about $45 half day or $70 full day, with a minimum of 4–6 persons.

GLEN CANYON
NATIONAL RECREATION AREA

This vast recreation area covers 1.25 million acres, most of which spreads northeast into Utah. Lake Powell stands as the centerpiece, surrounded by beautiful canyon country. Just a handful of roads approach the lake, so you'll need to do some boating or hiking to explore this unique land of water and rock. The recreation area also includes a beautiful remnant of Glen Canyon in a 15-mile section of the Colorado River from Glen Canyon Dam to Lees Ferry. Admission to Glen Canyon National Recreation Area is $5 per vehicle or $3 per pedestrian or bicyclist for seven days. There is no charge for passing through Page on Highway U.S. 89. For information on Glen Canyon National Recreation Area write: Superintendent, P.O. Box 1507, Page, AZ 86040, (520) 608-6404, www.nps.gov/glca.

Note that except for Navajo lands **Arizona does not observe daylight savings time.** This means that from April through October, the time in Page will be an hour earlier than time in Utah.

LAKE POWELL

Conservationists deplored the loss of remote and beautiful Glen Canyon of the Colorado River beneath Lake Powell. Today, we have only words, pictures, and memories to remind us of its wonders. On the other hand, the 186-mile-long lake now provides easy access to an area most had not even known existed. Lake Powell is the second-largest human-made lake within the United States. Only Lake Mead, farther downstream, has a greater water-storage capacity. Lake Powell, however, has three times more shoreline—1,960 miles—and holds enough water to cover the state of Pennsylvania a foot deep! Bays and coves offer nearly limitless opportunities for exploration by boaters. Nearly all of the lake lies within Utah. Only the lower part—Glen Canyon Dam, Wahweap Resort and Marina, Antelope and Navajo Canyons, and the lower parts of Labyrinth, Face, and West Canyons—extends

into Arizona. The elevation of the surface fluctuates 20–30 feet through the year and peaks in July. The Carl Hayden Visitor Center, perched beside the dam, offers tours of the dam, related exhibits, and an information desk for all the Glen Canyon National Recreation Area.

Climate
Summer, when temperatures rise into the 90s and 100s, is the busiest season for swimming, boating, and water-skiing. Visits during the rest of the year can be enjoyable, too, though activities shift more to sight-seeing, fishing, and hiking. Spring and autumn are the best times to enjoy the backcountry. Winter temperatures drop to highs in the 40s and 50s, with freezing nights and the possibility of snow. Lake surface temperatures range from a comfortable 80° F in August to a chilly 45° in January. Chinook winds can blow day and night for periods from February to May. Thunderstorms in late summer bring strong, gusting winds with widely scattered rain showers. Annual precipitation averages about seven inches.

Geology, Flora, and Fauna
The colorful rock layers that rise above the lake's surface tell a story of ancient deserts, oceans, and rivers. An uplift of the Colorado Plateau beginning about 60 million years ago started a cycle of erosion that has carved canyons and created delicately balanced rocks and graceful natural arches and bridges.

The desert comes right to the edge of the water because fluctuating lake levels prevent plant growth along the shore. Common plants of this high-desert country include prickly pear and hedgehog cacti, rabbitbrush, sand sagebrush, blackbrush, cliffrose, mariposa and sego lilies, globemallow, Indian paintbrush, evening primrose, penstemon, and Indian rice grass. Piñon pine and juniper trees grow on the high plateaus. Springs and permanent streams support sandbar willow, tamarisk, cattail, willow, and cottonwood. Look for hanging gardens of maidenhair fern, columbine, and other water-loving plants in small alcoves high on the sandstone walls.

Most animals here are secretive and nocturnal; you're more likely to see them in early morning or evening. Local mammals include pronghorn, mule deer, mountain lion, coyote, red and gray foxes, ringtail cat, spotted and striped skunks, bobcat, badger, river otter, beaver, prairie dog, Ord kangaroo rat, black-tailed jackrabbit, several species of squirrels and chipmunks, and many species of mice and bats. Some lizards you might see sunning on rocks are collared, side-blotched, desert horned, and chuckwalla. Snake species include common king snake, gopher, striped whipsnake, Western rattlesnake, and Western diamondback rattlesnake. Birds stopping by on their migrations include American avocet, Canada goose, and teal. Others, such as blue heron, snowy egret, and bald eagle, come for the winter. Birds you might spot any time of the year are American merganser, mallard, canyon wren, piñon jay, common raven, red-tailed and Swainson's hawks, great horned and long-eared owls, peregrine and prairie falcons, and golden eagle.

Recreation at Lake Powell

If you don't have your own craft, Wahweap and other marinas will rent a boat for fishing, skiing, or houseboating. Boat tours visit Rainbow Bridge (the world's largest natural bridge) and other destinations from Wahweap, Bullfrog, and Halls Crossing Marinas. Sailboats find the steadiest breezes in Wahweap, Padre, Halls, and Bullfrog Bays, where spring winds average 15–20 knots. Kayaks and canoes can be used in the more protected areas. All boaters need to be alert for approaching storms that can bring wind gusts up to 60 mph. Waves on open expanses of the lake are sometimes steeper than ocean waves and can exceed six feet from trough to crest.

Marinas and bookstores sell navigation maps of Lake Powell. You'll need an Arizona fishing license for the southern five miles of lake and a Utah license for the rest of Lake Powell. Obtain licenses and information from marinas on the water or sporting goods stores in Page. Anglers catch largemouth, smallmouth, and striped bass, northern and walleye pike, catfish, crappie, and carp. Smaller fish include bluegill, perch, and sunfish. Wahweap has a swimming beach (no lifeguards), and boaters can find their own remote spots. Scuba divers can swim underwater with the sizable bass. Hikers have a choice of easy day trips or long wilderness backpack treks. The canyons of the Escalante rate among America's premier hiking areas. Other good hiking spots within or adjacent to Glen Canyon NRA include Rainbow Bridge National Monument, Paria Canyon, Dark Canyon, and Grand Gulch. National Park Service staff at the Carl Hayden Visitor Center can suggest trips and supply trail descriptions. Several guidebooks to Lake Powell have detailed hiking, camping, and boating information. Most of the canyon country near Lake Powell remains wild and little explored—hiking possibilities are limitless! Be sure to carry plenty of water.

skimming the waters of Lake Powell

GLEN CANYON DAM

Construction workers labored from 1956 to 1964 to build this giant concrete structure. It stands 710 feet high above bedrock, and its top measures 1,560 feet across. Thickness ranges from 300 feet at the base to just 25 feet at the top. As part of the Upper Colorado River Storage Project, the dam provides water storage (its main purpose), hydroelectricity, flood control, and recreation on Lake Powell. Eight giant turbine generators churn out a total of 1,150,000 kilowatts at 13,800 volts. Vertigo sufferers shouldn't look down when driving across Glen Canyon Bridge; cold, green waters of the Colorado River glide 700 feet below.

Carl Hayden Visitor Center

Photos, paintings, movies, and slide presentations in the visitors' center show features of Glen Canyon National Recreation Area, including Lake Powell and construction of the dam. A giant relief map helps you visualize the rugged terrain surrounding the lake; look closely and you'll spot Rainbow Bridge. Guided tours inside the dam and generating room depart daily mid-April to mid-Oct. every half hour from 8:30 A.M. to 3:30 P.M. (4:30 P.M. Memorial to Labor Day weekends). National Park Service staff operates an information desk where you can find out about boating, fishing, camping, and hiking in the immense Glen Canyon National Recreation Area; general information: (520) 608-6404 or headquarters: (520) 608-6200. The Glen Canyon Natural History Association, (520) 645-3523, has a variety of books about the recreation area and its environs for sale next to the information desk. Souvenirs, snacks, and postcards can be purchased at a gift shop in the visitors' center building. The Carl Hayden Visitor Center is open daily 8 A.M.–7 P.M. mountain standard time in summer and 8 A.M.–5 P.M. the rest of the year. Tours, exhibits, and slide presentations are free. In summer, you can attend a campfire program several nights a week at nearby Wahweap Campground.

RAINBOW BRIDGE NATIONAL MONUMENT

Rainbow Bridge forms a graceful span 290 feet high and 275 feet wide; the Capitol Building in Washington, D.C., would fit neatly underneath. The easiest way to Rainbow Bridge is by boat tour on Lake Powell from Wahweap, Bullfrog, or Halls Crossing Marinas.

The more adventurous can hike to the bridge from the Cha Canyon Trailhead (just north across the Arizona-Utah border on the east side of Navajo Mountain) or from the Rainbow Lodge Ruins (just south of the Arizona-Utah border on the west side of Navajo Mountain). Rugged trails from each point wind through highly scenic canyons, meet in Bridge Canyon, then continue two miles to the bridge. The hike on either trail, or a loop with both (car shuttle needed), is 26–28 miles round-trip. Hikers must be experienced and self-sufficient; these trails cross wilderness. Because the trails are unmaintained and poorly marked, hikers should consult a Navajo Mountain (Utah) 15-minute topo map or the newer 7 1/2-minute Navajo Begay and Chaiyahi Flat maps.

No camping is allowed at Rainbow Bridge and no supplies are available. You may camp a half mile east of the bridge at Echo camp. The Dangling Rope Marina and National Park Service Ranger Station are 10 miles away, by water only. The best times to go are April to early June, September, and October. Winter cold and snow discourage visitors, and summer is hot and brings hazardous flash floods. The National Park Service offers "Hiking to Rainbow Bridge" trail notes; Glen Canyon NRA, P.O. Box 1507, Page, AZ 86040; (520) 608-6404.

The National Park Service cannot issue hiking permits to Rainbow Bridge. Obtain the required tribal hiking permit ($5 one person, $10 group of 2–10, $20 group of 11 or more) and camping permit ($2 per person per night) from the Cameron Visitor Center (not always open) or Navajo Parks Department, P.O. Box 9000, Window Rock, AZ 86515; (520) 871-6647. Both offices are open Monday–Friday about 8 A.M.–5 P.M.; the Cameron office is also open weekends from April to September.

The only road access to the Navajo Mountain area is Indian Route 16 from AZ 98, between Page and Kayenta. To reach the east trailhead, drive north 32 miles on Indian Route 16 past Inscription House Trading Post to a road fork, and then turn right six miles to Navajo Mountain Trading Post. Continue on the main road 6.5 miles (go straight at the four-way junction) to an earthen dam. Drive straight across the dam, take the left fork after a half mile, and then go 1.6 miles to Cha Canyon Trailhead at the end of the road.

You can reach the west trailhead by driving north 32 miles on Indian Route 16 and turning left and driving about six miles at the road fork to the Rainbow Lodge Ruins. Always lock vehicles and remove valuables at trailheads. Because Navajo Mountain is sacred to the Navajo, you need permission to climb from the Navajo Parks Department.

Boat Tours to Rainbow Bridge

By far the most popular way to visit Rainbow Bridge is to sign on with a boat tour and take a half- or whole day trip to see the national monument. Most tours leave from Wahweap Marina, off U.S. 89. In high season, there are six departures daily for Rainbow Bridge on a five-hour trip. There's at least one trip a day throughout the year. Cost is $75 adult, children $55. One day-long trip (includes lunch) departs daily from April through October; $99 adult, $69. Minimum numbers required on all trips.

Once at Painted Arch, tour boats park at a floating dock, and you can walk to a viewing area beneath the arch, a distance of about half a mile.

Reservations are strongly suggested. Call the marina at (520) 645-1070 for information.

MARINAS

The **National Park Service** provides public boat ramps, campgrounds, and ranger offices at most of the marinas. Rangers know current boating and back-road conditions, primitive camping areas, and good places to explore. **Lake Powell Resorts & Marinas** operates marina services, boat rentals, boat tours, accommodations, RV parks, and restaurants; contact them for information and reservations (strongly recommended in summer) at P.O. Box 56909, Phoenix, AZ 85079, (800) 528-6154 (602-278-8888 in greater Phoenix), fax (602) 331-5258. All the marinas stay open year-round; you can avoid crowds and peak prices by coming in autumn, winter, or spring. Private or chartered aircraft can fly to Page Airport, San Juan County Airport near Bullfrog, or an airstrip near Halls Crossing.

Wahweap

The name means "bitter water" in the Ute Indian language. Wahweap Lodge and Marina, Lake Powell's biggest, offers complete boaters' services and rentals, guided tours, deluxe accommodations, an RV park, and fine dining. Wahweap is seven miles northwest of Page, five miles beyond the visitors' center. **Wahweap Lodge** is a very large complex of motel rooms, restaurants, and public areas. There are a number of different kinds of rooms, starting at $165 (single or double) from April 1 to October 31, $105 (single or double) in winter; lake-view rooms cost about $10 more. Contact Lake Powell Resorts & Marinas for reservations at P.O. Box 56909, Phoenix, AZ 85079, (800) 528-6154, www.visitlakepowell.com. Wahweap Lodge & Marina can also be reached at P.O. Box 1597, Page, AZ 86040, (520) 645-2433. **Lake Powell Motel,** at Wahweap Junction (four miles northwest of Glen Canyon Dam on U.S. 89), has less expensive rooms, starting at $79. Information and reservations are through Lake Powell Resorts, above.

Wahweap Campground is operated on a first-come, first-served basis by Lake Powell Resorts & Marinas; tent sites have drinking water but no showers or hookups; $12; campers may use the pay showers and laundry facilities at the RV park (sites with hookups are $27). The RV park, campground, and a picnic area are located between Wahweap Lodge and Stateline. Primitive camping (no water, $8) is available at **Lone Rock** in Utah, six miles northwest of Wahweap off U.S. 89; cars need to be very careful not to stray into loose sand areas. Boaters may also camp along the lakeshore, but not within one mile of developed areas. A free picnic area and fish-cleaning station are located just west of Wahweap Lodge. Public boat ramps are located adjacent to the lodge and at Stateline, 1.3 miles northwest of the lodge and just into Utah. During summer (June 1–Sept. 30), you can also obtain recreation information from the **Wahweap Ranger Station** near the picnic area; at other times see the staff at Carl Hayden Visitor Center.

The marina offers six **lake tours,** ranging from an hour-long paddle-wheel cruise around Wahweap Bay ($11) to trips to Rainbow Bridge, 50 miles away ($75–99). The marina also offers a full range of watercraft rentals, including houseboats. For information on tours, call (520) 645-1070.

Antelope Point

Antelope Point, just northeast of Page, has complete boating facilities, plus a swimming beach.

Dangling Rope

This floating marina lies 42 miles uplake from Glen Canyon Dam. The only access is by boat. Services include a ranger station, store, minor boat repairs, gas dock, and sanitary pump-out station. A dangling rope left behind in a nearby canyon, perhaps by uranium prospectors, prompted the name. The dock for Rainbow Bridge is seven miles farther uplake in Bridge Canyon, a tributary of Forbidding Canyon.

San Juan

Boats can be hand-launched at **Clay Hills Crossing** at the upper end of the San Juan arm. An unpaved road branches 11 miles southwest from UT 276 (road to Halls Crossing) to the lake; don't attempt the road after rains. River-runners on the San Juan often take out here; no facilities.

Halls Crossing–Bullfrog Ferry

The ferry *John Atlantic Burr* can accommodate vehicles of all sizes and passengers for the short, 25-minute crossing between these marinas. Halls Crossing and Bullfrog Marinas lie on opposite sides of Lake Powell about 95 lake miles from Glen Canyon Dam, roughly midway up the length of the lake. Sections of paved UT 276 connect each marina with UT 95. The ferry's daily schedule has six round-trips from May 15 to September 30, then four round-trips the rest of the year; no reservations needed. You can pick up a schedule from the marinas. Fares are $9 for most cars and vehicles under 20 feet in length (includes all passengers and driver), $2 for bicycles and foot passengers. Service is suspended for a brief time annually, usually in November, for maintenance; signs at the UT 276 turnoffs will warn you when the ferry is closed. Low water in late summer can also affect service; the ferry may have to use the boat ramps instead of ferry docks.

Halls Crossing

In 1880, Charles Hall built the ferry used by the Hole-in-the-Rock pioneers, who crossed the river to begin settlement in southeast Utah. The approach roads were so bad, however, that he moved the ferry 35 miles upstream to present-day Halls Crossing in the following year. Business continued to be slow, and Hall quit running the ferry in 1884.

Arriving at Halls Crossing by road, you'll first reach a small store offering rooms in trailer houses and an RV park. Coin-operated showers and laundry at the RV park are also open to the public. The separate National Park Service **campground**, just beyond and to the left, has sites with a good view of the lake, drinking water, and restrooms; $12. Continue a half mile on the main road to the boat ramp and **Halls Crossing Marina.** The marina has a larger store (groceries and fishing and boating supplies), tours to Rainbow Bridge, a boat rental office (fishing, ski, and houseboat), gas dock, slips, and storage. The **ranger station** is nearby, though rangers are usually out on patrol; look for their vehicle in the area if the office is closed. Contact Lake Powell Resorts & Marinas for accommodation, boat rental, and tour reservations at P.O. Box 56909, Phoenix, AZ 85079, (800) 528-6154 (602-278-8888 in greater Phoenix), fax (602) 331-5258. The marina can also be reached at UT 276, Lake Powell, UT 84533, (435) 684-2261.

Stabilized Anasazi ruins at **Defiance House** in Forgotten Canyon make a good boating destination 12 miles uplake; a sign marks the beginning of the trail to the ruins.

Bullfrog

Before the days of Lake Powell, Bullfrog Rapids gave boaters a fast and bumpy ride. Bullfrog Marina has the most extensive visitor facilities of Lake Powell's Utah marinas. If driving in on the highway, you'll come to the **visitors' center,** on the right, (435) 684-2243; open daily 8 A.M.–5 P.M. The **clinic,** (435) 684-2288, is here, too; open May 15–Sept. 30. A large **campground** lies on the left; sites have drinking water and restrooms for $12. Continue on the main road to a junction; a service station, store, and marine

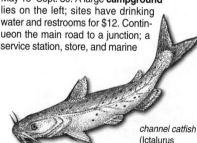

channel catfish
(Ictalurus
punctatus)

LOUISE FOOTE

service here offer repairs and supplies. Continue straight at the junction for a picnic area and the boat ramp; turn right at the service station for Defiance House Lodge and Restaurant, Trailer Village, Bullfrog Painted Hills RV Park, and Bullfrog Marina.

All-day **Rainbow Bridge tours** usually leave daily from April 15 to October 31 and stop on request to pick up passengers at Halls Crossing Marina. **Canyon Explorer tours** depart in the evening for two hours in nearby canyons during the same season. **Bullfrog Marina** has a store, snack bar, boat rentals (fishing, ski, and houseboat), gas dock, slips, and storage. Contact Lake Powell Resorts & Marinas for accommodation, boat rental, and tour reservations at P.O. Box 56909, Phoenix, AZ 85079, (800) 528-6154 (602-278-8888 in greater Phoenix), fax (602) 331-5258. Bullfrog Resort & Marina can also be reached at P.O. Box 4055-Bullfrog, Lake Powell, UT 84533, (435) 684-2233.

Defiance House Lodge, (435) 684-3000 or (800) 528-6154, offers luxury accommodations and the **Anasazi Restaurant** (open daily for breakfast, lunch, and dinner). Rooms begin at $103 (single or double) in summer (Apr. 1–Oct. 31) and $79 (single or double) in winter. The front desk at the lodge also handles **housekeeping units** (trailers) and an **RV park** (both located nearby with the same rates as those at Halls Crossing) and **tours** to Rainbow Bridge and local canyons. Showers, laundry, a convenience store, and a post office are at **Trailer Village.** The RV park has showers. Ask visitors' center staff or rangers for directions to primitive camping areas with vehicle access elsewhere along Bullfrog Bay.

Hite

In 1883, Cass Hite came to Glen Canyon in search of gold. He found some at a place later named Hite City and set off a small gold rush.

Cass and a few of his relatives operated a small store and post office, the only services for many miles. Travelers wishing to cross the Colorado River here had the difficult task of swimming their animals across. Arthur Chaffin, a later resident, put through the first road and opened a ferry service in 1946. The Chaffin Ferry served uranium prospectors and adventurous motorists until the lake backed up to the spot in 1964. A steel bridge now spans the Colorado River upstream from Hite Marina. Cass Hite's store and the ferry site are underwater about five miles downlake from Hite Marina.

The uppermost marina on Lake Powell, Hite lies 141 lake miles from Glen Canyon Dam. From here boats can continue uplake to the mouth of Dark Canyon in Cataract Canyon at low water or into Canyonlands National Park at high water. Hite tends to be quieter than the other marinas and is favored by some anglers and families. The turnoff for the marina is from UT 95 between Blanding and Hanksville. On the way in, you'll find a small **store** with gas pumps, **housekeeping units** (trailers; same rates as at Halls Crossing), and a primitive **campground** (no drinking water; free). Primitive camping is also available nearby off UT 95 at Dirty Devil, Farley Canyon, White Canyon, Blue Notch, and other locations. **Hite Marina,** at the end of the access road, has a small store, housekeeping units, gas dock, boat rentals (fishing, ski, and houseboat), slips, and storage. Hikers can make arrangements with the marina to be dropped off or picked up at Dark Canyon. A **ranger station** is occasionally open; look for the ranger's vehicle at other times. Contact Lake Powell Resorts & Marinas for accommodation and boat rental reservations at P.O. Box 56909, Phoenix, AZ 85079, (800) 528-6154 (602-278-8888 in greater Phoenix), fax (602) 331-5258. Hite Marina can also be contacted at P.O. Box 501, Lake Powell, UT 84533, (435) 684-2278.

PAGE, ARIZONA

Only sand and desert vegetation lay atop Manson Mesa in far northern Arizona, where Page now sits, until 1957. In that year the U.S. Bureau of Reclamation decided to build a giant reservoir in Glen Canyon on the Colorado River. Glen Canyon Dam became one of the largest construction projects ever undertaken: the 710-foot-high structure created a lake covering 250 square miles with a shoreline of nearly 2,000 miles. Workers hastily set up prefabricated metal buildings for barracks, dining hall, and offices. Trailers rolled in, one serving as a bank, another as a school. And thus was born the town of Page. The Bureau of Reclamation named it for John C. Page, who served as the bureau's commissioner from 1937 to 1943.

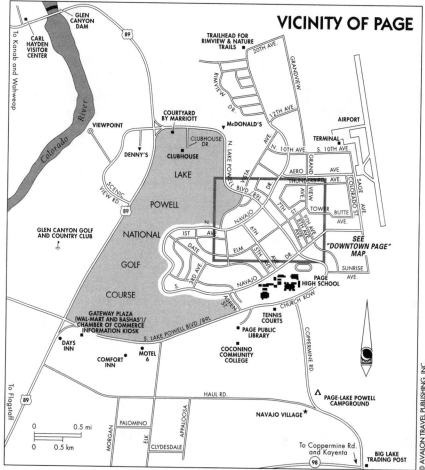

VICINITY OF PAGE

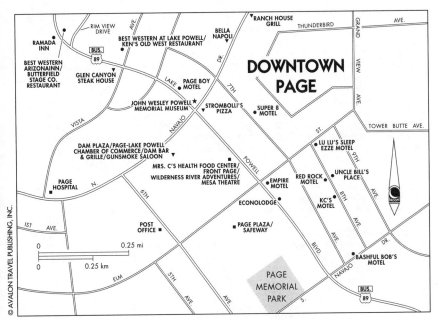

The remote desert spot (elev. 4,300 ft.) gradually turned into a modern town with schools, businesses, and churches. Streets were named and grass and trees planted so that Page took on the appearance of an American suburb. Today, the town still looks new and clean. Though small (pop. 9,500), it's the largest community close to Lake Powell and offers travelers a variety of places to stay and eat.

Wedged between the Arizona Strip to the west, Glen Canyon National Recreation Area to the north, and the Navajo Reservation to the east and south, Page makes a useful base of operations for visiting all of these areas. The town overlooks Lake Powell and Glen Canyon Dam; the large Wahweap Resort and Marina lies just six miles away.

SIGHTS AND HIKES

Powell Museum

This collection honors scientist and explorer John Wesley Powell. In 1869 Powell led the first expedition down the Green and Colorado River canyons, then ran the rivers a second time in 1871–72. It was he who named the most splendid section the Grand Canyon.

Old drawings and photographs illustrate Powell's life and voyages. Fossil and mineral displays interpret the thick geologic sections revealed by the canyons of the Colorado River system. Other exhibits contain pottery, baskets, weapons, and tools of Southwestern Indian tribes, as well as memorabilia of early river runners, Page's pioneers, and Glen Canyon Dam. Related videos are shown on request. Regional books can be purchased. Staff offer travel info and can book Lake Powell boat tours, all-day and half-day float trips, Corkscrew/Antelope Canyon tours, and scenic flights.

In summer (June–Aug.), the museum is open Monday–Friday 8:30 A.M.–5:30 P.M.; spring and autumn hours are Monday–Friday 9 A.M.–5 P.M.; it's closed mid-December–mid-February. Admission is $1 adult, $.50 children kindergarten–8th grade. The museum is in downtown Page at the corner of 6 N. Lake Powell Blvd. and N. Navajo Dr., (520) 645-9496 or (888) 597-6873, www.powellmuseum.org.

Navajo Village

Navajo offer cultural programs about their beliefs and traditional skills at this living museum on the edge of town. **An Evening with the Navajo** begins with a horse-drawn wagon ride to the recreated village where you'll see demonstrations of cooking, weaving, and silversmithing. Your hosts will also explain features of the sweat lodge and two types of hogans here. You'll enjoy a dinner of traditional foods, watch song and dance performances, and hear stories. The four-hour evening presentations cost $50 adults and $35 children 6–13 plus tax. You can also sign up for a shorter evening program or just visit the exhibits during the day. Contact the Page/Lake Powell Chamber of Commerce; (520) 645-2741 or (888) 261-7243, www.navajovillage.net.

The Best Dam View

An excellent panorama of Glen Canyon Dam and the Colorado River can be enjoyed just west of town. It's reached via Scenic View Road behind Denny's Restaurant off U.S. 89; turn west at the junction of U.S. 89 and N. Lake Powell Blvd. or west beside the Glen Canyon NRA headquarters building and turn at the sign for "scenic overlook." A short trail leads down to the best viewpoint.

Rimview Trail

An eight-mile trail for walkers, joggers, and cyclists encircles Page with many views of the surrounding desert and Lake Powell. The unpaved route has some sandy and rocky sections that will challenge novice bike riders. If you find yourself more than 30 vertical feet below the mesa rim, you're off the trail. You can pick up a map from the chamber office. A popular starting point is at the short nature trail loop near Lake View School at North Navajo Drive and 20th Avenue in the northern part of town.

Corkscrew/Antelope Canyon

You'll see photos around town of the beautifully convoluted red rock in this canyon, so narrow in places that you have to squeeze through. Sunshine reflects off the smooth Navajo sandstone to create extraordinary

light and colors. Beams of light enter the canyons at midday, further entrancing visitors. It's also very dim. Photographers don't wish to spoil the effect with a flash, so most bring a tripod to help capture the infinite shapes and patterns.

Antelope Canyon has a wider upper section known as Corkscrew and a narrower lower section. The shallow wash in between that you see from the highway gives no hint of the marvels up or downstream. Both can easily be reached from Page by driving south on Coppermine Road or east on AZ 98 to the junction at Big Lake Trading Post, then continuing east one mile on AZ 98 toward the power plant. Turn right into the parking area for the upper canyon, or stay on AZ 98 just 0.15 mile farther and then turn left half a mile at the sign on paved Antelope Point Road for the lower canyon. At either place you'll pay $5 for a tribal entry permit (good for both sections) plus shuttle or tour fees. The upper section has a $12.50 shuttle charge for the 3.5-mile drive to the trailhead and a one-hour visit; no walk-ins or private drive-ins are permitted. The shuttle cost increases to $17.50 for a two-hour visit, $22.50 for 3–4 hours, and $32.50 for all day. The lower canyon can be visited on self-guided hikes of $12.50 plus the $5 entry fee. Children pay less. You can also take a guided excursion from Page. Sightseers can tour either section easily in an hour; photographers will probably wish to spend more time.

The upper canyon ticket booth is usually open daily 8 A.M.–5 P.M. April–October; you can also obtain Rainbow Bridge hiking permits here. The lower canyon closes by 4 P.M. For information and off-season access, call the Antelope Canyon Navajo Tribal Park at (520) 698-2808; the office is 4 miles south of Page in Leche-e. From early April to late October, the canyon hours run on the Navajo Reservation's daylight saving time (when it's 4 P.M. in Page, it's 5 P.M. at Antelope). Late starts also run the risk of canyon access closing early if business is slow. In winter (Nov.–Mar.) you may need to telephone ahead to arrange a visit. Check the weather forecast before heading out, as slot canyons are deadly during a flash flood.

Horseshoe Bend View

The Colorado River makes a sharp, 180-degree bend below this spectacular viewpoint. Look for the parking area just west of U.S. 89, 0.2 mile south of Milepost 545; it's 2.5 miles south of Page's Gateway Plaza. A three-quarter-mile trail leads from the parking to the overlook. Photographers will find a wide-angle lens handy to take in the whole scene. Mornings have good light for pictures; afternoons can be dramatic if the sky is filled with clouds.

ACCOMMODATIONS

Nearly all Page motels lie on or near Lake Powell Blvd./Hwy 89L, a 3.25-mile loop that branches off the main highway. Page is a busy place in summer, however, and a call ahead is a good idea if you don't want to chase around town looking for vacancies. Expect to pay top dollar for views of the lake. The summer rates listed here drop in winter (Nov.–Mar.). The Eighth Avenue places lie in Page's historic district, a quiet residential area two blocks off Lake Powell Boulevard. These apartments date back to 1958–59 when they housed supervisors and foremen for the dam; today some of the buildings have been fixed up as pensions and motels.

Under $50

Uncle Bill's Place at 117 Eighth Ave. features a quiet garden in back; you have a choice of rooms with shared bath and kitchen (under $50) or private suites (over $50); (520) 645-1224, www.thedam.com/unclebill. KC's Motel at 126 Eighth Ave. offers rooms with private bath; (520) 645-2947. Red Rock Motel has private baths and some kitchens (under $50) plus two-bedroom suites (over $50) at 114 Eighth Ave.; (520) 645-0062, www.redrockmotel.com. Bashful Bob's Motel around the corner at 750 S. Navajo Dr. offers mostly two-bedroom apartments, all with kitchens; (520) 645-3919, www.page.az. net/bashfulbobsmotel. Navajo Trail Motel has rooms at two downtown locations and on the southern outskirts; contact the office for all three places at 800 Bureau, (520) 645-9508; the other motel units are at 630 Vista, behind Glen Canyon Steak House, and at 524 Haul Road.

$50–75

Lu Lu's Sleep EZZe Motel at 105 Eighth Ave. has some of the most luxurious rooms on this street; (520) 608-0273 or (800) 553-6211. Page Boy Motel offers a swimming pool at 150 N. Lake Powell Blvd.; (520) 645-2416. Econo Lodge is at 121 S. Lake Powell Blvd.; (520) 645-2488 or (800) 553-2666. Empire Motel features a swimming pool at 107 S. Lake Powell Blvd.; (520) 645-2406 or (800) 551-9005. Farther south from downtown, you'll find the Motel 6 with a pool at 637 S. Lake Powell Blvd.; (520) 645-5888 or (800) 4MOTEL6.

$75–100

Best Western at Lake Powell has views, a pool, spa, and exercise room at 208 N. Lake Powell Blvd.; (520) 645-5988 or (800) 528-1234. The nearby Best Western Arizonainn provides fine views, swimming pool, and adjacent restaurant at 716 Rim View Dr. and N. Lake Powell Blvd. (across from Ramada Inn); (520) 645-2466 or (800) 826-2718. Super 8 Motel is at 75 S. Seventh Ave.; (520) 645-2858 or (800) 800-8000. Comfort Inn is south of downtown at 649 S. Lake Powell Blvd. with a pool and spa; (520) 645-5858 or (800) 228-5150. Next door, Holiday Inn Express offers two-bedded rooms, pool, spa, and continental breakfast at 751 S. Navajo Dr.; (520) 645-9000 or (800) HOLIDAY. Lake Powell Day's Inn & Suites lies on the south edge of town beside U.S. 89 with an outdoor pool and spa; (520) 645-2800 or (877) 525-3769.

Canyon Colors Bed & Breakfast has a pool, patio, and fireplaces; (520) 645-5979 or (800) 536-2530, www.canyon-country.com/colors. Sunrise View Bed & Breakfast offers not only views but a shaded backyard and other extras; (520) 608-4763, www.canyon-country/ sunrise.

$100–125

Ramada Inn features a swimming pool, restaurant, and great views over Lake Powell from 287 N. Lake Powell Blvd.; (520) 645-8851 or (800) 261-6702. Courtyard by Marriott offers views, a restaurant, a pool, spa, exercise room, and adjacent 18-hole golf course at 600 Clubhouse Dr.; (520) 645-5000 or (800) 321-2211.

Campgrounds

Page–Lake Powell Campground offers sites for tents ($17) and RVs ($20–26 w/hookups) with an indoor pool and spa, store, laundry, and showers; non-guests may use the showers or dump station for a small fee; the campground is 0.7 mile southeast of downtown on Coppermine Road; (520) 645-3374. Other campgrounds, an RV park, and motels are in the Wahweap area (see Wahweap under Glen Canyon National Recreation Area).

OTHER PRACTICALITIES

Food and Entertainment

Ranch House Grill is a handy place for breakfast and does American lunches too; open daily at 819 N. Navajo Dr., (520) 645-1420. **Dam Bar & Grill** serves up steak, barbecue, seafood, pasta, and sandwiches daily for dinner at 644 N. Navajo Dr. in the Dam Plaza, (520) 645-2161; it also has a sports bar. The adjacent **Gunsmoke Saloon** features country bands and a variety of other music Wednesday–Saturday, (520) 645-2161. **Family Tree Restaurant** in the Ramada Inn offers a varied menu daily for breakfast, lunch, and dinner; in summer, you can choose a buffet for breakfast, lunch (usually just on Sun.), and dinner (seafood on Fri.); 287 N. Lake Powell Blvd., (520) 645-8851. **Butterfield Stage Co. Restaurant** serves American food daily for breakfast, lunch, and dinner at 704 Rim View Dr. next to Best Western ArizonaInn, (520) 645-2467; dinner choices include steak, prime rib, and seafood. **Pepper's Restaurant** at the Courtyard by Marriott offers American and continental cuisine with a Southwestern touch and is open daily for breakfast (also a buffet), lunch, and dinner at 600 Clubhouse Dr., (520) 645-1247. **Denny's** is open 24 hours and serves popular American fare for breakfast, lunch, and dinner at 669 Scenic View Dr. (turn west at the U.S. 89-N. Lake Powell Blvd. Junction, (520) 645-3999.

For Chinese cuisine, try **Mandarin Gourmet Restaurant,** open daily for lunch and dinner in Gateway Plaza, (520) 645-5516. **Padre Bay Cafe & Grill** does Mexican food, steaks, seafood, and sandwiches; it's open daily for lunch and dinner at 635 Elm St., (520) 645-9058. **Bella Napoli** offers fine Italian cuisine daily for dinner in summer and Monday–Saturday for dinner the rest of the year, except closed late December–mid-February, 810 N. Navajo Dr., (520) 645-2706. **Strombolli's Pizza** is open daily for lunch and dinner except in winter at 711 N. Navajo Dr., where diners have a choice of indoor seating or the outdoor deck, a popular gathering spot for boaters in the summer, (520) 645-2605. Pizza, spaghetti, and other Italian fare are also served daily for lunch and dinner by **Pizza Hut,** 6 S. Lake Powell Blvd. in Dam Square, (520) 645-2455 and **Little Caesar's** (carry-out only), Page Plaza near the corner of S. Lake Powell Blvd. and Elm St., (520) 645-5565.

You can buy **groceries** at Safeway (Page Plaza at corner of S. Lake Powell Blvd. and Elm St.), Bashas' (Gateway Plaza), or at Mrs. C's Health Food Center (32 S. Lake Powell Blvd.). Catch movies at **Mesa Theatre,** 42 S. Lake Powell Blvd.; (520) 645-9565.

Events

In March, Fishermen test their skills in the Bullfrog Open bass tournament. Indian Nights Pow Wow in early June has amazing dances, drumming, and music.

On July 4th, there's a parade followed by fireworks that light the sky over Glen Canyon Dam. Mr. Burfel's Softball Tournament plays in September. In October, Air Affaire takes off over Page with airplane acrobatics and parachutists.

Bullfrog's Festival of Lights Parade takes place on the Saturday after Thanksgiving. In December, the Here Comes Santa Parade marks the holiday season in Page. Wahweap Festival of Lights Parade on Lake Powell glides by on the first Saturday.

For more information on any Lake Powell event, ask at the marina where it's held. To learn about other events, contact Page/Lake Powell Chamber of Commerce, (520) 645-2741.

Services and Recreation

The **post office** is at 44 Sixth Ave, (520) 645-2571. **Page Hospital** stands at the corner of 501 N. Navajo Dr. and Vista Ave, (520) 645-2424. In **emergencies**—police, fire, medical—dial 911.

Page High School features a year-round indoor **swimming pool** near the corner of S. Lake Powell Blvd. and AZ 98; (520) 608-4100. Play

tennis at the courts on S. Lake Powell Blvd. (Church Row). **Lake Powell National Golf Course** offers an 18-hole championship golf course that wraps around the west side of the mesa; turn in on Clubhouse Dr. adjacent to the Courtyard by Marriott, (520) 645-2023. **Glen Canyon Golf and Country Club** has a 9-hole golf course west across U.S. 89 from the 18-hole course, (520) 645-2715. **Twin Finn Diving Center** offers a variety of diving activities and classes and rents diving equipment and kayaks (both touring and sit-on-top) at 811 Vista Ave., (520) 645-3114, www.twinfinn.com.

Information

The **Page/Lake Powell Chamber of Commerce** offers information about area sights and services and books lake and river tours, Corkscrew/Antelope Canyon tours, and scenic flights; open Mon.–Sat. 8 A.M.–8 P.M. and Sun. 9 A.M.–6 P.M. May 16–October 16, then Mon.–Fri. 9 A.M.–5 P.M. the rest of the year. The office is at 644 N. Navajo Dr. in the Dam Plaza (Box 727, Page, AZ 86040), (520) 645-2741 or (888) 261-7243, www.pagelakepowellchamber.org.

The semi-circular **Page Public Library** rises impressively from the mesa rim at 479 S. Lake Powell Blvd.; it has an Arizona/Native American collection, internet computers, and fine views; it's open Monday–Thursday 10 A.M.–8 P.M. and Friday–Saturday 10 A.M.–5 P.M., (520) 645-4270. **Front Page** has regional titles, general reading, and office supplies at 48 S. Lake Powell Blvd., (520) 645-5333.

Tours

You can obtain information and make reservations for many area tours through the Page/Lake Powell Chamber of Commerce (www.pagelakepowellchamber.org) or Powell Museum (www.powellmuseum.org).

Lake Powell Jeep Tours offers regular and photographer's tours to Corkscrew Canyon in Antelope Wash year-round, weather permitting; 104 S. Lake Powell Blvd., (520) 645-5501, web: www.jeep-

tour.com. **Roger Ekis' Antelope Canyon Tours** goes to both upper and lower Antelope Canyon except in winter; (520) 645-9102 or (435) 675-9109, web: www.antelopecanyon.com. **Scenic Tours** does 90-minute trips to Corkscrew Canyon year-round, weather permitting; (520) 645-5594. **J&C Outfitters** takes visitors on ATV tours in the Page and Kaibab Plateau areas; beginners receive instruction; (520) 645-9557, www.atvtours.net.

Wilderness River Adventures offers raft trips down the Colorado River from just below Glen Canyon Dam to Lees Ferry, traveling over 15 miles of smooth-flowing water through the beautiful canyon of Navajo sandstone. You'll stop to inspect some fine petroglyphs, and you're likely to see condors, blue herons, ducks, and other birds. Half-day trips leave once or twice daily March–October, weather permitting; the cost is $55 adults, $47 children 12 and under. All-day trips have more time on the water and include a lunch buffet; they run May 15–September 15 and cost $77 adults, $69 children 12 and under. Kayakers and canoeists can arrange for rafts to take them from Lees Ferry upstream to the dam. Contact the company at 50 S. Lake Powell Blvd., (520) 645-3279 or (800) 528-6154.

Classic Helicopter Tours takes to the air with a variety of tours: 10 minutes for Tower Butte ($39), 15 minutes for Tower Butte & Antelope Creek ($59), about 30 minutes for Rainbow Bridge ($95), and 50–55 minutes to Rainbow Bridge and Escalante ($160); there's a four-person minimum; (520) 645-5356, www.helicoptours.com. **Boat tours** to Rainbow Bridge and other destinations leave from nearby Wahweap Marina.

Transport

Wahweap Lodge operates **Page Shuttle** frequently to Page and the airport, (520) 645-2433. Most area motels also provide transportation for guests to and from the airport. Check with the chamber or a travel agent to see if scenic flights and fixed-wing air tours operate out of Page. **Avis** rents cars, (520) 645-2024 or (800) 331-1212.

BOOKLIST

DESCRIPTION AND TRAVEL

Angus, Mark. *Salt Lake City Underfoot.* Salt Lake City: Signature Books, 1996; 209 pages, $12.95. Walkers' Guide to Salt Lake City history and neighborhoods.

Bannan, Jan Gumprecht. *Utah State Parks: A Complete Recreational Guide.* Mountaineers Books, 1995; 207 pages, $14.95. A guide to all of Utah's state parks, complete with maps, hiking routes, campground evaluations, and other recreational information.

Barnes, F.A., and M.M. Barnes. *Cameo Cliffs: Biking-Hiking-Four-Wheeling.* Moab: Arch Country Books, 1992; 160 pages, $10.95. Canyons, arches, and panoramas attract visitors to this little-known area east of U.S. 191. Author Fran Barnes named the area Cameo Cliffs because the pink cliffs reminded him of an old-fashioned pink-and-white cameo locket. (You're not likely to see this unofficial name on maps, however.) Barnes describes the area, divided by UT 46 into Cameo Cliffs North and South, in this small guidebook and separate map ($4.50) of the same name.

Barnes, F.A., and M.M. Barnes. *Canyon Country's Canyon Rims Recreation Area.* Moab: Arch Hunter Books, 1992; 216 pages, $18. Comprehensive, large-format guide to this vast area south and east of Canyonlands National Park-or, as the author's subtitle explains, "The rest of Canyonlands National Park. Park-quality land that was left out of Canyonlands National Park." You'll find good background information on geology, flora, fauna, archaeology, and history. Practical advice will help you prepare for this remote region and enjoy the viewpoints, scenic drives, hiking, and mountain biking. Well illustrated with black-and-white photos, but you'll need the separate *Off-Road Vehicle Trail Map: Canyon Rims Recreation Area* to follow the road and trail descriptions.

Barnes, F.A. *Canyon Country Off-Road Vehicle Trails.* Moab: Arch Hunter Books. A series of backcountry driving guides to the canyon areas of southern and eastern Utah. This series originally had over 25 slim volumes, but only seven are currently in print (many are still available locally in Utah bookstores). Current volumes cover Arches and La Sal areas, the Maze, Needles, Island and Canyon Rims areas in Canyonlands National Park (three books), and a volume dedicated to the Moab area. Prices are usually $8 per book.

Bezy, John. *Bryce Canyon: The Story Behind the Scenery.* Las Vegas: KC Publications, Inc., 1988; 48 pages, $7.95. Large color photos illustrate Bryce's creation, wonderful erosion forms, winter scenery, history, wildlife, and flora.

Bickers, Jack. *The Labyrinth Rims: 60 Accesses to Green River Overlooks.* 4-WD Trailguide Publications, 1989; 80 pages, $8. Maps and descriptions lead you to more than 60 overlooks in this deep, meandering canyon between the town of Green River and the confluence of the Green and Colorado Rivers.

Carr, Stephen L. *The Historical Guide to Utah Ghost Towns.* Salt Lake City: Western Epics, 1987; 174 pages, $16.95. Excellent book about Utah's fading ghosts. The historic photos, well-written text, good directions, and maps will add to the pleasure of back-road travel. Check for this at a library, as it's hard to find.

Casey, Robert L. *A Journey to the High Southwest.* Old Saybrook, CT: Globe Pequot Press, 2000; 464 pages, $19.95. Introduction, history, and travel in southern Utah and adjacent Arizona, New Mexico, and Colorado.

Cunningham, Bill and Polly Burke. *Wild Utah.* Helena, MT: Falcon Publishing Company, 1998; 352 pages, $19.95. Utah contains more than a million acres of legally protected wilderness. This book provides the information needed to get off the beaten track and into 45 different roadless areas. The authors' comprehensive descriptions thoroughly discuss the land, ecosystems and habitats, and opportunities for exploration and recreation.

DeLorme. *Utah Atlas & Gazeteer.* Freeport, ME: Delorme Mapping, 2000; 64 pages, $19.95. This atlas is composed of topographic maps covering the entire state. The small scale of the maps may limit some uses but the maps are helpful in understanding the terrain of places you may wish to travel.

Eardley, A.J., and James W. Schaack. *Zion: The Story Behind the Scenery.* Las Vegas: KC Publications, 1992; 48 pages, $7.95. Large color photos illustrate descriptions of Zion's rock layers, canyons, prehistoric peoples, settlers, and ecology.

Hagood, Allen. *Dinosaur: The Story Behind the Scenery.* Las Vegas: KC Publications, 1990; 48 pages, $7.95. Introduction to the dinosaurs, fossil excavation, geology, and canyons of Dinosaur National Monument in northeastern Utah; has 65 color photos.

Huegel, Tony. *Utah Byways: 65 Backcountry Drives for the Whole Family, Including Moab, Canyonlands, Arches, Capitol Reef, San Rafael Swell and Glen Canyon.* Wilderness Press, 2000; 208 pages, $16.95. If you're looking for off-highway adventure, then this is your guide. The book includes detailed directions, human and natural history, outstanding photography, full-page maps for each of the 65 routes and an extensive how-to chapter for beginners.

McClenahan, Owen. *Utah's Scenic San Rafael.* Self-published (P.O. Box 892, Castle Dale, UT 84513), 1986; 128 pages, $8.95. The author, a local "desert rat," takes you on driving tours through the scenic San Rafael region of east-central Utah. About half the trips can be done by car; the others need high clearance or four-wheel drive.

Porter, Eliot. *The Place No One Knew: Glen Canyon on the Colorado.* San Francisco: Sierra Club Books, 2000; 192 pages, $29.95. Beautiful color photos show a world now lost to the waters of Lake Powell. Thoughtful quotations from many individuals accompany the illustrations.

Powell, Allan Kent. *The Utah Guide.* Golden: Fulcrum Publications, 1995; 534 pages, $18.95. Comprehensive and well-written guide to the state, with strong historical bent.

Roylance, Ward J. *Utah: A Guide to the State.* Utah: A Guide to the State Foundation, 1982; 779 pages, $15. An updated version of the book published by the W.P.A. Writers Program in 1941. Much of the original material and format have been preserved. The comprehensive introduction to Utah's people and history is followed by 11 tours of the state.

Rutter, Michael J. *Fun with the Family in Utah: Hundreds of Ideas for Day Trips with the Kids.* Globe Pequot Press, 2000; 288 pages, $12.95. Comprehensive guide to events, recreation, history, and activities with the family in mind.

Sierra Club. *Desert Southwest: The Sierra Club Guides to the National Parks.* New York: Random House, 1996; 352 pages, $17.95. Beautiful color photos illustrate the wildlife and scenic beauties of Utah's five national parks. The other parks described are Mesa Verde in Colorado, Grand Canyon and Petrified Forest in Arizona, Carlsbad Caverns in New Mexico, and Guadalupe Mountains and Big Bend in Texas. The text tells of the history, geology, wildlife, and flora. Maps and trail descriptions show hiking possibilities.

Stegner, Wallace, ed. *This is Dinosaur: Echo Park Country and its Magic Rivers.* Niwot, CO: Roberts Rinehart, Inc., 1985; 128 pages, $8.95. Essays on this rugged land—its geology, dinosaurs, wildlife, Indians, explorers, river-running, and visiting Dinosaur National Monument.

Utah Division of Wildlife Resources. *Lakes of the High Uintas.* Utah Division of Wildlife Resources (1596 W. North Temple, Salt Lake City, UT 84116), 1981–1985; 14–45 pages each, $1 each plus postage. Anglers headed for the Uintas will find this series of 10 booklets of detailed lake descriptions very useful. Also has practical advice on camping, hiking, and horse travel.

Utah Writers' Program of the Work Projects Administration. *Utah: A Guide to the State.* Hastings House, 1941; 595 pages. This classic guidebook to Utah still makes good reading. A lengthy introduction followed by detailed descriptions of towns and natural features provide rich historical background. The book offers a look at Utah before the postwar industrialization. Although it is out of print, libraries usually have a copy and some used bookstores carry it. Much of the material has been incorporated in the 1982 guide of the same name by Ward J. Roylance.

Wharton, Gayen and Tom Wharton. *Foghorn Outdoors: Utah Camping.* Avalon Travel Publishing, 2001; 400 pages, $17.95. The best guide to public and private campgrounds across the state. A great resource if you're planning on doing any backcountry exploration.

Wharton, Tom. *Utah! A Family Travel Guide.* Salt Lake City: Wasatch Publishers, Inc., 1999; 224 pages, $11.95. How to enjoy Utah's great outdoors with the kids. Also suggests museums, parks, and ski areas that the younger set will like. The well-illustrated guide contains many clever bits of wisdom.

Zwinger, Ann. *Wind in the Rock: The Canyonlands of Southeastern Utah.* Tucson: University of Arizona Press, 1986; 258 pages, $9.50. Well-written accounts of hiking in the Grand Gulch and nearby canyons. The author tells of the area's history, archaeology, wildlife, and plants.

HIKING, BICYCLING, SKIING, AND CLIMBING

Adkison, Ron. *Best Easy Day Hikes Grand Staircase-Escalante and the Glen Canyon Region.* Helena, MT: Falcon Publishing Company, 1998; 120 pages, $6.95. Features 19 hikes in south central Utah Canyon Country, including the newly created Grand Staircase Monument; also includes Paria Canyon.

Adkison, Ron. *Hiking Grand Staircase-Escalante and the Glen Canyon Region.* Helena, MT: Falcon Publishing Company, 1998; 320 pages, $14.95. The vast Escalante/Glen Canyon area of southern Utah is nearly roadless, and hiking is about the only way you'll have a chance to visit these beautiful and austere canyons. This guide includes detailed information on 59 hikes, including Paria Canyon and Grand Gulch, in addition to the new Grand Staircase Monument.

Allen, Steve. *Canyoneering the San Rafael Swell.* Salt Lake City: University of Utah Press, 1992; 256 pages, $17.95. Eight chapters each cover a different area of this exceptional, though little-known, canyon country. Trail and route descriptions cover adventures from easy rambles to challenging hikes. The author provides some climbing notes, too. Detailed road logs help you get there, whether by mountain bike, car, or truck.

Barnes, F.A. *Canyon Country Hiking and Natural History.* Salt Lake City: Wasatch Publishers, Inc., 1977; 176 pages, $7. Introduction to the delights of hiking amongst the canyons and mountains in southeastern Utah.

Barnes, F.A., and Tom Kuehne. *Canyon Country Mountain Biking.* Moab: Canyon Country Publications, 1988; 145 pages, $11. Authors tell how to get the most out of biking the canyon country of southeastern Utah. Trail descriptions take you through Arches and Canyonlands National Parks, the La Sal Mountains, and Canyon Rims Recreation Area.

Barnes, F.A. *Canyon Country Slickrock Hiking and Biking.* Moab: Canyon Country Publications, 1990; 289 pages, $14. "An illustrated guide to a completely different kind of hiking and mountain biking in the canyon country of southeastern Utah." A good introduction, areas to explore, personal anecdotes, and many black-and-white photos make this book fun to read and use.

Barnes, F.A. *Hiking the Historic Route of the 1859 Macomb Expedition.* Moab: Canyon Country Publications, 1989; 49 pages, $8. Captain John Macomb led the first expedition to explore and write about what's now Canyonlands National Park. Adventurous hikers can retrace part of Macomb's route, thanks to the descriptions, maps, and photos in this little guide.

Bicycle Vacation Guides. *Bicycle Utah.* Bicycle Vacation Guides, Inc. (P.O. Box 738, Park City, UT 84060; 801-649-5806); $5. This series of booklets describes 20 mountain-bike routes, one booklet for each of Utah's nine travel districts. The booklets are: *Bridgerland, Canyonlands, Castle Country, Color Country, Dinosaurland, Golden Spike Empire, Great Salt Lake Country, Mountainland,* and *Panoramaland.* Each book gives locations of trails on a map and gives full trail descriptions including a graph of the trail's vertical component. Booklets are found at many visitors' centers and bookstores.

Bomka, Gregg. *Mountain Biking Utah.* Helena, MT: Falcon Publishing Company, 1999; 256 pages, $19.95. Detailed route descriptions of over 100 rides, from the Salt Lake City area through Moab and Brian Head. Easy-to-use maps and elevation profiles included.

Brereton, Thomas, and James Dunaway. *Exploring the Backcountry of Zion National Park: Off Trail Routes.* Natural History Association, 1997; 112 pages, $7.50. Leave the crowds behind and discover Zion's backcountry.

Brinkerhoff, Brian. *Best Easy Day Hikes Salt Lake City.* Helena, MT: Falcon Publishing Company, 1999; 88 pages, $6.95. More than 20 short hikes in the Wasatch Front canyons near Salt Lake City.

Campbell, Todd. *Above and Beyond Slickrock.* Salt Lake City: Wasatch Publishers, Inc., 1999; 281 pages, $19.95. Exploring the slickrock country of Southeastern Utah.

Crowell, David. *Mountain Biking Moab.* Helena, MT: Falcon Publishing Company, 1997; 232 pages, $10.95. A handy guide to the many trails around Moab, from the most popular to the little explored, in a handy size: small enough to take on the bike with you.

Davis, Mel, and John Veranth. *High Uinta Trails: A Hiking & Backpacking Guide to the High Uintas Wilderness.* Salt Lake City: Wasatch Publishers, Inc., 1999; 160 pages, $13.95. Guide to hiking, backpacking, camping, and fishing in the High Uintas Wilderness of northeastern Utah.

Green, Stewart M. *Rock Climbing Utah.* Helena, MT: Falcon Publishing Company, 1998; 336 pages, $26.95. Amazingly comprehensive guide to climbing routes throughout the state. Route maps are superimposed over photographs to make sure climbers find the right route. Topo maps also included, as well as info on camping and travel.

Grubbs, Bruce. *Hiking Great Basin National Park.* Helena, MT: Falcon Publishing Company, 1998; 88 pages, $9.95. A guide to 21 high-country hikes in this little visited national park on the Utah-Nevada border.

Hall, David. *Hiking Utah.* Helena: Falcon Press, 1996; 254 pages, $14.95. Good selection of 60 trips within Utah. The day and overnight hikes range from easy to difficult. An introduction will help you get started hiking.

Jensen, Michael. *Skiers Guide to Utah.* Gulf Publishing Company, 1995; 212 pages, $16.95. A guide to downhill-skiing areas throughout the state.

Kals, W.S. *Land Navigation Handbook.* San Francisco: Sierra Club Books, 1983; 288 pages, $15. This handy pocket guide will enable you to confidently explore Utah's extensive backcountry. Not only explains how to use map and compass but also other navigation methods such as altimeter and using the sun and stars.

Keilty, Maureen. *Best Hikes in Utah With Children.* Seattle: The Mountaineers, 2000; 240 pages, $14.95. This guide describes 75 child-tested trails in all parts of Utah including hikes of easy, moderate, and difficult challenges, plus a few hikes that offer wheelchair access. Maps and photographs let readers know what to expect of hikes.

Kelsey, Michael R. *Canyon Hiking Guide to the Colorado Plateau.* Provo: Kelsey Publishing, 1999; 288 pages, $15.95. One of the best guides to hiking in southeastern Utah's canyon country. Geologic cross sections show the formations you'll be walking through. The book has descriptions and maps for 64 trips in Utah, 38 hikes in adjacent Arizona, 13 in Colorado, and two in New Mexico. The author is ahead of his time in using just the metric system, but the book is otherwise easy to follow.

Kelsey, Michael R. *Hiking and Exploring Utah's Henry Mountains and Robbers Roost.* Provo: Kelsey Publishing, 1990; 224 pages, $9.95. You'll find adventure and scenic beauty in this little-known region of high mountains and rugged canyons. Descriptions and maps cover 37 destinations. The book provides an excellent background of the region's history, mining, geology, and wildlife. Fascinating stories relate the escapades of Butch Cassidy. Uses metric system.

Kelsey, Michael R. *Hiking and Exploring Utah's San Rafael Swell.* Provo: Kelsey Publishing, 1990; 160 pages, $8.95. Motorists driving across I-70 in east-central Utah get just a glimpse at the massive rock fold called the San Rafael Swell. This book presents the area's fascinating history and shows the way to hidden canyons with 30 hikes. Good maps and geologic cross sections. Uses metric system.

Kelsey, Michael R. *Hiking, Biking and Exploring Canyonlands National Park and Vicinity.* Provo: Kelsey Publishing, 1992; 320 pages, $14.95. The author's newest guide emphasizes hiking and local history. He used his mountain bike and hiking boots to explore the backcountry, rather than a four-wheel-drive vehicle. Uses metric system.

Lambrechtse, Rudi. *Hiking the Escalante.* Salt Lake City: Wasatch Publishers, Inc., 1999;

189 pages, $11.95. "A wilderness guide to an exciting land of buttes, arches, alcoves, amphitheaters, and deep canyons." Introduction to history, geology, and natural history of the Escalante region in southern Utah. Contains descriptions and trailhead info for 42 hiking destinations. The hikes vary from easy outings suitable for children to a highly challenging four-day backpack trek.

Probst, Jeffrey. *High Uintas Backcountry.* Outland Publishing, 1996; 295 pages, $13.95. The number one selling guide to the Uinta highcountry, with nearly 100 hiking trails from easy to long-distance, and information on the area's 600 lakes.

Ringholz, Raye Carleson. *Park City Trails.* Salt Lake City: Wasatch Publishers, Inc., 1999; 104 pages, $8.95. Hikes and cross-country ski tours in the mountains and canyons surrounding this old mining town. Includes a walking tour of Park City.

Schneider, Bill. *Best Easy Day Hikes Canyonlands and Arches.* Helena, MT: Falcon Publishing Company, 1997; 74 pages, $6.95. Twenty-one hikes in this popular vacation area, geared to travelers who are short on time or aren't able to explore the canyons on more difficult trails.

Schneider, Bill. *Exploring Canyonlands and Arches National Parks.* Helena, MT: Falcon Publishing Company, 1997; 202 pages, $14.95. A hiking guide to these two Moab-area parks. Includes 63 easy and more difficult hikes.

Trails Illustrated. *Moab Bike Routes.* Evergreen, CO: Trails Illustrated, 1995; $7. Plasticized, handy topo map with Moab-area routes. Trails Illustrated also produces trail guides to the various national forests in Utah ($8.99).

Utesch, Peggy, and Bob Utesch. *Mountain Biking in Canyon Rims Recreation Area.* Moab: Canyon Country Publications, 1992; 89 pages, $8. An illustrated mountain bikers' guide to exploring this vast and beautiful area south and east of Canyonlands National Park. You'll need the separate map *Canyon Country Off-*

Road Vehicle Trail Map: Canyon Rims Recreation Area by F.A. Barnes.

Utesch, Peggy. *The Utah-Colorado Mountain Bike Trail System, Route I—Moab to Loma: Kokopelli's Trail.* Moab: Canyon Country Publications, 1990; 81 pages, $9. Learn about desert bicycling, then take off with the detailed descriptions in this well-illustrated guide. The 130-mile trail twists over spectacular terrain between Moab, Utah, and Loma, Colorado.

Waterman, Laura, and Guy Waterman. *Backwoods Ethics: Environmental Issues for Hikers and Campers.* Woodstock, VT: Countryman Press, 1993; 280 pages, $14. Thoughtful commentaries on how the hiker can visit the wilderness with the least impact. Case histories dramatize the need to protect the environment.

BOATING AND RIVER-RUNNING

Abbey, Edward. *Down the River.* New York: E.P. Dutton, 1991; 256 pages, $14. Abbey's love for the wilderness comes through in thoughtful descriptions of travels along rivers through deserts of the West.

Evans, Laura, and Buzz Belknap. *Dinosaur River Guide.* Evergreen, CO: Westwater Books, 1973; 64 pages, $16.95. Topo maps show the canyons and points of interest along the Green and Yampa Rivers in Dinosaur National Monument of northeastern Utah and adjacent Colorado. Includes Lodore, Whirlpool, and Split Mountain Canyons of the Green River. Notes and photos provide historical background.

Goldwater, Barry M. *Delightful Journey: Down the Green & Colorado Rivers.* Tempe, AZ: Arizona Historical Foundation, 1970; 209 pages, $50. Fewer than 100 people had run the entire Grand Canyon in 1940, when Goldwater joined a 47-day, 1,463-mile expedition from Green River, Wyoming, to Lake Mead in Arizona.

Kelsey, Michael R. *River Guide to Canyonlands National Park.* Provo: Kelsey Publishing, 1991; 256 pages, $11.95. How to do a trip on the Green and Colorado Rivers and the many hikes and things to see along the way. Lots of local lore, too. Begins at the town of Green River on the Green and Moab on the Colorado; coverage ends at the confluence area (there's not much on Cataract Canyon). Uses metric system.

Nichols, Gary. *River Runners' Guide to Utah and Adjacent Areas.* Salt Lake City: University of Utah Press, 1986; 168 pages, $14.95. A comprehensive guidebook to running Utah's many rivers—the little-known ones as well as the popular Green and Colorado. Maps, photos, safety info, and difficulty ratings let you know the excitement and hazards of what you're getting into.

Tejada-Flores, Lito. *Wildwater: The Sierra Club Guide to Kayaking and Whitewater Boating.* San Francisco: Sierra Club Books, 1982; 329 pages, $12. Comprehensive introduction to river-running: choosing boats and equipment, river techniques, safety, practical advice on trip planning, overview of river possibilities in the United States, and history of white-water boating.

Zwinger, Ann. *Run, River, Run: A Naturalist's Journey Down One of the Great Rivers of the American West.* Tucson: University of Arizona Press, 1984; 317 pages, $17.95. An excellent description of the author's experiences along the Green River from its source in the Wind River Range of Wyoming to the Colorado River in southeastern Utah. The author weaves geology, Indian ruins, plants, wildlife, and her personal feelings into the text and drawings.

MEMOIRS

Abbey, Edward. *Desert Solitaire.* Ballantine Books, 1991; 337 pages, $6.99. A meditation on the Red Rock Canyon Country of Utah. Abbey brings his fiery prose to the service of the American outback, while excoriating the commercialization of the West.

Stegner, Wallace. *Mormon Country.* University of Nebraska Press, 1982; 362 pages, $15. Stegner tells the story of the early Mormon experience in this highly readable near-epic.

Williams, Terry Tempest. *Refuge: An Unnatural History of Family and Place.* Vintage Books, 1992; 303 pages, $13. A memoir of a family devastated by cancer (caused by federal government atomic testing), overlain with a natural history of birdlife along the Great Salt Lake. Haunting, deeply spiritual, and beautifully written.

HISTORY AND CURRENT EVENTS

Alexander, Thomas G., Richard Sadler, and Susan A. Whetstone. *Utah, the Right Place: The Official Centennial History.* Gibbs Smith Publisher, 1996; 487 pages, $29.95. A good overview of the state's history, with an understandable focus on the Mormon experience. Lots of good photos and illustrations.

Bennet, Cynthia Larsen. *Roadside History of Utah.* Mountain Press Publishing Co., 1999; 417 pages, $18. A very readable account of the state's history organized by driving tours. Full of great stories, yarns, and amazing human stories.

Colbert, Edwin H. *The Great Dinosaur Hunters and Their Discoveries.* Mineola, NY: Dover Publications, 1984; 283 pages, $9.95. Discovery of the "terrible lizards" in England during the 1820s and the worldwide fossil searches that followed. Includes early digging in what's now Dinosaur National Monument. Many photos and drawings illustrate the lively text.

Dellenbaugh, Frederick S. *A Canyon Voyage: The Narrative of the Second Powell Expedition.* Tucson: University of Arizona Press, 1984; 277 pages, $16.95. Well-written account of John Wesley Powell's second expedition down the Green and Colorado Rivers, 1871–1872. The members took the first Grand Canyon photographs and obtained much valuable scientific knowledge.

Goodman, Doug and Daniel McCool. *Contested Landscape: The Politics of Wilderness in Utah and the West.* University of Utah Press, 1999; 320 pages, $19.95. A collection of essays that frame the contentious political debate over land-use policy in Utah.

McCormick, John S. and Rod Decker. *The Gathering Place: An Illustrated History of Salt Lake City.* Signature Books, 2000; 250 pages, $39.95. Fascinating guide to history of the City of Zion, with excellent photos.

Miller, David E. *Hole-in-the-Rock.* Salt Lake City: University of Utah Press, 1959; 229 pages, $12. Detailed account of pioneers struggling to build a 200-mile wagon road to the remote southeastern corner of Utah in 1879–1880. A group of about 250 men, women, and children in 80 wagons navigated some of the West's most rugged country to become the first white settlers in San Juan County.

Peterson, Charles S. *Utah, a Bicentennial History.* New York: W.W. Norton & Co., 1977; 213 pages, $7.95. Good popular history of Utah's exploration, Mormon settlements, economic changes, and politics up to modern times.

Powell, John Wesley. *The Exploration of the Colorado River and its Canyons.* Mineola, NY: Dover Publications, reprinted 1997 (first published in 1895); 400 pages, $10.95. Powell's 1869 and 1871–1872 expeditions down the Green and Colorado Rivers. His was the first group to navigate through the Grand Canyon. A description of the 1879 Uinta Expedition is included, too.

ARCHAEOLOGY

Lister, Robert, and Florence Lister. *Those Who Came Before.* Southwest Parks and Monuments, 1983; 184 pages, $16.95. A well-illustrated guide to the history, artifacts, and ruins of prehistoric Southwest Indians. The author also describes parks and monuments containing archaeological sites.

Slifer, Dennis. *Guide to Rock Art of the Utah Region: Sites with Public Access.* Albuquerque: University of New Mexico Press, 2000; 245 pages, $15.95. The most complete guide to rock-art sites, with descriptions of over 50 sites in the Four Corners region. Complete with maps and directions, and with an overview of rock-art styles and traditions.

UTAH INDIANS OF TODAY

Dedera, Don. *Navajo Rugs: How to Find, Evaluate, Buy and Care for Them.* Cody, WY: Northland Press, 1996; 128 pages, $14.95. Dedera gives the history of Navajo weaving, illustrates how it's done, shows regional styles, and offers practical advice on purchasing.

Gilpin, Laura. *The Enduring Navajo.* Austin: University of Texas Press, 1994; 505 pages, $34.95. Excellent book about the Navajo—their homes, land, ceremonies, crafts, tribal government, and trading posts.

Locke, Raymond F. *The Book of the Navajo.* Holloway House Publishing, 1992; 512 pages, $6.95. Navajo legends, art, and history from early to modern times.

Zolbrod, Paul G. *Diné bahane': The Navajo Creation Story.* Albuquerque: University of New Mexico Press, 1988; 431 pages, $16.95. Deities, people, and animals come to life in this translation of Navajo mythology.

NATURAL SCIENCES

Baars, Donald L. *The Colorado Plateau: A Geologic History.* Albuquerque: University of New Mexico Press, 1994; 279 pages, $14.95. Written for the layperson, this book takes you on a tour of the Four Corners area geology from the ancient twisted rocks at the bottom of the Grand Canyon to the fiery volcanism and icy glaciations of the Pleistocene epoch.

Craighead, John J. (and others). *A Field Guide to Rocky Mountain Wildflowers.* Boston: Houghton Mifflin Co., 1998; 275 pages, $18.

Handy guide takes in Utah's high country. A plant key and detailed descriptions make identification easy. Illustrated with line drawings and color photos.

Chronic, Halka. *Roadside Geology of Utah.* Mountain Press Publishing Company, 1990; 325 pages, $16. This layperson's guide tells the story of the state's fascinating geology as seen by following major roadways.

Dodge, Natt N. *100 Roadside Wildflowers of Southwest Uplands in Natural Color.* Southwest Parks and Monuments Association, 1989; 64 pages, $4.95. Introduction with a brief description and color photo for those flowers usually found in southern Utah above 4,500 feet.

Fagan, Damian. *Canyon Country Wildflowers.* Helena, MT: Falcon Publishing Company, 1998; 192 pages, $17.95. A comprehensive field guide to the diverse flora of the Four Corners area.

Fleischner, Thomas Lowe. *Singing Stone: A Natural History of the Escalante Canyons.* University of Utah Press, 1999; 237 pages, $17.95. A former Outward Bound instructor who has guided many city people through the Escalante Canyons, Fleischner knows the area well and lends first-hand vitality to his information on the area's plants, animals, ecology, geology and pre-history.

Halfpenny, James, and Elizabeth Biesiot. *A Field Guide: Mammal Tracking in Western America.* Boulder: Johnson Books, 1988; 163 pages, $14.95. No need to guess what animal passed by. This well-illustrated guide shows how to read trails of large and small wildlife. More determined detectives can study the scatology chapter.

Hamilton, Wayne L. *The Sculpturing of Zion: Guide to the Geology of Zion.* Springdale: Zion Natural History Association, 1984; 132 pages, $14.95. Outstanding book explaining geologic forces and history. Clear graphs, drawings, and beautiful color photography illustrate the nontechnical text.

Kappele, William A. *Rockhounding Utah.* Helena, MT: Falcon Publishing Company, 1996; 180 pages, $12.95. Informative and comprehensive guide to 86 rock-collecting sites. Each description includes concise information on the material to be found there, the tools to bring, the best season to visit, and what vehicle to drive.

McIvor, D.E. *Birding Utah.* Helena, MT: Falcon Publishing Company, 1998; 410 pages, $19.95. A guide to 100 areas of bird-watching interest throughout the state, plus black-and-white photos of common species, checklists, plus a good compendium on the state's ecoregions and vegetation communities.

MacMahon, James A. *Deserts.* New York: Alfred A. Knopf, The Audubon Society Nature Guides, 1985; 638 pages, $19. Comprehensive naturalist's guide to the Great Basin, Colorado Plateau, and other arid regions of the West. Many color photos help identify the birds, mammals, fish, insects, reptiles, amphibians, and flora.

Olin, George, and Dale Thompson. *Mammals of the Southwest Deserts.* Southwest Parks and Monuments Association, 1982; 97 pages, $6.95. Well illustrated with black-and-white and color drawings.

Perry, John, and Jane Greverus Perry. *The Sierra Club Guide to the Natural Areas of Colorado and Utah.* San Francisco: Sierra Club Books, 1985; 317 pages, $9.95. A reference source with addresses, recreation possibilities, plant and animal checklists, and road directions for 189 different areas.

Stokes, William L. *Geology of Utah.* Salt Lake City: Utah Museum of Natural History Occasional Paper, No. 6, 1989; 309 pages, $12. A comprehensive overview of Utah's geologic history, rock layers, fossils, and landscapes.

Sweet, Muriel. *Common Edible and Useful Plants of the West.* Happy Camp, CA: Naturegraph Publishers, 1976; 64 pages, $5.95. Nontechnical descriptions of plants and trees that have food, medicinal, and other uses. Most of these were first discovered by Indians and used later by pioneer settlers.

Welsh, Stanley L., and Bill Ratcliffe. *Flowers of the Canyon Country.* Moab: Canyonlands Natural History Association, 1995; 85 pages, $15.95. Beautiful color photography makes this book a pleasure to use while traveling in southern Utah. Each flower has a photo and nontechnical description.

VIRTUAL UTAH: WEB RESOURCES

Although a Virtual Visit to Utah cannot replace the real thing, you'll find an enormous amount of helpful information on the Internet's **World Wide Web.** Thousands of web sites interlink to cover everything from ghost towns to the latest community news.

Up-to-the-minute weather and news reports lie at your fingertips 24 hours a day. E-mail links let you write to many of the tourist offices and other people who can provide additional information. The web sites will save you time and money by quickly providing information that you would otherwise have to write or call for. Web "surfing" will have choppy waves at times, however, due to out-of-date sites and missing links. Also, don't expect to find every topic that's covered in *Moon Handbooks: Utah!*

Note that many Internet addresses begin with "http://" but most web browsers need only the part of the address that follows, which usually begins with "www." Internet addresses must have the correct capitalization, though they're usually all lower case; e-mail addresses can be entered in either lower or upper case. Forward slashes separate directories of some web addresses.

Where to Start

The **Yahoo** site will take you almost anywhere in Utah with its well-organized offerings. Enter www.yahoo.com and select Regional, U.S. States, then Utah or go directly to dir.yahoo. com/Regional/U_S__States/Utah and select "cities" or such topics as arts, government, libraries, news, recreation and sports, and travel. Other search engines work well too. The **utah.citysearch.com** is great for finding a community's news arts, entertainment, and Internet links. **Official City Sites** at officialcitysites.org/utah.htm also takes you directly to the place of interest for the links there. The **Church of Jesus Christ of Latter-Day Saints** at www.lds.org explains the Mormon religion.

Travel

The **Utah Travel Council** at utah.com takes you around the state to sights, activities, events, maps, and Internet links to local tourist offices. The **University of Utah** www.utah.edu in Salt Lake City and **Brigham Young University** www.byu.edu in Provo offer museums and sporting events to visitors. **Ghosttowns.com UTAH** at www.ghosttowns.com provides many descriptions of lonely places.

The Great Outdoors

The **National Park Service** offers pages for all their areas at www.nps.gov or enter this address followed by a slash and the first two letters of the first two words of the place (first four letters if there's just a one-word name); for example www.nps.gov/gosp takes you to Golden Spike National Historic Site and www.nps.gov/zion leads to Zion National Park. You'll find lots of hiking and other outdoor info at **Great Outdoor Recreation Pages** www.gorp.com/gorp/location/ut/ut.htm including national forests and wilderness areas. Visit **Utah State Parks** at parks.state.ut.us for details on the large park system. If you're interested in learning about Utah's highly scenic desert areas, check the state's listings in **Desert USA's** www.desertusa.com for places to visit and what plants and animals you might meet there. **Utah Guide** at www.americansouthwest.net/utah provides an overview of national parks, national recreation areas, and some state parks.

News and Sports

You can read news from Salt Lake City's big papers, **The Salt Lake Tribune** www.sltrib.com and **Deseret News** www.deseretnews.com to learn of local and world happenings. The **State of Utah Website** at www.state.ut.us has travel info, agencies, programs, and what the legislature is up to. If you're thinking snow, glide over to **SKIUTAH.COM** at www.skiutah.com where you'll also find summer activities at the ski resorts. And you can follow the countdown and news for the **XIX Olympic Winter Games** at www.slc2002.org to be held in Utah February 8–24, 2002.

INDEX

CAMPING/CAMPGROUNDS

HIKING

NATIONAL PARKS

STATE PARKS

ABOUT THE AUTHORS

Back in school, Bill Weir always figured he'd settle down to a career job and live happily ever after. Then he discovered travel. After graduating with a B.A. in physics from Berea College in 1972, Bill wound up as an electronic technician in Columbus, Ohio. But the very short vacation times just weren't enough for the trips he dreamed of. So in 1976 he took off with his trusty bicycle "Bessie" and rode across the United States from Virginia to Oregon with Bikecentennial '76. The following year he did an even longer bicycle trip—from Alaska to Baja California. Then the ultimate journey—a bicycle cruise around the world! That lasted from 1980 to 1984, with most of the time spent in the South Pacific and Asia. Naturally Bill used Moon's excellent *South Pacific Handbook* and *Indonesia Handbook*. Correspondence with the authors led to some text and photo contributions for their books and the idea of doing a guidebook of his own. From New Delhi in India, Bill returned to his home base of Flagstaff, Arizona, and set to work researching and writing the *Arizona Handbook*. The immense project took one and a half years of writing and nearly another year of production.

As soon as the writing of the Arizona book came to an end, Bill headed north across the Grand Canyon to the Beehive State. The *Utah Handbook* turned out to be a big challenge, too, though the rewards of travel there matched his efforts. Now it's time for this sixth edition, thoroughly updated from the last one.

Still free and single, Bill's major interests continue to be exploration of the inner and outer worlds along with writing and photography. The diverse worlds of the American West and Asia remain his favorites. Visit Bill at www.arizonahandbook.com to see his photos of Utah and Arizona along with text excerpts, updates, and the latest news of his world travels.

Bill McRae was born and raised in rural eastern Montana, on a traditional cattle and sheep ranch. Although he was brought up with one foot in the saddle, from an early age his real passion was for the culture of Europe, a taste that he evolved from stories of his grandparents' native Scotland. He made his first trip to the United Kingdom at 18 and awakened a serious urge to travel. This was the 1970s and much of the world seemed like a well-meaning and courteous place to have a party. And so he did. He used his college years as an excuse to travel, attending universities in England, Scotland, France, Canada, and the U.S. He finished his education at the University of Kent, with an M.A. in Modern Literature. All this traipsing around didn't make for much of an academic career, but it was a great education in life.

After seemingly unending years at university, Bill moved to Portland, Oregon, which is still his home. Since moving to Portland, Bill has worked at a number of jobs, including university teacher, waiter and bartender, journalist, and tile-setter. He has his name on other travel guides, including the *Montana Handbook* (Moon Publications), *Pacific Northwest USA: A Travel Survival Kit* and *Seattle City Guide* (Lonely Planet), and Frommer's *Canada* and Frommer's *BC and the Canadian Rockies*. He has also worked as an editor and contributor for Expedia.com, GORP.com, *National Geographic*, and the Mobile Guides series. Between travel writing junkets, he makes his money by technical writing. You can always interest Bill in a hand of bridge, a camping trip, or cooking up something French and full of calories.

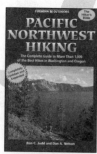

FOR TRAVELERS WITH SPECIAL INTERESTS

GUIDES

The 100 Best Small Art Towns in America • Asia in New York City
The Big Book of Adventure Travel • Cities to Go
Cross-Country Ski Vacations • Gene Kilgore's Ranch Vacations
Great American Motorcycle Tours • Healing Centers and Retreats
Indian America • Into the Heart of Jerusalem
The People's Guide to Mexico • The Practical Nomad
Saddle Up! • Staying Healthy in Asia, Africa, and Latin America
Steppin' Out • Travel Unlimited • Understanding Europeans
Watch It Made in the U.S.A. • The Way of the Traveler
Work Worldwide • The World Awaits
The Top Retirement Havens • Yoga Vacations

SERIES

Adventures in Nature
The Dog Lover's Companion
Kidding Around
Live Well

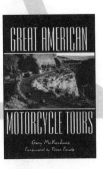

MOON HANDBOOKS provide comprehensive

coverage of a region's arts, history, land, people, and social issues in addition to detailed practical listings for accommodations, food, outdoor recreation, and entertainment. Moon Handbooks allow complete immersion in a region's culture—ideal for travelers who want to combine sightseeing with insight for an extraordinary travel experience.

USA

Alaska-Yukon • Arizona • Big Island of Hawaii • Boston
Coastal California • Colorado • Connecticut • Georgia
Grand Canyon • Hawaii • Honolulu-Waikiki • Idaho • Kauai
Los Angeles • Maine • Massachusetts • Maui • Michigan
Montana • Nevada • New Hampshire • New Mexico
New York City • New York State • North Carolina
Northern California • Ohio • Oregon • Pennsylvania
San Francisco • Santa Fe-Taos • Silicon Valley
South Carolina • Southern California • Tahoe • Tennessee
Texas • Utah • Virginia • Washington • Wisconsin
Wyoming • Yellowstone-Grand Teton

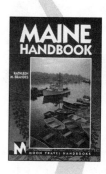

INTERNATIONAL

Alberta and the Northwest Territories • Archaeological Mexico
Atlantic Canada • Australia • Baja • Bangkok • Bali
Belize • British Columbia • Cabo • Canadian Rockies • Cancún
Caribbean Vacations • Colonial Mexico • Costa Rica • Cuba
Dominican Republic • Ecuador • Fiji • Havana • Honduras
Hong Kong • Indonesia • Jamaica • Mexico City • Mexico
Micronesia • The Moon • Nepal • New Zealand • Northern
Mexico • Oaxaca • Pacific Mexico • Pakistan • Philippines
Puerto Vallarta • Singapore • South Korea • South Pacific
Southeast Asia • Tahiti • Thailand • Tonga-Samoa • Vancouver
Vietnam, Cambodia and Laos • Virgin Islands • Yucatán Peninsula

www.moon.com

$Rick\ Steves$ shows you where to

travel and how to travel—all while getting the most value for your dollar. His Back Door travel philosophy is about making friends, having fun, and avoiding tourist rip-offs.

Rick's been traveling to Europe for more than 25 years and is the author of 22 guidebooks, which have sold more than a million copies. He also hosts the award-winning public television series *Travels in Europe with Rick Steves*.

RICK STEVES' COUNTRY & CITY GUIDES
Best of Europe
France, Belgium & the Netherlands
Germany, Austria & Switzerland
Great Britain & Ireland
Italy • London • Paris • Rome • Scandinavia • Spain & Portugal

RICK STEVES' PHRASE BOOKS
French • German • Italian • French, Italian & German
Spanish & Portuguese

MORE EUROPE FROM RICK STEVES
Europe 101
Europe Through the Back Door
Mona Winks
Postcards from Europe

WWW.RICKSTEVES.COM

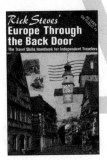

ROAD TRIP
USA

Getting there is half the fun, and Road Trip USA guides are your ticket to driving adventure. Taking you off the interstates and onto less-traveled, two-lane highways, each guide is filled with fascinating trivia, historical information, photographs, facts about regional writers, and details on where to sleep and eat—all contributing to your exploration of the American road.

"Books so full of the pleasures of the American road, you can smell the upholstery."
~ BBC radio

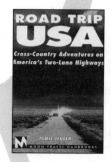

THE ORIGINAL CLASSIC GUIDE
Road Trip USA

ROAD TRIP USA REGIONAL GUIDE
Road Trip USA: California and the Southwest

ROAD TRIP USA GETAWAYS
Road Trip USA Getaways: Chicago
Road Trip USA Getaways: New Orleans
Road Trip USA Getaways: San Francisco
Road Trip USA Getaways: Seattle

www.roadtripusa.com

TRAVEL ✦ SMART

® guidebooks are accessible, route-based driving guides. Special interest tours provide the most practical routes for family fun, outdoor activities, or regional history for a trip of anywhere from two to 22 days. Travel Smarts take the guesswork out of planning a trip by recommending only the most interesting places to eat, stay, and visit.

"One of the few travel series that rates sightseeing attractions. That's a handy feature. It helps to have some guidance so that every minute counts."
~ San Diego Union-Tribune

TRAVEL SMART REGIONS

Alaska
American Southwest
Arizona
Carolinas
Colorado
Deep South
Eastern Canada
Florida Gulf
Coast
Florida
Georgia
Hawaii
Illinois/Indiana
Iowa/Nebraska
Kentucky/Tennessee
Maryland/Delaware
Michigan
Minnesota/Wisconsin
Montana/Wyoming/Idaho
Nevada
New England
New Mexico

New York State
Northern California
Ohio
Oregon
Pacific Northwest
Pennsylvania/New Jersey
South Florida and the Keys
Southern California
Texas
Utah
Virginias
Western Canada

Foghorn
Outdoors

guides are for campers, hikers, boaters, anglers, bikers, and golfers of all levels of daring and skill. Each guide contains site descriptions and ratings, driving directions, facilities and fees information, and easy-to-read maps that leave only the task of deciding where to go.

"Foghorn Outdoors has established an ecological conservation standard unmatched by any other publisher."
~ Sierra Club

CAMPING Arizona and New Mexico Camping
Baja Camping • California Camping
Camper's Companion • Colorado Camping
Easy Camping in Northern California
Easy Camping in Southern California
Florida Camping • New England Camping
Pacific Northwest Camping
Utah and Nevada Camping

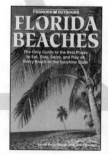

HIKING 101 Great Hikes of the San Francisco Bay Area
California Hiking • Day-Hiking California's National Parks
Easy Hiking in Northern California • Easy Hiking in Southern California
New England Hiking • Pacific Northwest Hiking • Utah Hiking

FISHING Alaska Fishing • California Fishing • Washington Fishing

BOATING California Recreational Lakes and Rivers
Washington Boating and Water Sports

OTHER OUTDOOR RECREATION California Beaches
California Golf • California Waterfalls • California Wildlife
Easy Biking in Northern California • Florida Beaches
The Outdoor Getaway Guide For Southern California
Tom Stienstra's Outdoor Getaway Guide: Northern California

WWW.FOGHORN.COM

CiTY·SMaRT™

The best way to enjoy a city is to get advice from someone who lives there—and that's exactly what City Smart guidebooks offer. City Smarts are written by local authors with hometown perspectives who have personally selected the best places to eat, shop, sightsee, and simply hang out. The honest, lively, and opinionated advice is perfect for business travelers looking to relax with the locals or for longtime residents looking for something new to do Saturday night.

A portion of sales from each title
benefits a non-profit literacy organization in that city.

CITY SMART CITIES

Albuquerque	Anchorage
Austin	Baltimore
Berkeley/Oakland	Boston
Calgary	Charlotte
Chicago	Cincinnati
Cleveland	Dallas/Ft. Worth
Denver	Indianapolis
Kansas City	Memphis
Milwaukee	Minneapolis/St. Paul
Nashville	Pittsburgh
Portland	Richmond
San Francisco	Sacramento
St. Louis	Salt Lake City
San Antonio	San Diego
Tampa/St. Petersburg	Toronto
Tucson	Vancouver

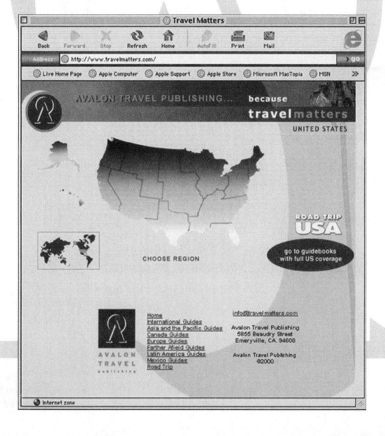

www.ricksteves.com

The Rick Steves web site is bursting with information to boost your travel I.Q. and liven up your European adventure. Including:
- The latest from Rick on what's hot in Europe
- Excerpts from Rick's books
- Rick's comprehensive Guide to European Railpasses

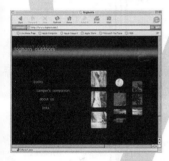

www.foghorn.com

Foghorn Outdoors guides are the premier source for United States outdoor recreation information. Visit the Foghorn Outdoors web site for more information on these activity-based travel guides, including the complete text of the handy *Foghorn Outdoors: Camper's Companion*.

www.moon.com

Moon Handbooks' goal is to give travelers all the background and practical information they'll need for an extraordinary travel experience. Visit the Moon Handbooks web site for interesting information and practical advice, including Q&A with the author of *The Practical Nomad*, Edward Hasbrouck.

U.S.~METRIC CONVERSION

1 inch = 2.54 centimeters (cm)
1 foot = .3048 meters (m)
1 yard = 0.914 meters
1 mile = 1.6093 kilometers (km)
1 km = .6214 miles
1 fathom = 1.8288 m
1 chain = 20.1168 m
1 furlong = 201.168 m
1 acre = .4047 hectares
1 sq km = 100 hectares
1 sq mile = 2.59 square km
1 ounce = 28.35 grams
1 pound = .4536 kilograms
1 short ton = .90718 metric ton
1 short ton = 2000 pounds
1 long ton = 1.016 metric tons
1 long ton = 2240 pounds
1 metric ton = 1000 kilograms
1 quart = .94635 liters
1 US gallon = 3.7854 liters
1 Imperial gallon = 4.5459 liters
1 nautical mile = 1.852 km

To compute celsius temperatures, subtract 32 from Fahrenheit and divide by 1.8. To go the other way, multiply celsius by 1.8 and add 32.

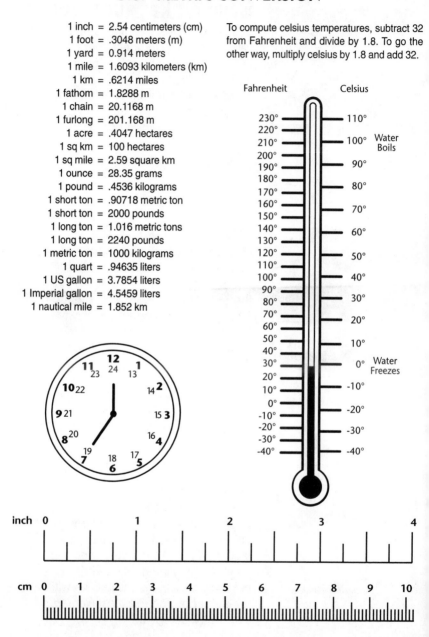

Will you have enough stories to tell your grandchildren?

Yahoo! Travel

DO YOU YAHOO!?

©2001 Yahoo! Inc.